Slanguage

A Dictionary of Slang and
Colloquial English in Ireland

Slanguage

A Dictionary of Slang and Colloquial English in Ireland

Bernard Share

Gill & Macmillan

Gill & Macmillan Ltd
Goldenbridge
Dublin 8
with associated companies throughout the world

© Bernard Share 1997

0 7171 2353 7 hard cover
0 7171 2683 8 paperback

Print origination by Peanntrónaic Teoranta, Dublin
Printed by Mackays of Chatham plc, Kent

A catalogue record is available for this book from the British Library.

5 4 3 2

This book is typeset in MBembo 10pt on 10.5pt.

In memoriam
MAXIMILIAN FRIEDRICH LIDDELL
sometime lecturer in Anglo-Saxon,
Trinity College, Dublin,
who would have been scandalised
by much of what follows

Contents

Introduction

I was daft about her and she about me. In the 'slanguage' of
the 'twenties, she was my 'big moment' and I was hers!

Lar Redmond, *Emerald Square*

Some time in the early 1960s, when I was working in advertising in Dublin, I
felt the need to evolve a Hiberno-English equivalent for the British slang term
'nit', then enjoying general currency. If the motivation for this experiment in
lexicography has long vanished into the mists of the past, the methodology
adopted has remained fresh in my mind simply on account of its banality. The
agency which employed me had thoughtfully acquired a copy of Tomás de
Bhaldraithe's seminal *English–Irish Dictionary*, published in 1959 — and to
which I am immeasurably indebted in what follows. At that time, I simply
looked up 'nit', discovered that its equivalent in Irish was both terse and easily
accommodated on the tongue, and launched it on its new career.

Snig, somewhat to my surprise, rapidly achieved a common currency in the
tight little world of Janus Advertising. In the context of what was then a
cheerfully innovative discipline, unburdened by subsequent accretions of
'market research' and other curbs on creativity, this might have been expected.
What I had not anticipated, however, was the manner in which this modest
neologism took upon itself a life of its own. From its original and intended
connotation as a term of mild abuse, it developed a transitive verbal form and,
with it, a new meaning. *To snig*, in our circle, came to mean 'to play a practical
joke upon' — a practice to which we were, then, lamentably addicted — and
from there took on the more abstract signification of 'messing' (see **messer**) in
general. Under the influence of this development the original noun–form itself
underwent modification, coming to mean any act, or behaviour, designed to
embarrass or confuse.

I would like to be able to confirm that this new coinage, launched
somewhere on the top floor of number 53 Parnell Square West, took off from
the window ledge on which we used to feed passing seagulls and winged its
way to general acceptance in the outside world. If this is the case, I have not
heard or, more pertinently, read of it: thus, though you will find *snig* in the
body of this work, it is not defined in terms of its Janus usage for the reason
that, as far as I am aware, no evidence in the public domain exists. Nevertheless
I live in hope, one day when I am sitting quietly minding my own business
over a pint, of hearing it on the lips of someone of another generation and with
no possible connection with the old firm.

The short history of *snig*, as far as I am aware of it, may, however, serve to
illuminate a number of matters relevant to the concept and compilation of this
dictionary. According to a *New York Times* estimate of 1989, words were being
added to the English language at the rate of from 15,000 to 20,000 per annum

— and this figure, presumably, referred to those employed in formal, as opposed to slang or colloquial, usage. But whereas words introduced into the scientific, legal, literary or other conventional vocabularies will most commonly submit themselves to lexicographical scrutiny and adumbration, slang and colloquialisms inhabit a much less well-defined area. Whereas an ostensibly bizarre locution such as *quark*, borrowed by its coiner from Joyce's *Finnegans Wake*, quickly established itself as an unexpendable neologism in the field of cosmic physics, many slang and colloquial accretions, coined for local and immediate reasons and highly subject to the effects of fashion, can fall into disuse — as in the case of *snig* — before they have achieved the status of a formal record. Further, this area of speech — for slang and colloquialisms are essentially verbal in provenance — can shift meaning both rapidly and unaccountably, so that the establishing of a sense history and verifiable antecedents often proves an impossible task.

I have therefore adopted as a criterion for inclusion that the usage of a word or phrase must be confirmed by recorded evidences, whether printed, broadcast or otherwise placed in the public domain. It is only relatively recently, of course, that many slang terms which must have been on the lips of our ancestors for generations have been, as the result of changing attitudes, thus publicly acknowledged; and even now it is not uncommon to find in a single edition of a 'family' newspaper 'four-letter' words appearing modestly adorned with asterisks on one page and in all their naked glory on another. Against this background it is thus virtually impossible, for large areas of this genre of vocabulary, to establish dates of first usage, and no attempt has been made to do so in the present work.

On the other hand, since slang and colloquial communication is very much a matter of *context*, substantive illustrative quotations have been supplied, providing examples of usage drawn from a wide variety of sources and periods, with the secondary intent of locating this dictionary in the category of a book that can be read for pleasure as well as simply consulted. The fact that many slang terms and colloquialisms have only recently been 'liberated' to the extent of being accepted in print and other media accounts for the high proportion of citations from contemporary and near-contemporary sources, a bias reinforced by the belief that the majority of readers will find this period of more immediate interest.

The nineteenth century, by contrast, figures less generously. The low level of Irish publishing in this period meant that the greater proportion of Irish writing was published abroad and with a non-Irish audience principally in mind: hence the pervasive Paddyisms, the patronising (and inaccurate) attempts to represent Hiberno-English pronunciation ('childher'; 'shpind it loike a man', etc.). This practice persisted into the first quarter at least of the twentieth century, for example in the work of Lynn Doyle. As Tom Paulin observed in *A New Look at the Language Question*, 'Until recently, few Irish writers appear to have felt frustrated by the absence of a dictionary which might define those words which are in common usage in Ireland, but which do not appear in the OED. This is possibly because most writers have instinctively moulded their language to the expectations of the larger audience outside Ireland.' With the revival in Irish publishing and the liberalised freedom of expression this state of affairs has been substantially remedied; though a comprehensive dictionary of Hiberno-English is still awaited.

If the terms and locutions defined herein have anything in common, it is that they exhibit qualities of irreverence, humour, satire, wit, sarcasm, indecency and indelicacy — to name but a few — that set them apart from the language of the liturgy or the law report, and especially from the mind-deadening cliché, which in the late 1990s could offer nothing beyond a view through a window of opportunity of the grass roots of a level playing field. Happily, Hiberno-English is continuing to respond vigorously to such moronic onslaughts on the idiosyncrasy of expression. As Joe O'Connor put it (*Sunday Tribune*, 15 October 1995), 'ever since English was forcibly introduced to this island, the people who live here have defiantly spoken it in their own way, with their own rhythms and cadences and meanings and nuances'. It is with such meanings and nuances that the present work is concerned.

The formal definition of slang is a matter which has confused and divided linguists ever since the phenomenon was first recognised as a category in its own right. As Alan Bliss, in *Spoken English in Ireland 1600–1740*, put it: 'It is a dangerous thing to challenge any word as slang nowadays. Determination of the precise elements in the vocabulary which can properly be characterised as slang is extremely difficult, partly because of rapid fluctuation in the status of colloquial expressions and partly because of the deficiencies in the record of informal speech.' *The Irish Times* complained on 22 August 1936: 'Language has been made safe for democracy. Words that are accused of a vulgar origin are shown to possess pedigrees that go back to Anglo-Saxon times.' This difficulty of definition is compounded when the field is extended — as it is here — to embrace the wider area of colloquial usage. Jacques Cellard and Alain Rey offered one solution in entitling their lexicon *Dictionnaire du français non conventionnel* — embracing the concept of a layer, or stratum, of usage which lies somewhere below the accepted levels of formal usage; though, it must be said, these levels are constantly shifting and redefining themselves. Thus while I have largely adopted the methodology of Cellard and Rey (and of G.A. Wilkes in *A Dictionary of Australian Colloquialisms*) for the purposes of the present compilation, I am aware of many grey areas — as between colloquialisms proper and dialect, for example — with the added complication, in the case of Hiberno-English, of its drawing its material from two distinctive language sources. If I have erred on the side of inclusion rather than exclusion, my justification would be not only the *embarras de richesses* which characterises colloquial Hiberno-English but the importance of recording as much as possible in a world of rapid linguistic levelling and — at least in terms of the Anglophone world — internationalisation. Not so long ago, in a very basic Dublin bar (pubs provide excellent locales for linguistic study), I overheard a middle-aged man — from his accent patently a local — use the term 'ear-bashing', a locution I had not then encountered outside Australia. Returned emigrant or soap addict, he constitutes a warning, if any were needed, that such colonisation offers a serious threat to our survival as a distinctive linguistic community. Much will be lost in the inevitable progress from clicking a mot to clicking a mouse.

In spite of this internationalisation the Hiberno-English linguistic community is, for the moment at least, still very much a reality; and in respect of slang and/or colloquial usage many people, though they would find it difficult to define, still clearly possess a discriminating sense of 'fitness' over a range of situations. One has only to listen to a radio interviewee, who might in many social situations employ the word **fuck** (q.v.) and its derivatives with the unthinking frequency which has led to the Irish being regarded, by startled visitors, as the most foul-mouthed nation in Europe, struggling to edit the word out of his conversational norm: **like** (q.v.) and **like you know** being commonly summoned into service as enclitics. In 1995 the then Tánaiste, Dick Spring, aroused unfavourable comment through the use, in a speech to the annual conference of the Labour Party, of the nickname **the Cruiser** (q.v.) in a reference to Dr Conor Cruise O'Brien. It was not the nickname itself, which had been common currency for decades, but the context. On the other hand McCann-Erickson Dublin ran an advertisement in *The Irish Times* on 26 July 1996 seeking an 'Account Director who doesn't miss a trick'. This appeared under the heading 'CUTE HOOR' (q.v.).

On another level, the wide response to popular investigations of language usage, such as RTÉ's *The Odd Word* and Diarmaid Ó Muirithe's *Irish Times* series *The Words we Use* — to both of which I stand gratefully indebted — affords ample evidence of an enduring public interest in the intricacies and felicities of the second national language — an interest which has extended beyond the insular boundaries. 'The English chattering classes have been wrapping their ironic air quote marks around Celtic colloquialisms of late,' the *Independent on Sunday* (London) suggested on 12 January 1997: '*Craic* [q.v.] abuse abounds, particularly in literary and media circles...'

This extension, of course, long antedates contemporary fashion: Irish and Hiberno-English locutions are common in the colloquial repertoire of other Anglophone countries, especially Australia (**good on you!** (q.v.); **Kathleen Mavourneen** (q.v.)) and North America (**phoney**, <British slang *fawney* <Irish *fáinne*, ring, 'referring to a swindle in which the *fawney-dropper* drops a cheap ring before the victim, then is persuaded to sell it as if it were valuable' (DAS)). The temptation to relate Ulster **nyam** (q.v.) with West Indies **nyam**, eat, or **fozy** (q.v.) with German slang **fotze**, pudendum, is perhaps better resisted.

If the Irish language currently occupies an equivocal position as a vernacular, its influence upon the vocabulary and usage of Hiberno-English is a matter not only of historical record but of demonstrable actuality. 'The syntax of Gaelic [Irish] still survives in the speech of many Irish people,' wrote Bob Quinn in *Atlantean*, '...this half-life of Gaelic in English speaking people can be seen as a linguistic substratum'. And this is true not only of syntax but of vocabulary. 'The number of actual Irish words used in Southern Hiberno-English is small, even in rural areas,' wrote Alan Bliss in 1984, 'Educated people do not use them at all, except by way of conscious rusticism.' But this view can be challenged on a number of counts, even if one ignores significant changes that have taken place since it was formulated.

Though few would assert that the attempt to revive Irish as the vehicle of everyday communication has been conspicuously successful, exposure to the language over successive generations and in a range of contexts from the schoolroom to the nomenclature of political office-holders and state-sponsored bodies has inevitably resulted in a 'leaking' of Irish words and phrases into predominantly Hiberno-English contexts. This infiltration, as the instances here collected will indicate, has, in the contemporary context, very little to do with 'rusticism'. The example of *ceol agus craic* is a case in point — an incontestably Irish word linked to a neologism coined from one long current in British dialects and in common use in its 'unIrishised' form in Ulster (**crack** (q.v.)). The term, brought into use to attempt to express a concept for which no adequate equivalent was felt to exist, has, interestingly, moved on another linguistic stage by assuming, in some instances, the 'Americanised' form *ceol 'n' craic*.

Another example of this process is the **cúpla focal** (q.v.). As one ill-disposed observer put it (John Boland in *The Irish Times*, 21 August 1995), 'And this new middle-class *Éire Nua* even absorbs the hitherto-unfashionable Irish language into everyday Irish life...with the result that we get restaurants called "Tá Sé Mohoganí Gaspipes" [see **mahogany gaspipe**] and fashion shops called "Sé Sí"...' In historical terms, one has only to glance at the derivations of many of the earlier slang and colloquial elements of our vocabulary to find confirmation for Polly Devlin's assertion that 'Gaelic words run all through our language, an old faded strand among the English tongue.' And bright — if sometimes garish — new strands are consistently being added to the tapestry. The as yet unassessable impact of Teilifís na Gaeilge, the Irish-language TV channel, is counterpointed by the bilingual cartoons of Tom Matthews, in one of which George Harrison greeting Ringo Starr is captioned with the proverbial *Aithníonn ciaróg ciaróg eile* (one beetle recognises another).

For the purposes of this dictionary I have regarded nearly all instances in which Irish locutions appear in Hiberno-English contexts as evidence of slang or colloquial usage. The same standards have been applied in the case of 'Paddyisms' (see Appendix) — words and phrases used by other nationalities to represent their concept of Irish speech which, though often long-established Anglicisations, have acquired a patina of stage-Irishism to the extent that when employed by the Irish themselves they frequently appear, as it were, in inverted commas. There are, inevitably, borderline cases in both these categories: Irish words or Anglicisations which may in one context be regarded as conventional Hiberno-English whilst appearing in another as carrying that edge of self-consciousness or even self-mockery which signifies the colloquial usage. When in doubt I have, as I have said, included rather than excluded, providing as far as possible examples to assist the reader in making his or her own judgment.

Similar considerations have been applied to definitively dialect words and phrases (though again the point at which a purely dialect term becomes accepted in a more widely colloquial context is very difficult to determine) from the Forth and Bargy, Shelta, and, in particular, Ulster Scots vernaculars. The latter element, apart from contributing substantially to the body of the work, is so distinctive as to lead some to claim for it the status of a language in its own right. The assertion by the Ulster Scots Language Society, founded in 1992, that there were 100,000 speakers in Cos. Antrim, Down and Donegal was not accepted as a valid criterion in this respect by the European

Commission's Dublin-based Bureau for Lesser-Used Languages; but the publication of *A Concise Ulster Dictionary* (see References in the Text and *passim*) has lent credibility to an argument that was given further reinforcement in April 1997 by the publication by the Democratic Unionist Party of sections of its election manifesto in Ulster Scots. 'Ulster folks', it asserted, 'haes a muckle cloud hingin abune [q.v.] us aa, like we hinnae sen before.' The cloud was more specifically identified as a 'Yin-cleekit Airlann'. But if a united Ireland remains a matter of political contention, it patently exists in the manner and spirit in which Hiberno-English, from whatever linguistic source, is deployed — and enjoyed — throughout the length and breadth of the island.

Acknowledgments

I am indebted to many people who will have remained unaware that they were, through a chance remark or reference overheard, enriching the texture of what follows: to these unwitting contributors I can offer only a general, if heartfelt, acknowledgment. More specifically I am indebted to Vincent Caprani, Richard Connolly, Anne Coughlan, Seán Diffley, Jonathan Williams, Seamus Kearns and Colm Swan for their assistance, and to Elizabeth — not only for suffering the protracted genesis with forbearance and sympathy but for making a substantial contribution in her own right. I must also acknowledge my indebtedness to the staff and resources of the National Library of Ireland and Naas Branch Library, Co. Kildare. My overriding debt, however, is to my old friend and former fellow alumnus Leslie Matson, without whose enthusiastic, sympathetic and scholarly collaboration this work would have been immeasurably the poorer, and whose persistence in following elusive etymologies up apparently blind alleys frequently resulted, to mangle the metaphor, in philological light at the end of the tunnel. Finally, the meticulous, painstaking and sympathetic labours of my copy-editor, Angela Rohan, have averted many a potential embarrassment and significantly refined the text. Any errors or omissions remain, of course, my sole responsibility.

Guide to Using the Dictionary

Head-word The order is *strictly alphabetical*, thus phrases beginning with 'go' will not all appear grouped under that word, but in their appropriate alphabetical position. This method has been adopted in view of the nature of the material, which presents few instances of substantial entries under one key headword. However, where an article appears at the end of an entry, it is not considered for alphabetical purposes. So, for example, **boxman** precedes **box, on the** and **wirrasthrue** precedes **wirra! wirra!** but **da, the** is found before **dab**.

Spelling The fact that much of this material existed in oral tradition long before being codified in print means that many words present themselves in a wide variety of spellings (see e.g. **yellow yalderin**). In these cases it has been the aim to offer the most common usage, i.e. **wan and wan** as against **one and one**, particularly where this reflects the pronunciation (see below). Where distinctively varied spellings have been accessed, they have been separately entered and cross-referenced. Transliterations of obscure spellings, especially in early texts, are enclosed in square brackets. In the interest of non-specialist readers the two Anglo-Saxon characters, 'thorn' and 'eth', have been rendered by **th**.

Part of speech/grammatical definition See Abbreviations and Symbols.

Pronunciation Given the diversity of regional pronunciation of the same word no attempt has been made to indicate this, except where it is necessary to comprehension or characterises a particular usage.

Etymology The term *Hiberno-English* is employed to represent the totality of English spoken in Ireland, irrespective of origin. *Anglo-Irish* is applied in its social context, as referring to the former Ascendancy, its successors and imitators. A line drawn roughly from Dundalk, Co. Louth to Tullaghan, Co. Leitrim marks the dividing line of the northern area in which the influence of Ulster Scots is predominant. The linguistic map of Ireland remains a matter of continued investigation and academic dispute, and no attempt has been made here to enter into these controversies, nor to indicate a first usage of a particular word or phrase, except in the rare instances where definitive evidence exists. In most cases it will be clear that demotic usage must substantially pre-date available published evidence.

Etymologies are not supplied in cases where they add little of interest or where they are patently obvious. The sign <? has been adopted to indicate both derivations of generally admitted obscurity and those concerning which I have personally been unable to satisfy myself. 'We philologists', said my former mentor Professor Liddell, generously including us neophytes in his first person plural, 'never guess: we make hypotheses.' I have endeavoured to follow this precept, in doubtful cases suspending judgment by supplying divergent

etymologies the merits of which I leave the reader to consider. The often ephemeral and arbitrary nature of slang and colloquial usage means that some of these etymological puzzles may never be conclusively determined, and it would thus seem in this context more interesting to supply the posited alternatives.

More common linguistic sources are supplied in abbreviated form (see Abbreviations and Symbols). In the case of words/phrases of Irish origin, definitions are taken from Ó Dónaill (see References in the Text) unless otherwise indicated.

Geographical location Where there would appear to be strong evidence that usage of a word/phrase is confined to or predominantly related to one particular area this has been indicated, though in the light of continuing research such criteria must be regarded as tentative. In this context *Ulster* refers to the traditional nine-county province.

Meaning Related senses are grouped; polysemous entries are indicated by numeric sequence.

Examples Unless otherwise indicated, quotations are from first published editions, which may, of course, substantially post-date the year of composition. Where this discrepancy is significant it has been noted. Newspapers, periodicals, etc. are to be taken as Dublin-published unless otherwise indicated. In instances where no appropriate quotations have been forthcoming, other authorities are cited as the source (see References in the Text).

Abbreviations and Symbols

<	from	Ger.	German
abbrev.	abbreviation; abbreviated	Gk.	Greek
		Hib.E	Hiberno-English
abst.	abstract	Hindust.	Hindustani
adj.	adjective; adjectival	Icel.	Icelandic
adv.	adverb(ial)	*idem*	'the same'
affect.	affectionate	imper.	imperative
art.	article	indef.	indefinite
attrib.	attributive(ly); attributed; attribution	infl.	influenced
		intens.	intensitive
Austral.	Australian	interj.	interjection
Brit.	British	interrog.	interrogative
C	century	intrans.	intransitive
c.	circa	invar.	invariably
cf.	compare	Ir.	Irish
Co.	County	Ire.	Ireland
cogn.	cognate	iron.	ironic(ally)
colloq.	colloquial(ly); colloquialism	It.	Italian
		joc.	jocular
cond.	conditional	Lat.	Latin
conj.	conjunction	lit.	literal(ly)
d.	died	masc.	masculine
Dan.	Danish	MDu.	Middle Dutch
def.	definite	ME	Middle English
deriv.	derivation	Med.	Medieval
derog.	derogatory	milit.	military
dial.	dialect	Mod.E	Modern English
dimin.	diminutive	Mod.F	Modern French
Du.	Dutch	n.	noun
Dub.	Dublin	neg.	negative
ed./eds.	editor/s	Norweg.	Norwegian
edn	edition	NZ	New Zealand
Eng.	English; England	obsc.	obscure
esp.	especially	OE	Old English
et al.	*et alii* ('and others')	OF	Old French
etym.	etymology	OGer.	Old German
euphem.	euphemism; euphemistic	OIr.	Old Irish
exclam.	exclamatory; exclamation	ON	Old Norse
		onomat.	onomatopoeic
fem.	feminine	p.	past
fig.	figurative(ly)	palat.	palatalised
fl. floruit	('flourished')	part.	participle
Flem.	Flemish	phr.	phrase
Fr.	French	pl.	plural
freq.	frequent(ly)	pop.	popular(ly)
GAA	Gaelic Athletic Association	poss.	possible; possibly
		prep.	preposition(al)
Gael.	Gaelic	pres.	present
gen.	general(ly)	pron.	pronoun

pronun.	pronunciation	Std	Standard
prop.	proper	Swed.	Swedish
q.v.	*quod vide*, 'which see'	TD	Teachta Dála (member
ref.	reference		of lower house of
rhym.	rhyming		parliament)
RTÉ	Radio Telefís Éireann	trans.	transitive
	(national broadcasting	unpalat.	unpalatalised
	service)	usu.	usually
Sc.	Scottish	var.	variant
Scand.	Scandinavian	vb.	verb(al)
sing.	singular	voc.	vocative
sl.	slang	WW	World War
s.o.	someone	Yidd.	Yiddish
Sp.	Spanish		

A

aaba-knot [n., <?] (Ulster). Charm used in healing cattle. 'A knotted string is passed three times over cattle afflicted with the batts' (Traynor).

abane/abeen/aboon/abune [adj., cf. Sc. *aboon*, above] (Ulster). As thus.

ABC [n.]. Scorch marks on the legs. **1927** Peadar O'Donnell, *Islanders*: '"it's the ashes bes on yer toes, an' the ABC on yer shins with toastin' them in the fire"'. See also **measle**.

abeen see **abane**

ablach [n., <Sc. *idem*, dwarf; insignificant, worthless person] (Ulster). Insignificant/slovenly person.

able as in **can you spell able?** [vb. phr.] (Ulster). Are you sure you can substantiate your claims?

ablins [adv., <Sc. *ailbins*, maybe, perhaps] (Ulster). As thus.

aboon see **abane**

abstrakerous [adj., cf. Sc. *abstraklous*, bad-tempered, obstreperous] (Ulster). As thus.

abune see **abane**

ach/ack [exclam., cf. Sc. *och*] (Ulster). 'Expression of frustration, impatience, annoyance' (Pepper).

act the jinnit [vb. phr., see **jinnit** 1.]. Act foolishly, irrationally.

act the lapwing [vb. phr., <habit of the bird (*Vanellus vulgaris*) of leading an intruder away from its nest]. Deliberately lead astray. **1845** William Carleton, *Tales and Sketches of the Irish Peasantry*, 'Bob Pentland': 'This manoeuvre of keeping in reserve an old or second set of [poteen (q.v.) making] apparatus, for the purpose of acting the lapwing and misleading the gauger, was afterwards practised with success...'

act the lig see **lig**

act the linnet [vb. phr.]. Engage in amorous dalliance. **1987** Lar Redmond, *Emerald Square*: '...Sloppy Molly was nuts about her father's new assistant. Nobody ever caught them acting the linnet or anything like that, but it was the very lack of any bit of flirting in public that put them on to Molly.'

act the maggot (q.v.) [vb. phr.]. Behave in a humorously irrational manner. **1986** Bob Geldof, *Is That It?*: 'To everyone else I was always "acting the maggot"... "They're laughing at you, Geldof, not with you," I was told.' **1995** Maureen Potter, RTÉ TV, *Super Trooper*, 30 Oct: 'I miss the panto most. But I can't charge around, dance or act the maggot like I used to.' **1995** Patrick Boland, *Tales from a City Farmyard*: '"Who said I ever smoked?" said I. "Don't act the maggot, you've been smoking since you were knee-high to a grasshopper..."' See also **cod**, **jack-act**, **jig-act**, **trick-acting**.

act the mowhawk [vb. phr.]. Behave badly. **1966** Patrick Boyle, *At Night All Cats are Grey*, 'The Betrayers': 'Still the pony refused to budge. "Get up there, you silly girl! Stop acting the mowhawk!" he pleaded, shaking the reins very gently in time with his words.'

acushla [exclam., <Ir. *a chuisle mo chroí*, my heart's beloved]. Term of endearment. **1899** E.Œ. Somerville & Martin Ross, *Some Experiences of an Irish RM*: '"Come here to me, a cushla," say I to him. "I suppose it's some way wake in the legs y'are."' **1913** Alexander Irvine, *My Lady of the Chimney Corner*: '"I've got four panes broke, Anna." "Well, they're just like four doores." "Feeries can come in that way, too." "Ay, but feeries can't sew up a broken heart, acushla."' **1922** James Joyce, *Ulysses*: 'OLD GUMMY GRANNY (*Thrusts a dagger towards Stephen's hand*.) Remove him, acushla. At 8.35 a.m. you will be in heaven and Ireland will be free.' See also **macushla**.

addle [n., <Sc. *idem* <OE *adela*, cow urine, liquid filth] (Ulster). Stagnant, foul-smelling pool.

adlins [n., cf. Sc. *ochtlins*, anything at all] (Ulster). Small earnings (MON).

affront [vb., <Sc. *idem*, disgrace, put to shame] (Ulster). Embarrass acutely,

mortify. **1983** *John Pepper's Illustrated Encyclopaedia of Ulster Knowledge*: '"Poor Minnie. There's one thing — the family didn't affront her. Look at them handles on the coffin — they're as long as your arm."'

after-clapps [n. pl.]. Unexpected results. **1675–95** Anon., *Purgatorium Hibernicum*: 'I never tought [thought]/Mee company had ever brought/Such after-clapps!'

Aga McCann, the [nickname]. J.J. McCann, newspaper man, founder of *Radio Review*. **1983** Hugh Oram, *The Newspaper Book*: 'At the time the *Sunday Review* was being launched [3 Nov 1957] J.J. McCann (often compared with the Aga Khan, the great socialite of the time) was crowning a colourful career in publishing by joining *The Irish Times*.'

agee [adj., <Sc. *agley*, awry, crooked] (Ulster). As thus; slightly mentally unbalanced.

aginner [n., <'agin' (prep.), against + endearment suffix]. One who opposes or criticises out of envy, resentment, etc.; begrudger (q.v.).

agra/agraw [exclam., <voc. of Ir. *grádh* (n.), love]. Term of endearment. **1702** George Farquhar, *The Twin Rivals*: 'TEAGUE I am prishoner in the Constable's house be me shoule, and shent abrode to fetch some bail for my maishter; but foo [who] shall bail poor Teague agra...'

a-hasky see **haisge**

ahaygar! [exclam., <Ir. *a théagar*, my dear!]. Term of endearment (OTF).

ahint [prep., <Sc. *idem*, behind] (gen. Ulster). As thus. **1943** George A. Little, *Malachi Horan Remembers*: '"It was ahint that fence," said Malachi, indicating his right-hand field, "that the men escaping after the Battle of Tallaght threw their blunderbusses..."' **1951** Sam Hanna Bell, *December Bride*: '"Well, put this lamp somewhere and get in ahint wi' the brother."'

ail [vb., <OE *eglan*, afflict; in Hib.E gen. interrog.]. Be wrong with. **1913** Alexander Irvine, *My Lady of the Chimney Corner*: '...Kitty Coyle gave vent to a scream of terror that brought the mourners to the door and terrified those outside. "What ails ye, in the name of God?" Anna said.' **1951** Frank O'Connor, *Traveller's Samples*, 'The Man of the House': 'She was through with me now. It was my cough bottle she had been after all the time. I began to weep despairingly. "What ails you?" she said impatiently.'

aims-ace [n., <ME *ambs-ace* <OF *ambs as*, double ace, the lowest throw at dice, hence bad luck]. A small amount, quantity or distance. 'Applied in the following way very generally in Munster: "He was within an aim's-ace of being drowned"' (PWJ). **1800** Maria Edgeworth, *Castle Rackrent*: '"I never saw him in such fine spirits as that day he went out — sure enough he was within aims-ace of getting quit handsomely of all his enemies..."' **1916** James Joyce, *A Portrait of the Artist* (q.v.) *as a Young Man*: '"One of the Crokes [hurling team] made a woeful wipe at him one time with his caman [hurley stick] and I declare to god he was within an aim's ace of getting it at the side of his temple."'

airishin [pres. part., <Ir. *arís* (adv.), again]. Mimicking s.o.'s speech (OTF).

airlock [vb.] (Ulster). Stop in one's tracks. Hence **airlocked** [p. part. as adj.]. The worse for drink.

airneal [n., <Ir. *airneál*, friendly night visit]. As thus. **1939** Patrick Gallagher (Paddy the Cope (q.v.)), *My Story*: '"What is an airneal?" said Jane. I said that it was a gathering of all the people of the townland into one house, for dancing, singing and storytelling.'

airt/art [n., <Ir. *aird*, point of compass] (Ulster). Direction. **1913** Alexander Irvine, *My Lady of the Chimney Corner*: '"Morra, bhoy!" says I. "Luks like snow," says he (it was July). "Ay," says I, "we're goin' t'have more weather; th'sky's in a bad art..."' Hence **all airts and parts** [n. phr., commonly **all arts and parts**] (Ulster). Everywhere; (less commonly) everything. **1938** Seumas MacManus, *The Rocky Road to Dublin*: 'The fair-day was a wonderful day...the hucksters and the gamesters gathered from all airts and

parts to make the countryside a holiday.' **1979** John Morrow, *The Confessions of Proinsias O'Toole*: '"I niver wanted any art or part of the bastard. He wallops in here slabberin' about 'Meaningful Dialogues' an' 'Power Bases' an' things…"'

airy [adj.]. 1. [<Ir. *aerach*, eerie, haunted]. As thus; (of person) mentally unbalanced. **1850** William Allingham, *Poems*, 'The Fairies': 'Up the airy mountain,/Down the rushy glen,/We daren't go a-hunting,/For fear of little men.' **1932** Seán O'Faoláin, *Midsummer Night Madness*, 'The End of the Record': '"After he died she went a bit airy so they had to bring her to us."' 2. [<Sc. *idem*, vain, conceited]. As thus. **1914** George Fitzmaurice, *The Pie-Dish*: 'FATHER TROY …wasn' there a strain of lunacy in the Pringles of Lisroe? MARGARET (*hotly*) Indeed there was not, but they being a little airy in themselves the same as the Carmodys of Moinveerna…'

aish [n., <Ir. *aos*, people] (Cork). Person, individual (Beecher).

aisy riz see **riz** 2.

aizel [n., <Sc. *aizle*, hot ember] (Ulster). Cinder, as in **burnt to an aizel** (adj. phr.).

alanna [exclam., <voc. of Ir. *leanbh* (n.), child]. Term of affection. **1886** Patrick Kennedy, *Legendary Fictions of the Irish Celts*: 'So she went over and soothered [q.v.] him, and said "Come, alanna, let me dress you, and we'll go and be christened."' **1962** Brendan Behan, *Quarryman* (Cork), 'That Woman': '"Mother, get the full of your eyes of that one [q.v.]." "Where, alanna?" asks Ria. "There," said Maire, pointing to a tree behind us.' **1991** James Kennedy, *The People who Drank Water from the River*: '"What do they do with the old moons, Daddy?" Billy Gleeson, our nearest neighbour, shot back, "They make stars out of them, alanna."'

alcfeatures [n. pl., portmanteau word, see **holliers**]. **1995** Pádraig O'Rourke, RTÉ Radio, *Music Choice*, 23 July: 'That concert…will send the National Symphony Orchestra off on their annual alcfeatures.'

alickadoo [n., poss. <book by *Alec Kadoo* being read on train journey by player who on that account refused to play cards with Ernie Crawford (Lansdowne & Ireland, 1920s–1930s)]. Rugby club official or committee member, esp. as referred to by younger players. **1995** Jack Mannion, *Irish Times*, 12 Aug: 'Sir — In all the media coverage of impending professionalism in Rugby Union, no mention has been made of the most important species in the game, namely the Alickadoo. To date, the proposed sponsorship of this elite body has not been clarified.'

Alie/Ally Daly, the real [catchphrase, <Alice Daly, *fl.* early C19 (Bernadette Lee, her great-great-granddaughter, quoted DOM); from the quality of her butter]. The sine qua non. **1916** James Joyce, *A Portrait of the Artist* (q.v.) *as a Young Man*: 'Stephen looked at the plump turkey…he remembered the man's voice when he had said "Take that one, sir. That's the real Ally Daly."'

all a baa! [exclam.] (Cork). Uttered when grabbing stake money in card games etc., with a view to making off with it (Beecher); throwing something 'up for grabs'. **1997** Greg Delanty, *Irish Review* (Belfast), 'The Lost Way', Winter/Spring: 'the tatters of a torn exercise page that correcting/Brother Dermot, Sister Benedict or any of the poetry heads [q.v.]/tore in disgust and cast all abaa'. Hence **ba-ing the stake** [vb. phr.].

allaghashtees [n. pl., cf. Ir. *áilleagán*, geegaw, frippery]. Tawdry clothing/ jewellery; geegaws (q.v.).

all airts and parts see **airt**

all behind like the cow's tail [vb. phr.]. Running very late.

all done and dusted [adv. phr.]. Satisfactorily completed. **1996** Catherine Cleary, *Irish Times*, 15 June: 'A smiling Mr Sexton solemnly took the five pieces of paper and added them to his bundle. Two minutes into the court sitting it was all done and dusted.'

all gab and guts (like a young crow) [adj. phr.] (Ulster). Of a raucous and incessant chatterer.

Allied Irish [n. phr., <rhym. sl. 'Allied Irish Bank' = wank]. Masturbation — in this example for a charitable purpose: **1994** Joe O'Connor, *Sunday Tribune*, 27 Nov: 'You turn up, sign a few forms. Then, a quick indulgence in what is known to devotees of rhyming slang as a bit of Allied Irish, and hey presto, there you are 10 quid richer...'

all together like Brown's cows [adv. phr.] (Ulster). In a disorderly gathering, jumble (Patterson).

allyaun [n., cf. Ir. *áilleánach*, dressed-up useless person]. Fool (EW).

Ally Daly, the real see **Alie Daly, the real**

Aluminium, the [nickname]. The ersatz Dub. 'Millennium' of 1988, justified on highly questionable historical grounds. **1994** Patrick O'Leary in Kevin C. Kearns, *Dublin Tenement Life*: 'They [the Liberties dwellers] had fantastic wit. And they absolutely *vandalised* the English language. Do you remember the Millennium? That was the "aluminium year"...Maybe that's just their way of getting back at the English. To make a shambles of their language.' **1996** *Sunday Tribune*, 10 Mar: 'Who would have thought, even before the "aluminium year" as the Millennium was called, that dear old dirty Dublin could rival Paris or Rome as a prime location for a weekend away.'

Alumnach [nickname, term of contempt, <Ir. *Albanach* (n.), Scotsman: Scots were first Protestant planters in Donegal] (Ulster). Englishman.

amadaun/amadan/amadán [n., <Ir. *amadán*, fool]. As thus, invar. masc. **1979** Jack McBride, *Traveller in the Glens* (of Antrim): 'Now an "amadaun" is a foolish person, and so is a "gulpin" [q.v.], but the difference between the two is that the "gulpin" is, in addition to being a bit of a fool, also conceited and self-assertive.' See also **oanshagh**.

ambaist/im bhaiste [exclam., <Ir. *im bhaiste*, by my baptism]. Employed to preface evasive answer or show perplexity.

American lad [nickname]. Unpopular imported US fatty bacon. See **lad** 1.

American Wake [n. phr.]. Farewell celebration for departing emigrants to that continent. **1986** Padraic O'Farrell, *'Tell me, Sean O'Farrell'*: 'The strange thing was that there was no fuss about emigration. No "American Wakes", or anything that you read about. You see, nearly every family had a son or daughter leaving for America.' **1991** John B. Keane, *Love Bites and Other Stories*: 'they journeyed to Ballybunion...and they were graciously received and given credit and presented with cold plates for it so happened that there was an American wake in progress.' **1996** Leslie Matson, *Méiní, The Blasket Nurse*: 'in all probability they would never see their home and people again. On the [Blasket] island there would have been an "American Wake" on the eve of departure...'

amossa/mossa/musha [exclam., <Ir. *Muise! Mhuise!*, Well! Well!]. As thus; and as enclitic. **1981** Victor O'D. Power, *Kitty the Hare* (q.v.): ''Twas nearly dark, mossa, by the time I came to the bend of the road...'

amplish/amplush [n. & vb., <Ir. *aimpléis* (n.), trouble, difficulty; cf. Lat. *non plus*, nothing more]. Disadvantage; place at a disadvantage. **1833** William Carleton, *Traits and Stories of the Irish Peasantry*, 'Going to Maynooth': ''Like I'm not often at a loss for something to say but thon boy had me teetotally amplushed!'' Hence **at an amplish** [adj. phr.]. At a loss (to know).

amsha/emsha [n., cf. Ir. *aimseach* (adj.), accidental, unfortunate]. Misfortune.

ancient [adj., <Sc. *idem*, precocious (of children)] (Ulster). As thus; cunning (of animals); picturesque (of scenery).

andramartins/andremartins [n. pl., poss. <individual 'Andrew Martin', renowned for irresponsible/frivolous behaviour]. As thus. **1995** Phil O'Keeffe, *Down Cobbled Streets, A Liberties Childhood*: '''You'll have my good kitchen floor possin' wet [see **poss out**] with your andremartins,'' and she wedged me on a chair and dried my hair till the scalp tingled...' Hence **andrew martining** [pres. part.] in same sense.

Andytown [nickname, abbrev.]. Republican suburb of Andersonstown, Belfast. **1995** Eamonn McCann, *Sunday Tribune*, 1 Oct: 'It's understandable that a warm-hearted southern nationalist of romantic bent should be bowled over by the activists of Andytown.' **1995** Anon. (Belfast drug dealer), *Irish Times*, 4 Oct: '"It scares the f... out of me that some day the Provos will bundle me into the back of a car and bring me to be tortured in some house in Andytown..."'

angashore/angishore [n., <Ir. *ainciseoir*, peevish person]. As thus. **1866** Patrick Kennedy, *Legendary Fictions of the Irish Celts*: '"Well, he said nothing till he and his mother were up at the fire, and the *angashore* (wretch) of a child in his bed in the room."' **1948** George Fitzmaurice, *Dublin Magazine*, 'There are Tragedies and Tragedies', July/Sept: 'GEOFFREY What signifies anything now but the picture we see before us of these two angashores, stricken in their misery...' **1966** Patrick Boyle, *At Night All Cats are Grey*, 'The Metal Man': 'It takes the folding dough to put manners on a publican. "That poor angashore is on my conscience," says Tailor.'

animal gang [nickname]. Members of the Fascist Blueshirt movement, 1920s– 1930s; violent street gang in gen., esp. Dub. **1936** *Irish Times*, 15 Feb: 'The recent riot at Donnybrook between the "Animal" and "Tiger" "gangs"...marks a recrudescence of certain characteristics that, as short as seventy years ago, rendered it unsafe for the unarmed and unwary to wander round the city after nightfall.' **1961** Dominic Behan, *Teems of Times and Happy Returns*: '"Well," Mr Devoy was saying, "accordin' to the way I heard it, the 'animal' gang thought it'd be a good idea to take over the stalls from the Liverpool boys, so they piled into the boat at the North Wall, armed with razors and iron bars..."' **1962** Eamonn Martin, *Globe* (Toronto), 15 Sept: 'Then, through the drizzling rain, appeared a large and ugly mob organised by the Irish Christian Front, otherwise known as the Blue Shirts, or Animal Gang, which supported Generalissimo Francisco Franco.'

ankle-spring warehouse [n. phr.]. The stocks. **Late C18** Anon., *Lord Altham's Bull*: 'Oh! boys, if de mosey [q.v.] was keeper of de ancle-spring warehouse, you cud not help pitying him; his hide smoked like Ned Costigan's brewery...'

annahydion [n., <?] (Ulster). 'Ignorant, ill-informed person' (Pepper).

Annie no rattle [n. phr.] (Ulster). 'One who pipes up at the end of the conversation' (TT).

annoy [vb., gen. passive, <OF *anoeir*, become distressed, <Late Lat. *mihi in odio est*, it is hateful to me (DOM)] (Ulster). Upset, distress. **1991** Shane Connaughton, *The Run of the Country*: '"That Rinty Reilly, he'd annoy a nation. He once sold me husband, RIP, a jacket and when he got it home it only had the one sleeve."'

anonder/anunder [prep., <'in under', <Sc. *idem*, beneath] (Ulster). As thus. **1925** Louise McKay, *Mourne Folk*: '"Ye're welcome, mem. Any frien' of Miss Gilmour's is welcome 'anondher' this roof."' See also **inanunder**.

any-which-way [adv.]. Randomly, in disorderly manner. **1989** Hugh Leonard, *Out after Dark*: 'I packed, ramming my clothes any-which-way into a suitcase...'

Ape, the [nickname]. Thomas Fitzgerald (C13). **1824** Thomas Crofton Croker, *Researches in the South of Ireland*: 'The other abbey [North Abbey, Youghal, Co. Cork] was founded by Thomas Fitzgerald, commonly called the Ape, a name bestowed on him in consequence of the tradition that a tame baboon or ape, at his father's castle in Tralee, had snatched him from his cradle, and, ascending the highest part of the walls, carried the infant about in his arms for a considerable time...'

apt [adv.] (Ulster). Certainly. **1966** Patrick Boyle, *At Night All Cats are Grey*: '"You certainly picked a choice spot," I say. "Bloody apt I did. Yer man[q.v.]'ll stay roosting down there till the crack of dawn."'

arcan [n., <Ir. *arcán*, smallest piglet of litter] (Ulster). Stunted adult/child; lively, light-hearted fellow (CUD).

ardhews [n. pl., <Ir. *ardú*, exaltation, excitement]. 1. (Ulster). Antics, capers (CUD). 2. Male erection (DOM).

arklooker/dark looker [n., <Ir. *earc luachra*, lit. lizard of the rushes]. Lizard, newt. **1904** George Bernard Shaw, *John Bull's Other Island*: 'PATSY I was afeerd o forgetn it; and then may be he'd a sent the grasshopper or the little dark looker into me at night to remind me of it. (*The dark looker is the common grey lizard, which is supposed to walk down the throats of incautious sleepers and cause them to perish in a slow decline.*)' Also **dearg–luchra** [n., Ir. *idem*, red lizard]. **1943** George A. Little, *Malachi Horan Remembers*: '"My shirt was open, and I felt something as cold as death stealing over my breast. I leapt to my feet, and there was dearg-lucra [*sic*] making off as fast as his legs could carry him…"' See also **athlukard, mankeeper**.

armory [n., <Fr. *armoire*, cupboard] (Ulster). Sideboard.

arnaun [n., <Ir. *airneán*, sitting up late at night]. As thus.

aroo/aroon/eroo [exclam., <voc. of Ir. *rún* (n.), love]. Term of endearment. **1829** Gerald Griffin, *The Collegians*: '"Run into the gentleman, Mike, eroo," she exclaimed, without even laying aside the candle…' Also **roon** in same sense. **1689** Anon., *The Irishman's Prayers*: 'O brother Teague, and Teague my roon,/ Arra [see **arrah!**] what shall we do quickly and soon…'

around/round the world for sport [adv. catchphrase]. In an unnecessarily circumambient or disorganised/excessive fashion.

arrah! [interj., <Ir. *ara*, but now! Really! Truly!]. As thus. 'Used at the beginning of a clause in an expostulatory or deprecating sense…' (Dinneen). **1705** John Michelburne, *Ireland Preserved*: 'DERMOT Arrah Joy [q.v.], cozen Teigue, fill [will] you let de trooparr lie at my house, and keep my wife faarme [warm] in de cold morning.'

arrangement see **awkward arrangement**

arse about face [adv. phr.]. Backwards, the wrong way.

arse over kick [adv. phr.] (Dub.). Head over heels. **1987** Lar Redmond, *Emerald Square*: '[I] nearly went arse over kick into the quarry. The strong cane I held bent over, as one of the cannibal trout fought for his life.'

arseward [adj. & adv.]. 1. [adj.] (Ulster). Obstinate. 2. [adv.]. In reverse motion, as in **arseward backwards** [adv. phr.].

art see **airt**

article [n.]. Small (female) person; gen. term of affection or derog. both sexes. **1966** Patrick Boyle, *At Night All Cats are Grey*, 'Suburban Idyll': '"A common article from the back streets of some foreign city," she said.' **1968** Myles na gCopaleen, *The Best of Myles*: 'the wife is a Cork girl, a right [see **right** 1.] flighty article'.

artist [n., derog.]. Rogue. **1944** James Joyce, *Stephen Hero*: 'Stephen told her to apply to McCann who was the champion of women. She laughed at this and said with genuine dismay "Well, honestly, isn't he a dreadful-looking artist?"' **1991** Bob Quinn, *Smokey Hollow*: '"So you're not?" "Not what?" "An artist." His father suspended his concentration to consider the small nuisance interrogating him. He made an effort. "Maybe I'm a quare [q.v.] artist."'

ashipet/ashypot [n., cf. Sc. *ashie-pet*, idle slattern, kitchen drudge] (Ulster). Person who always stays at the fireside, 'hugging the fire'; mollycoddle.

ask me arse see **axe me arse**

assel teeth [n. pl., <Sc. *idem*, molars] (Ulster). As thus.

Assembly's College [nickname]. Presbyterian College, Belfast. **1983** J.A. Todd, foreword to W.F. Marshall, *Livin' in Drumlister*: 'In the autumn of 1980, he [Marshall] and his elder brother, R.L., began their theological course at The Presbyterian College, Belfast, familiarly known as Assembly's College.'

Assembs, the [nickname]. Meeting room and theatre, latterly cinema, South Mall, Cork. **1970** Pádraig Mac Póilín, *Cork Holly Bough*: 'a famous Cork cinema of yesteryear, the Assembly Rooms — or as it was in the vernacular, the "Assembs"'.

ass's gallop [n. phr.]. Brief period of time. **1995** Brendan O'Carroll, *The Chisellers* (q.v.): 'Mr Wise had certainly perked up a lot in the initial months of his working in the shop, this had been as short and sweet as an ass's gallop.'

ass's roar [n. phr.] as in **within an ass's roar of** [catchphrase, more gen. in neg.]. In close proximity. **1995** Patrick Boland, *Tales from a City Farmyard*: 'Then my Dad was clearly heard by all within an ass's roar of him: "That fucking cat will be in the dung heap today, with his head stuck up his arse."' **1995** Phil O'Keeffe, *Down Cobbled Streets, A Liberties Childhood*: '"God forbid the fever ever comes knockin' at my door." "They slake the walls with lime, and then put sticky tape over the bedroom door and nobody's let within an asses roar 'f it."' **1995** Shane Connaughton, *A Border Diary*: 'What he did do was call the RUC [Royal Ulster Constabulary]. Normally the RUC would not have come within an ass's roar of the place.' See also **donkey's bray**.

as the fellow said see **fellow**

asthore/store [exclam., <voc. of Ir. *stór* (n.), treasure]. Term of endearment. **1958** Frank O'Connor, *An Only Child*: '"But, my store, I have no home now."'

astray in the head/mind [adj. phr.]. Very worried; mentally deranged. See **away**.

atallatall [adv. phr., latterly Paddyism]. Not at all. **1996** John S. Doyle, RTÉ Radio, *Morning Ireland*, 'It Says in the Papers', 2 Dec: 'One yellow line means no parking at all; two yellow lines means no parking atallatall.'

ate-the-bolts [n.] (Ulster). Glutton for work.

ate-your-bun [n.]. term of contempt. **1997** Joe O'Donnell, *Independent on Sunday* (London), 'Seraphim Preening', 9 Mar: '"Yeh little git [q.v.]. You told me you wanted to write your bleedin' memoirs, and I believed you, didn't I? Foolish ate-your-bun dat I am."'

a thaisge see **haisge**

Athens of Ireland, the [nickname]. Cork city. **1975** Davis & Mary Coakley, *Wit and Wine*: 'At this period [early C19] Cork had so many literary men that the city became known as "the Athens of Ireland".'

athlukard [n., <Ir. *earc luachra*, lit. 'lizard of the rushes', newt]. As thus. Swallowing an athlukard was believed to induce wasting etc. The cure was to hang oneself upside down over a dish of bacon which attracted it. See **arklooker**, **mankeeper**.

athra [adv., <Sc. *athraw*, off the straight, crosswise, <ON *um thvert*, transversely] (Ulster). The wrong way.

athrimmel [adj., <Sc. *trimmle* (vb.), tremble]. Confused, out of countenance. **1943** George A. Little, *Malachi Horan Remembers*: '"He had the heart of corn [q.v.]. You could learn from him; he did not put you all of 'athrimmel' like Hughes…"'

atomy [n., <'anatomy' <Sc. *idem*, skeleton, term of contempt] (Ulster). As thus.

at oneself [adj. phr.] (Ulster). Healthy; prosperous.

attercap/ottercop/ettercap [n., <Sc. *idem*, irascible person, <OE *attorcoppa*, spider — lit. poison cap] (Ulster). 'Person who is very easily annoyed' (SH); upstart, cheeky person; small, insignificant person. **1948** John O'Connor, *Come Day — Go Day*: '"How you're going to kneel down at the Altar tomorrow morning I do not know. Where's the other wee [q.v.] ottercopp [*sic*]?"'

Atty Hayes's goat [n. phr.] as in **as old as Atty Hayes's goat** [catchphrase] (Cork). Very old. **1996** *Irish Times*, 6 May: 'To be as old as Atty Hayes's goat is still, in Cork, an indication of great antiquity and recalls an animal beloved of the father of Sir Henry Brown Hayes, who built Vernon Mount [Corraghcon-way, near Douglas] in 1780.'

aul', auld for words and phrases beginning thus see also under **old, oul', ould**

aul-farrand/farrant [adj., <Sc. *idem*, old-fashioned, precocious] (Ulster). Cunning; precocious.

aumlach [adj. & adv., cf. Ir. *amlóireacht* (n.), awkwardness]. Awkward; awkwardly.

Auxies [nickname, abbrev.]. Auxiliary division of the Royal Irish Constabulary, recruited from Brit. army ex-officers, 27 July 1920. **1975** Séamus de Burca, *Dublin Historical Record*, 'Peadar Kearney (1883–1942)', Mar: 'Peadar was ordered to get up and dress. The Auxie remarked on the fresh wound on his cheek and sneered at the terse explanation of how he came by it.' **1993** Paddy Tuohy in Michael Verdon, *Shawlies* (q.v.), *Echo Boys* (q.v.), *the Marsh and the Lanes* (q.v.): *Old Cork Remembered*: 'As the night wears on, the city [Cork] continues to burn... One Auxie, menacing and hysterical, screams he will kill every Sinn Féin bastard in Cork.' **1995** Eoin Neeson, *Irish Times*, 21 July: 'I would be grateful for any data confirming makeshift uniforms so far as the Auxies were concerned.'

avic [form of address, <voc. of Ir. *mac* (n.), son]. **1995** Aidan Higgins, *Donkey's Years*: 'sending the dun-coloured ball down the field to where a pile of discarded clothes served for goal posts. "Now Tom avic, into him!"'

avourneen see **mavourneen**

awa [n., <'away'] (Ulster). Substitutes for proper name, word, etc. in lapses of memory. Cf. Fr. *Monsieur Un Tel* etc.

a-waitin' on see **waited on**

away [adv.]. Taken by the fairies; not right in the head (see **right** 2.). **1907** J.M. Synge, *The Aran Islands*: 'He had seen two women who were "away" with them [the fairies], one a young married woman, the other a girl.' **1938** Seumas MacManus, *The Rocky Road to Dublin*: 'Roisin, looking at him with pain in her eyes, said to her husband, "He's *away*. He must have met the mist [the *ceo draíochta*, druid mist] and been taken in it.' Hence **away with the fairies** [adj. phr.]. Out of this world. **1996** Lise Hand, *Sunday Tribune*, 1 Dec: 'So, while I was in the shop, I had an oul free flick through *Hello!* God Maggie, that magazine's away with the fairies, isn't it?' Also **away in the head/mind** [adj. phr.] (Ulster). Mentally deranged.

away for slates [adv. phr.]. Heading for success, satisfied. **1966** Séamus Murphy, *Stone Mad*: 'then after rubbing it on a bit of Yorkshire Flag you're away for slates'.

awayon! [exclam.] (Ulster). Precedes request to desist, lay off.

away on a hack [adv. phr., <abbrev. of 'hackney', usu. contemptuous but also = a saddle-horse; freq. incorrectly **...in a hack**]. Lucky, successful. **1954** Benedict Kiely, *Honey Seems Bitter*: 'Putting down the receiver, he said: "Boy, you're in the swim. You're away on a hack."' **1965** Lee Dunne, *Goodbye to the Hill*: 'I knew that if I could get talking to him, I'd be away in a hack.' **1996** Paul O'Kane, *Irish Times*, 28 Jan: 'In the mid-1980s, there seemed to be one [Italian restaurant] every few steps. At the time most were unlicensed, so patrons would buy bottles from a nearby "offy" [off-licence premises] and be away in a hack as they say in the North.'

away to the hills = away in the head (see **away**)

away with oneself [adj. phr.] (Ulster). Proud, happy.

away with the band [adj. phr.] (Ulster). The worse for drink.

away with the donkey [adj. phr.] (Ulster). Lost.

awkward arrangement [n. phr.]. Clumsy individual.

axe/ask me arse [exclam. & nickname]. 1. [exclam.]. Vigorous rebuttal. **1975** John Ryan, *Remembering How We Stood*: 'I might have got off with a simple "Axe me arse" — but even that I was in no mood to relish.' **1991** Bob Quinn, *Smokey Hollow*: 'She drew a breath, looked at them impatiently, and said: "Ah, ask me arse."' 2. [nickname]. Homophonic rendering of Acme Arch (now Dame Lane) off Dame St, Dub.

ayre [n., <Ir. *oighear*, sore produced by chafing or cold]. As thus. See **drab**.

aytin'-house see **eatin'-house**

a zed [exclam., <letters of alphabet] (Ulster). 'Sarcastic answer to question "why"' (TT).

B

ba/baa [n. & vb.]. 1. [n., <ME *baban*, babe]. Child. 2. [n., <ME *baban*, babe]. Cry-baby. **1975** Eilís Brady, *All In! All In!*: 'we have at some time all been called a big baa when we cried over something trivial'. See also **all a baa!**

babby house [n. phr.] (Ulster). Child's playhouse. **1993** Sam McAughtry, *Touch & Go*: 'There were neat, tidy cupboards, a shining new sink, and a ritzy-looking cooker. This is what my mother would have called a babby house...' **1994** Vonnie Banville Evans, *The House in the Faythe*: 'Our babby houses were moveable feasts and when one palled after days, weeks or hours depending on our humours...we upped stakes, prised our chainies [q.v.] out of their resting places...and set off for fresh fields and pastures new.' **1995** Monica Carr in Seán Power (ed.), *Those were the Days, Irish Childhood Memories*: 'It [the tree] grew tall over the wall behind which we had a marvellous "babby house", entrance to which was effected by pulling back a lovely springy branch...'

babe [n., <*Babe*, Austral. film featuring a pig]. Term of abuse. **1996** *Irish Times*, 26 Mar: 'An eight-year-old girl...burst tearfully into the staffroom to announce that a certain boy...has called her "Babe". Mild surprise all round, until we discover that the word has not been used Bogart-style as a term of endearment; rather it is a reference to the eponymous pig of current cinema fame...'

Baby Power [nickname, <John Power & Sons, whiskey distillers, formerly of Dub.]. Popular small bottle containing a 'glass' (q.v.) not uncommonly carried on the person as a readily accessible restorative. **1970** Christy Brown, *Down All the Days*: '"Two dozen, John...a baby Powers and God bless you boy...put that on the slate, me little dote [q.v.]..."' **1989** Hugh Leonard, *Out after Dark*: 'I peered behind one of the shelves [of Parsons bookshop] and was in time to see him [Patrick Kavanagh] draining a Baby Power as fast as it would empty.' **1991** James Kennedy, *The People who Drank Water from the River*: 'Some of us took a few drags of a cigarette. One or two I knew had a slug out of a baby Power.'

bachle see **bauchle**

back in one's box [prep. phr.]. Deflated, reduced to a proper sense of one's own importance, as in **put s.o. back in his/her box** [vb. phr.].

Back of/Behind God Speed [n. phr.]. 'A place...so far off that the virtue of your wish of *God-Speed* to a person will not go with him so far' (PWJ). Cf. Austral. sl. 'beyond the Black Stump' in same sense. **1986** Padraic O'Farrell, *'Tell me, Sean O'Farrell'*: 'My father, also called Sean...hailed from a place at the back of God speed in the County Roscommon, called Four-Mile-House.'

backset [n.] (Ulster). Relapse.

backspang [n., <Sc. *spang*, spring, bound, leap] (Ulster). 'Impromptu back somersault' (YDS); underhand trick. **1983** W.F. Marshall, *Livin' in Drumlister*, 'The Runaway': 'She has no backspangs in her either,/No harm in her more than a hen,/If I take maybe wan or two half-wans [see **half-one**]/She niver gets up on her en' [see **up on one's end**].'

backy [adj., <Ir. *bacach*, lame]. As thus.

badach see **boddagh**

bad cess [n. phr., poss. <'cess', assessment, levy, or abbrev. of 'success' (DHS); *c.*1850–]. Invocation of misfortune. **1879** Charles J. Kickham, *Knocknagow*: 'her smile is before me every hour uv the day; an' bad cess to me but I think, this blessed minit, 'tis her hand I have a hoult of instead uv this flail'. **1995** Eanna Brophy, *Sunday Tribune*, 6 Aug: '*Dinny*: Well, bad cess to them anywa', sure they haven't even topped the TAMs once yet and we're [the TV serial *Glenroe*] always doing it!'

badinas [n., <'bathing' (local pronun.) + endearment suffix] (Cork). Bathing suit.

bad lad see **lad** 2.

badly done [adj. phr.] (Ulster). Embarrassed.

Bad Man Below [nickname]. The Devil. **1938** Seumas MacManus, *The Rocky Road to Dublin*: 'The question arose whether the Bad Man Below used turf for fuel.'

bad scran see **scran**

bad swally [n. phr.] (Ulster). Fast eater.

bad with the bravelies [adj. phr.] (Ulster). Not ill at all. See **bravely**.

bag [n. & vb.]. 1. [n.] as in **give s.o. the bag** [vb. phr., deceive, abandon (a thing), slip away from s.o. (C16–17), dismiss, cf. give s.o. the sack (C18–19)]. As thus. **1675–95** Anon., *Purgatorium Hibernicum*: 'And den, fen dou has play'd de vagge [wag],/To give me, as before, de bagge!' 2. [vb.]. Poach (fish). **1968** John Healy, *The Death of an Irish Town*: 'We used bag the Moy, at the back of the house, and in the snug kitchen we'd pour out the gleaming, wriggling haul of brown trout…'

bageen cloth [n., <'bag' + Ir. dimin. *ín*]. Cloth made from flour bags. **1995** Éamon Kelly, *The Apprentice*: 'There was a bageen cloth on the table. This was a couple of flour bags opened out, sewn together and washed and ironed, but the brand of flour was still plain to be seen. "Pride of Erin 120 lbs".'

bagging can [n. phr., cf. Brit. sl. *bagging*, food taken between meals (DHS)]. Receptacle. **1997** Mary Manley, *Irish Times*, 19 Feb: 'Back then [World War II] there weren't many cafes around, and we couldn't afford the ones that were there, so I used to be sent down with a "bagging can" full of tea for all the [Moore St, Dub.] traders…'

baghal see **bauchle**

bagle/beagle [n., <OF *bé-gueule*, open throat] (Ulster). Noisy, ill-mannered person. Also **bagle's gowl, a** [n. phr., <'beagle', hunting dog + *gowl* <Sc. *idem* <ON *gaula* (vb.), bark, howl]. Proximity, as in 'he wasn't within a beagle's gowl of the price I was asking' (Pepper). Cf. ass's roar (q.v.).

bags [n.]. 1. [n., in sing. sense] as in **oul' bags**. Despicable individual, gen. male. **1977** Flann O'Brien, *The Hair of the Dogma*: 'Wasn't that a dirty one, th'oul bags?' Also **make a bags of** [vb. phr.]. Make a mess of. **1996** Hugo Duffy, *Irish Times*, 24 Feb: 'In fact Mala means an eyebrow, so must we sympathise with the citizens of Eyebrow [Mallow, Co. Cork] because at a passing glance the name may be taken to mean a bag? Certainly this method of double translation is well fitted to make a bags of our language.' 2. [n. pl.] (Ulster). Intestines, guts.

bail/bale out [vb.] (railway). Clear locomotive firebox of detritus of inferior wartime (WWII) fuel. **1963** Martin Whyte, *Journal of the Irish Railway Record Society*, 'Fifty Years of a Loco Man's Life', Spring: 'many are the tales that could be told of the strenuous efforts made to keep the trains running. "Baling out" became part of the footplate man's vocabulary, and a regular practice on most trains…' **1978** Bernard Share, *The Emergency*: 'For drivers on the Great Southern Railways …"bailing out" had become a regular and unwelcome part of the daily routine. It meant cleaning out the fire, sometimes after a journey of only five miles or so, and relighting it with timber from any available source.'

bake/bakes [n.]. 1. [<?] as in **make a bake/bakes of** [vb. phr., <?; cf. *bags* (q.v.)] (Cork). Make a mess of. Also **it's a bakes** (Cork). It's useless, disappointing. 2. (Ulster). Bees'/ants'/wasps' nest (YDS). 3. See **beak**.

baldy [adj.]. In compounds **baldy-conscience**, **baldy nopper**, **baldy peelo**, **baldy sconce** jeer at child with head shaved on account of ringworm etc.

bale out see **bail out**

bales of briquettes [n., <turf (peat) briquettes]. Platform-soled shoes.

ball-hop [n., <Gaelic games]. Rumour, unsupported theory, deliberate deception/ fabrication. **1973** Noël Conway, *The Bloods* (q.v.): 'They kept pumping the questions but Oglesby, who'd only been trying to cheer them up with a ball-hop,

kept his lip buttoned tight.' Hence **ballhopper** [n.]. **1996** Christy Kenneally, *Maura's Boy, A Cork Childhood*: '"Mam, is me hem straight?" "You could tug it down a small bit." "Auntie Noreen, you have a ladder." "Where? Go 'way, ye ballhopper. Hold up the mirror for me."' See also **hop ball**.

ball in the decker [n. phr.]. Children's street game. **1939** Sean O'Casey, *I Knock at the Door*: '"Let's have Ball in the Decker first," said Johnny, "An' afterwards, Duck on the Grawnshee [q.v.]..." Then they all laid their caps in a row at an angle against the wall of a house. They took turns...trying to roll a ball into one of the caps...'

ball of malt (q.v.) [n. phr.]. Measure of whiskey. **1975** John Ryan, *Remembering How We Stood*: 'But all these things could be...ameliorated by a good laugh, a charitable act, a kind thought or, better again, a ball of malt.' **1979** Frank Kelly, *The Annals of Ballykilferret*: 'The heavy drinker receives a book of green coupons from the manager at the local labour exchange...Each coupon can be exchanged at the local public house for one pint of stout...in exceptional cases the applicant is issued with a book of red coupons, which he can exchange for balls of malt.'

balloon [n.] (Ulster). Talkative person, one full of 'hot air'.

Ballygobackwards [n.]. Epitome of rural backwater from urban perspective. **1997** John Boland, *Irish Times*, 7 June: 'Alas, the asking price of £16,000 [for Joyce's birthplace] was a thousand more than I could come up with at the time. Nowadays you wouldn't get a lean-to in Ballygobackwards for that price.'

ballyhays [n.] as in **make a ballyhays of it** [vb. phr., poss. <*hames* (q.v.)] (Cork). Make a mess of.

ballyhoo [n., cf. US *idem*, advertising or publicity, esp. of a raucous or colourful sort (DAS), poss. <place name, e.g. *Ballyhoo*, Screen, Co. Wexford, but not proven]. Exaggeration, 'hype'.

Ballyhooly [n., <village near Fermoy, Co. Cork, formerly notorious for faction fights]. Bad trouble. **1879** Charles J. Kickham, *Knocknagow*: 'muttering curses on Mr Beresford Pender...for being the cause of sending him upon a journey, that would be sure to entail "Ballyhooly" upon his devoted head when he got home'.

Ballymena anthem [n. phr., <Co. Antrim town, & pun on 'mean'] (Ulster). Begrudging complaint of 'what's in it for me?' (Pepper). Cf. **1983** Alice Kane, *Songs and Sayings of an Ulster Childhood*: 'If you weren't so Ballymena/And you had some Ballymoney/You could buy a Ballycastle/To be your Ballyhome.'

ballyrag [vb., poss. <Oxford University sl., 1750s–]. Abuse, revile, scold.

balmed out [p. part. as adj.] (Cork). Exhausted, 'flaked out'. **1996** Christy Kenneally, *Maura's Boy, A Cork Childhood*: 'The men were in their shirts and braces, reading the paper or "balmed out" under it.'

Baluba [n., <Katangan tribe, former Belgian Congo]. Term of generalised contempt. On 9 Nov 1960 eleven Ir. army soldiers serving with the UN were ambushed by Balubas with the loss of nine lives. **1977** Wesley Burrowes, *The Riordans*: 'Batty said that no one but himself was entitled to call her [Minnie] a miserable oul faggot [q.v.] and called Johnny a lump of lard. Johnny called Batty an oul Baluba, one word borrowed another and the coats came off.' **1984** Fergal Tobin, *The Best of Decades*: 'The word "Baluba" passed into Irish colloquial speech as a synonym for barbarism, savagery, or plain oafishness.' **1996** RTÉ TV serial, *Glenroe*, 10 Mar: 'STEPHEN Everyone thought that Shirley would go to pieces when the Balubas murdered George...'

balyor/balyore/baulyor etc. [vb. & n., <?] (Ulster). 'Shout and roar in a state of great agitation' (YDS); such an outcry; loud, noisy individual.

bamer/beamer [n., <?]. Straw hat. **1939** James Joyce, *Finnegans Wake*: 'still berting dagabout in the same straw bamer, carryin his overgoat under his

schulder, sheepside out'. **1975** Eilís Brady, *All In! All In!*: 'When men wore straw bamers in the summer, children used to try to count a hundred of them and so get their wish. The first to catch sight of one claimed it with the words: "My straw bamer one, two, three,/ Nobody has one only me."'

ban! [interj., cf. Ir. *banbh* (n.), piglet]. Call to pigs. See **hurish!**

banafan [n., <Ir. *banbhán*, piglet]. Chubby youngster.

Banaghan as in **he beats Banaghan** [erroneously given by Grose: 'an Irish saying of one who tells wonderful stories. Perhaps Banaghan was a minstrel famous for dealing in the marvellous.']. See **beat Banagher**.

Banagher see **beat Banagher**

banatee [n., <Ir. *bean a' tí*, woman of the house]. As thus; housewife. **1961** Flann O'Brien, *The Hard Life*: 'The banatee up at six in the morning to get ready thirteen breakfasts out of a load of spuds...' **1991** James Kennedy, *The People who Drank Water from the River*: 'My mother was a *bean a' tí*. This does not mean that she was a housewife in the modern sense. *Bean a' tí* means *the* woman of *the* house, a title which has some respect built into it.' Also **vanithee** (with aspiration of initial & medial consonants). **1866** Patrick Kennedy, *Legendary Fictions of the Irish Celts*: 'The Vanithee washed their feet, and rubbed them with an ointment that took all the soreness out of their bones...'

band–house player [n. phr., <Old Band House in the Mardyke, where old men played cards (Beecher)] (Cork). Bad card–player.

bang Banagher see **beat Banagher**

Bang! Bang! [nickname]. Tommy Dudley (d. Jan 1981, aged 75), Dub. street character (see **character** 1.). **1981** *Irish Independent*, 12 Jan: 'He was an institution in Dublin during his lifetime. He carried a huge jail key with him around the city, mockingly pointing it at strangers and shouting "Bang Bang".' **1981** Paddy Crosbie, *Your Dinner's Poured*

Out!: 'Bang! Bang! appeared on our scene in the Twenties, but he belonged to the entire city. His favourite hunting-ground was the trams, from one of which he jumped, turning immediately to fire "Bang Bang" at the conductor.' **1987** Lar Redmond, *Emerald Square*: 'Or, if you were lucky, a running gunfight with that famous gun-slinger from the Liberties, Bang-Bang, who, imaginary gun smoking, would shoot it out with half a hundred kids...'

bangers [n. pl., cf. Brit. sl. 'bang' (vb.), have sexual intercourse with]. Testicles. **1987** Lar Redmond, *Emerald Square*: 'For gas [q.v.] I looked up "testicles". "Male reproductive glands" it said. So now I knew. Your bangers!'

bang of the latch [n. phr.]. Last quick drink after time has been called. **1989** Hugh Leonard, *Out after Dark*: 'a long-suffering publican asked them if they had no homes to go to and refused their pleas for "a bang of the latch"'. See **latch**.

bangtail [n.]. Racehorse of questionable ability. **1995** Michael Finlan, *Irish Times*, 3 Aug: 'You may well wonder what Bertie Ahern was up to at the Galway races yesterday laying out good money on the bangtails pounding across the hallowed turf...'

banished [p. part. (as adj.)] (handball), (Cork). Said of ball struck in error out of the court; hence any ball struck out of bounds. **1996** Christy Kenneally, *Maura's Boy, A Cork Childhood*: 'Then he'd open his coat dramatically and all the rubber balls that had been "banished" into his yard from the Quarry would bounce merrily around our front room.'

banjax [vb., 'probably formed by association with "banged", bashed, smashed...' (ODMS)] (Dub.). Injure, ruin, destroy. **1956** Samuel Beckett, *Waiting for Godot*: 'VLADIMIR That seems intelligent all right. But there's one thing I'm afraid of. POZZO Help! ESTRAGON What? VLADIMIR That Lucky might get going all of a sudden. Then we'd be banjaxed.' **1977** Flann O'Brien, *The Hair of the Dogma*: '"Did you not hear? He banjaxed the humorist [humerus]. I thought that was well known."' **1994** Ferdia Mac Anna, *The Ship Inspector*: "'The country's banjaxed," the woman said. "We're a banana republic without the bananas."'

banker [n. & vb., <Fr. *banc* (n.), bench; stonemasons' sl.]. Bench, raised place; provide with same. **1966** Séamus Murphy, *Stone Mad*: "Tis many a boy I bankered in this shed.'

Banks, de/the [abbrev.] (Cork). 'The Banks of My Own Lovely Lee', unofficial Cork anthem, words/music by J.C.S. Hanahan; hence the Lee/Cork city. **1995** Arthur McAdoo, *Cork Holly Bough*: 'if I caught an early train, I was home by the "Banks" in the early hours of the following morning'. See also **down the banks**.

bannalanna [n., <Ir. *bean na leanna*, woman of the ale]. Woman who sells beer over the counter.

Banner County [nickname, <support displayed at monster meeting, 1828, to nominate Daniel O'Connell as parliamentary candidate]. Co. Clare, esp. as applied to representative GAA teams. **1995** *Irish Times*, 8 Aug: 'The shouts of "Come on the Banner" were deafening as the team made its way through the crowd...' **1995** *Irish Air Letter*, Oct: 'Recent charter activity has included a Shannon–Dublin charter...carrying the Clare team to the All-Ireland final in Dublin. The flight used the radio callsign "Banner 4094".'

bannock [n., <Ir. *bonnóg*, homemade cake]. As thus.

banny [vb., <Ir. *beannaigh*, bless; greet]. Treat gently; cajole.

banshee [n., <Ir. *bean sí*, lit. woman of the fairies]. Spirit the appearance of whom foreshadows a death in the family; any female figure of menace. **1986** Patricia Lysaght, *The Banshee*: 'The knowledge shared by all native Irish speakers and by many people with minimal Irish that *bean sí* meant "fairy woman" is likely to have coloured beliefs and narratives about the death-messenger...' **1988** Gabriel Byrne,

Magill, Mar: 'she said she hoped I wouldn't be afraid of the next picture because the Banshee was in it, but so was Jimmy O'Dea and he was great gas [q.v.]'.

banter [vb., cf. Sc. *banters* (n. pl.), rebukes, admonitions] (Ulster). Challenge to fight, taunt. **1908** Lynn Doyle, *Ballygullion*: 'An' wi' that off he goes like a shot; for he was afeared I might banther him intil buyin' bether.'

banty/bendy [adj. & n.] (Ulster). Bow-legged (individual). **1948** John O'Connor, *Come Day — Go Day*: "'Hello, Pachy," Neilly greeted, "we were down at the score [see **score** 1.] there." "Ah, were you? Where's the banty?"'

bap [n., <Sc. *idem*, small, flat, diamond-shaped bread roll (CSD)] (Ulster). 1. As thus, popularised by Belfast baker Bernard Hughes. 2. Head, as in **lose the bap** [vb. phr.]. **1979** John Morrow, *The Confessions of Proinsias O'Toole*: 'He'd lost the bap completely. Having bounded out of his seat, he stood shaking a trembling fist under my nostrils, orbs birling [q.v.] in an unco-ordinated way...' **1983** *John Pepper's Illustrated Encyclopaedia of Ulster Knowledge*: "'Ye'll have to turn the caar rount and go on to the bottom of the hill...Then if you don't lose the bap ye'll get there soon enough."' See also **lose the head**, **off one's bap**.

bar [n.]. 1. [<?]. Shilling (pre-decimal coin). 2. [metonym, <musical notation]. Song. **1961** Dominic Behan, *Teems of Times and Happy Returns*: 'Whether she was down or up, Mrs Behan always had a bar to give the company, always singing, always gay.' Also **bar of a song**. See also **stave**. 3. [<Ir. *bárr nuachta*, strange news (Dinneen)]. As thus, as in **all the bars** [n. phr.]. All the news and gossip.

barbadoes [vb., <Caribbean island to which Cromwell transported many thousands following the Drogheda massacre, 1649]. **1992** Robert McCrum, William Cran & Robert MacNeil, *The Story of English*: 'A letter of 1655 describes Cromwell as "a terrible Protector...He dislikes shedding blood,

but is very apt 'to barbadoes' an unruly man — has sent and sends us by hundreds to Barbadoes, so that we have made an active verb of it…'"

Barcelona [nickname, <the Sp. city]. Imported silk scarf. **1811** Edward Lysaght, *Poems of the late Edward Lysaght*, 'The Sprig of Shillelah': 'His clothes spick and span new without e'er a speck;/A neat Barcelona tied round his white neck.'

bardicks/bardhiz/bardix [n., <Ir. *pardóg*, pannier: metonym for contents, cf. *brat* (q.v.)]. Belongings. **1983** W.F. Marshall, *Livin' in Drumlister*, 'The Runaway': 'So sez I, "I'll not stan' it no longer,/Ye can take me or lave me, an' min'/Here's the cowlt can take me in the seddle,/With you an' yir bardhiz behin'."'

bareaas [adj., as n. pl., <'bare' + endearment suffix] (Cork). Bare feet, as in **in their bareaas** [adj. phr.]. Going without shoes.

barge [n. & vb., cf. Sc. *bargle* (vb.), squabble, bandy words]. [n.]. Cantankerous woman. **1991** Ferdia Mac Anna, *The Last of the High Kings*: '"I don't want to go to any crummy *barby-cue* anyway. If you're having it, it's bound to be crap." "Fucken barge."' [vb.]. Scold, abuse. **1907** J.M. Synge, *The Shanachie* (q.v.), 'The People of the Glens': 'After prolonged barging he got a glass of whiskey, took off his hat before he tasted it…' **1913** Alexander Irvine, *My Lady of the Chimney Corner*: '"The road's been gey [q.v.] rocky an' we've made many mistakes." "Ay," I said, "we've barged (scolded) a lot, Anna."' **1926** Sean O'Casey, *The Plough and the Stars*: 'CLITHEROE (to Nora) What's wrong, Nora? Did she say anything to you? NORA She was bargin' out of her…'

barking irons [n. pl.]. 'Pistols, from their explosion resembling the bow-wow or barking of a dog. *Irish*' (Grose).

barley-buggle/boggle [n., <Sc. *bogle*, apparition, scarecrow] (Ulster). Scarecrow.

barley play [n. & vb., <Sc. *barley*, call for a truce, poss. <'parley'] (Ulster). 'Call for truce in boys' games' (Patterson).

barmbrack [n., <Ir. *bairín*, loaf + *breac* (adj.), speckled]. Rich fruit loaf. Freq. abbrev. to **brack**. **1951** Sam Hanna Bell, *December Bride*: 'In a short time she was back with a tray on which sat two cups and saucers, buttered barmbrack, and their intimate little supper teapot…' **1995** Éamon Kelly, *The Apprentice*: 'Especially for Hallowe'en night my mother bought a barmbrack. Three objects were hidden in the cake: a pea, a stick and a ring. Whoever got the pea would be forever poor. The finder of the stick would be master over all and the one who got the ring would be the next to marry.'

barney [n. & vb.]. 1. [n.]. Mind, head as in **don't bother your barney** [vb. phr., poss. metonym <rhym. sl. *Barnet Fair* = hair]. 2. [vb., <?]. Chat, collogue.

barney balls [n. phr., <?] as in **make a barney balls of oneself** [vb. phr.]. Make a fool of oneself. **1948** Patrick Kavanagh, *Tarry Flynn*: '"Ah, dry up and don't be making a barney balls of yourself. A person would think you were a missioner."'

barrack room [nickname]. Large bedroom with a number of beds for casual visitors. **1800** Maria Edgeworth, *Castle Rackrent*: '"Is the large room damp, Thady?" said his honor. "Oh, damp, your honor! how should it but be as dry as a bone (says I) after all the fires we have kept in it day and night — it's the barrack room your honor's talking on."'

barrel [vb.]. Move/travel rapidly. **1986** Peter Sheridan, with Jean Costello, *Shades of the Jelly Woman*: 'Larboy said he knew a place off the quays where we could get free cakes. We all barrelled down and Larboy had to get in this window to open the door for the rest of us.'

basket job/turn [n. phr., <woven flexible willow or osier basket in which food was carried] (railway). 'Double home turn' of duty involving night away from home. **1974** P.J. Currivan, *Journal of the Irish Railway Record Society*, 'Engineman's Son', Oct: 'Many enginemen were excellent cooks, being forced to spend at least every second night away from home. They carried

their food supply in a wicker basket; from this comes the name "basket turns" to nights away from home.' **1994** Dan Renehan, *Journal of the Irish Railway Record Society*, 'Basket Jobs', Oct: 'Though men still say "basket job" most use modern travel bags. The last driver to use an actual basket, to my knowledge, was Colbert Dunne of Inchicore.'

baste [vb., <OF *bastir*, sew lightly] (Ulster). Tack, stitch roughly (Todd).

bat [n. & vb.]. 1. [n.]. Hard slap. Also **on the bat of** [adv. phr.]. Approximately. 2. [vb., <ME *bate*, flutter eyelids] as in **I didn't bat an eye** [vb. phr.]. I didn't close my eyes. 3. [n.] as in **bats and bands** [n. pl.] (Ulster). Rude hinges.

bate [n., <?] (Cork). Piece or slice of bread. **1996** Christy Kenneally, *Maura's Boy, A Cork Childhood*: 'Any door on the lane could be opened by a child's push and "bates" of bread and jam were automatically offered and casually accepted.'

batter [n., <Ir. *bóthar*, road] as in **on the batter** [adj. phr.]. Engaged in serious drinking. **1927** Peadar O'Donnell, *Islanders*: '"An' Mary Manus is goin' to keep Manus off the batter."' **1989** Claude Robinot in Michel Sailhan (ed.), *Irlande, 'Le Pub, mode d'emploi'*: 'Les ouvriers agricoles, dès qu'ils étaient en fonds, s'achetaient un tonnelet de poteen et ne desaoulaient pas de la semaine. Ce sport national est connu sous le nom de *batter*.' ('Agricultural workers, when they found themselves in funds, used to buy a cask of poteen [q.v.] and remain drunk for a week. This national sport is known as a *batter*.')

battered [p. part.]. (Of children) More or less forcibly bathed, deloused and dosed on a Saturday night. **1985** Máirín Johnston, *Around the Banks of Pimlico*: 'The same ritual went on in all families and was colloquially known as "being battered". As each child was "battered" a drop of hot water was added [to the galvanised bath], and the same water was used again for the next victim.'

battering [n.]. Dance step. **1971** Breandán Breathnach, *Folk Music and Dances of Ireland*: 'In Limerick it was considered unladylike for a girl to do the grinding step or any other heavy or robust battering and drumming steps...' **1986** Bob Quinn, *Atlantean*: 'Even the typical Conamara dancing called "the battering" is the nearest thing possible to Spanish flamenco.'

battle in, battle out [n. phr.]. Children's game. **1995** Billy French in Mary Ryan et al. (eds.), *No Shoes in Summer*: '"Battle In, Battle Out" was also known as "Relieve-Eh-Oh" [see **relievio**] and had a den which was always strategically placed under the village [Crumlin, Dub.] lamp. The game consisted of two teams — the pursued and the pursuers.'

Battle of Baltinglass, the [nickname]. Confrontation in Co. Wicklow village occasioned by dispute over appointment of postmistress, 1950. **1996** John S. Doyle, *Sunday Tribune*, 13 Oct: 'The Battle of Baltinglass, presented [on TV] by Cathal O'Shannon...was the story of how public pressure in a small Wicklow town overturned the jobbery of a Labour government minister.' **1996** Paul Gorry, *Irish Times*, 29 Oct: 'The Battle of Baltinglass was a shameful episode in the history of Baltinglass; one not spoken of publicly when I was growing up.' See also **the Joy**.

baucagh-shool [n., <Ir. *bacach siúil*, itinerant beggar]. As thus. See **sleeveen**.

bauchle/bachle/baghal [n. & vb., <Sc. Gael. *bachall* (n.), old shoe] (Ulster). 1. [n.]. Down-and-out person, awkward person; messy piece of work. 2. [vb.]. Jilt; treat with contempt; wear shoes out of shape.

baukie [n., cf. Sc. *baukie-bird*, bat] (Ulster). Louse.

baulyor see **balyor**

baurna [n., <Ir. *báirne*, spectre] (Connacht). As thus (DOM).

bawl off [vb., cf. Brit. & US 'bawl out' in same sense] (Cork). Reprimand or rebuke severely. **1966** Séamus Murphy, *Stone Mad*: 'when he got angels to carve he would put boots on their feet!...I've seen those angels myself and when I joked him about them he bawled me off properly.'

baw-ways/wise [adv., cf. Sc. *baugh* (vb.), look/be confused (CSD); ON *bagr* (adj.), awkward, clumsy]. Askew. **1922** James Joyce, *Ulysses*: 'Little Alf was knocked bawways. Faith [q.v.], he was.' **1991** Bob Quinn, *Smokey Hollow*: '"Look at Picasso. They hang his pictures bawways and nobody knows the difference. Chancers [q.v.] that can't even draw a straight line."' **1995** Phil O'Keeffe, *Down Cobbled Streets, A Liberties Childhood*: '"Will ye go out to play like a good child and let me get on with the job. I'll put the sole on baw-wise if I'm not careful."'

Bayno, the [nickname, <Dub. pronun. of 'beano']. Iveagh Play Centre, Francis St (later Bull Alley), 1909–59. **1985** Máirín Johnston, *Around the Banks of Pimlico*: 'Tip-toe to the Bayno,/Where the kids go,/For to get their bun and cocoa,/Tip-toe to the Bayno with me.'

bayrie [n., <Ir. *béire*, goal]. Goal in football or hurling (OTF).

baythur/baytur [n., poss. <'beater'] (Cork). Penis; foolish person (Beecher).

bazer [n., <?] (Cork). Blow (Beecher).

bazz [n., <?] (Cork). Female pubic hair. Also **bazzer** [n.] (Cork). Haircut for men; '[Cork is] Where young Seánie, Gunk and Chaazer/Ask the barber for a bazer [*sic*]…' Niall Tóibín, 'Cork', quoted Beecher. Cf. **1990s** 'Bazzers' hairdressing salon in Washington St, Cork.

beagle see **bagle**

beak/bake [n., cf. Brit. sl. *idem*, nose]. Mouth; face. **1979** John Morrow, *The Confessions of Proinsias O'Toole*: 'I gave him a drag of my fag and inquired: "What have you been up to? Singing off-key?" "You'll laugh on the other side of yer bake some of these days, Francie Fallis," he girned [q.v.] ungratefully…' **1996** Joe O'Connor, *Sunday Tribune*, 9 June: '"Dey are ownee fookin baloobas [see **baluba**] de young wans [q.v.] now, yeh'd want to hear the talk ourra dem in de backa de cab…Picked up one de rubber nigh…Frock up to her wishbone and de langwich ouwa her beak. I blame Madonna."'

beaky lady/man [n. phr.] (Ulster). Truancy officer. Also **beak off** [vb.]. Play truant.

beal/beel/bield [vb., <Sc. *biel*, fester]. As thus; suppurate; throb with pain. **1943** George A. Little, *Malachi Horan Remembers*: '"Till the crack of day it never stopped bealing and throbbing till I thought it must burst. 'I'm fairly knackered [see **knacker**] this time' I thought."' **1985** Máirín Johnston, *Around the Banks of Pimlico*: 'These were chilblains caused by lack of calcium aggravated by the cold. As soon as the heat got at them they went mad throbbing, a condition we called bealing.'

béal bocht [n. phr., Ir. *idem*, poor mouth (q.v.)]. As thus. Hence **béal bochtery** [n. phr.]. **1968** John Healy, *The Death of an Irish Town*: 'it [Charlestown, Co. Mayo] remembers no past, glories in no past, is apathetic of the present and looks to the future with a fearful beal bochtery'.

beamer see **bamer**

Beamer [nickname, <abbrev. + endearment suffix]. BMW motor car. See **mortaller**.

bean-jacks [n., <Ir. *bean*, woman + *jacks* (q.v.), privy, punning imitation of *banjax* (q.v.)]. A female convenience.

bear in the air! [exclam.] (Belfast). Used by prisoners in Long Kesh to warn of the approach of a warder. **1983** Bobby Sands, *One Day in my Life*: '"Bear in the air," someone shouted, warning that there was a screw in the wing outside the cells. That was the call we used when someone detected the jingle of a key, the squeak of a boot or a passing shadow.'

beat/bang Banagher as in **that beats Banagher** [catchphrase, <town in Co. Offaly; or, more probably, Banagher Glen, Roe Valley, Co. Derry]. Said of something that excels or exceeds the norm, as in **that bates Banagher and Banagher bates the divil**. **1913** Alexander Irvine, *My Lady of the Chimney Corner*: '"thin I towld him I'd seen the Banshee [q.v.]! 'That bates Bannagher [*sic*]!' says he. 'It bates the divil,' says I."' **1969** Tom Mac Intyre, *The*

Charollais: '"M'lord — congratulations." "Oh — you've seen the —" "Glimpsed it this evenin', m'lord — doesn't it bate Banagher?"' **1983** William Trevor, *Fools of Fortune*: '"Would you credit that? Well that beats Banagher."'

beaten docket [n. phr., cf. 'strike a docket. To cause a man to become bankrupt: legal and commercial' (DHS)]. S.o. with all resources exhausted. **1995** Shane Connaughton, *A Border Diary*: '"Two days ago I was in Leicester Square and they were handing out invitations in the street. England is a beaten docket. No, Germany is the place."' **1996** Lise Hand, *Irish Times*, 29 Dec: 'But the minister [Ivan Yates] was a beaten docket (strictly equinely speaking, you understand). "I haven't had a good day. I'm a bit behind," he muttered despondently.'

beat the lard out of s.o. [vb. phr.]. Chastise severely. **1952** Bryan MacMahon, *Children of the Rainbow*: '"You'd what?" she said. "I'd beat the lard out of you!" I said. "Once on weekdays and twice on Sundays for good measure!"'

beat the little dish/wee (q.v.) **wheel** [vb. phr., <?]. Cogn. with beat Banagher (q.v.). **1927** Peadar O'Donnell, *Islanders*: '"Well, glory be to God," the mother exclaimed, "if that doesn't beat the wee wheel."' **1948** Patrick Kavanagh, *Tarry Flynn*: '"Jabus [q.v.], that's a dread [q.v.]," said Eusebius, "that bates the little dish as the fellow [q.v.] said."'

bedad [expletive, euphem. for 'by God']. **C.1910** Anon., *Irish Wit and Humour*: '"Come now, sir, did you not come direct from these men to Dublin on Monday last?" "Bedad, I did so," promptly answered the witness.' Also **be the dad**. **1961** Flann O'Brien, *The Hard Life*: 'Be the dad, Mr Hanafin said smiling, Marius will be delighted.'

beddies see **piggybeds**

beddy [adj., <Ir. *beadaí*, fussy about food] (Ulster). As thus; conceited, self-satisfied; interfering, greedy, covetous; forward, cheeky.

bedfast [adj.] (Ulster). Temporarily confined to bed.

beds see **piggybeds**

bedther [n., <Ir. *bodhar* (adj.), numb (of limb)]. Cripple.

beef to the heels like a Mullingar heifer [catchphrase, <Mullingar, Co. Westmeath, centre of a prosperous cattle-raising area]. Said (gen. by males) of a female with sturdy rather than elegant legs. **C19** Pop. ballad, 'The Mullingar Heifer': 'There was an elopement down in Mullingar,/But sad to relate the pair didn't get far,/"Oh fly," said he, "darling, and see how it feels."/ But the Mullingar heifer was beef to the heels.' **1908** Lynn Doyle, *Ballygullion*: 'She had her skirts well kilted up for the runnin', and she made no great sight, I can tell ye; for she was beef to the heels like a Mullingar heifer...'

beel see **beal**

beelie [n., <?] (Ulster). Domestic cat.

beelybatter see **bullia-batter**

beero hour [n. phr.]. Dockers' morning 'tea break'. **1994** Timmy 'Duckegg' Kirwan in Kevin C. Kearns, *Dublin Tenement Life*: 'dockers were the best pint drinkers in the world...They'd drink about five pints before they'd go to work and come out and down to the pub again at beero hour, that's ten in the morning.'

bee's toe [n. phr.] as in **neat as a bee's toe** [adj. phr.] (Ulster). Very neat.

beeswisp see **peaswisp**

bee-up [n.] (Cork). Game similar to **feck** [n.] 1.

beezer [n., poss. <US 'bee's knees', connoting excellence]. As thus.

begannies see **begomentays**

begob/begog [expletive, euphem. for 'by God']. **1650** *Páirlement Chloinne Tomáis*: 'Adubhairt Roibín, "I thanke you, honest Thomas, you shall command all my tobaco." "Begog, I thanke you," *ar Tomás*.' **1946** Myles na gCopaleen, *Irish Writing No. 1*, 'Drink and Time in Dublin', May: 'Another man, I say to meself, would ask people, make a show of himself and maybe get locked up. But not me. I'm smart. Then begob I nearly choked.'

begomentays/begommany/began-nies [exclam., cf. Brit. sl. 'by gum']. Expressive of amazement, affirmation, surprise. **1981** Victor O'D. Power, *Kitty the Hare* (q.v.): 'he told him all about the matter from start to finish, and a droll story it was, begannies'. **1983** W.F. Marshall, *Livin' in Drumlister*, 'John the Liar': '"The Lord bliss me," sez I, "what's wrong?" sez he,/"Be gomentays, I went an' killed two pigs…"'

begor/begorra/begorah/begorrah [expletive, euphem. for 'by God', latterly Paddyism]. **1969** Frank O'Connor, *Masculine Protest*, 'The Teacher's Man': '"I hear the old master was sick again, Tom," said the curate. "Begor he was, Father," said the cobbler.' **1993** Paddy Tyrrell in Joe O'Reilly & Sixth Class, Convent School, Edenderry, *Over the Half Door*: 'Now there's one thing I always remember about Johnny Keane and that was he had real curly hair and if the curl was hanging down you were in trouble for that day. Begor, you would get slapped.'

begrudger [n.]. S.o. who consistently and jealously belittles the achievements of others, cf. Austral. *cut the tall poppies*. **1995** Katie Donovan, *Irish Times*, 31 May: 'Deborah Troop believes it is a good sign that we freely use the term "a nation of begrudgers" to describe ourselves; "It shows an awareness that has grown out of the wound of Irish history."' **1996** Raymond Deane, *Irish Times*, 24 Sept: 'Originally the word "begrudger" accurately described a peculiarly Irish phenomenon: the person who resents another's success. There was a nuance to this: the begrudger often encourages the other person to strive after success, but once that has been achieved, seeks to pull the other down…' Also **begrudgery** [abst. n.]. **1996** Roderick O'Connor, *Sunday Tribune*, 14 Jan: 'There would be no begrudgery if The Corrs [pop group] didn't have something to begrudge, such as their good looks and their commercial sound.' **1996** David Hanly, *Sunday Tribune*, 4 Aug: 'The very idea of the Irish accusing anybody on earth of begrudgery makes one shiver with mirth…I would

put it forward as a tenable theory that it is an entirely Irish invention.' See also **fuck the begrudgers!**

be heaventers!/be hehivins!/be hivinders! [exclam.]. Mild oath. **1927** Peadar O'Donnell, *Islanders*: '"Wasn't I a Home Ruler since the first day I mind [q.v.]?" "He was, be heaventers," Manus said.' **1983** W.F. Marshall, *Livin' in Drumlister*, 'John the Liar': 'I wos mad,/Behivinders ye niver seen a man/As mad as me: I near driv over him…'

Behind God speed see **Back of God speed**

behind the door [adj. phr., gen. in neg.]. Tardy, deficient. **1913** Alexander Irvine, *My Lady of the Chimney Corner*: '"Yer spakin' ov clothes, Jamie; I'm spakin' ov mind, an' ye wor behind the doore whin th' wor givin' it out…"' **1920** Seumas O'Kelly, *The Leprechaun of Kilmeen*: 'Tom Kelleher wasn't behind the door when they were giving out the wits and the craft.' **1995** Phil O'Keeffe, *Down Cobbled Streets, A Liberties Childhood*: 'The decision, as in all these things, would be my mother's…Father was her sounding-post. I never heard him oppose any decision she made in our regard, but he was not behind the door in pointing out the pitfalls.'

be hivinders! see **be heaventers!**

bejabers/bejapers [expletive, euphem. for *bejasus* (q.v.); latterly Paddyism]. **C.1910** Anon., *Irish Wit and Humour*: '"Pat's a-writin' — he's got a quill in his fist." "So he has, be jabers!"' **1925** Louise McKay, *Mourne Folk*: '"Bejabers," said old Hughie, "how will the bed be got inside?"' **1979** Frank Kelly, *The Annals of Ballykilferret*: 'Perhaps he would not have taken the job offered to him if he had heard Norbert mutter: "Be japers I have ye now, ye shite [q.v.]!"' Also, rarely, **jabbers/ jabez**.

bejaminty [expletive, euphem. for 'by Jesus'] (Ulster). **1925** Louise McKay, *Mourne Folk*: '"The biggest trees in Mourne were blew down an' hurled about. Bejaminty, that was a storm!"'

bejapers see **bejabers**

bejasus/bejaysus [n., <expletive, see **Jaysus!**]. Life, vital essence, as in **beat the bejasus out of s.o.** [vb. phr.]. **1991** Roddy Doyle, *The Van*: 'He always used two [tea]bags, squeezed the bejasus out of them.' **1987** Vincent Caprani, *Vulgar Verse & Variations, Rowdy Rhymes & Rec-im-itations*, 'The Baptism of Gershon': '"St Patrick with the big loopy stick and he whackin' the bejasus out of all the devil's dirty snakes…"' **1995** Conal Hopper, *Irish Times*, 20 Jan: 'Perhaps there should be a BJ (Bachelor of Joyceana) or even a BJS (Bachelor of Joycean Studies) which might become known as a "Bejaysis".'

belch an oyster (q.v.) [vb. phr.]. Spit gob of phlegm. **1675–95** Anon., *Purgatorium Hibernicum*: '"Belching an oyster in her fist —/"I care not dis for all de grist [flattery]!"'

bellourin [pres. part., <Ir. *béal* (n.), mouth]. 'Crying aloud without tears' (OTF).

belly-bachelor [n.] (Ulster). Man who shows interest in a girl prompted by the financial prosperity of her family.

belly-buster see **red-belly**

belt of a/the crozier [n. phr.]. Episcopal censure. **1993** Tim Pat Coogan, *Dev* (q.v.): *Long Fellow* (q.v.), *Long Shadow*: 'The backlash created by this combination of duplicity and vacillation…was summed up in another notable "belt of the crozier" directed at the Irish Parliamentary Party by the Bishop of Derry…' **1996** Eanna Brophy, *Sunday Tribune*, 3 Mar: '2nd Pub Dub [see **Dub** 1.]:…So why did the Bishop go through Bangkok? 1st Pub Dub: To get to the other Thais. 2nd Pub Dub: Boom, boom! 1st Pub Dub: What was that? 2nd Pub Dub: Probably the belt of a crozier.' **1996** Michael O'Regan, *Irish Times*, 25 Nov: 'There rests the saga of the Bishop and the Nightie. Gaybo [q.v.], as we know, survived the belt of the crozier and still presents the [Late Late] show three decades on.'

bendy see **banty**

bengil [n., <?] (Ulster). 'A most uncomplimentary epithet denoting an unspeakably base cur' (YDS).

beresk [adj., <'berserk' by metathesis]. As thus.

berl see **birl**

beroo see **broo**

best thing since sliced bread/pan [cant phr.]. Epitome of excellence. **1996** George Keating, *Irish Times*, 20 Apr: 'Sir — Would you agree that the apartments under construction on the site of the former Johnston, Mooney & O'Brien bakery are the best thing since sliced bread?'

bet [vb. as adj.; solecistic strong p. part. of 'beat']. 1. Exhausted, overcome. **1958** Frank O'Connor, *An Only Child*: '"The Corkies has me bet at last."' **1987** Lar Redmond, *Emerald Square*: '"Bet from the drink," Mag whispered. He did not drink much now because he had no money, but he was bet anyway.' 2. Beaten, very tight (of clothes) as in **bet into s.o.** (adj. phr.).

be/by the hokey [expletive, contraction of *holy poker!* (q.v.)]. Mild oath. **1925** Louise McKay, *Mourne Folk*: '"I must be tellin' my woman how well ye look. Be the hokey, ye stan' it well, Sally…"' **1959** George Buchanan, *Green Seacoast*: 'we step among them [the targets] to pick up some of the bullet-cases that litter the grass. "Let's have a shot," I say. "Not today, sonny. By the hokey, you'd shoot yourself!"' Also **be the hokey-fly** [<?]. **1975** John Ryan, *Remembering How We Stood*: '"As black as the riding boots of the Err-ill [earl] of Hell — be the hokey-fly, damn me sowl, that's a good wan…" he [Patrick Kavanagh] murmured happily.' **1980** Bernard Farrell, *Canaries*: 'DAD Be the hokey — if I didn't know better I'd swear you were hearing his confession, father.'

be the holies! [expletive]. Mild oath.

betten pad (q.v.) [n. phr., <'beaten path']. **1948** Patrick Kavanagh, *Tarry Flynn*: '"Wonder who the devil it is." "Might be the bailiffs coming from Carlin's. They have a betten pad up to them."'

betty [n., <?]. Fireguard. **1979** Michael O'Beirne, *Mister, A Dublin Childhood*:

'We had a high-barred fire with a betty round it…'

between melts and rounds [concessive phr., <milt and roe of herrings]. Between one thing and another.

between the jigs and the reels [concessive phr.]. Between one thing and another. **1966** Séamus Murphy, *Stone Mad*: 'Anyway, between the jigs and the reels, somewan made a protest about it, and the result was that a bush was planted in front of the Modest man…'

beverage [n., <Sc. *idem*, kisses, or drink, demanded of anyone on the first wearing of new clothes (CSD)] (Ulster). As thus. **1979** Jack McBride, *Traveller in the Glens* (of Antrim): 'This is what happens when a Glens girl enters a room wearing a new hat for the first time: the young man who spots her is entitled to "gie her the beverage o'it…"'

bewildered [p. part. as adj., euphem.]. Mentally incapacitated, esp. as in **Home for the Bewildered** [n. phr.]. Lunatic asylum/mental institution. **1996** Lise Hand, *Sunday Tribune*, 29 Dec: 'As the Diary checks into the nearest Home for the Bewildered for some much-needed post-festive recuperation, here is a personal guided tour to some of the social (or sociable) highs and lows of 1996.'

bewitches as in **youse** (q.v.) **go on: I'll bewitches in a mina'** (minute) [joc. rendering of Dub. pronun. in answer to question 'Put "bewitches" into a sentence'].

beyond the beyonds [adj. phr.]. Beyond belief, excessive. **1966** Patrick Boyle, *At Night All Cats are Grey*, 'The Betrayers': '"an array of decoy ducks ringed round you like a squad of peeping Toms and you in the company of a black-avised Judas the like of yon —" He shook his head slowly. "It's beyond the beyonds."'

Bian [nickname, <Charles Bianconi, 'King of the Roads' (q.v.)]. Long car drawn by four horses, introduced by Bianconi in 1815 when inaugurating his transport network; Bianconi himself. **1962** M. O'C. Bianconi & S.J. Watson,

Bianconi, King of the Irish Roads: 'It proved too difficult for the country people to say "Bianconi cars", so they simply called them "Bians"…it was only logical that the owner himself should be called affectionately "Bian", which he always regarded as a great compliment.'

bibbling [pres. part. as adj., cf. 'bibber, imbibe']. Intoxicated. **1907** Joseph Guinan, *The Soggarth Aroon* (q.v.): 'an inveterate bibbling ne'er-do-well!'

biddy [n., abbrev. of 'Bridget'; gen. derog. and as in **old biddy**]. Meddlesome old woman.

Bidet Mulligan [nickname]. An alternative, based on the character Biddy Mulligan created by the actor and entertainer Jimmy O'Dea (1899–1965), applied to the Floozie in the Jacuzzi (q.v.).

bield [n., cf. OE *byldan* (vb.), defend, shelter] (Ulster). Shelter. **1817** James Orr, *The Posthumous Works of James Orr of Ballycarry*, 'The Irish Cottier's Death and Burial': 'If e'er he doze, how noiselessly they tread!/An' stap the lights to mak the bield be black.' See also **beal**.

BIFFO [n., acronym]. Big ignorant fucker from Offaly. **1996** Seán Mac Réamoinn, *Foinse*, 15 Dec: 'A Chara, Ag tagairt do Chúléisteacht (8 Nollaig) bhí orm mo chara David Hanly a cheartú faoin téarma BIFFO — ní mé a chum.' ('Dear Sir, With reference to Eaves-dropping (8 Dec) I had to correct my friend David Hanly about the term BIFFO — I did not invent it.') Also **BUFFALO**. Big ugly fucker from around Laois/Offaly.

Big Fella/Fellow, the [nickname]. Michael Collins, revolutionary leader (1890–1922). **1987** Lar Redmond, *Emerald Square*: 'He smiled and took my brother up on his knee as the door below crashed open. The raid for "The Big Fella" was on in earnest.' **1990** Tim Pat Coogan, *Michael Collins*: 'women of his own class found him "cheeky", his "Big Fellow" sobriquet indicating swollen-headedness as much as height, just under six feet'. **1994** Vonnie Banville Evans, *The House in the Faythe*: 'in her view the

Big Fellow was the good guy and the Long Fellow [q.v.] the bad guy and I tried never to disagree on any subject dear to Aunt Nan's heart'. Also the Martynside aircraft which Collins had on standby during the 1921 Treaty negotiations in London to effect a quick retreat should it be required. It was not. **1980** Liam Byrne, *History of Aviation in Ireland*: 'The aircraft was affectionately named *The Big Fella*, after Collins, and arrived at Baldonnel in June 1922 to become the first aircraft of the Irish Air Service.' Also applied by analogy to J.T. Lang (1876–1975), Premier of NSW, who exhibited similar personal characteristics (Wilkes).

big house [n. phr.]. Generic term for residences of the former Ascendancy. **1995** Rona Currey in Mary Ryan et al. (eds.), *No Shoes in Summer*: 'my friend Mrs Reddington, the full-time washerwoman employed at the Big House. A special hut had been built for her in the stable yard…' **1996** Dick Hogan, *Irish Times*, 12 Mar: 'Ms Glendinning said part of the ambiguity in Ireland could stem from the fact that she [Elizabeth Bowen] was of the "Big House" tradition.'

big-made [adj.]. Well-built. See **pick** 1.

Big Milestone, the [nickname]. Wellington Monument (1817), Phoenix Park, Dub. **1907** Samuel A. Ossory Fitzpatrick, *Dublin*: 'On the left is the massive granite obelisk of the Wellington Memorial, sarcastically termed "The Big Milestone"…'

big moment [n. phr.]. Chief object of affection. **1987** Lar Redmond, *Emerald Square*: 'In the "slanguage" of the 'twenties, she was my "big moment" and I was hers!'

bill see **true bill**

billy balls [n. pl., <?]. House dances. **1996** RTÉ TV, *Ear to the Ground*, 28 Oct: 'The big events were the house dances or billy balls as they were called here in Kerry.'

Billy Boys [nickname, <King William III of Eng., pop. 'King Billy' (q.v.)]

(Ulster). Members of the Orange Order and kindred loyalist organisations. **1995** Cal McCrystal, *Independent on Sunday* (London), 9 July: 'it is the first march of the "Billy Boys" since the Northern Ireland peace process began last September'. **1997** Susan McKay, *Sunday Tribune*, 9 Feb: 'There was no ignoring them last night. "We are, we are, we are the Billy Boys," they roared, "Up to our necks in Fenian [q.v.] blood."'

Billy Harran's dog [n. phr.]. Equivocating canine out of the same trap as Lanna Macree's dog (q.v.), Lanty McHale's dog (q.v.) and O'Brien's dog (q.v.). **1938** Seumas MacManus, *The Rocky Road to Dublin*: 'Every time she found him too ready to fall in with the ways of each latest adviser, it was "Hagh! Billy Harran's wee [q.v.] dog, who went a bit of the way with everyone."'

binder [n.] (Ulster). S.o. who behaves rashly/illogically.

bing [n., <ON *bing-r*, heap] (Ulster). Large quantity. **1908** Lynn Doyle, *Ballygullion*: '"an' if he wanst gets her he's a made man. The ould hussy has bings av money, I'm tould."'

binlid [n.] (Ulster). Stupid individual.

binner/binder [n. & vb.]. 1. [n. & vb., <Sc. *binner* (n.), quick movement, noisy dash] (Ulster). [n.]. As thus, as in **full binder** [adv. phr.]. **1908** Lynn Doyle, *Ballygullion*: 'There was a tinklin' of broken glass an' a rattle in the sthreet, an' thin whir-r-r! away goes the alarm full bindher.' [vb.]. Move quickly, rush. 2. [n.]. Parting glass. **1943** George A. Little, *Malachi Horan Remembers*: '"A binder", the last drink before going home, so called from the last sod of turf forced into a creel to bind the load.'

binnerer/bintherer/binntherer [n., cf. Sc. *binn*, strength, excellence] (Ulster). 'Anything very large and good of its kind' (Patterson).

birces/birse [n., <Sc. *idem* <OE *byrst*, bristle, by methathesis] (Ulster). Anger, as in **get one's birces up**.

birdalone [adj.]. Completely alone. **1974** John Hewitt, *Out of my Time*, 'The

Fairy Thresher': 'Thereat the brother at this hint began/a rambling story of a man he knew/dead twenty years or more, lived *birdalone*…'

Bird Flanagan [nickname, early C20]. Dub. eccentric. **1974** Éamonn Mac Thomáis, *Me Jewel and Darlin'* (see **jewel**) *Dublin*: '"The Bird Flanagan" got his name from the time he went to a fancy dress ball dressed as a bird. When he didn't win a prize, he went up onto the stage where the judge sat, laid an egg, and then threw it at the judge.' **1975** John Ryan, *Remembering How We Stood*: 'the "Bird" Flanagan was considered to have been the patron saint of Dublin characters [see **character** 1.]'. **1977** Flann O'Brien, *The Hair of the Dogma*: 'Shades of the Old Crowd! There we were in a lump… myself in the lead — Henry James, Bernard ("Barney") Kiernan, Hamar Greenwood, Melfort Dalton, the Bird Flanagan, Jimmy Joyce…all heading into the Scotch House for hot tailers [q.v.] of malt [q.v.]…'

birdie [n.]. Kiss. **1996** Christy Kenneally, *Maura's Boy, A Cork Childhood*: '"Would you look at the white head on him. Hello, blondie, will you give us a birdie?"'

birdmouth/ed [n. & adj., <ME *burde* (n.), woman, lady, confused with 'bird'] (Ulster). Unassertive, timid person; very shy.

bird never flew on one wing, a [cant phr.]. Most freq. employed in response to the offer (self-induced or otherwise) of a second drink. **1993** Deirdre Purcell, *Falling for a Dancer*: '"Well, a bird never flew on one wing, did it? No point in having only one…" Elizabeth felt his fingers creep round to the other suspender…' **1995** Éamon Kelly, *The Apprentice*: 'I'd venture to say that they had two pints a man, reminding each other that a bird never flew on one wing…' **1996** Hugh Leonard, *Sunday Independent*, 7 Apr: 'A gentleman pauses on his way out to say that he enjoys this column…This is so civil and well-mannered that…I am on the point of ordering the second wing that birds are supposed to fly on.'

birl/burl/berl/borl [n. & vb., <Sc. *idem*, poss. onomat., whirring sound; revolve, twirl] (Ulster). [n.]. Turmoil, row; spin, whirl. **1983** W.F. Marshall, *Livin' in Drumlister*, 'The Runaway': 'When weemin gets wicked they're tarra [q.v.],/Ye'll not intherfair if yir wise,/For ten townlan's wudn't settle/The birl that two weemin can rise.' [vb.]. Revolve, spin [trans.]; dance expertly; make buzzing sound. **1948** John O'Connor, *Come Day — Go Day*: 'They stood quite still, their heads raised, listening to the sweet berling of the music and the deep, lively voice of old Mick…' **1993** Sam McAughtry, *Touch & Go*: '"If you like you can birl your card so that it ends up the wrong way round," I said.'

birse see **birces**

birsey/bursy [n., <Sc. *birsy*, nickname for a pig (CSD)] (Ulster). Patronising term for farmer, country yokel; s.o. who looks depressed/unwell.

biscake [n., <Sc. *idem*, small round cake of flour] (Ulster). Biscuit. **1925** Louise McKay, *Mourne Folk*: 'on went the tin teapot, and I was despatched to Mrs McIntyre's for half a pound of biscakes'.

bisim/bisom/bizzum [n., <'besom', brush, <OE *besma*, broom] (Ulster). Cheeky/forward/cantankerous woman. **1951** Sam Hanna Bell, *December Bride*: 'But the women…would hear nothing in Sarah's favour, and the men, for peace's sake, agreed that she was a shameless bisom…'

bit [n., cf. *piece* (q.v.)] (Ulster). School pupil's or worker's packed lunch. **1938** Seumas MacManus, *The Rocky Road to Dublin*: 'Underneath the desks…there was a rich commerce in trogging [q.v.] of all the various merchandise transported in boys' pockets — even to their *bit*…'

bit, the [with def. art. specifically Hib.E]. Sexual intercourse. **1993** John Banville, *Ghosts*: 'where it seems every other cottage harbours a canny bachelor on the lookout for a secondhand mate, one well accustomed to the bit, as Mr Tighe the shopman put it to me'.

bite 'n' sup [n. phr., cf. Ir. *greim agus bolgam*, bite and swallow]. Sustenance.

biting at a bare hook [adj. phr., gen. neg.]. Financially straitened. **1996** Séamus McCloskey, RTÉ Radio, *Sunday Miscellany*, 10 Mar: 'They [North Monaghan people] have a very good way of describing a well-off lady when they say, "She's not biting at a bare hook."'

bittle [vb., <'beetle' <OE *beatan*, beat]. Wash clothes on flat flag in a river. **1879** Charles J. Kickham, *Knocknagow*: 'Honor ...set off to town in a very excited state of mind, a proceeding which caused every soul of a pretty numerous female crowd, who were "bittling" in the little stream, to "wonder" where she was going.' **1982** Edmund Lenihan, *Long Ago by Shannon Side*: '"Another thing I heard about is bittling. I s'pose this would happen before the soap came out for washing clothes."' Hence **bittle-to** [n.]. Implement used to pound washing. **1982** Edmund Lenihan, *Long Ago by Shannon Side*: '"'Twas a handle about 4 feet long, an' at the lower ends of it there was a round piece o' timber, say, about a foot in diameter...with the lower surface of this bit of timber curved."'

bizzum see **bisim**

blab [n.] (Ulster). Swelling on tyre/football resulting from material weakness.

black see **black Protestant**

Black and Tans [nickname, <hounds of a Co. Limerick hunt owing to their khaki and black uniforms]. Former Brit. army troops recruited as reinforcements to the Royal Irish Constabulary (1920). **1922** Anon., *Tales of the RIC*: 'The magic words "Black and Tan" have the same effect on an Irish crowd as the name of Cromwell had during a previous period of Irish history...' **1983** William Trevor, *Fools of Fortune*: 'A force of British soldiers known as the Black and Tans ...had been sent to Ireland to quell the spreading disobedience. By reputation they were ruthless men, brutalised during the German war, many of them said to have been released from the gaols in order to perform this task.' Also abbrev. to **Tans**. **1993** John Walsh in Michael Verdon, *Shawlies* (q.v.), *Echo Boys* (q.v.), *the Marsh and the Lanes* (q.v.): *Old Cork Remembered*: 'Let's not make the mistake that this was some glorious rebellion. War never is. We were fortunate that the Tans were unleashed upon us. Very fortunate indeed. Otherwise we might never have gained our independence.'

blackas [n. pl., <abbrev. of 'blackberry' + endearment suffix] (Cork). Blackberries.

black babies [n. pl.]. African infants, the object of Catholic missionary endeavours supported by regular collections in schools and elsewhere. **1973** Noël Conway, *The Bloods* (q.v.): 'Oglesby summed up his Congo experiences succinctly to Milligan when they were once again in the safety of a Newbridge pub. "Not another penny for the black babies — they grow up into big black bastards..."' **1994** Vonnie Banville Evans, *The House in the Faythe*: 'No matter how many pennies I brought the black baby never materialised. I was assured that I owned one all right, out in the depths of darkest Africa. We were also told that every baby we bought was given our name and so I can assume that there are legions of middle-aged African ladies today sporting the unlikely name of Ann Veronica Mary.' **1995** Phil O'Keeffe, *Down Cobbled Streets, A Liberties Childhood*: 'Our classroom in the Far East, nicknamed after the missions towards which we put our pennies in the nodding black-babies boxes, was the vantage point...'

Blackfeet [nickname]. Members of the early C19 Ribbonmen (q.v.) opposed to the Catholic priesthood.

blackfoot [n. & vb., <?]. Individual assisting in courtship ritual; providing such assistance. **1925** Louise McKay, *Mourne Folk*: 'the suitor, when he went "a-wooing", took with him a man to introduce the subject to the bride-elect's family. The "blackfoot" usually brought a bottle of whiskey...' Also **blackfooting**, **black man** in same sense. **1866** Patrick Kennedy, *Legendary Fictions of the Irish Celts*: 'Well, the black man never let him open his mouth all the time the coortin' was goin' on; and at last the whole party...were gathered into the priest's parlour.'

blackguard [vb.]. Abuse, vilify. **1943** George A. Little, *Malachi Horan Remembers*: 'She threw herself on the pillion behind her man, and he jolly, and blackguarded him all the way home...' **1952** Bryan MacMahon, *Children of the Rainbow*: '"I thought you were going strong there!" I said. "Leave off your bla'guardin," he replied angrily.'

Black Lead [nickname, poss. <lead rubbed into the skin to keep out the cold]. Wexford street character [see **character** 1.]. **1994** Vonnie Banville Evans, *The House in the Faythe*: 'even though he was threatened on us all by harassed mothers, we had no fear, and the cry of: "Black Lead will get you", left us all unmoved. I suppose he was Wexford's answer to Dublin's "Johnny Forty-Coats" [q.v.].'

black man see **blackfoot**

Black man [prop. n.] (Ulster). Member of Imperial Grand Black Chapter of the British Commonwealth, Orange organisation founded 1797. **1966** Robert Harbinson, *No Surrender*: 'To us Belfast boys, the Black men we looked for in the [12 July] procession were not negroes, but the most respected holders of the highest rank within the hierarchy of the Order. Purple men followed them in precedence...' **1976** R.M. Arnold, *The Golden Years of the Great Northern Railway*: 'Inter-railway specials of an even more interesting nature occurred on 31.8.35 and 11.12.36. On the former the invaluable [locomotive no.] 40 conveyed "Blackmen" from Comber to Ballyward...'

blackmouth [n.] (Ulster). Presbyterian.

black neb (q.v.) [adj. & n. phr., <Sc. *neb*, snout; <ON *nef*, beak, derog.] (Ulster). Presbyterian. **1915** L.J. Walsh, *The Pope at Killybuck*: 'ALEX Come on, man, a ten poun' note never raired [q.v.] ye. And before I wud let wan o' these black-nebbed, sour-faced Prisbyterians into a place I wanted, I wud either have it myself or wud make that man that bought it over my head pay dear for it.'

black out with [adj. phr.]. Antipathetic towards. **1939** Sean O'Casey, *I Knock at the Door*: 'even when I try to make up to her she'll shake her head and say No, Johnny, I'm black out with you for what you done in church'. **1975** Eilís Brady, *All In! All In!*: 'Little girls who have quarrelled and consequently are "not speaking" say they are "black out" with each other.' **1995** Aidan Higgins, *Donkey's Years*: '"I'm black out wiff yew!" Rita Phelan screeched naggishly at Grogan.'

black Protestant [n. phr., <Ir. *dubh* (adj.), black-hearted, malevolent, bigoted]. Term of sectarian disparagement. **1970** Christy Brown, *Down All the Days*: '"She was supposed to turn [see **turn** 2.] when she married poor Paddy Kerrigan, but anyone can see she's still a black bloody Protestant at heart."' **1982** Edmund Lenihan, *Long Ago by Shannon Side*: '"there was a townland called Mount Baylee an' in that townland there was a family of Baylees who were black Protestants"'. **1995** Michael Hand, *Sunday Tribune*, 27 Sept: 'Garret Patton from Bessbrook chipped in: "I'm what they call a black Prod [q.v.] and I'm all for the ceasefire."' Also **black** [adj.] in same sense. **1997**, *Observer* (London), interview with children on the Garvaghy Road, Belfast, 13 July: '"I was proud that a Portadown feller shot a policeman," says John, getting louder. "Yep, cos they're all black bastards."'

Blacksmith of Ballinalee, the [nickname]. Seán MacEoin, soldier (1893–1973). **1988** Henry Boylan, *A Dictionary of Irish Biography*: 'Became known as "the Blacksmith of Ballinalee" after holding the village of Ballinalee [Co. Longford] against superior British forces in February 1921.'

black stuff, the [n. phr., echoic of 1980s Brit. TV serial, *The Boys from the Black Stuff*]. Stout, esp. Guinness. **1965** Lee Dunne, *Goodbye to the Hill*: 'She didn't eat much but she was putting the black stuff away as quick as I was myself.' **1995** *Big Issues*, 26 Oct: '"Mine's a pint," in Ireland traditionally meant "yer man" [q.v.] wanted a pint of the black stuff — the bottles of lager and glasses of ale being considered more suited to "herself" [q.v.].' **1996** *Irish Times*, 5 Jan: 'Owned and run by a man with obvious Irish roots — Bjorni Omar — it [Iceland's first Ir. pub] apparently sold 100,000 pints of Guinness in its first two weeks. A Bjorn again market for the black stuff.'

black swop [n., <Ir. *dubh* (adj.), unknown]. Exchange 'sight unseen' (PWJ).

blad [n., <Sc. *blaud*, large fragment] (Ulster). 1. As thus. 2. Useless thing.

bladdoch [n., <Sc. Gael. *bláthach*, buttermilk] (Ulster). As thus.

blade [n.] (Ulster). Bizarrely dressed woman, a 'sight'; sharp-tongued woman. **1983** Polly Devlin, *All of us There*: 'Any other young woman wearing a hat, or any other garment not considered suitable, is...called a "blade" or "tackle".'

bla-flum/fum [n., <Sc. *idem*, nonsensical talk] (Ulster). 'Something said to mislead' (Patterson).

blah-faced [adj., <Ir. *bleathach* (n.), oatmeal cake; 'soft, spongy, delicious little flat cake of bread' (DOM)] (Leinster). Moon-faced.

blaich/bleach [n. & vb., <Sc. *bleach*, blow, strike a blow] (Ulster). As thus. See **father and mother of**.

blarge [n. & vb., <combination of 'blunder' & 'barge'] (Ulster). 1. [n.]. 'Powerful but unstylish kick of a football' (TT). 2. [vb.]. Do anything noisily and without ceremony. **1979** Paddy Tunney, *The Stone Fiddle*: '"Patrick," he told me solemnly, "if you want a pheasant or two in season, you'd be a fool to go out with a gun and start blarging at them."'

blarney [n., <Blarney Castle, Co. Cork]. Loquacious eloquence. **1824** Thomas Crofton Croker, *Researches in the South of Ireland*: 'A stone in the highest part of the castle wall is pointed out to visitors, which is supposed to give to whoever kisses it the peculiar privilege of deviating from veracity with unblushing countenance whenever it may be convenient — hence the well-known phrase of "Blarney".' **1948** *Cork Examiner*, 21 Sept: 'History has it that the

word "blarney"...originated when one of the Carthy clan found one thousand and one excuses for not surrendering his castle to Queen Elizabeth's troops, Elizabeth finally exclaiming impatiently that she had had enough of Blarney.' **1981** R.M. Arnold, *The County Down*: 'the BCDR [Belfast & Co. Down Railway] dispatched at least eighty trains each weekday from its Queen's Quay terminus at Belfast, which left little time for "blarney" about how to reach anywhere not in the timetable'.

blate [adj., <Sc. *idem*, shy]. As thus. **1911** Adam Lynn, *Random Rhymes from Cullybackey*, 'A Country Lad's Observations at the Hiring Fair in Ballymena': 'The toon assumed its usual gait,/Folk mashing roon at nae wee [q.v.] rate,/Each luckin' for their ain dear mate/In blank despair;/An so may I if I keep blate/To the next Fair.'

blather/blether [n. & vb., <ME *blather* (n.), nonsense (Sc. form *blether* more common in Ulster), <ON *blathra* (vb.), talk nonsense; Ir. *bladar*, flatter(y), coax(ing)]. [Talk] loquacious nonsense; one who indulges in such. **1925** Louise McKay, *Mourne Folk*: '"Och, Dandy, ye're a blether; but I forgive ye, for ye're too ould to take any notice of."' **1955** James Plunkett, *The Trusting and the Maimed*, 'Mercy': '"What are you blathering about?" Toner asked in terror.' Also **blatherskite/blatherumskite** [n.]. S.o. who talks thus, or the talk itself. See **skite** 2. **1904** George Bernard Shaw, *John Bull's Other Island*: 'DORAN There's too much blatherumskite in Irish politics, a dale too much.' **1938** Seumas MacManus, *The Rocky Road to Dublin*: 'a gathered group of neighbours, discussing the fight in Dainey Gillespie the cooper's, were drowned out by a deluge of blatherskite from Dainey's gabbler wife'. **1986** Padraic O'Farrell, 'Tell me, Sean O'Farrell': 'He [the priest] knocked a poor strammel (thin man) into a big bin of flour in Jones's public house in Clane one night. Belted him right [see **right** 1.] into it for giving some ould bletherumskite.' Hence **blathery** [adj.]. **1996** Djinn Gallagher, *Sunday Tribune*, 28

Apr: 'Having first made his imprint on the Irish psyche in the shape of Father Trendy [q.v.], purveyor of blathery platitudes to the multitudes, Dermot Morgan has now made his mark in Britain as Father Ted...' See also **Ted Head**.

blatter [vb., confused with 'batter', <Sc. *idem*, make rattling sound, talk loudly and noisily] (Ulster). Batter. **1979** John Morrow, *The Confessions of Proinsias O'Toole*: 'a red glow to the west that had fuck all to do with delighted shepherds — "Them Prods [q.v.] are blatterin' away like mad over there," he whinged.' **1995/6** Mark Kennedy, *Five Foot Three* (Belfast), 'Carriage and Wagon Report': 'CIÉ 1469: As one of the widest coaches in the Northern rake, it gets a good "blattering" from bushes every time it goes out.'

blaze o' whins [n. phr.] as in **like a blaze o' whins** [adv. phr.] (Ulster). Quickly.

blazes Kate! [interj., <?]. **1989** Hugh Leonard, *Out after Dark*: 'Suddenly he jumped up, bellowed "Blazes Kate, I'm destroyed [q.v.]!" and went tearing out.'

bleach see **blaich**

bleenge [n., cf. Sc. *breenge* (vb.), move impetuously] (Ulster). Badly aimed kick/blow, as in **play bleenge at s.o.** [vb. phr.].

bleerie-tea [n., <'bleary'] (Ulster). Very weak tea.

blemm [vb., <?]. Travel at speed. **1990** Roddy Doyle, *The Snapper* (q.v.): '"How'd it happen?" Jimmy Sr asked him. "I was blemmin' down Tonlegee Road." "Jaysis [q.v.]! Was it a race?"' Also **blemmed up** [p. part. as adj.] (Dub.). Dressed to the nines. **1987** Lar Redmond, *Emerald Square*: 'some blemmed-up "jazzers", who...were heading for the Fountain Picture House in James's Street for a session of cinema and sex and an exercise in "grope therapy"'.

blemt [n., <solecistic p. part. of 'blame']. Blame. **1987** Vincent Caprani, *Vulgar Verse & Variations, Rowdy Rhymes & Rec-*

im-itations, 'The Shawlie' (q.v.): '"there's no bloody way I'd put the blemt on her. Living all them years with Oul' Onion-Sack must've made the Crucifixion of Our Lord look like a nixer [q.v.]..."'

blert see **blirt**

blether see **blather**

bley [adj., <ON *blé*, dark blue, livid; Sc. *blae*, same sense] (Ulster). Pale and wan-looking.

blind [n.] as in **put the blind on s.o.** [vb. phr.]. Curse, invoke bad luck on s.o.

Blind Billy's bargain [n. phr., <Limerick hangman]. Bargain which proves to be no bargain at all 'by either overreaching yourself or allowing the other party to overreach you' (PWJ).

blind hays/blem hize/blun hize [n. phr., cf. Sc. *blind fish*, lesser spotted dogfish]. As thus. See **gubog**.

blink [n. & vb., cf. Sc. *blinkit* (p. part. as adj.), bewitched, soured, spoiled]. Unlucky individual; exercise malign influence by a glance of the 'evil eye' — 'when butter does not come in churning, the milk has been *blinked* by some one' (PWJ). **1913** Alexander Irvine, *My Lady of the Chimney Corner*: '"Tell me, Willie," Anna said, "is it thrue that ye can blink a cow so that she can give no milk at all?"' **1974** John Hewitt, *Out of my Time*, 'The Fairy Thresher': 'to rhyme and ramble through familiar stories/of ghosts and fairies, witches, *blinks* and spells'.

blirt/blert [n. & vb., <Sc. *idem*, storm of wind and rain; weep] (Ulster). 1. [n.]. Untrustworthy individual, loudmouth; gen. term of abuse. **1966** Patrick Boyle, *At Night All Cats are Grey*, 'Go Away, Old Man, Go Away': 'The accumulation of rage that had been festering in him all morning broke out at last. "Ye little blirt," he roared. "I'll put manners [q.v.] on ye."' **1977** Sam McAughtry, *The Sinking of the Kenbane Head*: 'I made my way to the far side of the pitch. "Come on North Star," I yelled in my boy's contralto, "ye can ate them dirty blirts..."' **1979** John Morrow, *The Confessions of Proinsias O'Toole*: '"You

realize what you've just done?" I asked quietly...that cross-eyed blirt is about the most dangerous —'" 2. [vb.]. Weep. **1913** Alexander Irvine, *My Lady of the Chimney Corner*: "'If ye'll lie very quiet, 'Liza — just cross yer hands and listen...' "Ay, bless ye. I'll blirt no more; go on!'" **1948** John O'Connor, *Come Day — Go Day*: "'Quit your whinging [*sic*]," Neilly shouted at him in a rage. "What are you blerting [*sic*] about?'"

blister [n.] (Ulster). Annoying person (Patterson).

blithero [adj. & adv.]. Very, extremely. **1952** Bryan MacMahon, *Children of the Rainbow*: 'Twice, as he was on the point of pitching us to hell, we made him blithero drunk; twice also we stole his breeches.'

blitter [vb., <Sc. *idem*, rattle] (Ulster). Fart.

blone [n., <OE *blowen*, woman; whore, poss. <Romany; or Ger. *blühen* (vb.), bloom, blossom (DOM)]. Woman. **1968** John Healy, *The Death of an Irish Town*: 'She's lost in the evening crowd when he turns to the man on the next stall: "a rager blone — four horses and two sprassies [q.v.]. Wide with the makes [q.v.]. Still." (In translation: "A country woman — four half crowns and two sixpences...she's careful with her money.")'

blood an' ounkers/ounds/ouns [expletive, euphem. for '(Christ's) blood and wounds']. Mild oath. **1879** Charles J. Kickham, *Knocknagow*: "'Blood-an-ounkers, Mat," he exclaimed..."I believe you are able to read writin'.'" **1920** Seumas O'Kelly, *The Leprechaun of Kilmeen*: "'When they come to the river the man says to your great-grandfather: 'Blood an' 'ounds, Kelleher, but you're beaten at last! You'll never try to leap the Shannon,' says he.'" Also **blood in ounce**. **1950** Liam O'Flaherty, *Insurrection*: "'Blood in ounce!" he whispered at length. "It's a soldier's rifle!'"

blood 'n' bandage [n. phr., <sporting colours] (Cork). Cork hurling team. **1993** Tommy Cronin in Michael

Verdon, *Shawlies* (q.v.), *Echo Boys* (q.v.), *the Marsh and the Lanes* (q.v.): *Old Cork Remembered*: 'Cork was called the blood 'n' bandage. That's because the jersey is red and white. The Cork supporters would shout "Come on, the blood 'n' bandage!"'

Bloods, the [nickname, <alleged freq. use of 'bloody' by Commandant General Bernard Sweeney, commanding 1st Northern Division, IRA, 1922, forerunner of 3rd Infantry Battalion, oldest infantry unit in Regular Army, formed 1924]. As thus. **1973** Noël Conway, *The Bloods*: 'The angel eyed him coldly. It was the first time since his creation he'd had that epithet [bloody] spat in his face. "I was going to ask you why they are called The Bloods, but I think I can see it...'"

Bloody Sunday [nickname]. 1. Dub., 21 Nov 1920, 14 Brit. secret service agents killed by IRA unit, subsequently avenged by Brit. milit. opening fire on GAA crowd in Croke Park (see **Croker**). **1990** Tim Pat Coogan, *Michael Collins* (see **the Big Fella**): 'The account given to the [Brit.] Cabinet of the events of Bloody Sunday, not for the first time in the Anglo-Irish war, makes one wonder how much the Government were kept informed by the military of what was really happening in Ireland...' 2. Derry, 30 Jan 1972, 13 civil rights demonstrators killed by Brit. troops. **1984** Bruce Arnold, *What Kind of Country*: 'Events such as Bloody Sunday, and the H-Block hunger strikes, can raise ancient animosities and provoke apparent hatreds which do not seem all that far beneath the surface.'

Bloomsday [nickname, <fictional character *Leopold Bloom*]. 16 June 1904, date of the events chronicled in James Joyce's novel *Ulysses*. Since *c*.1954 an annual celebration. **1975** John Ryan, *Remembering How We Stood*: 'He [Myles na gCopaleen] and I worked on several projects...Another of our ventures was to organise the first "Bloomsday"...we decided to commemorate it by covering as much of the original ground as the book had charted.' **1976** Anthony

Cronin, *Dead as Doornails*: 'June 16th was of course Bloomsday, though that word was not much used then; and June 16th 1954 would be the fiftieth anniversary ...Our celebration would be the first.'

blooter/bloother [n. & vb., <Sc *bluiter*, coarse, clumsy fellow; make a rumbling noise, work clumsily, etc.] (Ulster). [n.]. 'Clumsy blundering rustic' (Patterson); silly/noisy person; error in use of Eng., esp. as retold; heavy blow. [vb.]. Verbal equivalents of foregoing. Also **blootered/ bloothered/bluthered** [p. part. as adj., cf. ON *blautr*, soaked] (Ulster). Very drunk.

blow/blowhard [n.]. Methylated spirits for consumption purposes.

blow-in [n.]. Recent (2 days–25 years) arrival in a village, town or district, not yet accepted by the natives. **1995** Renagh Holohan, *Irish Times*, 29 July: 'He [Pádraig Flynn] had always taken the view, he said, that blow-ins should never be underestimated, but he was now afraid the whole concept might be dying out.' **1996** Andy Pollak, *Irish Times*, 19 Feb: 'From the beginning many senior priests in his [Dr Comiskey's] new diocese were suspicious of the flamboyant, media-friendly "blow-in" who had been sent to rule over them.' **1996** *Irish Times*, 6 Apr: 'In the hotel at the top of the town [Mountshannon, Co. Clare], the "blow-ins" sit around a television watching Ajax play the Greek side Panathinaikos...In the Bridge Bar...locals cheer Liverpool to victory over Newcastle.' See also **runner-in**.

blowout [n.] (Dub.). Cream cake. **1979** Éamonn Mac Thomáis, *The 'Labour' & the Royal*: '"What kept yis [q.v.]?" he roared and then he spotted the remains of the blowouts on my lips.'

blow-up [n.]. Signal for work break. **1966** Séamus Murphy, *Stone Mad*: 'When the Gaffer shouts "Blow-up" at one o'clock, the atmosphere improves slightly...'

Blue Blouses [nickname, <colour of uniform]. Female members and supporters of Blueshirts (q.v.). **1995** Éamon Kelly, *The Apprentice*: 'These followers of General Eoin O'Duffy

arrived in force...They were dressed in their military type shirts and were accompanied by their women, the blue blouses as we called them.'

blue-eye [n.] (Ulster). Favourite.

Blueshirts [nickname, <fascist political movement, Apr. 1933– which adopted blue shirts as uniform]. (Derog.) Fine Gael party and members thereof; those espousing right-wing views. **1991** Ferdia Mac Anna, *The Last of the High Kings*: 'the local Fine Gael TD, whom Ma called "a pig-ignorant [q.v.] blueshirt bastard who wasn't fit to suck cowshite through a straw"'. **1996** Renagh Holohan, *Irish Times*, 6 Apr: '"If he can sell the farmers, he can certainly sell the Blueshirts," said a hack on hearing...that IFA press officer, Niall Ó Muilleoir, is moving to Fine Gael.'

blug [n., nonce-word]. Low fellow. '[O]wld Beamish and two blugs, and the hounds and I had gone on a little fruitless excursion up and down and round a precipice' (S&R).

blur-an-agers [exclam., corruption of *tare an' ages* (q.v.)]. As thus. See **ninny-hammer**.

bluthered see **blooter**

B man [nickname] (Ulster). Part-time member of the Ulster Special Constabulary (established 1920), otherwise **B-Special**. **1969** Bernadette Devlin, *The Price of my Soul*: 'Most of the Protestant men in our district were B men, or Specials — members of the civilian militia in Northern Ireland which was formed to fight the IRA.' **1993** Sam McAughtry, *Touch & Go*: '"OK, the B men are doing ordinary police work now, but you know and I know why we're really here, it's to protect what we have when the balloon goes up."'

boadie/bodie [n., <Sc. *bodie*, small copper coin] (Ulster). Worthless person/thing, as in **not worth a bodie** [adj. phr.].

boak see **boke**

boast [adj., cf. Sc. *boss*, hollow] (Ulster). As thus, weak.

bobbery [n., <Hindust. *bap re!* (exclam.), O father!, expression of surprise/grief] (Munster). Noise, row.

bob's your rudd [cant phr., poss. <Brit. 'Bob's your uncle' + Ir. *rud* (n.), thing]. Indicating that everything's fine, that the job's oxo (q.v.). **1955** J.P. Donleavy, *The Ginger Man*: 'you just pull it back until the board jams up against the door frame and bob's your rudd'.

bocketty/bockedy/bockety [adj., cf. Ir. *bacach*, halting, imperfect]. Physically unstable or impaired (of person or thing). **1966** Patrick Boyle, *At Night All Cats are Grey*, 'The Metal Man': '"I'll give that bocketty hoor [q.v.] a drink he'll not forget in a hurry," he says.' **1991** James Kennedy, *The People who Drank Water from the River*: 'We inflated them [pigs' bladders] with a goose's quill and then kicked them around although they were a bit bockety like a rugby ball.' **1995** Joe O'Connor, *Sunday Tribune*, 27 Aug: 'he (or she) would unveil the latest wonky shelf, bockety wardrobe or baw-ways [q.v.] kitchen tiling'. Also **bockady** [n.]. Lame person.

boddagh/badach [n., <Ir. *bodach*, churl, lout]. As thus. Also **bodeaugh breene** [n., <Ir. *bodach bréan*, rotten lout]. As such; term of abuse. **1605** Anon., *Captain Thomas Stukeley*: 'Fate [what] is the token, bodeaugh breene? That I sall see ovare the valles [walls] of this Toone of Dundalke.' **1922** James Joyce, *Ulysses*: 'Swindled them all, skivvies and badhachs [*sic*] from the county Meath, ay, and his own kidney too.'

bodice [n., <?] (Cork). Pig meat, spare ribs (Beecher).

bodie see **boadie**

bogey [n., <?] (Ulster). Hardened mucus in the nose (SH).

boggin' [adj.] (Ulster). X-rated (of film).

bog Irish [n. phr., <perceived qualities of those working on peat bogs or living in proximity thereto; see **bogman**, **bogtrotter**]. Gen. term of racial contempt. **1986** Bob Geldof, *Is That It?*: '"Oi will not be physically abused..."

mimicked the make-up men...in awful bog-Irish accents in the background."'

bog Latin [n. phr., incorrect Lat. as allegedly taught in hedge schools (q.v.)]. **1922** James Joyce, *Ulysses*: 'he was a lefthanded descendant of the famous champion bull of the Romans, *Bos Bovum*, which is good bog Latin for boss of the show'. **1994** Vonnie Banville Evans, *The House in the Faythe*: 'We were convinced for years that my father could speak German and a smattering of what he called bog-Latin.'

bogman [n., see **bog Irish**]. Term of contempt. Hence **bog persons**. **1997** Damien Enright, *Examiner* (Cork), 3 May: 'the rich from all over are welcome [to membership of the Old Head of Kinsale Golf Club] but no resident bog persons need apply'.

bogtrotter [n., see **bog Irish**]. Term of contempt. **1989** Hugh Leonard, *Out after Dark*: 'When the Jacobs died they had taken not only their own world with them, but his. Bog-trotters like the schoolmaster were the new Quality [q.v.]...' **1992** Sean O'Callaghan, *Down by the Glenside, Memoirs of an Irish Boyhood*: 'a real bastard, a bog-trotter from the West'. **1992** Moya Roddy, *The Long Way Home*: '"Where's your mammy and daddy?" Loretta put on a country accent as she said it. "Go back to the bog. You don't belong around here." Other kids gathered round, egging Loretta on. "Bogtrotter!"' Hence **bogtrotting** [pres. part. as adj.]. **1996** Anthony Cronin, *Samuel Beckett, The Last Modernist*: 'The withdrawal of the O'Casey play and the subsequent events...would be instanced by him for many years as an example of Ireland's bog-trotting obscurantism...'

boke/boak [vb., <Sc. *idem* <OE *bealcan*, belch, throw up; cf. 'puke'] (Ulster). Retch.

Boker, the [prop. n., <Ir. *bóthar*, road] (Leinster). Street name, Wexford. **1995** Patrick Comerford, *Irish Times*, 1 Nov: '[Playwright] Billy Roche, with...his eulogising of the Boker Poker Club, has given literary grandeur to The Boker... more likely to be used by Wexford

people when referring to both Joseph Street and the Christian Brothers School there.'

bold [adj., gen. of children]. Naughty; *idem* with sexual connotation. **1987** Lar Redmond, *Emerald Square*: 'My poor mother had to spread her ration of love out too thinly and sometimes when I was bold — and that was often — there was none left over for me at all.' **1996** 'Drapier', *Irish Times*, 27 Jan: '"Bold boy" Pat Rabbitte was quickly brought back into line. It remains to be seen whether or not his *faux pas* has cost him and his Department dearly.' **1996** *Leinster Leader* (Naas, Co. Kildare), 23 May: 'he found his son crying outside his house. He said that his son told him that Peter Flood was "being bold to mammy inside".'

bold thing, the [n. phr., see **bold**]. Sexual intercourse. **1986** Tom McDonagh, *My Green Age*: 'I told her athletes weren't much good at the bould thing. They used up their juices in other ways.' **1996** *Irish Times*, 22 Oct: 'A group of pro-chastity campaigners are roving round the country in an effort to dissuade young people...from doing the bold thing until marriage.'

bollix [n., <'bollocks', testicles]. Despicable/unsavoury individual, invar. male. **1990** Roddy Doyle, *The Snapper* (q.v.): 'Jimmy Sr laughed. "He was an oul' bollix, tha' fella. A right [see **right** 1.] oul' bollix. I bought tha' fucker a brandy at the weddin'."' **1995** Patrick Boland, *Tales from a City Farmyard*: 'At that stage, the Arse, having earlier learned as to how I came a cropper, told me that I was a stupid little bollix...' **1995** Fiona Looney, *Sunday Tribune*, 11 June: '"We come in peace," David Attenborough will say. "Get up the yard [q.v.], ya old bollix," the [South American tribal] chief will laugh, for they have been listening to *Book at Bedtime* on shortwave radio, and they too know all about the crack [see **crack** 1.].' Hence **me bollix!** [exclam.]. Expressive of disbelief/scorn. See **messer**.

Bolshies [nickname, <alleged Marxist/Leninist sympathies]. Those who took the Republican side in the Civil War (1922–3). **1993** Tom O'Hannelly in Joe O'Reilly & Sixth Class, Convent School, Edenderry, *Over the Half Door*: 'I remember seeing lorry loads of soldiers and civilians going through the town. The civilians I got to know were republican prisoners and were often referred to at that time as Bolshies.'

bombed out [p. part. as adj.]. Jilted, given walking papers.

bona see **boney**

bona fide [nickname, originally <Brit. Defence of the Realm Act (WWI) which applied to Ire. A genuine traveller, under the terms of the DORA Act, was entitled to be served drink on licensed premises at any hour of the day or night, providing that he or she had travelled at least 3 miles. As amended, effectively restricted to a couple of hours drinking 3 miles beyond the city limits after the normal closing time of 22.00. Abolished 4 July 1960. Pronounced to rhyme both with 'feed' & 'tide'.]. Customer in such premises; the premises themselves. **1968** Joseph Cole, *Meanjin Quarterly* (Melbourne), 'Night Out in Dublin', Sept: 'It was therefore understandable that not one of the company — and least of all Brendan [Behan]...wanted the night to end so soon. "Let's do the *bona fide*?", he suggested, when all the glasses were empty.' **1975** John Ryan, *Remembering How We Stood*: 'A few of us set out on bicycles and, having pedalled the all-important three miles, sought, and nearly obtained, comfort under the old Act. This necessitated the knocking-up of Matt Smith of Stepaside...in the wee [q.v.] hours..."What do yeez [see **youse**] want?" "Weez is bonafeeds." "Let yeez get the hell outa here or I'll call the guards." "We can't. Weez is travellers. Really, weez is." "Yeez will not hop that ball [q.v.] here...Yeez have yez'r glue [q.v.]."' **1985** Máirín Johnston, *Around the Banks of Pimlico*: 'The stories Uncle Paddy told were very long...Strange things were always happening to him and Uncle Christy on their many journeys out to "do the bona fide" after the city pubs had closed.'

bone [n. & vb.]. 1. [n.] as in **keep the bone green** [vb. phr.] (Ulster). Delay in settling dispute. 2. [vb.] (Ulster). Confront s.o. (YDS).

boney [n., <*bone-fire*, funeral pyre, <'bonfire'. Ulster speech retains original pronun.]. As thus. **1995** Geoffrey Beattie, *Sunday Tribune*, 9 July: 'We always had guards stationed in the boney to make sure that no Taig [q.v.], or even no Prod [q.v.] from any of the neighbouring streets, tried to set fire to it before the Eleventh [of July: see **the Twelfth**] night.' Also **bona** [<abbrev. + endearment suffix] (Cork) in same sense. **1996** Christy Kenneally, *Maura's Boy, A Cork Childhood*: 'Jaded [q.v.] from our efforts, we lit a "bona" and reviewed the trailers for the coming week [at the cinema]...'

bonny-clabber [n., <Ir. *bainne*, milk + *clábar*, mud, thick liquid]. Clotted sour milk; many variations, **banny clapp**, **bonny-clapp**, **bannaclab**, etc. **1689** Anon., *The Irish Hudibras*: 'I'de give it, fait [see **faith**], vid all my heart,/T'njoy my Land, or any part,/My Banniclabber and Pottados...' **1692** Anon., *Brief Character of Ireland*: 'Bonny-Clabber and Mulahaan, alias Sowre Milk, and Choak-Cheese, with a dish of potatoes boiled, is their general Entertainment...'

booch/boogh [n., onomat.] (Ulster). Hit or slap (SH).

boodle [n.] (Ulster). Glass marble.

boodyman [n.] (Munster). Bogeyman. **1995** Éamon Kelly, *The Apprentice*: 'We were threatened with him when we were smaller. If we weren't good the boodyman would come with his bag and take us away.'

boogh see **booch**

book [n.]. 1. [<textbook containing a year's material]. Class in primary school. **1995** Phil O'Keeffe, *Down Cobbled Streets, A Liberties Childhood*: 'face to face with the women in the parlour, we came under close scrutiny. "And what book are you in now?"' 2. Lone parents' allowance. **1995** Nuala O'Faolain, *Irish Times*, 14 Nov: '"She leaves the name of

the father off the birth certificate, so she can go on the 'book'."'

bookeran [n., <Ir. *buachar*, cow dung]. Dried cow dung (as fuel).

booley/boolie [adj., <Sc. *boolie*, crooked] (Ulster). Bandy-legged.

boolia-botha see **bullia-batter**

boon [n.]. 1. [<ON *bún*, prayer, confused with OF *bon*, *bone* (adj.), fortunate, prosperous; &/or <Ir. *buan* (adj.), enduring, long-lived]. Drinks to celebrate a marriage. **1966** Séamus Murphy, *Stone Mad*: 'If at all possible, the "boon" was given on a Monday evening, that being a thirsty day for the Dust [q.v.].' 2. Also **boone** [cf. Sc. *idem*, voluntary help given to farmer by neighbours; Ir. *buíon fhómhair*, harvesting gang]. As thus. **1866** Henry M'D. Fletcher, *Poems, Songs and Ballads*, 'The Churn': 'A boone attacks a golden field/ In bright September's morn...'

boone see **boon** 2.

boortreebush/bootry-bush [n., cf. Sc. *butt'rie*, butterfly]. Elderberry tree.

boozle [vb., <'bamboozle', deceive, outwit (obsc.)]. As thus. **C.1780** Anon., *Luke Caffrey's Kilmainham Minit*: 'For Luke he was ever the chap/ To boozle de bull-dogs [sheriff's officers] and pinners [q.v.]...'

borgeegle [n., <Ir. *barrghalach*, refuse (Dinneen)]. Mess.

borl see **birl**

borrie [n., <Ir. *barraí*, superior/arrogant person, bully]. As thus.

borstal mark/spot [n. phr.]. Evidence of prison record. **1994** Paddy O'Gorman, *Queuing for a Living*: 'He had a blue dot, what's called a borstal spot, tattooed on his cheek. It signified a period in borstal or prison.' **1997** Alan Roberts, *The Rasherhouse* (see **rasher**): '"Will I give ya a borstal mark, Mags? T'would look great on ya, honest."'

bossman [n.]. Head of household/ business etc., gen. assumed to be male. **1995** Jack Boothman in Seán Power (ed.), *Those were the Days, Irish Childhood*

Memories: 'the mare started to dance sideways. But the "Bossman", with a considerable amount of skill...managed to keep the mare from going forward.' **1997** *Irish Times*, 10 Apr: '"It's a disgrace," declared a woman cleaning the windows of a pub in tiny Rathgormack [Co. Waterford]. "The bossman here was trying to get hold of the TDs last night and couldn't get any of them."'

bosthoon/bostoon [n., <Ir. *bastún*, lout]. Fool or blockhead. **1914** James Joyce, *Dubliners*, 'Grace': '"Is this what we pay rates for?" he asked. "To feed and clothe these ignorant bosthoons..."' **1932** (first published 1992) Samuel Beckett, *Dream of Fair to Middling Women*: 'On two counts, subsequently, by the Civic Guards, those plush bosthoons, they were indicted: breach of turbary and cruelty to the ass.' **1960** John O'Donoghue, *In Kerry Long Ago*: 'my mother would usually dismiss my explanations with some curt remark like the following: "Shut up, you old *bosthoon*, and don't be bothering me."'

bother [n. & vb., <Ir. *bodhar* (adj.), deaf; bothered, confused, cf. OIr. *buadrim* (vb.), vex. Grose erroneously derives **bothered** from 'both-eared: talked to at both ears by different persons at the same time']. 'Used both as a noun and a verb in English (in the sense of deafening, annoying, troubling, perplexing, teasing' (PWJ). **C.1735** Jonathan Swift, *A Dialogue in Hybernian Stile*: 'Lord, I was so bodderd t'other day with that prating fool Tom!' **1970** Christy Brown, *Down All the Days*: '"Amn't I after telling you a dozen times?" roared Father. "Is it bothered as well as stupid you are?"' Also **botheration** [exclam. & n.]. **1927** Peadar O'Donnell, *Islanders*: '"The devil take them for hens," Manus growled... "They're only a botheration," Charlie said. "A botheration? They're a curse!"' Hence **bother one's head** [vb. phr., in neg. usage] worry oneself with; **bother one's arse** [vb. phr., in neg. usage] take the trouble to do something; **not a bother on s.o.** [adj. phr.] expressing unconcern or contentment. **1996** Kitty Holland, *Irish Times*, 25 July: 'First to burst his able way

for this a member of the Slippery Fish. Not a bother on him. He quicksteps precisely through the nine laid-out tyres...' **1996** Brenda Power, *Sunday Tribune*, 18 Aug: 'Frank went next door for a couple of bags of chips. How's Jessica, the woman in the chipper [q.v.] wanted to know. Not a bother on her, Frank said.'

Bots, the [nickname]. Botanic Gardens, Dub. (1795), restored 1990s. **1995** Frank McDonald, *Irish Times*, 30 Sept: '[Authenticity] has been achieved in Glasnevin, and there could be no better way of celebrating the bicentenary of "The Bots".'

bottle [n.] (thatching). Handfuls of straw. **1985** Olive Sharkey, *Old Days Old Ways*: 'He pitched it [the straw] up to Jack who placed it alongside him on the roof, preparatory to working with it in manageable amounts known as yolms. These were barely handfuls, and the first few were often referred to as "bottles"...'

bottler [n.]. Itinerant musician's travelling companion. **1996** Pat Borrane, RTÉ Radio, *Sunday Miscellany*, 25 Feb: 'My friend Dick decided to travel with me as what the busking community call a bottler...'

bouchal/boughal [n., <Ir. *buachaill*, boy]. As thus. **1913** Alexander Irvine, *My Lady of the Chimney Corner*: '"Who gethered th' nettles?" Anna pointed to me. "Did th' sting bad, me boughal?"'

bouchalaun see **buachalán**

'bout ye see **how's about you?**

bowjanther [n., poss. <Fr. *pot*, 'pot', but second element is obsc.] (Munster). Pint bottle of Guinness; creamery churn; funnel for straining creamery milk.

bowl [n., <local game of road bowls] as in **a long bowl** [n. phr.] (Cork). Provocative remark (Beecher).

bowler [n., <?]. Dog, usu. of unpretentious pedigree. **1977** James Plunkett, *Collected Short Stories*, 'The Scoop': '"They got it too," Harmless said with relish, "shot it above at Eagle Rock."..."That's the photograph you see in front of you," John Joe said. "The

boys setting off to get the bowler.'" **1981**
Paddy Crosbie, *Your Dinner's Poured Out!*:
'How I longed for a sheep-dog of my
own. "Hey, mister, give us that oul'
bowler."'

bowsie/bowsy [n., gen. deriv. <Ger.
bös-e (adj.), bad, evil, malicious; obsolete
in Eng. 1700]. Gurrier (q.v.), lout. **1914**
James Joyce, *Dubliners*, 'Ivy Day in the
Committee Room': '"Sure, amn't I
never done at the drunken bowsy ever
since he left school?"' **1961** Flann
O'Brien, *The Hard Life*: 'Well, damn the
cardboard shields the Dominicans used in
Spain, those blood-stained bowsies.'
1995 *Leinster Leader* (Naas, Co. Kildare),
15 June: 'He denied suggestions by
solicitor Mr Conal Boyce that he was "a
bit of a thug", or that he "acted the
absolute bousy [*sic*]".'

Box in the Docks, the [nickname, on
formulaic model of Floozie in the Jacuzzi
(q.v.), Chime in the Slime (q.v.), Hags
with the Bags (q.v.), etc. <shape and
location] (Dub.). Waterways Interpretative
Centre, Ringsend.

boxman [n.]. Co-organiser of pitch-
and-toss game with tosser (see **tosser** 1.).
1985 Máirín Johnston, *Around the Banks
of Pimlico*: 'Sartini was one of two
boxmen who ran the toss-school up in
the Greenhills, beyond Griffith Bridge
[Dub.].' See also **feck** [n.] 2., **jack**,
jockey, **rider**.

box, on the [vb. phr.] (Cork). Engaging
in sexual intercourse.

box the fox [vb. phr., <?]. Rob an
orchard. **1991** Bob Quinn, *Smokey
Hollow*: '"Boxing the fox" was the term
for robbing an orchard. This was not a
solo job; it required three thieves in
tandem, one for climbing, one for
gathering, one for lookout.' **1994** Mary
O'Neill in Kevin C. Kearns, *Dublin
Tenement Life*: '"Then in summer they
used to go up to the canal and then 'box
the fox', rob apples from the orchard."'
1995 Patrick Boland, *Tales from a City
Farmyard*: 'we had the usual adventures
like "boxing the fox", getting into fights,
going on picnics'.

boxty [n., <Ir. *bacstaí*, bread made of raw
potatoes]. As thus; dish of potato and
flour. **1991** Seán Ó Ciaráin, *Farewell to
Mayo*: 'During the War we experienced
shortages of many things in Ireland. Flour
for baking was a problem to get and often
we had to do with the boxty bread made
entirely from potatoes.' **1995** Kathleen
Sheehan in Mary Ryan et al. (eds.), *No
Shoes in Summer*: 'it is a favourite with my
grandchildren today, made in the same
way [as *c.*1900–20], as follows: well
washed unpeeled potatoes, raw and
grated, with flour added to the
consistency of pancakes, and also a little
salt; baked by dropping onto a hot pan'.

boy [n.]. 1. (Cork). Film hero. **1996**
Christy Kenneally, *Maura's Boy, A Cork
Childhood*: 'At last, the picture. Oh the
groans when "de boy's" gun clicked on
an empty chamber!' See also **chap**. 2.
[euphem., cf. **lad** 2.] (Ulster). Cold or
influenza. 3. [euphem., cf. **lad** 2.]
(Ulster). Death.

Boy Jones [nickname, after Bernard
Duggan, known as 'the Trinity boy
Jones', alleged informer and associate of
Robert Emmet, executed 1803].
Informer.

Boyle Balderdash, Sir [nickname, <his
colourful employment of 'Irish bulls']. Sir
Boyle Roche, 1743–1807, politician.
1797 *Memoirs of Mrs Margaret Leeson,
Written by Herself*, Vol. III: 'Another day
as I was riding in the [Phoenix] Park,
with a little diminutive dwarf-looking
servant trotting after me, Sir B—
Balderdash accosted me with "yarrow
Piggy, what's that behind you?" "My
A—e, Sir B—," said I.'

boyo [n., <'boy' + endearment suffix].
Lad, cute hoor (q.v.). **1966** Séamus
Murphy, *Stone Mad*: 'But of course it
wouldn't suit this boyo at all..."That's not
the way we do it in Carlow," if you
please.' **1968** Myles na gCopaleen, *The
Best of Myles*: 'he was down in a certain
public house one night last week with
some hop-off-my-thumb from the
County Wicklow on a rogues errant [*sic*]
with two softies that have a quarry out on
the south side, the pair of them being

bested out of their property by the two boyos with the kind assistance of General Whiskey and Major Porter [q.v.]'. **1982** Edmund Lenihan, *Long Ago by Shannon Side*: 'could the local boyos and tricksters have been fooling him, knowing that he was disposed to be credulous...?'

Boys, the [nickname]. 1. Revolutionaries, esp. Republicans 'on the run', cf. the Lads (q.v.). **1925** Liam O'Flaherty, *The Informer*: '"Not that I didn't do me bit to help the boys...but 'tisn't the boys that done the fightin' that get the jobs."' **1975** John Ryan, *Remembering How We Stood*: 'when the Black and Tan [q.v.] war was at its fiercest, some of the "boys" on the run were given refuge in the house of a Mrs Clougherty'. **1987** Lar Redmond, *Emerald Square*: '"an' the Boys must think we live on fresh air". The "boys" referred to were the Shinners [q.v.]...' 2. Hilton Edwards and Micheál MacLiammóir, founders of the Dub. Gate Theatre, 1928. **1994** Christopher Fitz-Simon, *The Boys*: 'In the summer of 1933 "the Boys", as they were now generally known, visited Seville, Paris, London and Stratford on Avon...' See **Sodom and Begorrah**.

boys-a-boys!/boys-o-boys! [exclam.]. Expressive of amazement, disbelief. **1943** George A. Little, *Malachi Horan Remembers*: 'every townland had on everything a different way of going and a different way of living — Boys-o-boys — boys-o-boys."' **1966** Patrick Boyle, *At Night All Cats are Grey*, 'The Betrayers': '"Boys-a-boys, thon's a queer looking yoke [q.v.]," she said, out of the side of her uptwisted toothless mouth.' Also **boys-a-dear** (Ulster) in same sense.

brackery [adj., <Ir. *breac*, spotted, speckled]. As thus, brindled (OTF).

brada [n., <Ir. *bradach*, thief, plunderer]. Scoundrel. **1991** Shane Connaughton, *The Run of the Country*: '"Where's your brada of a son? And his sidekick? I haven't time for blather [q.v.] or plamas [q.v.]."'

braid feet [n. phr., <'broad'] (Ulster). 'Large turf cut with a spade' (SH).

brallion/breallan [n., <Ir. *breallán*, blunderer, fool] (Ulster). 'Good-for-nothing oaf' (YDS).

bramlah/brammelah [n., <'bramble'] (Ulster). Garden rubbish. Also **brammelly** [adj.]. Bow-legged.

Brandy Pad [nickname; see **pad**] (Ulster). Smugglers' route, C19–20. **1990** Mick Matthews, quoted in Walter Love, *The Times of our Lives*: 'The Brandy Pad was the smugglers' route through the [Mourne] mountains. They'd have loaded up in Kilkeel off the boats and come up the Pad to Hilltown...'

brash [n.]. 1. [<Ir. *brais*, bout, turn]. Motion involved in churning butter; any spell of work; helping in the work of churning milk, as in **giving a brash** (vb. phr.) (OTF). **1938** Seumas MacManus, *The Rocky Road to Dublin*: 'Every passing caller took part, as a matter of course, in whatever was proceeding under the roof. If eating, he sat down to the meal; churning, he took his *brash*...' 2. [<Sc. *idem*, illness] (Ulster). As thus.

brasser [n., cf. 'brassy' (adj.), impudent, shameless, & rhym. sl. 'brass nail'/'tail', prostitute]. Hussy, woman of dubious sexual morals, hence term of gen. denigration. **1970** Christy Brown, *Down All the Days*: '"Did you ever have to put up with being called hoor [q.v.] and brasser and fornicator as he put child after child into you...?"' **1987** Lar Redmond, *Emerald Square*: 'Was he another from the bog with "the little divil dancin' in his laughin' Irish eyes" while he sold a naggin [q.v.] to a brasser?' **1991** Roddy Doyle, *The Van*: '"Don't misunderstand me, compadre," he said. "Not just women. All men are brassers as well."'

brat [n., <Ir. *idem*, cloak, robe, garment; metonym for thing contained]. Badly behaved child (wrapped in shawl etc.).

brattle [n., <Sc. *idem*, peal of thunder] (Ulster). As thus.

bratwalloper [n.] (Ulster). Schoolteacher (YDS).

brave [adj., cf. It. *bravo*] (Ulster). Fine, handsome, great; also used ironically.

1979 Jack McBride, *Traveller in the Glens* (of Antrim): 'in our country "brave" means a fine young man or a good sort of girl or a well-developed child. There is, of course, a "brave day" which is not altogether a good day, but fair to middling.' Also in phrases **brave and often** etc.

bravely [adv. as adj.] (Ulster). 1. In good health. **1925** Louise McKay, *Mourne Folk*: '"Och, is that yerself, Peter? An' how are ye Peter, an' how's Mary Ann an' the childer [q.v.]?" "Och, we're all bravely, Sally."' **1948** John O'Connor, *Come Day — Go Day*: '"It's as long as I mind [q.v.] since I seen you. Are you bravely?"' 2. Moderately under the influence.

bread–earner [n.]. Knife used by shoeblacks. **1802** Maria & Richard Lovell Edgeworth, *Essay on Irish Bulls*: '"I out's with my bread–earner, and give it him up to Lamprey in the bread basket." John Edward Walsh, *Ireland Sixty Years Ago* (1847) comments: 'All the knives were then made by the famous cutler by the name of Lamprey, which was impressed on the blade. The true reading is, "up to de Y in the bread basket", the name being always formed with the L to the point and the Y to the handle, so that not only the blade, but the very name...was buried in the body.'

breadsnapper [n.] (Ulster). Child, esp. 'young lad who can eat his weight in groceries' (YDS). **1997** Alan Roberts, *The Rasherhouse* (see **rasher**): '"Ahh, a bread snapper, ah God help ya. How old?"... "Six months." "Ahhh Jasus! [q.v.] Boy or a child [q.v.]?"' See **snapper**.

break [vb.] (Ulster). Embarrass.

break a pudding [vb. phr.]. Belch. **1979** Michael O'Beirne, *Mister, A Dublin Childhood*: 'Granny nodded and said "Onions often repeat." (This was known as "breakin' a pudden".)'

break one's melt [vb. phr., see **melt**] (Cork). Try beyond one's patience.

breallan see **brallion**

breedog [n., <Ir. *Brídeóg*, little Bridget]. Figure dressed to represent St Bridget.

1943 George A. Little, *Malachi Horan Remembers*: 'Oh, the Bride Oge [*sic*]? A celebration in honour of St Bridget...It was held...from 2 February to Shrove. Brittas is the great place here for it.'

breeks [n. pl., <Sc. unpalat. form of 'britches', <OE *brec*] (Ulster). Britches, trousers. **1925** Louise McKay, *Mourne Folk*: '"many's the time I put him in my bed till I wud patch his bits of breeks"'.

brength [n., <'breadth', infl. by 'length'] (Ulster). Size.

brew see **broo**

brillauns [n. pl., <Ir. *brealláin*, rags, scraps]. '[A]pplied to the poor articles of furniture in a peasant's cottage' (PWJ).

brillo [adj., cf. Brit. sl. 'brill', wonderful, exciting + endearment suffix]. As thus. **1997** Alan Roberts, *The Rasherhouse* (see **rasher**): '"Jasus [q.v.], that's brillo, Betty. Ya sure but [q.v.]?" "Yea! How many times do I have ta bleedin' well tell ya?"'

bring home [vb. phr.]. Deliver a child. **1994** Mary Corbally in Kevin C. Kearns, *Dublin Tenement Life*: 'When your mother went into labour the handywoman [q.v.], like Mrs Dunleavy, would get everything prepared. She brought us home for my mother.'

brissle/bristle [vb., <Sc. *idem*, broil, scorch] (Ulster). Scorch one's shins at the fire; toast boiled potatoes golden brown.

broad pieces [n. pl.] (Ulster). Foreign coins, C17–18. **1953** *Belfast Telegraph*, 'Crawfordsburn — The Ulster House once sold Smugglers' Wine', 5 Aug: 'So many foreign coins were changed here or hereabouts [North Co. Down] in the seventeenth and eighteenth century that there was an accepted rate for "broad pieces", as the local inhabitants termed the pistoles and moidores.'

broc/brock [n. & vb.] (Ulster). 1. [n. & vb., cf. Ir. *broc*, leavings, refuse; spoil, mess; Sc. *idem* <Old High Ger. *brochân* (vb.), break into bits]. Food scraps, leavings; mess up food. **1938** Seumas MacManus, *The Rocky Road to Dublin*: 'When one sits down to eat from a pot of stirabout [q.v.] it is good form to take it

"out of a face" — working one's way across the pot spoonful by spoonful in an orderly way. An unmannerly fellow, however, is as like as not to broc the pot, digging here, there, everywhere.' **1995** Seamus Martin, *Irish Times*, 28 Nov: 'Johnny Orr would be approaching his 130th year now if the vicissitudes as a collector of brock — domestic rubbish to you — had not caught up with him.' 2. [n., <Ir. *broc*, badger]. 'One who has a bad smell' (Patterson).

broddle/brodle [n., cf. Sc. *bodle*, small copper coin] (Ulster). Pre-decimal twopenny piece.

broganeer/broganier [n., <'brogue']. 'One who has a strong Irish pronunciation or accent' (Grose). **1797** *Memoirs of Mrs Margaret Leeson, Written by Herself, Vol. III*: 'Mrs B— appeared to be a little termagant, a vulgar Munster broganeer vixen, with nothing to recommend her but her complexion...'

broo/buroo/brew/beroo [n.]. 1. [prop. n., by metathesis <'borough'] (Ulster). Employment exchange; unemployment benefit. **1939** Denis Ireland, *Statues round the City Hall*: 'He [the unemployed Belfast man] has no philosophy of leisure, and no means of acquiring one; and the "buroo" upon which he depends for his sixpences for the bookies, the pictures or the dance hall, still hands him his money as if it were a charity...' **1991** Carol Coulter, *Web of Punishment*: '"They ask you, 'Are you sure you're taking the kids over [to Britain]?' You go down with the doctor's letter to the brew, then to the travel agent..."' **1993** Sam McAughtry, *Touch & Go*: '"Jack's a clerk in the buroo," Mary explained. I was impressed. In our society buroo clerks were big stuff.' 2. [n., <Sc. *idem*, good opinion; inclination, liking] (Ulster). As thus. Also **broo with** dealings with. 3. [n., <?] (Ulster). Witch who can turn into a hare. 4. [n., <Ir. *bruach*, bank of river]. As thus; also **water-broo** in same sense.

brooghled [p. part. as adj., <Sc. *broggle* (vb.), bungle, botch] (Ulster). Badly executed.

Brophys, the [n., <?] (Dub.). Venereal disease. **1987** Lar Redmond, *Emerald Square*: 'mercurial ointment (Navy Blue Butter) for the treatment of crabs or their more fearful cousins, "the Brophys", who not alone bit a piece out of your balls but ran up your arse to eat it'.

brose [n., cf. Sc. *brosey, brosy* in same sense] (Ulster). Very fat person.

brosna/brosny [n., <Ir. *brosna*, decaying twigs, kindling]. As thus. **1938** Seumas MacManus, *The Rocky Road to Dublin*: 'His pockets were full to bursting, and he was trying to fill also the last available hold-all, his stomach, when the sound of *brosna*, breaking underfoot, told him he was caught.' **1936** Frank O'Connor, *Bones of Contention and Other Stories*, 'The Majesty of the Law': 'Old Dan Bride was breaking down brosna for the fire when he heard a step on the path.'

broth of a boy [adj. & n. phr., cf. Sc. *broth of a sweat*, violent perspiration]. Outstanding individual, latterly Paddyism. **1979** John Morrow, *The Confessions of Proinsias O'Toole*: 'just one short interview at a barricade...had established him as the spokesman for the New Ireland — a broth of a bhoy, strong but merciful, articulate, humorous, tolerant'. **1995** Jerome Reilly, *Sunday Independent*, 31 Dec: 'I reckon Daniel O'Donnell to appear on *Top of the Pops* in 1996 at 33-1 is a mighty attractive bet. The broth of a boy from Kincasslagh has to be worth a fiver of anyone's disposable income.' **1996** Katie Donovan, *Irish Times*, 9 Nov: '[Michael] Collins [see **the Big Fella**] was more than just a broth-of-a-boy swashbuckler. He had a serious philosophy about how Ireland was going to be...'

broughan [n., <Sc. *brochan/broughan*, thin gruel; Ir. *brachán*, porridge] (Ulster). Porridge. Also **spill the broughan** [vb. phr.]. Doze off.

browl [n., <Ir. *breall*, oaf]. Stupid or foolish person.

browlt [adj., cf. Sc. *bowltest*, most bent or crooked (CSD); cf. MDu. *boghelen* (vb.), curve] (Ulster). Deformed or bowed in the legs.

brown gargle [n., see **gargle**]. Stout. **1955** J.P. Donleavy, *The Ginger Man*: 'Soles of the feet warming deliciously and the brown gargle as they say putting the mind afloat.'

brown, in one's as in **you do in your brown** [cant phr., poss. ref. to excrement]. Expression of disbelief. **1991** Roddy Doyle, *The Van*: '"Do none of yis [q.v.] go up to the Hikers at all?" "I do," said Kenny. "You do in your brown," said Anto.'

Broy Harriers [nickname, <Eamonn Broy (1887–1972), Garda Commissioner]. Members of the Garda Síochána nominated by Fianna Fáil and recruited by Broy in the 1930s. **1971** Maurice Manning, *The Blueshirts* (q.v.): 'the government's decision to set up a reserve Volunteer force and the setting up of the "Broy Harriers" had attracted members and potential members from the IRA'. **1992** Sean O'Callaghan, *Down by the Glenside, Memoirs of an Irish Boyhood*: 'It is ironic to note that the men who asked these questions, the Broy Harriers, had been his comrades-in-arms in the old days.' **1996** Katie Donovan, *Irish Times*, 9 Nov: 'The real Ned Broy, incidentally, lived on to found Dev[q.v.]'s version of the Special Branch in the 1930s, called the Broy Harriers.'

bruckle sayson [n. phr., <OE *brucol* (adj.), brittle] (Ulster). Very unsettled weather.

bruillment/brulliagh/bruilliment [n., <OF *brouiller* (vb.), put in disorder] (Ulster). Row, noisy scuffle.

brumf [adj., poss. <'bluff'] (Ulster). 'Curt or short in manner' (Patterson).

brus [n., <Ir. *idem*, broken, crumbled bits]. As thus; fragments of boiled sweets sold cheaply. **1995** Phil O'Keeffe, *Down Cobbled Streets, A Liberties Childhood*: '"It's all *brus*," I complained to Jennie when we opened the bag outside the shop...Maybe it was, but it had pieces of brown aniseed rock, pink candy-striped rock, broken "glassy" fruit sweets and chunks of Peggie's leg [q.v.]...'

brush [n. & vb., cf. 'have a brush with a woman; to lie with her' (Grose)]. 1. [n.]. Female pubic hair. 2. [vb.]. Copulate with. **1797** *Memoirs of Mrs Margaret Leeson, Written by Herself, Vol. III*: '[when] Saunders's newspaper was handed about, which announced the marriage of a Mr and Mrs Brush, the witty and facetious councellor [John Philpot] Curran instantly produced the following: Now Brush with Mrs Brush, a Brush may take,/And Brush her Brush, so little Brushes make'.

brutal [adj.]. Very bad. **1991** Ferdia Mac Anna, *The Last of the High Kings*: 'away from Frankie who had annoyed him this morning by taunting him that his "old cowboy books were brutal"'. **1994** Mary Doolan in Kevin C. Kearns, *Dublin Tenement Life*: 'And I'll tell you, they weren't the "good old days". *Not at all!* They were *brutal* days.' **1996** Lise Hand, *Sunday Tribune*, 1 Dec: 'Howarya [see **howaya!**] — God, Maggie, sorry I'm dead late, but the traffic was only brutal around town...'

B-Special see **B man**

buachalán/bouchalaun [n., <Ir. *buachalán*, ragwort]. As thus. **1968** John Healy, *The Death of an Irish Town*: 'The land declined, subject to flooding and the annual sneaking crop of the whirlwind of thistledown and rushes and buachalláns [*sic*]...' **1992** John M. Feehan, *My Village, My World*: '"We'd have to do that [walk the land] to satisfy my man that he wasn't getting a pig in a poke, and that the land was well fenced and watered, with no ragworth [*sic*], thistles or bouchalauns."'

buala bos [n. phr., Ir. *idem*, 'putting the hands together', applause]. As thus. **1996** Headline, *Sunday Tribune*, 27 Oct: 'A big buala bos for TnaG [Teilifís na Gaeilge]'.

bubbelizer [n.] (Ulster). Stammerer (Todd).

buck [adj. & n.]. 1. [adj., <n., 'rare: *c*.1720–30, a forward, daring woman' (DHS)]. As thus. **1948** Patrick Kavanagh, *Tarry Flynn*: 'Nothing kills me only these buck nuns that make out they wouldn't look at a man.' Also **buckijit** [n.] (Ulster). 'Extreme type of idiot' (Pepper). See **eejit**. 2. [n., <Hindust. *bak*, *bahk*, conversation, 1895, poss. brought back

by Ir. soldiers in Brit. army in India] (Cork). Garrulity, chat. **1993** Aine de Courcy in Michael Verdon, *Shawlies* (q.v.), *Echo Boys* (q.v.), *the Marsh and the Lanes* (q.v.): *Old Cork Remembered*: '"No more ould buck out of you, you ignorant bostoon [q.v.]," said Finbarr. "I'll learn you respect for your betters!"' **1966** Séamus Murphy, *Stone Mad*: '"No more old buck out of you now," said Nedgill, "if you're not interested the other men are."' 3. [n., <OE *buc*, male deer; and as title]. Gentleman of eccentric habits; rake. **1847** John Edward Walsh, *Ireland Sixty Years Ago*: 'Among the gentry of the period was a class called "Bucks" whose whole enjoyment and the business of whose life seemed to consist of eccentricity and violence. Many of their names have come down to us. "Buck English", "Buck Sheehy"...' 4. [n., with def. art.]. Tuberculosis. **1968** John Healy, *The Death of an Irish Town*: '"Galloping consumption" was the fear of those 1940 days: when you heard someone had "the buck" it seemed almost a death sentence and all too often was.' 5. [n.] as in **run a buck** [vb. phr.]. 'To poll a bad vote at an election' (Grose).

buckaugh [n., cf. Ir. *bocaire*, beggar]. Itinerant beggar. **1824** Thomas Crofton Croker, *Researches in the South of Ireland*: 'Deeply conversant with character, this singular class of mendicants are quick, artful and intelligent, but assume a careless and easy manner...I have heard instances of the almost chivalrous honour of a poor buckaugh.'

bucked [p. part. as adj., euphem.]. Finished; done for. **1995** Shane Connaughton, *A Border Diary*: 'Albert gives the emotions full value. He has to say the line "We're bucked now, me boyo [q.v.]. She's dead."'

buckeen [n., <Ir. *boicín*, dimin. of *boc*, rake, playboy]. Bully; rake. **1797** *Memoirs of Mrs Margaret Leeson, Written by Herself, Vol. III*: 'Another day as I was riding on the Rock Road [Blackrock, Co. Dub.], a *Buckeen* accosted me with "By G— Peg, I wish I was st—g [strapping? stroking? strumming?] you."' **1843** W.M. Thackeray, *The Irish Sketch Book*: 'At

Ennis, as well as everywhere else in Ireland, there were of course the regular number of swaggering-looking buckeens, and shabby-genteel idlers...' **1866** Patrick Kennedy, *Legendary Fictions of the Irish Celts*: 'So the buckeens that were coortin' the eldest ladies, wouldn't give peace or ease to their lovers, nor to the king, till they got consent to the marriage...'

bucket [vb.]. Rain very heavily.

buckies [n. pl., <Sc. *buckie*, wild rosehip] (Ulster). Wild roses.

buckled [p. part. as adj.]. Intoxicated. **1990** Roddy Doyle, *The Snapper* (q.v.): '"I was drunk," said Sharon..."I know. So was I. I'd never've — God, I was buckled."' **1995** *Irish Times*: 'The accused man said by 9 p.m. he was "buckled drunk" and was at the staggering stage...'

bucklep [n. & vb., <'leap']. Ostentatious action/gesture; behave thus. Hence **bucklepper** [n.]. **1993** Seamus Heaney, *The Midnight Verdict* (translation of Brian Merriman, *Cúirt an Mheán Oíche*): 'A star bucklepper, the very man/You'd be apt to nickname "merry man"...'

buckle-the-beggars [n. C17–19]. Individual who performed illegal marriage ceremonies.

bucknyay [n., <?] (Ulster). Term of contempt.

bucko [n., <Ir. *boc*, buck, playboy + endearment suffix]. **1922** James Joyce, *Ulysses*: 'That's the bucko that'll organise her, take my tip.' **1980** Padraic O'Farrell, *How the Irish Speak English*: '"You have no call to carry on like that," says a father..."Oh, how bad you are," the daughter might well answer, "and not a word do you ever say to that bucko of a brother of mine."' **1991** Bob Quinn, *Smokey Hollow*: '"I'm warning you, me bucko. Next time you won't have your mother to save you. I'll take your solemn life, I swear."'

bucky wire [n. phr., cf. Sc. *buckie*, wild rosehip] (Ulster). Barbed wire.

buddaree [n., <Ir. *bodaire* = *bodach*, churl]. Rich, vulgar farmer. **1939** James Joyce, *Finnegans Wake*: 'Banalanna [see **bannalanna**] Bangs Ballyhooly [q.v.]

Out Of Her Buddaree Of A Bullavogue [q.v.].'

buddhelin [pres. part., <?]. Dabbling the hands in water; noise and action of ducks searching for food in shallow water (OTF).

buddley [n., <Ir. *bodalach*, big ungainly young person] (Ulster). Sausage; fat person.

buddy [n., <'body'] (Ulster). Man, person. **1972** Florence Mary McDowell, *Roses and Rainbows*: 'Adam McMeekin owned the Cogry Mill...Behind his back he was the "Wee (q.v.) Buddy", this last being merely Ulster for "man" and certainly *not* American for "friend".'

budget [n., poss. <*idem*, 'title for a journal' (OED)]. As thus. **1922** James Joyce, *Ulysses*: 'he wanted to milk me into the tea well he's beyond everything I declare somebody ought to put him in the budget'.

budion [n., <Ir. *boidín*, penis] (Ulster). As thus, but undersized (YDS).

buff [n.]. 1. Self-important individual. 2. Also **buffer** [derog.]. Countryman. **1968** John Healy, *The Death of an Irish Town*: 'If you were born beyond the edge of the town you were "a buffer". You wore clogs with yellow metal strips on the toe.' See also **sham**.

BUFFALO see **BIFFO**

buffer [n.]. 1. '[I]n Ireland it signifies a boxer' (Grose). 2. See **buff** 2.

bug [nickname]. 'A name given by the Irish to Englishmen; bugs having, as it is said, been introduced into Ireland by the English' (Grose).

bugle [n., <?]. Erection. **1991** Roddy Doyle, *The Van*: '"Caramba, lads, I nearly broke the counter with the bugle I had on me."'

bulkies [n. pl.] (Ulster). Royal Ulster Constabulary. **1979** John Morrow, *The Confessions of Proinsias O'Toole*: '"Twenty-five poun' of gelly buried in his back garden an' an anonymous tip-off to the bulkies. No go. The gelly disappeared and the next night the Prods [q.v.] blow the Hibernian hall."'

bullagadaun [n., <Ir. *bolgadán*, fat person or animal]. Stout, pot-bellied individual (PWJ).

bullaphants [adj., var. of Brit. rhym. sl. *elephants* = elephant's trunk, drunk]. As thus.

bullavaun/bullavogue [n., <Ir. *balbhán*, dumb/silent person, stammerer]. 'Strong, rough fellow' (PWJ).

bull-dragging [adj., <weight and resistance of bull]. Very laborious. **1948** Patrick Kavanagh, *Tarry Flynn*: '"How did you get on on the day, Tarry?" "Nearly finished." "Ye shouldn't try to do a bull-dragging day. Isn't there more days than years."'

bullet [n.] (Ulster/Munster). Projectile used in game of road bowls. **1948** John O'Connor, *Come Day — Go Day*: 'Lazily he picked up the bullet and walked back a few paces with downcast eyes.'

bullia-batter/boolia-botha/beely-batter [n., <Ir. *buaileadh bata*, blow with a stick] (Ulster). 'Noisy free-for-all' (YDS).

Bull's-Eye Day [nickname]. Day for payment of Brit. army pensions. **1993** Aine de Courcy in Michael Verdon, *Shawlies* (q.v.), *Echo Boys* (q.v.), *the Marsh and the Lanes* (q.v.): *Old Cork Remembered*: 'Every Wednesday in Ireland was called Bull's-Eye Day because that's when the soldiers got their pensions. Pappy [Coleman] would go on the drink and then go mad [q.v.] drunk down the street.'

bull's lick see **cow's lick**

bull's look/s [n. phr./pl.]. Angry glance/s. **1965** Lee Dunne, *Goodbye to the Hill*: 'as I got near the old Canon, who was a right [see **right** 1.] crochety old bastard, he gave me a bull's look'.

bully [adj., <MDu. *boele* (n.), sweetheart] (Ulster). Excellent, outstanding. **1927** Peadar O'Donnell, *Islanders*: '"You're a bully girl," Mary Manus concluded. "Are ye wan of the Paddy Andy's," Mary Doogan asked.'

bum [vb., <Ir. *bomannach* (adj.), bragging, boastful]. Boast. **1970** Seán O'Faoláin, *Stories of Seán O'Faoláin*, 'The End of the

Record': "'Ghosts?...My ould divil of a tailor is forever and always talkin' about 'um...Bummin' and boashtin' he is from morning to night...'" Hence **on the bum** [adj. phr.] in same sense.

bumbee work [n. phr., <'bumble-bee' <ME *bumme* (vb.), buzz] (Ulster). Nonsense.

bum clock [n. phr., <Sc. *idem*, flying beetle; see **clock** 4.] (Ulster). As thus. **1925** Louise McKay, *Mourne Folk*: "'Begob [q.v.],'" said John, "ye haven't as much [poteen (q.v.)] there as wud drown a bum clock. Will you have a thimbleful, Ned?'"

bummer [n., <ME *bumme* (vb.), buzz] (Ulster). Child's toy, 'made with a piece of twine and a small circular disc, usu. of tin' (Patterson).

bumper [n.] (horse racing). Amateur flat race. **1990** Raymond Smith, *Vincent O'Brien, The Master of Ballydoyle*: 'The race that he [O'Brien] chose for his first gamble was the Sportsman's Plate, an amateur flat race — or "bumper", as styled in Ireland on 8 May 1941...' **1996** *Leinster Leader* (Naas, Co. Kildare), 24 Oct: 'Usually producing good competitive fields, Bumpers are very popular with the betting public...'

bunched [p. part. as adj.]. Physically exhausted; stymied. **1977** James Plunkett, *Collected Short Stories*, 'A Touch of Genius': 'Naturally, there was no sense at all in singing to a house as poor as that. "You're bunched, Danny," I said.'

bundie [n., <'bun']. Child's backside.

bungalow [nickname]. S.o. of limited intelligence — with 'nothing on top'.

bungalow bliss [n. phr., <success of Ted McCarthy's *Irish Bungalow Book* (1976) popularising this invasive phenomenon]. Iron., somewhat derog. ref. to modest and architecturally obtrusive rural 'bungalow blight' and the perceived lifestyle of the incumbents. **1984** John McGahern, *Oldfashioned*: 'He is a young priest and tells them that God is on their side and wants them to want children, bungalow bliss, a car, and colour television.'

bunk out [vb., cf. Brit. sl. 'bunk off' in same sense]. Play truant, mitch (q.v.). **1986** Bob Geldof, *Is That It?*: 'Lahiffe and I bunked out and went to the shop across the road for sweets. This was forbidden.'

bunser [n., poss. <'bun' + endearment suffix] (Dub.). Pet name for a child. **1975** Eilís Brady, *All In! All In!*: 'a little girl can bask in the security of being "her Daddy's little hen"...or his "little bunser"'.

bunse up [n. & vb., poss. <'bonus'] (Ulster). Commission paid to s.o. who brings buyer and seller together at flax market (CUD); pool resources.

bunt [vb., <'bun(ny) rabbit'] (Ulster). Run away like a rabbit.

bunty [adj., <?] (Ulster). Short and stout (of person).

burgoo [n., <?] (Dub.). Porridge.

burl see **birl**

Burma Road [nickname, <notorious WWII construction by prisoners of war] (railway). **1995** Greg Ryan, *Irish Times*, 'Timber on the Train', 25 Oct: 'the remainder of the branch, from Claremorris through Swinford and Kiltimagh to the main Sligo line...was known by generations of railwaymen as "The Burma Road" because of its rough condition'.

burned out [adj., cf. Brit. sl. 'browned off']. Annoyed, irritated. **1992** Pauline Bracken, *Light of Other Days, A Dublin Childhood*: 'we played with such vigour and enthusiasm that we carried off second prize. Others who had practised dutifully for many weeks...were somewhat burned out.'

burn-shin-da-eve [n.] (Ulster). 'Term for a woman who is fond of crouching over the fire' (Patterson).

burn-the-gully [n., <*gully* (q.v.)] (Ulster). Careless/rough/unskilled workman.

buroo see **broo**

burst [vb. trans., cf. Brit. sl. 'bust']. Inflict significant injury on. **1987** Lar Redmond, *Emerald Square*: "'You're a gas [q.v.] man," he said...."After bursting two Crumlin villagers...'"

bursted churn [n. phr.] (Ulster). 'When the sun sets before the grain is all cut on the last day of reaping...there is said to be a bursted churn' (Patterson).

bursy see **birsey**

Burton books [n. pl., <?]. Cheap reprints used in hedge schools (q.v.). **1847** John Edward Walsh, *Ireland Sixty Years Ago*: 'They were small octavos, bound in cheap white basil, the paper and type of the coarsest kind, and full of typographical errors, illustrated occasionally by plates of the most "uncouth sculpture".' **1968** P.J. Dowling, *The Hedge Schools of Ireland*: 'Carleton is particularly critical of the reading books used by school children ...[and] gives a long list of these books. Most of them were probably the cheap reprints issued at Dublin, Limerick and Cork, and known as the "Burton Books" or "sixpenny books".'

bury the baldy fella [vb. phr.]. Achieve vaginal penetration. **1991** Ferdia Mac Anna, *The Last of the High Kings*: '"The Yank's a bit of all right," Hopper said. "Tell us, are ye burying the baldy fella then?"'

busk [vb., <ON *buask*, prepare oneself]. Dress up.

but [transposed conj. employed in colloq. Hib.E for emphasis at end of phrase or sentence, cf. Craig McGregor, *Profile of Australia* (1966): 'Ending a sentence with "like" [q.v.] and "but" is a common habit']. **1991** Roddy Doyle, *The Van*: '"No hang on Jim," said Bimbo, "I'll get this one." "It's my round but."' **1995** Shane Connaughton, *A Border Diary*: '"Holy God [q.v.]," I say to John Rudden, "what if your sow had died of a heart attack?" He looks at me like I'm mad. "She didn't but."'

butt [n.]. 1. (Cork). Horse or donkey cart (PWJ). 2. Core of apple. **1995** Gay Byrne in Seán Power (ed.), *Those were the Days, Irish Childhood Memories*: 'if you're going to be a successful bandit or major criminal, you have to keep your wits about you...I was inexperienced, and went into the house with the butt of the apple (core, to you) still in my hand.' Hence **butts on you!** [exclam.]. **1995** Phil O'Keeffe, *Down Cobbled Streets, A*

Liberties Childhood: 'We turned into Thomas Court, and there the young thief was. "Butts on ye!" he yelled and he swiped the apple from Betty's hand.' 3. Mark or boundary line from which competitors start in road bowling, marbles, horse jumping, etc.

buttons, make [vb. phr., <buttons (n. pl.), lumps of excrement; 'his a-se makes buttons' (Grose)]. Befoul oneself through fear. **1689** Anon., *The Irish Hudibras*: 'The *Dear Joys* [q.v.] strait began to quake,/Stinking for fear, did Buttons make.'

butty [n., <Ir. *bodach*, churl, lout]. Short person/animal; short-handled tool/implement. See also **boddagh**.

buyer [n.]. Cattle dealer. **1913** George A. Birmingham, *General John Regan*: '"Buyers", men whose business it is to carry the half-fed Connacht beasts to the fattening pastures of Meath and Kildare...'

by- for words and phrases beginning thus see also under **be-**

by-ball [n.] (Belfast). Reprieve. **1994** Paddy O'Gorman, *Queuing for a Living*: '"They gave me a by-ball you know. A by-ball that's like a second chance."'

by gaineys! [exclam., cf. *Janey Mac!* (q.v.)]. Expression of surprise. **1950** Liam O'Flaherty, *Insurrection*: '"By Ganeys! [*sic*] That looks like the king of all guns."' **1954** George Fitzmaurice, *Dublin Magazine*, 'The Terrible Baisht', Oct/Dec: 'DALY ...let the wife say what she likes, by gannies [*sic*], I'll go and have a couple of good balls of malt [q.v.] for myself.'

by the neck [adj. & adv. phr.]. Descriptive of bottle of beer/stout consumed or served without benefit of a glass. **1994** Greg Dalton, *My Own Backyard, Dublin in the Fifties*: '...whenever the notion took him. All in all about twice a year and no more than two half pint bottles of stout by the neck.'

by the new time [catchphrase, <pop. term for daylight saving or 'summer' time]. Without delay; at a great pace.

C

cabbage-patch rebellion [nickname, derog.]. Abortive rising by William Smith O'Brien, Ballingarry, Co. Tipperary, 29 July 1848. **1993** R.F. Foster, *Paddy & Mr Punch*: 'The climax of these tasteless jokes...was the so-called "cabbage-patch rebellion" of 1848, which gave cartoonists and satirists another heaven-sent opportunity for Irish ridicule.'

Cabbage-Stump Night [nickname] (Leinster). Hallowe'en. **1994** Vonnie Banville Evans, *The House in the Faythe*: 'the excitement of banging the paint off our neighbours' front doors with cabbage stumps on cabbage stump night. This was the name we had for Hallowe'en.'

cabber [n., cf. Eng. dial. *cab* (vb.), clog with dirt] (Ulster). Ring of dirt around the neck (YDS).

cabby-car [n.]. Hand-propelled railway trolley. **1996** Dermot Healy, *The Bend for Home*: 'The cabby-car, known as the up-and-downer or back-breaker...now sat in a shed at the disused station in Swellan.'

cabby/cobby house [n., <?; see **babby house**]. Child's playhouse. **1993** Isabel Healy in Seán Dunne (ed.), *The Cork Anthology*, 'A Cork Girlhood': 'We had "cabby-houses" and imaginary friends.'

cabin-hunt [vb., cf. Ir. *ag dul sna bothánaibh*, frequenting neighbours' houses, <*bothán* (n.), hut, cabin]. 'Go about from house to house to gossip' (PWJ). **1920** Seumas O'Kelly, *The Leprechaun of Kilmeen*: 'I noticed herself [q.v.] going out a good deal and travelling all over the parish, and I wondered at this, for she was never the one to do much cabin hunting or the like.' **1952** Bryan MacMahon, *Children of the Rainbow*: 'Although it was a night for cabin-hunting, Hibe was very diffident about going into Font'a.'

ca-ca [n., see **cack**]. Shit. 'King James II of England was known to the Irish as "Séamus a' Caca"' (YDS).

cack [n., <Ir. *cac*, excrement, poss. <Lat. *cacare* (vb.), void excrement, hence Eng. sl. 'cack-handed', left-handed]. As thus. **1979** Michael O'Beirne, *Mister, A Dublin Childhood*: '"Coming here to raise a row, you oul cack you. Blasted oul cow!"' Also **cackie-knuckle** [n.] (Leinster). Shot in children's marbles game. **1994** Vonnie Banville Evans, *The House in the Faythe*: 'There were various shots; one with the peculiar name of "cackie-knuckle" comes to mind...'

caddy/cadday [n.]. 1. [<Sc. *caddie*, errand boy, young fellow, <Fr. *cadet*, youngest of family]. Young boy; boy hired as servant; sharp-witted individual. **1939** Patrick Gallagher ('Paddy the Cope' (q.v.)), *My Story*: 'The mistress came to the door and spoke to the horse. "Lizzie," he said, "what do you think of the caddy I brought you?"' 2. (Ulster) 'Rather smelly old man' (YDS). 3. [abbrev.]. Catholic catechism.

cadge/cadger [vb. & n., cf. Sc. *cadger* (n.), carrier] (Ulster). Hawk goods for sale; professional distributor of poteen (q.v.), or illicit whiskey. **1938** Seumas MacManus, *The Rocky Road to Dublin*: 'He couldn't have been more than six or seven when he tried to help Eddie Quinn dispose of the old horse that time out of mind had served him for cadging fish from door to door...' **1978** John McGuffin, *In Praise of Poteen*: 'In Derry around 1800 the cadgers were so confident that the poitín was brought to town from Inishowen...in open tubs on donkeys.'

cadgy [adj., <Sc. *idem*, cheerful, in good spirits] (Ulster). As thus.

caffler [n., cf. Ir. *cafaire*, prater (Dinneen)] (Munster). 'Contemptible little fellow who gives saucy, *cheeky* foolish talk' (PWJ). **1951** Frank O'Connor, *Traveller's Samples*, 'First Confession': 'Nora came skeltering madly down the church. "Lord God!" she cried, "The snivelling little caffler! I knew he'd do it! I knew he'd disgrace me!"' **1978** T. Hallisey, *Cork Holly Bough*: '"You caffler, you scut [q.v.], you trickie [q.v.], you tally-boy [q.v.]," he roared.' **1992** Sean O'Callaghan, *Down by*

the Glenside, Memoirs of an Irish Boyhood:
'Another problem [driving cattle] was that
young "cafflers" (layabouts) often took
gates off their hinges on the road to the
fair...' Also **caffling** [pres. part.].
Gossiping, idle chattering. **1991** James
Kennedy, *The People who Drank Water
from the River.* 'I heard my father talk
about the caffling that went on when
many of the Brackile people had a garden
in Bobby Ryan's of Newtown.'

cagey-cannon [n.] as in **play cagey-
cannon** [vb. phr.]. Be cautious or 'cagey'.
1968 Myles na gCopaleen, *The Best of
Myles*: '"I would play cagey-cannon while
that gentleman is in the offing because he
would take the shirt off one's back."'

Caitlín ní Houlihan see **Cathleen ní
Houlihan**

caldera [n., <Ir. *cealdrach*, wretched-
looking creature, spiritless person,
coward]. As thus.

caleery/kileery [n. & adj., <?]. Giddy,
hysterical person; full of mischief. Hence
caleeried [adj.] scatterbrained, giddy;
caleeriness [abst. n.] frivolity, mischief.

callig/calligaleen see **colligoleen**

camac [n., nonce-word, <Revs. Ryan
& Camac, hanged at Wexford, C19, for
uttering false halfpennies]. 1. Any
unnecessarily complicated/costly contrivance for effecting a simple purpose. 2.
'Equivalent for any substantive' (S&R).

camalough [n., <Ir. *ceamalach*, ungainly
person or animal, lout]. Ill-mannered
individual.

canary/canaries [n.] as in **have a
canary/canaries** [vb. phr.]. Have a fit
(metaphorically) (EW).

canat see **kinat**

candlesticks [n. pl.]. Drips of mucus
from the nose. **1995** Patrick Boland,
Tales from a City Farmyard: 'There was a
kid who lived in Chamber Street [Dub.]
called Snotty O'Doherty, so named
because of the ever-present "candlesticks"
between his nose and upper lip...'

candy [adj., <?, mid. C18–early C19
(DHS)]. Drunk.

cant [vb. & n.]. 1. [vb., <OF *invuant*
<Med. Lat. *quantum*, how much. Cf. Ir.
ceant (n.), auction, <same sources]. Sell
by auction. **1729** Jonathan Swift, *A
Modest Proposal*: 'They were everywhere
canting their land upon short leases.' 2.
[n., cf. Low Ger. *kant* (adj.), lively,
cheerful]. Sport, enjoyment. **1996**
Dermot Healy, *The Bend for Home*: 'the
night finished with beetroot sandwiches,
Jacob's marsh-mallows and tea. We had
great cant.' Hence **cantie/canty** [adj.].
Pleasant, cheerful (of person); very
tidy/neat; thorough. **1987** Thomas
Beggs, *The Poetical Works of Thomas Beggs*,
'The Auld Wife's Address to her
Spinning Wheel': 'Now fare thee weel,
my cantie wee [q.v.] wheel,/In age an'
youth my staff an' my stay...'

canted [p. part., <Lat. *canthus* (n.), tyre
of a wheel] (handball, Munster/Leinster).
Of ball struck by mistake out of court.
See also **banished**.

cappy/cappy pig/caup pig [n., <Sc.
cap, shallow wooden bowl, <ON *koppr*,
bowl] (Ulster). Pet pig hand-reared from
bowl.

Captain Fantastic [nickname]. Mick
McCarthy, captain of Ir. soccer team
under Jack Charlton, 1980s–1990s,
succeeding him as manager, 1996. **1996**
Gerry Thornley, *Irish Times*, 6 Feb:
'Having played for the Republic 57
times, earning the soubriquet Captain
Fantastic, his Charltonesque candidness
and honesty will add to his popularity.'

car [n., <Ir. *cár*, mouth (showing teeth,
grin, grimace)]. As thus; forced smile.

Caravat [nickname, <Ir. *caravat*, cravat]
(Leinster). One of two hostile factions,
early C19. **1824** R.H. Ryland, *The
History, Topography and Antiquities of the
County and City of Waterford*: 'The
following extract from a report of a trial
which took place before a special
commission at Clonmel, in the year
1811, will give the reader some
explanation of the names by which these
formidable factions were distinguished
...Q. Why were they called Caravats? A.
A man of the name of Hanly was hanged:
he was prosecuted by the Shanavests

[q.v.] and Paudeen Car said he would not leave the place of execution till he saw the *caravat* about the fellow's neck: and from that time they were called Caravats.' **1824** Thomas Crofton Croker, *Researches in the South of Ireland*: 'The associations of Caravat and Shanavest have since the Rebellion disturbed the Southern Counties.'

Carder [nickname]. Revolutionary association, late C18. **1824** Thomas Crofton Croker, *Researches in the South of Ireland*: 'In the Central Counties, the Carders...(a name derived from their inhuman practice of inflicting punishment on the naked back with a wool-card) were in great measure inflamed by a desire to punish informers...'

care [n.]. Family. **1932** Seán O'Faoláin, *Stones*, 'An Enduring Friendship': '"And yourself? And the missus? All the care doing well?"'

carleycue/carlique/curlicue [n.]. Thing of little value; small coin (PWJ). Esp. as in **not give a carlique for** [vb. phr.] (Ulster). Not care in the least.

carlin [n., <Sc. *idem*, old woman, <ON *kerline*, (old) woman] (Ulster). Aggressive old woman.

carlique see **carleycue**

carnaptious [adj., <Sc. *idem*, irritable, quarrelsome] (Ulster). As thus. **1908** Lynn Doyle, *Ballygullion*: 'wi' the eatin' av so much cheese he got as carnaptious as a clockin' [see **clock** 3.] hen'. **1969** Robert Greacen, *Even without Irene*: 'A touch of cantankerousness goes down well in these parts: "carnaptious" as the dialect has it. St John Ervine is a founder member of that lot.'

Caroline [nickname, <?]. Tall hat or beaver. **1879** Charles J. Kickham, *Knocknagow*: 'Nellie took the hat...and immediately set to work to dry the inside. "A fine new Car'line," said she...'

caroogh [n., <Ir. *cearrbach*, card-player, gambler]. As thus.

carried-away [adj.] (Ulster). **1979** Jack McBride, *Traveller in the Glens* (of Antrim): '"a carried-away lookin' crathur

[q.v.]" is used to refer to a baby that looks unlovely and underfed, like one the fairies had left — a changeling in fact'.

carried story [n. phr.] (Ulster). Second-hand gossip (YDS).

carrying [pres. part. as n.]. In the money. **1966** Patrick Boyle, *At Night All Cats are Grey*, 'The Metal Man': 'Now when Tailor is carrying he will buy with the best of them. And sure enough he produced a sheaf of crinklers [q.v.]...'

carry-on [n., cf. Brit. sl. 'carryings on']. Unlooked-for or unacceptable behaviour. **1991** Seán Ó Ciaráin, *Farewell to Mayo*: 'And if you were to see the carry on of Duffy, the antics of him behind the inspector's back...' **1993** James Quirke in Joe O'Reilly & Sixth Class, Convent School, Edenderry, *Over the Half Door*: 'In the Mater I got to know the nurses pretty well. I was a teenager then and was interested in that sort of carry on!' **1996** Carol Coulter, *Irish Times*, 12 July: 'They came to see the destruction [in Belfast]. "They've gone too far," said Diane. "It's an excuse to start up the carry-on again."'

case o' pistles [n., <'case of pistols'] (Ulster). Arse.

cassey/cassy/causey [n., <'causeway', cf. Fr. *chaussée*, paved road]. As thus, path across bog etc.

cast clothes [n. phr.]. Second-hand garments. **1952** Bryan MacMahon, *Children of the Rainbow*: 'When the cast-clothes man held up a man's under-pants, the gathered countrywomen began to laugh.'

Castle Catholic [nickname, derog., <Dublin Castle, former seat of Brit. rule]. One who evinces sycophantically pro-Brit. sympathies and seeks to profit therefrom. **1938** Seán O'Faoláin, *King of the Beggars*: 'He [Robert Peel] began in Ireland a policy that many of his successors copied and developed — the formation of a class that became known as "renegade Catholics" or, in mockery of their affected half-English accents, "Cawstle Catholics".' **1979** C.S. Andrews, *Dublin Made Me*: 'The Castle

Catholics played golf, rugby, cricket, tennis, hockey and croquet...They lived cheek by jowl with the Protestants on Mountjoy Square, Fitzwilliam Square and Merrion Square...'

Castle hack [nickname, derog., <Dublin Castle, former seat of Brit. rule]. Informer. **1914** James Joyce, *Dubliners*, 'Ivy Day in the Committee Room': '"O, but I know it for a fact," said Mr Henchy. "They're Castle hacks..."'

Castle money [n., <Dublin Castle, former seat of Brit. rule]. Money paid to informers. **1966** Patrick J. Flanagan, *The Cavan & Leitrim Railway*: 'Dissension was fostered by a flow of money to informers from Dublin Castle...to some, "Castle money" was always acceptable.'

cast the creels [vb. phr.] (Ulster). Quarrel.

cast up [vb.] (Ulster). Remember unkindly; remind s.o. of past faults. 'He's a divil and a half. He even cast up the trousers I didden give him for his birthday' (Pepper).

cat [adj., adv. & n.]. 1. [adj., cf. Brit. sl. *idem* (vb.), 'vomit' (Green); Ir. *cat marbh* (n. phr.), mischief, calamity (Dinneen); poss. also <'catastrophic']. Shocking, rough, unpleasant. **1993** John Hurley in Michael Verdon, *Shawlies* (q.v.), *Echo Boys* (q.v.), *the Marsh and the Lanes* (q.v.): *Old Cork Remembered*: ''Twas a terrible time, really and truly. The poverty was cat.' Also **cat melodeon/ melodium** [adj.]. Terrible, catastrophic. **1996** Victoria White reviewing Ciaran Carson, *Last Night's Fun*, *Irish Times*, 4 May: 'Carson even attempts to find a history for the greatest expression in Hiberno-English, namely "cat melodeon". This, he suggests, is a conjunction of the Irish "cat marbh" or "cat mara", a "dead cat" or a "sea cat" which means a mischief or calamity, with the tendency of the piano-accordion players (who often refer to their instruments as melodeons) to play two notes at once.' 2. [adv.]. Very. **1961** Tom Murphy, *A Whistle in the Dark*: 'HARRY ...So many. So worried. All them clever blokes, cat smart, so worried about it all.' 3. [n., poss. <Sc. *idem*, stick used to strike ball or piece of wood in certain games (CSD)]. Slap of the hand to seal a bargain/deal. **1943** George A. Little, *Malachi Horan Remembers*: 'The Curragh officers came to Valleymount and saw Captain Kelly. He heard the conditions and agreed to them. The Captain gave them "the cat"...and the match was made.'

Catacombs [nickname] (Dub.). Extensive derelict basement of Georgian house, resort in late 1940s and early 1950s of Brendan Behan, Anthony Cronin, J.P. Donleavy and their circle. **1975** John Ryan, *Remembering How We Stood*: 'the generic name given to a large rambling basement of a Georgian house in Fitzwilliam Street, not far from Jack Yeats' studio...The principal inhabitant of these subterranean warrens was Richard (Dickie) Wyeman, a person of exquisite sensibilities...' **1976** Anthony Cronin, *Dead as Doornails*: 'Most of this company assembled in McDaid's every day under the benevolent aegis of one of the great barmen of all time, Paddy O'Brien, and almost every night the entire assemblage moved on to the Catacombs.'

cat breac [n. phr., <Ir. *idem*, speckled cat, <cover picture on schoolbook]. Protestant teacher in 'souper' (q.v.) mission schools in Ir.-speaking areas. **1979** Paddy Tunney, *The Stone Fiddle*: 'He was now safe from demons and heathens and the cat-breachs [*sic*] he had told me about.' **1987** Muiris Mac Conghail, *The Blaskets*: 'One of the publications which came from [the] Achill [Missionary Settlement] was a reading primer which had a picture of a speckled cat on the opening page, with an Irish text describing the cat — *an cat breac*...'

catch oneself on [vb. phr., poss. distinctive Hib.E usage] (Ulster). Come to a realisation of something, adopt a normal view. **1995** Gerry Moriarty, *Irish Times*, 11 July: 'There's a fervent wish that after the last ember of the Twelfth [q.v.] bonfires has been extinguished that people will settle...stay cool, and, as they say up here, catch themselves on.' **1996** Frank Caddy, *Irish Times*, 12 Oct:

'Anyone considering further violence [in the North] should catch themselves on. It would be disastrous.' See also **cop-on**.

cat got your tongue, has the? [cant phr.]. Asked of s.o. who refuses to answer a question. **1987** Lar Redmond, *Emerald Square*: 'I could not tell them, only smile when they asked me if the cat had got my tongue.'

Cathleen Mavourneen see **Kathleen Mavourneen**

Cathleen/Caitlín/Kathleen ní Houlihan [prop. n.]. Legendary personification of Ire., latterly ironic. **1929** Liam O'Flaherty, *A Tourist's Guide to Ireland*: 'The love of woman in the flesh may lead man to grave excesses. But the love of a mystical woman like Caitlín Ni Houlihain [*sic*] does untold harm.' **1973** Noël Conway, *The Bloods* (q.v.): 'They [the Bloods] were, like the rest of the Army they had helped to train, neutral, serving the most ungrateful Lady in Irish history — Cathleen ní Houlihan.'

cat melodeon see **cat**

Cats, the [nickname, from gen. attrib. *Kilkenny Cats* (q.v.)]. Kilkenny Gaelic football/hurling teams. **1995** Peadar O'Brien, *Irish Press*: 'Take Eamonn Morrissey and Denis Byrne; add in Adrian Ronan and the Kilkenny defence. They were the reasons why the "Cats" won their way to their ninth league title...'

catskin [n.]. Shiny outer layer on newly baked bread; heel of a loaf. **1970** Christy Brown, *Down All the Days*: 'hot gravy into which they dipped thick cuts of dry bread and the hard "heels" off loaves which were also called "catskins"'. **1995** Phil O'Keeffe, *Down Cobbled Streets, A Liberties Childhood*: 'the catskin we were told to avoid could be foisted on us by a seemingly helpful assistant who would slide the four loaves into our bag before we would realise it...Secretly I liked the rubbery feel of the catskin, but as often as not it was a slice which my mother discarded...'

cat's lick [n. phr.]. Perfunctory cleaning, as in **cat's lick and a promise**. See also **Scotch lick**.

Catty [nickname, derog.]. Catholic. **1963** Leslie Daiken, *Out Goes She* (Dub. street rhymes): 'Catty Catty go to Mass/ Ridin' on the Divil's ass,/When the Divil rings the bell/All good Catties go to Hell'. **1975** William Trevor, *Angels at the Ritz*, 'Mr McNamara': '"Proddy[q.v.]-woddy green guts," the Catholic children cried at us in Curransbridge. "Catty, catty, going to mass," we whispered back, "riding on the devil's ass."'

cat went a pound, if the [cant phr., <?]. Expressive of impossibility. **1995** Éamon Kelly, *The Apprentice*: 'The night began to freeze and after a while he woke up still tipsy but if the cat went a pound he couldn't find his clothes.'

caub/caubeen [n., <Ir. *cáibín*, old hat]. As thus. **C.1798** Pop. ballad, 'The Wearing of the Green': 'When laws can stop the blades of grass from growing as they grow,/And when the leaves in summertime their colours dare not show,/Then I will change the colour that I wear in my caubeen,/But till that day, please God, I'll stick to wearin' o' the Green.' **1922** James Joyce, *Ulysses*: 'Stephen looked down on a wide headless caubeen, hung on his ashplant handle over his knee.' **1977** Flann O'Brien, *The Hair of the Dogma*: 'Remember please, that the mate of the PEN on the Liffey is the COB...So far as Ireland is concerned, let me assure our visitors that here the CAUB is mightier than the PEN' (ref. is to Poets, Playwrights, Editors, Essayists and Novelists Club).

cauboge/caubogue [n., <Ir. *cábóg*, fool, clown]. As thus. **1960** John O'Donoghue, *In Kerry Long Ago*: 'So I suppose the Gurthagreenane girls decided that they might as well have their share of the good things...even if they had to lower their dignity by mixing up with country *caubogues* at the wedding in Glanlea.' **1966** Séamus Murphy, *Stone Mad*: '"I'm one of the most extraordinary men that ever lived an' the louts and cauboges of this country don't seem to realise that I'm a seer among them."'

caudy [n., <Sc. *caddy/caudy* <Fr. *cadet*, younger son] (Ulster). Boy; shrewd,

crafty boy; boy hired as servant. **1830** William Carleton, *Traits and Stories of the Irish Peasantry*, 'The Lianhan Shee': '"*Musha* [q.v.], never heed what the likes of him says; sure he's but a *caudy*, that doesn't mane ill, only the bit of divarsion [q.v.]..."'

caught rapid! see **rapid!**

caup pig see **cappy**

causey see **cassey**

cauthie [n., <?]. Irresponsible, untrustworthy person (OTF).

caving [n., cf. Sc. *cave* (vb.), push, drive backward and forward]. Beating, thrashing.

cawhake [n., <?] (Cork). Jinx (Beecher).

ceilidh/kailey/ceili [n. & vb., <Ir. *céilí* (n.), friendly call, visit, social evening, dancing session]. As thus; pay such a call. **1983** W.F. Marshall, *Livin' in Drumlister*, 'Ceilidth': 'Better crack [see **crack** 1.] when the latch lifts,/And the decent neighbour men/Make their kailey as like as not/Till the wag [see **wag/wag-at-the wall**] is striking ten.' **1990** Tom O'Kane, quoted in Walter Love, *The Times of our Lives*: 'They used to ceilidh years ago. That's when they used to sit round the fire and they would have a great night.' **1995** Joe McManus in Mary Ryan et al. (eds.), *No Shoes in Summer*: 'Your father is on his kailey and some neighbour is saying to him, "Where's John? I didn't see him this long time."'

Celtic Tiger see **Emerald Tiger**

ceolán [n., <Ir. *idem*]. Cry-baby; 'trifling contemptible little fellow' (PWJ).

cess see **bad cess**

chainies see **chaney**

chalk [vb. & n.]. 1. [vb., <?, C18–19]. Strike, slash. **1847** John Edward Walsh, *Ireland Sixty Years Ago*: 'while the punishment for "chalking" is made in the highest degree severe, it is provided that the offence shall not corrupt the offender's blood'. Also **chalker** [n.]. (a) In the same sense. (b) Child's marble. See also **glasser**, **steeler**. 2. [n., <?] (army). Battalion subdivision. **1996** Jim Cusack, *Irish Times*, 24 Apr: 'The entire battalion,

of just over 600, rotates in three such contingents, known as "chalks", a term whose derivation is a mystery to the present generation of soldiers. The staggering of the rotation in this way prevents the depletion of ranks in south Lebanon...'

Chalk Sunday [nickname, <chalk used to mark the backs of people remaining unmarried at the beginning of Lent]. First Sunday in Lent. **1986** Padraic O'Farrell, *'Tell me, Sean O'Farrell'*: 'It was called Chalk Sunday in some places because single people were marked with chalk by some joker — usually kneeling behind the person at mass.' See also **Puss Sunday**.

champ [n., cf. Sc. *idem* (vb.), mash, crush]. Mashed potatoes with milk, scallions, etc. **1996** Mary Gallagher, *Irish Times*, 30 Sept: 'Dear old Champ, which had departed in a casket of memory with those emigrants from Cobh, leaving an Ireland devoid of the unblighted potatoes needed to make it.'

chance one's arm [vb. phr., ascribed, on scant evidence, to a feud (1492) between the Ormondes and the Kildares, ended by the Earl of Kildare's cutting a hole with his sword in the door of St Patrick's Cathedral, Dub., and thrusting his hand through in the hope that it would be grasped by that of his enemy within rather than amputated in anger. His hope was, happily, fulfilled.]. Take a risk, engage in conduct the outcome of which is uncertain. **1980** Bernard Farrell, *Canaries*: 'DAD (*Looking over at the Contessa*) You know, I might chance me arm with that oul' wan [q.v.]. TOMMY Ah, will you give that up.' **1987** Lar Redmond, *Emerald Square*: 'If this Gorey priest had chanced his arm like that in Francis Street...the reaction would have been immediate and derisive.' **1994** Tim Magennis, *Ireland of the Welcomes*, 'Ireland and the Irish', Nov/ Dec: 'An ancient door, now reduced to four and a half pine planks...faces visitors entering Dublin's famed St Patrick's Cathedral. It tells the story of the expression "to chance your arm" and the key to the story is the hole, thirty inches by six, where there was once a panel.'

chancer [n., 'liar, one too confident of his ability; tailors' slang' (DHS)]. S.o., gen. male, with an eye to the main chance. See also **chance one's arm**. 1966 Liam Ó Cuanaigh, *Evening Press*, 21 Nov: 'hard chaws [q.v.] differ from chancers in so far as they will risk jail for love of their profession, whereas chancers always come away with a dividend; they keep on the safe side of the law and will only slag the Duke of Edinburgh on St Patrick's Day'. **1989** Hugh Leonard, *Out after Dark*: 'Those who had done business with him called him a chancer, or, less charitably, a hook [q.v.].' **1993** Sam McAughtry, *Touch & Go*: 'She wasn't one of those chancers who look away as the line's being shot. As she spoke, Annie Longley's eyes were on mine...'

chancy [adj., cf. Sc. *idem*, lucky, fortunate, happy] (Ulster). Good-looking, well endowed. **1983** W.F. Marshall, *Livin' in Drumlister*, 'Sarah Ann': '"Jist let him keep his daughter, the hungry-lukin' nur [q.v.],/There's just as chancy weemin in the countryside as her."'

chander/channer/chanter [vb., <Sc. *channer* (onomat.), grumble, mutter] (Ulster). As thus; bicker, quarrel, scold. Hence **channering** [pres. part. as adj.] in same sense.

chaney/cheney [adj. & n., cf. Sc. *cheeny*, china, <Persian *chini* (adj.)]. As thus. **C.1735** Jonathan Swift, *A Dialogue in Hybernian Stile*: 'Your Cousin desires you will buy him some Cheney cups. I remember he had a great many...' **1908** Lynn Doyle, *Ballygullion*: 'First he made a glam [q.v.] at the table, an' pulled off the cloth, wi' two or three bottles, and a pair of chaney dogs.' Also **chainies/chanies** [n. pl.]. Broken china fragments used in children's games. **1922** James Joyce, *Ulysses*: 'Silly-Milly burying the little dead bird in the kitchen matchbox, a daisychain and bits of broken chainies on the grave.' **1975** Eilís Brady, *All In! All In!*: '"Playing shop" is always great fun ...chanies are used for money...'

channer/chanter see **chander**

chap [n.] (juvenile). Cinema or other fictional hero. **1991** Bob Quinn, *Smokey Hollow*: 'They were thrilled that he might be going to take on the bad guy next door, just like the pictures. As Mr Toner was obviously the "chap", they had no fears for him...the chap never gets killed in the pictures.' **1995** Patrick Boland, *Tales from a City Farmyard*: 'When Errol Flynn was Robin Hood, we all made bows and arrows, and fought pitched battles in our farmyard. We all wanted to be the "chap" — the leading man — in our plays...'

chap-fallen [adj., with lower jaw hanging] (Ulster). Extremely hungry.

character [n.]. 1. Individual slightly larger than life, or existing at a perceptible angle to it. **1965** Lee Dunne, *Goodbye to the Hill*: 'He was a real person too, whereas Redmond was more of a character.' **1975** John Ryan, *Remembering How We Stood*: 'The gist of their [Myles na gCopaleen, Sean O'Sullivan and Brendan Behan's] dialogue was that they were deploring the absence from the Dublin scene of any *real* "characters"... Here you have the essence of the Dublin "character"; complete unawareness of the fact that he is one himself.' **1995** Patrick Boland, *Tales from a City Farmyard*: 'When we describe somebody as "a real character", we mean that the person is either entertaining in a show-off sort of way, or is not the full shilling [q.v.].' 2. Slightly derog. equivalent of fellow, individual, invar. male; cf. your man (q.v.). **1986** Bob Geldof, *Is That It?*: 'By this time Fachtna O'Kelly had left his newspaper. He was a frail-looking character, thin and gaunt...'

charge [n., palat. form of Anglo-Norman *kark*, burden]. Lazy/uncouth/ gross individual; loud-mouthed woman (see **targe**).

charley [n., abbrev. of *Charley Whitehouse*, chamber pot (Green)]. As thus. **1925** Liam O'Flaherty, *The Informer*: '"They'd take the charley from under a pope's bed."'

Chas Mahal [nickname, play on *Taj Mahal*; see also **Taj Micheál**]. Government Buildings, Merrion St, Dub., as restored 1990 under the aegis of

Charles J. Haughey (1925–) as Taoiseach. **1995** Lorna Siggins, *Irish Times*, 1 June: 'One question lingered in the air as officials awaited the arrival of Prince Charles at Government Buildings...Would anyone dare welcome him to "Chas Mahal"?'

chassie-boo [n., <?] (Cork dock sl.). Thingamagig, any undifferentiated object, yoke (q.v.).

chat [n.]. 1. [poss. reflects Sc. *idem*, gallows]. Methylated spirits as consumed by alcoholics. **1939** James Joyce, *Finnegans Wake*: 'a half sir [q.v.] from the weaver's almshouse who clings and clings and chatchatchat clings to her'. 2. [<'chit']. Small, inferior potato.

chavelled [p. part. as adj., <OE *ceafl* (n.), jaw]. Roughly cut at the edges.

chaw see **hard chaw**

chay! see **chegh!**

cheep [n., onomat.]. Sound, as in **not a cheep out of you!** Hence **cheeper** [n.]. Mouth. **1948** John O'Connor, *Come Day — Go Day*: '"if your father comes in now, you'll be stiffened! You'll never open your cheeper again."'

chefeneer [n., <Fr. *chiffonnier*, chiffonier]. As thus. 'Most homes had one which held your mother's prize china' (EW).

chegh!/chay! [interj. & vb., <Ir. *téigh* (vb.), go] (Ulster). Call to herd a cow/quieten a dog.

cheney see **chaney**

cherry [n., <?]. Look, as in **give us a cherry** (EW).

chest of tools [n. phr.]. 'A shoeblack's brush & wig, etc.' (Grose).

chew–chew [n.]. Toffee. **1983** *John Pepper's Illustrated Encyclopaedia of Ulster Knowledge*: 'In the *shap* were such delights as "chew–chew", toffee of a delicate rose pink and exquisite flavour...'

chick nor child [n. phr., gen. in neg. sense]. Nobody. **1995** Phil O'Keeffe, *Down Cobbled Streets, A Liberties Childhood*: '"Loaded, she is." "And why wouldn't she be? Not a chick nor child to

trouble her and two men under the clay before her."'

child [n.]. Female newborn infant. **1995** Phil O'Keeffe, *Down Cobbled Streets, A Liberties Childhood*: '"What is it?" I said as I turned to follow her. "A child," she said, "another little girl. God bless and preserve her."'

childer [n. pl., <OE pl. *childru*, ME *childre*, retained in Sc. etc. as *childer*]. Children. See **chiseller**.

childybawn [<'child' + Ir. *bán*, darling (hypocoristic)]. Term of affection. **1932** Seán O'Faoláin, *Midsummer Night Madness and Other Stories*, 'Childybawn': '"Oh, childybawn, they're the first natural [see **nature**] words you've said to me in six months."'

chiller [n., <OE *ceolor*, throat] (Ulster). Jowl; [n. pl.] double chin.

Chime/Time in the Slime, the [nickname] (Dub.). Countdown clock installed, Mar 1996, at O'Connell Bridge in River Liffey to celebrate forthcoming Christian millennium; withdrawn shortly after and not replaced. **1996** Frank Kilfeather, *Irish Times*, 20 Mar: 'The "Time in the Slime" is now the Clock in Dry Dock...Dubliners had barely got used to the unique National Lottery clock when there it was — gone.' **1996** Eanna Brophy, *Sunday Tribune*, 24 Mar: 'Is there some department of Dublin Corporation...whose job it is to think up fresh soubriquets for each new item of street furniture, sculpture or public clock? If not, who is it that comes up with them? Most Dubliners know instantly where you'd find the Floozie in the Jacuzzi [q.v.], the Tart with the Cart [q.v.] (Molly Malone in Grafton Street), and the Hags with the Bags [q.v.] (Liffey Street). Now of course we have (oh no we haven't) the Chime in the Slime, also known as the Clock in the Dock...'

chincough [n., <OE *cincian* (vb.), gasp & cough]. Whooping cough; spasm of crying/laughing. **1974** John Hewitt, *Out of my Time*, 'The Fairy Thresher': 'But suddenly the sister swept the talk/From *charms* and hedgerow cures dropped out

of use,/for *chin-cough* and for cleaning of the blood.'

chinies [n. pl., <'shinies']. Child's marbles (EW).

chinks, the [n. pl., <?, cf. 'the creeps']. As thus. **1932** (first published 1992) Samuel Beckett, *Dream of Fair to Middling Women*: 'Douceurs...! Ugh that word gives me the chinks doesn't it you?'

chinstrap [n.] (Ulster). 'Black ring round child's neck caused by failure to wash' (TT).

chippens [n. pl., <?]. Money. **1966** Patrick Boyle, *At Night All Cats are Grey*, 'The Metal Man': '"He was free with his chippens all right, but he was a proper nuisance with a few jars [q.v.] on him."'

chipper [n.]. [Fish and] chip shop. **1976** Neil Jordan, *Night in Tunisia*: '"Let's go inside," he said, just as it was getting dark and the last of the queue filed from the chipper.' **1996** Victoria White, *Irish Times*, 9 Oct: 'This writer would have murdered a canapé by this time, having spent tea-time [q.v.] tantalisingly across the way from Burdock's chipper on Werburgh Street...'

chirm [vb., <Sc. *idem*, murmur, fret, complain] (Ulster). Complain, whine. Also **chirm in** [vb.]. Intrude into conversation, 'chip in'.

chirpaun [n., <Ir. *tiarpán*, small load carried in hip-sack (Dinneen)]. Love child. **1993** Dick Kennedy, quoted in Tim Pat Coogan, *Dev* (q.v.): *Long Fellow* (q.v.), *Long Shadow*: 'Pat Coll never married but he had nine Chirpauns... Dev's mother was the first.'

chiseller/chisler [n., corruption of *childer* (q.v.), but used in sing. sense]. Affect. term for child. **1970** Christy Brown, *Down All the Days*: '"Still and all, for the sake of the chisellers, I mean," said the brown-booted kindly man, rubbing a small curly head...' **1977** Flann O'Brien, *The Hair of the Dogma*: '"Ah yes. The two is in the one grave." Observe the unique Dublin dual number in full flight. "The two is in the one grave and I am back above in Heytesbury Street in digs with the young chisler Nicholas."'

1995 Aidan Higgins, *Donkey's Years*: 'Mumu had gone very red and said it was quite unsuitable reading for a chissler [*sic*] and would I please stop reading her books.'

chitter [vb., <Sc. *idem*, complain constantly; chatter]. **1939** James Joyce, *Finnegans Wake*: 'Can't hear with the waters of. The chittering waters of. Flittering bats, fieldmice bawk talk.'

chocolate soldier [nickname, <comic opera by Oscar Strauss; colour of uniform] (Munster). Traffic warden, Waterford city.

choicer [n.] as in **for choicer** [n. phr.] (Cork). For choice (Beecher).

choker [n.]. 1. [cf. Brit. sl. *idem*, disappointment]. One who fails to deliver. **1996** Liam Griffin, *Irish Times*, 15 July: 'Bridesmaids, chokers and perennial losers. We have been called all these. I grew up in the '50s and '60s when Wexford were one of the giants of hurling.' 2. [cf. Brit. sl. *chokey*, prison]. Prison cell for solitary confinement. **1997** John Maher, *Irish Times*, 18 Feb: '[At Spike Island prison]...there is what staff call a "cooler" and prisoners the "choker"...'

Cholesterol Coast [nickname]. Coast of Co. Antrim. **1994** Michael Palin, *Great Railway Journeys*, 'Derry to Kerry': 'Along these fine, languid headlands and wide bays are dotted a string of hotels and guest houses whose preference for breakfast delicacies like the Ulster Fry have earned this stretch the name of the Cholesterol Coast.'

choo! [exclam., <Sc. *chew*, command to call off a dog]. As thus.

chook chook!/chuck chuck! [exclam., <Ir. *tiuc*, same sense (PWJ — but this deriv. is challenged)]. Call to hens; hence Austral. 'chook', chicken? **1966** Patrick Boyle, *At Night All Cats are Grey*, 'Go Away, Old Man, Go Away': 'Unbarring the door he flung it open. "Chook! Chook! Chook!" he called in a loud aggressive voice. There was a flutter of startled wings...' **1986** Padraic O'Farrell, *'Tell me, Sean O'Farrell'*: 'Then there

were calls for domestic animals or birds. "Chuck, chuck" — from the Irish "tioch" — to hens. "How-up" to drive cows, "Prug, prug" [q.v.] to coax them. "Suck-suck" to calves or pigs.'

chookie-egg see **guggy**

chrissie [n., <character in *Liffey Lane*, play by Maura Laverty (1951)]. **1994** Christopher Fitz-Simon, *The Boys* (see **the Boys** 2.): 'A "chrissie" became a word for a lower-class person with delusions of grandeur, and the phrase, "It suits ya, Chrissie!"...is still used to compliment someone wearing an item of clothing which patently does *not* suit them.'

chub [n., <?] (Maynooth College). First-year student. **N.d.** (unpublished) Neil Kevin, *'Ad Vota Saecularia'*: 'I am walking on the outside of a batch of seven or eight, for I am but a junior chub, and according to immemorial custom, must "thresh" (slang for walk on the outside), yielding place of honour to the Logs (slang for second-year students resident in Logic house)...'

chuck chuck! see **chook chook!**

Chuckie Armani [nickname, <Ir. *tiocfaidh ár lá*, our day will come, IRA slogan/graffito, 1970s–]. Gerry Adams (1949–), politician, president Sinn Féin (1983–), <his adoption of an 'upmarket' image particularly reflected in his choice of suits.

Churchman [n.] (Ulster). Adherent of the Church of Ireland. **1913** Alexander Irvine, *My Lady of the Chimney Corner*: '"Ye know, no doubt, Anna, that Misther Gwynn is a Churchman an' I'm a Presbyterian."'

Churchy and One Over [nickname]. Children's game. **1990** Harry Currie, quoted in Walter Love, *The Times of our Lives*: 'There was "Churchy and One Over", where you leant on a window sill or against a wall and your mates jumped on your back to see how many you could carry.'

cimeen/kimeen [n., <Ir. *síom*, prank, trick + dimin. *ín*; gen. in pl.]. As thus.

1953 Frank O'Connor, *My Oedipus Complex and Other Stories*, 'The Uprooted': '"Musha [q.v.], will you stop your old cimeens," boomed Tom, "and tell us where's Cait from you?"'

ciotóg see **kithogue**

cipín/kippeen/kippen [n., <Ir. *cipín*, little stick]. As thus; kindling. 'Often used as a sort of pet name for a formidable cudgel or shillelah [see **shillelagh**] for fighting' (PWJ). **1829** Gerald Griffin, *The Collegians*: '"An' if a poor boy...goes to a fair to thry it out with a little kippen, 'Oh, the savages!' the gentlemen cry at once..."' **1991** James Kennedy, *The People who Drank Water from the River*: 'His fire was never much more than a handful of cipíns and the cottage was always draughty and cold.' **1995** Éamon Kelly, *The Apprentice*: '"Bring in a few kippens..." my mother said. We did and the fire lit up and in no time at all the kettle was boiling...'

ciste [n., <Ir. *idem*, cake]. 'Delicacy of dough sprinkled with raisins and placed on top of a stew' (EW).

cittah/cittogue see **kithogue**

City of the Broken Treaty [nickname, <Treaty of Limerick, 1691]. Limerick. **1990** Michael Hannon, *Cork Holly Bough*: 'It was in the classroom too I had learned all about "The City of the Broken Treaty". Now here I was walking down the main thoroughfare.'

clab/claub [n., <Ir. *clab*, open mouth]. Gaping grin; blabber, one who cannot keep a secret. **1948** Patrick Kavanagh, *Tarry Flynn*: '"Oh, look at her now with the claub of laughing on her face."' See also **olagon**.

clabber [n., <Ir. *clábar*, mud; Sc. soft, sticky mud (CSD)]. As thus. **1995** Brigid O'Donnell in Mary Ryan et al. (eds.), *No Shoes in Summer*: 'We all went to school barefoot from April...When the roads were wet how much we enjoyed seeing the clabair [*sic*] (muck) coming up between our toes.' **1983** Polly Devlin, *All of us There*: 'In the declension of earthiness, mould is relatively clean and thin, clabber is thick and dirty, and glaur

[q.v.] is the ultimate...' **1983** W.F. Marshall, *Livin' in Drumlister*, 'Sarah Ann': 'The kitchen's like a midden, an' the parlour's like a sty,/There's half a fut of clabber on the street outby.' Also **bonny-clabber** (q.v.), **clabbery** [adj.].

cladyin [n., <?] (Ulster). Big, fat, useless person (CUD).

claim [n.]. Girl picked up or shifted (see **shift** 1.) at a dance etc. (EW).

clait see **cloot**

clamper [n., <Ir. *clampar*, noise, dispute, wrangle, poss. <Low Ger. *klampern* (vb.), make a noise, via Eng. dial.]. As thus. **1689** Anon., *The Irish Hudibras*: 'Only I pray dee now, my Dear,/Let not dy Ars make a Clam-peer,/Lest vid [with] a Fart dou blow it from me...' See also **esta clamper!**

clanjaffrey [n., <Sc. *clamjafry*, mob, vulgar crowd, riff-raff] (Ulster). Unexpected gathering of extended family circle (YDS).

clap see **cowclap**

clappers [n.] as in **like the clappers** [adv. phr., poss. <wooden implements for shaping butter; apparently not <Eng. dial. *idem*, wooden rattles]. In great haste. **1987** Lar Redmond, *Emerald Square*: 'and Roy [Rogers]'d jump into the saddle and he'd be off like the clappers, firing two hundred and forty nine shots...' **1995** Patrick Boland, *Tales from a City Farmyard*: 'Having reached the inner field, and waited until the bull had turned away from us at the top of it, we then ran like the clappers...' **1996** Tom Humphries, *Irish Times*, 24 Feb: 'Takes off like the clappers. Dead by lap three. Runs four minutes, 32 seconds in his first mile.'

clap till [prep. & vb.] (Ulster). 1. [prep.]. Joined on to. 2. [vb.]. Close (door).

Clare hearse [n. phr., <?] (Munster). Ten of clubs. **1991** John B. Keane, *Love Bites and Other Stories*: 'Fortunes are told by the casting of cards and beware if you fall foul of the ace of spades or the ten of clubs! The latter used to be called the "Clare hearse" when I was a gorsoon [q.v.].'

clarry [n. & vb., <Sc. *idem*, dirt, mess; make dirty, messy] (Ulster). As thus.

clart [n., <Sc. *idem*, sticky mud, dirt] (Ulster). Untidy girl/woman. **1979** John Morrow, *The Confessions of Proinsias O'Toole*: '"...I just called her a dirty clart and shattered her eardrums with the loudest tongue-fart I could muster"'.

clash (on) [vb., <Sc. *idem*, gossip] (Ulster). Tell tales (on). Hence **clashbag/ clashbeg** [n.]. Busybody, tell-tale.

clashmaclaver/clashmaclabber [n., see **clash**] (Ulster). Idle talk, gossip.

class [n.]. Kind, as in **a class of** [adj. phr.]. **1946** Mervyn Wall, *The Unfortunate Fursey*: '"You're some class of a monk?" "No, I was once, but not now."' **1977** James Plunkett, *Collected Short Stories*, 'Finegan's Ark': '"It struck me that a Noah's Ark is a very Protestant class of a toy — that's all," Casey said...' **1995** Eanna Brophy, *Sunday Tribune*, 6 Aug: '*Miley*: It says here that Glenroe never has anything about single mothers, or drugs or adultery, or any of that class of carry-on [q.v.].'

clatter [n. & vb.]. 1. [n. & vb.]. Physical chastisement, usu. of children by parents. **1994** Paddy O'Gorman, *Queuing for a Living*: '"I got enough clatters meself when I was growing up."' **1995** Tom Widger reviewing RTÉ Radio programme *A Fifties Boyhood*, *Sunday Tribune*, 5 Mar: 'He honestly couldn't see the reason for the commotion, nor the reason why his mother clattered him out of the church.' 2. [n.]. Large number. **1995** Phil O'Keeffe, *Down Cobbled Streets, A Liberties Childhood*: '"I want to send the children to the nuns," she told my father. "Well, ye have a chance now," he said; "there's a right [see **right** 1.] clatter of them around us for you to choose."' 3. [n. & vb.]. Gossip, chatter. **1939** Patrick Gallagher ('Paddy the Cope' (q.v.)), *My Story*: '"Every one of the Committee... would tell it to their women and they would clatter it all over the parish."' Hence **clatterbox** [n.] (Ulster). Gossip, tell-tale.

clatty [adj. & vb.]. 1. [adj., cf. Sc. *clattie*, nasty, muddy, obscene; Ir. *cladach*, dirty, miry (Dinneen)] (Ulster). As thus; slovenly, untidy. **1983** W.F. Marshall,

Livin' in Drumlister, 'Me an' me Da': 'An' if me shirt's a clatty shirt/The man to blame's me da.' **1995** Shane Connaughton, *A Border Diary*: 'Referring to the muck and mud Shamie said, "Ah now, it's a long go through and clatty dirty."' 2. [vb.]. Wash badly.

claub see **clab**

claw-hammer [n.] (Ulster). Pig's foot.

claw mould [vb. phr.] (Ulster) as in **away and claw mould on yourself!** Keep your nose out of my business!

cleek [n. & vb., <Sc. *idem*, hook; seize/clutch, <OE *claec(e)an* (vb.), clutch] (Ulster). 1. [n.]. Legal complication. 2. [vb.]. Catch hold of; wheedle. Also **cleeked/cleekit** [adv.]. Arm in arm.

cleft see **clift**

cleg [n.] (Ulster). Horsefly (*Haematopota plurialis*), hence unwanted hanger-on. **1966** Patrick Boyle, *At Night All Cats are Grey*, 'Myko': '"I'm just as glad you returned this bloody horse-box. No one but a hungry cleg would have let it out of here in the first place."'

clemmed [p. part. as adj., <OE *clamm* [n.], fetter, cramp] (Ulster). Perished with cold/hunger.

clever [adj.] (Ulster). 1. Roomy, generously cut (of garment). 2. Tall, well made (of man).

cleverality [n.]. Gratuitous display of learning, real or assumed. **1987** Vincent Caprani, *Vulgar Verse & Variations, Rowdy Rhymes & Rec-im-itations*, 'My Grandfather's Pint': 'intellectuals who come swaggering in about ten minutes to closing time and with a flourish of cleverality loudly proclaim that "a nocturnal libation assists wonderfully in unbending the mind"'.

clevy/clevvy [n., cf. Ir. *cliabh* (genitive *cléibhe*), basket, creel]. Small open cupboard. **1960** John O'Donoghue, *In Kerry Long Ago*: 'So I tied the straps on the side of the melodeon and put it up on the clevvy out of the way.' **1995** Éamon Kelly, *The Apprentice*: 'Between the window and the door was an open-shelved piece of furniture called a clevvy.

A hanging piece, it carried a display of tin mugs, lustre jugs and highly-polished saucepan covers...'

click [vb. & n.]. 1. [vb.]. Pick up a member of the opposite sex. **1961** Dominic Behan, *Teems of Times and Happy Returns*: '"They're [nuns] all shaven," said Piggy Cunliffe, "so as they won't start clickin' fellas."' **1985** Máirín Johnston, *Around the Banks of Pimlico*: 'Going downtown for a walk was a favourite [Sunday] pastime and hordes of factory girls with arms linked together would traipse around sporting their Sunday best, clicking fellas and window-shopping.' **1994** May Hanaphy in Kevin C. Kearns, *Dublin Tenement Life*: 'Oh, clicking then [1920s] was very popular ...We'd go clicking along mostly O'Connell Street or maybe down Henry Street, you know...and two fellas'd come along and say "There's two mots [q.v.]."' 2. [n., cf. 'clicker', foreman shoemaker]. Sole of shoe. **1961** Dominic Behan, *Teems of Times and Happy Returns*: 'Poor Frank! With the click of his shoe worn to shreds from touring builders' yards...'

clifft [vb.]. Throw over a cliff. **1906** E.Œ. Somerville & Martin Ross, *Some Irish Yesterdays*: '"He'll run to the say [sea] with him!" says Dan, "the two o' them'll be cliffted!"'

clift/cleft [n., <?] (Ulster). Very foolish person. Hence gradations: **quarter clift** [adj. & n.]; **three-quarter clift** [adj. & n.]; **the two ends of** (q.v.) **a clift** [n. phr.] complete fool.

clinic [nickname]. Open meeting, freq. on licensed premises, at which the local TD meets his constituents to address their wrongs, actual and imagined. **1984** John McGahern, *Oldfashioned*: 'A politician lives outside the village, and the crowd that once flocked to the presbytery now go to him instead. Certain nights he holds "clinics"...They come to look for grants, to try to get drunken driving convictions quashed, to get free medical cards...to get children into jobs. As they all have votes they are never "run" [q.v.].' **1988** John Healy, *Magill*, 'The Wild One', Mar: 'He [Donogh

O'Malley] took the best part of his Dáil allowance and changed it into silent ten-shilling notes and one pound notes before opening his "clinic" in Limerick of a Saturday.'

clink [n. & vb.]. 1. [n., <?] (Ulster). Mischievous child. 2. [vb.] (Ulster). Stub one's toe.

clinker/clinking [n. & adj.]. Excellent person or thing; exhibiting such a quality.

clinkers [n. pl.] (Ulster). Testicles. **1993** Sam McAughtry, *Touch & Go*: 'It wasn't as if I'd always been a pain in the clinkers to him. There'd been a time when he was an OK brother...'

clinking see **clinker**

clip/clipe [n. & vb., <ON *clippe* (vb.), cut]. Smart blow; deliver such a blow. **1983** Polly Devlin, *All of us There*: 'we would speedily get what Ellen, our young housekeeper...calls a "quare clipe" on the ear'. **1996** Patricia O'Reilly, RTÉ Radio, *Sunday Miscellany*, 18 Aug: 'I got one clip on the ear for not having it [the bread] wrapped and another for taking so long.' Hence **clipped** [p. part.]. **1990** Iris Brennan, quoted in Walter Love, *The Times of our Lives*: 'I was the only one that cursed, but I didn't do it at home or I'd have been clipped.'

clipe/clype [n. & vb.]. 1. [n.] (Ulster). Sizeable portion. 2. [vb., <Sc. *idem*, gossip, <OE *cleopian* (vb.), name] (Ulster). Tell tales. Hence **clipe-clash** [n.]. Tale-bearer.

clipping [adj.]. Excellent, outstanding. **1927** Peadar O'Donnell, *Islanders*: '"The way ye clouted through them waves was clippin'. I'd be makin' up to ye myself, if I was as young as some of the boys."'

clippings of tin [n. phr.]. Nugatory quantity. **1986** Padraic O'Farrell, *'Tell me, Sean O'Farrell'*: 'Some of the "bean a tighes" [see **banatee**] who got grants for housing students in the Gaeltacht at that time [WWII] fed them on the clippin's of tin.' **1991** James Kennedy, *The People who Drank Water from the River*: 'He and his auntie lived, so to speak, on the "clippings of tin".'

clisheerum [n., cf. Ir. *clisiam*, noise at play, uproar]. As thus. **1960** John O'Donoghue, *In Kerry Long Ago*: '"In the name of the devil then," says she, "what do you want waking the whole house with all the *clisheerum*?"'

clock [vb. & n.]. 1. [vb., gen. as pres. part., cf. Brit. sl. *idem*, punch in the face]. Beat, thrash. **1968** John Healy, *The Death of an Irish Town*: 'With lights-out was the rule of solemn silence, the slightest infraction of which was punishable by a "clocking" from the dormitory prefect.' 2. [vb.]. Sit, squat. 3. [vb.]. (Of hen) Lay away from nest. **1966** Patrick Boyle, *At Night All Cats are Grey*, 'Odorous Perfume her Harbinger': '"Are you trying to tell me that Granny is craving to clock?" "No need to worry, Jim. Her nesting days are over."' **1995** Phil O'Keeffe, *Down Cobbled Streets, A Liberties Childhood*: '"The red hen," she said, "will have to be watched. She's clocking." Convinced that the red hen was laying out, she told us to watch the ditches and the orchard...' Hence **clocker** [n.]. Laying hen. **1983** W.F. Marshall, *Livin' in Drumlister*, 'The Drumnakilly Divil': 'Then it wasn't long we tarried till the two of us were married,/An' home the donkey carried us — the presents made a load,/An' on them Sarah sittin' with a clocker an' a kitten,/As we jingled like a flittin' [q.v.] up the Drumnakilly road.' 4. [n., <Sc. *idem*, beetle] (Ulster). Beetle, cockroach. Hence **watch clocks in a basket** [vb. phr.]. Do something nearly impossible.

clod [n. & vb.]. 1. [n.]. Pre-decimal penny (Beecher, EW). **1968** John Healy, *The Death of an Irish Town*: 'You remember Jimmy Foley, the baker, who was always good for "the odd clod" to make up fourpence.' Also **clodhopper** (in same sense). 2. [vb.] (Ulster). Hit, throw at. **1946** Helen Waddell in Robert Greacen (ed.), *Irish Harvest*, 'Seisin': 'In the old burying grounds Catholic and Protestant lie together with little heaps of stones at the head of the graves, and we all know that these are there to be handy for "cloddin' other" in the Resurrection.' **1966** Florence Mary McDowell, *Other*

Days Around Me: 'with a strange mixture of his "English" voice and his Ulster background: "Will you please stop clodding!" This, after he had received a wet slice of currant-loaf on the back of his neck.'

clogher [n. & vb., <Sc. *clougher*, freq./ violent cough; cough thus] (Ulster). As thus. See also **clouter**.

Clonakilty-God-Help-Us [nickname, <euphem. for large workhouse for sick poor, as in 'he's gone to Clonakilty, God help us']. Clonakilty, Co. Cork. **1993** William Trevor, *Excursions in the Real World*: 'yellow furniture vans...carted our possessions off, westward through Cork itself and through the town people called Clonakilty-God-Help-Us...'

Clondyke [nickname] (Cork). Jeremiah Healy (*fl.* 1930s/1940s). **1993** Mick Long in Michael Verdon, *Shawlies* (q.v.), *Echo Boys* (q.v.), *the Marsh and the Lanes* (q.v.): *Old Cork Remembered*: 'Then there was *Clondyke*. He was probably the most famous of characters [see **character** 1.]. The man wasn't, as they say, the full shilling [q.v.]. His famous achievement was that he got the women's toilet built on the Coal Quay [q.v.]...his slogan for building the ladies' toilet was "Other nations are spending millions on arsenals. Can we not spend a few pounds on one urinal?"'

cloomin [n., cf. Eng. dial. *cloam* (vb.), daub with mud, <OE *clam* (n.), mud] (Ulster). Beating/thrashing.

cloot/clait [n., <Sc. *idem*, division of the hooves of cattle etc., human foot] (Ulster). Hand; left hand. Hence **clutey/clootie/clitty/cleety** [adj.]. Left-handed, awkward. Also **clootie-fisted/handed** in same sense.

clootie-dumpling [n., <'clout'] (Ulster). Pudding boiled in a cloth (SH).

clotty [n., <?]. Term of abuse. **1978** Tom Murphy, *A Crucial Week in the Life of a Grocer's Assistant*: 'Heeding that hussy of a clotty of a plótha of a streeleen [see **streel**] of an ownshock [see **oanshagh**] of a lebidjeh [see **lebbidha**] of a girleen that's working above in the bank.'

clouster [vb., <Ir. *clabhstar* (n.) as in *clabhstar éadaigh a chur ort*, encumber oneself with clothing]. 'Cover the head and shoulders with clothing as protection from the weather' (OTF). Also **cloustered** [p. part. as adj.]. Spoilt (of children). **1995** Phil O'Keeffe, *Down Cobbled Streets, A Liberties Childhood*: '"Don't coddle them; you have them cloustered. Harden them up a bit," my father would say when one or the other of us was kept home from school.'

clouter [n., cf. Sc. *cloiter*, disgusting wet mass; MDu. *claeteren* (vb.), besmear; poss. infl. by *clogher* (q.v.)] (Ulster). Cough, thick mucus. See also **glouter**.

clown [n., <Ir. *caille abhainn*, river maiden] (Leinster). Small sea trout. **1995** Éamon de Buitléar in Seán Power (ed.), *Those were the Days, Irish Childhood Memories*: 'These smaller sea trout, which were returning to the Dargle for the first time, were always known in the Bray area as "clowns".'

clunch [n., <?]. 'Thickset lusty person inclined to corpulency' (OTF).

clype see **clipe**

Coal Quay, the [nickname, pronun. 'Kay']. Cornmarket St, Cork, location of traditional market. **1881** *Shaw's Tourists' Picturesque Guide*: 'The Coal Quay — this is a part of the city amusing enough to strangers, yet far too unfashionable for the respectable citizens to take much interest in...coal is not sold within its precincts.' **1958** Louis Marcus, *Quarryman* (Cork), 'A Chapter from Work in Progress': '"There's a woman further down," said Harry..."who got her face from Da Vinci and her bearing from the Coal Quay."'

coarse [adj.] (Ulster) as in **coarse Christian** [n. phr.] rough diamond; **coarse shoes** [n. phr.] everyday work shoes.

coaxyorum [n., <'coax' + pseudo-Lat. ending]. 1. Individual alive to the main chance. 2. 'Cake prepared by prospective mother-in-law to show esteem for daughter's suitor' (RTÉ Radio, *The Odd Word*, 31 July 1995).

cobble [vb., cf. Sc. *cabble*, quarrel, dispute; Gothic *kaupatjan*, insult, affront; but poss. <ON & Icel. *kaupa*, buy, purchase] (Ulster). Bargain, haggle.

cobby house see **cabby house**

cockaninny [n., <Sc. *cockernony*, gathering of woman's hair into the 'snood' or fillet (CSD)] (Ulster). As thus; odd hat; young girl with high opinion of herself.

cocked hat [n. phr.] as in **drive into a cocked hat** [vb. phr., <US 'knock into a cocked hat', damage considerably, <officer's cap which could be flattened for carrying (DAS)]. Infuriate, exasperate. **1995** Maeve Binchy, *Irish Times*, 25 Nov: 'There are those who can't decide where to go on a holiday — they would drive you into a cocked hat.'

cock pheasant [n.] (Munster). Haymaking machine. **1995** Mick Doyle in Seán Power (ed.), *Those were the Days, Irish Childhood Memories*: 'When the hay was cut, it was aerated by tossing and turning with the sward-turner — referred to as the "cock pheasant". This ingenious machine, like a series of lawn-rakes on wheels, did a great job of drying wet hay.'

cock's step (along) [n.]. Lengthening spring daylight, associated with 12th day after Christmas. **1943** George A. Little, *Malachi Horan Remembers*: 'The fun would be kept going every night till Cock-step-along — that is Twelfth Day.' **1952** Bryan MacMahon, *Children of the Rainbow*: 'We had watched spring come, each day lengthening by the scarcely perceptible "cock's step".'

Cock Tuesday [nickname]. Shrove Tuesday. **1938** Seumas MacManus, *The Rocky Road to Dublin*: 'Cock Tuesday, the eve of Lent, was then the great day of the year for marriages.'

cod [adj., n. & vb., poss. <'codger' (n.), old fool, but poss. also <*cods* (n.), scrotum; 'somewhere between 1800 and 1900 a cod seems to have begun to mean a joke — but a practical one rather than a Rabelasian one' (Nicholas Bagnall, *Independent on Sunday*, London, 6 Nov 1994)]. In Hib.E, emphasis is on

deception, deceit or stupidity rather than practical jokes. **1995** Michael Noonan, RTÉ TV news, 12 May: 'that's a cod argument: everyone knew what they were voting for'. **1996** Justin Comiskey, *Irish Times*, 17 May: '[Brian] O'Nolan's satirical targets, principally people he considered pretentious, those in whom he discerned dishonesty of character and assumptions not borne out by their abilities, or what he called "cods" for short...' Hence **cod-acting** [vb. n.]. Foolish behaviour. **1952** *Kavanagh's Weekly*, 14 June: 'Ah James [Dillon], jewel and darlin' [see **jewel**], what kind of cod-actin' were you at?' See also **act the maggot, codology, jack-act, jig-act, trick-acting**.

coddle [n., <*idem* (vb.), boil gently, parboil, stew, 1588 (OED)] (Dub.). Dish of ham/bacon, sausages, onions and potatoes. **1961** Dominic Behan, *Teems of Times and Happy Returns*: '"The Behans are havin' a sausage coddle for dinner. Pork ones too! Far below her ladyship's dignity to boil beef."' **1983** Theodora FitzGibbon, *Irish Traditional Food*: 'Combining two of the earliest Irish foods, this has been a favourite dish since the eighteenth century. It is said to have been much liked by Dean Swift.'

codology [n., cf. Brit. sl. 'codswallop'; see **cod**]. Nonsense. **1928** 'Leo' (Lionel Fleming), *TCD, A College Miscellany*, 'The Irish Mail', 25 Oct: '"Yerrah [see **yerra**], Cosgrave? That's all codology. Now, when we get Dev [q.v.]..."' **1989** Hugh Leonard, *Out after Dark*: 'what the know-alls affected to look upon as art was known by plump and plain everyday people to be no more than old codology'. **1995** Vincent Browne, *Irish Times*, 12 Apr: 'The judges and barristers are all dressed up in their scruffy wigs ...gowns and stiff white shirts. And some of them actually believe that all this codology is essential...'

cod-on [n., see **cod**]. Practical joke. **1979** John Morrow in David Marcus (ed.), *Body and Soul*, 'Beginnings': 'Father ...had warned me about "cod-ons" — the apprentice sent traipsing [q.v.] from shed to shed in search of "the rubber-headed hammer" or "a bucket of blue steam"...'

coduter [n., <'coadjutor']. Adviser (EW).

coffin–cutter [n.]. Devil's coach horse beetle (*Staphylinus olens*).

coffin roller [n.] (Dub.). Mangle. **1975** Eilís Brady, *All In! All In!*: 'an ungainly but very efficient affair, consisting of a large box-like wooden frame, for all the world like a coffin...the clothes were laid on...rollers which were operated by a huge handle placed mid–way on the frame'.

cog [vb., poss. <*idem*, cheat at dice, colloq. Eng. *c*.1650]. Copy surreptitiously, crib. **1992** Brian Leyden, *Departures*: 'Witness, too, the same poor scholars [q.v.] every year who come in early to cog the homework.' **1996** Brendan Glacken, *Irish Times*, 9 June: 'I am going to cog some stuff from the wonderful world of stand-up comedy just to show you what you missed, unless you actually attended the Cat Laughs comedy festival in Kilkenny...' Also **cogging** [adj.]. Deceitful. **1623** Anon., *The Welsh Embassador.* 'CLOWN Come in. Oh, Mr Mac Teage, this may be cronicled to see you here. EDMUND Sawst thou Reece, datt coggin rascalls?'

coggle [vb., <Sc. *idem*, totter, wobble] (Ulster). As thus. Hence **cogglesome**, **coggley** [adj.]. Rickety; changeable (of weather).

coldoy [n., <?] (Munster). Bad halfpenny; worthless article.

coldrifed [adj., <Sc. *idem*, shivery, sensitive to cold] (Ulster). 1. As thus. 2. Hesitant, reluctant to take a risk. **1948** John O'Connor, *Come Day — Go Day*: '"Ah, I never seen such a pack of cold-rifed craythurs [q.v.] in my life," Neilly blurted.' **1993** Seamus Heaney, *The Midnight Verdict* (translation of Brian Merriman, *Cúirt an Mheán Oíche*): '"You hardened chaw [see **hard chaw**],/I've waited long, now I'll curry you raw! You've had your warnings, you cold-rifed blirt [q.v.].""'

colf [vb., <Sc. *idem*, cram, <Fr. *calfater*, caulk] (Ulster). Cram one's mouth with food, eat greedily. Also **colfed** [p. part. as adj.]. Constipated.

collar, Roman see **Roman collar**

colleen [n., <Ir. *cailín*, girl]. As thus, latterly ironic.

colley/colly [n., <Eng. dial. *coll(ey)*, coal]. Specks of coal dust; fluff that gathers under furniture etc.

colligoleen/calligaleen/gollagoleen/callig etc. [n., <Ir. *cuileog an lin*, lit. insect of the flax]. Earwig.

collogue [vb., poss. <Fr. *colloque* (n.), conference, communication, colloq. Eng. *collogue* (vb.), confabulate, *c*.1810–]. Gossip. **1966** Patrick Boyle, *At Night All Cats are Grey*, 'The Betrayers': 'Cassie turned at the pantry door, pointed dramatically at the calling voice and whispered: "He shouldn't be collogueing with the kitchen staff, should he, Ma'am?"'

collop [n.]. 1. [<Ir. *colpa*, (a) unit of grazing land; (b) calf of the leg]. As thus. 2. [<Sc. *idem*, slice of meat; bacon & eggs, cf. Swed. *kalops* (n. pl.), slices of stewed beef] (Ulster). Slice of meat; (fig.) large piece of anything. Also **Collop Monday**, day before Shrove Tuesday, when bacon & eggs were traditional fare.

colly see **colley**

colour/colourin' [n.]. Small amount, tincture, esp. of milk for the tea. **1967** Bryan MacMahon, *The Honey Spike* (q.v.): '"What do you want?" the woman asked. "A drop o' colourin' ma'am." Breda held out the pint bottle.'

comber/cumber [n., <OF *encombrer* (vb.), encumber] (Ulster). Encumbrance, inconvenience, burden.

combo [n.] (Dub.). Football practice.

combustibles [n. pl.] (Ulster). Comestibles, rich fare (YDS).

come-all-ye/you [n., <typical first line]. Sentimental ballad. **1916** James Joyce, *A Portrait of the Artist* (q.v.) *as a Young Man*: 'He got up quickly to dress, and when the song had ended, said, "That's much prettier than any of your other *come-all-yous.*' **1992** Sean

O'Callaghan, *Down by the Glenside, Memoirs of an Irish Boyhood*: 'The local poet was also a man of exceptional talent; his ballads were sung at fairs and markets, at dances and in public houses. They were called "Come all ye's," as the first lines usually ran "Come all ye good people, and hark to my song..."'

Come-Home Yankee [nickname]. Returned emigrant. **1938** Seumas MacManus, *The Rocky Road to Dublin*: 'Sometimes from the lads who came to school from all airts [q.v.] he heard of a Come-Home Yankee having brought a book with him...'

come-tae-me-go-aff-me [n.] (Ulster). Accordion. See also **frae-me-come-tae-me**.

comether [n., <'come' + Hib.E pronun. of 'hither']. '[A] sort of spell brought about by coaxing, wheedling, making love, etc.' (PWJ). **1922** James Joyce, *Ulysses*: 'Ann hath a way. By cock, she was to blame. She put the comether on him, sweet and twentysix.'

come up on the last load [vb. phr., invar. neg.]. Expressive of 'not being born yesterday'. **1995** Patrick Boland, *Tales from a City Farmyard*: 'The Ma [q.v.]...then smiled at me and said, "...Did you gang of toughs think I came up on the last load?"' Many vars. include: **come up the river on a bike**. **1995** *Leinster Leader* (Naas, Co. Kildare), 31 Aug: 'We've all heard the expression "I didn't come up the river on a bike," meaning "I'm no fool." Well, Arthur Lynch is no fool either, but he ...undertook to travel the river Barrow from Athy to Wexford on a specially made "aqua-bike"...' Also **come up the Foyle in a bubble** (Ulster) (TT).

comeuppance [n., <?]. Just deserts. **1993** James Quirke in Joe O'Reilly & Sixth Class, Convent School, Edenderry, *Over the Half Door*: 'like everything else you only get away with it for so long. I was out on the Belfast road coming back to Dublin one night and at a place called Greemore met my comuppence [*sic*]... That was the end of my motorbiking career.'

commit oneself [vb.] (Ulster). Soil with faeces (gen. of children).

comnoro [n., <Ir. *comóradh*, sign of respect (Dinneen); gathering, assembly, wake]. Gift at a wake. **1995** Kathleen Sheehan in Mary Ryan et al. (eds.), *No Shoes in Summer*: 'It was the custom to pay one shilling "comnoro"...If not a shilling, then some tea or something of that value. The Priests were very much against this and eventually it was abolished.'

company car [n.]. Old vehicle bought communally by group of youths for joyriding, esp. Dub. **1995** RTÉ TV news, 7 Apr: 'what are called company cars — bangers bought for about £50'.

comsleesh see **cumsloosh**

cond [n., <Ir. *canta*, chunk, hunk]. Hunk, crust (of bread). **1990** Edmund Lenihan, *In the Tracks of the West Clare Railway*: 'So hard was the work [digging a cutting] that it is yet claimed in the locality that there were no breaks during the working day, not even for meals: "You had to eat and work at the one time, picking away at a cond o' bread out o' your pocket."'

confirmation money [n. phr., <practice of giving money to children for their confirmation] as in **he still has his confirmation money**. Said of a miserly individual. **1991** John B. Keane, *Love Bites and Other Stories*: 'he had about a hundred acres of land and numerous other properties. It was rumoured too that he had his confirmation money.'

conjun box [n., <Tamil *kanjee*, water in which rice has been boiled — staple nourishment for prisoners in India; poss. imported by returning Munster Fusiliers] (Cork). Lock-up, hence small secure box, money box.

conn [n., <?] (Ulster). The ace of diamonds.

connihaly [n., 'may refer to an individual named Connie Healy who had a small penis' (Beecher)] (Cork). Penis.

conniption [n., <?]. Seizure. **1996** David Hanly, *Sunday Tribune*, 7 Apr: 'I casually mention to my editor that I have

left my press card at home. The young man nearly has a conniption in the middle of the street.'

conny [adj., <'canny' (Sc.), quiet, gentle]. As thus. **1975** Eilís Brady, *All In! All In!*: 'Somebody may say in praise of a neighbour's child "You'd steal her...She's a conny little thing."'

conny bun/dodger [n., <Cornelius Lucey, Catholic bishop of Cork & Ross, d. 1982] (Cork). Type of bread bun accepted as part of a 'collation' rather than a meal during Lent.

connysure [n. & vb., <?]. Gossip. **1996** Christy Kenneally, *Maura's Boy, A Cork Childhood:* 'Nan could be a formidable figure in the face of complaint and had little time for that particular coven of connysures.'

conny wobble [n., <?, Anglo-Ir., C18–19 (DHS)]. Eggs and brandy beaten up together.

consatey/consaty [adj., <'conceit'] (Ulster). Self-satisfied, 'stuck-up'. Also **fall in consate with** [vb. phr.]. Take a fancy to.

convoy [n.]. Gathering to speed departing emigrant. **1938** Seumas MacManus, *The Rocky Road to Dublin*: 'Often and often he went to the going-off party, the Convoy — when friends and neighbours gathered to the home of the departing boy or girl, and sat through the last night with them...' **1939** Patrick Gallagher ('Paddy the Cope' (q.v.)), *My Story*: 'The night of Mary's convoy I was very much ashamed of myself staying at home and my sister going away to a foreign country.'

cook [n., <?]. Hairstyle. **1994** Paddy O'Gorman, *Queuing for a Living*: 'True traveller women put their hair up in what I think they called a cook.'

cooker [vb., cf. Shetland *kukker*, cheer up/comfort s.o.] (Ulster). Spoil, pamper (child). Hence **cookered** [p. part. as adj].

coolican [n., <Ir. *cúl cinn*, back of the head]. As thus (OTF).

coolin [n., cf. Ir. *bheith i gcúil aon chinn*, be in a quandary]. Setback, deflation.

coolygullen [n.]. Ulster var. of colligoleen (q.v.).

coonagh [adj. & n.]. 1. [adj., <Ir. *cuain* (n.), band, company]. Friendly, on good terms. 2. [n., <Ir. *cúnamh*, help]. Savings, nest egg.

cooter/coulter [n., derog., <OE *culter*, ploughshare] (Ulster). Long nose.

cope [vb.]. 1. (Ulster). Defecate. 2. **cope/coup/cowp** [<OF *couper*, strike]. Overturn; be overturned; knock s.o. down. **1979** John Morrow, *The Confessions of Proinsias O'Toole*: '"'Lave that down, you kinky thing," says I, couping her onto the sofa.' Hence **cope-curley/cope/coup-carlie** [vb., <OF *couper* + *carl*, countryman, boy, fellow, <OE *ceorl*, man, ON *karl*, *idem*] (Ulster). Turn head over heels. **1979** Paddy Tunney, *The Stone Fiddle*: 'he had often seen trout rise so high for a sedge or a daddy-long-legs that they cope-carlied in the air'.

cop-on/cop on [n. & vb., poss. <Lat. *capere* (vb.) seize; gen. neg.]. (Possess) understanding, streetwise knowledge, esp. as in **he hasn't much cop-on**; **cop on to yourself**. **1997** Brendan Glacken, *Irish Times*, 15 May: 'The current test assesses literacy and numeracy but apparently gives few clues to the personality. "It wouldn't tell you if you had any cop-on," one garda was quoted as saying.'

coppul-hurrish [n., <Ir. *capall*, horse + poss. *thairis*, 'over it' (CUD)] (Ulster). Game of see-saw.

corbie [n., <OF *corbe*, crow]. Miserly, grasping individual.

corner boy [n.]. Loiterer without intent. **1981** Paddy Crosbie, *Your Dinner's Poured Out!*: 'The lowest name one could be called in my young days was "a corner-boy". The real corner-boy hung around corners, but grown-ups applied the term to all youngsters who formed into groups or gangs and shouted insults and rhymes after their elders.' **1987** Vincent Caprani, *Vulgar Verse & Variations, Rowdy Rhymes & Rec-im-itations*, 'Gough's Statue': 'My late father — though there was no better man [q.v] for a joke...strongly disapproved of cornerboy language.' **1991** John B. Keane, *Love Bites and Other Stories*: 'I will concede he is a first-rate corner boy. He never obstructs passers-by. He never answers people who seek directions. He disappears at the first sign of trouble. He looks into space all day long...'

coronations [n. pl.] (Cork). Brit. coins (Beecher).

corp [n., <'corpse'] (Ulster). Useless person.

Corpo [n., <abbrev. + endearment suffix]. (Dublin) Corporation. **1995** Ciara Dwyer, *Sunday Independent*, 26 Nov: '...Agnes Browne, a widow and Moore Street dealer, brings up her large family alone. The Corpo has moved them from their inner-city home, out to the country — Finglas.'

Corporation hairoil [n.]. Water. **1991** Bob Quinn, *Smokey Hollow*: 'He was the first to use "Corporation hairoil", or water, to achieve a quiff in his hair and was called a mickeydazzler [q.v.] because of it.'

corrie/corry-fisted [adj., cf. Ir. *cearr*, left-handed]. As thus, clumsy.

cosy/cosie [n. & adj., <'co-driver'] (Dub. taxi drivers). Co-driver. **1995** *Irish Times*, 26 Aug: 'A plate owner will often take on co-drivers...to drive the taxi while the owner is resting. The most common arrangement is for the cosy to rent the car and [licence] plate from the owner for 12 hours out of the 24...' **1996** Emmet Oliver, *Irish Times*, 17 Dec: 'He explains that many taxi drivers are "cosie" drivers — they don't own their plate (or licence) but rent one from someone else.'

cotamore [n., <Ir. *cóta mór*, overcoat]. As thus. **1943** George A. Little, *Malachi Horan Remembers*: 'He would wear a "trusty", or, as you would call it, a cotamore — the name the people had on it hereabout was a "bang-up".' **1993** Anon. in Seán Dunne (ed.), *The Cork Anthology*, 'Old Skibbereen': 'I wrapt you in my cotamore at the dead of night unseen.'

cough see **soften the cough**

coult [n., <'colt', young or inexperienced person, ME (OED)] (Cork). Half-trained worker. **C.1820** Peter Lynch, handbill: 'P.L. contaminates [*sic*] coults and their rotton [*sic*] work and all belonging to them which are only fit for workhouses and Auction Buzars [*sic*].'

coulter see **cooter**

country cute [adj. phr.]. Descriptive of rural deviousness as perceived by city-dwellers. **1914** James Joyce, *Dubliners*, 'The Dead': 'She had often spoken of Gretta as being country cute.' **1995** *Irish Times*, 1 July: 'Small wonder that Mildred Fox has been described by opponents as "country cute". She certainly had much of rural Wicklow on her side...'

coup see **cope** 2.

court [n., <'court' (vb.), pay amorous attention to; pronun. *coort*]. Close sexual contact; one providing such contact. **1948** Patrick Kavanagh, *Tarry Flynn*: '"I'm dead with the drouth [see **drooth** 2.]," he cried ever so casually. "And a pain in your head for want of a court," said Molly.' **1989** Hugh Leonard, *Out after Dark*: 'To be punished for my faith ...made a nice change from being told that I could not dance for skins [q.v.] or was a rotten court...' Also **bad court** [n. phr.] lacking in amatory prowess; unsatisfactory suitor; **cool court** [n. phr.] undemonstrative lover. **1978** Tom Murphy, *A Crucial Week in the Life of a Grocer's Assistant*: 'MONA ...You didn't tell me where you were for the past few nights. It seemed like...ages...Do you know? You *are* a very bad court...John Joe.' See also **hoult, scrape**.

cove [n., poss. <Romany *cova/covo*, that man]. Form of address; male individual (cf. Austral. usage). **1968** John Healy, *The Death of an Irish Town*: '"I had a new suit that John Bermingham made for me, all very snazzy, cove."' See also **sham**.

cowclap/clap [n. & vb., poss. <'crap']. Cow dung; deposit such. **1948** John O'Connor, *Come Day — Go Day*: 'great flurries of it [rain] kept blowing in at both sides of the bridge, forcing the crowd to step back uneasily through the clammy cowclap on the ground'. **1951** Sam Hanna Bell, *December Bride*: 'He set down his glass and shook his head appreciatively ..."That clears the cow-clap out o' your throat, all right"...'

cowhibble [n., <?]. Twist of arm and wrist when throwing (OTF).

Cowjack [nickname, <*Kojak*, US TV character, 1970s–1980s]. Michael Dillon, farmer and regular 1980s broadcaster on farming affairs. **1995** *Leinster Leader* (Naas, Co. Kildare): 'The body in the boot: was this a case for "cowjack"?'

cowp see **cope** 2.

cow's/bull's lick [n., 1st ref. in *Book of the Dun Cow* (*Leabhar na hUidhre*), *c*.1100 (PWJ)]. Hair slicked back at the front, quiff; or 'a bit of hair that wouldn't stay out of your eye' (EW). **1936** Frank O'Connor, *Bones of Contention and Other Stories*, 'Uprooted': 'Keating was a slow, cumbrous young man with dark eyes and a dark cow's-lick that kept tumbling into them.'

cowstails [n. pl.] (Ulster). Pigtails.

craags [n. pl., <Ir. *crág*, large hand]. Fat hands; large handfuls.

crab [n.]. 1. [poss. <Du. *krabben* (vb.), scratch]. Unpleasant child; '[a] cute precocious little child is often called an *old crab*' (PWJ); fit of the sulks. **1975** Eilís Brady, *All In! All In!*: 'it's bad enough to be bold [q.v.] but it's much worse to be a "crab" — old beyond your years and usually of small build'. Also **crabby** [adj.], **crabjaw** [n.] in same sense. 2. [cf. Brit. army sl. *crab wallah*, evil man (DHS)]. Term of contempt. **1989** John Healy, *Magill*, Aug: 'As one of the team put it to me in the vernacular "He [Bobby Molloy TD] is what he always was — a crab, a right [see **right** 1.] little crab."'

crabbed/crabbit [p. part. as adj., <Sc. *crabbit*, bad-tempered; see also **crab**]. As thus, upset. **1961** Tom Murphy, *A Whistle in the Dark*: 'BETTY My advice to you is don't get married at all. Honestly, Irishmen shouldn't...DES Is she crabbed?' **1991** Seán Ó Ciaráin, *Farewell to Mayo*:

'They had grown up and married, and matured, or become crabbit and contrary under the same bosses or their descendants.'

crab shells [n. pl.]. Shoes (Grose).

crack [n. & vb.]. 1. [n. & vb., <Sc. *idem*, brisk talk, news, poss. <OE *cracian*, crack, hence make loud sound (onomat.)]. (Ulster). As thus, but absorbing idea of informal entertainment as represented by Ir. neologism **craic**, as in cliché phrase **ceol agus craic**, esp. with ref. to pub entertainment. **1925** Louise McKay, *Mourne Folk*: 'Then she axed me to sit down, so we sut [*sic*] an' cracked for long enough about wan thing an' another...' **1995** Railway Preservation Society of Ireland, *Newsletter* (Belfast), Apr: 'The music from a piano in the vestibule of [coach no.] 50, and the crack from a cast of local radio and television personalities, kept the group of hopeful lovers happy as we travelled.' **1995** Peter Cunningham, *Independent on Sunday* (London), 29 Oct: 'Because no word existed to convey the particular sense of esprit produced by the confluence of drink, romance and music, the Irish invented the term "craic"...' 2. [vb., onomat.]. Fart. **1996** Dermot Healy, *The Bend for Home*: 'The fellow in front lifted his arse as the nun turned to the board. He cracked in my face.'

crackawly [n., <Ir. *craiceálaí*, stupid person] (Munster). As thus.

cracksome [adj.] (Ulster). Full of crack (see **crack** 1.). **1938** Seumas MacManus, *The Rocky Road to Dublin*: 'Ellen was jolly and cracksome in spite of her affliction...'

cradlebird [n.]. Bird trap. **1995** Nellie Ryan in Mary Ryan et al. (eds.), *No Shoes in Summer*: 'We saw a robin caught in a cradlebird. (A cradlebird was used to catch birds for people's dinners.) My sister opened the cradlebird and let the bird go free.'

craic see **crack** 1.

craik/crake [vb., onomat.] (Ulster). Grumble, complain, nag, talk incessantly.

Crank on the Bank, the [nickname] (Dub.). Memorial to poet Patrick

Kavanagh on the Grand Canal. **1996** Renagh Holohan, *Irish Times*, 1 June: 'When the President, Mrs Robinson, unveiled the James Connolly Memorial [see **the Scut under the Butt**]...she referred to a similar occasion involving the Patrick Kavanagh Memorial...which soon afterwards became known as the Crank on the Bank.'

cranky [adj., cf. Austral. usage]. Cross, cantankerous.

crapper [n., <?]. Half-glass of whiskey.

crathur see **craythur**

crattle [n., <Sc. *idem*, noisy breathing in the chest] (Ulster). As thus.

cratur see **craythur**

crawling [pres. part., metonym]. Of gridlocked traffic. **1995** Dessie Hughes, letter to the *Irish Times*, 3 Feb: 'On several mornings recently, *AA Roadwatch* on RTÉ Radio has informed us "The Stillorgan Road is crawling all the way into Dublin." I have since scoured the pages of your paper for evidence of this truly remarkable phenomenon.'

crawnshawler [n., cf. Ir. *crannseileach* (adj.), emitting tough phlegm (Dinneen)]. 'Someone always trying to get on your good side' (EW).

crawsick [adj., see **crawthumper**]. Suffering a hangover; sick to the stomach. **1922** James Joyce, *Ulysses*: 'I am among them, among their battling bodies in a medley, the joust for life. You mean that knockkneed mother's darling who seems to be slightly crawsick?' **1981** Brendan Behan, *After the Wake*: '"Tomorrow morning, when you wake up, craw-sick, you'll be down on your knees, praying for the wrath of God to be averted from a sinful old man."'

crawthumper [n., <ME *crawe*, Norse *krage*, neck; derisive 1573; obsolete in Std Eng. *c*.1800: the stomach]. Ostentatiously pious/religious individual. **1922** James Joyce, *Ulysses*: 'And just imagine that. Wife and six children at home. And plotting that murder all the time. Those crawthumpers, now that's a good name for them, there's always something shifty looking about them.' **1954** Benedict

Kiely, *Honey Seems Bitter*: '"She married a queer boy," he said, "a craw thumping yellow-hammer [q.v.]."' **1995** Eanna Brophy, *Sunday Tribune*, 9 July: 'THE CRAW THUMPER. Not as numerous as it once was, this noisy menace to public health has made a bit of a comeback lately...often congregates around the houses of rural ministers.' See also **voteen**.

craythur/crathur/cratur/creature [n.]. 1. [<'creature': strong drink (joc.) 1614]. Whiskey, more gen. illicitly distilled poteen (q.v.). Most commonly in phrase 'a drop of the craythur'. **1824** Thomas Crofton Croker, *Researches in the South of Ireland*: 'when he swears by all he considers holy, to drink "not a drop at all at all [q.v.]", he surmounts his difficulty by eating the bread he has sopped in "*the cratur*"'. **1925** Louise McKay, *Mourne Folk*: '"Ye must have a drop of the cratur with us afore ye go, jist to show that we're all on friendly terms."' **1978** John McGuffin, *In Praise of Poteen*: 'in our large cities school labs, hospital labs and back garden sheds and garages are being used for making their own version of "the cratur"'. 2. [<'creature', human being ME]. Expression of affection and/or pity, as 'The craythur!' **1906** E.Œ. Somerville & Martin Ross, *Some Irish Yesterdays*: '"Well, well! The cratures [*sic*]! An' they come to this lonesome place to ate their dinner..."'

creased [p. part. as adj.]. Severely maltreated. **1975** Eilís Brady, *All In! All In!*: '"Just wait till you're got in! You're going to be creased! killed! massacred!"'

creash/creesh [n. & vb., <Sc. *idem*, grease, <OF *craisse*, Fr. *graisse*, grease] (Ulster). 1. As thus. Hence **creashy** [adj.]. **1844** Robert Huddleston, *A Collection of Poems and Songs on Rural Subjects*, 'The Lammas Fair (Belfast)': 'Here gangs a wife sae laden'd doon,/Wi' mony a creashy treasure...' 2. Beating, thrashing; beat up, thrash. Hence **creeshin** [n.]. Thrashing.

creature see **craythur**

creecrator! [exclam., <Ir. *croí cráite ort*, a broken heart to you!]. As thus. **?1727**

Anon., *The Pretender's Exercise*: 'SERGEANT ...disgrace pon de Pretender and de fole [whole] Nashion, *Viry Creecrator Scrashtee Vodee brane* [**bodeaugh breene**: see **boddagh**] *Granagh Clootough...*' (succession of terms of abuse in Anglicised Ir.).

creepie/creepy (stool) [n., cf. Sc. *creepie-chair/stool*, 'stool of repentance' (CSD)] (Ulster). Low 3-legged stool, enabling user to move close in to turf fire avoiding smoke. **1908** Lynn Doyle, *Ballygullion*: 'the poor ould chap, startin' back, thrips over a creepie stool an' goes slap on the floor'. **1925** Louise McKay, *Mourne Folk*: 'The arm-chair was brought in double-quick time. Not only an arm-chair, but a "creepy" for my feet...'

creesh see **creash**

cregg [n., <Ir. *cnag*, blow]. Light blow on the head with knuckles of partly closed fingers (OTF).

crib/cribbin [n. & vb.] (Ulster). 1. [n., <Sc. *crib-stane*, kerb-stone]. As thus, pavement, footpath. **1948** John O'Connor, *Come Day — Go Day*: 'The bullet struck the cribben and glanced into the centre of the road again, still travelling very fast...' 2. [vb.]. Stub toe on kerb. See **crig** 2.

crig [n. & vb.]. 1. [n., poss. <Ir. *creag/creig*, rock, cf. Brit. sl., 'get one's rocks off']. Testicle. 2. [n. & vb., cf. Ir. *cnag*, knock, strike]. Blow, stub (toe). See **splank** (p. 319, Addenda).

crilly [n., cf. Ir. *crith-eagla*, fear causing trembling]. Glossed in Irish Folklore Commission ms., 1935, as 'a shivering sort of person, one who appears to be cold and bent down with misery' (DOM); hence use as term of abuse.

Crimbo [n.]. Christmas. **1996** Joseph O'Connor, *The Irish Male at Home and Abroad*: 'Your friends, whom you have not seen since last Crimbo...have decided that it is your turn to have them over for "supper", whatever that is.'

crinkler [n.]. Currency note. See **carrying**.

crith [n., <Ir. *cruit*, hump]. As thus. 'A person with shoulders hunched in wintry weather is described as having "a crith on him"' (OTF).

croaked [p. part. as adj., cf. 'croaker', one who forebodes evil]. Doomed to death, from croaking of the raven associated with imminent death in a family.

croak park [nickname; see **Croker**]. Glasnevin Cemetery, Dub. **1975** John Ryan, *Remembering How We Stood*: 'We were bound for Glasnevin Cemetery, the large metropolitan Necropolis, grave of our heroes, pantheon of our gods — *croak park*.'

crockety-crock [n., onomat.]. Sound of wheels on road. **1947** Seán O'Faoláin, *Teresa and Other Stories*, 'The Silence of the Valley': 'Once a farm cart made a crockety-crock down the eastern road and he wondered if it was bringing the coffin.'

Croker [nickname, <abbrev. + endearment suffix, <Archbishop Thomas William *Croke* (1824–1902), strong supporter of the Gaelic Athletic Association (GAA)]. Croke Park, Dub., national GAA headquarters. **1973** Noël Conway, *The Bloods* (q.v.): 'Small little things that he'd miss in Heaven increased his doubt: small things like the pint in Newbridge, an all-Ireland at "Croker"...' **1995** Paul O'Meara, *Leinster Leader* (Naas, Co. Kildare), 24 Aug: 'Lilies [see **Lillywhites**] in Croker.'

crole see **crowl**

cronebane [n., <halfpenny copper token circulated by Associated Irish Mines, Cronebane, Co. Wicklow, *c*.1790 (DOM)]. As thus, as in **not worth a cronebane** [adj. phr.].

croobs [n., gen. pl. with def. art., <Ir. *crúb*, foot]. Feet — usu. with some sense of disparagement. **1977** Flann O'Brien, *The Hair of the Dogma*: 'tellin' me I can spend sixteen hours a day behind this counter wearin' the croobs off me down to the shanks, thanks very much'.

croonawn/crownawn [vb., <Ir *crónán* (n.), (act of) humming, murmur]. Sing (of kettle). **1960** John O'Donoghue, *In Kerry Long Ago*: 'The kettle soon began to sing a teeny-weeny song...till it finally ended in a rough "Thur,r,r,r,r..." when

it could stand the heat no longer to keep up its first *croonawning...*' **1964** Mannix Joyce, *Capuchin Annual*, 'Eamon de Valera [see **Dev**], Bruree Man': 'By winter firesides, where crickets chirped, and where the kettle hung crownawning on the crook...'

croost/cruist/cruste [vb., <Ir. *crústa* (n.), blow, cast]. As thus. **1992** Sean O'Callaghan, *Down by the Glenside, Memoirs of an Irish Boyhood*: 'Lar saw this and "cruisted" (hit) Mick with a sod of earth...'

croppen for all corn [adj. phr.] (Ulster). Said of person expecting a free meal (Pepper).

Croppy [nickname, <short-cropped hair favoured by 1798 insurgents, following the French revolutionary model]. Rebel; and (Ulster) gen. denigratory term for Catholics. **C.1798** Pop. ballad: 'Croppies Lie Down': 'We'll fight for our country, our king and our crown,/And make all the traitors and croppies lie down./Down, down, croppies, lie down.' **1922** James Joyce, *Ulysses*: 'Hoarse, masked and armed, the planters' covenant. The black north and true blue bible. Croppies lie down.' **1989** John Healy, *Magill*, Sept: 'The mock-field of Scarva had come to Stormont and the Croppies were now to play the traditional role of lying down, only it was for real and it was everyday...'

crowl/crowlie/croul/crole etc. [n., cf. Ir. *cróilí*, disablement, infirmity]. Small, stunted person. Hence **crowled up** [adj.] in same sense. **1948** John O'Connor, *Come Day — Go Day*: 'An old crowled up woman, with a coat pulled round her, sidled up to the counter.'

crownawn see **croonawn**

crowner [n., <'coroner', by metathesis, obsolete in Std Eng.] (Ulster). As thus. **1908** Lynn Doyle, *Ballygullion* : '"I don't want to waste a day on a Crowner's jury, an' the potatoes comin' out."'

crozier, belt of a/the see **belt of a/the crozier**

crub [vb., cf. Ir. *crap*, contract, shrink]. Contract the body by bending. Hence

crubbed up [adj.]. Said of s.o. bent in the shoulders and at the knees (OTF).

crubeen [n., <Ir. *crúibín*, pig's trotter]. As thus in sense of edible delicacy. **1922** James Joyce, *Ulysses*: 'Florence MacCabe takes a crubeen and a bottle of double X [stout] for supper every Saturday.' **1996** John McKenna, *Irish Times*, 28 Nov: 'It seems that there was once a shop on Brown Street [Carlow]...which plied its trade selling boiled sheep's heads and crubeens, those deliciously yummy and fatty pig's trotters.' **1996** Christy Kenneally, *Maura's Boy, A Cork Childhood*: 'The fresh-meat shop was a shop of horrors. Crubeens were stacked like firewood on a plate, drisheen [q.v.] swam in a milky dish...'

Cruiser, the [nickname]. Conor Cruise O'Brien (1917–), diplomat, politician, academic, historian and latterly prophet of doom regarding the strife in Northern Ire. **1995** Dick Spring, Address to the Labour Party Annual Conference, 8 Apr: (following ref. to the Shannon–Erne waterway) 'Imagine that other Cruiser so well known to us never again predicting a bloodbath on this island.' **1995** Eanna Brophy, *Sunday Tribune*, 24 Sept: 'After the massive 1977 Fianna Fáil election win (84 seats) the broadcaster [Frank Hall] became a bit nervous when one day he was walking down the Bull Wall and saw none other than the Cruiser coming the other way...'

cruist see **croost**

Crum, the [nickname, abbrev.]. Crumlin Road gaol, Belfast. **1993** Sam McAughtry, *Touch & Go*: 'In fact, of all the screws in the Crum, he was the obvious one for O'Hare to use in order to make contact with me.'

cruste see **croost**

cry crack [vb.]. Give in. **1939** James Joyce, *Finnegans Wake*: 'They were on that sea by the plain of Ir nine hundred and ninety nine years and they never cried crack or ceased from regular paddlewicking...'

cuairt [n., <Ir. *idem*, visit]. As thus. **1995** Brian Farrell in Seán Power (ed.), *Those*

cub   cúpla focal

were the Days, Irish Childhood Memories:
'Friends visited on what I later came to
recognise as the *cuairt*. There would be
cups of tea and chat and...an impromptu
concert of ballads and come-all-yes [q.v.].'

cub [n.] (Ulster). Young boy. **1974** John
Hewitt, *Out of my Time*, 'The Fairy
Thresher': 'For instance when a *cub*, the
man himself/joined with his brother to
herd cattle in...'

cuckoo potatoes [n. phr.]. Potatoes
planted in May.

cuckoo's lachter [n. phr., <Ir. *lachtar*,
clutch of eggs, <ON *latr/lattr*, place
where animals lay their young] (Ulster).
Only child. Also **cuckoo's bird** in same
sense, esp. if a girl.

cuddy/cutty [adj. & n.]. 1. [adj. & n., cf.
Sc. *cutty*, short; short-handled horn
spoon] (Ulster). Short, short-stemmed/
handled (implement). **1913** Alexander
Irvine, *My Lady of the Chimney Corner*.
'He took a live coal and stoked up the
bowl of his cutty-pipe.' **1925** Louise
McKay, *Mourne Folk*: '"all we had in the
house was one knife for the whole crowd
of us, an' two or three cutty spoons"'. 2.
[n., <'cut'] (Ulster). Small, undersized
horse; small, cheeky person. **1981** R.M.
Arnold, *The County Down* (Belfast &
County Down Railway): 'Bob Clements
has provided most valuable data about the
1917 situation when the "cuddies" (0-4-
2 tanks) were described as the "Ardglass
engines".' 3. [n., <Sc. *idem*, girl, hare].
Young girl. **1966** Patrick Boyle, *At Night
All Cats are Grey*, 'The Metal Man': '"A
hedgehog wouldn't be safe with Tailor
around and there's bloody few quills on
Scroggy's young cuddy of a wife."' 4. [n.,
<Sc. *idem*, simpleton]. Left-handed
person. 5. [n., <Ir. *cuid oíche*, share for the
night]. As thus.

culchie [n., <?; most gen. received
etym. is <*Coillte Mach* (Kiltimagh), Co.
Mayo; others include: <Ir. *coillte* (n. pl.),
woods (CUD); *cúl a' tí*, rear entrance to
the big house (q.v.), as used by social
inferiors (*The Odd Word*, RTÉ Radio, 31
July 1995) — but the stress would not
argue in its favour; word coined in
University College Galway *c*.1940s to

refer to students of agriculture (Kevin
Flanagan, *Irish Times*, 28 Jan 1997)].
Derog. term for countryman/woman as
perceived by city-dweller, esp. Dub.
1991 Bob Quinn, *Smokey Hollow*: 'It was
the last leg of an amazing journey [to
Arklow, Co. Wicklow], the furthest
anybody had ever been from home...
They had never seen culchies in their
native habitat before.' **1993** Jim Martin
in Joe O'Reilly & Sixth Class, Convent
School, Edenderry, *Over the Half Door*. 'It
was shortly after this [1942] that the first
men came to the midlands under the
Turf Development Board. Many came to
Edenderry...They came from Kiltimagh
in Co. Mayo and the people referred to
them as "culchies".' **1995** Paul Gallagher,
Irish Times, 24 Aug: 'A true culchie "is a
shrewd individual capable of turning the
tables on those who underestimate his
abilities," according to Mr Rock, who
points out the [Culchie] festival is "pure
craic [q.v.]"...' See also **mulchie**.

cullagreefeen [n., <Ir. *codladh grifin*, pins
and needles]. As thus, numbness.

cultar [n., accent on second syllable,
<?] (Ulster). Argument, frightening
commotion.

cumber see **comber**

cumsloosh/comsleesh [adj., n. & vb.,
cf. Sc. *cumsleesh* (n.), severe scolding]
(Ulster). Flattering; flatterer, obsequious
person; curry favour.

cunniespeak [n., <'Connemara']. Rural
converse as perceived by town-dwellers.
1996 Bernie Ní Fhlatharta, *City Tribune*
(Galway), 2 Feb: 'this time the writer has
used some archaic language in an effort
to be "theatrical" when it is really
"cunniespeak" — it was the way the
townies do be thinking Connemara
people spake!'"

cúpla focal [n. phr., Ir. *idem*, a couple of
words; freq. & inaccurately seen in pl.
form *focail*: *cúpla* takes sing. n.].
Smattering of Ir. **1995** *Irish Times*, 20
May: 'Addressing the forum with an
opening cúpla focail, the British Labour
MP, Mr Roger Stott, said that the inter-
parliamentary body did not seek to write
anyone's agenda.' **1995** Mary Lyons,

RTÉ Radio, *Sunday Miscellany*, 'William Bedell', 6 Aug: 'valuable scholarships had been dished out to friends and relations with rather less than the statutory cúpla focal'. **1996** *Sunday Tribune*, advertisement for 'Seachtain na Gaeilge' (Ir. language week): 'The events are organised to encourage us all to use the cúpla focail we have, wherever possible.'

curate [n.]. 1. Assistant barman. **1914** James Joyce, *Dubliners*, 'Grace': 'These two gentlemen and one of the curates carried him up the stairs and laid him down again on the floor of the bar.' **1938** Samuel Beckett, *Murphy*: 'He did not speak to the curates, he did not drink the endless half-pints of porter [q.v.] that he had to buy.' **1968** Myles na gCopaleen, *The Best of Myles*: 'the curate behind the bar has opened his face into so enormous a yawn that the tears can be heard dripping into the pint he is pulling'. 2. 'Common little poker kept in use to spare the grand one' (PWJ).

curlicue see **carleycue**

curly water [n. phr.] (Ulster). Sugar and water mixture alleged to make hair curl (TT).

currney cake [n., <'currant']. Fruit cake. **1993** Mrs Geoghegan in Joe O'Reilly & Sixth Class, Convent School, Edenderry, *Over the Half Door*: 'I never remember a bad Christmas. We'd have a big currney cake and then there'd be rice and currants in it. That'd be a special treat.'

curse of Cromwell [n. phr., <the massacres/devastation for which he was responsible while in Ire., 1649–50]. Gen. as imprecation. **1866** Patrick Kennedy, *Legendary Fictions of the Irish Celts*: '"Oh, the curse of Cromwell on yourself an' the midwife!" says the poor man...' **1980** Robert Kee, *Ireland, A History*: 'with this final humiliation of the Irish Catholic landowners — their banishment to a remote corner of their own country in the beautiful sad lands of the west — what came to be known as "the curse of Cromwell" was complete'.

cut [n. & vb.]. 1. [n., <'cut a (fine, poor, etc.) figure', *c*.1760–]. Appearance, gen.

derog. **1948** George Fitzmaurice, *Dublin Magazine*, 'There are Tragedies and Tragedies', July/Sept: 'GEOFFREY ...didn't we think they had some intelligence left. But, look at the cut of them now!' **1980** Séamus de Faoite, *The More we are Together*, title story: '"I'm a soldier on short leave from Sam's Army in Berlin," the Yank said. "You have the cut of an officer," Miah told him.' **1991** John B. Keane, *Love Bites and Other Stories*: 'Haven't you all seen the cut of stray tomcats returning from forays into strange, moonlit territories? Scratched and bleeding they have paid the price for seductive meeeowing in the principalities of other cats.' 2. [vb.] (Maynooth College). Abandon the priestly calling. **N.d.** (unpublished) Neil Kevin, '*Ad Vota Saecularia*': 'In our college to *cut* meant to leave the college, to give up the idea of going for the Church.'

cute hare-beater [n. phr.]. Said of a bold (q.v.) child.

cute hoor see **hoor**

cutline [n., <'where the linotype operator "cut" or finished his last line of setting when stopping for a break' (WS)] (printing). Lunch or tea break etc.

cut the gutter [n.] (Ulster). Errand boy.

cutting/cutting up [pres. part. as n., <Ir. *gearradh*, cutting] (Ulster) as in **there's great cutting in him** [adj. phr.]. He is very positive, incisive. **1948** Patrick Kavanagh, *Tarry Flynn*: '"Lord," she exclaimed, "starting to puff at the curse-o'-God fag at such an hour of the morning. Have you any cutting-up in you at all?"' See also **how's she cuttin'?**

cutty see **cuddy**

cuttycub [n., <**cuddy** 2. + **cub**] (Ulster). Cissy, esp. young boy who plays with girls.

cyavie [n., <Sc. *cauve*, calf] (Ulster). Coward.

cygginets [n., with epenthetic vowel, common esp. in Dub. speech. Cf. *cathedral*, *severial*, *Westminister*, Moore St traders' street cry 'Fifty pence a pound the *musherooms*.']. Cygnets. See **scoops**.

D

da, the [n.]. Affect./respectful form of ref. by both adults and children. **1965** Lee Dunne, *Goodbye to the Hill*: 'even when the other oul' fella [q.v.] fell down, out to the world, the Da was still putting the boot in'. **1987** Vincent Caprani, *Vulgar Verse & Variations, Rowdy Rhymes & Rec-im-itations*, 'Gough's Statue': 'It happened quite accidentally when the four of us — the Da, Noel, Jack and myself — were having a pleasant pint in Conways...'

dab/dab hand [n. phr., <Sc. *dab haun*, expert, poss. <ME *dab* (vb.), strike sharply or abruptly; cf. Grose: 'a dab at any feat or exercise. Dab, quoth Dawkins, when he hit his wife on the a-se with a pound of butter.']. As thus. **1971** Seán O'Faoláin, *The Talking Trees and Other Stories*, title story: '"He's what they call a mender and turner...you can see he's very good at his job, he's a real dab..."' **1987** Vincent Caprani, *Vulgar Verse & Variations, Rowdy Rhymes & Rec-im-itations*, 'How Jem the Dancer Fought and Died for Ireland': 'Meself and the mot [q.v.] had won a coupla gold medals for our gyrations...She was a dab hand at the tango...'

dab out [n. phr.] (Dub.). Game of marbles. **1979** C.S. Andrews, *Dublin Made Me*: 'With "dab-out", the players each put an agreed number of marbles in a ring drawn with chalk...A "thaw" [taw] was thrown by each player and each marble knocked out of the ring belonged to the thrower.'

daddle [n., cf. 'doddle']. Gait (EW).

dado/daddo [n. & term of address]. 1. [n. & form of address, cf. Ir. *daideo*, grandfather (affect.)]. As thus, not necessarily affectionate. **1933** Muiris Ó Súilleabháin (translated by Moya Llewelyn Davies & George Thomson, *Twenty Years A-Growing*), *Fiche Bliain ag Fás*: 'My grandfather and I were lying on the Castle Summit. "Isn't it a fine healthy life those fishermen have, daddo?" said I.'

1950 Liam O'Flaherty, *Insurrection*: 'The butcher's wife thumped the old man in the back and said: "Shut your mouth, dado."' 2. [n., <?] as in **sighting the dado** [vb. phr.] (Listowel & Ballybunion elevated monorail, 1888–1924). **1952** Bryan MacMahon, *Children of the Rainbow*: 'Pat Gillick, one of the two train guards...stood at the rear of the train and ran his eye along the carriages ("sighting the dado", Old Carpenter Font called this operation) to see if they were in equipoise.' See also **the Lartigue**.

daff [n., <?]. Excrement. **1961** Tom Murphy, *A Whistle in the Dark*: 'MICHAEL Let him talk for himself. HARRY Go on, Des, tell him he's the colour of his daff.'

dag [n. & vb.]. 1. [n., <?, cf. Austral. *idem*, dashing individual, humorist; 'conventional youth, "square"' (Wilkes)] (Ulster). Unflattering term for a man (Todd). 2. [n., <ON *dagg*, dew] (Ulster). Fog, mist; sudden heavy downpour. 3. [vb.]. Slash. **1995** Edward McNerney in Mary Ryan et al. (eds.), *No Shoes in Summer*: 'a fellow that was dagging rushes in the bottoms would rise several hares'.

Dagenham Yank [nickname, <location of Ford plant in Dagenham, Essex, UK] (Cork). **1993** Michael Verdon, *Shawlies* (q.v.), *Echo Boys* (q.v.), *the Marsh and the Lanes* (q.v.): *Old Cork Remembered*: 'Leaving behind a skeleton workforce the American employer moves the greater part of its [Cork] operation to Dagenham in England as another war is looming on the Continent. Most of the foundry workers move with the company. These Corkmen become known as "Dagenham Yanks"...'

dailygone/dayligone [n., <Sc. *dayligaun* <OE *daeg* + *leocht* + *gan*, day + light + go, twilight] (Ulster). As thus. **1925** Louise McKay, *Mourne Folk*: '"So I chapped [chopped] away, an' before day-li-gone there wasn't a thorn left on the fort."' **1983** W.F. Marshall, *Livin' in Drumlister*, 'Ceilidh' (see **ceilidh**): 'It's dayligone, when the stars peep./And the cans clink in the byre...'

dainty [n., <*idem* (adj.)] (Ulster). Titbit.

daisy-picker [n.]. Chaperone, 'person who accompanies two lovers in their walk' (PWJ).

dale [n., <Sc. *deil*, devil] (Ulster) as in **dale a one** [emphatic neg. phr.]. No one.

dale-clock [n., <Ir. *daol*, beetle + Sc. *clock*, *idem*] (Ulster). Cockroach. See also **clock** 4.

dallapookeen [n., <Ir. *dalladh*, blinding + *púicín*, blind over eyes]. Game of blind man's buff. **1952** Bryan MacMahon, *Children of the Rainbow*: 'a braddy [see **brada**] — utterly mischievous cow. The cow had a dallaphookeen [*sic*] or blindfold fixed across her eyes.'

daltheen [n., <Ir. *dailtín*, brat, impudent fellow]. As thus.

dambut/damn-but [exclam., intens.] (Ulster). Expressing affirmation. **1939** Patrick Gallagher ('Paddy the Cope' (q.v.)), *My Story*: 'He handed it to James, saying, "Read that. Damn-but, I think whoever sent it to me sent me money too."' **1948** John O'Connor, *Come Day — Go Day*: '"How're ye, Malachey?" he greeted. "Wild class [q.v.] of a day that." "Hello, Johnny! Dambut is it yourself?"'

damn-it-skin [exclam., <?] (Ulster). Mild oath. **1951** Sam Hanna Bell, *December Bride*: 'Carspindle caught him by the arm. "Damn-it-skin," he said in a low voice, "ye can't have the lady sitting there!"'

Damn-the-Weather [nickname]. Dub. character (see **character** 1.), 1950s. **1995** Patrick Boland, *Tales from a City Farmyard*: 'There were plenty of characters around when I was growing up. Some were well-known like "Bang-Bang" [q.v.] and "Damn-the-Weather"...'

dance Jack Lattin/Latten see **Jack Lattin**

dander [n. & vb.]. 1. [n., colloq. US 1837, poss. fig. use of *dunder* (vb.), 1793, corruption of Sp. *redundar* (vb.), overflow, but <?]. Angry temper. **1939** Flann O'Brien, *At Swim-Two-Birds*: 'There wasn't a thing left for me to do but go off again and choke down my rising dander.' **1994** Sean Doyle, letter in *Irish Times*, 30 Sept: 'At the recent PD

conference in Cork, Mr Michael McDowell informed the assembled delegates that the party's "gander" was now up...Perhaps it was intended as a humorous rejoinder to those who believe that the party's goose is about to be cooked. Or perhaps Mr McDowell does not know his gander from his dander.' 2. [n. & vb., <Sc. *idem*, *daunder* (vb.), stroll]. As thus. **1922** James Joyce, *Ulysses*: 'they dandered along past by where the empty vehicle was waiting without a fare or a jarvey'. **1932** (first published 1992) Samuel Beckett, *Dream of Fair to Middling Women*: 'She must build herself up a little first, she must lead a simpler life, Benger's and a dander daily in the gardens.' **1995** Nuala Haughey, *Irish Times*, 27 July: 'I dandered home at around midnight to the Salmon Weir Hostel in Woodquay Street [Galway].'

dandy [n., <?]. Small drink of whiskey or punch; glass suitable for the purpose.

dandy cap [n. phr.]. Women's headdress. **1995** Éamon Kelly, *The Apprentice*: 'She had a white apron and on her head a lace affair with a starched linen front, what my mother used to call a dandy cap.'

dangler [n.]. Hanger-on. **1795** *Memoirs of Mrs Margaret Leeson, Written by Herself, Vol. II*: 'He was a mean looking ugly old fellow, and the dirtiest wretch I ever sat in company with. He was one of my danglers for a time, but had no chance of pleasing me.' Hence **dangle** [vb.]. 'To follow a woman without asking the question' (Grose).

Danny Boy [nickname]. Daniel Cohalan, Bishop of Cork & Ross 1916–52, who excommunicated (12 Dec 1920) those who were taking part in IRA attacks on the British during the War of Independence. **1961** Frank O'Connor, *An Only Child*: 'The bishop, Daniel Coholan [*sic*] — locally known as "Danny Boy" — was a bitter enemy of all this pretence...'

darby [n., <?] as in **small darby** [n. phr.]. Glass of whiskey. **1892** Robert Day, *Journal of Cork Historical and Archaeological Society*: 'Tom [Green] had one failing — whiskey. In these old times

a glass of whiskey, familiarly known as "a small darby", could be purchased for a penny...'

Dargle see **waxy**

dark [adj.]. Blind. **1967** Bryan MacMahon, *The Honey Spike* (q.v.): '"I'm dark," the old man quavered. "We'll give you six young eyes." "I'm as dark as midnight," the old man said...'

dark looker see **arklooker**

darling [adj.]. Exceptional, remarkable. **1925** Sean O'Casey, *The Plough and the Stars*: 'JOXER Give us that poem you writ t'other day...Aw, it's a darlin' poem, a daarlin' poem.' **1959** Joseph O'Connor, *The Iron Harp*: '"Surprise — what a darling understatement. Yes, we'll lift their eyebrows for them!"' See also **jewel**.

darrol [n., <Ir. *dearóil* (adj.), feeble, puny, insignificant]. 'Smallest of the brood of pigs, fowl, etc.' (PWJ).

DART/dart [adj., n. & vb., acronym, Dublin Area Rapid Transit]. Electrified suburban rail system, 1984. Hence **DART accent/dortspeak** [n. phr.], aka **Roadwatch accent**, <speech of some presenters of RTÉ Radio slot, characterised by *ou* phoneme ('The Red Cow Roundabout'). **1994** Kevin Myers, *Irish Times*, 21 July: 'The basis of Dortspeak is the middle-class Irish accent which has now been substantially overlaid by an Anglo-American argot, in which most vowel sounds seem to be based on an heroic but largely unsuccessful imitation of the English Home Counties...' Hence **Dortland** [nickname]. **1996** Joseph O'Connor, *The Irish Male at Home and Abroad*: 'He strutted about the hall like a peacock on steroids barking "yeah" and "I loik it"...in his Dortland accent...'

dashlin [n., <?] (Ulster). Second-best clothes (SH).

dauncey/doncy/donsey [adj., <Sc. *donsie*, weak, sickly; Ir. *donas* (n.), misfortune, affliction, misery] (Ulster). 1. As thus. **1925** Louise McKay, *Mourne Folk*: '"I helped to bring him into the world; his mother was very dauncey for a long time, so I took him to my own

house..."' See also **dawney**. 2. Dishonest (SH).

dauny see **dawney**

daw [n., abbrev. of *gobdaw* (q.v.); gen. in neg.]. Fool. **1986** Padraic O'Farrell, *'Tell me, Sean O'Farrell'*: 'I started off with the usual bedside small-talk...But J.J. was no *daw*. He had a bit of business to discuss — "in case anything happens".' **1991** Teddy Delaney, *Where we Sported and Played*: 'I...asked Ursula if she'd go for a spin on the bike to Guagán Barra next day. She said she'd see. I liked that. It meant that she was no daw.'

dawk [n., <Dan. *dalk*, thorn]. Prickle or spine of a thorn (OTF).

dawney/dawny/dauny/donny [adj., <Ir. *donaí*, wretched, miserable. 'This appears to be a Fingallian word. At the present day it is widely used in north Leinster and the extreme south of Ulster, but not elsewhere' (Bliss).]. As thus; pale, sickly-looking. **1663** Richard Head, *Hic et Ubique*: 'KILTORY Sirrah? PATRICK The donny fellow make buse [abuse] for my Moister.' **1938** Seumas MacManus, *The Rocky Road to Dublin*: '"The dark's only droppin', and as we have a long night afore us...it will be mighty *dauny* work on our part, if we can't collect a wife from some house or other..."' **1995** Phil O'Keeffe, *Down Cobbled Streets, A Liberties Childhood*: 'I was coddled and cosseted for months afterwards... Neighbours shook their heads and referred to me as the dawney one.'

daylight [n.] (Ulster). Bare necessities (Todd).

dayligone see **dailygone**

dayr [n., poss. <'dear' (q.v.)] as in **dayr a bit** [emphatic neg. phr.]. Not a bit (OTF).

daza see **me daza**

dead [adj.]. Completely, very, as in **dead flick** [adj. phr.]. Very desirable. See also **dead spit**.

deadbell [n.] (Ulster). Ringing in the ears.

dead end [n. phr.] (Ulster) as in **I tuk my dead enn at him** (Pepper). React with astonishment.

deader [n.]. Corpse. **1961** Dominic Behan, *Teems of Times and Happy Returns*: "'Seamus an' Brian were up to have a look at the deader an' got cake an' fizzy stuff. I got nothin' at all.'"

dead man [nickname & n. phr.]. 1. [nickname]. Individual collecting weekly funeral insurance. **1993** Con O'Donoghue in Michael Verdon, *Shawlies* (q.v.), *Echo Boys* (q.v.), *the Marsh and the Lanes* (q.v.): *Old Cork Remembered*: 'They'd call the fellow collecting the insurance the "dead man". "Did the dead man call to you yet?" Or, "I have to keep the money for the dead man."' 2. [n. phr., gen. pl., cf. *dead marine* (Austral.); *dead soldier* (US)]. Empty bottle of beer/stout/spirits.

dead spit [n. phr., <OE *spittan* (vb.), spit, colloq. 1825]. Exact resemblance. **1936** *Irish Times*, 7 Nov: 'a big department store has got from them (for a special window display) the "dead spit", as we say, of Long John Silver, a man with a wooden leg'. **1995** Phil O'Keeffe, *Down Cobbled Streets, A Liberties Childhood*: "'She's the livin' image of her father." "She's the dead spit of her mother." "Indeed she's not, she's the image of herself, aren't ye, pet?"'

dear [adj. for n., euphem. for 'Dear Lord', <confusion of Ir. *Fiadha*, God & *fiadh*, deer, carried into Hib.E]. As thus. **1830** William Carleton, *Traits and Stories of the Irish Peasantry*, 'The Lianhan Shee': "'Tisn't that I want to know anything at all about it — the dear forbid I should; but I never heard of a person bein' tormented wid it as you are."' **N.d.** Traditional ballad: 'I know where I'm going,/I know who's going with me,/I know who I love,/But the dear knows who I'll marry.' **1927** Peadar O'Donnell, *Islanders*: "'When are ye expectin' to get flour?" he demanded. "The dear knows," she said, running a knitting-needle through her hair.'

dear joy (q.v.) [n. phr.]. Form of address; Irishman (see also Appendix). **1689** Anon., *The Irishmen's Prayers*: 'O den we must leave all our Citys Dear-Joys/And yield them unto those *Ingalish* brave boyes.' **1702** George Farquhar, *The Twin*

Rivals: 'SUBTLEMAN And how do you intend to live? TEAGUE By eating, dear joy, fen I can get it; and by sleeping when I can get none: 'tish the fashion of Ireland.'

Dear Summer [nickname]. 1818, when cost of living rose following the Napoleonic wars. **1938** Seumas MacManus, *The Rocky Road to Dublin*: "'I went to Mickey's funeral myself, me father holdin' me by the hand...That was the second winter before Waterloo — and five before the Dear Summer.'"

deave/deeve [vb., <Sc. *deave*, deafen, <OE *adeafian*, become deaf]. Deafen; bewilder, bore. **1908** Lynn Doyle, *Ballygullion*: 'kept talkin' away wi' big long words that nobody knowed the manin' av but himself, till we were near deaved'. **1966** Patrick Boyle, *At Night All Cats are Grey*, 'The Betrayers': 'For the next three days Willie had me deeved with enquiries about Cassie...'

debble [vb., <Sc. *daible*, wash clothes (by hand)] (Ulster). As thus.

decent skin see **skin**

decline, the [n., euphem.]. Tuberculosis. **1909** Canon Sheehan, *The Blindness of Dr Gray*: "'the finest family in the parish... an' look at 'em now. Wan dying of decline, another up in Cork madhouse...'"

dee [for *d*, indicating a pre-decimal penny or pence]. **1965** Lee Dunne, *Goodbye to the Hill*: "'Two bob," he [the taxi driver] said, trying it on. "Ah," I said in my best poor mouth [q.v.], "I only have nine dee.'"

deeve see **deave**

deffo [adv., <abbrev. + endearment suffix]. Definitely. **1994** Greg Dalton, *My Own Backyard, Dublin in the Fifties*: 'the perfume in their room'd knock you over, not natural deffo'.

delira' and excira' [catchphrase, representing Dub. pronun.]. Overjoyed. **1995** Deaglán de Bréadún, *Irish Times*, 27 Nov: 'Mags O'Brien, of the Divorce Action Group...was delira and excira, as Gay Byrne [see **Gaybo**] would say.'

delph [n.]. False teeth. **1995** Patrick Boland, *Tales from a City Farmyard*: 'a few years later Tommy married a very nice woman, also sporting a set of "delph"'.

de paper [nickname]. The *Cork Examiner* newspaper, the spelling thus of the def. art. being cited, largely by non-Corkonians, as evidence of an inability to pronounce the dental fricative. (From 29 Mar 1996 'De Paper' was retitled the *Examiner*). **1994** Gerry Moriarty, *Irish Times*: 'Buying a *Cork Examiner* on the way to his digs in the Metropole Hotel... his eyes lit up when he spotted the banner headline on *de paper's* lead story.' **1995** Thomas McCarthy, *Sunday Tribune*, 6 Aug: 'He [Seán Dunne] was soon offered a staff job with the Cork Examiner...Seán thrived at *de Paper*.'

deshort/dishort [n., <Sc. *dishort*, disappointment, disadvantage] (Ulster). Sudden interruption, surprise.

Desocrats [nickname, pun]. Progressive Democrats party, founded 21 Dec 1985 by Desmond O'Malley. **1987** *Phoenix*, 25 Sept: 'Appearances are everything to a yuppie party like the Desocrats. Party leader Des O'Malley has decided to give himself a new facelift...'

desperate [adj.]. Very bad. **1983** *John Pepper's Illustrated Encyclopaedia of Ulster Knowledge*: '"Desperate weather" can embrace gales in June and snow in July, and "a desperate job" connotes a lawn constantly in need of cutting...' **1994** John O'Dwyer in Kevin C. Kearns, *Dublin Tenement Life*: 'And drovers used to come in [to the pub] and they'd put a glass of whiskey into a pint of porter [q.v.]. Desperate people they were.' **1995** Ann Burns in Mary Ryan et al. (eds.), *No Shoes in Summer*: 'Then of course came the food rationing. It was desperate. Ration books for everything.'

Desperate, Mrs see **Maud Gone Mad**

destroyed [p. part. as adj., cf. Ir. *sáraigh* (vb.), violate; harass, worry]. Harassed, exhausted.

deuce/juice [n., 'mostly among vagrants and Dublin newsboys' (DHS); 'Dews Wins' or 'Deux Wins' (Grose), twopence in pre-decimal coinage]. As thus. **1926** Sean O'Casey, *The Plough and the Stars*: 'FLUTHER What's the bettin'? PETER Heads, a juice. FLUTHER Harps, a tanner.' See also **heads or harps**. **1965** Lee Dunne, *Goodbye to the Hill*: 'I used it [the boxcart] to carry sacks of turf for old women...This was usually worth a deuce or even threepence...'

Dev [nickname]. Eamon de Valera (1882–1975), revolutionary and statesman. **1993** Tim Pat Coogan, *Dev: Long Fellow* (q.v.), *Long Shadow*: 'It was in Rockwell [College] that he was first christened "Dev" — by one of the other teachers on the staff, Tom O'Donnell.' **1995** Éamon Kelly, *The Apprentice*: 'There were... tributes to the tall gaunt man with the foreign name who stood against the might of Empire. Amid the wild cheers and cries of "Up Dev!" a poor travelling woman, the worse for drink, threw her black shawl on the bonfire.'

devalve [vb.] (Ulster). Desist from talking (YDS).

devil/divil a/the bit [adv. phr., cf. Ir. *deamhana bhfuil air*, there's nothing the matter with him, & similar constructions]. Not at all; in no way. **1952** Michael McLaverty, *Truth in the Night*: '"Your poor daughter will be at a loss this moment," he interrupted..."Devil the bit of her!"'

devil/divil an' all [n. phr.]. Expressing excellence, connoting an optimum quantity. **1977** Flann O'Brien, *The Hair of the Dogma*: 'The squad cars...have gigantic aerials, wireless valves, the divilanall machinery inside the bonnet to apprehend criminals.' **1979** Frank Kelly, *The Annals of Ballykilferret*: '"Young fellas [q.v.] has the divil an' all of a time nowadays," he thought as he straightened up from his back-breaking labours...'

devileen/divileen [n., 'devil' + Ir. dimin. *ín*]. Little rogue.

devil mend you! [exclam.]. Mild oath. **1797** *Memoirs of Mrs Margaret Leeson, Written by Herself, Vol. III*: '"Upon my vord I tell de truth [said the French Captain]: me phas only F——g [I was only fucking], and Mr T——d can vouzch for me if he pleases." This set the table in a roar...and obliged the ladies with a smothered laugh to withdraw; Ned T—d vociferously roaring out, — "The devil mend you girls, the devil mend you."' Also **devil/divil moan you** in same sense. **1908** Lynn Doyle, *Ballygullion*: "'...I'd be a nice hound to ask her to marry me on two hundhred and fifty a year." "Divil moan her," sez I, "if she nivver gets a man wi' more."'

devilment/divilment [abst. n.]. Mischief. **1965** Lee Dunne, *Goodbye to the Hill*: "'There's plenty here," she said, and her eyes sparkled with devilment.' **1991** James Kennedy, *The People who Drank Water from the River*: 'I still can't remember whether it was my own bravado...or whether it was the devilment in Paddy who wanted to see if such a co-operative youngster got loaded.' **1995** Roisín Ingle, *Sunday Tribune*, 10 Sept: 'Advertisers admit, however, that there is a certain amount of disingenuousness — or, as one put it, "divilment" involved [in observing ethical standards].'

devil's cure [exclam.]. Mild oath. **1925** Louise McKay, *Mourne Folk*: "'Fairy or divil, come down out of that [tree] with ye." The stone struck Denis and he gave a great yell. "Divil's cure t'ye," sis I...' **1953** Frank O'Connor, *The Stories of Frank O'Connor*, 'Peasants': 'When Michael John Cronin stole the funds of the Carricknabreena Hurling, Football and Temperance Association...everyone said: "Devil's cure to him! 'Tis the price of him [q.v.]!"'

devil's half-acre [nickname, cf. *idem*, 'the rough area of a town' (Green)]. Dublin Castle, seat of Brit. power. **1996** Justin Comiskey, *Irish Times*, 2 July: 'Dublin Castle — or the Devil's Half Acre as Michael Collins once called it — has undergone some £10 million worth of structural development since 1994.'

devil's needle [n., <Ir. *snáthaid an diabhail*, *idem*]. Crane-fly, daddy-long-legs.

devil thank ye [exclam.]. Mild oath. **1948** Patrick Kavanagh, *Tarry Flynn*: "'The divil thank ye and thump ye,

Bridie, ye whipster [see **whipster** 1.] ye."'

dhera see **yerra**

Diceman, the [nickname, <his employment advertising Grafton St (Dub.) shop of same name as 'sandwich man']. Thom McGinty, Dub. street entertainer (1954–95). **1995** Frank McNally, *Irish Times*, 23 Feb: 'The man known to a generation of Irish people as the Diceman, Mr Thom McGinty, died in his sleep yesterday morning after a relatively short battle with AIDS.' **1995** Renagh Holohan, *Irish Times*, 3 June: 'He [Richard Wentges] wants one of the new squares being built in Dublin's Temple Bar to be called "McGinty Square"...But given that McGinty was more popularly known as The Diceman, wouldn't "Diceman Square" have a better ring to it?'

diddle [vb., onomat.]. Make traditional 'mouth music'. **1995** Phil O'Keeffe, *Down Cobbled Streets, A Liberties Childhood*: 'My father stood his glass of porter [q.v.] on the floor beside him and diddled a few bars until she was satisfied he had the speed and the rhythm, and then she began.'

diddly/didley [adj. & n.]. Small 'but with overtones of affection' (Todd); small, insignificant; small payment. **1994** Mary Doolan in Kevin C. Kearns, *Dublin Tenement Life*: 'Back then everyone run the didley clubs for saving money...My mother was always in the didley...A didley starts with a ha'penny a week and it went to a penny, from a penny to three, and, you know, up to about five shillings.' **1995** Phil O'Keeffe, *Down Cobbled Streets, A Liberties Childhood*: "'The Aunt Bridie was up Saturday. She just got her summer diddly and she was handin' out money like snuff at a wake [q.v.]."'

diddy [n., <Ir. *dide*, nipple; more usu. pl.]. Woman's breast; nipple (both sexes). **1970** Christy Brown, *Down All the Days*: "'She goes and pawns thirty-five bleeding pound for thirty-five lousy clap-happy shillings, the fat-arsed, big-diddied oul madwoman..."' **1991** Roddy Doyle,

The Van: 'if Sophia Loren came up to yeh an' stuck her diddies in your face'. **1993** Sam McAughtry, *Touch & Go*: '"In Dublin's fair city, I searched for her diddy,/But I'm frigged if I found one on Molly Malone./With her chest flat and narrow, she wheels her wheelbarrow..."'

didgeen see **dudeen**

dido [n., <?]. 1. 'Dressed-up girl' (PO'F). 2. Trick, antics [pl.]. 3. [pl.] Luxuries, extravagances. **1952** Michael McLaverty, *Truth in the Night*: '"She's getting notions now about her food, if you please," Vera said impatiently. "Didoes and fiddle-faddles she wants..."' See also **dado**.

diet [n., <ME *idem* in same sense, cf. OF *diete* <Lat. *diaeta*]. Food in daily use, hence board/keep. **1975** Séamus de Burca, *Dublin Historical Record*, 'Peadar Kearney (1883–1942)': 'Paddy Heeney... was employed as a bagman in Hickey's drapery establishment in North Earl Street at a salary of eight shillings a week and his diet.'

differ [n., abbrev.]. Difference. **1995** Phil O'Keeffe, *Down Cobbled Streets, A Liberties Childhood*: '"D'ye think they'd know the differ if we went to one of the shops and brought back shop milk?"'

digging [pres. part., poss. <straight left in boxing, 1815–]. Fighting. **1982** Éamonn Mac Thomáis, *Janey Mack* (q.v.), *Me Shirt is Black*: 'we never knew who caused the Civil War but we did know that if the digging broke up the meeting, we got no ginger beer'.

digs, the [nickname] (Dub.). Red-light district. **1979** C.S. Andrews, *Dublin Made Me*: 'Immediately below the house was Joyce's famous "Nighttown", known locally as "Monto" [q.v.] or "the digs".'

dig with the right/left/other/wrong foot [vb. phr.] (Ulster). Sectarian characterisation of an individual of another religious persuasion (gen. Catholic/Protestant). **1957** E. Estyn Evans, *Irish Folk Ways*: 'in Ireland the majority of diggers use the right foot...In Eastern Ireland, on the other hand, and particularly in Protestant districts of the

north-east, the left foot is usually the digging foot...' **1969** Robert Greacen, *Even without Irene*: 'He used to talk about a "Father Poland"...he had been friendly with in those days, although father was normally somewhat suspicious of those who "dug with the wrong foot".' **1983** Robert Johnstone, *Images of Belfast*: 'My family would present a headache for any student of social class and religion...I don't think any of us turned [see **turn** 2.] to "dig with the other foot" but I probably wouldn't have heard about it if they had.' Also **dig with the same foot**, be of the same persuasion; **dig with both feet**, said of a clever/unscrupulous person.

dildo [n., cf. *idem* (vb.), 'to exchange sexual caresses with a woman' (DHS)]. Woman of easy virtue. **1995** Circuit Court, Dub., *Butler* v. *Four Star Pizza*, Mar: 'A pizza courier had been sexually harassing a more senior employee over a seven-month period — grabbed her chest, slapped her bottom...called her a slut, a slag and a dildo.'

dilsy [n., <?] (Ulster). Foolish individual, usu. female; affected, overdressed woman; social climber.

dindle see **dinnel**

ding-dust [adv. & n., <ON *dengja* (vb.), beat, thrash] (Ulster). 1. [adv.]. Fast, speedily: 'he drove ding-dust down the lane' (CUD). 2. [n.]. Din, racket (YDS).

dinge [n. & vb., cf. Icel. *dengji* (vb.), hammer] (Ulster). Dent.

dinger [n., poss. abbrev. of US 'humdinger', 'a person or thing that is remarkable' (DAS)]. 1. As thus. **1978** *Cork Holly Bough*: 'The messenger bicycle was brand-new, a real dinger...' **1982** Éamonn Mac Thomáis, *Janey Mack* (q.v.), *Me Shirt is Black*: 'Some priests were real dingers at giving out the ashes. Dead [q.v.] straight, right in the centre...' 2. (Ulster). Indicative of speed, rapidity (Pepper).

Dingley-Cooch/Cootch [n., <*Daingean Uí Chúis* (Dingle), Co. Kerry, 'from the remoteness and inaccessibility of that place' (EDD)]. Unimaginable location;

cf. 'beyond the Black Stump' (Austral.). As in **send s.o. to Dingley-Cooch** [vb. phr.]. Send s.o. to Coventry.

dinnel/dindle [n. & vb., onomat.] (Ulster). 1. [n. & vb.]. Throbbing or tingling pain (Pepper); throb with pain. 2. [vb.]. Vibrate, shake (SH). Hence **dinneling** [pres. part. as n.] in same sense.

dint/dunt [vb. & n., <OE *dynt*, cogn. with ON *dyntr/dyttr* (n.), blow, shock]. 'To strike or butt like a cow or goat with the head' (PWJ); such a blow. **1879** Charles J. Kickham, *Knocknagow*: '"well, the big, black bottle was split in two with the fair dint of the frost"'. *C*.**1910** Anon., *Irish Wit and Humour*: 'An Irishman, in describing America, said: "You might roll England through it, an' it wouldn't make a dint in the ground"...' **1981** Paddy Crosbie, *Your Dinner's Poured Out!*: 'At last we reach the gallery,/We rush down to the front,/Last year our Mossy slipped an' fell,/An' he got an awful dunt.'

dip [n. & vb.] (Ulster). 1. [n.]. Fried bread. **1983** *John Pepper's Illustrated Encyclopaedia of Ulster Knowledge*: 'A Belfastwoman told a neighbour, "When we were in Malta last year I asked the waitress could we have dip and she gave me a look."' 2. [n.]. 'Hot gravy or an egg to dip in' (Todd). 3. [vb.]. Work, be occupied: 'he never dipped all day' (YDS). Also **dippity** [n.]. Milk in a saucer with a pinch of salt. **1939** Patrick Gallagher ('Paddy the Cope' (q.v.)), *My Story*: 'The main seasoning with potatoes was "dippity"...We dipped the potato for each bite. If there was no milk we used water.'

dirt bird [n., skua (*Stercorarius spp*.), from its habit of forcing other birds to regurgitate their stomach contents; cf. US *dirt bag*, *dirt ball*, contemptible individual]. As thus; loose woman/man; gen. derog. **1997** Brian Kerr, quoted *Irish Times*, 8 July: '"You [Bertie Ahern] were a dirt-bird, always looking to give someone a kick [in amateur soccer]...I only jest."'.

dirty elders [exclam., poss. <*elder*, cow's udder]. Term of abuse. **1989** Hugh Leonard, *Out after Dark*: '"We don't want them and their sort here...dirty elders."'

(A derisive Dublin term I have never been able to track to its source.)' See **elders**.

Dirty Shirts, the [nickname]. 1st Battalion, then 101st Foot, of the Royal Munster Fusiliers of the Brit. army, which fought without tunics at Delhi during the Indian Mutiny, 1857.

Dirty, Slow and Easy [nickname, <initials]. Dublin & South Eastern Railway, 1907–25. Also, less commonly, **Damn Slow and Easy**. **1996** Anthony Cronin, *Samuel Beckett, The Last Modernist*: 'The line by which they travelled was the DSER...known, though not in earshot of the children, as the "Damn Slow and Easy" Railway because of its frequent stops and delays.'

disciple [n.]. 'Miserable-looking creature of a man' (PWJ).

dishabells/dizybels [n., <Fr. *déshabiller* (vb.), undress]. 1. Working clothes, cf. 'undress uniform'. 2. (Ulster). Underclothes (Pepper).

dishort see **deshort**

Disneyland [nickname]. Ballymena, Co. Antrim. **1983** *John Pepper's Illustrated Encyclopaedia of Ulster Knowledge*: 'Sometimes called "Disneyland" because of the constant references to it heard there, as in "The child disney like her breakfast."'

disremember [vb.]. Forget, fail to recollect; pretend to forget. **1879** Charles J. Kickham, *Knocknagow*: '"I disremember if them lines isn't in 'Lalla Rookh'."' **1952** Peter Smythe (aka Patrick Kavanagh), *Kavanagh's Weekly*, 'Graftonia', 26 Apr: 'a play by Daniel Corkery was on — a fabulous piece about a sculptor or something, we disremember'. **1977** Tom Mac Intyre, *The Charollais*: '"You recall the incident, no doubt?" "I disremember," W — weakish on history — admitted.'

distasted [adj.] (Ulster). Tainted or spoiled (food).

ditch, hurler on the see **hurler on the ditch**

divarshin/divarsion [n., <Hib.E pronun. of 'diversion']. 'Any contrivance

or activity that makes for idle amusement' (YDS). **1836** Francis Sylvester Mahony ('Father Prout'), *The Reliques of Father Prout*, 'The Attractions of a Fashionable Irish Watering-Place': 'The town of Passage/Is both large and spacious.../The hake and salmon,/Playing bagammon [*sic*],/Swim for divarsion/All around this "hulk".' **1982** Thomas Gallagher, *Paddy's Lament*: 'One grandmother, asked when she first took to the pipe, replied, "I tuk to it as a bit of divarshion after me poor old maan was tucked under the daisies."'

divil for words and phrases beginning thus see under **devil**

dizybels see **dishabells**

do a line see **line** 2.

dob [vb., <?] (Ulster). Play truant, gen. of boys.

docken/dockin [n., <OE *docce*] (Ulster). Common dock (*Rumex obtusifolius*). **1983** W.F. Marshall, *Livin' in Drumlister*, 'The Big Trout': 'We cocked big worms/Before his nose/And the grub that you get/Where a dockin' grows.'

dod [n.]. 1. [<Ir. *idem*, sullenness, anger] (Ulster). Sulks, huff. 2. [<Sc. *daud*, large piece]. Lump. **1995** Shane Connaughton, *A Border Diary*: 'Cissie heaps burning turf on to the lid of an iron pot in which is a round of baking bread. "Ah now, it's only a wee [q.v.] dod."'

doedel [n., poss. = *dote* (q.v.)]. Darling. **1960** John O'Donoghue, *In Kerry Long Ago*: '"Isn't he the *doedel*, God bless him," says she, after pushing the little shawl aside to see his face.'

dog and divil see **every dog and divil**

dog's abuse [n. phr.]. Severe verbal abuse, insults. **1925** Liam O'Flaherty, *The Informer*: '"Yer ol' man gev me dog's abuse and drov' me outa the house..."' **1995** Interviewee (anon.) in *Sunday Tribune*, 19 Mar: '"We got dogs abuse. I was also approached by members of his family. His mother came to me and started giving out [q.v.]..."' **1996** Kathy Sheridan, *Irish Times*, 23 Sept: 'After years of dogs' abuse directed at "the

feminists" for saddling women in the homes with a terrible inferiority complex, suddenly the shoe is on the other foot. Hail, Norma [Major], the standard bearer.'

dogs in/on the street, the [n. phr.]. Everyone, the whole world. **1997** *Irish Times*, 15 Apr: 'Do the dogs on the street know that the question on an Anglo-Irish poet is usually the toughest poetry question on the paper?' See **street**.

dog's mushroom [n. phr.] (Ulster). Toadstool.

dog's tail [n. phr.] as in **send a letter on the dog's tail** [vb. phr.] (Ulster). Not send a letter at all (CUD).

dog's tongue [nickname] (Ulster). 'One side of a soda farl [q.v.]' (YDS).

doh-doh [n.]. Baby's dummy or soother (q.v.). **1985** Máirín Johnston, *Around the Banks of Pimlico*: 'The mouth organ was the most popular instrument in Pimlico when I was young...Nearly every child at one time or another was given a mouth organ to suck and blow as a substitute for the doh-doh.'

Doheny & Nesbitt School of Economists [nickname, <pub in Lower Baggot St, Dub.]. Ad hoc right-wing talking shop. **1988** John Waters, *Magill*, Sept: 'a few extremely tedious economic types who had suddenly appeared out of nowhere. These people seemed preoccupied with what they insisted was excessive government spending and borrowing for non-productive purposes ...These fellows came to get mentioned in the course of serious conversations as "the Doheny and Nesbitt School of Economists".' **1996** John Bowman, RTÉ Radio, *Bowman's Saturday 8.30*, 14 Dec: 'there was even what was called a Doheny & Nesbitt school of economics'.

doit [vb., <Sc. *doit*, foolish person] (Ulster). Stupefy. Hence **doitery** [adj.]. Feeble (SH).

doiter/doughter/dooter [vb., <Sc. *doiter*, potter about aimlessly; see **doit**] (Ulster). As thus; walk unsteadily; be senile (dote); annoy with noise etc. **1925**

Louise McKay, *Mourne Folk*: '"...I'm beginning to feel very lonely in that wee [q.v.] house of mine since my ould mother died. I'm 'doughterin' in and 'doughterin' out..."'

Dolan's ass [n. phr., <?]. Time-server, sycophant. **1961** Frank O'Connor, *An Only Child*: 'My fight for Irish freedom was of the same order as my fight for other sorts of freedom. Still like Dolan's ass, I went a bit of the way with everybody.' See **Billy Harran's dog**, **Lanna Macree's dog**, **Lanty McHale's dog**, **O'Brien's dog**.

doll [vb., cf. Ir. *dall*, dazzle, stupefy]. Confound. **1914** George Fitzmaurice, *The Pie-Dish*: 'JACK ...It's roused entirely the old grey shandanagh [q.v.] is in himself, and it's dolled entirely I am on account of him...'

dollies [n. pl.]. Female breasts. **1970** Christy Brown, *Down All the Days*: '"often he said a roll on my dollies was as good as the other thing [see **the other**], and he would play with them like they was toys or something'.

dollop [vb.]. Adulterate.

dolly [vb., <'doddle'/'dawdle']. As thus.

doncy see **dauncey**

donkeys [n., abbrev. of 'donkey's years'] (Ulster). Long period of time. **1983** *John Pepper's Illustrated Encyclopaedia of Ulster Knowledge*: 'A motorist, upset at the non-delivery of a new car, will complain to the dealer, "I'm fed up. I've been asking you for donkeys."'

donkey's bray [n. phr.] as in **within a donkey's bray** [prep. phr.]. In close proximity to. **1994** Joseph O'Connor, *The Secret Life of the Irish Male*: '"...I am prepared to say you have some dreadfully infectious venereal disease that will surely rot the very fundament off anyone misfortunate [q.v.] enough to come within a donkey's bray of you"'. See also **ass's roar**.

donkey's gudge [n. phr., <?] (Cork). 'Cake baked from remnants of previous day's unsold cakes with a layer of pastry on top and at bottom' (Beecher). Hence

donkey's wedding cake [n. phr.]. As thus, with cream topping.

donkey's lugs [n. phr.] (Ulster). A type of loaf. See **sore head**.

Don 'n' Nelly [nickname] (advertising). **1992** Pauline Bracken, *Light of Other Days, A Dublin Childhood*: 'The Donnelly's sausage sign was probably Dublin's first neon sign, and it was also the cause for excitement. The name Donnelly had been split into two names, Don and Nelly and these exciting and original characters tossed a skinless sausage back and forth between two frying pans.'

donny see **dawney**

donnybrook [n., <faction fights at Donnybrook fair, Dub., 1204–1855; latterly exclusively US usage]. Fight.

donovan [n., <common surname, 1830–]. Potato.

donsey see **dauncey**

don't be talking! [exclam.]. Expressive of strong agreement. See **knacker** 1.

doodoge [n., <Ir. *dúdóg*, tobacco pipe, pinch of snuff]. Large pinch of snuff.

doofer [n., <'do for...']. Nameless object, cf. yoke (q.v.), Fr. *machin*, etc. **1979** John Morrow, *The Confessions of Proinsias O'Toole*: 'I...found myself looking down the wrong end of my Japanese fountain pen. He held it, cocked, level with his right little-red-eye — "Mustn't forget your wee [q.v.] doofer, Francie," he said, the bastard.'

Doog, the [nickname, abbrev.]. Derek Dougan (1938–), Northern Ireland soccer player. **1996** Peter Byrne, *Irish Times*, 7 Dec: 'Coincidentally or otherwise, the man known to millions as The Doog has just published his life story...'

doorach/duragh [n., <Ir. *dúthracht*, goodwill offering, favour]. Small extra amount. **1913** Alexander Irvine, *My Lady of the Chimney Corner*: 'I stood beside her on a creepie [q.v.], watching the process and awaiting the end, for at the close of each batch of bread I always had my "duragh"...'

doorshay–daurshay [n., <Ir. *dúirt sé*, he said + nonsense doubling]. Hearsay, gossip.

dooter see **doiter**

dootsie [adj.] (Ulster). Childish; old-fashioned.

dose [n.]. 1. (Ulster). Crowds of people. 2. Bad attack (of flu etc.). 3. Sight, spectacle. **1995** Shane Connaughton, *A Border Diary*: 'Later, in the pub, people look at me and laugh. "Holy God [q.v.], you look a dose."'

dosed [p. part. as adj., gen. in neg. context]. Impressed.

doss [vb.]. Play truant. See also **mitch** and **lang, on the**.

dote [n., <ME *dotien* (vb.), to be excessively fond of]. Lovable, appealing (child), gen. employed by females. **1995** Aidan Higgins, *Donkey's Years*: '...I tottered across the nursery to be received into the open arms and scent of Mumu who assured me warmly that I was a little dote'. Hence **dotey/doty** [adj. & n.]. **1960** Edna O'Brien, *The Country Girls*: '"Ask me nicely, Hickey, and call me dotey." "Dotey. Ducky. Darling. Honeybunch, do you want a white or brown egg for your breakfast?"' **1994** Maeve Binchy, *Irish Times*, 10 Dec: 'but try telling that to the hundreds of dotey little Chinese children on their school outings'. **1995** Anne Marie Hourihane, *Sunday Tribune*, 17 Dec: 'she said helpful things like "Now they're nicer" and "But what would they be like with trousers?" I ended up with a dotey pair of sling-backs in metallic leather...'

do the trick see **trick**

doty see **dotey**

double barrel [n. phr.]. Repeated orgasm (male). **1997** Alan Roberts, *The Rasherhouse* (see **rasher**): '"But inanyway [q.v.], he used to pay me three hundred pound, so he did. For nuttin' special like [q.v.], just a double barrel."'

double-decker shawl [n. phr.] (Cork). Superior garment, esp. as commanding higher value when pawned.

doublings see **singlings**

douce [adj., <Fr. *douce*, fem. of *doux*, sweet, pleasant] (Ulster). Gentle, sedate, sober; tidy, neat; prosperous.

doughter see **doiter**

dowey/dowie [adj., <Sc. *dowie*, sad, dismal, <OE *dol*, foolish] (Ulster). Dismal, sorrowful.

downblow [n.]. Disaster. **1948** George Fitzmaurice, *Dublin Magazine*, 'There are Tragedies and Tragedies', July/Sept: 'GEOFFREY Nothing left to them now but the four old cows and the bare little farm. A downblow wouldn't so much matter if they were big people.'

downie [adj. & n., cf. Ir. *donaí* (adj.), wretched, miserable]. As thus, small, weak person. See also **dawney**.

down-sit/sitting [n.] (Ulster). Establishment, property; financial provision, esp. marriage settlement. **1925** Louise McKay, *Mourne Folk*: 'So her mother would relate the splendour of Mickey, and the grand [q.v.] "downsitting" she would have — a farm of her own.'

down the banks as in **I gave him down the banks** [adv. phr., poss. <*Banks* (q.v.)]. Reprimand. **1968** John Healy, *The Death of an Irish Town*: 'I was standing there idly listening to the Chairman giving it down the banks to Fianna Fáil...' **1996** Bill O'Herlihy, RTÉ TV coverage of Ire.–Russia soccer match, 27 Mar: 'We haven't any interviews at the moment because Mick McCarthy [see **Captain Fantastic**] is giving them down the banks in the dressing room.'

dowse [vb.]. Overcome, do for. **1943** George A. Little, *Malachi Horan Remembers*: '"he told me the cure was frog-spawn. 'Well,' says I, 'I may as well try it, for this pain will dowse me anyway.'"'

dozed [p. part. as adj.] (Ulster). Decayed, rotten; stupid with age/drink.

dozer [n., gen. in neg., as in **he's no dozer**]. Of s.o. alert to the main chance. **1979** John Morrow, *The Confessions of Proinsias O'Toole*: '"as you request, I'll zoom to the point — Francie O'Fallis, you are no dozer...I — and others — have decided that you are ready for better things."' **1995** Sam Smyth, *Irish Independent*, 21 Dec: 'No dozer when it comes to spotting a good yarn, Deputy O'Keeffe says the media should realise what may seem to be a good story can hurt those who depend on pigs for a living.'

drab [n., <Fr. *drap*, cloth]. Rough cloth. **1927** Peadar O'Donnell, *Islanders*: '"the hem of yer skirt'll be up to yer houghs [see **hough** 1.] an' yer legs red with the ayres [q.v.] from the drab"'.

drachy [adj., <Sc. *dreich*, dull, monotonous] (Ulster). As thus. Also **dreech** [n. & adj.] in same sense (SH).

drack [vb., unpalat. cf. Icel. *drukna* (vb.), be drowned; OE *drencan*, *idem*] (Ulster). Drench, soak. **1911** Adam Lynn, *Random Rhymes from Cullybackey*, 'A Country Lad's Observations at the Hiring Fair in Ballymena': 'Weel, freens, A gat me tae the toon,/Although big clouds were hoverin' roon,/An while an odd yin [one] did come doon/Tae we got drack'd...'

drass [n., <Ir. *dreas*, turn, spell]. As thus.

drauchy see **drawky**

draw [n., cf. *idem* (vb.), 'lift or raise (the fist) for the purposes of attack' (CUD)]. Blow. **1899** E.Œ. Somerville & Martin Ross, *Some Experiences of an Irish RM*, 'Lisheen Races, Secondhand': '"Hah!" says I, givin' her a couple o' dhraws o'th'ashplant acriss the butt of the tail...'

drawky/drauchy/drooky/drookit [p. part. as adj., <Sc. *droukit*, soaked, cf. ON *drakkja* (vb.), submerge] (Ulster). Wet, drizzling, dull, murky (of weather). **1938** Seumas MacManus, *The Rocky Road to Dublin*: 'the blood that had evaporated entirely from his body in the drear, drooky, frosty potato-field, now flew back from the great sky to which it had gone'. **1979** Jack McBride, *Traveller in the Glens* (of Antrim): 'In the Glens a miserable, wet day is a "drauchy" day, or in frosty weather it "has a gye [see **gay** 2.] shart air in it".' **1995** Shane Connaughton, *A Border Diary*: '"The spring this year was late and we had a drawky summer. With rain and ojus [q.v.] hasky [q.v.] winds."'

draw the twine [vb. phr., <?]. Engage in profitable activity. **1993** Joe Hannon in Joe O'Reilly & Sixth Class, Convent School, Edenderry, *Over the Half Door*: 'Any kid going to school could make a man's wages "footing" [see **foot**] turf. So when you're young and fit — to hell with the training, "draw the twine".'

dread [n.]. Object of pity/disgust/distaste, as in **that's a dread**. **1996** Dermot Healy, *The Bend for Home*: '"What happened you?" asked Lila Little. "I was in a fight." "You look a dread," she said.'

dreech see **drachy**

dree your weird! [exclam., <Sc. *idem* <OE *dreogan* (vb.), suffer; *wyrd* (n.), fate] (Ulster). Be patient; hold your horses!

drench [n., palat. form of OE *drenc*, drink]. Love potion (PWJ).

dribble [n., <ME *drib*, small quantity] (Ulster). As thus. Also **dribs and drabs** [adv. phr.] (gen. usage) in same sense; gradually, by degrees. **1951** Sam Hanna Bell, *December Bride*: 'The brothers had been lifting their potato crops in "dribs and drabs", as they say in the townlands...'

drink [n., <ON *drengt*, a young married man, cf. Icel. *drengur*, boy, lad] (Ulster). Person too tall for his age.

drink-a-penny see **willie-hawkie**

drink Lough Erne dry [vb. phr.]. Said of s.o. endowed with an inordinate thirst. **1995** Aidan Higgins, *Donkey's Years*: 'My aunty is the famous horsewoman who rode champions...mucked out stables at cockcrow, could drink Lough Erne dry.' **1995** Éamon Kelly, *The Apprentice*: '"you'll never see a good shoe on a mason. And another thing: there never was a man of them yet but wouldn't drink Lough Erne dry!"'

drink of water [n. phr.] (Ulster). Milksop, pain in the neck.

drink taken as in **he had drink taken** [adj. phr.]. Moderately under the influence. **1996** *Leinster Leader* (Naas, Co. Kildare), 10 Oct: 'Judge Thomas Ballagh at Newbridge District Court was told that Gerard Wickham...had "a lot of drink taken" on the night in question.' Also **a drop taken** in same sense. **1969** Frank O'Connor, *Collection Three*, 'An Act of Charity': "'Well they're as good as the next, Your Holiness," says I. "Except when they'd have a drop taken."'

drink the cross off an ass [vb. phr.]. Said of s.o. with an inordinate capacity for alcohol. See **drouth** 3.

drisheen [n., <Ir. *drisín*, animal intestine] (esp. Munster). Blood sausage containing tansy. **1916** James Joyce, *A Portrait of the Artist* (q.v.) *as a Young Man*: 'Mr Dedalus [on visit to Cork] had ordered drisheens for breakfast...' **1980** Colm Lincoln, *Cork at the Turn of the Century*: 'The blood from the many slaughter houses was the chief ingredient of the well-known local dish, "drisheen".' **1989** Margaret O'Brien, *Cork Holly Bough*: 'Her voice erupted in a high-pitched shriek. "Tansy drisheen? Erra [see **arrah!**] girral I didn't see a tansy drisheen since St Finbarr left Barrack Street!"'

driver [n.]. Man employed by landlord to drive tenants' cattle to the pound against rent due. **1800** Maria Edgeworth, *Castle Rackrent*: 'Then fining down [q.v.] the year's rent came into fashion — any thing for the ready penny, and with all this, and presents to the agent and the driver, there was no such thing as standing it...'

drizzen [n., <Sc. *idem*, cf. MDu. *druysschen* (vb.), make a hollow roaring sound]. 'Sort of moaning sound uttered by a cow' (PWJ); cry (of child).

drogh/droich [n., <Ir. *droch* (prefix), bad, evil]. 1. Smallest, weakest bonham (piglet) of a litter. 2. Term of abuse. **1927** Peadar O'Donnell, *Islanders*: "'I was wonderin' who she was. The other wan's some droich I don't know.'"

droit [n., cf. Ir. *dreoigh* (vb.), decompose, decay] (Ulster). Small, deformed piglet (YDS).

droleen [n., <Ir. *dreoilín*, wren]. As thus; smallest/youngest in family/litter. **1961** Frank O'Connor, *An Only Child*: 'On Christmas Day they raised the country-

side killing wrens...Everyone knew that it was the droleen's chirping that had alerted the Roman soldiers in the Garden of Gethsemane...' See **the wren**.

drookit/drooky see **drawky**

drooth/drouth/druth [n., cf. OE *drugian* (vb. intrans.), dry] (esp. Ulster). 1. Dryness; drying (for washing). **1943** George A. Little, *Malachi Horan Remembers*: "'Well, beyont in Nazareth the grain does be growing and it mortal [q.v.] short in the straw. That is because of the druth, do you see!"' 2. Thirst; hence **droothy** [adj.] thirsty. **1940** Richard Rowley, *Ballads of Mourne*, 'Newry': 'Good-day yerself, sez I till him,/An' will ye take a dram?/I'll not say no, sez the sailor,/For it's drouthy that I am.' 3. One too fond of alcohol. **1921** (first published 1983) Patrick MacGill, *Lanty Hanlon*: "'I knew a man, a great drouth, and one day his wife saw smoke coming from his mouth.'" **1966** Patrick Boyle, *At Night All Cats are Grey*, 'The Metal Man': "'He was a powerful [see **power**] drouth. He would drink the cross off an ass [q.v.].'"

drop [n.] as in **he has a bad drop in him**. Bad strain in the blood (fig.). See also **drink taken**.

drop asunder [vb.] (Ulster). Give birth (of woman).

drop of the craythur see **craythur** 1.

dropsey [n.]. 1. [n., <'drop']. Payment exacted from hotels, restaurants, souvenir shops and other tourist facilities by tour bus drivers for delivering custom. **1996** Michael Ryan, RTÉ TV, *Nationwide*, 19 Feb: 'This kind of backhander is known in the business as a dropsey.' 2. **dropsies** [n. pl.] (Ulster). Game formerly played with cigarette cards, involving dropping one on top of another from a distance to cover it. **1983** *John Pepper's Illustrated Encyclopaedia of Ulster Knowledge*: '[The windy stool (q.v.) was] Formerly used for the popular children's game of "dropsies", played with cigarette cards. The object was to touch as many cards as possible with the one you dropped.'

drouth see **drooth**

drownded [solecistic p. part. as adj.]. Soaking wet from rain. **1925** Louise McKay, *Mourne Folk*: '"Come in, come in, mem; ye're fairly drownded!" she said, as she relieved me of my dripping umbrella.'

drown the shamrock [vb. phr.]. Celebrate St Patrick with generous libations.

Drum [nickname, poss. <patronage by the milit., C18] (Cork). Social assembly in Cork city. **1824** Thomas Crofton Croker, *Researches in the South of Ireland*: 'there were weekly meetings termed Drums, which are said to have been extremely social and agreeable, the admission was trifling, the company danced, played cards, talked or promenaded without restraint'.

Drumcondra medallists [nickname, <Dub. suburb]. **1994** Christopher Fitz-Simon, *The Boys* (see **the Boys** 2.): 'the minor parts [in the Gate Theatre productions] were taken by students...As well as these sources of unpaid talent, there were the "Drumcondra medallists" — the originator of the epithet is unknown — who appear to have been members of a section of society which habitually entered for competitions in verse-speaking, ballad-singing and step-dancing, all of whom (it would seem) resided in the exceedingly dreary and genteel suburb of that name.'

druth see **drooth**

drutheen [n., <Ir. *drúchtín*, white slug, supposed to trace out initials of a future lover, cf. *Chuaigh sí ar lorg a drúchtín*, She went to the track of a white slug (to seek her marriage prospects)]. As thus.

dry drizzle [n. phr.]. Very fine shower of rain.

dry money [n. phr.]. Ready money. **1907** Joseph Guinan, *The Soggarth Aroon* (q.v.): 'the loss of all their "dry money" through the failure of the bank'.

dry nod [n. phr.] (Ulster). 'Disapproving indication of recognition' (Pepper).

dry rub [n. phr.] (Ulster). Heavy-handed hint (YDS).

dub [n., <Low Ger. *dobbe*, pool of stagnant water]. Puddle, pool; mud, dirt. **1844** Robert Huddleston, *A Collection of Poems and Songs on Rural Subjects*, 'The Lammas Fair (Belfast)': 'Yeir basket Kates are skelpin' [q.v.] on,/An' passin' a' they're seein';/Their petticoats weel kilt ahin,/Nor dub or stoure [see **stour**] mismay 'em.'

Dub [nickname, abbrev.]. 1. Native of Dublin. **1995** Seamus Martin, *Irish Times*, 25 Sept: 'While some "Dubs" consider provincials less than the full civilised shilling [see **full shilling**] — "muck-savages" is a phrase which comes to mind — some provincials appear to consider Dubliners less than fully Irish: "Jackeen" [q.v.] in its etymology is a form of "Shoneen" [q.v.], a sort of working-class "West Brit" [q.v.].' See also **Molly Malones**. 2. Member of Royal Dublin Fusiliers, former regiment in Brit. army. **1979** C.S. Andrews, *Dublin Made Me*: 'They [the have-nots of the city] supplied the rank and file of the Dublin Fusiliers, known in the British Army as "the Dubs"...' See also **Old Toughs**.

dúchas [n., <Ir. *idem*, heritage, patrimony, traditional connection]. Native pride. **1997** Mary Gallagher, *Irish Times*, 3 Feb: 'There was dúchas in the air, the same dúchas and hope that was in Mayo in 1986 when...the people gathered to open an international airport that economists damned.'

duchill/ducle [n., <'dunghill'] (Ulster). Term of disparagement.

duck-house door [n. phr.] (Ulster). Very thick slice of bread, 'doorstep'.

duck nebs [n. pl., <OE *nebb*, bird's beak] (Ulster). Broad-toed boots. Also **duck's neb** [n. phr.] (Ulster). Vienna roll.

duck on the grawnshee [n. phr., <Ir. *gráinseach*, grange, granary, farm (Dinneen)]. Children's game. **1939** Sean O'Casey, *I Knock at the Door*: 'Then followed Duck on the Grawnshee in which a marble was placed on a slight depression making it look like a squatting duck. Round the resting marble, a chalk circle was drawn. The boy who owned

the duck on the grawnshee stood, with one foot within the chalk circle, watching the other boys...trying to knock the duck off the grawnshee.'

duck's meat [n.] (Ulster). Mucus formed in the eyes during sleep.

ducle see **duchill**

dudeen/didgeen [n., <Ir. *dúidín*, short-stemmed clay pipe]. 1. Smoking pipe in general. **1887** Bernard Magennis, *Lámh Dearg or the Red Hand*, 'The Boys of our Day': 'See that urchin who out from his pocket doth draw/An old dhudeen pipe which he sticks in his jaw!/He wants with *men's* age, not his own to keep pace...' **1939** James Joyce, *Finnegans Wake*: 'And didn't she up in sorgues and go and trot doon and stand in her douro, puffing her old dudheen...' **1956** Samuel Beckett, *Waiting for Godot*: 'POZZO What can I have done with that briar? ESTRAGON He's a scream. He's lost his dudeen.' (Poss. a play on 2.) 2. Penis.

Duff, Time of the [nickname, <fuel resorted to by the railways during WWII in the absence of steam coal]. As thus. **1963** Martin Whyte, 'Fifty Years of a Loco Man's Life', *Journal of the Irish Railway Record Society*, Spring: 'When the supply of steam coal became exhausted, a new type of fuel appeared, known technically as "duff" or "slurry", a very fine form of slack. I well remember the first day it was used; practically all the trains were reduced to a crawl...' **1975** P.J. Currivan, 'Engineman's Son', *Journal of the Irish Railway Record Society*, June: 'We now come to "The Time of the Duff" which is the manner in which all footplatemen and their successors refer to the period of the second World War, or "The Emergency" as it was officially called in this country.'

duggins [n. pl., <Sc. *deugs*, rags]. As thus.

duggy [n., <'dug', udder] (Cork). Boiled cow's udder. **1997** Eilís de Barra, *Bless 'em All, The Lanes* (q.v.) *of Cork*: 'Nowadays, of course, nobody eats duggy because people have become too grand...'

dug out of [vb. phr.]. Separated from s.o. by force. **1989** Hugh Leonard, *Out after Dark*: '"What was that all about? ...What ailed [q.v.] you? I thought you'd have to be dug out of him."'

duke see **juke**

dullamoo [n., <Ir. *dul amú* (vb.), go wrong, make a mistake]. Wastrel, ne'er-do-well.

dulling [pres. part., <*dull* (n. & vb.), 'loop or eye on piece of string' (SH); make such a loop] (Ulster). Poaching.

dumfounder [vb., <Sc. *dumfouner*, amaze, stun] (Ulster). As thus.

dummy tit [n. phr.] (Ulster). Child's comforter or soother (q.v.).

dumpy level [n., cf. *dumper*, post rammer for firming earth round fence posts (CUD)]. As thus. **1987** Lar Redmond, *Emerald Square:* 'men with wooden pegs, sledge hammers, tape measures and dumpy levels appeared at the top of Emerald Square'.

duncey [adj., cf. Ir. *donas* (n.), ill luck, misfortune]. **1927** Peadar O'Donnell, *Islanders:* '"It was a heartbreak for ye to lose Hughie the duncey way you did, if it was God's will," Mary Doogan said.'

dunch [n. & vb., <Sc. *idem*, push, bump, jog]. As thus. **1913** Alexander Irvine, *My Lady of the Chimney Corner:* 'I "dunched" my brother, who lay beside me, with my elbow. "Go an' see if oul' Hughie's livin' or dead," I said.' **1914** F.F. Moore, *The Ulsterman, A Story of Today*: 'Mr Alexander's eyes gleamed, his mouth twitched as if he were licking his lips. "A clout? Yon was no clout, it was a dunch — man, but I hit him a quare [see **quare** 1.] dunch that day."'

duncher [n., <?] (Ulster). Man's cloth cap. **1993** Sam McAughtry, *Touch & Go*: 'Civilians walked past with their heads down...the men in grey or brown raincoats and duncher caps.'

dundeen [n., <?]. Lump of bread without butter (PWJ).

dunder/dunner [n. & vb., <Sc. *dunner*, clatter]. Loud rumble; loud noise caused

by heavy blow; hence the blow itself; reverberate. **1908** Lynn Doyle, *Ballygullion*: 'the masther was away down the loanin' like a hare, splashing through the gutthers [see **gutter**], wi' the wee [q.v.] keg dundherin' on his backbone cruel'. **1913** Alexander Irvine, *My Lady of the Chimney Corner*: '"I got up and ran like the red shank t'McShane's house. I dundthered at his door till he opened it..."' **1979** John Morrow, *The Confessions of Proinsias O'Toole*: '"Would y'ever wait till he [the dog] gits this length an' hit him a good dunder up the balls, Francie?"' See **sotherer**.

dunderin-in [n., <*dunner* (q.v.)] (Ulster). 'Place that is falling apart' (Todd).

dunnage [n., <?, cf. *idem*, light packing to protect ships' cargo] (Ulster). Odds and ends, baggage, etc.

dunner see **dunder**

Duns Stocious [nickname, <Johannes Duns Scotus, *c.*1266–1308]. From his depiction on £5 currency note, introduced 1 Nov 1976. See **stocious**.

dunsy [adj., <'dunce'] (Ulster). 'Slow-witted, dopey-looking' (YDS).

dunt see **dint**

dunty [n., see **dint**] (Ulster). Awkward/useless unreliable person/animal. **1986** Charles McGlinchey, *The Last of the Name*: 'One day Máire was down along the road somewhere and she was attacked by a dunty cow, and nearly killed, till some Clonmany man was passing and drove the cow off.'

duragh see **doorach**

Durationist [nickname]. Individual enlisting in defence forces for the duration of the Emergency (WWII). **1973** Noël Conway, *The Bloods* (q.v.): 'So the year [1943] dragged towards a weary close and the Bloods...turned all of their unspent energy into making a right [see **right** 1.] merry Christmas. To the durationists the question was often asked of themselves: how many more?' **1991** John P. Duggan, *A History of the Irish Army*: 'On 7 June 1940 the government declared that a state of emergency existed. The Defence Forces Act was

amended to authorise the enlistment of personnel for the duration of the Emergency ("Durationists" or "E-men" [q.v.]).'

during ash/oak/soot [adv. phr.] (Ulster). For a long time; for ever. **1948** Patrick Kavanagh, *Tarry Flynn*: '"Oh, never during soot was there such a family as mine, one worse than the other."'

durlogues [n., gen. pl., <Ir. *duirleog/doirneog*, round stone]. Stone setts or cobbles. **1981** Paddy Crosbie, *Your Dinner's Poured Out!*: 'We used to call the stones durlogues and, of course, the traffic was very noisy, what with iron-rims on all wheels.'

durn/durnock [n., <?] (Ulster). Stupid/slow-witted/fat/lazy person.

durnawny [n., <Ir. *durnánaí*, dense, obtuse person]. As thus. **1914** George Fitzmaurice, *The Pie-Dish*: 'JACK ...every minute I'd think of my old durnawny here of eighty years and more...'

dusheen [n., cf. Sc. *dush* (vb.), strike, push forcibly, hence *dushing*, beating, with *-ing* infl. by Ir. dimin. *ín*] (Ulster). Deserved punishment; just deserts.

duskus [n., <'dusk'] (Ulster). Eventide.

dust [vb., <OE *dúst* (n.), *idem*, cf. Ger. *dunst* (n.), vapour; disturbance, row, shindy, 1753]. Abuse. **1847** John Edward Walsh, *Ireland Sixty Years Ago*: 'When the criminal was turned off, and the "dusting of the scrag-boy" began, the hangman was assailed, not merely with shouts and curses, but often with showers of stones.'

Dust, the [nickname]. Stonemasons. **1966** Séamus Murphy, *Stone Mad*: 'the right to have beer at 11 o'clock in the morning...is still held by the "Dust"'.

dust house [n., <?] (Ulster). Child's playhouse. **1995** Catherine McAleavey in Mary Ryan et al. (eds.), *No Shoes in Summer*: 'At playtime the girls skipped and sang "Down on the Carpet" and "Jenny sits a Weeping". The boys played marbles and ran in and out of the wee [q.v.] girls' dust houses.'

Dutch Billy [nickname, <William, Prince of Orange, later King William III of Eng.]

(Dub.). C17 house style with curvilinear gables. **1985** Máirín Johnston, *Around the Banks of Pimlico*: 'it [Marrowbone Lane] dates from the time English woollen workers and the followers of William III or William of Orange settled in the district. Many of the houses in the area were built during this period and were nicknamed Dutch Billys, after the king.' **1987** Lar Redmond, *Emerald Square*: 'the Huguenots came, bringing their expertise in weaving with them, built their Dutch Billies on the banks of the Poddle'. **1991** Douglas Bennett, *Encyclopaedia of Dublin*: 'In about 1670 a housing development began in the area [the Coombe] with houses known as Dutch Billies with their gables facing the street.'

DV [acronym, <Lat. *Deo volente*, by God's will]. Pious qualification of expressed intention; all being well. **1996** Anthony Cronin, *Samuel Beckett, The Last Modernist*: 'As had been common in Ireland among Catholics and Protestants when he was growing up, he had always sprinkled his letters with "Thank Gods" and "Please Gods", even the occasional DV...which is more of a Catholic practice.'

dwable/dwible [n. & vb., <Sc. *dwable*, onomat.] (Ulster). Feeble/misshapen/spindly person/animal (YDS); walk feebly, totter.

dwam/dwammel [n., <Sc. *dwam*, faint] (Ulster). Fit of dizziness or abstraction; heavy and half-unconscious state resembling a coma (S&R).

dwible see **dwable**

dydee [n., cf. Ir. *daighsin/daighdin*, trinket]. As thus; but DOM quotes 'another correspondent [who] tells me that she heard a lady of the old school giving out [q.v.] about a young wan [q.v.] of her acquaintance frolicking in Brittas Bay "in nothing but the tiniest dydee of a knickers"'.

Dyke, the [nickname, abbrev.] (Cork). The Mardyke, tree-lined city walk, laid out 1719. **1951** Frank O'Connor, *Traveller's Samples*, 'Darcy in the Land of Youth': '"Don't talk to me about the Dyke," groaned Chris as if the very name of it filled him with nostalgia, "I think I'll never get back to it."'

E

earles [n., <Sc. *earl* (vb.), make a deposit on a purchase etc.] (Ulster). Deposit on purchase etc.

Earl of Cork [nickname, −1830 (DHS)]. Ace of diamonds.

ears see **hear one's ears**

earwigging [pres. part., Hib.E usage differs from Brit. sl. *idem*: 'synonym for *ear-bashing* (ODMS)]. Listening attentively to private conversations. **1966** Patrick Boyle, *At Night All Cats are Grey*, 'Myko': 'By this time all hands were earwigging. Drinks were sitting untouched on the counter...' **1995** Phil O'Keeffe, *Down Cobbled Streets, A Liberties Childhood*: '"It clears the system," I heard a woman say expansively. "What's the system?" I asked my mother. "You were ear-wiggin' again," she said, "to things that should be no concern of yours."'

Easter house [n. phr.] (Ulster). Children's playhouse where eggs are boiled at Easter.

Easter Lily [n., gen. name for *Lilium longiflorum* & others]. Worn by republicans subsequent to 1916 in commemoration of Easter rising and so referred to.

eat [vb. trans.]. Subject to verbal abuse/attack. **1995** 'B.C.', *Irish Times*, 18 Apr: 'He [Bishop Newman] called my secretary later to ask which edition of *Hotspur* I was referring to. When Fr Brennan gently suggested that it might be *Hot Press* instead of *Hotspur* Jeremiah "ate" him. He "ate" a lot of people in his time.' Also **eat the head off s.o.** [vb. phr.]. **1994** Ferdia Mac Anna, *The Ship Inspector*: '"I've a good mind to go round there now and eat the head off the lot of them."' **1996** Kathryn Holmquist, *Irish Times*, 23 Jan: '"If I ate the head off him, he'd beat me" is the cry which Ms Wall hears from the parents of many of the 30 children detained by order of the court at Oberstown.'

eat a farmer's arse (through a hedge) [vb. phr.]. Expressive of acute hunger. **1954** James Plunkett, *Bell*, 'The Eagles and the Trumpets', Aug: 'When they left Slattery's they tried Mulligan's and in the Stag's Head Higgins said he could eat a farmer's arse, so they had sandwiches.' Also **eat a baby's bottom through the monkey cage in the eZoo** (*sic*) (Dub.) in same sense (PO'F).

eatin'/aytin'-house [n.]. 1. Restaurant. **1951** Sam Hanna Bell, *December Bride*: 'When Hamilton had shaken up the horse's nosebag they went to a little eating-house close to the markets.' **1996** Headline, *Leinster Leader* (Naas, Co. Kildare), 19 Sept: '"Eating Houses" attacked over beef charges'. 2. Mouth. **1995** Shane Connaughton, *A Border Diary*: '"Fellah with the sign above the eatin' house." "Sign above the eating house?" I had no idea what he meant. Mickey explains — a moustache.'

eccer/eccker/ecker/ekker [n., <abbrev. of 'exercise' + endearment suffix]. School exercise. **1977** Noël Conway, *The Bloods* (q.v.): '[The corporal], when given the syllabus the previous night, had swotted up his subject...He wasn't going to let the previous night's "eccer" go to waste and he had a captive audience.' **1991** Roddy Doyle, *The Van*: '"Okay, love," said Jimmy Sr. "Good luck. D'yeh have all your eccer done now?"' **1991** Bob Quinn, *Smokey Hollow*: 'Their groceries were delivered by cocky young messenger boys...Parents warned about ending up in such dead-end jobs if they didn't do their eckers (homework) and study properly.'

Echo boys [nickname] (Cork). Street sellers of the Cork *Evening Echo*. **1970** Pádraig Ó Dálaigh, *Cork Holly Bough*: 'The Cork "Echo" boy is usually a lively, good-humoured piece of organism, quick with Cork wit and quick with the change.' **1975** S.F. Pettit, *This City of Cork*: 'To these traditional city cries there came another towards the end of the [19th] century when the "Echo" boys spilled onto the streets in the late afternoon.'

ecker see **eccer**

edgie [adj., <Sc. *idem*, quick-tempered] (Ulster). As thus.

eejit [n., <'idiot', phonetic spelling of pronun.; also **eeja'** (specifically Dub. pronun.)]. Fool, idiot, simpleton. **1958** Frank O'Connor, *An Only Child*: 'He had great contempt for our little [Cork] colony of German musicians, whom he spoke of...as "bleddy eejits".' **1983** William Trevor, *Fools of Fortune*: '"You're the biggest eejit this side of Cork," his old father used to say snappishly...' **1995** Anne Marie Hourihane, *Sunday Tribune*, 23 July: 'The adorable thing about John [Bruton] is that even when he's doing the right thing he looks like a complete eejit.' Also **eedjity/eeijity** [adj.]. 1. In same sense. **1967** Bryan MacMahon, *The Honey Spike* (q.v.): '"Martin! What are you doin'?" "Are women eedjity? She's standin' on the bank, an' I'm up to my thighs in water. An' she asks me what the hell I'm doin'!"' **1995** Patrick Boland, *Tales from a City Farmyard*: '"What is it, Ma?" said I. Rover sat bolt upright in the bed as if expecting another eejity attack...' 2. Drunk.

eelans/eelins [n. pl., <Sc. *eildins*, equals in age] (Ulster). As thus.

e'erawan [n.]. Anyone. **1939** James Joyce, *Finnegans Wake*: 'Small wonder He'll Cheat E'erawan our local lads nicknamed him.' See **ne'erawan**.

eerie [adj., <Sc. *idem* <ME *eri*, timid] (Ulster). Surprising, strange.

eervar [n., <Ir. *iarmhar*, remnant, remainder, last survivor of a race etc. (Dinneen)]. Last pig in a litter.

egg-nog [n.] (Ulster). Eggs scrambled without milk and fried in bacon fat.

eirog [n., <Ir. *eireog*, pullet]. Sprightly, comely girl.

ekes an' ens [n. phr., cf. Eng. dial. *eke* (n.), extra bit] (Ulster). Odds and ends; 'small scraps of things turned to account' (Patterson).

ekker see **eccer**

elder [n., abbrev.] (Ulster). Presbyterian eldership. 'They tuk the elder aff him' (CUD).

elders [n. pl., <MDu. *idem*, cows' udders]. Women's breasts. **1966** Patrick Boyle, *At Night All Cats are Grey*, 'Go Away, Old Man, Go Away': 'slooching around half-dressed, the bare ones scalded off her with the heat of the fire and the two elders swinging out of her like she was six months gone'. See also **dirty elders**.

elected [vb.]. Fortunate in being accepted. **1995** Deaglán de Bréadún, *Irish Times*, 2 Dec: 'The whole occasion [of the US presidential visit] could be summed up with a traditional Dublin phrase: "Bill, you're elected."'

elegant [adj.]. Excellent. **C.1910** Anon., *Irish Wit and Humour*: '"A family dinner is a mighty plisant thing. What have ye got?" "Och, nothing *by* common. Just an illigant pace of corned beef and potatoes."'

element [n.] as in **that's the element!** [exclam.] (Ulster). Expressive of approval.

elephant [n., euphem. abbrev. of 'elephant's turd'] (TCD). Solid and unpopular suet pudding formerly served on Commons for resident students. **1947** Anon., *TCD, A College Miscellany*, 'Victrix Magistra', 14 Nov: 'Whale steak in the future is sure to go down/When carved by a figure in hood, cap and gown,/And "Elephant"'s welcome as apricot tarts/If it comes from the hand of a Master of Arts.'

elf-shot [n.]. Disease in cattle supposedly caused by supernatural agency. **1938** Seumas MacManus, *The Rocky Road to Dublin*: 'In both christian and beast fairy doctors cured the mysterious ills induced by fairy power — such as heart-fever in one, and elf-shot in the other.'

elsin [n., <Sc. *idem* <MDu. *elsen*, shoemaker's awl] (Ulster). Sharp-tongued individual.

E man [nickname]. One of those volunteering for military service during the Emergency (WWII). **1996** Deasún Breathnach, *Irish Times*, 1 Apr: 'Volunteers after the declaration [of war] were known as E (for Emergency) men. I became one of them...' See also **Durationist**.

Emerald Isle, the [attrib.]. Ire., latterly ironic. **1965** T.P. O'Neill, *Irish Press*, 'Window on the Past', 5 Feb: '"The Emerald Isle" is a name so widely accepted for Ireland that it almost comes as a surprise to think that someone must have given it that name. That person was a medical doctor named William Drennan...' (1754–1820; in his poem 'When Erin First Rose'). **1995** Frank Fitzgibbon, *Sunday Tribune*, 6 Aug: 'A Burbank-based source claims that Disney is planning to shift all his movie production to the Emerald Isle, citing the country's natural beauty and a veritable army of extras.' **1996** A.J. Rous, *Irish Times*, 10 Apr: 'Sir...The latest set [of traffic lights] to appear is situated outside the new ferry terminal in Dún Laoghaire. We can only hope that visitors to the Emerald Isle are met by a green light.'

Emerald Tiger [n. phr., on analogy of 'Asian Tiger', booming economy, esp. Singapore, South Korea, etc. Coined by US magazine *Newsweek*, Dec 1996]. Ir. economy thus perceived. **1996** Fintan O'Toole, *Irish Times*, 28 Dec: 'What *Newsweek* magazine described...as the Emerald Tiger...was not so much on the prowl as on the razzle-dazzle.' **1997** Kieran Daley, *Independent on Sunday* (London), 19 Jan: 'We hear a great deal these days about the so-called "Emerald Tiger" meaning the allegedly booming Irish economy; in international rugby terms the "Emerald Famine" continues apace...' Also **Celtic Tiger** in same sense. **1997** Hugh Campbell, *Irish Times*, 2 July: 'Sir — A leopard may be unable to change its spots, but a *flaithiúlach* [see **flahool**] Celtic Tiger could all too easily lose its stripes and revert to over-weight pussyhood. Believe me, we know our cats here in Kilkenny [see **Kilkenny cats**].'

empty skite see **no empty skite**

emsha see **amsha**

end see **take one's end**

Endymion [nickname, <Greek shepherd allegedly loved by the Moon goddess & thus 'moonstruck', bestowed on him by Lord Cadogan, Lord Lieutenant]. James Boyle Tisdell Burke Stewart Fitzsimons Farrell, Dub. 'character' (see **character** 1.), *fl.* late C19–20. **1936** Oliver St John Gogarty, *As I was Going Down Sackville Street*: 'Dublin saw him only as a man gone "natural", and Dublin has outstanding examples in every generation. Endymion was preceded by Professor Maginnis, who turned himself into an Italian professor by eliding the two terminal letters of his name.'

Englified/Inglified [adj., <'English']. Said of s.o. who apes Eng. manners/speech, puts on airs. **1829** Gerald Griffin, *The Collegians*: '"Then to be watching yourself, an' spake Englified, an' not to ate half your 'nough [q.v.] at dinner..."'

enjain [n., <'engine'/'ingenious'] (Ulster). Clever contrivance or invention.

entermeddle [vb., <ME *entremedle*, interfere in] (Ulster). As thus.

entire [adj.] (Ulster). Financially independent.

erick's egg [n., <Sc. *errack* <Sc. Gael. *eireag*, pullet] (Ulster). Small egg.

Erin-go-bragh [n. phr., <Ir. *go breá* (adj. & adv.), well, fine). Patriotic slogan. **1969** Les A. Murray, *The Weatherboard Cathedral*, 'A Walk with O'Connor': 'At Waverley, where the gravestones stop at the brink,/Murmuring words, to the rebel's tomb we went,/An exile's barrow of Erin-go-bragh and pride/In grey-green cement.'

ern [n.] as in **have an ern for** [vb. phr.]. Be good at.

eroo see **aroo**

errand [n.] as in **on one end's errand** [adv. phr., cf. Ir. *i n-aonturas*, purposely] (Ulster). For the particular purpose of.

ersehole [n., <'Erse', Ir. Gaelic, latterly joc./derog.]. Fáinne (ring). **1996** Declan Kiberd, *Inventing Ireland*: 'He [Brendan Behan] spoke often and with jocular scorn of the silver and gold rings worn in lapels by officially-accredited Irish-speakers as "erseholes".' Also **erse** = 'arse' in other contexts: **1997** Gerry Dukes, *Irish Times*, 14 June: 'Joyce's knowledge of Irish was rudimentary but some of [Danis] Rose's corrections would give you sunburn on your Erse.'

esta clamper! [exclam., <Ir. *éist do chlampar*, hush your noise!]. As thus. **1605** Anon., *Captain Thomas Stukeley*: 'ONEALE Esta clamper, thou talkest too much, the English upon the vall [wall] will hear thee...' See also **clamper**.

ettercap see **attercap**

even [vb., <OE *efnan, idem*]. 1. (Ulster). Lower or demean oneself, as in **even one's wit to** [vb. phr.]. Lower oneself to argue with. 2. Liken to. 3. Hint at, impute. 4. Have one's name coupled with another's.

even-ash [n.] (Ulster). Ash leaf with even number of leaflets, used in divination. 'This even-ash I hold in my han',/The first I meet is my true man' (Patterson).

even-down [n.] (Ulster). Continuous downpour (of rain).

every dog and divil [n. phr.]. Absolutely everybody, *tout le monde*. **1977** Flann O'Brien, *The Hair of the Dogma*: 'Hardly a word appearing under his pseudonym [Myles na gCopaleen] is written by himself. To use a witticism, every dog and divil in the country writes it...' **1996** RTÉ TV serial, *Glenroe*, 21 Jan: 'DINNY Didn't I tell you? STEPHEN No you didn't. But you seem to have told every other dog and divil.'

example [n.] (Ulster). Term of contempt (Traynor); a 'sight'.

excira' see **delira' and excira'**

extortioners/extortions [n. pl., joc.] (Ulster). Nasturtiums.

eye-bright [adj.] (Ulster). Beautiful, handsome.

eye-fiddle/hifiddle [n., <Ir. *aghaidh fidil*, fiddle face]. Mummer's or wren-boy's mask. **1952** Bryan MacMahon, *Children of the Rainbow*: 'Almost all wore false faces, which we called hifiddles. A lazy minority had masks cut from dark cloth.' See **the wren**.

eye of one's arse [n. phr.]. Anus.

eyesweet [adj.] (Ulster). Handsome.

eyewinkers [n. pl.]. Eyelashes, blinkers. See **winkers**.

F

face [vb.]. Pay court to (gen. woman); accept marriage proposal. **1925** Louise McKay, *Mourne Folk*: "'D'ye think, Thomas, wud Miss O'Hara 'face'?" said John..."Ye know as well as me she's long past her market [q.v.].'" **1983** W.F. Marshall, *Livin' in Drumlister*, 'Me an' me Da': 'But cryin' cures no trouble,/To Bridget I went back,/An' faced her for it that night week/Beside her own thurf-stack.'

faddle [n., poss. <'fiddle'] (Ulster). Fool; mess, botched job.

fadge [n., <Sc. *idem*, rich loaf] (Ulster). Griddle bread; rich, fruity bread; potato bread. **1913** Alexander Irvine, *My Lady of the Chimney Corner*. 'Three kinds of bread she baked. "Soda" — common flour bread ..."pirta [q.v.] oaten", made of flour and oatmeal; and "fadge" — potato bread.'

faggot [n., <?, dial. 1591 (OED)]. Term of abuse applied to a woman, gen. as **oul' faggot**. **1908** Lynn Doyle, *Ballygullion*: 'The uncle stirs in his sleep, an' thin sits up in bed. "Ye ould faggot, ye," sez he...' **1922** James Joyce, *Ulysses*: 'doing his highness to make himself interesting to that old faggot Mrs Riordan that he thought he had a great leg of [q.v.]'. **1970** Christy Brown, *Down All the Days*: "'Essie, yeh greasy oul faggot yeh, the smell of snuff off yeh would kill a horse.'"

fags [exclam., poss. corruption of Sc. *faick/faicks*, faith (q.v.)]. **1925** Louise McKay, *Mourne Folk*: "'D'ye min' the night of the big win', Thomas?" asked John McCunningham. "Fags, I think I do," replied Thomas.'

fahal [vb., cf. Ir. *bathlach* (n.), lout, clumsy person] (Ulster). 'Fall over oneself in pointless, flustered activity' (YDS).

failed [p. part. as adj., <OF *faillir* (vb.), be wanting] (Ulster). In poor health.

fair [n. & vb.]. 1. [n.]. See **take to the fair**. 2. [vb.] (Ulster). Improve (of weather).

fair doos/dues [n. phr., cf. Austral. *fair dos, fair goes*]. Indication of agreement/admiration. **1973** Noël Conway, *The Bloods* (q.v.): 'it was the first time in his twenty years' service that he had heard the order to break step given. Fair dues to the lads, they licked up the step again and kept it...' **1983** Peter Heavey in Joe O'Reilly & Sixth Class, Convent School, Edenderry, *Over the Half Door*. 'There is an old school friend of mine still alive in there in Edenderry, in Fr Murphy Street, Joe Kelly. He does about eight miles a day walking, fair dues to him.' **1995** *Sunday Tribune*, 24 Dec: 'Fair dues to Guinness, they are now running an ad with a dancing reindeer...without mentioning the Uncle Arthur [q.v.] product at all.'

fairlie [n., cf. Sc. *fairley*, wonder; 'fairing'] (Ulster). Fairing, gift bought at a fair (Traynor).

fairy bit [n. phr.]. Portion of food left for the fairies. **1938** Seumas MacManus, *The Rocky Road to Dublin*: 'Her children from her learned, no matter how hungry they'd be at quitting the table, never to finish their portions — to leave nor plate nor bowl lacking what she properly called the fairy bit...'

fairy dress [n.]. Fancy dress. See **water rat**.

faith/faix [exclam., latterly gen. iron. or Paddyism]. **1879** Charles J. Kickham, *Knocknagow*. 'I forgot thankin' you for the fresh eggs...an' our own hens stopped layin' this I don't know how long." "Faix an 'tis the same story we'd have ourselves," replied Nelly.' **C.1910** Anon., *Irish Wit and Humour*. '"And what are your landlord's opinions?" "Faix, his opinion is, that I won't pay him the last half-year's rint; and I am of the same opinion myself."' **1995** Eoin Ó Súilleabháin, *Irish Times*, 3 Oct: '...I commenced student life. And faith and begorah [q.v.], 'twas not the demon I imagined...'

Faithful Annie [nickname] (Army Air Corps). Avro Anson aircraft, in service from 1937. **1994** Aidan McIvor, *A History of the Irish Naval Service*: 'a flight of four Avro Ansons mounted long coastal patrols...a physically arduous duty. The Anson, nicknamed "Faithful Annie", was a durable aircraft.'

Faithful County [nickname]. Co. Offaly, esp. as applied to its GAA teams. **1982** Vivienne Clarke, *Leinster Gaelic Games Annual*, 'How Offaly Earned the "Faithful County" Title': 'The title of the "Faithful County" generally attributed to Bob O'Keeffe, an Association President in the mid-Thirties, dates only from the Golden Jubilee era [1980s] and was no doubt prompted by his observations of the efforts of a small county to achieve some measure of success in both codes [football and hurling]...' **1995** *Offaly Independent*, 23 June: 'though it is sixteen years since they [Wexford] defeated Offaly in a championship match, a distinct air of caution prevails in hurling circles throughout the "Faithful County"'.

faix see **faith**

faize see **faze**

fake [n., cf. Ir. *féachadh*, examination, diagnosis (Dinneen)] (Ulster). Cancer.

falairy [adj., <'floury', by metathesis] (Ulster). Unpleasant (taste).

falloch [n., <Sc. *idem*, large lump of anything] (Ulster). As thus.

falls [n. pl.] (Ulster). Flies (of trousers).

falorey [n., <?] (Ulster). 'Lovable, mischievous person; implies harmlessness' (Pepper).

false [adj., <Ir. *falsa*, lazy]. As thus.

False Men see **Fir Bréaga**

famine grass see **hungry grass**

famous [adv.] (Ulster). Excellently.

fangle/fank/fankle [vb., <Sc. *fankle*, entangle, become entangled] (Ulster). As thus.

fanner [n., <?] (Dub.). Work-shy individual.

fardel/farl/farrel [n.]. 1. [<OE *fiortha dael*, fourth part]. Farthing. See **waxy**. 2. (Ulster). Quarter/portion of circular griddle scone etc. 3. [<OF *fardel*, Mod.F *fardeau*, baggage]. As thus, as in **pack and**

fardel [n. phr.]. Bag and baggage. 4. (Leinster). Book cover.

Far-Downer [nickname] (Ulster). Donegal man (Traynor).

farl see **fardel**

far-lands [n.] as in **fill the far-lands** [vb. phr.] (Ulster). Take an adequate quantity of food.

farley/ferley [n., <Sc. *farley/farlie* (adj.), strange, unusual, <ON *ferligr* (adj.), monstrous] (Ulster). Remarkable occurrence, strange sight; also term of contempt (iron.).

farntickles/ferntickles [n. pl., <Sc. *fairney/farn-tickles*, freckles] (Ulster). As thus.

far out as Kit Logue, as [adj. phr.] (Ulster). Way off the mark (TT).

farrel see **fardel**

farry [n., <Ir. *fara*, hen-roost]. Attic, loft over the hearth; small shelf, found one on each side of chimney; hayloft.

farteen [n., <'fart' + Ir. dimin. *ín*; nonce-word?]. Something insignificant. **1969** Tom Mac Intyre, *The Charollais*: 'C nodded towards the farteen of a bedroom. The door was shut.'

farthing face [n. phr., <low-value pre-decimal coin]. Pinched, wan look. Applied to child who is crabby (see **crab** 1.). **1995** Phil O'Keeffe, *Down Cobbled Streets, A Liberties Childhood*: '"You've a little farthin' face," she would declare as she wound the rags round my stubborn hair. "We have to try and make somethin' of you."'

far-through [adj., <Sc. *idem*, weak, near death] (Ulster). As thus. **1986** Charles McGlinchey, *The Last of the Name*: 'I said the *Confiteor* for him in Latin and in Irish, to let him see I wasn't as far through as the people made out.'

fash [n. & vb., <Sc. *idem* <Fr. *fâcher* (vb.), trouble, annoy] (Ulster). Trouble, annoyance; annoy. **1966** Patrick Boyle, *At Night All Cats are Grey*, 'The Betrayers': '"Could it be she's fashed about something?...Maybe it's because the pony won't take to her.'

fastened see **fessend**

Fasten's E'en [prop. n., <Sc. *idem*, Shrove Tuesday] (Ulster). As thus.

fasting–spittle [n.] (Ulster). Saliva of s.o. who has not eaten, believed to have healing powers.

father and mother of [adj. phr., intensifying what follows]. **1895** Seumas MacManus, *The Leadin' Road to Donegal*: 'For three fardins [farthings] I would take it from ye an' give ye the father an' mother of a good soun' blaichin' [q.v.].' **1922** James Joyce, *Ulysses*: '"Myler dusted the floor with him," says Alf... "Handed him the father and mother of a beating."'

Father Trendyism/Trendiness [abst. n., <bland, populist cleric created 1980s by broadcaster and humorist Dermot Morgan, on model of journalist Fr Brian D'Arcy]. Tabloid religion for the unthinking masses involving use of banal metaphors: 'In catchy, with-it language he spells out the real meaning of Life, Religion and the post-Einsteinian universe' (from blurb for Morgan, *Trendy Sermons*, 1981). **1995** John Waters, *Irish Times*, 8 Aug: 'If you will pardon the Father Trendyism, I sometimes think of the health of Irish Catholicism as being a bit like a torch battery. Once upon a time, batteries used to fade away gradually...' **1995** Eddie Holt, *Irish Times*, 6 Nov: 'Dr Daly...was furious that the authority of the conservative church was being challenged. His rigidity exposed the safe, cosmetic, functional unction of three decades of Father Trendiness.'

fat in the forehead [adj. phr.] (Ulster). Stupid.

faumera [n., <*Fomorians*, semi–mythical prehistoric invaders of Ire.]. Wandering beggar, idle individual. 'In Clare the country people that go to the seaside...are called *Faumeras*' (PWJ).

fause–face [n., <Sc. *idem*, mask, deceitful person] (Ulster). As thus.

favour [vb., <Sc. *idem*, resemble in features] (Ulster). As thus.

faze/faize/fiz [vb., cf. Sc. *faise*, disturb, put to inconvenience, <OE *fesian*, drive

away]. As thus; disconcert; gen. in neg. **1973** Noël Conway, *The Bloods* (q.v.): 'Even a little question from the Chief of Staff as to whether he thought a rifle the most appropriate implement to gap a hedge didn't faze him.'

fearful [adv., intens.]. Exceedingly, very.

feather see **take a feather out of s.o.**

feck [n.]. 1. [<?] (Cork). Card game (Beecher). See **all a baa!**, **bee-up**. 2. [<?]. Implement used in game of pitch and toss. **1982** Éamonn Mac Thomáis, *Janey Mack* (q.v.), *Me Shirt is Black*: '"Go wan now, sir," said yer man [q.v.], "I've the flyers on the feck. Put your horse where your mouth is..." The other man looked at his horse and cab, looked at the crowd who egged him on and looked back at yer man with the flyers. Flyers were two black Victorian ha'pennies... The feck was one half of an old blue-coloured comb.' **1985** Máirín Johnston, *Around the Banks of Pimlico*: 'The "feck" was a little bit of stick about the width of a ha'penny and the length of the fingers.' See also **boxman**, **jack**, **jockey**, **rider**, **tosser** 1. 3. [<Sc. *idem*, part, greater part] (Ulster). As thus. 4. [aphetic, <'effect'] (Ulster). Ability, as in **there's no feck in him** (Traynor).

feck [vb.]. 1. [<OE *feccan*, fetch, seek, gain, take; DOM suggests <Ger. *fegen*, plunder]. To take or steal. **1916** James Joyce, *A Portrait of the Artist* (q.v.) *as a Young Man*: '"But why did they run away, tell us?" "I know why," Cecil Thunder said. "Because they had fecked cash out of the rector's room."' **1960** Edna O'Brien, *The Country Girls*: '"Where are you going?" "To feck a few samples from the surgery."' 2. By mimesis a euphem. for **fuck** (q.v.). Similarly **fecker**, **feck off**, **feck-all**. **1989** Hugh Leonard, *Out after Dark*: 'I went on clinging to the wall until old Fanning appeared at his front window and made feck-off gestures of great savagery.' **1993** Deirdre Purcell, *Falling for a Dancer*: '"Fecker," said Hazel passionately. "That's all he is, a fecker. I can't stand the sight of him..."' **1995** Patrick Boland, *Tales from a City Farmyard*: 'After about fifteen minutes trying to get

my head out [of the railings]...while some little fecker of a kid pinched the bum off me, it was decided that the fire brigade should be called...'

feckless [adj., <Sc. *idem*, weak, weak-minded] (Ulster). As thus.

feedogue [n., cf. Ir. *fiodóir*, spider]. As thus.

fegary/figary/figgairy [n., var. of 'vagary'; cf. Lat. *vagari* (vb.), wander]. Departure from normal conduct; notion. **1928** E.Œ. Somerville & Martin Ross, *French Leave*: 'To have freedom and — what was it his mother used to say? — "to follow me own Figgairy O!"' **1966** Patrick Boyle, *At Night All Cats are Grey*, 'Oh Death Where Is Thy Sting-aling-aling': '"But that figayrey [*sic*] she had," he went on, "about the blood leaving your head if you slept with it raised too high..."' **1996** David Hanly, *Sunday Tribune*, 19 May: 'Some years ago I took a figary, as my mother used to put it, and started seriously to consider doing a degree.' Hence **figaried** [p. part. as adj., cf. Sc. *vaigrie* (n.), freak, piece of folly, poss. <Lat. *vagari* (vb.), wander] (Ulster). Dressed up, decked out. **1925** Louise McKay, *Mourne Folk*: '"...I cud see Miss O'Hara was laughin' up her sleeve at me all the time. She was all figaried up like a young wan [q.v.]."' Also **figario** [n.] in same sense. **1991** John B. Keane, *Love Bites and Other Stories*: 'People should try to remember that it is not the scenic drawings on a po or the figarios attached to it that matter. Rather it is the lasting powers of the pot in question.'

feint/fient a hate [exclam., <Sc. *feint*, devil] (Ulster). Divil a bit (q.v.). See **hate**.

feist [vb., <?]. Fart. **1705** John Michelburne, *Ireland Preserved*: 'he did bate my Wife, and did trow her down stairs, and did call her a Feisting, Farting, Stinking Shaad [q.v.]'.

fella see **fellow**, **fellow-me-lad**

fellow [n.] as in **as the fellow said** [concessive phr., cf. Ir. *mar a dheartar*, as is said]. Indicating use of colloq. or sl. phrase 'in inverted commas'; intensifying what it precedes or (more commonly) follows. **1948** Patrick Kavanagh, *Tarry Flynn*: '"Jabus [q.v.], that's a dread [q.v.]," said Eusebius, "that bates the little dish [see **beat the little dish**] as the fellow said."' **1991** Seán Ó Ciaráin, *Farewell to Mayo*: '"...I have relations, Toghers, around Ardmore yet, though they might not know it, or care. As the fella said, 'It's a bit far back now.'"' **1993** Mick McInerney in Joe O'Reilly & Sixth Class, Convent School, Edenderry, *Over the Half Door*: 'I remember when I went there first there was no roof on it [the mart] and it was very hard to work on it...But now it's covered and there is a bit of comfort in it, as the fellow says.'

fellow-me-lad [term of address, gen. affect., adult to boy]. **1965** George Buchanan, *Morning Papers*: 'John Shaw, the chief sub-editor, with a white moustache, pads about in carpet boots. "Now, young fella-me-lad, here's something for you to do. See what you can make of this story."' **1983** William Trevor, *Fools of Fortune*: '"Well, fellow-me-lad," a man would say and, finding it difficult to continue, would laugh and tap me on the head.'

fendy [adj., <Sc. *fendie/fendy*, resourceful] (Ulster). Cunning, cute.

Fenian [adj., prop. & common n., <Ir. *na Fianna*, legendary warrior-band led by Fionn Mac Cumhaill; hence member of the Fenian Brotherhood, revolutionary organisation founded New York 1859]. Term of abuse applied to Ulster Catholics/nationalists. **1913** Alexander Irvine, *My Lady of the Chimney Corner*: '"Anthrim's a purty good place fur pigs an' sich to live in," he told the travellers. "Ye see, pigs is naither Fenians nor Orangemen."' **1989** Eoin McNamee, *The Last of Deeds*: '"Keep your hands off her, Taig [q.v.] bastard," an unfamiliar voice said. "Fenian get [q.v.]," another one said...' **1996** Robin Livingstone, *Irish Times*, 28 Feb: 'Sir — The ceasefire's over, bombs are going off in London...and Kevin Myers...is getting worked up about Falls Road Fenians drawing the dole.'

ferley see **farley**

ferntickles see **farntickles**

ferrin [n., cf. Ir. *fírinneach*, truthful]. First mark made by plough. 'Should the "feerin" not be straight, the succeeding sods will also be "out of truth" as the local saying is' (OTF).

fessend/fessent/fezzent [adj., <Sc. *festen* (vb.), fasten] (Ulster). Set in one's ways; advanced in years. **1983** W.F. Marshall, *Livin' in Drumlister*, 'The Runaway': 'She's a fessend oul' thing, but her father,/Wee [q.v.] Robert, he's tarble well-off.' Also **fastened** in first sense (Traynor).

feur-gortach see **hungry grass**

fey [adj., <OE *faege*, doomed to death] (Ulster). Having second sight.

fezzent see **fessend**

fiddle-faced [adj.]. Long-faced.

fiddler's [n., abbrev. of 'fiddler's curse'; 'fiddler's money'. From poor status of itinerant musicians; cf. '*fiddler's pay*, thanks and wine' (Grose).]. Implying insignificance; small change. **1987** Lar Redmond, *Emerald Square*: 'if I got rattled I spoke Liberties style and just now I did not give a fiddlers'. **1995** Joe O'Connor, *Sunday Tribune*, 23 July: 'this is very ungrateful of me. But I don't give a fiddler's anyway.'

fidge [n. & vb., <Sc. *idem*, fidget] (Ulster). As thus, as in **it wouldn't take a fidge out of me**. I would have no difficulty in...

Field, the [n.] (Ulster). Venue for Orange demonstrations on the Twelfth (q.v.). **1951** Sam Hanna Bell, *December Bride*: 'Petie Sampson and his fife were the pride of Ravara's Loyal Sons, and the little man had led his Lodge to the Field and back for many years.' **1993** Muriel Breen, *Liquorice All-sorts, A Girl Growing Up*: '"If you're good," Mumper said, "and if it's a nice day, we'll all go to 'the Field' on the 12th of July." "What's 'the Field'?" I asked her, puzzled. "It's a wonderful picnic," she said. "Run by the Orange Order."'

fient a hate see **feint a hate**

fierce [adj.]. Gen. as intens., modifying 'bad', 'serious', 'acute', etc. **1993** Mick McInerney in Joe O'Reilly & Sixth Class, Convent School, Edenderry, *Over the Half Door*: 'The farmhouse was a big house...it had eight or nine rooms. There was a front way and a back way into it and in the yard there was a fierce lot of sheds.' **1995** Interview with Daniel O'Donnell, *Sunday Tribune*, 26 Feb: 'He admits to having two "fierce" hobbies — ceili [q.v.] dancing and going to whist drives.' See also **Paraic**.

fiery-edge [abst. n., <rough edge on knife; cf. 'take the edge off one's appetite'] (Ulster). Eagerness, keenness.

Fifteen Acres, the [nickname] (Phoenix Park, Dub.). Large open area. **1907** Samuel A. Ossory Fitzpatrick, *Dublin*: 'On the left of the main road is the fine review ground, curiously designated the "Fifteen" acres, its area being some 200, where formerly many notable duels were fought.' **1914** James Joyce, *Dubliners*, 'The Dead': 'The Wellington Monument wore a gleaming cap of snow that flashed westward over the white field of the Fifteen Acres.' **1936** *Irish Times*, 25 July: 'a good open-air bathing and swimming pool, with facilities for sun-bathing. For these purposes the Fifteen Acres, unthronged as they are, would be ideal.'

fifty [n., <?] as in **she gave me fifty** (Cork). She stood me up. Also **get (a) fifty** [vb. phr.]. **1987** Con Houlihan, *Dublin Opinion*, 'The Ball Hop' (q.v.), May: 'One sporting metaphor intrigues me specially...It was *getting a fifty*. It came apparently from Gaelic football, but by what route I couldn't even hazard a guess ...It signified that some lass had made an appointment to meet you in some rather public place but hadn't kept it. And the usage implied that her action was deliberate and meant to humiliate.'

figary/figgairy see **fegary**

fight with the nails on your toes/ your own toenails [vb. phr.]. Said of s.o. prone to aggression. **1995** Shane Connaughton, *A Border Diary*: '"Do you know what it is you'd fight with the nails on your toes." "Only when I'd be done stamping on yours."' **1995** RTÉ Radio,

'The GB [Gay Byrne] Show', 1 Nov: 'She says she knows you and the two of you would fight with your own toenails.'

figure [n., poss. <'cut a figure'] (Ulster). Light summer clothing, as in **out in one's figure** [adj. phr.]. Out without a coat.

filled up [p. part. as adj.] (Ulster). Greatly afflicted, ready to burst into tears (Traynor).

fillybeg [n., <Ir. *filleadh beag*, kilt]. As thus.

finagle [vb., <?, common in US]. Fix, contrive, arrange by dubious means.

fine down [vb.]. **1800** Maria Edgeworth, *Castle Rackrent*: 'When an Irish gentleman...has lived beyond his income and finds himself distressed for want of ready money, tenants obligingly offer to take his land at a rent far below the value, and to pay him a small sum of money in hand, which they call fining down the yearly rent.'

fine thing [n. phr.]. Sexually attractive woman, less commonly man. **1991** Ferdia Mac Anna, *The Last of the High Kings*: 'He and Nelson and Hopper were planning a massive bonfire with loads of booze and joints as long as your arm; every fine thing on the hill would be invited...' **1996** *Irish Times*, 30 May: 'During the function he had been introduced to another man's wife. He told her she was "a fine thing" but later called her "a dry bitch" because she would not accept a drink from him.' **1996** Patsy McGarry, *Irish Times*: 'A group of youths waved their cans at her and sang "Rose [of Tralee], give us a wave..." "Go 'way, you fine thing you," shouted one of them. And she did.'

finger [n.]. Five pips (any suit) on a playing card. See **five fingers**.

finger, put on the long see **long finger**

fink [n., <?] as in **dead fink** [n. phr.]. Good-looking girl.

finnickity [adj., <'finicky' + 'pernickety'] (Ulster). Excessively particular.

Fir Bréaga [nickname, <Ir. *idem*, false men] (archaeology). Standing stones.

1975 Peter Somerville-Large, *The Coast of West Cork*: 'Fir Bréaga is a general term for standing stones. Throughout the country many are known as False Men, possibly an indication of phallic association.' See also **mock man**.

fire [vb. trans.]. Throw. **1990** Iris Brennan, quoted in Walter Love, *The Times of our Lives*: 'We'd have played with stones, not firin' stones like [q.v.], just playin' building wee [q.v.] houses.' **1991** Seán Ó Ciaráin, *Farewell to Mayo*: 'The Ballyglass lads were a bad crowd for "firing" stones — pelting them after us when we parted from them at the crossroads.'

first shot [n. phr.]. First distillation of whiskey or poteen (q.v.). **1938** Seumas MacManus, *The Rocky Road to Dublin*: 'he withdrew the poteen, and gave the lad an egg-shell of First-shot'. See also **singlings**.

fissake [n., <*physog*, abbrev. of *physognomy*, corruption of 'physiognomy'] (Ulster). Hallowe'en mask.

fissle [vb., <Sc. *idem*, rustle (paper etc.); bustle] (Ulster). As thus. **1804** James Orr, *Poems on Various Subjects*, 'To the Potato': 'Creesh't [see **creash**] scons stan' pil't on plates, or brislin' [see **brissle**]/A' roun' the ingle,/While a fand *Wifie* fast is fislin,/An tea-cups jingle.'

fisty [n., <Sc. *idem*, left-handed person] (Ulster). Person lacking one hand.

fit-me-tight [n., derog.]. Journeyman tailor. **1966** Patrick Boyle, *At Night All Cats are Grey*, 'The Betrayers': 'You'd have thought it was the Fifty Shilling Tailor was buying the drink instead of a little drunken scut [see **scut** 1.] of a country fit-me-tight.'

fit to be tied [adj. phr.]. Very angry. **1943** George A. Little, *Malachi Horan Remembers*: '"There was a woman beyont and she after getting him to make her a churn...divil a drop of water she put in it to make the timbers swell. She was fit to be tied when she found it leaking..."' **1989** Eoin McNamee, *The Last of Deeds*: 'up to the hilt one night in the back of the car and she got a hold of him and wouldn't let go. The fanny muscles lock up. Fit to be tied so he was with her all sweetness...'

Fitz-Brassy [nickname]. Fritz Brase, Ger. founder of Army School of Music, Mar 1923. **1991** John P. Duggan, quoting *Irish Defence Journal*, in *A History of the Irish Army*: '"Fitz Brassy" learned his English from brother officers with amusing effect: "Good morning Mr Mulcahy isn't it a 'hure [q.v.] of a day'."'

Fitzgerald-Kenny's Cows [nickname]. Detectives acquitted of assault on IRA man T.J. Ryan, 1929. **1993** Tim Pat Coogan, *Dev* (q.v.): *Long Fellow* (q.v.), *Long Shadow*: 'the police said his injuries had been caused by being "kicked by a cow". The Minister for Justice, [James] Fitzgerald-Kenny...said that he accepted their explanation; as a result the detectives were known from that time onwards as "Fitzgerald-Kenny's Cows".'

five fingers [adj. & n.]. 1. [adj.]. Excellent, dependable. 2. [n.]. Five of trumps/hearts in card-playing.

fixture [n.]. Contrivance, gadget, yoke (q.v.).

fiz see **faze**

flaa/flah [n. & vb., <?] (Cork). 1. [n.]. Sexually active girl. 2. [vb.]. Have sexual intercourse with.

flaff [vb., <Sc. *idem*, wave about] (Ulster). As thus.

flah see **flaa**

flahool/flahoolach/flahooler/flaithiúl-ach [adj., <Ir. *flaithiúlach*, lavish, generous]. As thus, but gen. mildly derog. **1962** Brendan Behan, *Quarryman* (Cork), 'That Woman': 'All I could see was a poor middle-aged woman...dressed in the cast-off hat and coat of some flahool old one [see **oul' wan**] she'd been doing a day's work for.' **1996** Kathy Sheridan, *Irish Times*, 28 Dec: 'Meanwhile, as the seconds race tick-tock-tick-tock towards the new millennium, the most we can do is stare, saucer-eyed, at the flaithiúlach ways of our neighbours up North and across the Irish Sea as they gear up on lottery billions.' Hence

flahoola [n.]. 'A large loud woman of stupendous vulgarity' (S&R).

flake [vb.]. Beat, thrash; throw. **1932** Seán O'Faoláin, *Midsummer Night Madness and Other Stories*, 'Sinners': 'I once stole an apple in the nun's orchard ...they caught me and gave me a flaking.' **1996** Christy Kenneally, *Maura's Boy, A Cork Childhood*: 'The Quarry was a blizzard of boys and girls flaking half-made snowballs with purple fingers...'

flap/flapping meeting [n./n. phr.]. Unlicensed dog/horse race. **1993** Helga Grove-Knapp in Michael Verdon, *Shawlies* (q.v.), *Echo Boys* (q.v.), *the Marsh and the Lanes* (q.v.): *Old Cork Remembered*: 'There were also the races, the flapping meetings. That was an unlicensed race and if you were seen attending or you rode in a flap or you ran a horse in it, you weren't allowed on a proper race course.' Hence **flapper track** [n. phr.]. Clandestine venue where coursing greyhounds are 'blooded' with a kill. **1966** RTÉ TV serial, *The Riordans*: 'FR SHEEHY I want to write to him [the President of Leestown Coursing Club]. I want to ask him straight if he is aware of these Flapper Tracks, if he's aware of what goes on at them, and if he proposes to do anything to stop them.'

flats [n. pl.]. Playing cards.

flatter [vb., <Sc. *flaither*, use wheedling or fawning language (CSD)] (Ulster). Coax, persuade.

flaysome [adj., <Sc. *fleysome*, frightful, terrifying] (Ulster). As thus.

fleece [vb.]. Hit, beat. **1995** Kathy Sheridan, *Irish Times*, 12 Dec: 'Mr Collins, however, believes..."some of them just do it [throw rocks at buses] by nature or because of the home system, or social deprivation...I know if it was my son, I'd fleece him."'

fleech (at) [vb., <Sc. *idem*, coax, cajole, flatter] (Ulster). As thus.

fleer [vb., cf. Sc. *idem*, ogle, make a wry face] (Ulster). Act in a giddy manner.

flegged out [p. part. as adj., cf. Sc. *fleg* (n.), stroke, random blow; Brit. sl. 'flaked out'] (Ulster). Tired out.

flick see **dead**

flinch [n., <OF *flenchir* (vb.), turn aside] (Ulster). Upset, as in **it wouldn't take a flinch out of s.o.** It wouldn't have any effect on...

flindher(s)/flinner(s) see **flitter(s)**

flipe [n.]. 1. [cf. Sc. *idem*, 'contemptuous name for a person' (CSD)] (Ulster). Impudent, immoral girl (Traynor). **1983** W.F. Marshall, *Livin' in Drumlister*, 'Our Son': 'An' the wee [q.v.] back room it wud never do/For the flipe that was raired [q.v.] in the South.' 2. Piece, portion. 3. Brim of a hat.

flipper [n., <?]. Untidy/unkempt man.

flisky [adj., <Sc. *flisk* (vb.), switch, whisk] (Ulster). Skittish (horse).

flit [vb., <Sc. *idem*, move house, <ON *flytja*, migrate] (Ulster). Move house. **1913** Alexander Irvine, *My Lady of the Chimney Corner*: '"Maybe we're goin' t'flit, where there's a perch or two wi' the house!"' **1948** John O'Connor, *Come Day — Go Day*: 'So Tommy and Teasie had flitted, and Neilly was sent over to live with his granny to keep her company.' Hence **Saturday flit, short sit** [proverbial phr.]. Superstition related to moving house/leaving hospital on a Sat. **1983** *John Pepper's Illustrated Encyclopaedia of Ulster Knowledge*: 'Saturday is also considered a day of ill omen on which to move house. The basis...is the belief that "a Saturday flit means a short sit".' **1997** Alison O'Connor, *Irish Times*, 14 Feb: '"Saturday flit, short sit" is a phrase recognised by 58 per cent of Irish patients... "The superstition implies that leaving hospital on a Saturday is bad luck and will mean early readmission..." explained Dr Elizabeth Keane...'

flitter(s) [n. pl. & vb., <*fitters* (n. pl.), fragments, pieces, <? (1532)]. Tatters; reduce to tatters. **1927** Peadar O'Donnell, *Islanders*: '"Another summer I fished in Portnoo, I was near torn in flitters with fleas."' **1987** Lar Redmond, *Emerald Square*: '"Wait till Linda gets yeh," he whispered. "An' Sis...an' Maura ...an' Rosie...they'll flitther yeh."' **1989** Hugh Leonard, *Out after Dark*: 'It was common knowledge that Englishwomen, their morals in flitters from six years of war, were coming to Ireland...' Also **flitterjigs** [n. pl.] (Ulster). **1932** *Ulster Hiker* (Cushendall, Co. Antrim), 'The Ulster Dialect', June: 'We have "flinners" or "flindhers" for broken pieces, and the delightful "flitterjigs" for small broken pieces.'

flooster [vb.]. 1. Flatter, coax. 2. (Of dog) Play, romp. 3. Confuse, fluster. Hence **flusthration** [n.]. 'Fluster in a superlative degree' (S&R).

flooter/flute [vb., cf. Sc. *fluther*, confuse, agitate]. Dither around aimlessly. **1954** James Plunkett, *Bell*, 'The Eagles and the Trumpets', Aug: '"You're spoiling my drink." "You're spoiling mine too," Higgins said, "all this fluting around."' **1995** Patrick Boland, *Tales from a City Farmyard*: 'he couldn't find the key to open the padlock. While he flootered around looking for it, both performers in the stable were getting even more excited...' Also **floother-footed** [adj.] (Ulster). Awkward, unskilled, esp. of soccer player. See also **fluthered**.

Floozie/Floozy in the Jacuzzi, the [nickname]. Monument in O'Connell St, Dub., representing the River Liffey. **1989** Ann Morrow, *Picnic in a Foreign Land*: 'Who will save the old houses from being pulverised to make way for banks, hotels ...night clubs called Floozie in the Jacuzzi?' **1993** Vincent Caprani, *The Berlitz Travellers* [*sic*] *Guide to Ireland*: 'a 1988 Millennium presentation to the city — by well-known local businessman Michael Smurfit — is an elongated female figure ...reclining in a bubbling fountain; the wags quickly christened it "the floozie in the jacuzzi"'. **1996** Róisín Ingle, *Sunday Tribune*, 28 Apr: 'The "Floozy in the Jacuzzi" and the more recent "Chime in the Slime" [q.v.] will hardly put Dublin on the landmark map.' Aka **the Hoor** (q.v.) **in the Sewer**. See also **Bidet Mulligan**.

floptious [adj., iron.]. Generous (OTF).

flough [n., cf. Sc. *flow*, Icel. *flói*, bog, morass] (Ulster). Soft turf of poor calorific quality.

flowan/flowin [n., <'flow' (vb.)] (Ulster). Light dust, esp. in flax-scutching mill.

flower see **oul' flower**

flowering [n.] (linen industry) (Ulster). Embroidery. **1956** Sam Hanna Bell, *Erin's Orange Lily*: 'His daughter "took in flowering", that is to say, she acted as an agent for several of the linen firms in the city of Belfast, and distributed embroidery work to the needlewomen of the district.'

flowers/fun and frolics [n. phr., <rhym. sl. 'bollocks'/*bollix* (q.v.) (DHS)]. Testicles.

flowin see **flowan**

flug-fisted/handed, fluggy see **fyuggy**

fluke [n., cf. Brit. sl. *idem*, stroke of luck, <lucky billiard stroke (DHS)] as in **I haven't a fluke** [neg. phr.]. I have nothing.

flute [exclam., n. & vb.]. 1. [exclam., n. & vb.]. Expression of annoyance/surprise. 2. [n., cf. *idem*, fellator (Green)]. Penis. **1990** Roddy Doyle, *The Snapper* (q.v.): '"But it's his fault as much as Sharon's. Whoever he is — it was his flute that —" "Daddy!" "Well, it was."' 3. [vb.]. See **flooter**.

fluthered [p. part. as adj., cf. Sc. *idem* (vb.), confuse, agitate]. Intoxicated. **1996** Gene Kerrigan, *Sunday Independent*, 21 Apr: 'The women, loath to risk disturbing their makeup, kiss the air over each other's shoulders as they gingerly embrace. The men exchange reminiscences about the time they got fluthered at one sports event or another.'

flutter-guts [n.] (Ulster). S.o. excessively fussy/pernickety (YDS).

flyer [n.]. 1. Cup of tea in advance of 'high tea' or a quick cup at any time. 2. See **feck** [n.] 2.

flying column [n. phr.]. Mobile volunteer unit in nationalist cause in Anglo-Ir. war, 1919–21. **1931** A.W. Kward, *An t-Óglach*, 'Tales of a Flying Column', Dec: 'One cold night in the Spring of 1921, a cordon of scouts protected the Flying Column while it slept in Knocknaskeha House.' **1949** Tom Barry, *Guerrilla Days in Ireland*: 'Wanted men...had a far better chance of survival in a Flying Column.' **1986** David Marcus, *A Land not Theirs*: '...Flying Columns ambushing patrols, convoys blown up, hunger strikes, arrests — goodness knows what'.

flying snail [nickname, <visual suggestion]. Transport company logo designed by Frank Brandt, 1941. **1992** Tom Ferris, *Irish Railways in Colour*: 'She [locomotive no. 461] was at Dungarvan ...on a special train on June 6th 1961. The CIÉ [Córas Iompair Éireann, national transport company] logo on her tender was often referred to as the "flying snail".' **1996** *Nuacht CIÉ*, Aug: 'The winged wheel...refers to the old Dublin United Transport Company logo introduced in 1941 and adopted by CIÉ in 1945. It became known somewhat irreverently as the "Flying Snail".'

fly-the-kite [n.]. Boaster, chancer (q.v.). **1948** Patrick Kavanagh, *Tarry Flynn*: '"Here is none of your fly-the-kites, Mrs Flynn. He could go where there's more money but he's not looking for money."'

fodder [vb.] see **fother**

fog [vb., <Sc. *idem*, eat heartily; cf. 'fog' (n.), long grass left standing through the winter and fed to cattle] (Ulster). Eat greedily. Hence **fog feed/meal** [n. phr.]. Lavish meal.

foile [n., <?]. Frustration. **1675–95** Anon., *Purgatorium Hibernicum*: 'Butt I will vatch de vales [watch the walls], Nees [Aeneas],/ And putt foil on dee...'

folderol/foldherol [n., <Sc. *falderal*, useless ornament, trifle] (Ulster). As thus, geegaw (q.v.).

follow copy out the window [vb. phr.] (printing). 'Compositor's phrase for keeping religiously to the manuscript, even when mistakes are blatant in it, so as to achieve maximum speed' (WS).

follower-upper/follyer-upper/folly-inupper/folly-up [n. phr.]. Weekly cinema serial, of a type pop. with the younger generation of the 1940s/1950s.

Latterly gen. for sequel etc. **1965** Lee Dunne, *Goodbye to the Hill*: '...I'd buy twopence worth of broken biscuits and munch my way through the "folly an' upper" [*sic*].' **1989** Hugh Leonard, *Out after Dark*: 'Like the hero in the weekly follower–upper at the Picture House, he unfailingly broke free from his bonds an instant before the blazing roof crashed in.' **1995** Patrick Boland, *Tales from a City Farmyard*: 'I didn't go to the Lyric [James's St, Dub.] too often, but for a time...I went every week to see a follyinupper named *Don Winslow of the Coastguard*.'

fong [n., <?]. Blow, kick. **1961** Tom Murphy, *A Whistle in the Dark*: 'MUSH ...but Hugo got him a right [see **right** 1.] fong up in the arse as he was running out the passageway.'

foof [vb., onomat.]. Howl miserably (of dog).

foogragee [n., <Ir. *fógra*, notice, proclamation + *gaoth*, wind]. Garrulous individual who cannot keep a secret (OTF).

fooster [n. & vb., cf. Ir. *fústaire*, fusspot]. Fuss or dither. **1843** Repeal song: 'Then Tommy jumped about elate,/Tremendous was his fooster-O...' **1922** James Joyce, *Ulysses*: 'What is he foostering over that change for? Sees me looking.' **1926** Sean O'Casey, *The Plough and the Stars*: 'MRS GOGAN I wondher what he is foostherin' for now?' **1995** Tom Humphries, *Irish Times*, 21 Aug: 'For 22 minutes, Dublin fiddled and foostered and allowed their nerves to get the better of them.'

foot [vb.]. Stack turf sods to dry. **1957** E. Estyn Evans, *Irish Folk Ways*: 'After lying spread on the ground for a week or two the turves are footed, that is a dozen or so are put to lean together in the shape of a pitched roof, to catch the wind.' **1960** Edna O'Brien, *The Country Girls*: 'While Hickey was cutting or footing the turf, I used to wander over to the bog lake.' **1973** Noël Conway, *The Bloods* (q.v.): '"Someone asked me what 'footing' is. It is this. You rest three sods against each other in the same manner as you stack rifles. You then lay a fourth sod on top of

them like putting the lid on a bellied three-legged pot. That's what's known as 'footing' turf and don't ask me why it's called footing. If it was good enough for the Fir Bolgs it's good enough for you!'"

footer/futter [n. & vb., cf. Ir. *fuadar* (n.), rush, bustle; Sc. *fouter* (n.), clumsy person; & see **fooster**]. 1. [n.]. Clumsy person. 2. [vb.]. Potter, fidget, fiddle about. **1990** Willie Grey, quoted in Walter Love, *The Times of our Lives*: 'He was futterin' about and there was some bad language on my behalf...'

foother see **fother**

footing [n.] (Ulster). Sense, reason.

foot, in one's [intens.] as in **I am in me foot!** [exclam. phr.]. Expressive of rejection/denial.

footless [adj.]. 1. Of an awkward walker. 2. Drunk.

footless stocking without a leg [n. phr.]. Nothing (DHS).

footy [adj., <Sc. *idem*, low, mean] (Ulster). 1. As thus. 2. Very ill. 3. Of little value. **1908** Lynn Doyle, *Ballygullion*: '"But keep your mind aisy about us; we'll not soil our fingers wi' your footy money."'

forbidden fruit [n. phr.]. Adam's apple. **1943** George A. Little, *Malachi Horan Remembers*: '"Them are my lambs," I told him. He tried to brazen it out. But I seen his "forbidden fruit" and it lepping [q.v.] in his neck.'

fordersome [adj., <Sc. *idem*, expeditious] (Ulster). Manageable.

fore [n.] as in **to the fore** [adj. phr.] (Ulster). Alive.

forget [n., <Sc. *idem*, omission, neglect] (Ulster). As thus.

fornenst/fornent/forninst [prep., <Sc. *fornens/fornenst*, opposite to]. As thus. **1914** George Fitzmaurice, *The Pie-Dish*: 'LEUM ...'Tis little respect the pair of them have for your cloth and the way they are splitting big lies fornenst your face.' **1943** George A. Little, *Malachi Horan Remembers*: 'they would be standing fornent each other and they

with pistols and they trying to blow out each other's brains. The duel they called it.' **1996** Shane Kenny, *Sunday Tribune*, 26 Mar: 'The Newfoundland dictionaries list "forninst" as one of their Irish words — and in the south shore fishing village communities, which are almost exclusively Irish, the houses are built and described as "forninst the road" — Irish style.'

Forty-Coats [nickname] (Belfast/Cork/Dub.). Street characters (see **character** 1.). 1. **1983** *John Pepper's Illustrated Encyclopaedia of Ulster Knowledge*: 'Down the years Belfast has produced..."Forty Coats", so called because he went out with at least four or five ragged coats to keep him warm...' 2. (Cork). **1993** Aine de Courcy in Michael Verdon, *Shawlies* (q.v.), *Echo Boys* (q.v.), *the Marsh and the Lanes* (q.v.): *Old Cork Remembered*: 'If you have a picture in your mind of Father Christmas, white whiskers, pink skin, big bushy eyebrows and a shock of white hair, that was *Forty-Coats*. He got his name because he had a coat and another old coat pinned over it.' See also **Johnny Forty-Coats**.

fosy see **fozy**

fother/foother/fodder [vb., <Sc. *fother*, give fodder, <ON *fothr* (n.), fodder]. Feed farm animals. **1938** Seumas MacManus, *The Rocky Road to Dublin*: 'the ghost-fearing Ned Haran and wife, who...at bedtime fothered their cattle by flinging them a wap [q.v.] of hay — from their own open door'. **1983** W.F. Marshall, *Livin' in Drumlister*, 'Sarah Ann': 'I've fothered all the kettle [cattle], an' there's nothin' afther that/But clockin' [see **clock** 2.] roun' the ashes wi' an oul Tom cat.' **1993** Mick McInerney in Joe O'Reilly & Sixth Class, Convent School, Edenderry, *Over the Half Door*: 'In the winter time I'd spend most of my time in the yard foddering cattle.'

founder [n. & vb., <Sc. *idem* <OF *fondrer*, plunge to the bottom]. [n.]. Cold, chill, as in **catch a founder** [vb. phr.]. [vb.]. Become chilled, suffer from exposure. **1927** Peadar O'Donnell, *Islanders*: '"I was out there in Traighenna

a couple of winters, an' devil such a founderin' I ever got."' **1973** Sam Hanna Bell, *A Man Flourishing*: 'James surveyed him with a melancholy smile. "Away back to the counting-house and get yourself dried out. You'll be getting a founder, man."' **1983** W.F. Marshall, *Livin' in Drumlister*, 'The Runaway': 'Calves died on me, too, in the spring-time,/The kettle [cattle] got foundered in rain,/Hens clocked [see **clock** 3.], or they took the disordher,/An' me heart warmed till Sarah agane.'

found on [adj. phr., abbrev., <'found on the premises']. Discovered drinking on licensed premises outside the permitted hours. **1991** John B. Keane, *Love Bites and Other Stories*: 'This pub was always regarded as being relatively safe because it was so near the garda barracks. Anyway Canavan and Callaghan were "found on".'

four bones [n. phr.]. Human body. **1920** Seumas O'Kelly, *The Leprechaun of Kilmeen*: '"I only came up the tree to save my four bones from being broken," said the leprechaun.' **1922** James Joyce, *Ulysses*: 'It is between the lines of his [Shakespeare's] last written words, it is petrified on his tombstone under which her four bones are not to be laid.'

four-faced liar [nickname, <differing times shown on the clock faces] (Cork). Clock and, by association, steeple of St Anne's Church, Shandon. **1987** Colm Fehily, *Dublin Opinion*, May: 'without having to actually cross the Rubi...*sorry* ...Lee (both channels) to risk murder, mayhem and moral degeneration in that dangerous region dominated by the "Four-Faced Liar"'. **1992** Antóin O'Callaghan, *Cork Holly Bough*: 'The clock at Shandon, known to generations as "The Four-Faced Liar".' Also of many other similar clocks: **1991** Bob Quinn, *Smokey Hollow*: 'Then there was that four-faced liar, the Rathmines [Dub.] town hall clock...' **1996** Kathryn Holmquist, *Irish Times*, 22 Apr: 'Time is running out for Westport's town clock, a 1940s "monstrosity" so unreliable that locals refer to it as "the four-faced liar"...'

four o'clock eyes [n. phr.] (Ulster). Squint.

fourpenny rush [n. phr.]. Cheap children's admission to matinée cinema performances, 1950s. **1965** Lee Dunne, *Goodbye to the Hill*: 'The cheaper seats were eightpence for adults and fourpence for kids. Myself, I always went to the fourpenny rush.' **1982** Éamonn Mac Thomáis, *Janey Mack* (q.v.), *Me Shirt is Black*: 'In the cowboy pictures at the Fourpenny Rush an Indian statue stood outside the tobacco shop.' **1989** Hugh Leonard, *Out after Dark*: 'the street corners, the girls on the pier, the fourpenny rush with Charles Starret as the Durango Kid'. See also **penny rush**, **twopenny rush**, **sixpenny rush**.

four prices [adj.] (Ulster). Very expensive.

four-roads [n.]. Crossroads. **1908** Lynn Doyle, *Ballygullion*: '"I never seen three or four people gathered about a four-roads but they riz a bit of a laugh before they went home.'

four-square [adj.]. In one's usual good form.

Fox and the Goose, the [n. phr.] (Ulster). Game of noughts and crosses. **1966** Florence Mary McDowell, *Other Days Around Me*: 'Sometimes, slates and slate pencils were brought out for the playing of "The Fox and the Goose"...'

foxer [n.] (Cork). Employment in the black economy, nixer (q.v.). **1966** Séamus Murphy, *Stone Mad*: 'the old boy often has a foxer in hand'. **1996** Christy Kenneally, *Maura's Boy, A Cork Childhood*: 'On any Saturday night in the [confession] box they could hear that someone had been "connyshurin'" [see **connysure**], "doin' a foxer", or "slockin'" [q.v.]...'

fozy/fosy [adj., cf. Sc. *foze* (vb.), become fusty; *foziness* (n.), sponginess, <Du. *voos* (adj.), spongy]. Spongy, over-ripe. **1994** Dermot Healy, *A Goat's Song*: 'The fozy nest between her thighs. He stopled [q.v.] her.'

frae-me-come-tae-me [n.] (Ulster). Trombone (SH). See also **come-tae-me-go-aff-me**.

freak/frake [n., <OE *frician* (vb.), dance]. As thus; frolic.

freath [n., <Sc. *idem* <OE *freothian* (vb.), froth] (Ulster). 1. Soapy water. 2. Light wash (clothes etc.).

Free State [prop. n., abbrev. of Irish Free State, established 1922, superseded by new constitution 1937] (Ulster). Latterly derog. Unionist or extreme republican ref. to Republic of Ireland. **1969** Robert Greacen, *Even without Irene*: 'He received the news of my visit to foreign parts with some display of incredulity..."But that's in the Free State," he exclaimed, "Them mickeys'll [see **Mickey**] knock the s— out of you.'" Also **Free State Border!** [exclam., rhym. sl.] (Ulster). Order! Order!

freet/freit/froot [n., <Sc. *freet* <ON *frétt*, news, augury]. Spell; omen; old wives' tale. **1817** James Orr, *The Posthumous Works of James Orr of Ballycarry*, 'The Irish Cottier's Death and Burial': 'Cou'd [cold] he whose limbs they decently had stretch'd,/The followers o' freets awake an' mark,/What wad he think o' them...' **1974** John Hewitt, *Out of my Time*: 'The farmer launched into another tale/of how a man, a famous story-teller,/to whom all happened, who was always present/when freets appeared...'

freheen [nickname, <Ir. *fraoichíní* <*fraoch*, heather] (Munster). 'Men and women from the bogs who sold loads of turf in Cashel and Thurles...they bound the tops of their carefully-built loads with decorative bands of heather' (DOM).

freit see **freet**

French fiddle [n.]. Harmonica/mouth organ. **1968** Austin Clarke, *A Penny in the Clouds*: 'the men rowed on one side of the boat, while I played treasonable music on the mouth-organ, or as it is called here [Donegal], a "French fiddle"'.

Freney [nickname, <James Freney, C18 highwayman]. One-eyed individual. **1847** John Edward Walsh, *Ireland Sixty Years Ago*: 'Those who saw and conversed with him described him as a mean-looking fellow, pitted with the small-

pox, and blind of an eye, whence Freney became a *soubriquet* for all persons who had lost an eye.'

fresh lodger [n.]. Loaf of bread. **1983** *John Pepper's Illustrated Encyclopaedia of Ulster Knowledge*: 'An order for a "fresh lodger" indicates that a cylinder-shaped loaf marked off in half-inch slices is sought.'

friend [n.] (Ulster). Relation.

fright to God [n. phr.] (Cork). Enigmatic or extraordinary individual, thing or event. **1966** Séamus Murphy, *Stone Mad*: 'You'd get a most gracious salute and then he was off — a fright to God and the world.'

frimsy-framsy/frincy-francy [n., <Sc. *frim-fram*, nonsense]. Kissing game.

fringes see **riding the fringes**

from a height [adv. phr., intens.]. Immoderately. **1995** Patrick Boland, *Tales from a City Farmyard*: 'But Joe did not depart quietly. He "effed" my Dad from a height.' See also **read**.

froot see **freet**

frosty face [n. phr.] (Ulster). Joker in pack of cards.

frowsy [adj., cf. Eng. dial. *frowsty*, ill-smelling] (Ulster). As thus, musty, foetid (Patterson).

fuck [n. & vb., not distinctively Hib.E except, perhaps, in the context of intensity of enclitic usage & in specific usages noted below]. Act of sexual connection, so to connect. **1994** Helen Lucy Burke, *Sunday Tribune*, 6 Nov: 'the bus was crowded. In the seat behind me two young men...conversed loudly in exaggerated Dublin accents. "So I fucking told him I was going to bleeding Glasnevin." "You were fucking right." "I fucking well bleeding was and I told the bleeder that I would take the fucking car"...I turned in my seat...and addressed them in loud carrying tones..."It is so boring — fuck, fuck, fuck non-stop..." Warming to my work I discussed the word "fuck" first used in its slangy sense by Catullus, and best reserved...for its original sense of having sexual intercourse. "However," I added kindly, "there are occasions such as when you drop a concrete block on your toes. You are devaluing it by using it for such expressions as 'fucking Glasnevin'."' **1995** John Boland, *Irish Times*, 1 Nov: 'he [Elmore Leonard] found Irish idioms rich in irony and metaphor. He was especially taken by the way in which Irish people frequently use obscenities as terms of endearment ("You f....g eejit (q.v.)," "I'll f....g kill you" — that kind of thing).' Also **for fuck/'s sake** [exclam., poss. Hib.E coining]. **1990** Roddy Doyle, *The Snapper* (q.v.): 'Sharon screamed. "You!" "Yeah; why not. Don't tell da, for fuck sake."' **1991** Ferdia Mac Anna, *The Last of the High Kings*: '"You'd think she'd know by now that kaftans are out," he said. "This is 1977 for fuck's sake."' Also **fuck off with yourself/fuck away off with yourself** [gen. imper.] (latter = Ulster usage). Invitation to depart hastily. **1996** *Leinster Leader* (Naas, Co. Kildare), 26 Dec: 'Judge Brophy urged Garda Hannon to tell him exactly what Mr Lowe said to him on the night. "He said you have f— all on me so you can f— off with yourself," elaborated Garda Hannon.' See also **feck** [vb.] 2., **like**.

fuckation [n., on model of 'fornication'; nonce-word?]. Act of sexual intercourse. **1663** Richard Head, *Hic et Ubique*: 'Fuy [why] by St Patrick agra [q.v.], he put de fuckation upon my weef [wife].'

fuck the begrudgers! (q.v.) [catchphrase, cf. Fr. *emmerder*, as in *je vous emmerde tous*]. Expression of virulent scorn. **1987** Vincent Caprani, *Vulgar Verse & Variations, Rowdy Rhymes & Rec-imitations*, 'How Jem the Dancer Fought and Died for Ireland': '"so no doubt he'll bitterly begrudge the fact that you and me and Vinno can sit here...and drink no end of pints till closin' time. Amn't I right?" "Yes, I suppose so. Same again Jem?" "Sound man [q.v.] Vinno. And fuck the begrudgers!"' **1996** Raymond Deane, *Irish Times*, 24 Sept: '"F★★k the begrudgers!" became the battle-cry of those determined on celebrating success at all costs...'

fuillaloo!/pillaloo!/pullaloo!/whilla-lew!/whillaloo! [exclam., <Ir. *puillillú*, cry of distress]. Alas!; distressful cry. **1663** Richard Head, *Hic et Ubique*: 'Enter *Patrick crying*. PATRICK Fuillilaloo [*sic*]! KILTORY How now Sirrah?' **1865** Michael Banim, *The Mayor of Windgap*: 'Nothing could equal the surprise of the Murphys when she began pullalooing and crying peccavi for not giving them tick...' **1991** John B. Keane, *Love Bites and Other Stories*: 'She paused, looked from one of us to another and, aided by our sympathetic faces, provided us with a virtuoso if hasty re-hash of all her previous pillalooing.' See **ullilu!**

full [adj., <*idem* in same sense, Brit. colloq. C19, now obsolete; cf. Austral. sl. in same sense] (Ulster). Intoxicated. **1908** Lynn Doyle, *Ballygullion*: 'If iver he wint to bed sober, 'twas because the pubs was shut before he got right [see **right** 1.] full...' **1981** James Milroy, *Regional Accents of English: Belfast*: '"well, she walked out of the house to come to the party and she kept saying: 'Oh, our Nellie'll be coming soon — we'll have to get her full..."' **1983** W.F. Marshall, *Livin' in Drumlister*, 'The Runaway': 'We got dhrunk, an' we fell till the fightin',/ Be me sang [q.v.] oul' John's purty tough,/It wos prime how he leathered [q.v.] all roun' him/An' him jist as full as a shugh [q.v.].' Also **as full as the Boyne** (river) [adj. phr.] in same sense.

full of a door, the [adj. phr.]. Said of a big man. **1922** James Joyce, *Ulysses*: 'Digs up near the Mater. Buckled [q.v.] he is. Know his dona? Yup, sartin, I do. Full of a dure.'

full of oneself [adj. phr., cf. Ir. *tá sé lán de féin*, he is full of himself]. Displaying exaggerated self-esteem. **1943** George A. Little, *Malachi Horan Remembers*: 'Take the word you would say to him, and him so full of himself.'

full of one's shirt, in the [adj. phr.]. In good form.

full shilling [n. phr.] as in **not the full shilling** [adj. phr., <pre-decimal coin, = 5p]. Mentally handicapped, having a 'wee want' (see **want**). **1992** Pauline

Bracken, *Light of Other Days, A Dublin Childhood*: 'The first person I remember dying was a man in Blackrock who was not the full shilling and used to run after me...' **1995** Maeve Binchy, *Irish Times*, 3 June: 'But what's all the pretence about if you are all friends, I ask, and I know my face has taken on a not-quite-the-full-shilling look which is not deliberate.'

fum/fumm [n., <?]. 1. Light toffee. 2. Brown turf. **1995** Shane Connaughton, *A Border Diary*: '"John Agnew came to the red bog with two brand new wheelbarrows...At the end of the day he hid them under bushes. Man dear [q.v.], Jordan found them, threw oul fumm atop them and set them alight."'

fun [vb.]. Joke. **1948** John O'Connor, *Come Day — Go Day*: '"John Kelly, dead?" "Aye, dead asleep." They smiled. "Ah, you're only funning!"'

fun and frolics see **flowers and frolics**

Fungie [nickname, <fisherman's nickname for bearded colleague]. Dolphin resident in Dingle Bay, Co. Kerry, 1983-. **1991** Sean Mannion, *Ireland's Friendly Dolphin*: 'the dolphin's escapades at sea soon became such a talking point in the town that one day a visitor asked if it had a name. Not wishing to disappoint the enquirer, a Dingle citizen thought one up. "Fungie," he said.'

funky knuckles (Ulster). 'Awkward person, player who fails to use proper technique during a game of marbles' (Pepper).

funt [n., vb. & exclam.]. 1. [n. & vb., poss. <'punt'] (Cork). Kick. 2. [exclam., poss. <combination of 'fuck' & 'cunt'. Nonce-word?]. **1955** J.P. Donleavy, *The Ginger Man*: 'There is a word for it all; funt. Now if you say this word upon rising in the morning and before each meal, you will see things change.'

fur coat and no drawers [adj. phr.]. Descriptive of s.o. with delusions of grandeur. Also **fur coat and margarine sandwiches**.

fushion [n., <OF *foison*, plenty; nourishing power] (Ulster). Nourishment.

Hence **fusionless** [adj.]. 'Applied to fodder of inferior quality' (*Ballymena Observer*, 1892). Useless, lacking vigour.

fusted [p. part. as adj., <Sc. *fustit*, decayed] (Ulster). As thus.

futter see **footer**

fwid [n., <Sc. *whid* (vb.), run quickly] (Ulster). Quick run; hasty flight.

fyuggy/fluggy/fyug-handed/flug-fisted/handed [adj., cf. Sc. *fyeuch!*, exclam. of disgust, reflecting gen. dislike and mistrust of left-handed people] (Ulster). Left-handed, awkward.

G

gabberloony/gobberloony [n., <*gab*, mouth, Sc. form of 'gob', see **gabby-guts**, **gobshite**] (Ulster). 'Person who acts the fool and talks too much' (SH).

gabbleblooter [n., see **blooter**]. Windbag.

gabby [adj., poss. corruption of *gammy* (q.v.)]. Bad, malfunctioning. **1994** Jimmy McLoughlin in Kevin C. Kearns, *Dublin Tenement Life*: 'and this is how I got my bad eye, very gabby eye — there was this man, "Hopalong" Cassidy...he hit me with a belt, a buckle, and it knocked the pupil right across'.

gabby-guts [n., <*gab*, mouth, Sc. form of 'gob', cf. 'gabble', see **gobshite**]. Over-loquacious individual, gen. female. **1948** Patrick Kavanagh, *Tarry Flynn*: '"You were talking to gabby-guts," said Bridie. "What had *she* to say?"'

gabslick [n., <*gab*, mouth, Sc. form of 'gob', cf. 'gabble', see **gobshite**] (Ulster). Inveterate chatterer.

gache/gatch [n., <Ir. *geáitse*, affected manner]. As thus; swagger. [pl.]. Antics. **1866** Patrick Kennedy, *Legendary Fictions of the Irish Celts*: 'she sent him to Bunclody to buy a billhook to cut the furze. When he was coming back he kep' cutting gaaches [*sic*] with it round his head...' **1966** Séamus Murphy, *Stone Mad*: '"Isn't the boss a queer man to put up with that daft article [q.v.]? He wouldn't be kept in any job for five minutes when they'd see the gache of him."' See also **gaitch**.

gack see **geck**

gadderman [n., <Ir. *cadramán*, boor, awkward person] (Ulster). Rogue; s.o. too wise for his years (YDS).

gaff [n., onomat.] (Ulster). News, gossip. **1948** John O'Connor, *Come Day — Go Day*: '"Many out?" "It's packed! You missed the gaff. The preacher got threw in."'

gaffer [n.]. 1. [contraction of 'grandfather', 1575; in the sense 'foreman, headman', 1841] (railway). Shed foreman. **1974** P.J. Currivan, *Journal of the Irish Railway Record Society*, 'Engineman's Son', Oct: 'To turn this long locomotive...my father would resort to the expedient of taking off the front buffers, but if he was short of time he might cajole the MGWR [Midland Great Western Railway] "Gaffer" (the local name for Shed Foreman) to allow him to make use of the MGWR turntable.' 2. [<?]. Child. **1960** John O'Donoghue, *In Kerry Long Ago*: '"Tell me this, my good woman...have you any supper at all to give to these little *gaffers*?"'

gag/geg [n., poss. <ON *gaghals* [adj.], with neck thrown back] (Ulster). Joke, gag; joker, as in **he's a right** (see **right** 1.) **geg**. **1979** John Morrow, *The Confessions of Proinsias O'Toole*: 'Silver's big blue eyes, still heavy with liquor, lit on me. "Hiya, Francie oul' son! Fuck this for a geg."'

gager see **gouger**

gah [n., <initials GAA, Gaelic Athletic Association]. Gaelic football, gen. derog. **1989** David Walsh, *Magill*, Sept: '[John McCarthy's] earliest memories are of walking down Cappagh Road in Finglas West [Dub.] with his kit. The lads on the street would ask "was he still playin' that gah?"'

gaisce [n., <Ir. *idem*, feat (of arms)]. As thus, & figurative. **1996** Dick Hogan, *Irish Times*, 12 Aug: 'So great was the chase that Mr Joy and his fellow goatcatchers were moved to take a libation or two on the way home to Killorglin...The story of the great gaisce on the Reeks was well appreciated...'

gaishen see **gation**

gaitch [n., <Ir. *geáitse*, affected manner, pose, gesture]. Style, technique. **1996** Christy Kenneally, *Maura's Boy, A Cork Childhood*: 'The rules [of marbles] were simple and timeless but the "gaitch" or style was everything.' See also **gache**.

gak see **geck**

galeery/galeeried [adj./p. part. as adj., <?] (Ulster). Bird-brained (Pepper).

gallant [adv., cf. Ir. *galúnta*, fine, grand]. As thus. **1948** Patrick Kavanagh, *Tarry Flynn*: 'he stood up for a moment beside the poplar and took a breath. Man alive, he was getting on gallant.'

galley [n., cf. Sc. *galliard* (adj.), gay, cheerful, lively] (Leinster). Fun, crack (see **crack** 1.).

gallon [n., metonym, cf. Ir. *galún*, vessel]. Receptacle for liquids used by manual workers, gen. kept on site. **1991** John B. Keane, *Love Bites and Other Stories*: 'In capable hands a bucket or a gallon could be transformed into a most presentable po.' Hence **get one's gallon** [vb. phr.]. Be sacked, fired. **1966** Séamus Murphy, *Stone Mad*: 'If anyone is to get his gallon he is told at four o'clock — the agreed hour's notice.' **1993** Seán Beecher in Michael Verdon, *Shawlies* (q.v.), *Echo Boys* (q.v.), *the Marsh and the Lanes* (q.v.): *Old Cork Remembered*: 'Whacker was game ball [q.v.] now. After getting his gallon from Dunlop's, he picked up a great number.'

Galloping Hogan, (the) [nickname]. Michael (?) Hogan, who poss. entered the service of France/Portugal after the Flight of the Earls. **1979** Matthew J. Culligan-Hogan, *The Quest for Galloping Hogan*: 'I believe the Galloping Hogan was Michael Hogan. Readers, critics and cynics can believe that, or favour one of the alternatives: he was captured and killed by the English at Cashel; he was killed in a battle with other Raparees [see **rapparee**]; there was more than one Hogan using the identity of the Galloping Hogan.' **1990** Robert Shepherd, *Ireland's Fate, The Boyne and After*. 'Tradition has it that Sarsfield had been guided [on the ride to Ballyneety, Co. Limerick, 1690] by the legendary Galloping Hogan, a guerilla-style Irish resistance fighter who knew the terrain intimately.'

gallous/gallus [adj. & adv., <Sc. *gallows* (adj.), depraved, rascally]. 1. [adj.]. As thus; irresponsible; lively. 2. [adj. & adv., intens.]. Very, great. **1910** J.M. Synge, *In Wicklow and West Kerry*: 'I asked him where most of the tinkers came from that are met with in Wicklow. "They come

from every part," he said. "They're gallous lads for walking round through the world."'

galluses/gealasses [n., double pl., <Ir. *gealasacha*, men's braces, <OE *galga/ gealga*, gallows] (Ulster). As thus. **1991** Shane Connaughton, *The Run of the Country*: 'Prunty wore a good pair of tweed trousers tucked into wellingtons. The trousers were held up by gealasses.' Hence **do something at the slack of one's galluses** [adv. phr.]. Do something with ease.

galoot [n., cf. Ir. *gealt*, crazy person]. Uncouth, awkward man.

galvanise [n., <Luigi Galvani, electrical pioneer, 1737–98]. Galvanised metal; object made therefrom. **1993** Mick McInerney in Joe O'Reilly & Sixth Class, Convent School, Edenderry, *Over the Half Door*. 'He told me to go out the Carrick road to where the galvanise was standing on its side.' **1994** Vonnie Banville Evans, *The House in the Faythe*: 'the population of the town seemed to be gathered on the snowy slopes, sliding on everything from tin trays and sheets of galvanise to hastily-made toboggans'.

gam see **gom**

game ball [adj. phr., <last round in game of handball]. Excellent, in good form, OK. (See also **oxo**.) **N.d.** Children's street rhyme: 'How is your oul' wan [q.v.]/Game ball./Out in the back yard/Playing ball.' **1977** Flann O'Brien, *The Hair of the Dogma*: 'You ask him, "How is tricks?" and he says...that everything is game ball.' **1980** Séamus de Faoite, *The More we are Together*, 'Pictures in a Pawnshop': '"Sullivan here in the village have it tapped in barrels," Jack said. "'Tis a bit off colour from confinement, they say, but 'tis game ball when you blow the froth off."'

gamfral/gamfril/gamful see **gamph**

gammy [adj.]. 1. [<Ir. *geamhchaoch*, bleary-eyed]. Weak-eyed; crippled (OTF). 2. [<Shelta *idem*, bad]. As thus. 3. See **gamph**.

gam on [vb., cf. *gammon*, pretend, 1812 (OED)]. As thus. **1961** Tom Murphy, *A Whistle in the Dark*: 'HARRY   Them are the ones that gam on not to know you when they meet you. MUSH Even the ones was in your own class.'

gamph/gamfral/gamfril/gamful [n., <Sc. *gamf*, buffoon] (Ulster). Foolish individual. Hence **gammy** [adj.] in same sense.

gamshowgin [n., <Ir. *caimseach* (adj.), deceitful]. Playful deceit, trickery (OTF).

gamut [n.] (Ulster). Knack, ability.

gancanagh [n., <Ir. *geancánach*, 'one of the lower and more vicious kinds of fairies' (Dinneen)]. As thus.

ganch/gaunch [n. & vb., cf. Ir. *gaimse* (n.), fool, simpleton, Sc. *ganch* (vb.), 'to be very ugly' (CSD)] (Ulster). Ignoramus, s.o. who behaves badly; talk stupidly.

gansey/gansy [exclam. & n., <Ir. *gansaí*, <'Guernsey', source of original garment]. 1. [exclam.] (Ulster). Expression of approval (TT). 2. [n.]. Wool pullover, as formerly used by fishermen etc., latterly gentrified. **1927** Peadar O'Donnell, *Islanders*: 'They carried the curragh to the Point. Charlie kicked off his boots. "Take off the gansey," Manus advised.' **1961** Dominic Behan, *Teems of Times and Happy Returns*: '...I started to think of all sorts of words and they all sounded funny ...after a while they didn't sound funny at all only they wouldn't go back the way they had been before Sister Ita called my gansey a jumper.'

gant [vb., <Sc. *idem*, yawn] (Ulster). As thus. **1993** Seamus Heaney, *The Midnight Verdict* (translation of Brian Merriman, *Cúirt an Mheán Oíche*): 'It was awe-inspiring just to see her,/So hatchet-faced and scarred and sour —/With her ganting gums and her mouth in a twist...'

gap [vb., cf. *idem*, 'make notches in', 1847 (OED)]. Cut very roughly. **1982** Éamonn Mac Thomáis, *Janey Mack* (q.v.), *Me Shirt is Black*: '"I think yeh need a haircut. How much does yer man [q.v.] in Old Kilmainham charge?" "Thru'pence, ma, but he gaps ya."'

gap of danger see **man in the gap**

gar [n., <Ir. *gáir*, cry, shout]. Long-standing row.

Garden County/Garden of Ireland [nickname; esp. journalistic use as applied to GAA teams]. Co. Wicklow, noted for its many 'big house' (q.v.) gardens. **1995** Paddy Hickey, *Irish Independent*, 3 July: 'It was very much the case of the "Garden County" digging their own grave by indulging in some appallingly sub-standard play.' **1996** Róisín Ingle, *Sunday Tribune*, 11 Feb: 'The Chinese spy satellite which some experts predicted would plunge to earth somewhere in the Garden of Ireland within the next month may now land in Limerick instead...'

gargle [n.]. Alcoholic drink. **1991** Roddy Doyle, *The Van*: 'but it wasn't the gargle he was dying for: it was this...the lads here, the crack [see **crack** 1.].' **1994** Kevin C. Kearns, *Dublin Tenement Life*: 'he [Timmy 'Duckegg' Kirwan] would deliberately walk beneath the windows of certain kip [q.v.] houses where the prostitutes would be "roaring out the windows and they'd let down a can with a string on it and money'd be in the can to get cigarettes and matches or get them a gargle at the pub"'. **1995** Ronnie Drew, quoted in *Sunday Tribune*, 22 Oct: 'there are times when I get the urge for a pint, but I keep thinking of the horror days when I had too much of the gargle'. Also **gargled** [p. part. as adj.]. Drunk. **1987** Lar Redmond, *Emerald Square*: 'Her oul' fella [q.v.] came in shortly afterwards. Half gargled, he found a few blankets and doggedly started to cover the [bird] cages.' **1995** Brendan O'Carroll, quoted in *Sunday Independent*, 26 Nov: '"It's so important now that I don't f**k this up, it's so important now that I don't become a junkie, it's so important that I don't fall out of pubs gargled."'

Garlic/Garland Sunday [nickname]. Last Sunday in July. **1957** E. Estyn Evans, *Irish Folk Ways*: '...Lammas, originally 1st August, now held on Lammas Sunday... which is also known as Garland, Bilberry or Height Sunday'.

garraun [n., <Ir. *gearrán*, gelding]. Term of abuse.

Garrett Reilly as in **not for the world and Garrett Reilly** [catchphrase, <?]. In

no circumstances. Also **the world and Garrett Reilly** [catchphrase]. Everyone. **1985** Máirín Johnston, *Around the Banks of Pimlico*: 'I had never been to a party in my life and so I was quite excited. The world and Garrett Reilly were there...'

Garryowen [n., poss. <term for high kick forward, <Garryowen rugby club, Limerick] (army, Lebanon). State of alert. **1996** Jim Cusack, *Irish Times*, 27 Apr: 'The 79th Battalion members assembled in the camp's square to be addressed by a man with a megaphone who informed them that a state of "Garryowen" was in place — which meant that they must wear flak jackets and helmets at all times outdoors and in unprotected buildings.'

garsoon/garsun/gorsoon [n., <Ir. *garsún*, poss. <Fr. *garçon*, boy; see **gosoon**]. Boy, freq. derog. **1973** Sam Hanna Bell, *A Man Flourishing*: '"You've worked hard on that land all your life," said Kate..."I want none of it." She struck the table. "Half a farm, ye poor silly garsun!"' **1991** John B. Keane, *Love Bites and Other Stories*: 'When I was a gorsoon in Renagown in the Stacks Mountains there was no such thing as insomnia.'

gas [adj. & n., cf. US sl. *a gas*, something very impressive, pleasurable, effective (DAS)]. Funny or extraordinary; a lot of fun. **1965** Lee Dunne, *Goodbye to the Hill*: 'It was great gas, with me imagining I was Roy Rogers on Trigger, galloping after the outlaws.' **1969** Frank O'Connor, *Collection Three*, 'A Minority': 'Everything with Stein was "gas". His mother...let him have everything he wanted, so she was "great gas"...[his father] was gas, too, though not, Denis gathered, great gas.' **1995** Seán Moran, *Irish Times*, 22 July: 'It's gas the extent to which Galway have suddenly thrown off eight years of gloom and underachievement to become favourite for tomorrow's Connacht final...'

gashun see **gation**

gasoor [n., see **garsoon**, **gosoon**] (Connacht). Boy. **1991** Seán Ó Ciaráin, *Farewell to Mayo*: 'To our elders we were not known as "boys"; to them we were

"Gasoors", "the Gasoors of the village", never "garsoons", as I believe boys were called in some parts of Ireland.'

gasworks [nickname]. Inhaler for sufferers from asthma etc. **1995** Sam McAughtry, RTÉ Radio, *Sunday Miscellany*, 26 Nov: '"Have you tried the gasworks?" "No, the gasworks is for children with bronchitis, Mrs Henry..."'

gatch see **gache**

gather–'em–up/gather–up [n.]. Useless individual. **1979** Michael O'Beirne, *Mister, A Dublin Childhood*: '"That oul gather–em–up," mother said in disgust. "With his bike and his blarney [q.v.]."'

gation/gaishen/gashun [n., cf. Sc. Gael. *gaisean*, stalk, young boy; Ir. *gasúr*, *idem*] (Ulster). Very thin person.

gattle [vb., <?] (Cork). Chase girls (Beecher).

gaubey [n., <Ir. *gabhgaire*, onlooker (at cards), hanger–on]. 'A person who with an expression of intense curiosity rudely stares at others engaged in a game or occupation' (OTF).

gaug [n., <Ir. *gág*, crack in skin]. As thus. **1931** A.W. Kward, *An t-Óglach*, 'Tales of a Flying Column [q.v.]', June: 'Frank Ryan had worked hard since early youth to help to keep the roof-tree over his father and mother. The "gaugs" of labour seamed his hands...'

gauger see **gouger**

gaulder/gulder [n. & vb., <Sc. *gulder*, boisterous shout, shout thus] (Ulster). As thus. **1908** Lynn Doyle, *Ballygullion*: 'Thin down went the lookin' glass...An' ivery clatther there was a guldher av an oath from him, and a screech from her in the bed.' **1979** John Morrow, *The Confessions of Proinsias O'Toole*: 'humming and sawing like a claque of Uncle Toms round the old plantation door. I had two Powers [see **Baby Power**] down me and was starting on a third before they guldered the last stanza.' **1996** Martina Devlin, *Sunday Tribune*, 'Confessions', 2 June: 'There was too much screaming and guldering and I was concerned that all that tension would distress the baby.'

gaumaction see **gom**

gaunch see **ganch**

gauzer/gawzer [n., poss. <'gorgeous']. Beautiful girl, fine thing (q.v.).

gawk [n. & vb., <Sc. *idem* (n.), fool, lout, <OE *geac*, cuckoo]. 1. [n. & vb.]. Gape, stare. **1995** Phil O'Keeffe, *Down Cobbled Streets, A Liberties Childhood*: 'Mother gathered us tightly round her and told us to face forward and stop our gawking.' **1996** Uinsionn Mac Dubhghaill, *Irish Times*, 12 Sept: 'He reached Claremorris in a hired car at about 8 a.m. on the Monday [after Mayo's win in the 1936 football final]...A few of the farmers recognised O'Malley and his driver and came over to have a gawk at Sam [q.v.] before returning to more serious business.' 2. [vb.] (Cork). Vomit; be about to vomit. Hence **have the gawks**.

gawm see **gom**

Gawney Mac/Mack! [expletive, euphem.] (Dub.). Jaysus! (q.v.). **1982** Éamonn Mac Thomáis, *Janey Mack* (q.v.), *Me Shirt is Black*: 'The words "Gawney Mack" is the swanky way of saying "Janey Mack". You see the word "Gawney" suits the Rathgar accent, whereas the word "Janey" would sound downright vulgar when used by people who speak pound notes.'

gawp [n. & vb., <ON *gapa* (vb.), stare with mouth open]. One who stares vacantly, stare thus. **1991** Shane Connaughton, *The Run of the Country*: 'Prunty laughed. "You shoulda seen your face when your wan [q.v.] rode by." "My face? I was the only one didn't gawp."'

gawrey see **gorry**

gawzer see **gauzer**

gay/gey/gye/guy [adj. & adv., <Sc. *gey* <Std Eng. 'gay'] (Ulster). 1. [adj.]. Good (at something); fine, bright (of weather); large (in number, size, etc.). 2. [adv.]. Very. **1913** Alexander Irvine, *My Lady of the Chimney Corner*: 'Some said she would make "a gey good schoolmisthress", for she was fond of children.' **1951** Sam Hanna Bell,

December Bride: '"Martha," he said, "don't be harsh on the girl. She's gey sad at ye leaving."'

Gaybo [nickname, <first name + endearment suffix]. Gay (Gabriel) Byrne (1934–), pop. RTÉ Radio and TV presenter. **1995** Headline, *Sunday Tribune*, 27 Sept: 'RTÉ fearful of life after Gaybo'. **1995** Lise Hand, *Sunday Independent*, 3 Dec: 'Nor was Hillary [Clinton] entirely without any jokes; she had the temerity to scold a certain "prominent television talk-show host"...Poor old Uncle Gaybo, handbagged by Hillary.' **1995** Gay Byrne in Seán Power (ed.), *Those were the Days, Irish Childhood Memories*: 'And that's how Uncle Gaybo turned out to be the thieving rascal and general no-good layabout which he is today.'

Gaybrick [nickname, <Ir. *ar oibrigh sé?* did it work?] (Munster). **1989** Leslie Matson, *CARA*, 'Introducing Waterford', Mar/Apr: 'Tramore is a favourite destination for visitors from inland areas such as Tipperary — at one time they were known as "Gaybricks" because many went boating deliberately to get sea-sick, for their health's sake. Their friends would call to them in Irish "Ar oibrigh sé?"...'

gaza [n., <'gas' + endearment suffix] (Cork). Gas lamp. Hence, in dismissive sense, **go wax a gaza!** Go climb a gas lamp! **1985** R.T. Cooke & Marion Scanlon, *Guide to the History of Cork*: 'a common game among children in Cork was to "wax the gaza", meaning to climb the gas lamp poles'.

gazaybo/gazaybee/gazebo [n., poss. <Sp. *gazapo*, artful fellow, via US. sl. *gazebo*; cf. Austral. *gazob*, mug, fool]. Fool. **1983** W.F. Marshall, *Livin' in Drumlister*, 'The Runaway': 'Sez I, "Wull ye come for a half-wan [see **half-one**]?/ Ye'll not. Well, listen to this./Yon hirplin' [q.v.] gazaybo, yir father,/He'll say neither ay, naw nor yis.'

gazened/gizzened [p. part. as adj., cf. Icel. *gisna*, become leaky]. Cracked from heat/dryness, hence made uncomfortable by hot weather.

gealasses see **galluses**

geanc [n., <Ir. *geanc*, snub nose] (Cork). As thus (Beecher).

geatch [n., cf. Sc. *geck*, act of deception, Mid. Du. *geck*, jest]. Caper, misdemeanour. **1986** Padraic O'Farrell, *'Tell me, Sean O'Farrell'*: 'after that incident she couldn't get a neighbour to help with the sowing or the reaping or the threshing. She was shunned, the poor woman, for her daughter's "geatch"...'

geatled [adj., cf. Sc. *geetle* (vb.), spill over] (Ulster). Exhausted, worn out (YDS).

geck/gack/gak/geek [n. & vb.] (Ulster). 1. [n. & vb., <Sc. *geck*, toss of the head, scornful air; mock, deride, scoff at, <Mid. Low Ger. *gecken* (vb.), make a fool of]. As thus; s.o. who talks behind another's back. 2. [n.]. Weird-looking man (SH).

gee [n., poss. abbrev. of **gowl** 2.]. Vagina. **1991** Roddy Doyle, *The Van*: 'But he'd had to keep feeling them up and down from her knees up to her gee.' **1991** Bob Quinn, *Smokey Hollow*: 'Occasionally he would say "feck [see **feck** (vb.) 2.] it" or "a pain in me ah [arse]". His children could have expanded his vocabulary, with bollix [q.v.], cunt, gee and the rest of the normal everyday speech they heard...' **1996** Phone-tapping of conversation between paedophiles, *Sunday Tribune*, 25 Aug: '"I love the way the little one climbs across and sticks her butt out and shows her gee from the back, that's nice, isn't it?"'

geegaws [n. pl., <'gewgaw']. Flashy, meretricious ornaments etc. **1973** Sam Hanna Bell, *A Man Flourishing*: 'Kate looked up with candid eyes..."Will I give them back? Mr Gordon said they were but —" she hesitated over the unfamiliar word, "but *geegaws*."' **1991** Bob Quinn, *Smokey Hollow*: 'he and the other kids were doing the ceremonial parade down the stairs with their parents' presents: a packet of hairpins, six razor blades...cheap Woolworths geegaws with sentimental poems to the best mother and father in the world'.

geek [n. & vb., <Sc. *keek*, peep, cf. Ir. *caoch* (vb.), wink] (Ulster). 1. [n. & vb.]. Peep, cautious look; look thus. 'Take a wee [q.v.] geek and see if she's cummin' (Pepper). **1979** John Morrow, *The Confessions of Proinsias O'Toole*: '"But just now I'd like you to tell me the name of thon unfortunate cratur [see **craythur** 2.] over there and let me have a quick geek in your wee [q.v.] attaché case."' 2. [n.]. See **geek**.

geelig/geelug [n., cf. Sc. *gelloch/gellock*; Ir. *gailseach*, earwig] (Ulster). As thus.

geezer [n., <?] (Dub.). Cat. **1982** Éamonn Mac Thomáis, *Janey Mack* (q.v.), *Me Shirt is Black*: 'A woman was complaining one time, about the trouble she had trying to heat the washing water. "Why don't you get a 'geezer' [geyser]," said me Ma. "Sure what would I be doing with a cat?" said she, "and me with two dogs."'

geg see **gag**

General, the [nickname]. Dub. criminal Martin Cahill, murdered 1994. **1988** Michael O'Higgins, *Magill*, July: 'The *Sunday World* ran a front page story naming Martin Cahill as Dublin's top criminal, though they didn't say he was the man known as "The General". The *Sunday Tribune* went a step further and became the first to name the General as Martin Cahill.' **1995** Pádraig Yeates, *Irish Times*, 3 June: 'Martin Cahill, The General, Tango One were the various names by which a chubby, balding, shabbily dressed, middle-aged Dubliner with a benign smile and two families was known to his friends.'

Gentry, the [prop. n.]. Evil fairies. **1960** John O'Donoghue, *In Kerry Long Ago*: '"the Gentry are the people fond of pleasant pastimes, that sell their souls forever to the devil...In return they can have all the pleasures of the world until they die. They say they go about in batches when the darkness gives them cover, sweeping lovely girls to their mansions in the cities, leaving yellow, sickly changelings in their places..."'

get [n., <ON *geta* (vb.), <beget; abbrev. of *hoor's get* (q.v.)]. Despicable individual; gen.

term of abuse. **1965** Lee Dunne, *Goodbye to the Hill*: 'whether he's been a cheeky little gett [*sic*] or not, I was awful glad to have had him for my brother'. **1970** Christy Brown, *Down All the Days*: '"Fact is, ma'am, the young gets have scarpered — did a bunk."' **1987** Lar Redmond, *Emerald Square*: 'Ernie grinned. "Chapel, me arse," he said bluntly. "Not for that oul' get..." "Janey [see **Janey Mac!**], Ern," I said, genuinely shocked...' See also **git**.

getaffye [vb. phr., imper.] (Ulster). Get undressed, as in instruction to child, **go up and getaffye**. See **getonye**.

get away [vb., usu. in p. tense, euphem.] (Ulster). Die.

get/go away ou'/outa that! [exclam.]. Expression of derision/disbelief.

getherer [n., cf. Sc. *gaitherer*, 'one who collects corn for binding into sheaves' (CSD)]. Agricultural rake. **1991** James Kennedy, *The People who Drank Water from the River*. 'The four of us...stood round around the [potato] pit with hurleys, while my father carefully probed it with the blunted tooth of a "getherer".'

get off [vb. intrans.] (teenagers). Indulge in French kissing. **1996** Frances O'Rourke, *Irish Times*: 'The etiquette, apparently, is strict: no one attempts to "get off" at a disco unless permission has been granted. Among younger teenagers, this is generally arranged by friends. If someone fancies "getting off" with someone, their friends approach the object of desire. If he or she is agreeable, the pair proceed to the disco floor and French kiss each other for as long as they can keep breathing or until the music stops.' See also **shift** 1.

get one's eyes together [vb. phr.] (Ulster). Have a nap.

get one's pot scripped [vb. phr., <'scraped'] (Ulster). Go to (Catholic) Confession.

getonye [vb. phr., imper.] (Ulster). Get dressed. See **getaffye**, **put on**.

get them off ya! [catchphrase]. Invitation to lady to remove her knickers, gen. applied as term of jovial abuse; cf. get up the yard! (q.v.). **C.1950s** Overheard in a Dub. cinema: *Male voice from back row*: 'Get them off ya!' *Female voice from front stalls*: 'I haven't any on me!' *Male voice*: 'Where are ya?' **1977** Wesley Burrowes, *The Riordans*: 'The crowd, good-humoured and noisy, co-operated when told that we were about to shoot, but more would then arrive ...and would fire their contributions over the heads of the others: "The hard [q.v.] Benjy!" "Any news Minnie?" "Get them off you Maggie!"' **1996** Christy Kenneally, *Maura's Boy, A Cork Childhood*: 'the film was subtitled by shouts from the gallery. "He's behind ye, ye flipping gowl [q.v.]," was the advice to the hero and, "Get 'em off ya!" was the admonition to the heroine.'

get up the yard! [exclam., catchphrase]. Crude invitation to sexual congress or simply to 'get lost'. **1979** Frank Kelly, *The Annals of Ballykilferret*: 'Suddenly there was a cry, terrifying in its aloneness in the empty ether, "Get up the yard, ye silly bollocks [see **bollix**], yer flies is open!"' **1986** Gene Kerrigan, *Magill*, Jan: 'How often has one turned away in despair as one watched from the Dáil press gallery while Deputies stooped to such vulgarisms as "Gerrup the yard ya feckin [see **feck** (vb.) 2.] bowsie [q.v.]" or "Yer uncle was a B Special [see **B man**]"?' **1995** Tom Widger, *Sunday Tribune*, 1 Oct: 'after some featherweight frolics about a St Patrick's day edition and a feature on nude colleens [q.v.], "get up the yard, yeh girrul, yeh [see **yeh-boy-yeh!**]!" — O'Donnell was allowed rabbit on about the *Playboy* philosophy...'

gey see **gay**

ghost bus [nickname]. Unscheduled service, gen. returning to the garage at night. **1994** Gabriel Byrne, *Pictures in my Head*: 'so off we trudged, shoulders hunched, clinging tightly to each other, glancing behind now and again to see if the ghost bus might come'.

gibbets see **jibbets**

gick [adj. & n.]. Disgusting, unpleasant; excrement; nausea. **1996** Edna O'Brien, *Down by the River*: '"I'm disgusted...all you people with liberal tendencies is what's destroying the country...it gives me the gick.'" Also **gicky** [adj.]. Mildly unpleasant.

giddum [abst. n., <Ir. *giodam*, restlessness, liveliness] (Cork). High spirits; 'he has a lot of giddum in him today' (Beecher).

giff-gaff [n. phr.] (Ulster). Mutual giving. **1932** *Ulster Hiker* (Cushendall, Co. Antrim), 'The Ulster Dialect', June: 'An Ulster proverb says: Giff-gaff makes good friends...'

gig [n.]. 1. [poss. onomat.]. Fun, joke. **1996** Dermot Healy, *The Bend for Home*: '"Phone, said your mother, for the gig of the thing. And she started laughing.' 2. [<wheeled vehicle]. Children's pushcart. **1994** Greg Dalton, *My Own Backyard, Dublin in the Fifties*: 'if there were a set of wheels there [on the scrap heaps] for a gig they were our property and that was that'.

gillaroo [n., <Ir. *giolla rua*, red fellow]. Subspecies of trout found esp. in Lough Melvin, Co. Fermanagh. **1966** E.V. Malone, *Harp* (Guinness, Dub.), Christmas: 'In the booklet entitled *Angling in Northern Ireland*...the gillaroo is described as "handsome, golden trout indigenous to Lough Melvin. They are reputed to have a gizzard like that of a fowl."' **1990** Brian Inglis, *Downstart*: 'it was there my father had learned to fish for what he called "gillaroos", an indigenous Melvin species'.

gimp [n., cf. Sc. *idem* (adj.), elegant, slender, neat]. Swagger. **1996** Dermot Healy, *The Bend for Home*: 'Painted the outside of the house. Got terrible rubs from the house painters like Tom Dale and Dinny Brennan. Look at the gimp of him, said Dinny.'

gingle [n., <'jingle']. As thus. **1925** Liam O'Flaherty, *The Informer*: 'as soon as ye can smell yersel' after a good meal and there's a gingle in your rags, ye stick yer nose in the air an' you know nobody'.

ginnle [vb., <Sc. *idem*, 'tickle trout, by groping under stones with the hands' (CSD)] (Ulster). As thus. See **sprick**.

gipe/gype [n., <Sc. *idem*, awkward person, fool, cf. ON *geip*, nonsense] (Ulster). Fool, 'half-way between a lig [q.v.] and a shloother [q.v.]' (quoted DOM); clumsy/awkward person; long-legged person; silly girl.

girn/gurn [vb., <'grin' with metathesis of r] (Ulster). Moan, complain; become agitated; show teeth in rage, disappointment, etc. **1927** Peadar O'Donnell, *Islanders*: 'a glowering heavens, low and threatening, hanging over a sea beginning to gurn and toss'. **1983** W.F. Marshall, *Livin' in Drumlister*, 'Sarah Ann': 'A crooked, crabbit crathur that bees neither well nor sick,/Girnin' in the chimley corner, or goan happin' on a stick.' **1996** Hugh Leonard, *Sunday Independent*, 21 Apr: 'This is a lovely place for lunch, and you can always cross your eyes and do a spot of gurning at the passers-by who stick their noses against the window.' Also **girney gob** [n. phr.]. Constantly crying child.

girsha [n., <Ir. *girseach*, young girl]. As thus.

git [n., var. of *get* (q.v.)]. Term of abuse. **1995** Patrick Boland, *Tales from a City Farmyard*: 'The Da [q.v.] advanced slowly ...snarling though gritted teeth: "Get out of this yard, you snotty-nosed oul' git."' **1995** Roddy Doyle, *Irish Times*, 'One Last Hurrah', 16 Dec: 'He [Jack Charlton] wasn't a git after all. By the end of the 1990 World Cup I was ready to name my children after him — enter the Doyles: Jack, Jackie, Jacqueline, Jacqui, John and Jacques.'

git up [n., <Dub. pronun. of Brit. sl. 'get-up', dress, appearance]. As thus. **1994** Gabriel Byrne, *Pictures in my Head*: 'Twelve chin Doberman conductor with Santa Claus cheeks. "The git up of youse [q.v.]! I hope it keeps fine for youse!"'

give off/out [vb., abbrev. of 'give out the hour']. Expostulate, complain strongly. **1908** Lynn Doyle, *Ballygullion*: '"Wheesht [q.v.], fiddler, wheesht," sez Sammy in desperation; for he'd heard the fiddler givin' out the hour before, an' knowed his capacity.' **1970** Christy

Brown, *Down All the Days*: '"If I eat any more turnips I'll turn bleeding yellow." "Ah, don't be always giving out," said Mother.' **1996** Dermot Healy, *The Bend for Home*: 'Dermot, she said again, say something. Give off to me but don't stay quiet.' Also **give out the pay**, **give out yards** in same sense. **1966** Patrick Boyle, *At Night All Cats are Grey*, 'The Betrayers': 'Mrs Nesbitt, a bitter-tongued old wasp, gave out the pay as we stood at the gate watching.' **1968** Myles na gCopaleen, *The Best of Myles*: 'If you want to hear the pay given out in right [see **right** 1.] style, get the brother on to the doctors. Fierce [q.v.] language he uses sometimes!'

gizzened see **gazened**

glaik see **gleek**

glam/glaum/glawm [n. & vb., <Ir. *glám* (vb.), grab, clutch]. As thus. **1966** Séamus Murphy, *Stone Mad*: 'When her back was turned he put out his hand an' made a glaum at a piece.' **1983** W.F. Marshall, *Livin' in Drumlister*, 'The Runaway': 'Boys ye never seen sichin [q.v.] a han'lin' [see **handlin'**],/I wos thunnersthruck watchin' the birl [q.v.],/The oul' da limpin' out wi' the pitchfork,/An' the frens makin' glam for the girl.'

glar/glaur [n., cf. Sc. *glaur/glawr*, mud, dirt, ooze] (Ulster). As thus. **1925** Lynn Doyle, *Dear Ducks*: 'It was just like one of them sea lions...only instead of having a sealskin coat on him he was one solid mass of mud an' glar.' **1927** Peadar O'Donnell, *Islanders*: '"It'd be fine for her to have a day in the stran' there, where there's a glar, and she up to her waist in dirt and wet."' **1979** John Morrow, *The Confessions of Proinsias O'Toole*: 'pouring myself a jam–jar of blood–red tea. All the cups were coated with stout glaur from the last roulette school.'

glasheen/glawsheen [n., <'glass' + Ir. dimin. *ín*, gen. iron.]. Small glass of strong drink. **1968** Myles na gCopaleen, *The Best of Myles*: 'Between yourself, meself and Jack Mum [q.v.], Charley is a little bit given to the glawsheen.'

glass [n.]. Half-pint of stout or beer. **1989** Claude Robinot in Michel Sailhan (ed.), *Irlande*, 'Le Pub, mode d'emploi': 'Pour commander, énoncez le contenant suivi du contenu, par exemple "A pint of Harp" ou "A glass (on dit rarement 'half-pint') of Smithwicks..."' ('To order, state the container followed by the contents, for example "A pint of Harp" or "A glass (you rarely hear 'half-pint') of Smithwicks..."')

glasser [n., <'glass' + endearment suffix]. Glass marble. **1982** Éamonn Mac Thomáis, *Janey Mack* (q.v.), *Me Shirt is Black*: 'One big steeler [q.v.] was worth one hundred glassers and a thousand white chalkers [see **chalk** 1.].' Also **glassy** (Ulster). As thus.

glaum see **glam**

glaur see **glar**

glawm see **glam**

glawsheen see **glasheen**

gleed [n., <Sc. *idem*, glow, spark, red ember] (Ulster). 1. Glow, glimmer. **1811** Francis Boyle, *Miscellaneous Poems*, 'The Coal Hole, A Strange Tale': 'Let every matron wish guid speed,/That boils a pot, or harns [see **harning iron**] her bread,/Or hings the kettle owre a gleed/At close of day...' 2. Spark of intelligence, as in **the man hasn't a gleed**.

gleek/glaik [n. & vb.]. 1. [n. & vb., cf. Sc. *glee* (vb.), squint, look sideways] (Ulster). Peep. **1938** Seumas MacManus, *The Rocky Road to Dublin*: 'the good earnest man, determined to catch his victim in crime, gleeked into the very mouseholes, searching a pretext for reprimand and Report'. 2. [n. pl., cf. Sc. *glaik* (vb.), spend time playfully]. Rough play. **1986** Padraic O'Farrell, *'Tell me, Sean O'Farrell'*: 'there'd be Black Bottom Irish when I'd come back in because I'd have to trounce you for carrying on with your gleeks'.

gleg/gleggy [adj. & n., <ON *gleggr* (adj.), sharp-sighted, clever] (Ulster). [adj.]. As thus. [n.]. Gossip. **1844** Robert Huddleston, *A Collection of Poems and Songs on Rural Subjects*, 'The Lammas Fair

(Belfast)': 'There sits a tinker wi' his tins,/A turner wi' his ladles;/A gleg tongu'ed spunkie's [q.v.] cryin' spoons...'

glengorm [n., cf. Sc. *glengore*, venereal disease] (Ulster). Dirt, muck (TT).

glick/glic [adj., <Ir. *glic*, clever, crafty, cunning]. As thus, gen. derog. **1986** Padraic O'Farrell, *'Tell me, Sean O'Farrell'*: 'Taking advantage of the great number of Thomond-men lost in the battle [of Clontarf] the glick (wily) Desmonds demanded that one of theirs should assume the throne.' **1996** Dermot Healy, *The Bend for Home*: 'Well we don't want anyone else's leavings, she laughed sarcastically. We all know about you, you glick fucker.'

gligeen/glugeen [n., <Ir. *gligín*, babbler]. Empty-headed individual. **1960** John O'Donoghue, *In Kerry Long Ago*: '"Why didn't they travel along the road?" I asked in surprise..."They had no roads in those days, you *glugeen*," she said.'

glimmer-man [nickname, <glimmer of gas remaining in pipes when supply had been turned off]. Inspector employed to check on unauthorised use of domestic gas during 'Emergency' period (1939–45). Cartoon in *Dublin Opinion*: 'Glory be, the Glimmer Man!' (Housewife on opening oven to discover g.m. crouching inside.) **1978** Bernard Share, *The Emergency*: 'The Emergency threw up its quota of national bogeymen, amongst whom could be numbered...Glimmer Men. "Look out missus, here's the glimmer man!" echoed from street to street as that individual arrived...to lay hands on your jets to see were they still warm.' **1995** Seamus Martin, *Irish Times*, 18 Aug: 'One menu posted outside a Dublin restaurant mentioned that a certain item would be "glowfried", a term which brings thoughts of glow-worms or even the glimmer-man to mind.'

glit [n., <OF *glette*, slime, filth] (Ulster). As thus.

glorags [n. pl., cf. Ir. *meall a lárag*, his posteriors (Dinneen)]. Buttocks (Moylan).

glory hole [n. phr.]. Space under stairs in terrace-type houses. **1983** *John Pepper's*

Illustrated Encyclopaedia of Ulster Knowledge: 'Obstreperous children would be threatened: "If you don't be good you're for the glory hole."'

gloss/glose [n., <Sc. *glose*, 'act of warming oneself at a quick fire' (CSD), <ON *glossi*, blaze] (Ulster). Heat at a fire.

glouter [n., see **clouter**] (Ulster). Sticky, wet mess, hence tapioca.

glue, to have one's [adj. phr., <?]. Retort indicating rejection. **1988** Gabriel Byrne, *Magill*, May: '"And then I have to go out to Papua New Guinea to convert all the pagans out there. You can come out and visit me." "You have your glue," he said and walked on.' **1990** Roddy Doyle, *The Snapper* (q.v.): '"A bike's much too dear for a birthday," said Veronica. "God, yeah. He has his glue..."'

glugeen see **gligeen**

gluggar [n., <Ir. *ubh ghlugair*, rotten egg]. As thus, term of abuse.

glunch [vb., <Sc. *idem*, frown, grumble] (Ulster). As thus. **1913** Alexander Irvine, *My Lady of the Chimney Corner*: 'I handed out a handful of marbles. "Now don't glunch, dear, when I tell ye what I want thim fur." I promised.'

glundie/glundy [n., <Sc. *idem*, inert, awkward lout] (Ulster). Bad-mannered/clumsy/surly/blundering individual.

glype [n., <Sc. *idem*, stupid individual]. As thus. **1983** *John Pepper's Illustrated Encyclopaedia of Ulster Knowledge*: '"Alec's a porn [born] glype. Spoke back to his morr-in-law."'

go [vb. as n.]. One visit to a well, as in **a go of water**.

goal [n., poss. <Fr. *gaole/geôle*, prison]. As thus. **1867** Patrick Kennedy, *The Banks of the Boro*: 'Come pay for the whole, Or else you'll be first man in the goal'.

goamey see **gom**

goat's toe [n. phr.] (Ulster) as in **he's no goat's toe**. He's no fool.

go away ou'/outa that! see **get away ou' that!**

gobberloony see **gabberloony**

gobdaw [n., <Ir. *gabhdán*, gullible person]. **1968** Myles na gCopaleen, *The Best of Myles*: 'The ignorant self-opinionated soft-minded suet-brained ham-faced mealy-mouthed streptococcus-ridden gang of natural gobdaws.' **1989** Hugh Leonard, *Out after Dark*: '"What kind of gobdaws are yous [q.v.]," he said, "to be made eejits [q.v.] of be the English?"' **1996** Joe O'Connor, *Sunday Tribune*, 30 June: 'If you, major gobdaw who wrote in, knew anything at all about Myles [na gCopaleen] you would know that He was not exactly behind the door [q.v.] when it came to such borrowings Himself.' See also **daw**.

gobeen [n., <Ir. *gob*, beak, bill, mouth + dimin. *ín*.]. Term of abuse, gobshite (q.v.). **1939** Sean O'Casey, *I Knock at the Door*: '"The dirty dhrop's in him [Parnell: see **the Uncrowned King of Ireland**], or he wouldn't be rallyin' all the gobeens of the counthry against the interests an' comfort of the few decent people left livin' here."'

gobhawk [n., cf. Ir. *gobachán*, sharp-tongued, inquisitive or interfering person]. As thus. **1961** Flann O'Brien, *The Hard Life*: 'They'd [policemen] swear a hole in an iron bucket. They are all the sons of gobhawks from down the country.' See also **shitehawk**.

go-boy [n.]. (Juvenile) delinquent, chancer (q.v.). **1985** Máirín Johnston, *Around the Banks of Pimlico*: 'granny hung the bird up on the wall outside the window to get it out of her sight. She forgot all about it and at some time during the day didn't a few go-boys notice that the bird was unattended and they quietly whipped it off the wall.' **1994** Dermot Healy, *A Goat's Song*: '"Them lads are all go-boys," he complained, "they'll have my field destroyed."'

gobshite [n. & adj., <Ir. *gob*, beak, bill, mouth + *shite*, Ir. & NEng. form of 'shit', excrement]. [n.]. A gobbet of spittle, now principally and by association a despicable individual. Cf. PWJ: 'Gobshell, a big spittle direct from the mouth (Limerick). From Irish *gob*, the mouth, and *seile*, a spittle.' [adj.]. Parochial, petty, gen. derog. **1985** Hugh Leonard, *Leonard's Year*: 'I shall not mention the fellow's name, for it is only a few weeks since his moniker [q.v.] appeared in this column, and unless he is again elected Gobshite of the Year, I doubt if I can spare him any further panegyrics...' **1991** Roddy Doyle, *The Van*: 'on a bus or on the DART [q.v.], sitting there like a gobshite with a big picture on your lap, of a woman in her nip [q.v.] or something'. **1995** *Irish Times*, 24 Nov: 'The Labour TD, Mr Tommy Broughan, said that the constant raising of the Government jet issue was "gobshite politics".'

godless colleges, the [nickname]. Queen's Colleges at Belfast, Cork and Galway, opened Oct 1849. **1903** *Guide to Cork & the South-West of Ireland*: 'the "godless" colleges have never found favour with the Roman Catholic authorities, Queen's had never attracted a great number of students.' **1988** R.F. Foster, *Modern Ireland 1600–1972*: 'From 1884 Parnell [see **the Uncrowned King of Ireland**] took a forward line in condemning the "godless" Queen's colleges and calling for full provision for Catholic educational control at all levels...'

God's acre [n. phr.]. Grass on roadside verges providing free grazing. See also **long acre**.

godsamount [n.]. Large quantity. **1977** Flann O'Brien, *The Hair of the Dogma*: 'I seen bones and human skeletons in wan place...And any godsamount of swords and small hatchets.'

God's children [n., euphem.]. Those mentally retarded. **1987** Lar Redmond, *Emerald Square*: 'I felt strangely attracted to this man, even though he was supposed to be "not all there"...I would have a soft spot for "God's children" for the balance of my life.'

goffo [n., <?] (Dub.). Free ride on the back bumper of a car, unknown to the driver. See **scut** 2.

goghedsies/goghendies/gohendies etc. [exclam., <?]. Disguised oath

expressing surprise, astonishment. **1938** Seumas MacManus, *The Rocky Road to Dublin*: 'He had said bad words — *faith* [q.v.], *troth, bedad* [q.v.] — *goghedsies*, too, sometimes.'

going strong [vb. phr.] (Ulster). In a close relationship likely to end in marriage.

go in the moon see **go to the moon**

Goldie Fish [nickname] (Cork). Gilded salmon weathervane on church of St Anne's, Shandon, Cork city. **1995** Tom Widger, *Sunday Tribune*, 18 June: 'Elsewhere, the increasingly bizarre Cork soap *Under the Goldie Fish* would hardly be complete without a Bedouin.'

gollagoleen see **colligoleen**

gollier/gollyer [n., <?]. Gob of spittle. **1985** Máirín Johnston, *Around the Banks of Pimlico*: 'On Sundays Johnny Tynan never came around [selling papers], we had Gollier instead. He was a tall, skinny man with a permanently runny nose and he was always spitting.' **1991** Bob Quinn, *Smokey Hollow*: 'They loved being there except when their Granny hawked and dropped a big gollyer in the spitoon beside her chair.' **1995** Patrick Boland, *Tales from a City Farmyard*: 'in the traditional way that he sealed a deal with others, he spat a big gollier onto his toil-worn hand, and slapped it down on my scholarly hand'.

golly fishing [vb. phr., cf. Ir. *gabhlach* (n.), forked implement (to hold string of fish)] (Leinster). Fishing for small crabs with a bone on a piece of twine. **1995** Cathal O'Sullivan, RTÉ Radio, *The Odd Word*, 10 Sept: 'This week in the local regatta they had an event for the first time ever — golly fishing.' Also **golligor fishing**.

gom/gawm/goamey/gam [n., cf. Ir. *gamal*, lout, simpleton, fool]. As thus. **1966** Liam Ó Cuanaigh, *Evening Press*, 21 Nov: 'Goms are not famous for mental brilliance...it's not unusual to hear questions "What kind of gom is he?" or "Did you ever see a gom like that before?"' **1995** Phil O'Keeffe, *Down Cobbled Streets, A Liberties Childhood*:

'"I'm sure I'll get weak this morning," I repeated as I struggled with the chemise top. "Don't be a gom," Betty snapped...' **1996** Liam Mackey, *Irish Times*, 3 Feb: 'In *Bracken* [RTÉ TV serial], Pat Barry was the brooding sex symbol and Miley Byrne the wide-eyed gom, but the former went entirely to the bad afterwards...' Hence **gaumaction** [n.]. Horseplay, clownish tricks (OTF).

gombeen [n. & adj., <Ir. *gaimbín* (n.), usury, interest, <ME *cambie* (n.), barter]. Moneylender or trader who exploits the disadvantaged, esp. in rural areas; hence gen. term of contempt. **1922** Anon., *Tales of the RIC*: 'They [poor farmers] are thus forced to go to the gombeen wallah, who advances them so much money, according to the size of their farm and their capacity for drink, as a mortgage on the farm at a high rate of interest.' **1968** Myles na gCopaleen, *The Best of Myles*: 'Self-consciousness about 'Art', then, is the stamp of the gombeen-bourgeoisie.' **1996** Fintan O'Toole, *Irish Times*, 9 July: 'A society that is prepared to recognise those [minority] rights...is not an atavistic, gombeen republic, but a sophisticated and civilised democracy.'

gomer [n., poss. <*idem*, 'a large pewter dish' (DHS)]. Measure of drink. **1907** Joseph Guinan, *The Soggarth Aroon* (q.v.): 'he tossed off the second "gomer"'.

gomeral/gomeril [n., <Ir. *gomaral/gamal*, lout]. Fool. **1908** Lynn Doyle, *Ballygullion*: '"Two shillin's," sez he, "for a 'larmer clock; two cowld shillin's to that wee [q.v.] thief. Oh! Holy Biddy, but I married the right [see **right** 1.] gomeril."' **1913** Alexander Irvine, *My Lady of the Chimney Corner*: '"I was fixin' my galluses [q.v.] over Crawford's hedge, whin a gomeral luked over an' says, says he, 'Morra, Hughie!'"'

gone for its tea [adj. phr.]. Worn out, life-expired, of no further value; vanished. **1982** Éamonn Mac Thomáis, *Janey Mack* (q.v.), *Me Shirt is Black*: '"Well," says I, "you needn't worry about Sydney Parade and the Sandymount tram. The trams are all gone for their tea."'

gone for the milk [adj. phr.]. Dead. **1986** Padraic O'Farrell, *'Tell me, Sean O'Farrell'*: 'She knew who the culprit was, however, and when he was gone for the milk...the mother would shout through the cemetery gates..."Aha, me auld hayro [hero], your clapper won't ring much now."'

gone to the lake [vb. phr.] (Ulster). Said of s.o. who has committed suicide. **1995** Shane Connaughton, *A Border Diary*: '"her poor man walked into the lake and was found drowned standin' up in the water." "Gone to the lake" is a Cavan expression for suicide.'

gononstrips [n. pl., <?] (Cork). Arrangements. See **sawney**.

goo [n., <Sc. *idem*, taste, liking, <Fr. *goût, idem*] (Ulster). As thus.

good hand [n. phr.] (Ulster). Witty individual.

goodie see **goody**

goodle [n., <'good deal'] (Ulster). As thus. **1951** Patrick Kavanagh, *Envoy*, 'Diary', Mar: '"God, there's a goodle of blood in it still," say I, hoping that my cliché will help to establish me as a man of merit.'

good leg see **leg**

good on you! [exclam., cf. Ir. *rinne sé a mhaith orm*, lit. he made/did his good on me, poss. origin of Austral. usage]. Expression of approval/good wishes. **1986** Padraic O'Farrell, *'Tell me, Sean O'Farrell'*: 'The conclusion of such a recitation was greeted with calls of "More power [q.v.] to your elbow" or "Good on you" or "Me life on you."' **1996** *Irish Times*, 17 Sept: 'Christina [Murphy] used to provoke comments like "Did you see what she wrote this morning?"..."Good on her, she's putting it up to them now."' **1996** J.P. Duggan, *Irish Times*, 6 Nov: 'A chara [Sir] — The opening of T na G [Teilifís na Gaeilge] was withal swished through with verse, vivacity, pulse, pace and life...Sin é an slí is fearr [That's the best way]...Good on ye!'

good people [n. phr., <Ir. *na daoine maithe*]. Fairies, 'little people' (q.v.). **1824** Thomas Crofton Croker, *Researches in the South of Ireland*: 'to dig, or plough up, a rath or fort, whose construction the superstitious natives ascribe to the labour and ingenuity of the "good people", is considered as unlucky...' **1879** Charles J. Kickham, *Knocknagow*: 'it was generally believed that the "Good People" were wont to take their nightly journeys through the air to an' from Maurice Kearney's fort over the quarry'. **1982** Edmund Lenihan, *Long Ago by Shannon Side*: '"I knew another man, too, that wasn't the better of meeting the good people."'

goody/goodie [n.]. Bread and sugar softened in boiled milk. **1993** Tim Pat Coogan, *Dev* (q.v.): *Long Fellow* (q.v.), *Long Shadow*: 'In the cottage a young woman was feeding a baby "goody"...' **1993** Pat Tierney, *The Moon on my Back*: 'As well as changing their nappies and washing them, they would feed them bottles of milk and spoon "goodie" into them from a tiny mug.'

go off at the nail [vb. phr.] (Ulster). Become flustered, confused.

googeen [n., <Ir. *guaigín*, fidgety, capricious person]. As thus (usu. of female).

goosah as in **play the goosah** [n., <abbrev. of 'gooseberry' + endearment suffix] (Cork). Play gooseberry.

goosegreen [adj.] (Ulster). Yellowish-green.

gooter [n., <?]. Penis. **1991** Roddy Doyle, *The Van*: 'He put his hand in his pocket to adjust his gooter — the way she kept putting her mouth up to his ear...'

goozer [n., <?]. Kiss. **1991** Bob Quinn, *Smokey Hollow*: '"Hey, Oul' Jimmy, does your mother know you're out!" "Go on, give her a goozer." But the couple ignored them.' **1997** Tom Widger, *Sunday Tribune*, 22 June: 'When Dekko arrives at Pauline's gaff, she could be heard enthusiastically giving him a toe-curler of a goozer.'

gopin see **gowpen**

gorawar/s [exclam. & n. pl., <Ir. *goradh mhór* [n. phr.], great heat]. [exclam.]. Mild oath. **1943** George A. Little, *Malachi Horan Remembers*: "'Suddenly he heard a move in the kitchen. He went up and, Gor-a-war, but if there wasn't the fox with the buckskin breeches in his mouth!'" [n. pl.]. Stratagems. **1961** Flann O'Brien, *The Hard Life*: 'You know the gorawars you have to get him to drink his milk in this kitchen. He thinks milk is poison.'

gorb [n. & vb., <Sc. *idem* (adj.), greedy, voracious]. Glutton; eat ravenously. **1983** Polly Devlin, *All of us There*: 'Anyone who asks for more is called a "gorb".' Also **gorby-guts** in same sense.

Gorgeous Gael, the [nickname]. Jack Doyle (1903–78), boxer, entertainer and playboy.

Gorman, the [nickname, abbrev.]. Grangegorman Mental Hospital, Dub. (1816). **1996** John Waters, *Irish Times*, 27 Aug: 'Virtually everyone in Dublin has heard of St Brendan's, or "The Gorman", he [Ivor Browne] said once in an interview. But very few can tell you where it is.' **1996** Peter Kavanagh, quoted in *Sunday Tribune*, 1 Dec: 'I beg that he reports, not to me...but directly to the Superintendent of Grangegorman Lunatic Asylum, familiarly known as the Gorman.'

gornet [n., <'gurnet'] (Ulster). Stupid person.

gorry/gawrey [n., <?] (Ulster). Bonham (small pig). **1952** Anon. (Patrick Kavanagh?), *Kavanagh's Weekly*, 'I Went to the Fair', 21 June: 'How well I remember the Sparrow Madden. He was a dealer in gorries...'

gorseyjack [n., <?] (Leinster). Young man (DOM).

gorsoon see **garsoon**

gosha [n., <Ir. *gaisce*, voc. *a ghaisce*, hero, champion]. As thus. **1925** Liam O'Flaherty, *The Informer*: 'Who's comin' to bed with me," he cried, "before the bank is broke?" "I am, me bould son a gosha," cried Connemara Maggie.'

gosoon/gossoon [n., <Ir. *garsún*, poss. <Fr. *garçon*, boy, cf. Med. Lat. *garcio*, groom]. Young boy. **1925** Percy French, *Prose, Poems and Parodies*, 'Shlathery's Mounted Fut': 'An' down from the mountains came the squadrons an' platoons,/Four-an-twenty fightin' min, an' a couple o' sthout gossoons...' **1961** Flann O'Brien, *The Hard Life*: '"these County Council scholarships to the universities above in Dublin do more harm than good, young gossoons walking around with their Sunday suits on them weekdays'. **1995** Patsy McGarry, *Irish Times*, 5 Aug: 'Enter a slightly built gosoon [Jason Sherlock], small in stature, with speed, a nifty turn of foot...' See also **garsun**.

goster [n. & vb.; cf. Ir. *gasrán cainte* (n. phr.), conversation; PWJ has '*gastaire*, a chatterer, a prater']. Chat, conversation. **1914** James Joyce, *Dubliners*: 'Ivy Day in the Committee Room': 'I asked him again now, but he was leaning on the counter in his shirt-sleeves having a deep goster with Alderman Cowley.' **1994** Gabriel Byrne, *Pictures in my Head*: 'Every morning I collected letters...and delivered them to the big insurance companies around the city. This usually took about two hours, allowing half an hour for gostering and slingeing [q.v.].' **1995** Phil O'Keeffe, *Down Cobbled Streets, A Liberties Childhood*: '"Will you girls hurry up and stop gostering; we'll never get done."'

gotchie [n., <'got ye']. Park keeper or one in similar authority. **1994** Greg Dalton, *My Own Backyard, Dublin in the Fifties*: 'up to St Patrick's Park to pick flowers and run like Herb Elliot until you made it to the Naller [q.v.]...Sure the old groundsmen or gotchies hadn't a chance.'

go through s.o. for a short cut [vb. phr.]. Abuse, reprimand strongly. **1991** Roddy Doyle, *The Van*: 'and Veronica went through him for a short cut when she saw the paste in his hair'.

Go to God [exclam.]. **1989** Hugh Leonard, *Out after Dark*: 'He bowed and said: "Madam, I am German." She was thrilled to bits. "Ah, go to God," she said. "A Jerry.'"

go to/in the moon [vb. phr.] (Ulster). Be very angry. **1939** Patrick Gallagher ('Paddy the Cope' (q.v.)), *My Story*: 'She did not think much of me certainly, but she went clean to the moon when she found I could not milk.'

goudee hang see **guddy hang**

gouger, less commonly **gager/gauger** [n., cj. *gouge* (vb.), 'squeeze out a man's eye with the thumb: a cruel practice used by the Bostonians in America' (Grose); 'Dublin slang of the 1980s [sic]' (Thorne), but also Cork and elsewhere]. Lout, thug. **1966** Liam Ó Cuanaigh, *Evening Press*, 21 Nov: 'It seems the gouger is a cross between a chancer [q.v.], a bum, a waster and a gom [q.v.]; only worse. A very rare specimen in the pure state, his traits are inclined to rub off on average characters [see **character** 2.], hence "a bit of a gouger" or "a certain amount of the gouger". Beware when you get a tip on the elbow and a nod towards the corner with the warning "Your man [q.v.] over there is a *real* gouger." Hold onto your mug, old son [q.v.], in case there's trouble.' **1986** Bob Geldof, *Is That It?*: 'Gougers were cornerboys [q.v.], gurriers [q.v.], yobs, hooligans, streetwise kids who used to lay trails of seeds for the pigeons outside the Pavilion Cinema in Dun Laoghaire.' **1995** Catherine Cleary, *Irish Times*, 14 Nov: 'At 11.45 p.m. [bus inspector] Mr Mugan drops the garda back to the station. He suspects that the weather contributed to the relative calm. "You don't get gougers hanging about in the rain."'

gowan [n., <Sc. *idem*, daisy] (Ulster). As thus. **1983** W.F. Marshall, *Livin' in Drumlister*, 'The River': 'Back of there the sun is shining, and the riverside is cheery,/There are gowans for a carpet, and the moss to make a throne...'

gowdy [n., cf. Sc. *idem*, term of endearment]. As thus, ironic. **1952** Anon. (Patrick Kavanagh?), *Kavanagh's Weekly*, 'I Went to the Fair', 21 June: 'A poor woman and her gowdy of a son came up to me.'

gowl [n. & vb.]. 1. [n. & vb., cf. ON *gaula*, Icel. *gelta*, bark, roar; but poss. <'yowl'] (Ulster). Cry, howl, yell. **1908** Lynn Doyle, *Ballygullion*: 'an' if he'd been silent all his days before, be me sowl he made up for it that night for the gowls av him was lamentable'. **1913** Alexander Irvine, *My Lady of the Chimney Corner*: 'He stopped there. He could go no further for several minutes. "I hate a man that gowls, but —" "Go on," I said, "have a good one..."' **1983** W.F. Marshall, *Livin' in Drumlister*, 'John the Liar': '"Twos John the Liar with his two han's up/To keep the mare; ye'd hear the gowls of him/From far enough...' 2. [n., <Ir. *gabhal*, fork, junction]. Female genitals, and by extension, fool, idiot. Cf. Fr. *con*, Sp. *coño* etc. **1991** Teddy Delaney, *Where we Sported and Played*: 'Out it [the paint] flowed through the joining where the two sheets met and onto the lovely Turkish carpet. "Go away, ye gowl!" says I, "now we're rightly [see **right** 1.] up shit creek"...'

gowlogue [n., <Ir. *gabhlóg*, prop, support]. Large/strong drink.

gown soura [n. phr., <Ir. *gamhain samhraidh*, summer calf (reared on plentiful supply of milk)]. Milksop.

gowpen/gowpin/gopin [n., <Sc. *gowpen/gowpan/gowpin*, hollow of the hand] (Ulster). Handful; the full of two cupped hands held together. **1983** W.F. Marshall, *Livin' in Drumlister*, 'The Lad': 'Plenishment [q.v.] they'd have little or noan/Except for what they'd stale,/An' they'd make the childher [see **childer**] go out an' beg/Gowpins of oaten male.' Also **gowpinful** in same sense.

gowries [n., cf. Ir. *geamhraigh* (vb.), spring, sprout]. Wit, intelligence. **1996** Christy Kenneally, *Maura's Boy, A Cork Childhood*: 'In a loud whisper she confided the source of her happiness to her pal: "He's in from the country, girl. Sure he haven't a gowries, tank God."'

goyno see **guino**

grá/gradh [n., <Ir. *grá*, love]. Affection. **1943** George A. Little, *Malachi Horan Remembers*: '"I have yet to hear of a man who could care for a motor as any man

— that *is* a man — cares for his horse. Even for a work-horse you would get a 'grá'." **1987** Lar Redmond, *Emerald Square*: "'you'll make it all the harder with your *grá* for the women and the drink'". **1996** *Examiner* (Cork), 9 Oct: 'He [Bishop Murphy] loved the people of Cork, but he had a particular grá for the people of the northside...'

graal/grawl [n., <Sc. *grawl*, grilse (young salmon)] (Ulster). Growing lad; heavy, big-boned fellow.

graanogue [n., <Ir. *gráineog*, hedgehog]. As thus, also urchin, buffoon, jester. '[S]he might tell him to be off with himself adding that he was reared on the hind teat of a graanogue' (PO'F).

Grab All Association [nickname, <play on initials]. Gaelic Athletic Association. **1996** Seán Kilfeather, *Irish Times*, 21 Sept: "'That's typical of the GAA,'" was the immediate cry. The old "Grab All Association" *canard* was trotted out. "How do they expect people to pay once again for a replay"...'

grabber [n., abbrev. of 'land-grabber']. One who took possession of lands of evicted tenant, C18–19; anyone greedy for land. **1915** George Fitzmaurice, *The Moonlighter* (q.v.): 'PETER I'm no friend to grabbers, but God forbid I'd have your mind to damn my immortal soul for a bit of land!' **1991** Seán Ó Ciaráin, *Farewell to Mayo*: 'The weight of the Land League organisation was brought to bear against the newcomer. Branded as a grabber, which indeed he was, he was boycotted by the local community.'

gradh see **grá**

graith/greath [n. & vb., <Sc. *graith* (n. & vb.), equipment, horse harness, equip] (Ulster). As thus. See **guilderhead**.

grammel [vb., <'grabble']. Grope for, fumble.

grand [adj.]. Fine, first-class; just about all right. **1993** Joe Langan in Joe O'Reilly & Sixth Class, Convent School, Edenderry, *Over the Half Door*: 'There was a Miss Foy and a Miss O'Sullivan. O'Sullivan was the head teacher. Miss Foy was the grandest in the world.' **1994**

Christopher Fitz-Simon, *The Boys* (see **the Boys** 2.): 'after the television recording he [Micheál MacLiammóir] wrote from London to Maura Laverty to thank her for "one of the grandest parts I have played" — using the term "grand" in the Irish sense of "first-class"'. **1996** Nell McCafferty, *Sunday Tribune*, 27 Oct: 'Generally, in their marriage, they got on. "Fine, not great, but grand," she repeatedly summed up the four years of their relationship.'

grannuaile/granuaile [n., <Ir. *Gráinne Ní Mhaol*, more properly *Gráinne Umhaill*, aka Grace O'Malley (1530–c.1600), sea captain and pirate] as in **an old grannuaile**. Said of a child old beyond its years. See **crab** 1.

granny [n.] as in **me granny!** [exclam.]. Expressing disbelief. Also **on your granny!** in same sense. **1996** Martina Devlin, *Sunday Tribune*, 'Confessions', 2 June: 'Myles looked smug, as well he might. He muttered something about being deeply sorry — on your granny, I thought — and finally left...'

granny greybaird/mush-mush [nickname] (Ulster). Caterpillar.

granuaile see **grannuaile**

grapple the rails [n. phr., 'because after drinking it one had to do this to remain upright' (DHS)]. 'A cant name used in Ireland for whiskey' (Grose).

grass of a hen [n. phr.] as in **you haven't the grass of a hen** [neg. phr.]. Alleging stupidity. **1979** Frank Kelly, *The Annals of Ballykilferret*: '...Norbert asks him bitterly, "What the hell would you know ye stray oat ye? Sure you haven't the grass of a hen!"'

grauver [adj., <Ir. *grámhar*, loving, lovable]. As thus, sociable. **1960** John O'Donoghue, *In Kerry Long Ago*: "'Faith [q.v.], then, she's the fine *grauver* girl," said Dansel, earnestly.'

gravy ring [nickname] (Ulster). Doughnut with a hole.

grawl see **graal**

grawn bawn [n. phr., <Ir. *grán bán*, white grain; or poss. *gearrán bán*, white

nag, fig. reflection of moon on water (Dinneen)] (stonemasons' sl.). Hard flecks in stone. **1966** Séamus Murphy, *Stone Mad*: "'tis a bitch of a stone... There's a grawn bawn in it, boy, like the little bits of gristle you see in a rasher.'

greadal [n., <'great deal']. Large amount. **1943** George A. Little, *Malachi Horan Remembers*: 'But long ago there was a greadal of seriouser fighting.'

great [adj.]. Close, very friendly. **1990** Tom O'Kane, quoted in Walter Love, *The Times of our Lives*: 'he went up at about five or ten minutes to three to the bank. He and the cashier were very great, so he was able to walk behind the bank counter.' See **thick** 2. Also **great with, be** [vb. phr.]. Be close to; have an amorous understanding with. **1960** John O'Donoghue, *In Kerry Long Ago*: 'Johnnie O'Sullivan Corrig was to make music with a melodeon, borrowed from Kate Norrie, a girl he was great with at the time.' **1982** Edmund Lenihan, *Long Ago by Shannon Side*: "'There were two brothers of the MacNamaras...Finn an' Conn. Both of them were in love with the same girl, an' neither Conn knew that Finn was great with her, or Finn didn't know that Conn was great with her.'" **1993** Joe Langan in Joe O'Reilly & Sixth Class, Convent School, Edenderry, *Over the Half Door*. 'Miss O'Sullivan, the head teacher, was from Cork. She was a hard ould divil. She was great with some crowd down in Carbury...'

great gas see **gas**

greath see **graith**

Great Hunger, the [nickname]. Great Famine, 1845–50, caused by failure of staple potato crop. **1989** Cormac Ó Gráda, *The Great Irish Famine*: 'the "Great Hunger" has gained wider and more lasting notoriety than most famines. There are several reasons for this.'

great leg see **leg**

great wish for [n. phr.]. Great respect for; great hopes/ambitions for. **1914** James Joyce, *Dubliners*, 'The Sisters': "'The youngster and he were great friends. The old chap taught him a great

deal, mind you; and they say he had a great wish for him.'"

Green Army, the [nickname]. Followers of Jack Charlton's Ir. soccer team, 1980s–1990s. **1995** Liam Mackey, *Irish Times*, 11 Nov: 'Happily most of the legends bequeathed by The Green Army are memorable for all the right reasons — from the supporters in Bulgaria in 1988 who had to escort a couple of police officers back to their own car after inveigling them into a drinking session...'

greenhouses [n. pl., <exterior paintwork] (Dub.). Street urinals. **1922** James Joyce, *Ulysses*: 'All kinds of places are good for ads. That quack doctor for the clap used to be stuck up in all the greenhouses.'

greeshig/griosach [n., <Sc. *grieshoch/grieshach*, red, flameless fire, <Sc. Gael. *griosach*, hot ashes, embers]. As thus. **1983** W.F. Marshall, *Livin' in Drumlister*, 'Sarah Ann': 'The night the win' is risin', an it's comin' on to sleet,/It's spittin' down the chimley on the greeshig at me feet...' **1995** Joe McManus in Mary Ryan et al. (eds.), *No Shoes in Summer*. 'The roasted and mashed potatoes, gravied turnips, and sizzling rashers which awaited him in the pot oven on the griosach of the turf fire...'

greet [vb., <Sc. *idem* <OE *greotan*, weep] (Ulster). As thus. **1983** *John Pepper's Illustrated Encyclopaedia of Ulster Knowledge*: "'The wean [q.v.] went oot to school this mornin greeting buckets.'"

greg/grig [vb., <Ir. *griog*, tease, tantalise, annoy]. As thus. **1961** Flann O'Brien, *The Hard Life*: "'You don't believe in what you say at all. As they say in Ireland, you are only trying to grig me.'" **1987** Christopher Nolan, *Under the Eye of the Clock*: 'Yvonne...chatted, sang and gregged her brother about his not being able to eat toast in bed.'

grew/grue [vb. & n., <Sc. *grue*, shudder with fear/repulsion; feeling of horror] (Ulster). 1. [vb. & n.]. As thus. 2. [n.]. Term of abuse.

Grey Ghost, the [nickname] (Civil War). Armoured rail vehicle. **1963**

Martin Whyte, *Journal of the Irish Railway Record Society*, 'Fifty Years of a Loco Man's Life', Spring: 'A small armoured Lancia car, fitted with flanged wheels, and known as "The Grey Ghost", was patrolling the line between Clonmel and Thurles. The Irregular forces trapped the vehicle between two overbridges, and a concentrated attack was made on it.' **1978** W.J. Bergin, *An Cosantóir*, 'Ambush on the Grey Ghost', May: 'When fire ceased from the *Grey Ghost* the crew surrendered or as Sean Fitzpatrick says in his book "Recollection of the Fight for Irish Freedom by the 3rd Tipp[erary] Bde"..."they gave up the Ghost".'

grig see **greg**

grimacious [adj.]. Dire, dreadful. **1987** Vincent Caprani, *Vulgar Verse & Variations, Rowdy Rhymes & Rec-im-itations*, 'How Jem the Dancer was Mortally Wounded for the Cause': '"Grim times." "Extremely grimacious," Jem nodded.'

grind [n. & vb.]. Extra tuition for examinations; supply or receive such tuition. **1986** William Trevor, *The News from Ireland*: '"A fellow came up to me this morning," he said now, "a right [see **right** 1.] eejit [q.v.] from Monasterevin. Was I looking for grinds in Little-go Logic? Five shillings an hour."' **1996** *Irish Times*, 9 Apr: 'for thousands of Leaving Cert students, and some of their teachers, the real grinds are about to begin. Easter days are becoming known as Grindhog Days as students gravitate towards a week's grinding for their exams.'

griosach see **greeshig**

griosgeen/grisceen/griskeen [n.]. 1. [<Ir. *gríscín* (pl.), (broiled) giblets]. As thus. **1992** John McGahern, *The Collected Stories*, 'The Wine Breath': 'The butter melted on the fresh bread on the plate. There were sausages, liver, bacon, a slice of black-pudding and sweetest grisceens.' **1995** Eugene McGee in Seán Power (ed.), *Those were the Days, Irish Childhood Memories*: 'We used the word "griosgeens" for the tasty pieces of edible offal which were extracted from the pig.' 2. [poss. <ON *griss*, pig; or as 1?]. Loin of pork.

gripe [n., usu. pl., <OE *gripe*, grip, grasp, handful]. Hands. **C.1780** Anon., 'Luke Caffrey's Kilmainham Minit': 'When to see Luke's last jig we agreed,/We tipped him our gripes in a tangle...'

griper/gripper [n.]. Bailiff. **1800** Maria Edgeworth, *Castle Rackrent*: '"The execution came down, and every thing at Castle Rackrent was seized by the gripers, and my son Jason, to his shame be it spoken, among them."' **1948** Patrick Kavanagh, *Tarry Flynn*: '"They tell me the grippers were up at Carlins again...I was glad the oul' cow, the only four-footed animal they have about the place, wasn't taken."'

grisceen/griskeen see **griosgeen**

groak/growk [n. & vb., <Sc. *idem* (vb.), overlook watchfully (CSD)] (Ulster). Child who waits around in expectation of a treat; 'look at others eating in expectation of being asked to join them' (YDS).

grogger [nickname] (Boys' Brigade) (Ulster). Biscuit. **1990** Harry Currie, quoted in Walter Love, *The Times of our Lives*: 'The day ended at ten o'clock... The buglers sounded retreat, cocoa was served with "the grogger", a big slab of biscuit...'

ground hurling [n. phr., <sporting ploy]. Political in-fighting. **1996** 'Drapier', *Irish Times*, 2 Nov: 'Before this [food] board is established there will be plenty of what is called "ground hurling" between the Departments of Health and Agriculture...'

groundshels [n. pl., cf. Ir. *gráinseáil*, small portion of grain, small repast] (Ulster). Used tea leaves, dregs.

growk see **groak**

Growl [nickname]. Fund-raising organisation launched by Eamon de Valera (see **Dev**), Nov 1920. **1993** Tim Pat Coogan, *Dev* (q.v.): *Long Fellow* (q.v.), *Long Shadow*: 'Called the American Association for Recognition of the Irish Republic (AARIR), appropriately enough it became generally known as Growl.'

grue see **grew**

grug [n., <Ir. *grogaide/gogaide*, hunkers]. As thus; 'sitting on one's grug means sitting on the heels without touching the ground' (PWJ).

grulch [n.] (Ulster). 1. [cf. Sc. *idem*, thick, squat, fat person/animal]. 'Stocky, small fellow who is rather rough in his ways and perhaps a mite dour' (YDS). 2. Very small pig (Traynor).

grumah [adj., <Ir. *gruama*, gloomy, sad, morose]. As thus; frowning, dejected (OTF).

grumly/grummly [adj., <Sc. *grumly*, muddy, cf. Swed. *grujmmel* (n.), sediment] (Ulster). As thus. **1951** Sam Hanna Bell, *December Bride*: '"Sarah daughter, wet [see **wet** 2.] me a cup of tea, for my mouth's as grummly as a puddle."'

grush/grushie [n. & vb.]. 1. [n. & vb., cf. E. Frisian *grusen* (vb.), Sc. *gruss* (vb.), press, squeeze] (Dub.). Scramble for small change thrown to children, esp. after a wedding; throw or scramble for such change. **1981** Paddy Crosbie, *Your Dinner's Poured Out!*: 'We had seen blackmen in the pictures, but there was none in Dublin as far as I knew. He was "grushying" money in the shape of sixpences, threepenny bits, pennies, ha'pennies and farthings.' **1994** Mary Doolan in Kevin C. Kearns, *Dublin Tenement Life*: 'And the groom would throw out a few coppers in a brown bag to the kids. Ha'pennies and pennies. Oh, Yeah, that was called the "grushie".' **1995** Billy French in Mary Ryan et al. (eds.), *No Shoes in Summer*: 'we youngsters would congregate outside St Agnes' Church [Dub.] to see the weddings and join in the "grush" — this was the traditional throwing of money by the best-man.' 2. [n., <Ir. *gnúis*, sour expression]. As thus.

guarlya [n., <?]. Term of abuse. See **nudger**.

guban [n., <Ir. *gobán*, old-fashioned, incompetent tradesman]. Term of abuse; 'captious critic, who professes knowledge he does not always possess' (OTF). **1995** William Downey in Mary Ryan et al. (eds.), *No Shoes in Summer*: '"You're nothing but a guban to do that to the girl and she after doing a hornpipe for us and all.'

gubog [n., <Ir. *gobóg*, dogfish] (Ulster). As thus. **1995** Brigid O'Donnell in Mary Ryan et al. (eds.), *No Shoes in Summer*: 'He [my father] caught a different lot of fishes, sheelog, mackerel, gubog (known locally as rock salmon), grey fish, puckers (small fish), creilógs and blind hays [q.v.]...'

GUBU [acronym, derog., coined 1982 in respect of a political scandal involving the Attorney-General and Malcolm MacArthur, subsequently convicted of murder]. Major political mishap, extended to other fields. **1983** Joe Joyce & Peter Murtagh, *The Boss*: 'The MacArthur affair caused immense damage to [Charles] Haughey's government. Some of his own adjectives used to describe it — grotesque, unbelievable, bizarre, unprecedented — were apt, and led to the invention of a new word, GUBU, coined by one of his critics of old, Conor Cruise O'Brien [see **the Cruiser**]'. **1984** Bruce Arnold, *What Kind of Country*: 'The unlucky GUBU principle entered the Irish language and gave expression to a degree of public disquiet not justified by the facts.' **1995** Tom Humphries, *Irish Times*, 12 June: 'Inquiry points to GUBU virus. Five points dropped in eight days. Grotesque. Unusual [*sic*]. Bizarre. Unprecedented. Jack Charlton marches into his press conference...'

guddy/goudee hang [n. phr.]. Gallows bird, good-for-nothing person. **1663** Richard Head, *Hic et Ubique*: 'PATRICK He was no Sougare [soldier] nor Musketeer, but a greyshy [greasy] guddy hang of a Peek-man [pikeman].'

guff [n., poss. <Ir. *gaoth*, wind; or cf. Norweg. dial. *gufs*, puff of wind; Icel. *gufa*, mist, fog, smoke, etc; '? orig. US' (DHS)]. Humbug, empty talk. **1987** Lar Redmond, *Emerald Square*: 'I had been told to say please and thank you and mind my manners...and all the other guff...' **1995** Eddie Holt, *Irish Times*, 8

July: 'How else can his [Terry Wogan's] guff be explained? It began with a sniggering "Céad fáilte róimh arais" and ended with a mocking "Give the woman in the bed more porter [q.v.]."' **1995** Declan Lynch, *Sunday Independent*, 3 Dec: 'the Rev. Eric Smyth, DUP Lord Mayor of Belfast, followed on with a smattering of biblical quotations. The crowd gave him short shrift, roaring for Bill [Clinton] to be wheeled on and enough of that oul' guff.'

gug [n., cf. Ir. *gogach* (adj.), nodding, wavering]. Duck's waddle; jerky up-and-down motion.

guggy [n., <Ir. *gogaí*, child's name for egg]. As thus.

guilderhead [n., cf. Sc. *guldie*, 'tall, black-faced, gloomy-looking man' (CSD)] (Ulster). Stupid, clumsy individual. **1983** Polly Devlin, *All of us There*: '"And by Christ," Feley said, "it'll be the last [word he said] for I'll have the greath [q.v.] off the guilderhead fornenst [g.v.] it.' Also **guldy** [n.]. Rough but harmless individual.

guino/goyno [n., <?] (Dub.). Money. **1982** Éamonn Mac Thomáis, *Janey Mack* (q.v.), *Me Shirt is Black*: 'The only mid-Lent break was St Patrick's Day...On St Patrick's Day we could eat sweets and if we had the Guino (money) we could have the pics...'

gulder see **gaulder**

guldies [n., poss. <'goodies']. As thus. **1979** Michael O'Beirne, *Mister, A Dublin Childhood*: 'Mother would go out on Christmas Eve and get all kinds of guldies and toys and a cake...'

gullion [n., <Ir. *góilín*, inlet, creek] (Ulster). Muddy hole; open sewer.

gully [n., <Sc. *gully-knife*, large knife] (Ulster). As thus.

gullyer [n., cf. *gollyer* (q.v.)]. Child's marble. **1995** Phil O'Keeffe, *Down Cobbled Streets, A Liberties Childhood*: 'A gullyer was a large marble and a taw was a large earthenware marble. Leadeners [q.v.] could not be bought in the shops. They were ball-bearings, and a deadly weapon in the hands of a marble-player.'

gulpin [n., <Ir. *guilpín*, lout; cf. Sc. *idem*, 'raw, unwieldy fellow' (CSD)] (Ulster). As thus; gen. term of abuse. **1927** Peadar O'Donnell, *Islanders*: '"dirty gulpins of ducks, that I didn't get an egg out of since I don't know when"'. **1948** Patrick Kavanagh, *Tarry Flynn*: '"I'm the two ends of [q.v.] a gulpin," he said aloud to himself. And all through the day he kept cursing himself for his cowardice.' **1986** Padraic O'Farrell, *'Tell me, Sean O'Farrell'*: '"Why in the name of Jaysus [q.v.] would he want to be buried with his gateposts?" was the remark of a "gulpin" during the lunch-break...' See also **amadaun**.

gum [n., cf. Sc. *idem*, palate]. Desire, need, taste. **1991** Roddy Doyle, *The Van*: 'He'd be going past a pub in town and he'd have the gum for a pint...' Also **gumming** [pres. part.] as in **gumming for a cigarette**.

gunge [n.] (Ulster). 'Sweets, cakes, desserts' (SH).

guniog [n., cf. Ir. *goineog*, stab, sting, prick] (Ulster). Slap.

gunk [n. & vb., cf. Ir. *gonc* (vb.), snub, rebuff] (Ulster), esp. as in **quarely** (see **quare** 1.) **gunked**. [n.]. 'A shock or a mortifying and ludicrous disappointment' (MON). [vb.]. Shock, rebuff, let down. **1908** Lynn Doyle, *Ballygullion*: '"Ah, ye ould sarping [serpent]," sez I to meself, "is that your game? But I'll gunk ye."'

gunny [adj., <nickname *the Gun*, applied to the College chapel] (Maynooth College, 1950s). Romantic with the implication of matrimony. **1995** Eithne Tynan, *Sunday Tribune*, interview with Tom MacBride, 23 Apr: '"I had goodlooking sisters who used to come and visit me. A visit used to be known as a call. So when my sisters came the boys would be leaning out of the top windows and they'd say 'MacBride has a gunny call.'"'

gunterpake [n., <?] (Belfast). Stupid individual.

gur cake [n., poss. <Hindust. *gur*, molasses, poss. brought from India by Ir. regiments in the Brit. army; see **hooley**]

(Dub.). Cake favoured by schoolchildren when playing truant, or mitching (q.v.). **1965** Lee Dunne, *Goodbye to the Hill*: 'and she's red hot in bed. It's just that when they start on about wedding bells I want to get my gurcake and milk and get out of town.' **1995** Patrick Boland, *Tales from a City Farmyard*: 'My favourite cake was "gurcake", a dark brown slab full of currants, raisins and sultanas.' Hence **on (the) gur** [adj. phr.]. Mitching, staying away from home. **1943** George A. Little, *Malachi Horan Remembers*: '"A boy on gur that was given the candle to hold was shaking with the fright that was on him."' **1982** Éamonn Mac Thomáis, *Janey Mack* (q.v.), *Me Shirt is Black*: 'In all, Joyce lived in eighteen houses in Dublin, not counting Buck Mulligan's tower in Sandycove or the places he slept in when he was out on "Gur".'

gurly [adj., <Sc. *idem*, boisterous, threatening to be stormy] (Ulster). As thus; rough-tempered.

gurn see **girn**

gurrey [n., <?] (Cork). Children's steering car (Beecher).

gurrier [n., poss. <Fr. *guerrier*, warrior]. Street urchin, esp. Dub., and gen. derog. by extension. **1955** J.P. Donleavy, *The Ginger Man*: 'A girl pipers' band was rounding the front of Trinity College, all green and tassels and drumming... Followed by gurriers.' **1987** Lar Redmond, *Emerald Square*: '"that was a terrible belt you gave him." "Nothin' teh what I gev' the other bastard," I replied speaking gurrier style...' Hence **gurrierish** [adj.]. **1995** *Sunday Tribune*, 19 Nov: '"[Andy O'Mahony is] a surprisingly gurrierish interviewer," says journalist Emily O'Reilly. "He likes to make people squirm."'

gutter [n., gen. pl., & vb., <Sc. *idem* (n.), mud, filth, <OF *goutiere* (n.), gutter; cf. Ir. *guta* (n.), mud, filth]. 'Wet mud on a road' (PWJ); stain thus. **1908** Lynn Doyle, *Ballygullion*: 'I thought Mr Barrington would have died laughin' at him...for he was a shockin' sight wi' gutthers an' clay.' **1993** Sam McAughtry,

Touch & Go: 'she would stop and brush the black hair away from her eyes with the back of her hand; her arms were guttered to the elbows with dirt'. Also **guttery** [adj.].

guttie [n.]. 1. [poss. <Ir. *gótaire*, goatish fellow (Dinneen); cf. Sc. *guttie*, glutton, very fat person (DHS)]. S.o. with no redeeming features, gurrier (q.v.). **1979** C.S. Andrews, *Dublin Made Me*: '[He played a few holes] before the possible arrival of members who, at that time, would have regarded Kenny and his like as "gutties".' **1991** Bob Quinn, *Smokey Hollow*: '"Your young fella [q.v.] better watch his tongue, missus." "Is that so?" "It is so. Name-calling is only for gutties."' **1995** Con Costello, *Leinster Leader* (Naas, Co. Kildare), 'A Dub in the Great War', 6 Apr: 'His [Frank Laird's] fellow recruits included men who had been tea-planters in Malaya...and "two genuine Dublin gutties, who proved to be deserters, and who soon deserted again"'.' Also **guttiest** (adj.). **1975** John Ryan, *Remembering How We Stood*: 'Though her speech had lost its refined "blas" [accent] (for she had now substituted this with the "guttiest" Dublin accent this side of Moore Street)...' 2. [<*gutta-percha*, golfers' sl., *c*.1890 for golf ball] (Ulster). [n. pl.]. Plimsolls, runners (q.v.). Also **sink the guttie** [vb. phr.]. Drive at speed. [n.]. Bladder. **1986** Stephen Moore, quoted in *Magill*, Aug: 'I was interviewed by about four detectives ...My watch, my gutties (shoes) and a few bob in my pocket was taken.' **1994** Maurice Hayes, *Sweet Killough Let Go your Anchor*: 'he confessed that he had been playing football in gutties at a base camp called Deolali in India'. 3. [cf. Sc. *guttie*, minnow]. Small piece. **1983** Polly Devlin, *All of us There*: '"and the pair of them has each other kilt [q.v.]. Oh Jaysus [q.v.], they'll not leave gutties of each other."'

guy see **gay**

guzz-eye [n., <?] (Cork). Cast or squint in the eye. Hence **guz(z)-eyed** [adj.]. **1996** Christy Kenneally, *Maura's Boy, A Cork Childhood*: 'The shilling seats were always up front where you'd be guz-eyed after five minutes.'

guzzle [n.] (Cork). Party, social gathering (Beecher).

gwall [n., <Ir. *gabháil*, 'as much as can be taken between the outstretched arms' (Dinneen)] (Cork). Load, large amount (Beecher).

gwan! [exclam., <contraction of 'go on']. Expressing disbelief. **1925** Liam O'Flaherty, *The Informer*: '"Gwan," said another contemptuously. "There's no sojers [soldiers] goin' to come down here."'

gye see **gay**

gype see **gipe**

gyppo [n., <?] (army). Gravy. **1973** Noël Conway, *The Bloods* (q.v.): 'That was at Dinner on Christmas Day when, in his considered opinion, the Lieutenant serving him didn't give him enough "gyppo" on his ration of turkey.'

Gypsies, the [nickname] (Dub.). Bohemians soccer club. **1996** Emmet Malone, *Irish Times*, 18 July: 'at the final whistle, it was the Gypsies who had the greater cause for relief having escaped defeat'.

H

habermagallion [n., <Sc. *idem*, fool, useless person] (Ulster). As thus.

habu [n., <?]. Sleep, nap. As in **go for a habu** (EW).

hack [n., vb. & exclam.]. 1. [n., <OE *haccian* (vb.), cut in pieces] (Ulster). Sore, wound. 2. [n., cf. **crack** 1.] (Cork). Fun (Beecher). 3. [vb., <?] (Ulster). Tolerate (SH). 4. [exclam.] (Ulster). Command to horse to come (MON).

hack, away on a see **away on a hack**

hackle/heckle [n. & vb., <Sc. *heckle*, comb for dressing flax; dress flax thus] as in **put the box on the hackles** (Ulster). Complete a job.

haddick [n., <Eng. dial. *haddock/hattock* (n. pl.), 'imperfectly threshed ears of corn, discarded after winnowing' (EDD)] (Leinster). Friend or lover discarded or jilted.

hag [n. & vb.]. 1. [n., <ME *hegge*, evil spirit] (Ulster). Coward. 2. [vb., <ON *hoggva*, strike, fell trees]. Cut/chop wildly.

haggard [n., <ON *heygarthr*, hay yard]. Stacking or storage area. **1910** J.M. Synge, *Deirdre of the Sorrows*: '"It's well you know that it's this day I'm dreading seven years, and I fine nights watching the heifers walking to the haggard..."' **1952** Bryan MacMahon, *Children of the Rainbow*: 'Old wives doing mysterious chores in haggards straightened their backs and looked wistfully after us.' **1988** Alice Taylor, *To School through the Fields*: 'The haggard was the realm of the men and children to which the women, busy in the kitchen, rarely came.'

haggary/haggoty [adj., <*hag* (vb.), tire out, 1674] (Ulster). Tiring.

hagsmash [n., <'hog', pig] (Ulster). Botched piece of work; one who produces such.

Hags with the Bags, the [nickname]. Dub. street sculpture of two female shoppers, Liffey St. **1996** Renagh

Holohan, *Irish Times*, 1 June: 'We already have the Floozie in the Jacuzzi [q.v.], the Hags with the Bags, the Tart with the Cart [q.v.], the Chime in the Slime [q.v.] and, ahem, for the Joyce statue — the Prick with the Stick.'

hail/hale [vb., <'heal'] (Ulster). Enjoy oneself.

Hailer [prop. n., <abbrev. of 'hail' + endearment suffix]. 'Hail Mary' (prayer). **1987** Lar Redmond, *Emerald Square*: 'As regards prayers, I felt I had said enough Hailers to last me many a long day.' Also **Hailey Mary**. **1961** Dominic Behan, *Teems of Times and Happy Returns*: 'the priest would ask you not to do it again and tell you to go to the end of the chapel and say six Hailey Marys'.

hain/hane [vb., <ON *hegna*, hedge] (Ulster). Save or spare (oneself).

hair [n.] (Ulster). Fight between women (pulling hair).

hairpin [n.]. Carnaptious (q.v.) oul' wan (q.v.). **1966** Patrick Boyle, *At Night All Cats are Grey*, 'The Betrayers': '"No use wasting your sympathies on that old hairpin. Sure she might as well be out in pasture for all she's doing."'

hairy [adj.]. 1. (Ulster). 'Remarkable, conspicuous, exceptional' (Traynor). 2. Clever, wary. **1914** James Joyce, *Dubliners*, 'Two Gallants': '"She doesn't know my name. I was too hairy to tell her that. But she thinks I'm a bit of class, you know."'

Hairy Fairy [nickname, <beard & his interest in mysticism]. George W. Russell ('AE') (1867–1935), poet, painter and journalist. **1905** David Patrick Moran, *The Philosophy of Irish Ireland*: 'Shoneens [q.v.]: apers of English manners; Sour-faces: Protestants; West-Britons [q.v.]: Anglo-Irish; The Hairy Fairy: AE (George Russell).'

hairy mary/molly [n.]. 1. Caterpillar. **1966** Patrick Boyle, *At Night All Cats are Grey*, 'The Betrayers': '...I started combing through the curls on the back of her neck, watching them coil up again like the little furry caterpillars we call

Hairy Mollies'. 2. Female genitals. **1996** Katie Donovan, review of Aisling Maguire, *Breaking Out*, *Irish Times*, 25 May: 'Encountering a sympathetic nun, she realises that nuns have naked bodies too...She asks "Do you have a hairy molly between your legs?"'

haisge/hasky/a thaisge [exclam., <Ir. *a thaisce* (voc.), my dear!]. As thus. **1938** Seumas MacManus, *The Rocky Road to Dublin*: '"But Billy, *a thaisge*, why don't you take with you one of your own comrades and neighbours?"'

hait see **hate**

haith/heth [exclam.] (Ulster). Euphem. for 'faith' (q.v.). **1983** W.F. Marshall, *Livin' in Drumlister*, 'The Runaway': 'But we never thought what we were in for,/ Heth naw, we dhriv up at a throt,/But the welkim wos sharp, 'twos a pitchfork...'

hakit hands [n. phr., <Sc. *hack* (n.), break or crack in the skin] (Ulster). 'Hands chapped from exposure to cold' (Patterson).

hale [n. & vb.]. 1. [n., <'inhale' (vb.)] (Cork). Pull at a pipe. **1982** Pádraig Ó Clára, *Cork Holly Bough*, 'The Cork Shawlies [q.v.]': 'the ladies, their immense sacks backed up to the fence, reddening the dudeen [q.v.] and having a "hale"'. 2. [vb.]. See **hail**.

half and between [adj. phr.] (Ulster). 1. Slightly deranged (of individual). 2. Neither one thing nor the other.

half away [adj.] (Ulster). Mad.

half-car [n.]. Standard of transport accorded to junior government ministers as opposed to the limousine, most freq. a Mercedes, availed of by their seniors. **1995** *Sunday Tribune*, 31 Dec: 'New Year Resolve. Hugh Coveney...to get out of the half-car and back into the Merc.'

half-decent [adj.]. Acceptable, respectable. **1996** Conall Davey, *Sunday Business Post*, 27 Oct: 'Up to now any Irish chef who was wearing anything half-decent was buying it abroad.' **1997** Tom Widger, *Sunday Tribune*, 9 Mar: 'Pat [Kenny] would have been better had he

sat down Tuesday night and...thought up some half decent questions.'

half-natural [n.] (Ulster). Fool.

half-note [nickname]. Ten-shilling note in pre-decimal currency. **1879** Charles J. Kickham, *Knocknagow*: 'the doctor had lighted upon a page where sundry sums were entered, which he himself had received in the shape of half-notes'. **1975** John Ryan, *Remembering How We Stood*: 'Brendan [Behan] would come in for a fag, or "the lend of a loan" of a half-note, or any other reason why.'

half on [adj. phr.] (Ulster). Slightly intoxicated.

half-one [n.]. Half a glass of whiskey. **1936** *Irish Times*, 20 Mar: 'If help is near at hand "a half one" — in the vulgar vernacular — will be of benefit. It gives an artificial lease of life...'

Halfpenny Bridge see **Ha'penny Bridge**

halfroads [adv.] (Ulster). Halfway. **1979** John Morrow, *The Confessions of Proinsias O'Toole*: 'the next thing I knew I was half-roads across the polished table top at him, my tobacco knife well in advance'.

half-sir [n.]. Son of landlord/gentleman farmer. 'A landlord's son is referred to as a half-sir in Galway. He might be as dacent a man as ever wore shoe leather or he might be the two ends of [q.v.] a devil' (PO'F). **1992** Sean O'Callaghan, *Down by the Glenside, Memoirs of an Irish Boyhood*: 'he was what we call in Ireland a "half-sir" — the son of a gentleman farmer from a neighbouring parish'.

Half-time Jimmy [nickname, <?]. Chocolate bar. **1995** Phil O'Keeffe, *Down Cobbled Streets, A Liberties Childhood*: '"Thruppence is a lot to spend on chocolate," Ann said, a little shocked. "Ye could get a whole Half-time Jimmy for that." Half-time Jimmy was a chocolate bar that was only bought at Christmas or Easter.'

half-tore [adj.] (Ulster). Somewhat intoxicated.

Hallentide [prop. n.]. Feast of All Saints, 1 Nov. **1943** George A. Little, *Malachi*

Horan Remembers: '"But I knew a man on Killenarden here, who hadn't the cure when he needed it. One evening, nigh to Hallentide, he was driving up the Ardmore."'

hallion [n., derog., <Sc. *idem*, clumsy boy; irresponsible person; vulgar woman] (Ulster). As thus. **1993** Seamus Heaney, *The Midnight Verdict* (translation of Brian Merriman, *Cúirt an Mheán Oíche*): 'And steering towards me along the bay/This hefty menacing dangerwoman,/Bony and high, a terrible hallion.'

hames [n. sing., <two pieces of metal placed one on each side of a horse's collar, gen. as in **make a hames** (vb. phr.), cf. Brit. sl. 'make a hash' in same sense]. Mess, muddle. **1939** James Joyce, *Finnegans Wake*: 'Shun the Punman!: safely and soundly soccered that fenemine Parish Poser, (how dare he!) umprumptu rightoway hames...' **1989** Robert E. Tangney, *Other Days Around Me*: 'This was a good start: my first salaried job and I was making a hames of it.' **1995** Chris Glennon, RTÉ TV, *Farrell*, 28 May: 'He [John Bruton] made a dreadful hames of things when he admitted that he had the information...'

hammer a job [vb. phr.]. Engage in sexual act, gen. of male. **1950** Valentin Iremonger, *Reservations*, 'Icarus': 'But star-chaser, big-time-going, chancer [q.v.] Icarus/Like a dog on the sea lay and the girls forgot him,/And Daedalus, too busy hammering another job,/Remembered him only in pubs.' **1991** Shane Connaughton, *The Run of the Country*: '"Ah, good man yourself," Reilly said when he saw him. "I hear you hammered a job on Mrs Lee's daughter."'

hammers see **like the hammers**

hanch [n. & vb., cf. OF *hancher* (vb.)] (Ulster). Voracious snap (of dog etc.).

hand [n.]. 1. Butt, as in **make a hand of s.o.** [vb. phr.]. 'To make a hand of a person is to make fun of him' (PWJ); also destroy, make a mess of. Also **take a hand out of s.o.** (Ulster) in same sense (YDS). 2. [n. pl.] as in **have two hands alike** [vb. phr.]. Not pay one's way.

handbag [adj., <practice of groups of women dancing around their handbags]. Derog. as applied to pop music. **1995** Luke Clancy, *Irish Times*, 2 Sept: 'Way back at the beginning of the 1980s, when clubbing in Dublin was strictly "handbag" — the word recently adopted by one group of club-runners to signify the naff, plastic music from the 1980s...'

handle oneself see **hanle oneself**

handle one's feet [vb. phr.] (Ulster). Make good use of one's legs (in football etc.).

handless [adj.] (Ulster). Person useless with his/her hands.

handlin' [n.] (Ulster). Business, affair, as in **some handlin'!** **1990** Cover blurb, *Some Handlin', The Dialect Heritage of North Ulster*: 'They [the children of Ballyshrane Primary School]...entered with enthusiasm into this task [of the collection and transcription of local dialect], whose demands were such that they described it as SOME HANDLIN'!'

hand me down the moon/paper the moon [n. phr.] (Cork). Used of very tall person. **1993** Margaret O'Donovan in Michael Verdon, *Shawlies* (q.v.), *Echo Boys* (q.v.), *the Marsh and the Lanes* (q.v.): *Old Cork Remembered*: 'A tall person in Cork would be called *Hand Me Down the Moon* or *Paper the Moon*. That'd be traditional in Cork.'

hand shandy [n. phr.]. Act of (male) masturbation.

hand's stir [n. phr.]. A stroke of work; slight movement; very small distance.

hand-trot [n.] (Ulster). 'Rate between running and walking' (Traynor).

handy [adj. & adv.]. Not negligible. **1995** Deaglán de Bréadún, *Irish Times*, 2 Dec: 'As though reared in the Liberties, he [Bill Clinton] described Dublin as having a "handy" football team...' **1996** *Leinster Leader* (Naas, Co. Kildare), 4 July: 'His solicitor said that Mr Collins had "got in over his head". "He earned handy money on somebody else's heartache," Judge Brophy said.'

handywoman [n.]. Untrained midwife. **1994** Mary Corbally in Kevin C. Kearns, *Dublin Tenement Life*: 'Had to put up with it no matter how bad it was. Just hold on to the brass bed and the handywoman'd tell you what to do. She'd say to push or not to push.'

hane see **hain**

hang [vb., <OE *han* (n.), stone, poss. infl. by OE *hon* (vb.), hang] (Ulster). Hone. **1948** Patrick Kavanagh, *Tarry Flynn*: 'He was "hanging" a scythe in the kitchen the next morning to mow around the rocks and corners in the hay-field...'

hanging [adj., <?] (Cork). Drunk (Beecher).

hank [n.] (Ulster). Doubt/difficulty; mess/tangle.

hanky ball [n. phr.]. Children's ball made from handkerchief etc. **1951** Sam Hanna Bell, *December Bride*: '"It's a long time since you and me kicked a hanky ball coming home from school!" continued Skillen...'

hanle/handle oneself [vb. phr.] (Ulster). Hurry, exert oneself.

hannel [n., <?] (children's game). 'Blow with the spear or spike of a pegging-top (or "castle-top") down on the wood of another top' (PWJ). **1879** Charles J. Kickham, *Knocknagow*: 'Your castle tops came in for the most hannels.'

hap (aff) see **hop off** 2.

hap (up) [vb., <ME *happe*, wrap] (Ulster). Wrap up s.o., 'tuck them in bed' (SH).

ha'penny book [n. phr., <pre-decimal coin]. Cheap comic/story book. Hence **talk like a ha'penny book** [vb. phr.]. Talk rubbish. Also **penny book**, **tuppenny book** in same sense, reflecting inflation.

ha'penny boy [n. phr.]. Person of no account. **1966** Patrick Boyle, *At Night All Cats are Grey*, 'Myko': '"I'm not holding this against you, chum. I know you're only the ha'penny boy around here."' See also **penny boy**.

Ha'penny/Halfpenny Bridge [nickname, <toll formerly exacted] (Dub.). Wellington Bridge, footbridge across the Liffey, opened 1816. **1952** Maurice Craig, *Dublin 1660–1860*: 'the elegant, single-span cast-iron footbridge officially called Wellington Bridge...but in conversation always the Halfpenny or Metal Bridge'. **1993** William Trevor, *Excursions in the Real World*: 'On weekdays people hurried on the Ha'penny Bridge, not bothering to linger over the view.' **1996** Róisín Ingle, *Sunday Tribune*, 3 Mar: 'The Ha'penny Bridge on a sunny morning last week had two 10-year-old children with dirty faces camped at either side of the steps.'

ha'penny place [n. phr., <low-value coin]. Lowly position or condition. **1982** Éamonn Mac Thomáis, *Janey Mack* (q.v.), *Me Shirt is Black*: 'I think the cuff links thought their job was to escape rather than stay tied up to the shirt sleeve. Houdini was only in the ha'penny place to some cuff links I've had.' **1989** Hugh Leonard, *Out after Dark*: 'It [my book] would expose the venality of the gombeen [q.v.] men...it would for all time put Ibsen in the ha'penny place.' **1995** Declan Lynch, *Sunday Independent*, 17 Dec: 'It [sport] leaves every other religion in the ha'penny place. It is Catholicism and Protestantism, Islam and Buddhism...all rolled into one.'

hard [adj. & adj. as n.] as in exclam. **the hard!/the hard man!** Term of affection.

hard chaw [n. phr., see **hard**; cf. Eng. sl. *chaw*, yokel (DHS)] (Dub.). Irrepressible joker; tough individual. **1966** Liam Ó Cuanaigh, *Evening Press*, 21 Nov: 'A friend of mine was cycling home to Finglas with his wife on the crossbar, at the time the gardaí had been issued with new white uniforms. It was a hot day, so he pulled up beside the first man on point duty, handed him eightpence, and said "Give us two choc ices, please." He belongs to the group of Dublin characters [see **character** 1.] called "hard chaws".' **1970** Christy Brown, *Down All the Days*: '"I bet you won't put your finger in the fire, hard–chaw," he said triumphantly to Tony.' **1982** Éamonn Mac Thomáis, *Janey Mack* (q.v.), *Me Shirt is Black*: 'everyone knew I'd hired a dress suit... Some hardchaw would roar across the street, "Hey, you, come back with the dress suit."'

hard drop [n. phr.] as in **have the hard drop in one** [adj. phr.] (Ulster). Be miserly.

hard man! see **hard**

hard old/ould station [n. phr.]. Adverse condition or situation. **1964** Seán O'Brien, *Irish Press*, 'In Jail with Brendan Behan', 21 May: "Barr na maidhne [top of the morning (q.v.)], a Sheairi," he said, "and how are the balls of your feet? — What sort of an ould station is this?"..."Not bad," I said, "better nor the Glasshouse [area of solitary confinement] anyway." "'Tis not the station that matters," said he. "'Tis the station-master."'

hard root [n. phr., see **hard**] (Dub.). Devil-may-care individual. **1954** James Plunkett, *Bell*, 'The Eagles and the Trumpets', Aug: 'Maisie, who belonged to the establishment, giggled. "You're a terrible hard root," she said admiringly.'

hardshipping [adj.] (Cork). Difficult, arduous. **1966** Séamus Murphy, *Stone Mad*: 'It is hardshipping to try and skew-chisel a quarter of an inch off a bed.'

hard stuff, (the) [n. phr.]. Spirits, as opposed to beer etc. **1987** Lar Redmond, *Emerald Square*: 'A few bottles of stout and a drop of the hard stuff loosened their tongues...' Also **hard tack** [by analogy <nautical *idem*, ship's biscuit]. **1965** Lee Dunne, *Goodbye to the Hill*: 'and he rolled it around his tongue. Not getting much chance to drink the "hard tack", as he called it, he wasn't just slinging it down the hatch.'

hard ticket [n., see **hard**]. Natural humorist; eccentric individual; hard-natured individual. **1966** Liam Ó Cuanaigh, *Evening Press*, 21 Nov: 'A hard ticket is a conductor on the 79 to Ballyfermot, or any of the poorer runs where you can still use your sense of humour. The name may have come about as a result of the job, but that's a matter I leave to yourself and the "Pope" [q.v.] O'Mahony. A hard ticket says "Hurry up now, girls," to the mothers of fifteen children...' **1993** John O'Keefe in Michael Verdon, *Shawlies* (q.v.), *Echo Boys* (q.v.), *the Marsh and the Lanes* (q.v.): *Old Cork Remembered*: 'I was such a hard ticket. The master of the school, he'd always say to me: "Now, John, look after the boys until I come back." I was the tough man, you see.' **1994** Mary Doolan in Kevin C. Kearns, *Dublin Tenement Life*: 'And there was a woman, a hard ticket, a stuffy-nosed old thing — and we were such a poor gang — and she'd a young one [q.v.] going to a private school...'

hard word [n. phr.]. 1. 'A hint, an inkling, a tip, a bit of secret information' (PWJ). **1914** James Joyce, *Dubliners*, 'Two Gallants': 'Whenever any job was vacant a friend was always ready to give him the hard word.' 2. as in **put the hard word on...** 'expression for bringing matters to a point, but applied also to other requests that approach an ultimatum' (Wilkes, who also cites 'used most often of a man seeking sex (outside marriage)' — not common in Hib.E).

hardy [adj.]. Frosty (of weather).

hare [n.]. 1. as in **make (a) hare of** [vb. phr.]. Put down in argument; mock. **1889** A.P. Graves, 'Father O'Flynn': 'Don't talk of your Provost and Fellows of Trinity,/ Famous for ever at Greek and Latinity,/ Faix [q.v.] and the divels and all [see **devil an' all**] at Divinity —/Father O'Flynn'd make hares of them all.' **1937** Seán O'Faoláin, *A Purse of Coppers*, 'Admiring the Scenery': '"For," sighed the teacher, "he had no sense and people used to make a hare of him. He couldn't sing any more than I could."' **1988** John Healy, *Magill*, 'The Wild One', Apr: '"He would have loved to be called Doctor [Donogh] O'Malley," says [Desmond] McGreevy, "and I thought afterwards it was just as well he didn't because you, Healy, would have made a hare of him."' 2. [with def. art.] (Ulster). 'Last handful of growing corn cut at harvest' (Patterson); tiny piece, hence **damn the hare I care**.

harl [n. & vb., <Sc. *idem*, slattern, uncouth individual] (Ulster). 1. [n.]. As thus; quantity of something awkward to handle. Also **harl o' bones** [n. phr.]. Very lean person/animal (MON). 2. [vb.]. Heave, drag; peel skin from cooked potatoes without a knife.

harning iron [n., <'hardening'] (Ulster). Hardening board put on hearth to cool oatcakes. **1995** Ernest M.A. Scott in Mary Ryan et al. (eds.), *No Shoes in Summer*: 'Soda farls [see **fardel** 2.] and oatcake from the harning iron lifted/ With country butter over all, leaves each player well gifted.'

harns [n. pl., <Sc. *idem*, brains, <ON *hjarne*, brain] (Ulster). As thus.

harp see **quare harp**

harple see **hirple**

harp six [adv., <tail of Ir. coin, see **heads or harps**] (Ulster). Upside down. 'I went harp six on the frosty road' (Pepper).

Harriers [nickname, derog.]. Garda Síochána (police force). See also **Broy Harriers**.

Harry as in **be/by the Lord Harry!** See **Lord Harry**, **be the**.

harry hunner feet/legs [nickname] (Ulster). Centipede.

hash [adj. & n., <Sc. *idem* (n.), heavy fall of rain; foolish person]. 1. [adj.]. Unpleasant. 'That's a hash one — that's a horrid dirty day' (PO'F). **1943** George A. Little, *Malachi Horan Remembers*: '"he was a great poet, a mountain man, a 'hash' man to hurt, but a good friend"'. 2. [n.]. Lazy, untidy person. Also **hashter** [n. & vb.]. Mess and muddle; work in slovenly manner.

hasky [adj. & exclam.]. 1. [adj., cf. ME *harsk*, harsh; Norweg. *idem*, rough] (Ulster). Ill-natured, unsympathetic. **1983** W.F. Marshall, *Livin' in Drumlister*, 'The Runaway': 'So I went, an' if Robert was hasky,/Sarah Ann wos as nice as cud be...' 2. [exclam.]. See **haisge**.

hat see **my hat**

hate/hait [n., <Sc. *hae't*, have it, as in *Deil hae't!* Devil have it! Acquired sense of strong neg.]. Whit, smallest conceivable thing/quantity; also **sorra** (q.v.) **hate** not a whit. **1983** Polly Devlin, *All of us There*: '"I don't give a hait," is her way of expressing ostensible indifference...' **1995** Eileen Meehan in Mary Ryan et al. (eds.), *No Shoes in Summer*. 'But this one warm day, she was passing the custom man and he asked her had she anything to declare. She told him she hadn't a hate...He kept her there for ages and the butter started melting.' **1996** Séamus McCloskey, RTÉ Radio, *Sunday Miscellany*, 10 Mar: 'Everyone up here [North Monaghan] knows that a "hate" means absolutely nothing.'

hatherin/hutherin [adj., <Sc. *huther* (vb.), heap together untidily] (Ulster). Slovenly/untidy (woman).

hauch see **haugh** [vb.]

hauchle/houghle [vb., see **hough** (n.) 1.] (Ulster). Hobble, shamble, walk awkwardly. **1908** Lynn Doyle, *Ballygullion*: 'If there was word av law between two neighbours, Hughey would hauchle round to them both an' invite them down to talk it over.' Hence **hauchling** [pres. part. as adj.].

haugh/hauch/hough/hockle/haughal [vb., <Sc. *idem*, hawk, cough to clear the throat]. **1983** *John Pepper's Illustrated Encyclopaedia of Ulster Knowledge*: '"Ye should hear him haughal in the morning. You'd think it was claps of thunder."'

haugh [n.] see **hough**

haul home [vb. phr.]. Bring home the bride after the wedding to her husband's house (PWJ). See also **infair**.

haun [n., cf. Sc. *idem*, hand] (Ulster). Gen. with right (see **right** 1.) in neg. sense. A real mess. **1983** *John Pepper's Illustrated Encyclopaedia of Ulster Knowledge*: '"She had awful nice dark hair. Pity she made such a haun of herself."'

haunted [p. part. as adj.] as in **get haunted with** [vb. phr.] (Ulster). Become accustomed to.

have a mouth on one [adj. phr.] as in **he never asked me had I a mouth on**

me. Complaint of prospective drinker denied access.

have a notion of see **notion** 1.

have larks for breakfast/supper [adj. phr.] (Ulster). Said of s.o. preternaturally eloquent. **1913** Alexander Irvine, *My Lady of the Chimney Corner*: '"I don't mind a good bowl ov broth, Anna, but I'd prefer a bowl — jist a bowl of good broth!" "Ye've had larks for breakvist surely, haaven't ye, Billy?" Anna said.'

haver [n. & vb., <Sc. *idem*, nonsense; talk nonsense] (Ulster). As thus; hence **haverer**, **havering**.

haverel/haveril [n., <Sc. *haveeral*, half-witted/talkative/garrulous person]. Ignorant man; slatternly woman. **1996** Dermot Healy, *The Bend for Home*: 'He'd taken with him the only loaf of bread in the house and a pot of gooseberry jam. "The fecking [see **feck** (vb.) 2.] haverel," shouted Eileen.'

havverick [n., <?]. Rudely built house, or one roughly restored.

hay-foot, straw foot [adv. catchphrase, <ropes of hay tied to one foot and straw to the other to teach dancing pupils, army recruits, etc. to distinguish left from right: *Sí amach cos an ghiad agus crap cos an tsúgáin* — Stretch out the withie foot and withdraw the strawrope foot]. In great haste.

hazeler [n., <hazel rods carried by cattle drovers] (Dub.). Countryman, culchie (q.v.).

H-block [n., <shape as viewed from the air]. Prison building, esp. Belfast. **1983** Bobby Sands, *One Day in my Life*: 'The H-Block loomed up ahead of me on my right. I stood waiting for the gate to open — the gate to hell.' **1997** Frank McNally, *Irish Times*, 30 Apr: 'Loyalist prisoners remained in control of two Maze Prison H-blocks last night...'

head [n.]. 1. [poss. <Classical Gk.]. Familiar term for member of either sex, but more gen. male, also in greeting, as in **howaya** (q.v.), **head?** 1847 John Edward Walsh, *Ireland Sixty Years Ago*: 'A usual exhortation from a father to his son was,

"make your head, boy, while you're young," and certain knots of seasoned drinkers who had succeeded in this insane attempt, were called *kat' exochen*, "the heads", from their impenetrability to the effects of liquor.' **1992** Brian Leyden, *Departures*: 'Waistcoats, packet tobacco and roll-your-own heads with cowboy hats, leaky guitar cases and lanky girlfriends.' **1995** *Irish Times*, interview with Glen Hansard, 15 Dec: '[Van Morrison is] still a very important person in my life, because he...was the first person to make me believe I'd go places as a musician myself. He was like [q.v.] 15 years older, a real "head"...' 2. (Cork) as in **the head off** [n. phr.]. The image of. **1996** Christy Kenneally, *Maura's Boy, A Cork Childhood*: '"Who's dat now?" "He's poor Maura Hartnett's boy; sure you'd know him outta dem. Isn't he de head off Christy Hartnett?"'

headache [n., <effect of unpleasant smell]. Common red poppy. Considered obnoxious to females, 'the more so to unmarried young women, who have a horror of touching or being touched by them' (EDD).

headbin [n.] (Ulster). Unstable person; 'headcase'. **1996** Gary Arthurs, *Irish Times*, 26 Oct: 'we could have packed out eight or 10 [buses] with headbins and sent them out first to start a full-scale riot'.

headbombardier [n.] (Ulster). Foreman, any person in charge.

headbuckcat [n., <Ir. *buc*, he-goat, hence any virile male]. Person in charge. **1968** Austin Clarke, *A Penny in the Clouds*: '"Good God, man," I cried..."do you think the head buck cat is going to come down from Dublin in the middle of the night?"' **1979** John Morrow, *The Confessions of Proinsias O'Toole*: '"I mind [q.v.] you callin' him 'the chap with a stoppage in his Erse'...An' look at him now, eh? — Head buck-cat newsreader in RTÉ!"'

header [n., cf. Brit. & US sl. 'headcase']. Mentally deranged individual. **1965** Lee Dunne, *Goodbye to the Hill*: 'thinking they must all be virgins [in the Virgin Islands] and dying for it on account of the shortage of men. As I say, I was a right [see **right** 1.] header.' **1986** Tom McDonagh, *My Green Age*: 'There were plenty of "headers", as they were called: people who did not make sense, disturbed perhaps or of low mental ability.'

head lar [n. phr., cf. Austral. sl. *lair*, show-off, term of gen. contempt (Wilkes)]. Man in charge, gen. ironic.

head money [n. phr., 'Believed to derive from the eighteenth-century practice of printers meeting weekly each Saturday night in the Brazen Head and Carteret Head inns [Dub.]...' (WS)] (printing). Trade union dues.

head–piece [n.]. Intelligent individual. Also **have the head-piece on one** [adj. phr.]. Be well endowed with intelligence.

heads or harps [n. phr., <harp emblem on obverse of Ir. coinage, 1520–]. Heads or tails. **1965** Lionel Fleming, *Head or Harp*: '"Toss you for it, head or harp." "Harp?" "...when there was Irish money in the old days, there was the King's head on one side and the harp on the other..."' **1996** *Galway Advertiser*, 15 Feb: 'Galway City theatre company, Heads or Harps, have begun rehearsals for Brian Friel's acclaimed play "Living Quarters"...'

headstaggers [n. pl., <disease of horses]. Mental derangement, state of total confusion.

head–the–ball [n., derog.]. Fool. **1995** Opel Astra commercial, RTÉ Radio, Mar: 'What sort of head–the–ball would miss a chance like that?'

heap of decency [n. phr.] (Ulster). Excessive politeness.

hear one's ears [vb. phr., gen. neg.]. Hear oneself speak.

heart [adj. & n.]. 1. [adj.] (Ulster). Extremely. **1908** Lynn Doyle, *Ballygullion*: 'She wasn't far wrong there, for the ould fellow was heart miserable about money.' 2. [n.]. See **put the heart across**.

heart of corn [n. phr.]. Said of kind, generous person. **1943** George A. Little, *Malachi Horan Remembers*: '"But Kitty and Johnny (God will forgive them), they had the heart of corn."' **1990** Tom O'Kane,

quoted in Walter Love, *The Times of our Lives*: 'I went to Orange Halls myself and danced...and all the best of friends. The one would do anything for the other. They had a heart of corn all my early years...'

heart of the roul/rowl [n. phr., <Dub. pronun. of 'roll' (of tobacco)] (Dub.). (One of) the best (of an individual). **1964** Seán O'Brien, *Irish Press*, 'In Jail with Brendan Behan', 21 May: 'That gallant, reckless Brendan that never did a mean turn. He was "the heart of the Roul", as he might put it himself...' **1969** Tom Mac Intyre, *The Charollais*: 'Throw your mind back to that fine lump of a girl...*the prototype of her species, the handmaid of The Lord, and the heart of the rowl...*' **1982** Éamonn Mac Thomáis, *Janey Mack* (q.v.), *Me Shirt is Black*: 'Messrs. T.P. and R. Goodbody opened a factory in Tullamore, Co. Offaly, in the year 1843 to manufacture tobacco. Their first brand was Irish Roll, which gave its name to the saying...the centre of the Irish Roll tobacco was the freshest and juiciest.'

heart–scald [n., <Ir. *scall*, scald; cf. *an croí a scalladh ag duine*, lit. to scald s.o.'s heart; see **scald** 2.]. 1. Mortification, vexation. 2. Troublesome individual or situation. **1995** Phil O'Keeffe, *Down Cobbled Streets, A Liberties Childhood*: '"You said the doctor from the Coombe was coming. Is the baby sick?" "You're a right [see **right** 1.] heart-scald with your questions."' Hence **heart-scalded** [p. part. as adj.]. **1951** Frank O'Connor, *Traveller's Samples*, 'The Masculine Principle': 'She said it was all his fault for not standing up for her; that he knew she was heart-scalded at home...' **1968** John Healy, *The Death of an Irish Town*: 'And so I came home, thanking God and the American taxpayer and a lot of my heart-scalded school friends for my education.' Also **have one's heart scalded** [adj. phr.]. **1961** Dominic Behan, *Teems of Times and Happy Returns*: '"Larry Clancy! Come up this minit! Jasez [see **Jaysus!**], that young fella has me heart scalded."'

Hearts of Steel see **Steelboys**

heartsome [adj.] (Ulster). Cheerful; encouraging. **1883** David Herbison, *The*

Select Works of David Herbison, 'My Ain Native Town': ''Twas heartsome to see on a Saturday morn,/Before the red clouds o' their tassels were shorn,/Our blithe bonnie lassies come into the town.'

heatherbleat/heatherblade [n., <OE *haefer-blaete*, lit. goat-bleater, <noise of wind through the feathers when diving] (Ulster). Snipe (*Gallinago gallinago*). **1979** Paddy Tunney, *The Stone Fiddle*: 'May eves were full of the bleating of heather-blades and bitterns as they scythed across the swamps and slunks [q.v.]...'

heavy eye [n. phr.] (Ulster). Evil eye.

Heavy Gang [nickname]. Alleged element in Garda Síochána (police force) employing violent means to extract confessions etc., 1980s. **1996** Cathal O'Shannon, *Sunday Tribune*, 1 Dec: 'Which brings us to the Heavy Gang. This phrase was coined by Paddy MacEntee, SC...when he suggested to a witness that "the heavy gang came down from Dublin".'

heavy metal! [interj.] (Ulster). Expressing astonishment.

heck-a-beds [n., <?] (Leinster). Children's game, see **piggybeds**. **1994** Vonnie Banville Evans, *The House in the Faythe*: 'An excursion to the Rocks, the local quarry, saw us returning with pockets full of chalk...and then the heck-a-beds started.'

heckle see **hackle**

hedge school [nickname, implying rural location etc., hence 'poor, low-class school' (OED)]. Informal, usually open-air education for Catholics disadvantaged under the late C17–early C18 Penal Laws. **1847** John Edward Walsh, *Ireland Sixty Years Ago*: 'the only places of general instruction were "Hedge Schools", that is, benches laid loosely either in a waste cabin, or under a hedge by the wayside'. **1984** John McGahern, *Oldfashioned*: 'Race memories of hedge schools and the poor scholar [q.v.] were stirred, as boys...came long distances from the villages and outlying farms to grapple with calculus...' See also **Burton books**.

hedge up [vb.]. Move up to make more space. **1970** Christy Brown, *Down All the Days*: '"Hedge up there you inquisitive shower of bastards and let me behold my handiwork."'

heel-ball [n. as adj., <shoemaker's implement]. Full of business. **1995** Gregory Allen, RTÉ Radio, *Sunday Miscellany*, 15 Oct: (to a Garda) 'Look at your man [q.v.], all heel-ball. Who did you lock up today?'

heeler [n.] (Ulster). Working dog that drives cattle by nipping at their heels; 'Sharp, prying, managing woman' (Patterson); rapid worker.

heel of the hunt, at/in the [concessive phr.]. Eventually. **1938** Seumas MacManus, *The Rocky Road to Dublin*: 'the father, who was of a mordant humour, finished the man's story for him — "and at the heel o' the hunt you found the other calf here before you"'. **1977** Flann O'Brien, *The Hair of the Dogma*: 'At the heel of the hunt, after hopping and trotting he got paid.' **1995** Aidan Higgins, *Donkey's Years*: 'But "in the heel of the hunt", Mumu would say, meaning when all was said and done, they didn't go and sneak on me...' Also **in the heel of the reel** in same sense.

heels foremost [adv. phr.]. Dead. Cf. 'be carried out **feet first**'.

Heffo's Heroes [nickname, <abbrev. + endearment suffix, <Kevin Heffernan, captain of Dub. GAA team which won the All-Ireland football finals in 1974, 1976 and 1977]. **1989** David Walsh, *Magill*, Jan: 'the public, keen to personalise the success of the team, settled on Kevin Heffernan. The team became known as "Heffo's Heroes".' Hence **Heffo's Army** [nickname]. Supporters of the team. **1977** Wesley Burrowes, *The Riordans*: 'a Dublin weaver called Murph who drove a motorbike and spoke in a strange tongue about culchies [q.v.] and rednecks [q.v.] and belonged to a paramilitary group called Heffo's Army'.

hefted [p. part. as adj., <ON *hefta* (vb.), restrain] (Ulster). Full, as of cows needing to be milked; suffering from a full

bladder. **1921** (first published 1983) Patrick MacGill, *Lanty Hanlon*: 'The heavy udders of hefted cows trailed on the ground, dripping milk on the greensward.'

helping-stick [n.]. Crutch. **1938** Seumas MacManus, *The Rocky Road to Dublin*: 'he would be knocking, pounding, bumping and thumping with his *croisín* (as, back in Glen Ainey, they called the big helping-stick)'.

hen on a hot griddle, like a [catchphrase]. Very agitated. **1908** Lynn Doyle, *Ballygullion*: 'For all that I was like a hen on a hot griddle till the [Grand] National.' **1965** Lee Dunne, *Goodbye to the Hill*: 'Poor Ma was hopping about like a hen on a hot griddle, worrying if I had this, that and the other.'

hen's race [n. phr.] (Ulster). Very short distance.

hen-toe/d [n. & adj.] (Ulster). Pigeon-toe/d.

here's your hat and what's your hurry [catchphrase]. Employed to speed a parting guest. **1995** Sean Kilfeather, *Irish Times*, 14 Dec: 'the Irish fans were left to give [Jack] Charlton an affectionate reception on the pitch even if there was an element of "Here's your hat and what's your hurry," about what may yet prove to be a premature farewell'. See **Jack's Army**.

herring hogs [n. pl., <?] (Ulster). Harbour porpoise (*Phocaena phocaena*); bottle-nosed whale. **1995** Brigid O'Donnell in Mary Ryan et al. (eds.), *No Shoes in Summer*: 'I saw what my father described as herring hogs sticking their noses out of the water.'

herself [pron.]. Quasi-respectful ref. to wife; less commonly to any female. **1920** Seumas O'Kelly, *The Leprechaun of Kilmeen*: 'So up with Tom Donohoe into the box, and began to tell all about the diggins of the bush, and the assault of him by "Kelleher's wife" — that's the way the miserable tinker spoke of herself...' **1966** Séamus Murphy, *Stone Mad*: 'Herself is always in a good humour of a Friday morning.' **1994** Ferdia Mac Anna, *The*

Ship Inspector: '"This is for Herself," Butch Cassidy said, slipping me an extra chop with a big grin.' See also **himself**.

heth see **haith**

hi [enclitic] (Ulster). 'Much used but meaningless ending to most Derry speech' (TT).

hick [n. & adj., <Brit. sl. *idem*, simple countryman, <dimin. of 'Richard'; cf. Austral. & US usage]. Yokel; vulgar, shoddy, cheap. **1991** John B. Keane, *Love Bites and Other Stories*: '[The corner boy (q.v.)] is not as he has been so often mis-labelled a peasant or a churl or a bog trotter [q.v.]. He is neither a yokel or hick.' Also **hicky/hickey** [adj.]. Unfashionable, gimcrack.

hide/hilt nor/or hair [n. phr. <Sc. *idem*, nothing at all] (Ulster). As thus. **1925** Louise McKay, *Mourne Folk*: '"...Pat flung himself off the car into their midst, and they as quickly closed around him, so that neither hilt nor hair of Pat could be discovered"'. **1938** Seumas MacManus, *The Rocky Road to Dublin*: '"Why, Jaimie, you're a sight for sore eyes! Is it sick you've been for these five weeks, that I haven't seen hilt or hair of you?"' **1948** Patrick Kavanagh, *Tarry Flynn*: '"I sent Aggie up to see how you were getting on and she came back to tell me that hilt or hair of you wasn't to be seen and that the devil the damn the fence you did."'

hidey/hidy-hole [n., <Sc. *idem*, hiding place]. As thus. **1958** Frank O'Connor, *An Only Child*: 'He rooted about on top of the wardrobe, which was his hidey-hole, well out of reach.' **1993** Eilís Dillon in Seán Dunne (ed.), *The Cork Anthology*, 'In the Honan Hostel': 'big ramshackle houses, cold in winter but heavenly in summer, with wild gardens and all kinds of hidey-holes where one could escape from one's own kind'.

hifiddle see **eye-fiddle**

hig [n., cf. Sc. *hike* (vb.), 'move the body suddenly by the back joint' (CSD)] (Ulster). Helping hand, as in **I gave him a hig up**.

higgler [n., <'haggle' (vb.) with fronting of vowel]. Itinerant dealer. **1995** Shane Connaughton, *A Border Diary*: 'Every Saturday higglers, hucksters, tinkers and shopkeepers from all over Ulster gather here to sell their wares...'

high babies [n. phr.] (education). Senior infants, second year of school. **1994** Vonnie Banville Evans, *The House in the Faythe*: 'From the moment we were seated together in the same desk in high babies we became inseparable.' **1995** Des Cahill in Seán Power (ed.), *Those were the Days, Irish Childhood Memories*: 'I guess I was in "high babies" or maybe in first class — I would have been about six or so...' **1995** Phil O'Keeffe, *Down Cobbled Streets, A Liberties Childhood*: 'I liked school. In Babies and High Babies we sat snugly together and made funny shapes from *marla* [modelling clay]...' Also **low babies** (q.v.).

high Lizzie see **high Nellie**

highmadandy [n.] (Ulster). Individual with more money than education.

high Nellie/Maggie [n. phr.]. Old-style ladies' 'upstairs' bicycle. Also **high Lizzie**.

Higo [n., <Highland Light Infantry, 'a British regiment despised by Cork people' (Beecher)] (soccer supporters) (Cork). Coward, cowardice. As in **a touch of the Higos**. Also **HLI** in same sense.

hike! [exclam.]. Call to stop a horse. **1939** James Joyce, *Finnegans Wake*: 'Tuck up your sleeves and loosen your talktapes. And don't butt me — hike! — when you bend.' **1982** Éamonn Mac Thomáis, *Janey Mack* (q.v.), *Me Shirt is Black*: 'The sudden roar of the word "Hike, Hike, Hike," and the scraping of the horse's shoes was something terrible. The horseman stopped his charger an inch from me beard.' **1985** Máirín Johnston, *Around the Banks of Pimlico*: 'A runaway horse was as good as a cowboy film. It was hair-raising to watch the driver bent backwards like a rodeo rider straining and pulling on the reins, yelling "Hike, ho-there, ho-there..."'

hillsiders [nickname]. Rebels. **1914** James Joyce, *Dubliners*, 'Ivy Day in the Committee Room': '"Some of these hillsiders and fenians [q.v.] are a bit too clever if you ask me," said Mr Henchy.'

hilt nor/or hair see **hide nor hair**

himself [pron.]. The man of the house; quasi-respectful ref. to any male. **1979** Frank Kelly, *The Annals of Ballykilferret*: '"I think himself is after going to his Maker earlier this evenin', but I didn't like to tell ye when ye were busy with the customers."' See also **herself**.

hinch [vb., <Sc. *idem*, throw underarm while bouncing the hand off the upper thigh]. As thus.

hind-tit [adj., <tit offered by cow to weakest calf]. Disadvantaged; weak. **1997** Tom Mooney, *Carlow Nationalist*, 6 Feb: 'Carlow will continue to be Ireland's hind-tit county.'

hinogues [n. pl., <Ir. *fuinneog*, window]. 'Bits of broken window glass' (OTF).

hintin [n., <Sc. *hint* (vb.), plough up bottom furrow between rigs (CSD)] (Leinster). Last strip between the ridges. **1995** Edward McNerney in Mary Ryan et al. (eds.), *No Shoes in Summer*: 'One fellow might be dragging a drain to let the water away...Another fellow might be throwing in hintins in the hill field...'

hip-at-the-clinch [n.] (Ulster). Person with a limp.

hip buttons, to want the [n. phr.] (Ulster). 'Be not quite wise' (Traynor).

hippin [n.] (Ulster). Child's nappy.

hippity-tippity [adj., <Sc. *hippertie tippertie*, over-punctilious] (Ulster). Of person concerned with having things 'just so'.

hip-screwed [adj.] (Ulster). Having stiff hip joints.

hirple/harple/hirsel [vb., <Sc. *hirple*, hobble] (Ulster). Walk lame, move with difficulty. Hence **hirplin/g** [adj.] lame; **hirplin** [n.] lame individual.

hise/hize [vb., <Low Ger. *hissen*, hoist]. Raise, lift. **1966** Séamus Murphy, *Stone*

Mad: 'they caught the job as if 'twas a sack of meal and hised it into position'.

hiyis!/hiyiz! [exclam., <US 'hi!' + Hib.E pl. of 'you': see **youse**]. Form of greeting. **1990** Roddy Doyle, *The Snapper* (q.v.): 'Sharon came in. "Hiyis," said Sharon. "What're yiz laughin' at?"' Also **howayis/howyis** in same sense.

hize see **hise**

ho [n., <Ir. *chomh-*, equal; gen. with neg. & derog.]. As thus. 'A child spills a jug of milk and the mother says: "Oh Jacky, there's no ho to you for mischief"' (PWJ).

hoaching/hooching [pres. part. as adj., <?] (Ulster). Infested (as with rats).

hoag/hoger/hogo [n., <Fr. *haut goût*, high flavour] (Ulster). Strong smell.

hobbelty-causey see **hobbledy-curry**

hobble/hubble [n. & vb.]. 1. [n., <'hobble' (vb.), hamper]. Difficulty. **1888** Rosa Mulholland, *A Fair Emigrant*: '"But, sure, here's Misther Rory himself. Never fear but the masther'll pull ye out of the hobble."' **1943** George A. Little, *Malachi Horan Remembers*: '"Talking of Mathers and mares reminds me of the hobble that caught Father Dunne."' 2. [n.]. Term of abuse. **1952** Bryan MacMahon, *Children of the Rainbow*: 'When we had come up, Finn said to me, with undertone laughter: "Your sister Mary is a right [see **right** 1.] hobble!"' 3. [vb.]. Secure the right to moor a ship at the Dub. quays, hence **hobbler** [n.] one who acts thus. **1936** *Irish Times*, 23 Feb: 'The "hobbler"...must come close to the vessel he hopes to moor...Sometimes two or three "hobblers"' boats are waiting, and whoever secures the line first gets the mooring.' **1995** Denis Doyle, *Irish Times*, 13 Oct: 'We were fishermen, and, when that went, we were hobblers. We would go out and meet the ship, get the tying-up of her and the pigging-out of her.' Hence [vb.] (Cork). Acquire possession of. **1991** Teddy Delaney, *Where we Sported and Played*: 'We knew there was eating and drinking in a pint of stout and tried to hobble one each at the Guinness stand...'

hobbledy-curry/hobbelty-causey/hubbelty-curry [n., cf. Sc. *coggle* (vb.), wobble] (Ulster). See-saw.

hobby-horse [n., <ME *hobyn/hoby*, small horse, pony]. Foolish person, buffoon. **1630** Thomas Dekker, *The Honest Whore Part II*: 'BRYAN Pox on de gardens, and de weeds, and de fooles cap here...doest make a hobby-horse of me.'

hobby-horse manure as in **scarce as hobby-horse manure** [adj. phr.]. Very scarce. **1981** Paddy Crosbie, *Your Dinner's Poured Out!*: 'Although money was "as scarce as hobby-horse manure", my father managed to produce a bicycle for the three of us...'

hobnobs [n. pl., <Brit. sl. 'nobs', persons of rank, position or wealth, 1809] (Cork). As thus. **1991** Teddy Delaney, *Where we Sported and Played*: 'a row of chalets on the beach front, which the hobnobs from the city rented, shared a communal tap'.

hoch see **hough** [n.]

hochmagandy [n., see **hough** (n.) 1.] (Ulster). Fornication.

hockle see **haugh** [vb.]

hodal [vb., cf. Sc. *hoddle*, waddle] (Ulster). Ride a bicycle in a standing position.

hog [n.]. Pre-decimal shilling. **1806** Anon., *Ireland in 1804*: 'I must not omit the answer made me by the waiter at the coach inn, in Bolton-street [Dub.], when I asked her what I had to pay for breakfast. "Two hogs and a half"; and again on my staring in her face, "Two hogs and a tester [q.v.]," meaning in each case half-a-crown.'

hoger see **hoag**

hogger [n., <abbrev. of 'hogshead' + endearment suffix] (Dub.). Street idlers, corner boys (q.v.), C19–20. **1997** Richard Roche, reviewing Dervla O'Carroll & Seán Fitzpatrick, *Hoggers, Lords and Railwaymen*, *Irish Times*, 1 Mar: 'The "Hoggers" of the title...were a group of men who congregated on the North Wall outside the Custom House and who prided themselves on their

ability to drink the dregs from empty Guinness barrels left on the quayside.'

hogo see **hoag**

H.O.H.A. [abbrev., children's street challenge] (Dub.). Hit one hit all. **1946** Donagh MacDonagh, *Happy as Larry*: 'H.O.H.A., Hit one, hit all,/Here's when the wake becomes a spree.' **1963** Leslie Daiken, *Out Goes She* (Dub. street rhymes): 'Pronounced *Haitch Oh Haitch Ah*...a defensive challenge when a tough gang is menaced by a tougher gang. A powerful morale–booster, democratic but militarily weak. I have seen...the invocation and magic of H.O.H.A. fail miserably against brute strength and Monto [q.v.] cunning.'

hoke [vb., <Sc. *howk*, dig, burrow, <Low Ger. *holken*, make hollow] (Ulster). Dig, scoop out, rummage through. **1983** Polly Devlin, *All of us There*: 'He plunges about the waist and pockets of his ancient trousers and coats ...this kind of search is called "hoking".'

hokey see **be the hokey**

hold foot to [vb. phr.] (Ulster). Sustain, keep up with.

hold hard! [exclam.]. Wait a minute! Hold on! See **neb** 2.

hold one's whisht see **whisht**

hold/take your hour! [exclam., cf. Brit. sl. 'hold it!']. Wait a minute! Have patience! **1963** Brendan Behan, *Hold your Hour and Have Another* (book title). **1991** Bob Quinn, *Smokey Hollow*: '"You told him he was doing Nick wrong?" "Will you take your hour. That's not the way to approach these matters. You have to be circumspectual."'

holliers [n. pl., <abbrev. + endearment suffix]. Holidays. **1988** Gabriel Byrne, *Magill*, 'Fade In, Fade Out', Mar: 'On holliers on Sunday nights waiting under the town clock in Ballytore for a man on a bicycle bringing silver cans of film from Athy.' **1990** Roddy Doyle, *The Snapper* (q.v.): '"They're goin' on their holliers together," Mary told Sharon. "Dirty bitch," said Yvonne.'

holy alls [n. phr.]. End result. **1914** James Joyce, *Dubliners*, 'Grace': '"Such a sight! Oh, he'll do for himself one day and that's the holy alls of it. He's been drinking since Friday."' **1951** Frank O'Connor, *Traveller's Samples*, 'Old Age Pensioners': 'her view was that poetry, like drink, was a thing you couldn't have knocked out of you, and that the holy-all of it would be that Coleman would ruin the business on her'.

holyawn/uhlan [n., <Ir. *ɨeolán*, little thief; alternatively Ir. *uailán*, light-headed, skittish person; Sc. *hallion*, 'clumsy fellow, clown, idle, lazy scamp' (CSD); *Uhlan* (prop. n.), one of the Polish army lancers, from their atrocities in the 1798 rising (all quoted DOM)] (Leinster). Young hooligan.

Holy Farmer, by the [expletive, euphem., <'Holy Father']. Mild oath. **1922** James Joyce, *Ulysses*: 'by the holy farmer, he never cried crack [q.v.] till he brought him home as drunk as a boiled owl'.

holy father [nickname, <use of oath 'By the Holy Father']. 'A butcher's boy of St Patrick's Markets, Dublin, or other Irish blackguard' (Grose).

holy flip me pink! [exclam.]. Mild oath. **1995** Gerry Adams in Seán Power (ed.), *Those were the Days, Irish Childhood Memories*: 'Uncle Paddy's voice rose above the din. "Nearly there now, lads. Don't give up! Holy flip me pink! What did that signpost say?"'

holy fly! [expletive]. Mild oath. **1908** Lynn Doyle, *Ballygullion*: '"I'll not run afther her, not if she was 'my lady'. Be the holy fly," sez he..."I'll ask the first woman I meet!"' **1932** (first published 1992) Samuel Beckett, *Dream of Fair to Middling Women*: 'Lilly Neary has a lovely gee [q.v.] and her pore Paddy got his B.A. and by the holy fly I wouldn't recommend you to ask me what class [q.v.] of a tree they were under when he put his hand on her and enjoyed that.'

holy frost, by the [exclam.]. Mild oath.

Holy God! [expletive]. **1989** Hugh Leonard, *Out after Dark*: 'Holy God derived his nickname from his favourite expletive, employed promiscuously either to express amazement or simply to fill a void in conversation.'

holy hour [n. phr.]. Sixty-minute period of compulsory closing, 14.30–15.30, of licensed premises in principal cities — later limited to Dub. and Cork — introduced in 1927 and finally rescinded in 1960. By extension, the afternoon closure enforced on Sundays under the same legislation. **1953** Honor Tracy, *Mind You I've Said Nothing*: 'The pub was just closing for the Holy Hour as I came up to it and entry could only be gained by a subterfuge.' **1994** Senan Finucane in Kevin C. Kearns, *Dublin Tenement Life*: 'Certain places didn't see that the Holy Hour was observed...people could be *sneaky* in keeping out of sight and there could be thirty or forty people inside the public house during the Holy Hour.' Hence **1995** Frank McNally, *Irish Times*, 15 Aug: 'By 5 a.m. the cafe has grown quiet...The [Bewley's] staff...start the clean-up operation in advance of the official "holy hour".'

holy lamb [n. phr., iron.]. 'A thorough-paced villain' (Grose).

Holy Mary [n.]. Hypocrite, ostentatiously religious individual, male or female. **1961** Tom Murphy, *A Whistle in the Dark*: 'MUSH Us? We've no chance. Har? Too much back-handin', too much palm-oil, too many Holy Marys pulling strings...'

Holy Mother (of God) [exclam.]. Mild oath. **1996** Maureen Tatlow, *Sunday Tribune*, 21 Jan: '"Yes, people do tend to say, holy mother, 20 quid for a bottle of oil," Sean Gilley of Terroirs says.'

holy poker! [exclam., <supposed implement of punishment employed in purgatory; see **be the hokey**]. Mild oath. **1908** Lynn Doyle, *Ballygullion*: '"whin he tries to work the joint, — 'be the holy poker,' sez he, 'she's stuck.'"'

holy show [n. phr., iron.]. Cause/source of scandal/embarrassment, esp. as in **make a holy show of oneself** [vb. phr.]. **1995** Frank McNally, *Irish Times*, 26 Apr: 'Has anybody noticed the state of the new £5 note lately?...only a year after the Central Bank rather rudely stamped the £5 sign on Mother McAuley's forehead, the note has become something of a holy show.'

holy terror [n. phr.]. Undisciplined, misbehaving individual; figure of fear. **1989** Hugh Leonard, *Out after Dark*: '"Isn't your young lad a holy terror for talking on the altar."' **1992** Sean O'Callaghan, *Down by the Glenside, Memoirs of an Irish Boyhood*: 'before he came to the parish, people knew he was a "holy terror". At his first mass...he preached a sermon full of hell and damnation...' **1995** Aidan Higgins, *Donkey's Years*: 'He wore big brown boots and a wide-brim felt hat which he clutched to his head with one hand, the other reaching out towards me, summoning. I watched this holy terror come plunging towards me...'

homeboy [n.]. Former inmate of religious institution. **1963** John McGahern, *The Barracks*: 'labourers hired out for their lives from the religious institutions that reared them to farmers, homeboys, were known to have as few as 5 cars behind their deal coffins [i.e. few to mourn them]'.

home-rulers [nickname, <?]. Pint bottles of stout. 'Doneraile Walk [Tramore, Co. Waterford] will be like Finaghy Field tonight with all the "home-rulers"...that will be lying about' (PO'F).

hooch [n. & vb., cf. Sc. *hooing* (n.), loud shouting] (Ulster). Shout.

hooching see **hoaching**

hoofler [n., cf. *huffle*, 'a piece of bestiality too filthy for explanation' (Grose, 1785 edn)] (Cork). Scoundrel. **1966** Séamus Murphy, *Stone Mad*: 'The biggest hoofler I ever worked with...was a Carlow man. Oh, he was a thorough-going scoundrel.'

hook [n.]. Twister. **1967** Bryan MacMahon, *The Honey Spike* (q.v.): 'He had taken out the torn demand note and was searching the empty envelope. "Damn-all else here," he said. Reading from the back of the demand note: "This tinker is a hook.'" Hence **hookery** [abst. n.] in same sense. Also **hooky** [adj.]. Questionable. **1946** Myles na gCopaleen, *Irish Writing No. 1*, 'Drink and Time in Dublin', May: '"It's the late nights that's the killer, two and three in the morning, getting poisoned in shebeens [q.v.] and all classes [q.v.] of hooky stuff..."'

Hook and Eye, the [nickname, <type of centre-buffer railway coupling] (Cork). Cork & Muskerry Light Railway, 5 Aug 1887–29 Dec 1934. **1934** Anon., 'Lament for the Blarney Express': 'Goodbye, good-bye,/Old Hook-an'-Eye,/Farewell, O Harnessed Power!/We knew full well/The strain would tell/At fourteen miles an hour!' **1977** *Cork Holly Bough*: 'The public usually travelled to the Fair on the "Muskerry Tram", the narrow-gauge steam railway, often referred to as the "Hook and Eye".'

hook-em-snivey [n., <crook of thick iron wire on a wooden handle used to undo wooden door-bolts from outside: thieves' cant *c*.1800]. **1802** Maria & R.L. Edgeworth, *Essay on Irish Bulls*, 'The Dublin Shoeblack': 'An indescribable, though simple machine, employed by boys in playing at head and harp [see **heads or harps**]…"With that I ranged them fair and even with my hook-em-snivey up they go."'

hooley [n., poss. Hindust. *hoolie*, a Hindu festival, brought back by Ir. soldiers in Brit. army]. Extended celebration, usu. involving consumption of alcohol. **1955** Samuel Beckett, letter to Alan Simpson (Pike Theatre director), Nov: 'but I may be in Dublin next summer and look forward to a hooley with you all then'. **1981** Paddy Crosbie, *Your Dinner's Poured Out!*: 'My mother frowned on [the stage] and so he performed only at hooleys and parties…'

Hoops, the [nickname, <shirt design] (Dub.). Shamrock Rovers soccer club. **1988** Robert Allen, *Magill*, 'Not Fade Away', May: 'The thought for many Shamrock Rovers fans of a move to Tolka Park…was unthinkable. "Will Greed kill the Hoops?" said one of the protest banners.'

hoor/hure [n., <Late OE *hore*, whore; Hib.E phonetic spelling reproduces approximately the original OE pronun.; almost exclusively male or impersonal in attrib., cf. Austral. *hooer*, 'applied to men in a generally derogatory way, like "bastard"' (Wilkes)]. Derog., also term of grudging affection or respect. **1987** Vincent Caprani, *Vulgar Verse & Variations, Rowdy Rhymes & Rec-imitations*, 'The Irish Hoor': 'We're the only people on earth that refer to a man as "yeh hoor!"' **1989** Ann Morrow, *Picnic in a Foreign Land*: 'In his [Lord Altamont's] own case, the highest compliment he has been paid on the estate is to be called "a great auld whore", pronounced "whoer".' Also **cute hoor** [n. & adj., invar. male]. Term of denigration, implying (political) deviousness and lack of scruple. **1994** David McKittrick, *Independent on Sunday* (London), 20 Nov: 'It [Fianna Fáil] is the party of quiet deals, of smoke-filled rooms, of nudge and wink — in rural argot, of the "cute hoors".' **1995** Denis Coghlan, *Irish Times*, 12 Aug: 'It doesn't come across as a cute-hoor position; more a statement of how things are in day-to-day business.' Also **hoorin'/huaring** [adj.]. **1963** John McGahern, *The Barracks*: '"Some of the bog roads. Some place where not even Quirke's huaring car can get.' **1988** John Healy, *Magill*, 'The Wild One', Mar: 'he [Donogh O'Malley] gave me, as a gift, his bound copies of the Dáil debates covering his career in Leinster House. "You'll find some use for them," he said…"The hoorin' things are no use to me."' Also **a hoor of** [adj. phr.]. Disastrous, dreadful. **1966** Séamus Murphy, *Stone Mad*: 'Firies stone now, a hoor of a stone, a bitch of a stone, a treacherous bloody stone…'

Hoor in the Sewer, the see **the Floozie in the Jacuzzi**

hoor's/whore's/whoor's get [n. phr., *hoor* implying female + *get* (q v.), whore's bastard]. Term of abuse. **1939** Sean O'Casey, *I Knock at the Door*: 'the drover nearer to Johnny ran over to the tired cow, and began to hammer her with his stick. "Yeh whore's get," he shouted, slashin' away at her…'

hoor's/whore's/whoor's melt [n. phr., *hoor* implying female + *melt* <OE *milt*, spleen, offspring, spawn]. 1. Derog. term. **1961** Dominic Behan, *Teems of Times and Happy Returns*: "'Go on, yeh rotten whore's melt! Yer people turned [see **turn** 2.] Protestant for soup durin' the famine!'" **1989** Hugh Leonard, *Out after Dark*: "'An' sure God is good, and the whoor's melt won't have a minute's luck.' **1992** Sean O'Callaghan, *Down by the Glenside, Memoirs of an Irish Boyhood*: 'But it was of Parnell [see **the Uncrowned King of Ireland**] that he spoke most: "A king," he called him, "A hero who would have freed Ireland," but for the opposition of the black-hearted "hoors' melts".' 2. Complete mess, as in **make a hoor's melt of** [vb. phr.].

Hoor, the Long see **Long Hoor, the**

hoosh! see **hush!**

hooter [n.] (Ulster). Braggart, conceited person.

hop [n.]. as in **on the hop** [adj. phr.]. Playing truant.

hop and go constant [n. phr. & adj.] (Ulster). Uneven gallop of horse with leg cramps; steady worker. **1948** Patrick Kavanagh, *Tarry Flynn*: 'They still kept running along so that their hop-and-go-constant gait was like the progress of kangaroos or horses with itch in the heels.'

hop (the) ball [n. & vb., <method of starting Gaelic games]. Provocative remark or observation; make such remark. **1987** Con Houlihan, *Dublin Opinion*, 'The Ball Hop' (q.v.), May: 'Though as a people we are probably the world's leading sports-lovers, our *afición* has bequeathed few usages to the vernacular. *The hop ball* is almost certainly the most common...' **1991** John B. Keane, *Love Bites and Other Stories*: '"I know now," said a Waterford man, an elderly commercial who likes to hop balls, "why Kerry won so many All-Ireland finals." Dead silence ensued.' **1994** Joseph O'Connor, *The Secret World of the Irish Male*: 'Annoyin' me, yeh know? Hopping the ball she was, ourra badness.' See also **ball-hop**.

hop off [vb.]. 1. Attack with blows, strike violently. **1988** John Healy, *Magill*, 'The Wild One', Mar: 'a wild [Donogh] O'Malley night when, a bit the worse the wear for drink, he grabbed a fire extinguisher, hopped it off the bar counter to activate it and then proceeded to spray the bottles and end wall of the bar'. **1993** Pat Tierney, *The Moon on my Back*: 'The prospect of slipping off the tail light [of the motorbike] and hopping my arse several times off a Connemara road did not appeal to me in the slightest.' **1995** *Leinster Leader* (Naas, Co. Kildare), 9 Mar: 'the defendant denied the assault charge, claiming, "If anyone was assaulted I was assaulted." She told Judge Martin that Lorraine Holohan "hopped off me" and spat on her back.' 2. (Cork). Tease, as in **have a hop off s.o.** [vb. phr.] (Beecher). 3. [as exclam.]. Call to horse to turn to the right.

hopper [n.]. Vermin. **1994** Maggie Murray in Kevin C. Kearns, *Dublin Tenement Life*: 'And we had no bedclothes, we mostly slept with me daddy's overcoats over you. Sure, the bed was loaded with bugs and hoppers and you'd be scratching yourself.'

horchin/hurchin/urchin [n., <'urchin'] (Ulster). Unpleasant person.

horney [n., cf. *Oul Hoarny Cluty*, the Devil] (Ulster). Policeman. **1986** Tomás Ó Canainn, *Home to Derry*: "'Are you naval officers?" he asked. "No, we're not," Sean answered. He couldn't help feeling a certain elation that a dock "horney" had mistaken them for officers.'

horrid [adj.]. Extremely, very. **1995** Michael 'Gossie' Browne in Mary Ryan et al. (eds.), *No Shoes in Summer*: 'I made many friends at the fairs and on the road. They were horrid dacent men and would always do you a good turn...'

horse-protestant [n., mildly derog.]. Country gentry; Protestants in general. **1932** *Ulster Hiker* (Cushendall, Co. Antrim), 'The Ulster Dialect', June: 'The farmer who works hard all the week and neglects his stock on Sundays glories in the designation "horse protestant".' **1962**

Brendan Behan, *An Irish Sketch-Book*: 'It started off with top-hats and white ties and getting into the gentry and then to chatting about the servant problem with the Anglo-Irish Horse-Protestants...'

hot [vb., <solecistic p. tense of 'hit']. Abuse, beat. **1961** Dominic Behan, *Teems of Times and Happy Returns*: '"I don't want to go to school. The nun'll hot me for not having any money for the black babies [q.v.]."'

hot press [n.]. Domestic airing cupboard. **1997** Property advertisement for Drumboy House, Lifford, *Irish Times*, 12 June: 'Dining Room, Kitchen/ Breakfast Room, Back Kitchen, Utility Room, Mistress's Pantry, Maids' Pantry, Cloakroom, 5 Bedrooms, Hotpress Room...'

hot water, the [nickname] (angling). **1989** Ken Whelan, *The Angler in Ireland*: 'it finally snapped while I was spinning for bass at the outfall of the Ringsend Power Station near Dublin (known to generations of Dublin anglers as "the hot water"'.

hough/haugh/hoch/huff [n.]. 1. [<Sc. *idem* <ME *hogh/hough*, hollow behind knee joint] (Ulster). Back of (upper) leg, thigh. 'See her huffs? You could nearly see her navel!' (Todd). **1993** Sam McAughtry, *Touch & Go*: 'Weaving was clean work, not like spinning or doffing; weavers didn't stand in water with their skirts hoisted up to the houghs.' 2. [<?]. Mess. **1995** Phil O'Keeffe, *Down Cobbled Streets, A Liberties Childhood*: '"Well it looks to me as if he's makin' a hough of it. Look at him parin' all that stuff away from the horse's foot." "He couldn't make a hough of it, or the horse would kick him."' 3. as in **last haugh in the pot** [n. phr.] (Ulster). Said of s.o. invar. late (YDS).

hough [vb.] see **haugh**

Hougher [nickname, (see **hough** (n.) 1.)]. Member of the Whiteboy (q.v.) agrarian movement, mid C18, from their practice of hamstringing their victims.

houghle see **hauchle**

hoult [n. & vb., <Hib.E pronun. of 'hold'] as in **a fine/great/good hoult** (of a woman). With desirable sexual attributes, hence act of sexual intimacy; engage in such an act. **1991** Bob Quinn, *Smokey Hollow*: 'She was a stocky woman in her thirties, what Granda Hope would call "a fine hoult".' **1994** Gabriel Byrne, *Pictures in my Head*: 'He said he didn't think she was serious about anyone, but she was a great hoult as he himself knew...' **1995** Éamon Kelly, *The Apprentice*: 'she, struggling to free herself, said, "Bad luck to you! Isn't it hard up you are for your hoult and the priest coming in the front door!"' See also **court**, **scrape**.

houthern [n., <?] (Ulster). Untidy, slovenly (woman).

hoved out [p. part., <Sc. *idem*] (Ulster). Swollen with drink.

howanever [adv., <'however', cf. howsomever (q.v.)]. However, nevertheless. **1889** W.G. Lyttle, *The Royal Visit to Ireland* (letter from 'Robin' — pseudonym of W.G.L. — to Prince Albert Victor of Eng., subsequently Duke of Clarence. The mode is echoed in Percy French's *The Queen's After-Dinner Speech*: see **man in the gap**]. 'Hooaniver, pittin' that tae yin [one] side, A'm prood, as A said afore, that yer cummin' back tae Bilfast. It shews that ye likit it when ye wur there afore...' **1908** Lynn Doyle, *Ballygullion*: 'The crayther [see **craythur** 2.] was ready for the asylum as it was. Howaniver [*sic*], all I could think of, I could only give him cowld comfort...' Also **howasever** (Leinster) in same sense.

how are you! [exclam.]. Expression of denial, disbelief, dismissal. **1918** James Joyce, *Exiles*: 'BEATRICE ...Did he practise the piano when I was away? BRIGID (*laughs heartily*.) Practice, how are you! Is it Master Archie?' **1987** Vincent Caprani, *Vulgar Verse & Variations, Rowdy Rhymes & Rec-im-itations*, 'James Joyce': 'So there you are — three generations of double marriages of sisters celebrated. Guinness Book of Records, how are yeh!' **1991** Bob Quinn, *Smokey Hollow*: 'Mr Toner put a half-crown on the table and invited them to contribute some of their pocket money to the cause. Pocket money how are ye! Slowly and grudgingly the pennies and thruppenny pieces were produced.'

how are you blowing? [greeting, interrog., cf. Austral. *how're ya goin'?*]. How are you? **1922** James Joyce, *Ulysses*: 'who should I see dodging along Stoney Batter only Joe Hynes. "Lo, Joe," says I, "How are you blowing?"'

howaya!/howya! [exclam., <'how are you?']. Form of address; greeting. **1996** Desiree Shortt, *Irish Times*, 20 Feb: 'For the past 20 years, I have always been addressed as "howaya" by police, traffic wardens, builders, painters, electricians, plumbers, shopkeepers, and my most recent burglar.' **1996** Niall Moloney, *Irish Times*, 27 Feb: '"Howya" is not an address but rather a greeting. "There", however (as in "Howya there"), does qualify as a true salutation.' Also pl. form **howayis(/z)!/ howyis(/z)!** See **hiyis!**

howdy/howdie(-woman) [n., <Sc. *idem*, midwife; cf. Fr. *sage-femme, idem*] (Ulster). As thus.

howlt [n., <'hold'] (Ulster). Awkward situation. **1983** W.F. Marshall, *Livin' in Drumlister*, 'The Runaway': 'No falt till his daughter, I left her/But I foun' meself still in a howlt.' Also **in howlts** in same sense.

how's about you? (Belfast). How are you? **1994** Senan Molony, *Star*, 19 Oct: '"Hi-za-bowchee? A Bag Mock, azzat?" [Welcome. Would you like a Big Mac?]' Also **'bout ye**. **1995** *News Letter* (Belfast), 9 Dec: 'According to Gerard Rocks, who works for the Family Planning Association on the "Bout Ye" project, the most common concern of 13- to 16-year-olds is sexual health...'

howsomever/howsumdiver [adv., cogn. with 'howsoever', with *-sum-*, *-som-* elements <Dan., Swed. *som*, as, that, for 'so']. However, nevertheless. **1925** Louise McKay, *Mourne Folk*: 'It was evident Tim didn't relish the job. "Howsomever," he remarked, "polis is polis," and there was nothing for it but to go.' **1943** George A. Little, *Malachi Horan Remembers*: '"Who was the murderer, Mr Horan?" I asked. "I will not tell you that, but it is known," answered Malachi. "Howsomever," he continued, "suspicion was raised..."'

how's she cuttin'? [catchphrase, <agricultural machinery? Cf. Austral. sl. *how're ya goin'?*]. How are things? **1986** Gene Kerrigan, *Magill*, June: 'The driver, a man with a cheery grin, hopped out and ran over to Joey. "How's she cuttin', chief?" Joey gestured helplessly.' **1994** Gabriel Byrne, *Pictures in my Head*: 'a star in a white suit, under which the world famous muscles are bulging and contracting with a life of their own. How'ya [q.v.], how's she cutting, ya boy ya! [q.v.]' **1996** Joe O'Connor, *Sunday Tribune*, 21 July: 'Chat-up lines you might be better to avoid..."How's she cuttin, sweetychops? May I just inform you that I speak 18 languages and can't say no in any of them."' See also **cutting**.

how's your father [cant. phr.]. Sexual activity; 'it could describe anything' (EW).

howya! see **howaya!**

hubbelty-curry see **hobbledy-curry**

hubble [n. & vb.]. 1. [n., <'hobble' (vb.), hamper] (Ulster). Fuss and bother (SH). 2. [n. & vb.]. See **hobble**.

huckleback/hucklebuck [n. & vb.]. Lively dance. 'D'ye mine [see **mind**] the Charleston an the huckleback?' (Todd).

huff see **hough** [n.]

huffle [vb., onomat.]. (Of wind) Blow in sudden, strong gusts. **1583** Richard Stanihurst, translation of Virgil's *Aeneid*: 'To swage seas surging, or raise by blusterus huffling.'

hugita ugitas, iskey sollagh [exclam., <Ir. *Chugat! Chugat! Uisce salach!*, Watch out! Watch out! Dirty water!]. Charm against the fairies. **1995** George Sheridan in Mary Ryan et al. (eds.), *No Shoes in Summer*: 'if it was after sunset, she would say before she threw the water [outside the back door], "hugita ugitas, iskey sollagh"'.

hug-me-tight [n.] (Ulster). Shawl that can be fastened, woollen vest.

hulk [n., <Ir. *olc*, bad] (Ulster). Cross, stubborn individual.

Humanity Dick/Martin [nickname]. Richard Martin, politician & Connemara landowner (1754–1834). **1945** Robert Gibbings, *Lovely is the Lee*: 'Ballynahinch Castle, once the property of Richard Martin, MP, "Humanity Martin" they called him...' **1983** Martin Wallace, *100 Irish Lives*: 'In 1824, he was the founder of the (now Royal) Society for the Prevention of Cruelty to Animals...The Prince Regent (later George IV) nicknamed him "Humanity Dick".'

humbugg [n., <?]. Hoax. **1754** Thomas Sheridan, *The Brave Irishman*: 'he's as merry as he never was in his life. Phin [when] I'm by, he's sometimes pretty smart upon me with his humbuggs...'

hume [n., <?] (Ulster). Bad smell.

hummins [n. pl., cf. Sc. *hummel* (vb.), chew carelessly] (Ulster). Small pieces of chewed food (SH).

hump [n. & vb.]. 1. [n.] as in **take the hump** [vb. phr.] (Ulster). Take offence. 2. [vb., mild euphem. for fuck (q.v.)]. As thus. **1979** Éamonn Mac Thomáis, *The 'Labour' & the Royal*: '"And what about George," I said, "waiting for us up in Sarsfield's Place." "Ah hump George and hump Sarsfield too," he said.' Also **hump off** [exclam. & vb., cf. Eng. sl. *hump oneself*, hurry (DHS)]. Go away, get lost. **1997** Bertie Ahern, RTÉ Radio news, 8 July: 'I was told I should just have told him [Dick Spring] to hump off.'

hunch [vb. trans., <'hunch-backed', orig. 'bunch-backed; Brit. dial., 1689' (OED)]. Push, thrust, shove. **1985** Máirín Johnston, *Around the Banks of Pimlico*: 'The cattle drovers, wielding ashplants, hunched the cows, sheep and pigs, beating them mercilessly...'

hungry grass/feur-gortach [nickname, <Ir. *fear gortach*, *idem*]. Mountain grass supposed to induce weakness and hunger. **1938** Seumas MacManus, *The Rocky Road to Dublin*: 'in later days, on the mountains, the *feur-gortach* got him three times — only, luckily for him, each time help and food were near at hand'. **1943** George A. Little, *Malachi Horan Remembers*: '"That was the hungry-grass you trod on,' the neighbourman told me. 'Nobody but a fool tramps these hills without food in his pocket.'"' **1947** Donagh MacDonagh, *The Hungry Grass*: 'Crossing the shallow holdings high above sea/Where few birds nest, the luckless foot may pass/From the bright safety of experience/Into the terror of the hungry grass.' Also **famine grass** in same sense.

hunker [vb., cf. ON *húka*, squat] (Ulster). Toady to s.o. in authority.

hunker-slide [vb.]. 1. Slide on ice sitting on the hunkers. 2. Act with duplicity; shirk work. **1914** James Joyce, *Dubliners*, 'Ivy Day in the Committee Room': '"One man is a plain honest man with no hunker-sliding about him. He goes in to represent the labour classes."' **1970** Christy Brown, *Down All the Days*: '"You needn't come whining here for your grubstakes. There'll be no hunger[*sic*]-sliding as long as I'm head of this house."'

hunt [vb. trans.]. Drive away, see off s.o.

hunt-a-gowk [n., <Sc. *gowk* <ON *gaukr*, cuckoo] (Ulster). Person sent on fool's errand.

Hunting Cap [nickname]. Maurice O'Connell, uncle of Daniel O'Connell, the Liberator (q.v.). **1938** Seán O'Faoláin, *King of the Beggars*: '...Count O'Connell kept nagging at Dan's other uncle Maurice, called Hunting Cap — a shrewish, hard-fisted old smuggler — until he persuaded him to adopt Dan as his protégé'.

hupyaboya!/yup ya boy ya! [joc. exclam., <*hup!*, call to horse etc.]. Sporting adjuration. **1995** Eanna Brophy, *Sunday Tribune*, 9 July: 'THE HUPYABOYA. Harmless enough when on its own, but can be quite distressing when encountered in large numbers. It tends to flock to football and hurling grounds...but it is also a nocturnal creature whose eponymous call is often

heard late into the summer nights...'
1996 Anne Marie Hourihane, *Sunday Tribune*, 18 Feb: 'Charlie [Haughey]'s public appearances are always marked by men shouting "Yup, ya boy ya!" which is a nice cheerful sound.' See also **yeh-boy-yeh!**

hurchin see **horchin**

hurdies [n. pl., <Sc. *idem*, buttocks] (Ulster). As thus.

hure see **hoor**

hurish! [exclam., <?]. Call to a sow. **1960** John O'Donoghue, *In Kerry Long Ago*: '"Hurish! Hurish! Hurish!" she shouted as she threw out the food on the yard, for that was the usual call for a sow, as distinct from the "ban, ban, ban" which was meant for the other pigs.'

hurkle [vb., <Sc. *idem*, crouch over the fire] (Ulster). Sit idle when there is work to be done.

hurl [n., <Sc. *idem* (vb.), bowl along] (Ulster). (Car) ride.

hurler [n., <?]. Whiskey measure. **1975** John Ryan, *Remembering How We Stood*: '"Just a friend," replied Myles [na gCopaleen] quietly...meanwhile ordering another hurler of malt [q.v.]...'

hurler on the ditch [n. phr., <Hib.E *ditch* by palatalisation of OE *dic*, embankment, wall or fence]. 'Said in derision of persons who are mere idle spectators sitting up high watching the game...critics who think they could do better' (PWJ). **1996** Anna R. Quinn, *Irish Times*, 18 Sept: 'Sir — John Banville in his article about hurling...notices "the odd Mediterranean tan"...I wonder how Mr Banville knows the difference between a Mediterranean tan and an Atlantic or Irish Sea tan? Perhaps the best

way to get a tan is to be a hurler on the ditch.'

hurley [n., <shape of stick used in game of hurling] (Ulster). Shaped loaf of boxty (q.v.). **1982** Henry Glassie, *Passing the Time*: 'mix the potatoes with flour, about half as much as there is potato...then form it into puck-shaped, circular "hurleys", five inches across and one in depth'. Also **hurley foot** [n. phr.]. Club foot. **1943** George A. Little, *Malachi Horan Remembers*: '"Lanky Tom Callaghan of the Hurley Foot' was the name they had on him. He had a club-foot, you see."'

hurnish! [exclam., <?] (Munster). Call to hens. **1995** Éamon Kelly, *The Apprentice*: 'Two hens and a cock... seemed to complain bitterly that they were hungry and why weren't they getting something. With a "hurnish" from the woman of the house and a flapping of wings they were gone.'

hurt [n., <?]. Whortleberry. **1995** Éamon Kelly, *The Apprentice*: 'Her youthful days before when she went out working were all sunshine. Strolling by the river bank, gathering hurts...or courting on the grassy slopes of the railway...'

hush!/hoosh!/whush! [exclam.]. Cry to drive fowl.

hushoe/huzho [n. & vb.]. Lullaby, cradle song. **N.d.** Folk song, 'M'Kenna's Dream': 'The murmur of the ocean huzhoed me to sleep.' Also **put the husho on s.o.** Silence s.o.

hutherin see **hatherin**

huxter [n., cf. 'huckstery', 'huxtry', huxter's premises] (Ulster). Run-down house or property.

huzho see **hushoe**

I

idleset [n.] (Ulster). Idleness, idle time; large belly (as evidence of idleness).

ignorant [adj.]. Badly behaved, bad-mannered, uncouth. See also **pig-ignorant**.

ile see **oil**

ill-set [adj., <Sc. *idem*, evilly disposed] (Ulster). Bent on making trouble.

ill-willie [adj.] (Ulster). Disobliging.

im bhaiste see **ambaist**

immo [adj. & n., <abbrev. + endearment suffix]. Imitation, fake.

inagh!/inyah! [exclam., cf. Ir. *an eadh?* is it?]. Expression of surprise. **1866** Patrick Kennedy, *Legendary Fictions of the Irish Celts*: "'I'll go with you for your servant," says the other. "Servant *inagh* (forsooth)! Bad I want a servant...'" **1922** James Joyce, *Ulysses*: 'Jappies? High angle fire, inyah! Sunk by war specials. Be worse for him, says he, nor any Rooshian.'

inanunder/inunder [prep.] (Ulster). Underneath. **1938** Seumas MacManus, *The Rocky Road to Dublin*: 'She cursed barley, and kilty, and poteen [q.v.] likewise,/And cursed all the still-tinkers inunder the skies.' See also **anonder**.

inanyway [adv. & conj., <elided pronun. of 'and anyway']. Anyway. **1997** Alan Roberts, *The Rasherhouse* (see **rasher**): "'Don't mind her, Mags, it's not that bad arall [at all]." Betty tried to sound cheerful. "Better than I get outside inanyway."'

inching and pinching [vb. phr., <Sc. *idem*, living frugally] (Ulster). As thus.

income [n., <Sc. *idem*, 'ailment without apparent external cause' (CSD)] (Ulster). As thus.

indeed and doubles [adv. phr.] (Ulster). 'Strong way of saying indeed' (Patterson).

India/Indian-buck [n.]. Meal/porridge made from maize (Indian corn).

Indo [nickname]. *Irish Independent* newspaper. **1988** John Waters, *Magill*, Mar: "'In Independent House, 'gay' means happy," the [House Style] booklet cautions. Indo journalists, it urges, should use the word "homosexual" — "when this is what they mean".' **1995** Brendan O'Carroll in Seán Power (ed.), *Those were the Days, Irish Childhood Memories*: 'So if there are still any of those old codgers left from the Indo or the [Evening] Herald of '66, please accept a heartfelt "Thanks" from Benny, the lift boy...'

infair/infare [n., <'in' + OE *faran* (vb.), go]. Bringing home of the bride after marriage. See also **haul home**.

Inglified see **Englified**

Inishowen [nickname, <Inishowen peninsula, Co. Donegal, location for illicit distillation]. Illicit whiskey, poteen (q.v.).

in it [adv. phr., <Ir. *ann, idem*]. Alive, esp. as in **only in it**, marginally existing. **1914** James Joyce, *Dubliners*, 'The Sisters': "'Ah, poor James!" she said. "God knows we done all we could, as poor as we are — we wouldn't see him want anything while he was in it."'

innocent [n., euphem.]. Simpleton, idiot. **1800** Maria Edgeworth, *Castle Rackrent*: "'To be sure, to hear her talk, one might have taken her for an innocent, for it was "What's this, Sir Kit? and what's that, Sir Kit?"' **1943** George A. Little, *Malachi Horan Remembers*: "'One day and he coming across the Commons he came up with an 'innocent' carrying a churn...'Whose churn did you steal, *amadán* [q.v.],' shouted Hughes, very wicked.'"

innocent Amy! [exclam.]. Directed at s.o. simulating innocence. **1914** James Joyce, *Dubliners*, 'The Dead': 'Gabriel coloured and was about to knit his brows, as if he did not understand, when she said bluntly: "O, innocent Amy! I have found out that you write for *The Daily Express*."'

insense (into) [vb., <Sc. *idem*, convince] (Ulster). Instil, impress upon.

inside car [n. phr.]. One-horse public conveyance. **1847** John Edward Walsh, *Ireland Sixty Years Ago*: 'The addition of covers to the kind of cars called inside-cars, is an improvement made within the last few years, giving the vehicle most of the advantages of a coach...'

insleeper [n.] (Ulster). Visitor who will spend the night.

Inst. [nickname, abbrev.]. Royal Belfast Academical Institution. **1985** John Boyd, *Out of my Class*: 'Inst was very different from Mountpottinger. It had a well-kept lawn at the front and a muddy playing field and a bicycle-shed at the back.' **1996** BBC Radio, *Inside Ulster*, 31 Jan: 'Inst. came back in determined fashion and were unfortunate not to score.'

in the jigs [adj. phr., cf. Scand. *jigg* (n.), sediment; Brit. sl. *jiggered* (p. part. as adj.), 'made from a secret still, *c*.1880–' (DHS)]. In a serious state of intoxication/ delirium tremens. **1975** John Ryan, *Remembering How We Stood*: 'Shortly after departure, the plane was struck by lightning. Brendan [Behan], who was in the jigs anyhow, reacted in fear-shaken fashion.' **1977** Myles na gCopaleen, *The Hair of the Dogma*: '"You heard about the mad brother-in-law coming home on a visit out of the British army three quarters in the jigs?"'

inunder see **inanunder**

Invincibles, the [nickname, first appeared as 'Irish Invincibles', 6 May 1882]. Secret society. **1922** James Joyce, *Ulysses*: '"I heard that from the head warder that was in Kilmainham when they hanged Joe Brady, the invincible. He told me that when they cut him down after the drop it was standing up in their faces like a poker."' **1939** Sean O'Casey, *I Knock at the Door*: 'the damned English with their No Irish Need Apply after the [Phoenix] Park murders, even though it was well known that it wasn't the English protestant [Lord Frederick] Cavendish the Invincibles were after but the Irish catholic [T.H.] Burke'. **1973** León Ó Broin, 'The Invincibles' in T. Desmond Williams (ed.), *Secret Societies in Ireland*: 'the

assailants made their way back to the city [of Dub.] and left black-edged cards at the newspaper offices which said that the deed had been done by the Irish Invincibles. It was the first time the world had heard of this secret society.'

inyah! see **inagh!**

in your grannie's/granny's [adv. phr.]. Well contented. **1992** Hugh Leonard, *Rover and Other Cats*: 'There is a Dublin phrase for being totally at ease and in the kind of company where all may be said and all is understood. Achieve such a state and you are "in your grannie's".'

ire [n., <Ir. *oighear*, sore produced by chafing] (Cork). As thus; sexual arousal (Beecher).

Irish... for racist expressions thus prefixed see Appendix.

Irish solution to an Irish problem, an [catchphrase, coined by Charles J. Haughey, Minister for Health, introducing the Family Planning bill of 1978; latterly iron.]. Fudged solution to a political/religious/social dilemma. **1987** T. Ryle Dwyer, *Charlie*: '"This bill seeks to provide an Irish solution to an Irish problem," he said. "I have not regarded it as necessary that we should conform to the position obtaining in any other country."' **1988** John Healy, *Magill*, 'The Wild One', Apr: 'no new concert hall was ever built from the ground up: we took the Irish solution to an Irish problem and converted the abandoned UCD Earlsfort Terrace building'.

iron fool [n.]. **1966** Patrick Boyle, *At Night All Cats are Grey*, 'The Metal Man': 'You could safely say that Mr Bloody Doyle is a solid cast-iron hundred-per-cent Metal Man — what's known in other parts of the country as an "iron fool"...the title given to a wolf that has no need to wear sheep's clothing because it happens to have been born complete with fleece and double stomach.'

iron lung [n., <apparatus formerly employed in treatment of tuberculosis]. Aluminium keg containing draught stout, esp. Guinness, pop. at parties.

Irregular [adj. & n., euphem.]. Member of anti-Treaty force in Civil War, 1921–2. **1982** Robert Kee, *Ireland, A History*: 'Because communications across the south of Ireland were still being effectively harassed by republicans (soon to be known as "irregulars") Collins [see **the Big Fella**] sent Free State troops round by sea to take the city of Cork...' **1996** Patsy McGarry, *Irish Times*, 9 July:

'In the civil war he [Jim Rogers] was on the losing side. There was no future for "Irregular" drapers' assistants in the new State. He left for America...'

itchypoos [n. pl., <Sc. *itchy-coo*, rose-hip] (Ulster). As thus.

ithergates [adv., <Sc. *idem*, elsewhere] (Ulster). As thus.

it suits ya, chrissie see **chrissie**

J

jabble [vb., <Sc. *idem*, spill] (Ulster). Splash about, spill over (YDS).

jabus! [exclam., euphem.]. Jesus! See **fellow**.

jack [n.] Coin employed in feck (see **feck** [n.] 2.) game. See **boxman**, **jockey**, **rider**, **tosser** 1.

jack-act [vb.]. Play the fool. **1966** Patrick Boyle, *At Night All Cats are Grey*, 'Odorous Perfume her Harbinger': 'My fingers become deft. Often I pull ahead of Granpa and am forced to wait till he catches up. On these occasions I feel I am entitled to jack-act.' See also **act the maggot**, **cod**, **jig-act**, **trick-acting**.

jack-an-ory [exclam., <*Jackanory*, Brit. TV children's storytelling programme] (Ulster). 'Scornful statement of disbelief' (TT).

jack-easy [adj.] (Ulster). Very easy, no trouble (Todd).

jacked [p. part. as adj., cf. Austral. sl. *jack up* (vb.), give in, collapse]. Exhausted, tired out.

jackeen [n., <'Jack' + Ir. dimin. *ín*; *c*.1840–]. Dubliner, as opposed to culchie (q.v.). **1914** James Joyce, *Portrait of the Artist* (q.v.) *as a Young Man*: 'that he [Mr Dedalus] was an old Corkonian, that he had been trying for thirty years to get rid of his Cork accent up in Dublin and that Peter Pickackafax beside him was his eldest son but that he was only a Dublin jackeen'. **1987** Lar Redmond, *Emerald Square*: 'he [the teacher] had twice as many Jackeens to beat if they gave him a chance. He hated Dublin kids...' **1995** Patrick Boland, *Tales from a City Farmyard*: 'Then she added, "Don't you know, you Dublin Jackeen, that billy-goats — gentlemen goats to you — don't give milk?"' See also **Dub** 1.

jack-in-the-box [nickname] (Ulster). Wild arum *(Arum maculatum)*.

Jack, Jack, Show the Light [n. phr.]. Children's game. **1979** C.S. Andrews, *Dublin Made Me*: '...I spent the ample leisure time of my formative years... playing "Billy Rump Sticks", "Jack, Jack show the light", "Ball in the decker" [q.v.]...' **1995** Billy French in Mary Ryan et al. (eds.), *No Shoes in Summer*: 'the chase took place through the fields that surrounded the village. The object of the game was for Team B to capture Team A. Team A had a lamp, or a candle in a jam jar, and Team B had three chances to call on Team A by shouting "Jack, Jack, Show the Light".'

Jack Lattin/Latten as in **I'll make you dance Jack Lattin/Latten** ['John Lattin of Morristown House, Co. Kildare (near Naas) wagered that he'd dance home to Morristown from Dublin — more than twenty miles — changing his dancing-steps every furlong: and won the wager'(PWJ)]. Threat of chastisement. **1922** James Joyce, *Ulysses*: 'THE HONOURABLE MRS MERVYN TALLBOYS Very much so! I'll make it hot for you! I'll make you dance Jack Latten for that.'

Jack Mum [n.]. Generalised individual, as in **between you and me and Jack Mum** between you and me and the gatepost. See **glasheen**.

Jack Nod [n.] (Ulster). Sleep.

jacks/jax [n., cogn. with *jakes*, a privy, *c*.1530–, less common in Hib.E; poss. <'Jack's place']. Toilet. **1946** Myles na gCopaleen, *Irish Writing No. 1*, 'Drink and Time in Dublin', May: '"So I take one [sleeping pill]. But I know the doctor doesn't know how bad I am. I didn't tell him the whole story, no damn fear. So out with me to the jax another one."' **1991** Roddy Doyle, *The Van*: '"Anyway," asked Tracy, "why am I to put a tick on this piece of paper when I go to the jacks?"' **1995** Alan Stanford, *Sunday Tribune*, 7 May: 'I get very ill on opening nights, it seems to affect me in the bowel region and I have to have a direct line to the jacks...'

Jack's Army [nickname]. Followers and supporters of the Republic of Ireland soccer team under its manager Jack Charlton (1986–95). **1995** *Irish Times*, 12 Dec: '"This is one of the biggest airlifts ever of football fans," said a company

[Aer Rianta] spokesman. "Jack's Army has been very good to us."' **1995** Paul Kimmage, *Sunday Independent*, 17 Dec: 'Five years ago — on my first major assignment as a sportswriter — the editor of the *Sunday Tribune*, Vincent Browne, bought me a boat and rail ticket to Sicily and enlisted me in Jack's Army.'

Jacuzzi see **the Floozie in the Jacuzzi**

jaded [p. part. as adj., <*idem*, become tired/worn out, 1593]. Physically and/or emotionally exhausted. **1996** Joan Walsh, *Leinster Leader* (Naas, Co. Kildare), 1 Aug: 'As someone who gets jaded at the mere mention of the word aerobics I'm not likely to be rubbing trainers with the hundred-plus gearing up for a charity aerobathlon this weekend.' **1996** Christy Kenneally, *Maura's Boy, A Cork Childhood*: '"We'd be walking the floor at all hours of the night trying to pacify you...We were jaded from you."'

jaffler [n., <?] (Ulster). Cattle dealer who bids but does not intend to buy (Traynor).

jag [n. & vb.] 1. [n.] (Cork). Mild sexual activity, as in **have a jag with** [vb. phr.]. Date. **1993** Seán Beecher in Michael Verdon, *Shawlies* (q.v.), *Echo Boys* (q.v.), *the Marsh and the Lanes* (q.v.): *Old Cork Remembered*: 'He made a jag for the Statue [q.v.], even though he thought he'd get fifty [q.v.].' 2. [n. & vb., <Sc. *idem*, thorn, prick: onomat.] (Ulster). [n.]. Pointed remark. [vb.]. Irritate, annoy. **1966** Patrick Boyle, *At Night All Cats are Grey*, 'The Metal Man': 'All the time jagging at him about women — the women he must have met in foreign parts...'

jaggety [adj., <see **jag** 2.] (Ulster). Having rough or torn edges.

Jailic [n., pun, <'Gaelic']. Ir. learned in prison, specifically Long Kesh, Belfast, 1970s–. **1986** Derek Dunne, *Magill*, 'McFarlane, The Inside Story', Apr: 'As the men in H-Blocks [q.v.] began to be moved from cell to cell, they were learning from the writing on the wall. For example, the past tense of an Irish verb might be on one wall, the future on another..."Jailic" they called it.'

jakers! see **japers!**

jallup [n., <Sc. *idem*, strong purgative, <'jalap' <Sp. *purga de Jalapa* (Mexican city)] (Ulster). As thus.

jalouse [vb., <Sc. *idem*, suspect, guess; cf. Fr. *jalouser*, envy] (Ulster). Suspect, suppose.

jam [n., <initials: Junior Assistant Mistress]. Poor teacher (Todd). Also gen. of such teachers.

jamer [n., <?]. 'Someone buttering you up would be a jamer' (EW).

James's Street! [interj., euphem., <Dub. thoroughfare best known for the location, since 1759, of the brewery of Arthur Guinness, aka Uncle Arthur (q.v.)]. Jaysus! (q.v.). **1982** Éamonn Mac Thomáis, *Janey Mack* (q.v.), *Me Shirt is Black*: 'Men who didn't want to curse or use the holy name in vain used the name of James's Street and Jacobs instead. In their angry moments they cried out "Holy James's Street and Jacobs [biscuit factory], will you get off my back?"'

jammered [p. part. as adj.]. Jammed, congested. **1991** Roddy Doyle, *The Van*: 'He looked over at the bar. He'd never get near it; it was jammered.'

Janey Mac/Mack! [interj., euphem.] (Dub.). Jaysus! (q.v.). **N.d.** Dub. street rhyme: 'Janey Mack me shirt is black,/ What will I do for Sunday?/Go to bed and cover your head/And don't get up till Monday.' **1978** Tom Murphy, *A Crucial Week in the Life of a Grocer's Assistant*: 'MIKO I let you down? Well, bejingoes! Well, bejaney-mack tonight! Well, you're a nice one, anyway!' **1987** Lar Redmond, *Emerald Square*: '"Janey Mac," said Bay. "The bushes are dripping with berries."' See **Gawney Mac!**

janty [adj., <Sc. *idem*, cheerful] (Ulster). Jaunty, smart.

jap [n. & vb., onomat., <Sc. *idem*, 'dash in waves' (CSD)] (Ulster). Splash, spatter. **1993** Seamus Heaney, *The Midnight Verdict* (translation of Brian Merriman, *Cúirt an Mheán Oíche*): 'Her height, I'd say, to the nearest measure,/Was six or seven yards or more,/With a swatch of

her shawl all japs and glar (q.v.)/Streeling (q.v.) behind in the muck and mire.'

japers!/jakers! [exclam., euphem.]. Jaysus! (q.v.). **1977** Flann O'Brien, *The Hair of the Dogma*: 'The hard man [see **hard**]! *Good morning*, I said. Japers! Yerself? Well, by gor [see **begor**]. You'll have the usual?' **1993** Seán O'Neill in Joe O'Reilly & Sixth Class, Convent School, Edenderry, *Over the Half Door*: 'We landed at Kennedy Airport and I looked around me. There wasn't a sinner I knew. They disappeared like snow, melted away. "Japers," says I, "I must be on my own here."'

jar [n. & vb.]. 1. [n., metonym, <earthenware jars formerly used to hold beer and spirits]. Indeterminate measure of strong drink. **1977** Flann O'Brien, *The Hair of the Dogma*: 'A character [see **character** 1.]. I suppose I could call him my best friend. But a divil when he has a few jars on him.' **1980** Bernard Farrell, *Canaries*: 'FERGUS (*To Dad*) He told you this himself, did he? Hans? DAD Had a few jars on him admittedly, but there we were playing Find the Lady when out he comes with it. "She left me for another woman," sez he.' **1994** Pre-Christmas national advertising campaign slogan: 'Going for a jar? Leave the car!' Hence **jarred** [adj.]. Having drink taken (q.v.). **1970** Christy Brown, *Down All the Days*: '"I'm not jarred, Pop — true as God I'm not...just a few jars, that's all — but not jarred..."' **1995** *Irish Times*, 2 Mar: 'the woman said she had only one pint in the first pub. She denied they had gone to another pub and had been refused because they appeared "jarred".' Also **hot jar** [n. phr.]. Earthenware hot-water bottle. 2. [vb.] (Ulster). Broach an unpleasant or controversial matter (YDS).

jarbles [n. pl., <Sc. *jarble*, old, tattered garment] (Ulster). 'Loose, dangling tatters' (MON).

jarbox/jawbox [n., <Sc. *jawbox*, kitchen sink] (Ulster). As thus.

jare [n., <?] as in **on the jare** [adj. phr.]. Playing truant. **1981** Paddy Crosbie, *Your Dinner's Poured Out!*: '...I remember

being intrigued with the actions of a group of boys who used to go "on the jare" every Tuesday and Friday...'

Jasus! see **Jaysus!**

jaunder [vb., <Sc. *jander*, talk foolishly] (Ulster). As thus.

jawbox see **jarbox**

jaw-warmer [n.]. Stump of clay pipe (Moylan).

jax see **jacks**

Jay! see **Jaysus!**

Jays [nickname]. Members of the Society of Jesus, or Jesuits; the Order as such. **1995** Aidan Higgins, *Donkey's Years*: '[Clongowes Wood] Castle servants were sent out...to inform the Line Prefect of a call for Higgins. It was on formal occasions like these that the more theatrical of the Jays came into their own.'

Jaysus!/Jasus!/Jaysis! [exclam., <Hib. E. pronun. of 'Jesus']. As thus. Also abbrev. as **Jay!**, **Jayz!** **1961** Tom Murphy, *A Whistle in the Dark*: 'MUSH God, I don't know. I suppose he has no choice. HARRY Hah?... MUSH Aw jay, I didn't mean it like that.' **1994** Greg Dalton, *My Own Backyard, Dublin in the Fifties*: '...Uncle Joe "the painter" had come to paint the house inside and out. Jaysus, the colours, all mixes he'd left over from other jobs.' **1995** Eanna Brophy, *Sunday Tribune*, 6 Aug: '(...the door bursts open and A Stranger enters). **Stranger:** Jayz, wharrakip! Not much chance of any action around here.'

Jayz! see **Jaysus!**

jeeg [vb., <Sc. *idem*, creak] (Ulster). As thus.

jeetled [p. part. as adj., cf. Sc. *jeetle* (vb.), delay, be idle] (Ulster). Very tired (SH).

jehoe [vb., cf. *gee-ho*, call to horse to stop] (Ulster). Cease doing a thing (Traynor).

Jem [prop. n., cf. *jemmy fellow*, 'a smart, spruce fellow' (Grose)]. The generic Dubliner; also employed to avoid direct ref., cf. your man (q.v.). **1946** Donagh MacDonagh, *Happy as Larry*: 'when one of them dies [in India]/He's burnt to be buried in style;/Right up on the fire will go Jem...' Also **Jembo** in same sense. **1977** James Plunkett, *Collected Short Stories*, 'A Walk through the Summer': 'He stuffed a wad of crisps into his mouth. "I'm not offering jembo over there any. He drank enough free whiskey to satisfy a bishop."' **1989** Hugh Leonard, *Out after Dark*: '"What I'm saying is that Jembo here looks like him. Rory could have a cousin, couldn't he?"' **1996** Joe O'Connor, *Sunday Tribune*, 9 June: 'I was comin home from de pub wit de war department when sez she to me, Jembo, will we buy de papers? Do yeh no wor I sez to ur? Dew yeh? Yeh have yer *shy* [see **shite**], I sez...'

jenny/jinny [n. & vb., <familiar form of 'Janet'/'Jane'] (Ulster). 1. [n.]. Young cod (fish). 2. [vb.]. (Of a woman) Henpeck. Also **jenny longlegs** [n. phr.] daddy-long-legs; **jenny wren** [n. phr.] wren, esp. female. Also **Jinny/ Jinny Ann**. [n.]. Effeminate man. **1969** Robert Greacen, *Even without Irene*: '...I had not been truly a country boy, for my native place was Londonderry and earlier I had lived in Belfast. I steered a course between being a rough lad and a "cissy" or "Jinny".' Also **jenny-ass, jinny wing** in same sense. **1951** Frank O'Connor, *Traveller's Samples*, 'Legal Aid': 'Jackie was a little jenny-ass of a man with thin lips, a pointed nose and a pince-nez that wouldn't stop in place...' **1993** Sam McAughtry, *Touch & Go*: '"Why don't you go out and play like the other kids? Why are you always hanging about the house like a jinny wing?"'

jenny-wine [adj., <familiar form of 'Janet'/'Jane'] (Ulster). Not given to the drink. **1938** Seumas MacManus, *The Rocky Road to Dublin*: '"Wullie John hadn't a pair o'trousers fit to be seen in the fair, so borrowed yours to stand in. He'll have them home in good time, for my man's a jenny-wine Methodist who never lets night find him in a fair."'

Jerusalem [nickname]. Applied to Thomas or 'Buck' Whaley (1766–1800), who, for a wager, travelled to Jerusalem and returned in 2 years (1788–9). **1847**

John Edward Walsh, *Ireland Sixty Years Ago*: 'to the hour of his death, which occurred recently, he was called "Jerusalem Whaley"'.

jessie [n., <woman's name] (Ulster). Effeminate man.

Jesus Kate! [exclam.]. **1994** Noel Hughes in Kevin C. Kearns, *Dublin Tenement Life*: 'she robbed her husband's suit and pawned it...And she makes the run over to me mother and says, "Oh, jesus Kate, he'll f— kill me!"'

Jesus tonight! [exclam.]. Expression of surprise.

jewel [term of address]. Term of affection. **1847** John Edward Walsh, *Ireland Sixty Years Ago*: 'He [the hangman] called out at the door, so as to be heard by all the bystanders, as well as the criminal, "Mr O'Brien, jewel, *long life* to you, make haste wid your prayers..."' Also in phrase **me jewel an' darlin'** [adj. phr., intens.]. **1996** Headline, *Irish Independent*, 15 Nov: 'Me Jewel, Darlin' and Dear Dublin'.

Jewman [n.]. Moneylender, pedlar. **1961** Tom Murphy, *A Whistle in the Dark*: 'HARRY ...Well, when he [the teacher] came to my turn, and I was ready to say what I was going to be, he said first, "I suppose, Carney, you'll be a Jewman."' **1970** Christy Brown, *Down All the Days*: 'a car pulled up outside and on looking out old Essie suddenly shrieked and exclaimed "It's the Jewman!"' **1985** Máirín Johnston, *Around the Banks of Pimlico*: 'My mother's last involvement with the jew-men was when she borrowed for my Confirmation from Mr Glick...My mother said he was glic [q.v.] by name and nature, as *glic* is the Irish word for "clever".'

jib [nickname, *c.*1840–] (Trinity College, Dub.). First-year undergraduate. **1909** 'Nong', *TCD, A College Miscellany*, 'Fulfilment', 17 Mar: 'But, thank God, I never figured where the Commons-glutted jibs,/With their fatuous complacency parade...' **1922** James Joyce, *Ulysses*: 'I oughtn't to have got myself swept along with those medicals. And the Trinity jibs in their mortarboards.'

jibber [n., <'jib' (vb.), stop short, draw back]. Coward, one who hesitates, esp. as in **never reared a jibber**. **1987** Lar Redmond, *Emerald Square*: 'He grinned. "Never say your mother reared a jibber," he said...' **1991** Bob Quinn, *Smokey Hollow*: 'Granda Hope caught her in his arms, swung her around and cried, "I never reared a jibber."'

jibbets/gibbets [n. pl., <OF *gibet*, gallows (DOM)] (Leinster). Scraps, morsels, smithereens (q.v.). **1869** Patrick Kennedy, *Evenings in the Duffrey*: 'They'd have made gibbets of him only for Tony Whitty.'

jibble [vb., <Sc. *idem*, spill] (Ulster). Dribble, spill (SH).

jiddlins [n. pl., cf. Sc. *diddle* (vb.), busy oneself with trifles (CSD)] (Ulster). Odds and ends; household chores.

jig-act [vb.]. Play the fool, play up, act irresponsibly. **1950** Liam O'Flaherty, *Insurrection*: '"Where are they going?" he said to the shabby man. "Just jig-acting," the shabby man replied. "They are paid to make trouble."' **1963** John McGahern, *The Barracks*: 'She and they were involved together: they jigacted with millions of others across a screen's moment, passionately involved in their little selves and actions...' See also **act the maggot, cod, jack-act, trick-acting**.

jigger [n., <Sc. *jeeg* (vb.), trot, walk briskly] (Ulster) as in **have the jiggers up** [vb. phr.]. Be in a state of agitation.

jigs see **between the jigs and the reels, in the jigs**

jig time, (in) [adv. phr. & n.]. (In) no time at all. **1987** Lar Redmond, *Emerald Square*: 'So we came noiselessly down the stairs, out the back way...and were outside the fence in jig time.' **1995** Phil O'Keeffe, *Down Cobbled Streets, A Liberties Childhood*: '"Can I have shop socks?" "No." "Why?" "They're too expensive and don't last jig-time."' **1995** Peter Coogan, *Irish Times*, 29 Aug: 'Sir — Those who would resurrect Irish misunderstand our national psyche. Prohibition and "on the spot" fines for users would do it in jig time.'

jildy [vb., <*idem*, 'lively' (adj. & adv.), Brit. army, C19–20, poss. <Hindust. Verbal form is poss. Hib.E.] (army). Smarten up. **1973** Noël Conway, *The Bloods* (q.v.): 'The majority of the Bloods were seasoned regulars but the ranks now included many reservists and young recruits who had to be jildied into professional soldiers.' Hence **jildiness** [abst. n.].

jimmy-dog [n.]. Child's term for penis (Moylan).

jimp [adj., <Sc. *idem*, slender, neat, elegant; tight; scarce, deficient in quantity] (Ulster). As thus. Hence **jimply** [adv.]. Scarcely.

jingbang [n., emphatic] (Ulster). Total, as in **the whole jingbang**. **1983** W.F. Marshall, *Livin' in Drumlister*, 'The Hills of Home': 'Still, when I see, behin' the barn/The big, brown back of Mullagharn,/I'd let him [the Derryman] keep, while she's our own,/The whole jingbang outside Tyrone.'

jingle [n., onomat.]. Covered conveyance, late C18; 'one of Bianconi's long cars' (PWJ). Also Austral. usage. **1824** Thomas Crofton Croker, *Researches in the South of Ireland*: 'Of late, jingles, as they are termed, have been established between the principal towns. These are carriages on easy springs, calculated to contain six or eight persons. The roof is supported by a slight iron frame capable of being unfixed in fine weather...' **1847** John Edward Walsh, *Ireland Sixty Years Ago*: 'The next improvement was the "jingle", a machine rolling on four wheels, but so put together that the rattling of the work was heard like the bells of a waggon team.' See also **Bian; King of the Roads**.

jink [n. & vb., <Sc. *idem*, trick; play a trick on] (Ulster). As thus.

jinnit [n.]. 1. [cf. 'jennet', small Sp. horse, Sp. *jinete*, light horseman]. Mule. 2. [cf. 'gin and It.', nonce-word?]. Gin and Italian vermouth. **1994** Maurice Hayes, *Sweet Killough Let Go your Anchor*: 'One daring lady shook the moral foundations of Killough by calling instead for a "jinnit", which turned out not to be the crossbred mule we recognised, but the rudimentary ancestor of James Bond's Martini, stirred, not shaken.'

Jinny/Jinny Ann see **jenny**

jinny-go-up/jinnyjo [n., <?]. Thistle-down. **1939** James Joyce, *Finnegans Wake*: '"That's three slots an no burners. You're forgetting the jinnyjos for the fayboys."' **1975** Eilís Brady, *All In! All In!*: 'If you catch one and there's "an egg" (seed) in it, you put the "egg" in a matchbox. If there's no "egg" in it then you blow it away from the palm of your hand saying "Jinny-jo, jinny-jo, lay me an egg."' **1992** Pauline Bracken, *Light of Other Days, A Dublin Childhood*: 'she donned her pumps and set off across the floor, executing a slip jig that would have shamed a jinni-go-up [*sic*] for its lightness'.

jinny wing see **jenny**

jip/jip-job [n.] (Ulster). Poor treatment, abuse; said of something botched, in bad condition.

jirg [vb., <Sc. *idem*, creak] (Ulster). As thus, esp. of new boots.

JKL [nickname, <pseudonym]. James W. Boyle, Catholic bishop of Kildare & Leighlin (1786–1834), who published his *Vindication of the Irish Catholics* (1824) under the initials. **1985** Davis & Mary Coakley, *Wit and Wine*: 'During this period [John] Hogan's most distinguished creation was the famous *JKL* group which was commissioned to commemorate the famous Bishop Doyle of Kildare...still in Carlow Cathedral.' **1993** Annie Behan in Joe O'Reilly & Sixth Class, Convent School, Edenderry, *Over the Half Door*: 'I don't remember much about JKL St. We were young when we moved down to Fr Kearns St. In JKL St we lived where Bradys live now...'

jobby [n.]. Bowel motion. **1995** Patrick Boland, *Tales from a City Farmyard*: 'Once when I was in the Lyric [cinema], a little fellow in the corner next to the wall dropped his pants and did a jobby.'

job's oxo, the see **oxo**

jockey [n.] (Cork). Coin which lands on top of the jack (q.v.) in a feck (see **feck**

[n.] 2.) game (Beecher). See also **boxman**, **rider**, **tosser** 1.

joe maxi [n., <rhym. sl.]. Taxi. **1994** Joseph O'Connor, *The Secret World of the Irish Male*: '"I seen him ownee the other night outside Lillie's Bordildo [*recte* Bordello] and him being hurried into a joe maxi; blue mowldy [q.v.] with the drink..."'

johnny [n., poss. <'Johnny Walker', Scotch whisky]. Half-glass of whiskey (DHS).

Johnny Forty-Coats [nickname]. Dub. 'character' (see **character** 1.), *c.*1930s. **1994** Paddy Casey in Kevin C. Kearns, *Dublin Tenement Life*: 'Oh, I knew Bang-Bang [q.v.] well...Then there was "Johnny Forty Coats". And he *had* forty coats on him! And on warm days. He had so many coats on him that it was just unbelievable.' **1995** Frances O'Brien in Mary Ryan et al. (eds.), *No Shoes in Summer*: 'Johnny Fortycoats was a small man with a long white beard and about six overcoats, hat etc. He was a quiet man. Didn't speak much just looked for alms to keep himself.' **1995** Patrick Boland, *Tales from a City Farmyard*: 'I remember him walking along the street with a sack slung over his back, and a few kids running after him shouting out: "Johnny Forty-Coats" as if the poor devil didn't know his name, or the number of garments he had on.'

johnny-jump-up [n., <?]. Bottle of cider (EW).

Johnny Magorey [nickname, <Ir. *mogóir*, rose-hip]. As thus. **N.d.** Children's rhyme: 'I'll tell you a story about Johnny Magorey.'

Johnny-Nod [prop. n.] (Ulster) as in **Johnny-Nod is creeping** said to sleepy children (Traynor).

Johnny Wetbread [nickname, <Dub. beggar who dipped bread into a fountain before eating it]. Term of non-malicious mockery. **N.d.** Rhyme employed by old people dandling a child: 'In the dirty end of Dirty Lane/There lived a cobbler Dick McClane/He wore a coat of the old king's reign/And so did Johnny Wetbread.'

(This is a corruption of a Zozimus (q.v.) ballad, 'Dickey and the Yeomen'.)

join [n.] (Ulster). People pooling money to buy drink for a social gathering; money so collected, whip-round. **1979** Paddy Tunney, *The Stone Fiddle*: '"there was a right [see **right** 1.] lock [q.v.] of us sitting round so we made a 'join' and sent away to Carmichael's for the poteen [q.v.]"'.

joinin' [pres. part.] (Ulster). Chastising, rebuking.

jolly [n., <?] (Cork). Favourite in horse/dog race (Beecher).

joogins/juggins [n. pl., <Sc. *juggins*, rags] (Ulster). Pieces, scraps.

jook see **juke**

jookey [n., see **chook chook!**]. Hen on pre-decimal penny.

jook-halter [n., see **juke**] (Ulster). One who has narrowly escaped hanging.

jook-the-beetle [n., see **juke**] (Ulster). 1. Lumps in mashed potatoes, stirabout (q.v.) or colcannon. 2. Poor cook.

jook-the-bottle [n., see **juke**] (Ulster). Teetotaller (derog.).

jorey/jorry [n.] (Ulster). 1. [<?]. Small pet pig; smallest of brood/litter; anything small of its kind. 2. [cf. Ir. *deoraí*, pitiable person]. Sickly person/animal.

josies [n. pl., <?]. Breasts. **1976** Tom Murphy, *On the Inside*: 'MALACHY ...What's that? Look at the pair of josies on that! Look at little Willie wrapping himself around that!'

jotter [n.]. 1. Copybook (of poor-quality paper). **1995** Phil O'Keeffe, *Down Cobbled Streets, A Liberties Childhood*: 'In school [during WWII] jotters became the despair of our teachers...The pen would go through the paper, and we had to resort to pencils...' **1996** Pat Smyth, *Irish Times*, 29 Mar: 'On page seven of *The Irish Times* (March 21st) the statement appeared "copybooks, or jotters as they are known in the North". Does anyone in the North use the term "jotter" for a copybook? I have not come across it.' 2. (Ulster). Small quantity or dash of a liquid, esp. whiskey.

joult [n., cf. Ir. *seoltóir*, sailor, voyager (Dinneen)]. Journey. **1922** James Joyce, *Ulysses*: 'he was making free with me after the Glencree dinner coming back that long joult over the featherbed mountain'.

joulter/jowlter [n., cf. Ir. *seoltóir*, jolter (one who hawks fish etc.), jobber (Dinneen)] (Cork). As thus; also derog. (Beecher).

jow off! [exclam., <Hindust. *jana*, go, poss. introduced by Ir. serving with Brit. army in India]. Go away! Fuck off! **1987** Lar Redmond, *Emerald Square*: '"Ay... you!" The biggest of them was shouting at me. "Jow off!"'

joxer [n., poss. <*jock*, North Country (Eng.) seaman, collier (DHS) + endearment suffix]. Idler, unemployed individual. **1934** Samuel Beckett, *More Pricks than Kicks*: 'He was tolerated...by the rough but kindly habitués of the house, recruited for the most part from among dockers, railwaymen and vague joxers on the dole.'

joy [n., 'the great frequency of the word in Hiberno-English leaves no doubt that it represents an arbitrary substitution for some Irish endearment as *a chroidhe* or *a ghrá(i)dh* [see **agra**]' (Bliss)]. My friend. **1754** Thomas Sheridan, *The Brave Irishman*: 'CHEATWELL ...how is the old gentleman your father? I hope you left him in good health? CAPTAIN Oh, by my shoul, he's very well, joy; for he's dead and buried these ten years.' See also **Dear Joy**.

Joy, the [nickname, abbrev.]. Mountjoy prison, Dub. **1966** Patrick Boyle, *At Night All Cats are Grey*, 'The Lake': 'And when he wasn't in the Joy or the Glass-House [area of solitary confinement] or in Arbour Hill he was being kicked out of one job after another...' **1994** Christy Murray in Kevin C. Kearns, *Dublin Tenement Life*: 'Now I done four days in the "Joy" (Mountjoy) over the [newsboys'] licence — I wouldn't pay the five shillings for the licence.' **1996** RTÉ Radio, *Bowman's Saturday 8.30*, interview with Leo Maguire originally broadcast 1950s: 'I didn't want Leo Maguire being pilloried or put in the Joy' (on his adapting a pseudonym for his 1950 ballad 'The Battle of Baltinglass' (q.v.)).

jube [vb., poss. <Lat. *duius* (adj.), doubtful, doubting]. Be dubious, suspect. Hence **jubious/jubish/jubous** [adj.]. 1. Dubious. 2. Superstitious.

Jubilee mutton [n., <distribution of small quantities of free mutton to the poor of Dub. on the occasion of Queen Victoria's of Eng.'s diamond jubilee, 1897]. Very little. **1922** James Joyce, *Ulysses*: 'Dusty Rhodes. Peep at his wearables. By mighty! What's he got? Jubilee mutton.'

juggins see **joogins**

juice see **deuce**

juke/jook/duke, etc. [vb., <Sc. *idem*, peep, dodge, avoid] (Ulster). As thus; play truant; swindle. **1925** Lynn Doyle, *Dear Ducks*: '"Watch him, then, Billy," sez I, "till we see how he does — Juke down! There's a sthring of ducks comin' between us an' him..."' **1927** Peadar O'Donnell, *Islanders*: '"...I was duking round the stacks wan night, an' I saw herself [q.v.] an' him comin' home from a ceilidh [q.v.]..."' **1990** Harry Currie, quoted in Walter Love, *The Times of our Lives*: 'People just flew in whatever door was open. They flew up the hall and hid, then they'd juke out when the coast was clear.' Hence **jooker** [n.] dodger, one who evades his responsibilities; **jookery**, **jook-packery**, double-dealing.

jumm [n., cf. Sc. *jum*, 'clumsily-built, awkward-looking house' (CSD)] (Ulster). 'Something that is large and unwieldy and comparatively worthless' (MON).

jump [vb.]. Convert from Catholic to Protestant for material advantage. **1982**

Thomas Gallagher, *Paddy's Lament*: 'Their parents had escaped the poverty and serfdom of a tenant farmer's life by "jumping" from Catholicism, with its stigma, to Protestantism, with its job opportunities...' Hence **jumper** [n.] in same sense. See **turn** 2.

jump-jack [n.] (Ulster). Child's toy made from the breastbone of a goose (Patterson).

jump over the besom [vb. phr., cf. Eng. sl. *live over the brush* in same sense] (Ulster). Live together without being married.

junder/jundey/jundy [n. & vb., <Sc. *jundie*, jolt, push] (Ulster). As thus. **1938** Seumas MacManus, *The Rocky Road to Dublin*: 'The Master's elbow jundied Billy in the ribs, signifying, "Don't let her go — Engage her in conversation."' **1979** Paddy Tunney, *The Stone Fiddle*: 'Johnny could elbow and jundy his way through the Quadrilles and Lancers with the best of them.'

junk [n., <?]. Short, thickset man (Moylan).

junt [n., <Sc. *idem*, large piece of anything] (Ulster). As thus. **1939** Patrick Gallagher ('Paddy the Cope' (q.v.)), *My Story*: '...I drank a fine bowl of hen's soup...ate the breast of a real hen and had a fine bowl of tea and a junt of flour bread and butter'.

jute [n., cf. Sc. *joot*, 'used contemptuously of tea' (CSD)] (Ulster). Small quantity of tea (Patterson).

jybe [vb. trans., <'gibe' (vb. intrans.), taunt, sneer at]. As thus. **1961** Tom Murphy, *A Whistle in the Dark*: 'DES Two fellas in the — the, yeh know, of the pub ...Sort of jybin', well, sort of jybin' Iggy and Hugo.'

K

kahoole [vb., cf. Sc. *cahoo* (n.), game of hide-and-seek] (Ulster). Engage in amorous play.

kailey see **ceilidh**

kaks [n. pl., <?]. Testicles. **1991** Roddy Doyle, *The Van*: 'Bimbo grabbed him by the kaks; he was only wearing his runners [q.v.] and his underpants.'

Kate Mac [nickname, <?]. West Clare Railway, 1887–1961. **1990** Edmund Lenihan, *In the Tracks of the West Clare Railway*: 'the West Clare — "Kate Mac", as it was affectionately known by many Clare people — became one of the mainstays and shapers of the agricultural and social life of its hinterland'.

Kathleen/Cathleen Mavourneen (system) [nickname, <1830 Julia Crawford, 'Kathleen Mavourneen' (pop. ballad): 'Oh hast thou forgotten how soon we must sever!/Oh! hast thou forgotten this day we must part,/It may be for years and it may be for ever...', iron.; cf. Austral. sl. *idem*, indeterminate prison sentence]. Payment by instalments; the 'never-never'. **1960** John O'Donoghue, *In Kerry Long Ago*: 'but when he asked Peggy the Corner for a bottle of whiskey on the Kathleen Mavourneen system she politely refused to let him have it'. **1985** Máirín Johnston, *Around the Banks of Pimlico*: 'On the Kathleen Mavourneen system (the never-never) the tenement rooms were furnished and the walls elaborately decorated with gold-framed pictures of Pope Pius XII...' **1986** Padraic O'Farrell, *'Tell me, Sean O'Farrell'*: 'He [Robert Brooke] provided livestock for his tenants and stopped money out of their pay each week to recoup the cost — an early example of the Cathleen Mavourneen...'

Kathleen ní Houlihan see **Cathleen ní Houlihan**

katie hunkers, on one's [adj. phr., <Sc. *katie hunkers* (n. phr.), sliding on ice in a crouching position (CSD)] (Ulster). Sitting on one's heels (SH).

Kay river [nickname, <Waterford quay]. River Suir (EW).

keech/keegh/keek [n. & vb., <Sc. *idem*, excrement, defecate; cf. Ir. *cac* in same sense] (Ulster). As thus. **1979** John Morrow, *The Confessions of Proinsias O'Toole*: '"He'll not be able to go for a crap without the Liberals' say-so," stated Steffers graphically. "Say 'keek', my love, not 'crap'...it is our national duty to use the Erse whenever at all possible."'

keeho [n. & vb., poss. onomat.] (Ulster). Loud laugh (SH).

keek [n. & vb.]. 1. [n. & vb., <Sc. *idem* <ME *kike*, peep] (Ulster). As thus. **1819** John McKinley, *Poetic Sketches Descriptive of the Giant's Causeway and the Surrounding Scenery*, 'A Winter Night in the North of Ireland': 'The winsome matron at the wheel,/Wi' canny e'e keeks at the chiel/She thinks wad fit her Jenny weel...' **1951** Sam Hanna Bell, *December Bride*: '"Where would that be now," says God...St Peter takes a keek down. "Oh-ho," says he..."sure ye know rightly that's Belfast."' 2. [n.]. See **keech**.

keenagh-lee [n., <Ir. *caonach liath*, lit. 'grey moss', mildew]. As thus.

keeny [vb., <Ir. *caoin*, keen, lament]. Cry, wail.

keep dick [vb., <Eng. sl. *dick*, watch] (Ulster). Keep a lookout. **1979** John Morrow, *The Confessions of Proinsias O'Toole*: 'the "column" — Punchy Coyne and a couple of nippers to keep dick — would welcome a drop of fresh loot around the tumbling pennies up in the brickfields'.

keeping, on one's [vb. phr., <Ir. *ar mo choimhéad*, on my keeping (Dinneen)]. On the run, in hiding from authority. **1921** (first published 1983) Patrick MacGill, *Lanty Hanlon*: 'Kevin Roe was abroad, on his own keeping, a wanted man.' **1927** Peadar O'Donnell, *Islanders*: 'Manus was overjoyed to shelter the man that was "on his keeping".'

keeroge [n., <Ir. *ciaróg*, beetle]. As thus.

kell [n., cf. ME *idem*, northern form of *calle*, caul, web, cocoon of caterpillar] (Ulster). Ring of dirt (around unwashed neck). Hence **kelled** [p. part. as adj.].

kelp [n.] (Ulster). 1. [<ON *kjelp*, pot handle]. As thus, as in **that's right, hand the kelp**. Said to sulking child (DOM). 2. [cf. Sc. *gilpp*, young, growing girl]. Ungainly, self-conscious teenager, usually girl (CUD).

kelters [n. pl., <Sc. *kelter*, money]. As thus, coins (PWJ). See also **yellow kelters**.

kemp [vb., <Sc. *idem*, contend, compete, <OE *cempa* (n.), warrior] (Ulster). Compete.

keo [n. & vb., cf. Sc. *kiow-ow*, 'trifle in discourse or conduct' (CSD)] (Ulster). [vb.]. As thus; play tricks. [n.]. Such conduct. Hence **keo-boy/keowt** [n.]. Entertaining fellow; low contemptible individual (PWJ); trickster; ladies' man.

keolaun [n., <Ir. *coileán*, whelp, young pup]. Contemptible male individual (PWJ).

kep [vb., <Sc. *idem*, turn or head back an animal] (Ulster). As thus.

kepper [n.]. 1. [<'keep']. Person good at catching a ball. 2. [<Ir. *ceapaire*, slice of bread and butter]. As thus.

kerfuffle [n. & vb., <Sc. *carfuffle*, fuss, disorder; disarrange, disorder, tumble]. As thus; handle roughly (of man courting girl).

Kerry witness [n.]. 'One who will swear to anything' (DHS).

kevel/kevil [n. & vb., cf. Ir. *camadh* (n.), act of bending, making crooked; ON *cafa* (vb.), dip; Sc. *cave* (vb.), toss the head (of horse)]. 1. [vb.]. Jump awkwardly; toss the head. **1844** Robert Huddleston, *A Collection of Poems and Songs on Rural Subjects*, 'The Lammas Fair (Belfast)': 'They're dreamin' as they travel;/Wi' boots an' spurs their whipper-in,/Yet scarce can make them kevel,/Frae sleep that day.' 2. [n.]. 'Ungainly or slightly deformed foot' (OTF).

kib [vb., cf. Ir. *cipín* (n.), little stick].

Make holes with a stick for planting seeds, potatoes, etc. Hence **kibben** [n.]. Dibbler stick. **1938** Seumas MacManus, *The Rocky Road to Dublin*: 'Always was he roaming and exploring them [the woods] — always, that is, when a slave-driving father didn't have him kibbing potatoes...'

kibosh/kybosh [n., deriv. disputed but poss. <Ir. *caipín báis*, cap of death, or pitch cap, as employed by Brit. forces against 1798 insurgents; vb. usage of other origin and not gen. Hib.E]. Final destructive action/utterance, as in **put the kibosh on** [vb. phr.]. **1966** Séamus Murphy, *Stone Mad*: '"We'll get nothing done today. This will put the kybosh on everything."'

kick [n.]. Pre-decimal sixpence. **1948** Patrick Kavanagh, *Tarry Flynn*: '"Every man jack of that band gets a pound and a kick for his night."' **1968** Myles na gCopaleen, *The Best of Myles*: 'the writer... should never be paid less than five bar [see **bar** 1.] for a good job. (I could do it for four and a kick, Mr O'Faoláin, *but it wouldn't be a job*.'

kick in one's gallop [n. phr.] (Ulster). Weakness in ability or character; skeleton in the cupboard. Hence **put a kick in s.o.'s gallop** [vb. phr.]. Put a spoke in s.o.'s wheel.

kick up [vb.]. React unfavourably. **1968** John Healy, *The Death of an Irish Town*: 'The agent knew Patrick's father and knew he'd "kick up" for taking on his son.'

kiddhoge [n., <Ir. *cuideog*, wrap for the shoulders] (Ulster). 'A wrap of any kind that a woman throws hastily over her shoulders' (PWJ).

kidger [n., <'kid' + endearment suffix] (Dub.). Young lad. **1939** Sean O'Casey, *I Knock at the Door*: '"Eh there, kidger," shouted a drover from the end of the herd, "don't let the bastard dodge yeh!"'

kiffle [vb., onomat., cf. Sc. *kiffling-cough* (n.), a slight cough (CSD)] (Ulster). Move hesitatingly/uncertainly; potter about, do trivial jobs. **1983** W.F. Marshall, *Livin' in Drumlister*, 'Me an' me

Da': 'Well, I knowed two [women] I thought wud do,/But still I had me fears,/So I kiffled back an' forrit/Between the two, for years.'

Kildare side [n. phr., <?]. Right-hand side. **1939** James Joyce, *Finnegans Wake*: '...MacSmashall Swingy of the Cattleaxes, got up regardless, with a cock on the Kildare side of his Tettersull'. **1985** Máirín Johnston, *Around the Banks of Pimlico*: 'His accordion was strapped under this [cloak] from his shoulders, and on his head he wore a battered slouched hat, cocked on the "Kildare" side, which gave him a very rakish appearance.'

kileery see **caleery**

Kilkenny [n.]. 'An old frize [*sic*] coat' (Grose).

Kilkenny cats [n. phr.] as in **like Kilkenny cats** [adj. & adv. phr., <C17 'troop of Hessian soldiers, who amused themselves in [Kilkenny] barracks by tying two cats together by their tails and throwing them across a clothes line to fight. The officers...resolved to put a stop to the practice. The look-out man...did not observe the officer on duty approaching the barracks, but one of the troopers, seizing a sword, cut the two tails, and the cats made their escape. When the officer inquired the meaning of the two bleeding tails, he was coolly told that the two cats had been fighting and had devoured each other all but the tails' (Brewer, *Dictionary of Phrase and Fable*, 1895 edn]. Fierce(ly), confrontational(ly), argumentative(ly). **1909** Canon Sheehan, *The Blindness of Dr Gray*: '"In America," she said, "we're above such little things [as religious confrontation]. Seems to me, that you here in Ireland are going to keep up the Kilkenny-cats programme to the end."' **1925** E.L. Ahrons, *Railway Magazine* (London), 'Great Southern and Western Railway': 'when they were both at the main platform [at Limerick Junction] the two engines faced each other on the same line of rails, looking like a couple of cats — Kilkenny brand — which, had they been able to waggle their trains, would very likely have sprung at each other'.

killeen [n., <Ir. *cillín*, large sum of money]. As thus.

Kill 'ems and Ate 'ems [nickname, <alleged cannibalistic practices of wreckers on the Wexford coast, C19]. **1996** Lorna Siggins, *Irish Times*, 5 Feb: '"The Graveyard of a Thousand Ships" [off Carnsore Point] was also a source of income for some, according to Richard Roche, historian and author...There is no greater term of abuse to a Wexford person than to link their blood-line to the "Kill 'ems and Ate 'ems".'

Killinchy muffler [n. phr., <Killinchy, Co. Down]. Arm around one's neck; cuddle.

Killyman wrackers [nickname, <Ulster pronun. of 'wreckers'] (Ulster). 1. Yeomanry of the Killyman area, Co. Tyrone, who wrecked the houses of Catholics during the 1798 rising. 2. Variety of potato. **1932** *Ulster Hiker* (Cushendall, Co. Antrim), 'The Ulster Dialect', June: 'We used to have a variety of potato known as "Killyman wrackers", and the name originated from a company of Yeomanry!' See also **Yeo**.

kilt [solecistic p. part. of 'kill']. Mentally/physically overcome. **1800** Maria Edgeworth, *Castle Rackrent*: 'The mere English reader, from a similarity of sound between the words *kilt* and *killed*, might be induced to suppose that their meanings are similar, yet they are not by any means in Ireland synonymous terms. Thus you may hear a man exclaim — "I'm kilt and murdered!" — but he frequently means only that he has received a black eye, or slight contusion. — *I'm kilt all over* — means that he is in a worse state than being simply *kilt*.' **1843** W.M. Thackeray, *The Irish Sketch Book*: 'a whole troop on a hedge retreated backwards into a ditch opposite, where there was rare [q.v.] kicking, and sprawling, and disarrangement of petticoats, and cries of "O murther!" "Mother of God!" "I'm kilt," and so on.'

kiltie [n., <Sc. *idem*, one who wears a kilt or very short dress (CSD)] (Ulster). As thus; soldier of kilted army regiment. **1951** Sam Hanna Bell, *December Bride*:

"'We'll put a clean clout on it tae keep it from festering." She patted Hamilton's cheek. "Ye bore it like a kiltie, son."' **1979** John Morrow in David Marcus (ed.), *Body and Soul*, 'Beginnings': "'an' we had ice-cream an' chips an' cuckles [cockles]," I listed breathlessly..."An' paddled an' this wee [q.v.] kiltie tried to catch Aunt Minnie's diddies [q.v.]."' **1996** Jonathan Bardon, *Irish Times*, 27 Apr: 'Orange parades...are not what they were...Only a few of the magnificent silver bands are left and the "kilties" with skirling pipes are being supplanted by growing numbers of fife-and-drum "kick-the-Pope" bands.'

kimeen see **cimeen**

kimmel–a–vauleen [n., <Ir. *cuimil a' mháilín*, shake the bag]. 'Uproarious fun' (PWJ).

kinat/kinnat/kinnatt/canat [n., <Ir. *cnat* <'gnat']. Rogue; 'an impertinent, conceited, impudent little puppy' (PWJ). **1922** James Joyce, *Ulysses*: '...Gerty could see by her looking as black as thunder that she was simply in a towering rage though she hid it, the little kinnatt'. **1979** Michael O'Beirne, *Mister, A Dublin Childhood*: "'Well after *that*," my mother said, meaning there were no wonders left. "The clever kinat."' **1985** Máirín Johnston, *Around the Banks of Pimlico*: "'That bloody canat is never around when he's wanted," my mother would sigh as pots and pans slipped everyway.' Hence **kenatiness** [abst. n.]. 'An artful and dangerous person, capable of treacherous and flatigious acts' (S&R).

King Billy [nickname]. William III of Eng., icon of Orangeism. **N.d.** Nursery rhyme: 'If I had a penny/Do you know what I would do?/I would buy a rope/And hang the pope/And let King Billy through.' **1996** Michael Finlan, *Irish Times*, 20 May: 'It might be Rome Rule south of the border but up here it looked like King Billy was boss.' See **Billy Boys**.

Kingdom, the [nickname, esp. in Gaelic games context]. Kerry. **1996** John B. Keane, *Irish Times*, 4 Apr: '...John Philpot Curran commented adversely that the magistracy of the county of Kerry were

so opposed to the laws of the land that they were a law unto themselves, a Kingdom apart...In fact some Kerrymen say there are only two Kingdoms, the Kingdom of God and the Kingdom of Kerry.' **1996** Dick Hogan, *Irish Times*, 7 Sept: 'All around Tralee there are signs of the hand of Mr [Dick] Spring. The capital of the Kingdom is booming.'

King of the Roads [nickname]. Charles Bianconi (1786–1875), transport innovator. **1877** S.F. Pettit, *This City of Cork 1700–1900*: 'Clonmel was to be the centre of the nationwide horse transport enterprise of the "King of the Roads", Charles Bianconi.' See also **Bian**, **jingle**.

kink [n., <Sc. *idem*, bend, crease, fold] as in **in kinks (of laughing)**. Doubled up with laughter.

kinnat/kinnatt see **kinat**

kip [n., <Dan. *kippe*, hut, mean alehouse] (Dub.). Brothel. **1766** Oliver Goldsmith, *The Vicar of Wakefield*: "'My business was to attend him at auctions...and to assist at tattering [wrecking] a kip, as the phrase was, when he had a mind for a frolic."' **1954** Benedict Kiely, *Honey Seems Bitter*: "'So they caught him in a kip." "Was it a kip?" "Oh, the true native Irish bordello. Fleas, disease, and fights in the backyard."' **1994** Mary Corbally in Kevin C. Kearns, *Dublin Tenement Life*: 'Now we didn't call them "madams", the outsiders called them madams. We called them "kip-keepers"...The houses that they lived in were called kips.' Also **kip house** [n. phr.] in same sense.

kip of the reel [n. phr.]. Noisy argument (Moylan).

kippeen/kippen see **cipin**

kirower [n., <Ir. *creabhar*, gadfly, horsefly]. As thus (OTF).

kish of brogues [n. phr., <Ir. *cis*, wicker basket + *bróg*, shoe] as in **as ignorant as a kish of brogues**. Very stupid. **1966** Séamus Murphy, *Stone Mad*: 'Clever enough when it came to stone, but as ignorant as a kish of brogues when it came to anything else.'

kitchen [n. & vb.]. 1. [n.]. (Savoury cooked) food. **1913** Alexander Irvine, *My Lady of the Chimney Corner*: 'In nine cases out of ten, Sunday "kitchen" was a cow's head, a calf's head and pluck [q.v.], a pair of cow's feet, a few sheep's "trotters" or a quart of sheep's blood.' **1991** Seán Ó Ciaráin, *Farewell to Mayo*: 'Groceries bought by the country people were mainly tea, sugar and tobacco, with fish, usually herring or mackerel, for everyday kitchen.' **1995** Brigid O'Donnell in Mary Ryan et al (eds.), *No Shoes in Summer*: 'They [dried fish] served us during the winter as "kitchen". Kitchen was a term used locally [Co. Donegal] to describe food for dinners.' 2. [vb.]. Make a meal out of nothing.

kitchen house [n. phr. & adj.] (Ulster). Working-class 'two-up two-down' dwelling; working-class. **1993** Sam McAughtry, *Touch & Go*: 'The woman, kitchen house all over, in a headscarf, argued with the man, pleaded, then walked slowly to the train...'

kite [n., <?]. Anus. **1987** Lar Redmond, *Emerald Square*: 'We had often thought up tortures for Tella' Man. Such things as hanging him up on a butcher's hook by the nakers [testicles]...or shoving the rough end of a pineapple up his kite...'

kithogue/ciotóg/cittah/cittogue [n., <Ir. *ciotóg*, left-hand]. As thus; left-handed and/or awkward person. **1988** Alice Taylor, *To School through the Fields*: 'She was left-handed, and always referred to her left hand as "the *ciotóg*", almost as if it belonged to someone else.' **1994** Vonnie Banville Evans, *The House in the Faythe*: 'It [the Room (q.v.)] too ran from the front window, scene of my brother Jack's mysterious accident which turned him into a kitogue [*sic*], to the back window looking out into the yard.'

kitterdy [n., see **kithogue**, **kitter-fisted**] (Ulster). Left-handed and/or awkward person. **1983** Polly Devlin, *All of us There*: 'Anyone who through high spirits, talent, frustrations, ambition, desire to shock...breaches the behaviour barriers becomes the target of biting scorn and ire: he or she...is an "amadan" [q.v.] or a "kitterdy".'

kitter-fisted/handed [adj., <Ir. *ciotach*, left-handed, awkward; cf. Frisian *käitig*, left-handed]. As thus. See **kithogue**.

kittle [vb., <Sc. *idem*, have kittens] (Ulster). As thus.

kitty [n.] (Ulster). Children's game. **1995** Liam Bradley in Mary Ryan et al (eds.), *No Shoes in Summer*: 'a game we called "Kitty", which was played with a small stick, pointed at both ends, which we struck on the ground so that it flew up in the air. The object was to hit it as far as possible with a long rod...'

Kitty the Hare [nickname]. Fictional character of travelling woman created by C20 writer Victor O'D. Power. Hence gen. used of travelling woman. **1987** Lar Redmond, *Emerald Square*: 'I stuck my head out the window. "Kitty the Hare country," I told him. "Why don't you ask the headless coachman when he passes by?"' **1995** Patrick Boland, *Tales from a City Farmyard*: 'When...I turned around, half asleep, to see the lady in white with her white face standing there, I let out a scream thinking she was a banshee [q.v.] with a bit of Kitty the Hare thrown in for good measure.'

K.M.R.I.A. [expletive, acronym, play on *M.R.I.A.*, Member of the Royal Irish Academy]. Kiss My Royal Irish Arse. **1922** James Joyce, *Ulysses*: '"Will you tell him he can kiss my arse?" Myles Crawford said...**K.M.R.I.A.** "He can kiss my royal Irish arse...Any time he likes, tell him."' See also **póg mo thón**.

knab see **nab**

knacker [n., <*idem*, buyer of worn-out horses for slaughter, 1812, <ON *knakkur*, saddle, derog.]. 1. Tinker, itinerant; gen. term of abuse. **1991** Roddy Doyle, *The Van*: 'The trip into town was grand [q.v.]. A scuttered [q.v.] knacker and a couple having a row kept them entertained as far as Connolly [station].' **1994** Paddy O'Gorman, *Queuing for a Living*: '"when you go to England, you're a person. No one would come up to you and say you're a knacker or a tinker."' **1996** *Sunday Tribune*, 4 Feb: 'Grand Prix team boss Eddie Jordan...recalled his younger days...People then saw business-

men as "strokers [see **stroke** 3.], knackers or chancers [q.v.]", he said.' Hence **knackered** [p. part. as adj., pre-dating modern sl. usage]. Finished, killed. **1943** George A. Little, *Malachi Horan Remembers*: '"Was I frightened? Ah, don't be talking! [q.v.] Didn't I know it was a judgment, and but for somebody's prayer I was knackered."' 2. One who buys old houses for demolition and redevelopment of the site (DOM).

knacky/knackety see **nauky**

knauvshaul [vb., <Ir. *cnáimhseáil* (n.), act of complaining] (Munster). Complain; 'grumbling, scolding, muttering complaints' (PWJ). **1997** Greg Delanty, *Irish Review* (Belfast), 'The Lost Way', Winter/Spring: 'Suzanne Vega stereotyped "Calypso"/as we knawvshawled [*sic*] about our families...'

knawky see **nauky**

knee-cap [vb.] (paramilitaries) (Ulster). Punish suspected informers etc. by shooting in both knees.

knick-knocks [n.]. Children's street game. **1995** Des Cahill in Seán Power (ed.), *Those were the Days, Irish Childhood Memories*: 'We were discussing what to do, but couldn't really think of anything. There wasn't much point in doing "knick-knocks" (ringing a doorbell and running away)...'

knock-beetle [n., <Sc. *idem*, one who is severely beaten] (Ulster). S.o. who allows himself to be pushed around.

knock down/knock-down [vb. & n.] (printing). Mark s.o.'s completing his apprenticeship by his fellow workers

banging mallets, hammers, etc. on imposing stones and metal chases etc. (WS).

knock for score [n. phr. & vb.]. Timid knock at a door, as by s.o. seeking a favour etc. (Moylan).

knoit see **noit**

knowe [n., <Sc. *idem* <OE *cnoll*, hilltop] (Ulster). Knoll, hilltop. **1938** Seumas MacManus, *The Rocky Road to Dublin*: 'there was no man so sinful as to set spade or plow to the fairy rath, their pleasant green knowe on the hillside'.

knowin [n., <Sc. *knowing*, very small quantity] (Ulster). As thus.

knurr see **nur**

knyam! see **nyam!**

kouth [n., <Ir. *crabhait*, insignificant person (Dinneen)]. Wizened, miserable-looking person (OTF).

Kruger [nickname, bestowed on him for leadership of his gang, nicknamed 'The Boers' by a teacher, at his school in Dún Chaoin, Co. Kerry]. Muiris Kavanagh (1894–1971), film publicist in USA and subsequently, on his return in 1920, publican in his native place. **1994** Bo Almqvist in Tadhg Ó Dúshláine (ed.), *Is Cuimhin Linn Kruger*, 'Kruger, Some Memories': 'sa tslí chéanna, deinadh Kruger de Mhuiris, mar gur imir sé páirt... Uachtarán na mBórach, Paul Kruger' ('in the same way, Muiris changed to Kruger, because he played the part...of the President of the Boers, Paul Kruger').

kybosh see **kibosh**

L

laaban [n., <Ir. *lábán*, mud, mire]. Rotten, sterile egg.

lab [n., <'lob'] (Ulster). Game of marbles.

labb [vb., poss. cogn. with *labber* (q.v.)]. Stick out the tongue in contempt or defiance (OTF).

labber [vb., <Sc. *idem*, slabber, slobber] (Ulster). As thus.

lá breá [n. phr., Ir. *idem*, nice day]. Neophyte student of Ir., esp. in Gaeltacht (Ir.-speaking) areas. **1994** Leslie Matson in Tadhg Ó Dúshláine (ed.), *Is Cuimhin Linn Kruger* (q.v.), 'Kruger, Some Memories': '"He'll teach you all you need to know"...Mártan, I'm sure, was none too pleased at having a "Lá Breá" dumped on him...'

labscouse [n., <?] (Ulster). Stew, mess.

lace [vb., <Ir. *léas*, welt, thrash, poss. <OF *laz* (n.), Lat. *laqueus* (n.), noose (DOM)]. Beat, flog. **1987** Lar Redmond, *Emerald Square*: 'He gazed along the line of scared boys, looking for a chance to lace one of them, a Kerry expression we had come to understand without the aid of a dictionary.' Also **lace one's jacket** (Ulster) in same sense (Traynor).

lachter see **cuckoo's lachter**

lack [n., <?] (Munster). Girlfriend.

lacken day [n. phr., <'leak'] (Ulster). Wet day (Patterson).

lad [n.]. 1. [placeholder]. Applied with ref. to undifferentiated inanimate objects, usu. in terms of grudging affection; 'person or thing that's very good or very bad' (EDD). **1977** Myles na gCopaleen, *The Hair of the Dogma*: (castigating the new Penguin edn of James Joyce's *Dubliners*) 'but what word have we for this thing, on p. 128?: Mr Lyons sat on the edge of the table, pushed his hat towards the nape of his neck and began to swing his legs. "Which is my bottle?" he asked. "This, lad," said Mr Henchy." That comma after "this" — have we a word for it? Yes: BLASPHEMY.' **1995**

Aidan Higgins, *Donkey's Years*: 'injections for pernicious anaemia kept her alive. "Without those lads," the doctor had warned her..."you wouldn't walk the length of this room.' 2. [euphem.]. Cancer; TB. **1992** Pauline Bracken, *Light of Other Days, A Dublin Childhood*: 'Cancer was never mentioned by name. "The Lad" was the sympathetic form of allusion...' Also **bad lad** in same sense. **1995** Shane Connaughton, *A Border Diary*: 'I met a friend the other day who referred to cancer as "the bad lad". He wouldn't say the word.' 3. Penis. **1984** John McGahern, *A Ballad*: '"O'Reilly got Rachael to take his lad in her mouth," Ryan said. "Then he wouldn't let her spit it out."' 4. Fox. **1995** 'Y', *Irish Times*, 23 Dec: 'The latter activity [hunting] has spawned some interesting prose and verse, often respectful of the fox — known, for example, as "the lad".'

laddie-buck [n.]. As **lad** 1. **1995** Shane Connaughton, *A Border Diary*: 'Peter Reilly, who is lying full out, opens an eye and says, "There's a laddie-buck comin' up now."...Sure enough a cloud is daring to cross the field.'

ladeen [n., <'lad' + Ir. dimin. *ín*]. Term of affection. **1995** Michael Hand, *Sunday Tribune*, 13 Aug: 'Thoughts of music and song, women and hurling stirred the emotions. "Do you know something, ladeen," one said. "When we leave here there will be no one to give the Feakle roar [Clare football/hurling supporters' chant]."'

ladoose [n., <Ir. *ladús*, pert, wheedling or silly talk, cajolery]. As thus; also 'mildly erotic, flirtatious talk' (Cork) (DOM); self-importance (Munster).

Lads, the [nickname]. Members of an illegal organisation, gen. the IRA in its various manifestations. See also **Stick**. **1982** Trevor Danker, *Sunday Independent*, 7 Nov: 'At long last a legend about those Rabelaisian verses about "Gough's Statue" has been laid to rest. The verses were written the morning after the statue of Sir Hubert Gough in the Phoenix Park [Dub.] was dynamited by The Lads on July 23, 1957.'

lag/lag-lost [n., cf. Sc. *idem* (adj.), late, last of all] (Ulster). Lazy/idle person; s.o. always late. See also **lag-a-bag**.

lag!/leg! [exclam.]. Call to geese.

lag-a-bag [n., <Sc. *idem*, loiterer] (Ulster). Lazy, idle person. See also **lag**.

lagger/legger [n. & vb., <Sc. *lagger*, miry place, mud; bemire] (Ulster). Sticky substance, like grease/porridge; bespatter, wade through mud. Hence **laggered** [p. part. as adj.]. 'Thick with mud' (SH).

lagheryman see **loughryman**

lag-lost see **lag**

lagonish! [exclam., poss. <Ir. *leag as!* lay off! + *anois*, now] (Ulster). Mind your own business!

lahoach [n., <] (Ulster). Anything big and awkward; fat woman.

laid by [p. part. phr. as adj.] (Ulster). Said of chronic invalid, cf. 'laid up'.

laimeter/lamester/lameter/lamitor [adj. & n., <Sc. *idem* (n.), lame person] (Ulster). Not oneself, in poor condition; individual as thus. **1908** Lynn Doyle, *Ballygullion*: 'Up till then she'd been afeared he was goin' to be a lamitor all his days, an' she wasn't right [see **right** 1.] sure whether to face [q.v.] him or not.'

lair [vb., <Sc. *idem*, stick fast in mud, snow, etc., <ON *leir* (n.), mud] (Ulster). Get, or cause to get, bogged down; wallow.

Lake County, the [nickname]. Co. Westmeath, esp. in GAA teams context. **1996** *Westmeath Independent*, 14 June: 'While Barney's boys might have been full of optimism against Dublin...there was to be no fairytale ending to the Lake County's campaign of the last months.'

lal the ral the ra/raddy [exclam., poss. <Ir. *radaí* (n.), stroller, rake, flirt (Dinneen)]. Freq. as nonsense refrain in songs & ballads. **1922** James Joyce, *Ulysses*: 'To topboots jog dangling on the Dublin. Lal the ral the ra, lal the ral the raddy.'

lamester/lameter/lamitor see **laimeter**

lamp (along) [vb., cf. 'like a lamp-lighter' (DHS), at a great rate, *c.*1840–]. As thus.

Lamprey see **bread-earner**

land [n., <*idem* (vb.), land a blow, Brit. sl. 1888–]. Unpleasant surprise. **1995** Aidan Higgins, *Donkey's Years*: 'She had a regular repertoire of sayings...among which prominently featured: "A land", or "a bit of a land", meant an unexpected disappointment, a let-down.'

lane [n.] (Cork). Street or square of slum or near-slum housing in Cork city. **1993** Bridey Murphy in Michael Verdon, *Shawlies* (q.v.), *Echo Boys* (q.v.), *the Marsh and the Lanes: Old Cork Remembered*: 'All the lanes were occupied by people in small houses...I was born among the lanes. Crowley's Lane, Warren's Lane, Pickett's Lane...There was one called 98th Street. That's knocked down with the rest of them.'

lang [n. &, less commonly, vb., <?] as in **on the lang** [adj. phr.] (Cork). Playing truant, mitching (q.v.). **1951** Frank O'Connor, *Traveller's Samples*, 'The Thief': 'I saw that it wasn't the langing she minded but the lies..."Larry...went on the lang with Peter Doherty and my mother isn't talking to him..."' **1963** Seán O'Faoláin, *Vive Moi!*: 'our headmaster, a brother whom we called Sloppy Dan, had hauled into this room two boys... who had been, as we used to say, "on the lang", that is, who had been roving the fields outside the city for several days instead of attending classes'. **1991** Teddy Delaney, *Where we Sported and Played*: 'holding our books under drain pipes to convince our mothers that it was too wet to send us back...'Twould have been easier just to go on the lang.'

langel [n., <Sc. *idem*, tether for hobbling an animal] (Ulster). Tall, spindly man or boy.

langer [n., <?]. Penis. **1990** Roddy Doyle, *The Snapper* (q.v.): '"Dark an' tall an'" — "Exotic," said Bertie. "Exactly," said Bimbo. "An' a hefty langer on him," said Bertie.'

langered/langers [adj., joc., poss. <Sc. *langer* (n.), weariness, tedium, <OF *languour* (n.), listlessness]. Drunk. **1982** Éamonn Mac Thomáis, *Janey Mack* (q.v.),

Me Shirt is Black: 'Well, the packing and the pints went on until the twenty-four eggs were all in the box and your man [q.v.] was langers.' **1994** Ferdia Mac Anna, *The Ship Inspector*: 'he had seen our dad staggering out of the Tall Ships, langered out of his mind'.

lang fiel' [n. phr.] (Ulster). Long acre (q.v.).

Lanna Macree's dog [n. phr.]. Time-server. **1906** William Boyle, *The Eloquent Dempsey*: 'You're like Lanna Macree's dog — piece of the road with everybody.' (One of the pack of accommodating canines: see also **Billy Harran's dog**, **Lanty McHale's dog**, **O'Brien's dog**.)

lant/lanty [n. & vb., cf. Sc. *lant* (vb.), jeer at, <*lanterloo* (*loo*) (n.), card game, <Fr. *lanterlu* (n.), meaningless refrain to a song] (Ulster). Scold. Also as in **give s.o. lanty** give s.o. hell/a rough time. **1991** Shane Connaughton, *The Run of the Country*: '"There'll be me and you and the crowd from Wattlebridge agin the whole of them. We'll give them lanty, don't fret."'

Lanty McHale's dog [n. phr., <?]. Time-server. **1944** James Joyce, *Stephen Hero*: '"Put this in your diary," he said to transcriptive Maurice. "Protestant orthodoxy is like Lanty McHale's dog: it goes a bit of the road with everyone."' **1961** Dominic Behan, *Teems of Times and Happy Returns*: 'Not that I ever attempted to say anything about them, or keep away from them — like Larry [*sic*] McHale's dog, I'd go a step of the road with anyone.' Billy Harran's dog (q.v.), Lanna Macree's dog (q.v.), O'Brien's dog (q.v.) & Dolan's ass (q.v.) are similarly disingenuous.

lap [vb., <ME *lappe*, fold, wrap] (Ulster). Wrap, wrap up. **1948** John O'Connor, *Come Day — Go Day*: 'at length, unable to endure it any longer, she had lapped the child in an old shawl and come out'.

lappered [p. part. as adj., <Sc. *idem*, coagulated, clotted; cf. ON *hløypa* (vb.), curdle milk] (Ulster). As thus.

lapwing see **act the lapwing**

lard see **beat the lard out of s.o.**

larky-boy [n.]. One addicted to mischief.

larry [n., <Ir. *learaire*, lounger, loafer]. Fool (Moylan).

Larry Dugan's eye-water [nickname]. Blacking. 'Larry Dugan was a famous shoe-black at Dublin' (Grose).

Lartigue, the [nickname, <Charles François Lartigue, C19 inventor]. Listowel & Ballybunion elevated monorail, 1888–1924. **1989** A.T. Newham, *The Listowel & Ballybunion Railway*: 'In June 1889 it was revealed that numerous complaints had arisen concerning the noise of travel on the "Lartigue" (as the railway was popularly known)...'

lash [n.]. 1. [cf. Sc. *idem*, great number or quantity; *lash* (vb.), lavish, squander, –1657] as in **give it a lash** make an attempt; cf. Austral. sl. 'have a lash at'; 'give it a birl (q.v.)/go' in same sense. **1980s–1990s** Republic of Ireland soccer supporters' chant: 'Give it a lash, Jack [Charlton], give it a lash, Jack, never, never, never say no; Ireland, Ireland, Republic of Ireland, rev it up and here we go.' **1995** *Irish Times*, 12 June: 'He [Professor Frank Convery] also queried the "give it a lash" school of economic development.' **1996** John Boland, *Irish Times*, 20 Apr: 'Invited to open the forthcoming Writers' Week in Listowel, the former Taoiseach [Charles J. Haughey] replied as follows: "To open Listowel Writers' Week/Is an honour that many would seek./So without hesitation/But with some trepidation,/I will give it a lash, so to speak."' 2. [<?]. Sexy woman. See **lasher** 1.

lasher [n.]. 1. [<?] (Cork). Beauty. **1991** Teddy Delaney, *Where we Sported and Played*: 'I'd never have stuck it at all if it wasn't for the *craic* [q.v.]...Some of the women were right [see **right** 1.] lashers.' **1993** Seán Beecher in Michael Verdon, *Shawlies* (q.v.), *Echo Boys* (q.v.), *the Marsh and the Lanes* (q.v.): *Old Cork Remembered*: 'Whacker Murphy went shifting [see **shift** 1.] in the Arc [Arcadia ballroom] and clicked [q.v.] a dolly from Gurrane. She was a lasher with a pair of josies [q.v.] that would act as buffers for the *Innisfallen*

[vessel on Cork–Britain routes].' See **lash** 2. 2. (printing). 'An over-conscientious worker; one anxious to impress overseer by a show of fussy diligence...' (WS).

lash-in [n., cf. Brit. sl. 'lash out' (vb.), spend money freely] (printing). 'A pub get-together...A "lash-in" always follows a "knock-down" [q.v.]...' (WS).

lashings [vb. n., invar. pl., Hib.E 1829; also Austral. sl. in same sense]. Abundance, plenty (gen. of food or drink). **1920** M.E. Dobbs, *She's Going to America*: 'CASSIE ...What's going to America that it should fret ye?...This is a poor country, and out there there's plenty o' work and lashings of money, and why wouldn't they go!' **1925** Lynn Doyle, *Dear Ducks*: '"Pat," sez he, "is there any wild-duck about that a body could shoot handy [q.v.]?" "Lashins of them," sez I.' **1977** James Plunkett, *Collected Short Stories*, 'Dublin Fusilier': '"Marty Callaghan," his mother had said to him previously, "are you going to mass at all?" He said he was ready, he had lashings of time.' Also **lashings and lavings/leavings** [n. phr.]. Plenty and to spare. **1937** Seán O'Faoláin, *A Purse of Coppers*, 'Sinners': '"I did take the boots ...But I didn't steal them. Sure I haven't a boot on my foot and she has lashings and leavings of them."' **1938** Seumas MacManus, *The Rocky Road to Dublin*: 'A loafing life is mostly thought a losing life, but to our lad it was a mortal [q.v.] gainful one, almost every heaven-sent idle day of his boyhood piling in his lap lashin's and leaving's of yellow gold.' **1979** C.S. Andrews, *Dublin Made Me*: 'The meals were cooked before our eyes and there was always "lashins and lavins".'

lasty [adj.]. Enduring, long-lasting (of turf etc.).

latch [n.] as in **bang the latch** [vb. phr.]. Delay, dilly-dally. See **bang of the latch**.

latchico [n., cf. Sc. *latch*, indolent, idle person, poss. <OF *laschier* (vb.), relax; but many other etyms. suggested; 'Dockland slang for a waster or a rogue' (Vincent Caprani, *Rowdy Rhymes & 'Rec-im-itations'*,

1982); used on Brit. building sites by West of Ireland workers, poss. <unidentified Ir. (DOM)]. As thus; halfwit. **1970** Christy Brown, *Down All the Days*: '"They trust me, bejasus [q.v.]...They know I'm no fucking latchico or general foreman's lick-arse [see **lick**]."' **1989** Robert E. Tangney, *Other Days Around Me*: '"What did you let him in for?" roared the angry widow. "He's the biggest latchico in town."'

latitat [n., <Lat. *latitare* (vb.), lie concealed; legal term –C19]. Warning note/letter (gen. from solicitor).

latitude [n.] as in **out of one's latitude (for)** [adj. phr.]. Much in love (with).

lauchy/laughy [adj., <Ir. *lách*, pleasant, affable, friendly]. As thus. **1896** Michael Banim, *The Bit o'Writin'*: '"She'd make a nate [neat], an' a clane [clean], an' a lauchy wife."'

laugh [n.] as in **badly a laugh for** [adj. phr.] (Ulster). Greatly in need of. Also (gen. usage) **(just) for the laugh** [adv. phr.]. For the hell of it.

laughing [pres. part. as adj.] (Ulster). Said of skins of potatoes broken when cooked. **1938** Seumas MacManus, *The Rocky Road to Dublin*: 'and set him in front of a big beechen dish full of still-steaming taties [q.v.] that were laughing at him through their jackets'. **1995** Éamon Kelly, *The Apprentice*: 'We had whatever vegetables were in season, big laughing potatoes and home-made butter...'

laughing sport [n. phr., gen. neg.] (Ulster). (No) laughing matter.

laughy see **lauchy**

launa-vaula/launawalla [n., <Ir. *lán an mhála*, full of the bag (Dinneen)]. Full and plenty. 'There was launa-vaula at the dinner' (PWJ).

launeyday! see **lawnyday!**

laverock [n., infl. by Sc. *levrek*, OE *laweerce*, lark] (Ulster). Leveret. **1966** Patrick Boyle, *At Night All Cats are Grey*, 'The Pishogue' (q.v.): 'That ould cod [q.v.] Clancy. An' him preening himself like a newly-trod laverock.'

lawnmower [nickname] (army, Lebanon). Israeli pilotless observation aircraft. **1996** Jim Cusack, *Irish Times*, 27 Apr: 'They even sounded inoffensive, something like a diesel lawnmower or a moped. The Irish soldiers call them lawnmowers and hate them. "Those f**king lawnmowers," one officer said.'

lawny/launeyday! [exclam., <Ir. *láine Dé*, fullness of God]. Mild oath. Also **oh lawny!**, **lawny save us!**

lay a finger on [vb. phr., invar. neg.]. (Not) attack, hurt or harm.

lay down one's bone [vb. phr.] (Ulster). Work earnestly/hard (Patterson).

laying hen [n. phr.]. Farmer's working wife or partner. **1996** Seán MacConnell, *Irish Times*, 28 Sept: 'many of these [part-time farmers] rely for their cash on a working wife or partner, known in the politically-impolite language of the farmer as the "laying hen"'.

lay out [vb., <'clocking' (see **clock** 3.) hen]. Engage in sexual two-timing. **1977** Wesley Burrowes, *The Riordans*: 'Minnie believed for a while that he [Batty] had another woman, (or, as Francey put it, that he was layin' out), but it turned out that the only rival was the horse...'

lazy-bed [n.]. Spade-ridge for potatoes. **1957** E. Estyn Evans, *Irish Folk Ways*: 'The potato ridge presumably derives its name...from the fact that the sod under the ridge is not dug: the bed is built up on top of the grass...the ridge technique is certainly older than the potato in Ireland.'

leadener [n.]. Heavy marble used in children's game. **1995** Phil O'Keeffe, *Down Cobbled Streets, A Liberties Childhood*: 'As I nodded off I remembered where I had hidden the big leadener which I had won at marbles the week before...' See **gullyer**.

leadóg [n., <Ir. *idem*, slap, skelp (q.v.), clout]. As thus. **1991** Seán Ó Ciaráin, *Farewell to Mayo*: '"He has many a long day out before him and many a *leadóg* of the cane from Galligan."'

leaf, go off with the [vb. phr., *c*.1870–]. Be hanged. 'Criminals in Dublin being turned off from the outside of the prison by the falling of a board, propped up, and moving on a hinge, like the leaf of a table' (Grose).

leaky [adj., <Sc. *idem*, wet (of weather)] (Ulster). As thus.

lean into [vb.]. Bring pressure to bear on. **1990** Iris Brennan, quoted in Walter Love, *The Times of our Lives*: 'He [the headmaster] was a right [see **right** 1.] bugger, especially if he'd a drink in him. He just sat up at that desk and he leaned into you...'

leather [n. & vb., <Ir. *leadair* (vb.), beat, hack, strike; poss. infl. by 'leather' (n.) as in leather belt etc.]. Beating; beat, hence **a good leathering**. **1993** Michael Boland in Michael Verdon, *Shawlies* (q.v.), *Echo Boys* (q.v.), *the Marsh and the Lanes* (q.v.): *Old Cork Remembered*: 'I'd say if you punched your wife, there'd be three or four of us come in that night and we'd really leather you. The community had its own sanctions.' **1993** Pat Tierney, *The Moon on my Back*: 'the thought that I might get caught and brought back to St Joseph's suddenly dawned on me, as did the possible leathering I would get on my return'. **1994** Jimmy Owens in Kevin C. Kearns, *Dublin Tenement Life*: 'And school was very bitter, a hard, hard school...A load of us used to be lined up on a cold morning to get a few leathers.'

leather-head [n.]. Stupid individual.

leather-lungs [n.]. Loud-voiced individual.

leavings see **lashings**

lebbidha/lebidjeh [n., <Ir. *leibide*, slovenly person, softie]. As thus (PWJ).

leebeen [n., <Ir. *líbín*, minnow, small fry of any fish]. As thus. **1995** Stephen Collins in Seán Power (ed.), *Those were the Days, Irish Childhood Memories*: 'Pinkeens [q.v.], or leebeens as we called them, also nibbled at the bait but the strength of the bites showed that something much larger was lurking there somewhere.'

leecher [n., <'leech' + endearment suffix]. Moneylender (derog.). **1987** Lar

Redmond, *Emerald Square*: 'The leecher Byrne was a fat, tallow-coloured slug, a moneylender crippled by arthritis...'

lees [n., <'lease' <'leash' <OF *laisse*, leash, division of threads in a warp] as in **lose the lees** (Ulster). Lose the thread of an argument.

leet–tlee–lee! [exclam.]. Call to young ducks.

left [solecistic p. part. of 'let']. Allowed. **1953** Frank O'Connor, *The Stories of Frank O'Connor*, 'Christmas Morning': '"you went on the lang [q.v.] with Doherty. I wouldn't play with them Doherty fellows." "You wouldn't be left."'

Left Bank [topographical name, <cultural etc. character of Rive Gauche, Paris]. The right bank of the River Liffey at Dub., specifically the Temple Bar area. **1995** *Irish Times*, 31 Mar: 'Temple Bar, Dublin's developing Left Bank area, is to have its own brewery.' Similarly Athlone, in respect of the Shannon. **1995** *A Guide to the Tourist Attractions of the Irish Midlands*: '"ATHLONE LEFT-BANK". This area of Athlone is in the shadow of the Historic Castle [actually located on the right bank]...All in all, Athlone's left-bank is worth a visit.'

left-footer [n., see **dig with the right foot**] (Ulster). Roman Catholic. **1993** Sam McAughtry, *Touch & Go*: '"don't you agree that things have turned out right, with that left-footer only getting the jail for the same thing?"'

leg [n. & exclam.]. 1. [n.] as in **to have a good/great leg of s.o.** [vb. phr.]. To be well in with, have influence on. **1989** Hugh Leonard, *Out after Dark*: 'the local priests possessed what they called "a great leg" of the local undertaker and had conveyed us the sixteen miles from town by hearse'. 2. [exclam.]. See **lag!**

legger [n. & vb.]. 1. [n.] as in **do a legger** [vb. phr.]. Depart (on foot) in haste. **1991** Roddy Doyle, *The Van*: 'What he decided on was, one of them would do a legger back to Bimbo's...' 2. [n. & vb.]. See **lagger**.

leg-over [n.]. Assistance, aid.

lemoner [n., <sourness of lemon + endearment suffix]. Deflationary occurrence. **1980** Bernard Farrell, *Canaries*: 'DAD (*Laughs*) A good one, isn't it? His wife left him to go to Paris with a *woman*. That must've been a right [see **right** 1.] lemoner, what?'

length of one's tongue, give s.o. the [vb. phr.] (Ulster). Reprimand, scold.

lep [n. & vb., <Hib.E pronun.; <OE *hleapan* (vb.), leap]. Jump, leap, bound. **1991** Bob Quinn, *Smokey Hollow*: '"What's a 'lepper'?" "It's unfortunate people with a terrible disease that makes their limbs fall off." "How can they 'lep' if they're like that?" "They don't lep. They walk around slowly."' Hence **leppin'/lepping** [adj., adv. & pres. part.]. 1. [adj. & intens. adv.]. Angry, incensed. **1966** Séamus Murphy, *Stone Mad*: '"I needn't tell you we were lepping mad at the beating we got..."' **1986** Tomás Ó Canainn, *Home to Derry*: '"Father Chapman's leppin' in there," Barney said, as he pushed Sean in front of him towards the sacristy door.' 2. [pres. part.] (Ulster). Throbbing painfully.

leprechaun [n., <Ir. *leipreachán*, diminutive fairy, invar. male] as in **knee-high to a leprechaun**. Diminutive. Also as adj., characteristic of perceived Oirish (q.v.) qualities, gen. derog. **1996** Sammy Wilson, quoted in *Irish Times*, 14 Dec: 'I would never want to read anything Councillor Ó Muilleoir would write, especially in that leprechaun language [Ir.] he likes to spout...'

lethericks [n. pl., <?]. Slices, as in **I'll cut levericks off your backside!** (DOM).

let on [vb., gen. neg.]. Pretend. **1982** Éamonn Mac Thomáis, *Janey Mack* (q.v.), *Me Shirt is Black*: 'We all went into town, O'Connell Street, and bought colours... and "let on" we were up for the Match.' **1995** Phil O'Keeffe, *Down Cobbled Streets, A Liberties Childhood*: '"You're not going to the war. You're not, you're not." I began banging my father's legs until he caught me and lifted me high in the air. "We're only letting on," he said as he lowered me to the ground.'

let-out [n.]. Spree, entertainment. **1866** Patrick Kennedy, *Legendary Fictions of the Irish Celts*: 'she went to New Ross to buy sugar and tay, and beef and port, to give a grand let-out to welcome her husband'.

letter [n., <Sc. *idem* in same sense] (Ulster). 'Spark on the wick of a candle, supposed to denote a visitor' (Traynor).

let the priest say mass [vb. phr.]. Reprimand to s.o. intent on offering supererogatory advice.

Levellers [nickname, <practice of levelling ditches erected on common land]. Alternative name for Whiteboys (q.v.).

lezzer [n., <abbrev. + endearment suffix, cf. Brit. sl. *lezzie*, lesbian]. As thus. **1997** Alan Roberts, *The Rasherhouse* (see **rasher**): '"Are ya a lezzer, are ya but [q.v.]?" "Here, ya can pretend this is a cucumber any time, so you can."'

liatroidie [n. pl., <Ir. *liathróidí*, balls]. Testicles. **1991** Shane Connaughton, *The Run of the Country*: '"Ah, the hard men [q.v.]," he called jovially to them. "How's the liatroidie?" "Oh, dangling nicely," Prunty replied with a grin.'

libber/libbock/libe/lybe/lybber [n.]. 1. [gen. pl., <Ir. *liobar*, loose, hanging thing]. Ribbons or skeins of meat; small loose piece of anything; hanging underlip (OTF). **1991** James Kennedy, *The People who Drank Water from the River*: 'No bone was hacked. No piece [of the pig] went in with "libbers"...hanging out of it. It was a clinical packaging exercise.' 2. [<Ir. *leadhb*, strip; rag, clout; slovenly person; clown]. 'Untidy person careless about his dress and appearance' (PWJ).

Liberator, the [nickname, <his campaign for the repeal of the union with Britain]. Daniel O'Connell (1775–1847), statesman. **1938** Seán O'Faoláin, *King of the Beggars*: 'The cattle market butchers edged about them, their cleavers under their coats. "Give us the word, Liberathor," they begged, "and let us get at them."' **1966** Patrick Boyle, *At Night All Cats are Grey*, 'Odorous Perfume her Harbinger': '"Hush, John! You'll only..." "I'll not hush. Drink and women were

never the downfall of the Liberator."' **1975** Davis & Mary Coakley, *Wit and Wine*: '[John] Hogan set out to search in the caves of Saravezza for a block of marble suitable for his figure of the "Liberator".'

lick [n. & vb., cf. Sc. *idem* (n.), cheat]. [n.]. Sycophant, crawler. Hence **lick-me-lug** (Ulster); **lick-arse** [cf. US sl. *ass-licker*, sycophant] in same sense. [vb.] as in **lick up to s.o.** [vb. phr.].

lick (along) [vb. phr., Austral. −1889 (DHS)]. Move very swiftly; more gen. in adv. phr. **at a good/great lick**.

lick alike [adj. phr., intens.] (Cork). Identical. **1963** Frank O'Connor, *Sunday Independent*, 17 Feb: 'the proposed destruction of Fitzwilliam Place and the Paddy and the Pig dinners at Bunratty are, as we say in Cork, "lick alike"'.

lick-me-lug see **lick**

lick thumbs [vb. phr.] (Ulster). Come to an agreement, seal a bargain.

lie [n.]. Black speck on the teeth, supposedly indicating a liar.

lie heads and thraws [vb. phr., <Sc. *idem*, lie head to toe] (Ulster). As thus.

lie out [vb.] (Ulster). Play truant. **1939** Patrick Gallagher ('Paddy the Cope' (q.v.)), *My Story*: 'I went to Roshine school when I was about seven years. I was not very good at school, although I never "lay out" for a day.'

life of Larry [n. phr., poss. echoic of Austral. 'happy as Larry']. Ideal existence. **1969** Robert Greacen, *Even without Irene*: 'a troubled boyhood — dark and haunted, yet not without an innate belief that one day I would lead the life of Larry, far away from the Newtownards Road [Belfast]'.

life of Reilly/Riley [n. phr., <common Ir. surname, popularised in H. Pease's song 'My Name is Kelly' (1919) (ODMS)]. Carefree, hedonistic existence. **1981** Brendan Behan, *After the Wake*: 'It [famine food] was for the hungry Irish and it saved them the trouble of going any further with it. They had the life of Riley down on the quay while it lasted.'

Liffey water [nickname, <rhym. sl. for *porter* (q.v.) and <alleged constituent]. Guinness stout.

lift [n. & vb.]. 1. [n.]. Shoe support, gen. pl. **1995** Úna Claffey in Seán Power (ed.), *Those were the Days, Irish Childhood Memories*: 'There was the trip to get "lifts" on the soles of my shoes so I wouldn't grow up with flat feet...' 2. [vb.] (Ulster). Understand. 'She's onny two but that wee [q.v.] girl can lift me' (Pepper). 3. [vb.] (esp. Northern Ire.). Arrest. **1948** John O'Connor, *Come Day — Go Day*: '"if you don't leave that bottle down and get outside this house this minute, I'll have you lifted before night"'. **1951** Sam Hanna Bell, *December Bride*: '"[the wee (q.v.) dog'll] be kilt wi' all those people and motor-cars!" "Ach, not at all, the police'll lift him and keep him for ye."' See also **up in the lift**.

lifted and laid [adv. phr.]. Unfairly favoured. **1996** Suzanne Breen, *Irish Times*, 2 Nov: 'many Protestant officers [of the Royal Ulster Constabulary] harboured deep-seated sectarian attitudes towards their Catholic colleagues. They felt that Catholic recruits were "lifted and laid" by senior officers.'

lifting [adj., <Sc. *lifter* (n.), one who gathers cut corn] (Ulster). Starving with hunger.

lig/liggety [n. & vb.]. 1. [n., cf. Sc. *lug* & US *idem*, foolish man] (Ulster). Fool, prankster, rogue; clumsy individual. '"Lig" is often male and "liggety" female' (Traynor). **1948** John O'Connor, *Come Day — Go Day*: '"God knows where those two ligs have got to this time; away since Friday..."' 2. [n., <OE *lyge*, lie]. Reception etc. which could be gatecrashed. Hence **lig** [vb.] gatecrash, **ligger** [n.] gatecrasher. **1986** Derek Dunne, *Magill*, Aug: 'The ligger is a person who goes to everything, eats and drinks well, has very little right to be there, but who nonetheless takes a joy and delight in being there.'

light [vb.] as in **she never lights** (Ulster). She is always busy/working.

light (in the head) [adj. phr.]. Foolish.

light into/on s.o. [vb., gen. p. tense]. Attack; berate, as in **he lit on me**. **1977** James Plunkett, *Collected Short Stories*, 'A Touch of Genius': 'The kid lit into the biscuits right away and Danny went up to pay for them.' **1993** Eamon O'Neill in Joe O'Reilly & Sixth Class, Convent School, Edenderry, *Over the Half Door*: 'I got a pliers, a screwdriver and a phase tester stuck in my locker where I had left them. This electrician came over and lit on me. "You were doing our work last night."'

lig-lag [exclam., <Sc. *idem*, chatter loudly] (Ulster). 1. As thus. 2. Call to geese.

like [adv., modifying adj., redundant usage, cf. Craig McGregor, *Profile of Australia* (1966): 'Ending a sentence with "like" and "but" [q.v.] is a common habit']. As it were; & as terminal intens. **1995** Luke Clancy, *Irish Times*, 18 Oct: 'When a rogue "like" showed up in the everyday speech of suburban Dublin, it was as a substitute for "eh" or "um", a sort of patch to cover up a period of like ...mental lag. But now things have gotten, like...way out of hand.' Similarly **like you know**.

like Lord Thomond's cocks [adj. phr., <Earls of Thomond, O'Briens of Co. Clare]. Of professed allies who attack each other. 'Lord Thomond's cock-feeder, an Irishman, being entrusted with some cocks which were matched for a considerable sum, the night before the battle shut them all together in one room, concluding that as they were all on the same side, they would not disagree: the consequence was, they were most of them killed or lamed before the morning' (Grose).

like oneself [n. phr.] (Ulster). In unchanged state of appearance or health. **1966** Patrick Boyle, *At Night All Cats are Grey*, 'Oh Death Where Is Thy Sting-aling-aling': '"She's very like herself, isn't she?" his daughter asked. "Not a day over fifty she looks."' See **pass oneself**.

like snuff at a wake [adv. phr.]. With great rapidity; in large quantities. **1965** Lee Dunne, *Goodbye to the Hill*: 'And all over the place governments were coming and going like snuff at a wake...' **1985** Máirín Johnston, *Around the Banks of Pimlico*: 'Uncle Christy was a very quiet cheerful man who was everybody's favourite...especially in the pubs, where he threw money around like snuff at a wake.'

like the hammers (of hell) [adv. phr.]. With great speed. **1987** Lar Redmond, *Emerald Square*: 'I must have gone like the hammers of hell, for I was suddenly in Firhouse, on the road to the bridge...'

like you know see **like**

lilt [n. & vb.]. 1. [n. & vb., <Sc. *idem* (vb.), dance to music] (Ulster). [n.]. One who acts foolishly/irresponsibly; 'Bouncy, energetic woman' (SH). [vb.]. Cavort. **1951** Sam Hanna Bell, *December Bride*: '"And then she goes lilting round the house and making no shift to wipe the wean[q.v.]'s face."' Hence **lilty** [adj.]. Full of energy. 2. [vb.]. Provide wordless vocal accompaniment to traditional dancing. **1979** Paddy Tunney, *The Stone Fiddle*: 'Francey Bell could whistle like the blithest blackbird that ever piped on hawthorn bough, but his lilting was the most melodious I have ever heard.' See **puss music**.

Lilywhites [nickname, rarely sing., <colour of sports flag]. Co. Kildare GAA teams, and by association any Kildare inhabitant. **1986** Padraic O'Farrell, *'Tell me, Sean O'Farrell'*: 'the glow of cigarettes and pipes could be seen in the corner of the field as tales of the famous "Lily White" footballers were told'. **1995** Liam Kenny, *Leinster Leader* (Naas, Co. Kildare), 2 Feb: '"B" Company accounts for the largest number of Kildare lads in any unit in the Lebanon with 39 of the 122 strong company having Lillywhite roots.' Also **Lilliwhites, Lillies, Lilies**.

line [n.]. 1. Undercover communications route. **1993** Tim Pat Coogan, *Dev* (q.v.): *Long Fellow* (q.v.), *Long Shadow*: 'Using "the line", the general name for the multiplicity of routes whereby Irish political prisoners have traditionally smuggled messages in and out of prisons...' 2. Romantic association, as in

doing a line [vb. phr.]. **1977** Wesley Burrowes, *The Riordans*: 'Jane, played by Mary Larkin, had arrived before the summer break, and when we re-started, the line with Benjy was already going strong.' **1986** Tom McDonagh, *My Green Age*: 'I even did a line for a while with a nurse from Galway.' **1989** Hugh Leonard, *Out after Dark*: 'My friendship with Oliver was dying a natural death. He had begun what in those days [1940s–1950s] was known as a steady line...' 3. (Ulster). Certificate; doctor's prescription; referral to doctor. **1990** Tom O'Kane, quoted in Walter Love, *The Times of our Lives*: 'when the people had no money they would come for to see the Doctor. They would come into the bar and I would give them a line, a black line, and the doctor saw them for that. When they wanted to bring the doctor out to the house, they had to get a red line.' 4. Road between towns.

liner [n.]. Substantial meal (Moylan).

links [n. pl.] (Ulster). Sausages.

linney/linnie [n., <Ir. *lann eatha/iotha*, corn house] (Munster). 'Long shed – sort of barn – attached to a farm house' (PWJ); hence spare room. **1995** Mary Lyons in Mary Ryan et al. (eds.), *No Shoes in Summer*: 'some [hired workmen] resided in the farmhouse in a little room off the kitchen called a linney'.

lip [vb.] (Ulster). Eat, taste. **1908** Lynn Doyle, *Ballygullion*: '"Have ye any cheese in the house," sez he, "Pat?" "Divil a crumb," sez I; "it's a thing I niver lip."'

lip and laggin/lippin-leggin [adv., <Sc. *laggen* (n.), projection of staves at bottom of a barrel] (Ulster). Full to the brim.

lithing see **lythin**

little-dick [nickname]. Little finger.

little God's time [n. phr., <?]. Time immemorial; 'the year dot'. See also **old God's time**.

little people [n. phr.]. Fairies, latterly ironic. **1988** Alice Taylor, *To School through the Fields*: 'Mrs Casey had a healthy respect for the spirits of the dead and the "little people"...' **1995** Patsy McGarry, *Irish Times*, 2 June: 'Anyhow, in 1963 if anyone said "There's gold in them thar' hills" they would probably have assumed it belonged to "the little people" and should be left there.' See also **wee folk**.

live in s.o.'s ear [vb. phr.]. Form a very close association with s.o. **1979** Frank Kelly, *The Annals of Ballykilferret*: 'They find they cannot sustain their anger with him because he is "great crack [see **crack** 1.] and would live in your ear".' **1985** Máirín Johnston, *Around the Banks of Pimlico*: 'Among the people themselves there existed the most genuine support and neighbourly assistance. We lived in each other's ears.'

live on the skin of a rasher [vb. phr.]. Exist marginally. **1987** Lar Redmond, *Emerald Square*: '[During the Anglo-Ir. economic war] Calves were killed for their hides and the carcasses buried. Towns and cities lived on the skin of a rasher, while daily, herds of cattle were butchered and left to rot.'

load [n. & vb.] as in **get one's load** [vb. phr.]. Become intoxicated. Hence **loaded** [p. part. as adj.].

loaf [vb.]. Head-butt. **1991** Ferdia Mac Anna, *The Last of the High Kings*: 'A front tooth popped out...Sorry about that, said the boy, I meant to loaf you on the nose.'

lob [n., cf. Sc. *idem*, lump]. Large quantity (of money). **1986** Padraic O'Farrell, *'Tell me, Sean O'Farrell'*: 'a big cleft appeared in the mound. He saw lobs (large quantities) of treasure within and went home for a bag to collect some.'

lochrie man see **loughryman**

lock [n., <Sc. *idem* <OE *loc*, (usu. small) quantity of something] (Ulster). As thus. Also **brave** (q.v.) **lock**, **quare** (see **quare** 1.) **lock**, considerable quantity. **1914** St J. Ervine, *Mixed Marriage*: 'RAINEY A don't like Hughie goin' after Papishes [q.v.]. He knows a quare lock of them.' **1925** Louise McKay, *Mourne Folk*: '"Broccoli," said John, "is a vegetable much used in America." "Oh," replied Mary Anne, "ours is all done long ago, but we have a

'brave lock' of cabbages in the garden.'" **1982** Henry Glassie, *Passing the Time*: 'both women add flour, "a lock of salt, and a wee [q.v.] taste of soda" to make a pancake that you butter while hot'.

locked [p. part. as adj.]. Intoxicated. **1970** Christy Brown, *Down All the Days*: 'Their father had been drinking since he was twelve, when a pint of stout cost only a penny...so he often got "locked" on a shilling which he earned as a messenger boy.' **1996** Paul Howard, *Sunday Tribune*, 5 May: 'Why are we so obsessed with the sobriety or otherwise of our politicians? Was Dan Kiely locked? Was Sean Barrett locked? Was Ned O'Keeffe locked? Who cares?'

lodger [n.] (Ulster). Small uncut loaf.

Loft, the [nickname, <location]. Cork Shakespearean Society. **1996** M. Ó hA., *Irish Times*, obituary of Geoff Golden, 13 Dec: 'Eddie, an older half-brother, was the most famous boy-actor trained at Father O'Flynn's "The Loft"...'

log [n.] (Maynooth College). Second-year student. See **chub**.

logey [adj., <'log']. Heavy or fat individual (PWJ).

loggy [adj., cf. Sc. *luggy*, 'growing more to stem than to grain or root' (CSD)] (Ulster). Dull, clammy (of weather).

logie-hole [n., cf. Ir. *logán*, little hollow; Sc. *logie*, ventilating hole at the foundation of a stack] (Ulster). Hidey-hole.

loider [n., <Ir. *láidir* (adj.), strong] (Gaelic football). High kick. **1978** J.J. Comerford, *My Kilkenny IRA Days*: 'I kicked the ball for a while with the boys and enjoyed a few "loiders" or high kicks.'

lollion [n., <?] (Ulster). Fat, awkward person.

lomine!/lominty! [exclam., euphem.] (Ulster). Lord! See **slipe** 3.

lone, its [adv.] (Ulster). Alone, (on) its own. Also **my lone**, **their lone**, etc. in same sense.

long acre [n. phr.]. Grass roadside margins, providing free grazing. **1946**

Mary Lavin in Robert Greacen (ed.), *Irish Harvest*, 'The Story of the Widow's Son': 'It was for Packy's sake that she walked for hours along the road, letting her cow graze the long acre of the wayside grass...' **1973** Noël Conway, *The Bloods* (q.v.): 'They [farm horses] could also be very undisciplined on the long marches, dropping off to the side of the road whenever the mood got them to nibble at the Long Acre!' See also **God's acre**.

Long Fella/Fellow, the [nickname]. Eamon de Valera (1882–1975), statesman & politician. **1961** Dominic Behan, *Teems of Times and Happy Returns*: 'the result was something of a shock for his Fianna Fáil party. The expected landslide did not take place and the "Long Fella" was forced to count on support from Labour.' **1991** Bob Quinn, *Smokey Hollow*: 'Mrs Toner referred to him as "The Long Fellow" or "The Lanky Oul' Get [q.v.]" or "The Spaniard". She would never commit herself to saying who she actually voted for...' See **Dev**, **Long Hoor**.

long finger [n. phr.], gen. as in **put on the long finger** [vb. phr., <Ir. *cuir ar an méar fhada, idem*]. Postpone indefinitely. **1952** Letter from 'P.L.L.', *Kavanagh's Weekly*, 31 May: 'Often four unmarried folk, watching each other, hugging the corner, afraid to move, jealous of one another...No one to give advice, guidance, encouragement...just watching each other and the "long finger".' **1995** John Fleetwood, RTÉ Radio, *Sunday Miscellany*, 13 Aug: 'so the idea [of a railway between Listowel and Ballybunion] was put on the long finger until the arrival in 1885 of Charles Lartigue [see **the Lartigue**].' **1995** Doctor, BBC Radio Ulster news, 19 Dec: 'We're told chocolate[-flavoured barium] is a little more tricky, so we're putting it on the long finger.' Also **long-finger** [vb.] in same sense. **1995** Tom MacGinty, *The Irish Navy*: 'Again the topic [marine survey] was long-fingered, and there was no action until 1963...'

Longford Slasher, the [nickname]. Albert Reynolds (1932–), politician & businessman. **1995** Sean Duignan, *One Spin on the Merry-go-round*: 'Now, the so-called Longford Slasher, scything through the ranks of his erstwhile ministerial colleagues, was also demanding the head of their pal, PJ [Mara]...'

long grass, be in the [vb. phr.]. Lie low. **1986** Bob Geldof, *Is That It?*: 'We called the album *In the Long Grass*, an Irish expression. When you have not seen someone for a long time and you ask them where they have been they might reply, "Oh, I've been in the long grass..."' Also **wait for s.o. in the long grass** [vb. phr.]. Lie low.

long-headed [adj.]. Deep-thinking, intelligent. **1866** Patrick Kennedy, *Legendary Fictions of the Irish Celts*: 'bedad [q.v.] the long-headed neighbours took that opportunity to gain their ends of the fairy imp'.

Long Hoor, the [nickname]. Michael Collins's name for Eamon de Valera. **1937** Frank O'Connor, *The Big Fellow* (q.v.): 'But Collins put his foot down at last. "The Long Whoor [*sic*] won't get rid of me as easy as that," he said.' See **hoor**, **Long Fella**.

long-lippit [adj., <'lipped'] (Ulster). Sulky.

longnebbed [adj., <OE *nebb* (n.), nose] (Ulster). Over-inquisitive.

long streak/string of misery [n. phr.]. Tall, lanky individual. **1958** Frank O'Connor, *An Only Child*: 'John P...was a long string of misery, with an air of unutterable gravity, emphasised by the way he sucked in his cheeks.' **1991** Bob Quinn, *Smokey Hollow*: '"Dommo, you're not worth a shit. You should have got him, the long streak of misery."'

long tack [n. phr.] (Ulster). 'Long time spent in one place or at one employment' (MON).

long-tongue [n.]. Talebearer.

looby [n., poss. <'lubber'; cf. Dan. *lobbes*, clown]. Lout, awkward individual. **1577** Richard Stanihurst, 'Description of Ireland' in Holinshed's *Chronicles*: '"Sir, you take me short, as long and as verie a lowbie as you imagine to make me.'

172

looder/loodher/luder [n. & vb., <Ir. *liúdar* (n.), stroke, blow], Vicious blow; strike thus.

loodheramaun see **ludaramaun**

looka', lookat/it [interj. used to emphasise what follows or precedes]. **1946** Myles na gCopaleen, *Irish Writing No. 1* 'Drink and Time in Dublin', May: '"...I'm nearly too weak to walk and the shakes getting worse every day...Lookat here, mister-me-man [see **mister-me-friend**], I say to meself, this'll have to stop."' **1961** Dominic Behan, *Teems of Times and Happy Returns*: '"Looka here, Charlie Mac, if yer goin' to play Relievio [q.v.], stand in line."' **1996** Brendan Glacken, *Irish Times*, 9 June: 'There was an American female comic on the stage and she said, "You know that phrase about men seldom making passes at girls who wear glasses — well, most men I know would f★★★ a tree." Talent? Humour? Well lookit.'

look seven ways for Sunday [vb. phr.]. Squint.

loon see **loun**

loopy [adj.] (Ulster). Crafty, deceitful.

loose ball [n. phr., <soccer, Gaelic games]. Opportunity to cadge free drink. **1987** Con Houlihan, *Dublin Opinion*, 'The Ball Hop' (q.v.), May: 'A local man made good was whooping it up with a few friends; inevitably a loose ball gatherer quietly took up his station. Soon he had been co-opted into the company and was about to live happily ever after.'

loose leg, have a [adj. phr.]. Be free to act without impediment.

loose porter see **porter**

loothy [n., cf. Ir. *liútar*, big, ungainly man]. Slovenly, uncouth person (OTF).

lop [n., <?] (Cork). Pre-decimal penny; small sum of money. **1953** Frank O'Connor, *My Oedipus Complex and Other Stories*: '"If you give him a tanner you ought to give me a tanner," he yelled. "I'll tan you," she said laughingly. "Well, give me a lop anyway," he begged, and she did give him a penny...' **1993** Aine de Courcy in Michael Verdon, *Shawlies*

(q.v.), *Echo Boys* (q.v.), *the Marsh and the Lanes* (q.v.): *Old Cork Remembered*: 'Then Danny Hobbs would collect pennies. A *lop*. And they'd get lops off the people and every boy playing would get fourpence...'

lord/my lord [n.] (Ulster). Hunchbacked man.

Lord Harry, be/by the [exclam., <euphem. for the Devil]. Mild oath. **1922** James Joyce, *Ulysses*: 'by the Lord Harry green is the grass that grows on the ground'.

lorry/lurry (up) [vb., <Ir. *iúradh* (n.), beating or thrashing]. Beat, thrash. Also as in **lorry him up, he's no relation** [catchphrase]. **1946** Donagh MacDonagh, *Happy as Larry*: 'Lorry him up, he's no relation!/Give him a blow or two for me.' **C20** Dub. street rhyme: 'Lurry them up! Kick their shins! That's the way "Sycamore" [street soccer team] wins.' Also **lurry into** [vb.]. Attack. **1996** Joseph O'Connor, *The Irish Male at Home and Abroad*: '"I was sitting there lurrying into the breakfast with Jennifer. And she said, 'Would you pass the cornflakes please?' and I looked up at her. And I said "You've ruined my life, you wagon [q.v.]."'

lose the head [vb. phr.]. Lose one's temper or control. **1991** Shane Connaughton, *The Run of the Country*: '"Feck all [see **feck** (vb.) 2.] use losing the head," said Prunty. "Away to bed the pair of you."' **1996** Press advertisement for Hibernian Insurance Company, Aug: 'But little Boy says/"Sure why lose the head?/Hibernian cover/My humble homestead..."' Also **lose the bap** (Ulster) in same sense. See **bap** 2.

lose the run of oneself [vb. phr., cf. Ir. *ná bí ag rith leat féin mar sin*, lit. don't be running with yourself like that]. Lose control. **1994** Radio commercial for Power City, Oct: 'Youse [q.v.] are losing the run of yourselves, seems to me.' **1995** Vincent Browne, *Irish Times*, 16 Aug: '[Michael D. Higgins] Has lost the run of himself badly, though, since becoming a Minister...' **1995** Catherine Donnelly, *Sunday Independent*, 3 Dec: 'Obviously

David Hanly is becoming as nervy as I am...chairing a debate between Mervyn Taylor and William Binchy, he lost the run of himself entirely.'

lossenger see **lozenger**

lost [adj. & vb.] (Ulster). 1. [adj.]. Cold, wet, perished. 2. [vb.]. Lose. **1994** Paddy O'Gorman, *Queuing for a Living*: '"I have to run down every week with the child ...And she keeps losing my book [see **book** 2.] and they [Department of Social Security] won't give me a new book."'

loughryman/lagheryman/lochrie man [n., <Ir. *luchramán*, pygmy, dwarf, elf; confused with *leprechaun* (q.v.)] (Ulster). Small individual with magical powers: 'not a dwarf or an elf' (Todd); 'Race of small hairy people living in the woods' (Patterson). **1983** W.F. Marshall, *Livin' in Drumlister*, 'Absent': 'The holy thorns are dead now,/The Lochrie Man's a dream,/We've Santa Claus instead now,/And gramophones and steam.'

loun/loon [n., <MDu. *loen*, fool, lout] (Ulster). As thus; boy, youth. See **mense**.

loup the tether [vb. phr., <ON *hlaup*, OE *hleap* (n.), leap]. Ramble.

louser [n., <'louse' + endearment suffix]. Despicable individual, occasionally joc. **1961** Tom Murphy, *A Whistle in the Dark*: 'MICHAEL Are they coming?... MUSH The lousers must have stayed on for another one at The Lion.' **1975** John Ryan, *Remembering How We Stood*: 'Mrs Clougherty, having "foostered" [q.v.] for a moment in front of a mirror, gave them a last look as much as to say "shut up you lousers" and made straight for the hall door.' **1979** Frank Kelly, *The Annals of Ballykilferret*: '"Ah Mr Gilhooley, ye're a louser! Me pint isn't half finished, and the dogs has bitten the leg off me three times!"' Also **lousing** [pres. part.] in same sense. **1987** Lar Redmond, *Emerald Square*: 'by the time they were seventeen they were short-winded from smoking, slack from lousing at street corners'.

louzing/lowsing-time [n., <Sc. *lowse* (vb.), unyoke horses] (Ulster). Finishing time (work).

low [n., <ON *logi*, flame] (Ulster). Sudden blaze.

low babies [n. phr.] (education). Junior infants, first year of school. See **high babies**.

lower [vb.] (Connacht). Beat severely. **1995** *Sunday Tribune*, 17 Dec: 'Then, "they lowered me and lowered me", is how Patrick [Gardiner] describes the first beating, "they knocked me with their fists, they fleeced [q.v.] me around the head and they reefed [q.v.] up the room".'

lown [adj., <Sc. *idem*, calm, silent, <Norweg. dialect *logn/lugn*, calm] (Ulster). Calm, quiet, as in **lown day** [n. phr.]. Calm day.

lowset [adj.]. Small in stature.

lowsing-time see **louzing-time**

lozenger/lossenger [n., <'lozenge']. 1. As thus. **1983** W.F. Marshall, *Livin' in Drumlister*, 'The Drumnakilly Divil': 'So I went an' sat beside her, an' with tay and buns supplied her,/An' to soften her I tried her with a lossenger or two.' Also as in **not worth a lozenger**. Worth very little. 2. Penis. **1993** Pat Tierney, *The Moon on my Back*: 'One fellow might say to the other: "How's your mott[q.v.]'s belly fixed for a lodger?" and the other fellow might respond: "Your lozenger is not big enough to give a lodger to a flea!"'

luckpenny [n.]. Token amount returned to buyer/seller on completion of deal. **1936** *Irish Times*, 18 July: 'From the beginning of October next the private telephone service in England will be made a present of fifty local calls every quarter...By this move the Post Office has introduced the principle of the "luckpenny" into public finance.' **1991** John B. Keane, *Love Bites and Other Stories*: 'We were to receive no luck penny from the vendor as was the fashion but these bonhams [piglets] would make their own luck in the course of time.' **1995** Michael 'Gossie' Browne in Mary Ryan et al. (eds), *No Shoes in Summer*: 'I asked him what he was lookin for and he said "eight pound". I bid him five with a luckpenny of five bob an he agreed.'

lucky lumps [n. pl.]. Sweets in which one might — rarely — find a small coin (pre-decimal sixpence).

lucky stone [n. phr.] (Ulster). Small perforated stone found on a beach.

ludaramaun/ludramawn/loodheramaun etc. [n., <Ir. *liúdramán*, 'lanky, lazy person' (Dinneen)]. As thus. **1922** James Joyce, *Ulysses*: "'...Pisser Burke told me there was an old one [see **oul' wan**] there with a cracked loodheramaun of a nephew and Bloom trying to get on the soft side of her'". **1961** Flann O'Brien, *The Hard Life*: 'Adam was a damn fool, a looderamawn if you like. Afraid of nobody, not even the Almighty...Why didn't he tell that strap [see **strap** 1.] of a wife he had to go to hell.' **1986** Maurice Manning, *Magill*, 'The Pride of Ballaghaderreen', Mar: 'And then [James] Dillon in his stentorian voice boomed "All you ludaramans who are shouting 'Up Dev [q.v.]' can hardly know that the tri-colour presented by the French to the Young Irelanders was first hoisted by my grandfather, John Blake Dillon, at the Battle of Ballingarry in 1848, when at that time de Valera's grandfather was in all probability banging a banjo in the streets of Barcelona.'" Also **lúdram**, **lutherum** (Moylan). Gullible individual, fool; big, awkward man.

ludeen [n., <Ir. *lúidín*, little finger]. As thus.

luder see **looder**

ludramawn see **ludaramaun**

lug [n., cf. Sc. *luggie* (adj.), awkward, sluggish]. Awkward, unhandy individual, fool. See **lig** 1.

lumber [vb. & n.] (Ulster). Embrace, kiss. **1995** Glenn Patterson, *Sunday Tribune*, 9 July: 'The Eleventh [of July] night, rather than the Twelfth [q.v.] day, was the highlight of our year. In the weeks before, we stayed out late, kissed girls (lumbered, we said then, and it describes our technique perfectly)...'

lump [n.]. Good size, esp. as applied to a child. **1927** Peadar O'Donnell, *Islanders*: "'Best thing ye could do is settle down on the island: we'll get ye a brave [q.v.] lump of a lad..."' **1990** Tom O'Kane, quoted in Walter Love, *The Times of our Lives*: 'I was a lump of a lad about eight year old, and I'd a wee [q.v.] pool where the water'd go through but the fish weren't able to get out.'

lunatic soup [n., cf. Austral. & NZ *idem*, 'alcoholic drink of poor quality' (ODMS)]. Methylated spirits. **1993** Frank Casey in Michael Verdon, *Shawlies* (q.v.), *Echo Boys* (q.v.), *the Marsh and the Lanes* (q.v.): *Old Cork Remembered*: 'In those days some of the men went on benders. They'd go mad for the drink, absolutely mad...Some — not many — but some would even drink methylated spirits. They would. "Lunatic soup", we called it.'

lunder [n., <Sc. *lounder*, heavy blow] (Ulster). **1908** Lynn Doyle, *Ballygullion*: 'So I lifts a bit of a stick, an' hits the dog two or three lundhers wid it; but divil a bit [q.v.] would he let go.'

Lundy [n., derog., <Robert Lundy, governor of Derry, who recommended surrender during the Jacobite siege of 1689] (Ulster). Traitor. **1996** Jim Cusack, *Irish Times*, 3 Aug: 'The [Ulster Volunteer Force] statement used one of the most defamatory terms in the loyalist lexicon when it described the PUP [Progressive Unionist Party] leadership... as "Lundies".'

lunk [adj., cf. Norweg. dial. *lunken*, mild, tepid]. Close, sultry (day); having a sickly feeling.

lurcher [n., cf. Sc. *lurch*, 'a tricky way' (CSD)] (Ulster). 'Person who lurks about watching for timely advantage' (Traynor).

lured [p. part. as adj.] (Ulster). Happy; excited. Also **lured stiff**. Extremely or excessively thus.

Lurgan shovel/spade [n. phr.] as in **a face as long as a Lurgan spade** [n. phr., <Ir. *lorgán spáid*, handle of a shovel/spade]. Of gloomy countenance.

lurry see **lorry**

lusty [adj., <OE *lust* (n.), pleasure]. Pleasant. **1927** Peadar O'Donnell,

Islanders: 'It was a lusty evening. In the west the bronze-bordered sun glowed above the ocean.'

lybe/lybber see **libber**

L.Y.K.A.H. [acronym, 'popular among the *gorseyjacks* [q.v.] of my day' (DOM). Most freq. on the backs of letters addressed to young women.]. Leave Your Knickers at Home.

lyrakeen [n.] as in **lyrakeen peebora** [n. phr., <Ir. *laidhricín píobaire*, piper's little finger]. Useless individual.

lythin/lithing [n., <'lithe', mild, agreeable, mellow (OED)] (Ulster). 1. Onions, flour and water, pan-fried. 2. Thickening or congealing of jam, stew, etc. **1913** Alexander Irvine, *My Lady of the Chimney Corner*: 'Jamie was the family connoisseur in matters relating to broth. He tasted Ann's. The family waited for the verdict. "Purty good barley an' lithin'," he said, "but it smells like Billy's oul' boots."'

M

Ma, the [n., abbrev. of *the mammy* (q.v.)]. Mother. **1994** Greg Dalton, *My Own Backyard, Dublin in the Fifties*: 'The Ma decides to explain the need for religion to me. She tells me I'll never walk alone after me First Holy Communion.' Also (with endearment suffix) **the masey**. **1985** Máirín Johnston, *Around the Banks of Pimlico*: 'What we couldn't fit into the sacks we shoved down into the empty spaces in the pram ...the masey was going to be delighted with all this grub.'

McAlpine's Fusiliers [nickname, <Sir Robert McAlpine & Sons, Brit. building contractors]. Emigrants to Britain working in the construction industry, 1950s–. **1977** Wesley Burrowes, *The Riordans*: 'He [John Cowley] became, successively, a barman, a McAlpine Fusilier and a porter at St Pancras Station.' **1988** John Healy, *Magill*, 'The Wild One', Apr: 'Never mind MacAlpine's Fusileers [*sic*] — they were now the new army of [Donogh] O'Malley's Fusileers marching in the opposite direction, with grappling irons and climbing ropes instead of the pick and shovel.'

mack deawle [exclam., <Ir. *mac diabhail*, son of a devil]. Term of abuse. **1605** Anon., *Captain Thomas Stukeley*: 'ONEALE Mack deawle, marafastot [q.v.] art thou a feet [white] liver'd kana [whelp].'

macushla [exclam., <Ir. *mo chuisle*, my beloved, gen. voc.]. As thus; latterly ironic. **1965** Lee Dunne, *Goodbye to the Hill*: '"What's your name, macushla?" he asked the girl who was to be my partner.' See also **acushla**, **pulse**.

mad [adv., intens.]. Very.

made up [p. part. as adj.]. Endowed with good fortune. **1992** Pauline Bracken, *Light of Other Days, A Dublin Childhood*: 'She [the maid] did vast washings, cooked repasts of many courses...We thought we were made up for life.' **1996** Christy Kenneally, *Maura's Boy, A Cork Childhood*: '"Happy Christmas Dave," she said and pushed a ten-bob note into me pocket. Sure we were made up."'

mageegle [vb., cf. Sc. *maggle*, mangle, bungle] (Ulster). Confuse, bewilder (YDS).

maggie [n. & nickname]. 1. [n.] (card-playing) (Ulster). Ace or queen of hearts (Traynor). 2. [nickname]. Ex-inmate of the Magdalen Asylum, founded in Leeson St, Dub. in 1766 'for unfortunate females abandoned by their seducers ...who preferred a life of penitence and virtue to one of guilt, infamy and prostitution'. **1995** Thomas P. White in Mary Ryan et al. (eds.), *No Shoes in Summer*: 'O Maggie, hold your head up high,/Walk tall, and proud, and strong,/For you are worth a million more/Than those who did this wrong...'

Maggie Ryan [n.]. Margarine. **1982** Éamonn Mac Thomáis, *Janey Mack* (q.v.), *Me Shirt is Black*: 'But sure, even the Maggie Ryan that we did spread on our bread, it's called "Summer Country Freshness".'

maggot [n.]. Term of contempt. **1987** Lar Redmond, *Emerald Square*: '"Yeh dirty little maggot," sobbed Linda, "teh kick a woman!"' See also **act the maggot**.

maggoty [adj.]. 1. Intoxicated. **1986** Padraic O'Farrell, *'Tell me, Sean O'Farrell'*: 'The Clane man got maggoty, mouldy [q.v.], eejity [see **eejit**] and struck the earl with the red cap. At that all the fairies disappeared...' **1994** May Hanaphy in Kevin C. Kearns, *Dublin Tenement Life*: 'At that time all the [funeral] horse cabs stopped and drew up at the public houses and everyone would get their beer and come home *mouldy* [q.v.], *maggoty drunk*!' 2. Dirty, disgusting. **1993** Aine de Courcy in Michael Verdon, *Shawlies* (q.v.), *Echo Boys* (q.v.), *the Marsh and the Lanes* (q.v.): *Old Cork Remembered*: 'But the Luiwee [legendary monster] wasn't too keen on giving up the lake. The cattle were nice and fat, you see. "You maggoty-looking article [q.v.]," he told the saint [Finbarr]. "You'll have to make me leave."' **1996** Cathy Geogan, *Leinster Leader* (Naas, Co.

Kildare), 'Secondary Schools Forum', 27 Feb: 'Maggoty dirty and shattered,/So frustrated I could cry,/The things a babysitter goes through,/To keep the baby's bottom dry!'

maggyman/maggie-man [n., <Ir. *margadh*, fair]. Fairground huckster. **1910** Thomas MacDonagh, *Songs of Myself*, 'John-John': 'For there again were thimble men/And shooting galleries,/And card trick men and Maggie men/Of all sorts and degrees...' **1952** Bryan MacMahon, *Children of the Rainbow*: 'a toothless wheel-o'fortune mother nursing a pair of chalk chanticleers, a maggieman mounted in wall-eyed guard over his spy-holed barrel'. Hence **maggymore/margymore** [n., <Ir. *margadh mór*, big fair, market] (Ulster). As thus (Todd); exaggerated account (YDS).

magobbler [n. phr., <Ir. *mo ghobaire*, my chatterer, talebearer, busybody (Dinneen)] (Ulster). Form of address and ref. to a (naughty) child (Todd).

mahogany gaspipe [n. phr., macaronic]. Hib.E representation of intonations of Ir. **1968** Myles na gCopaleen, *The Best of Myles*: 'Taw shay [*tá sé* — it is] mahogany gas-pipe. An vill Gwayleen a gut? [*An bhfuil Gaolainn agat?* — Have you Ir.?]' **1981** Paddy Crosbie, *Your Dinner's Poured Out!*: 'In the beginning, we made fun of the whole scheme [of Ir. classes]: "Taw shay mahogany gaspipes/Ock neel shay [*níl sé* — it is not], taw shay muck the full of a handcart."' **1995** Eanna Brophy, *Sunday Tribune*, 2 July: 'He [Terry Wogan] rambles off into the sunset, muttering to himself "Sic transit gloria swanson...tá sé mahogany gaspipe...'tis the classical education from the Jesuits you know."'

Maiden City nickname, <its withstanding the Jacobite siege, 1690.] Derry/Londonderry (see **Stroke City**). **1996** Paul Routledge, *Independent on Sunday* (London), 18 Feb: 'Fewer than 500 protesters gathered to march into the heart of "the maiden city" but their autumnal walk had been banned by Stormont's hard-line home affairs minister William Craig.' **1996** *Journal of*

the Irish Railway Record Society, Oct: 'Crossing stops were made at Ballinderry and Antrim, from where the next crossing took place at Castlerock...The Maiden City was reached by 12.05.'

maigrum see **maygrum**

mailie, mailie! [exclam., cf. *Malle*, name of sheep in Chaucer's *Canterbury Tales*]. Call to pet sheep.

mainland [n. & adj.]. Term employed by those of unionist/loyalist sympathies with ref. to neighbouring offshore island.

maithgalors [adj., <Ir. *maith go leor*, good enough, all right; euphem.]. Excessively intoxicated. **1995** Donal Byrne, *Sunday Tribune*, 2 Apr: 'And if you are stupid enough to be completely maithgalors at over 151 mgs then you will be off the road for two years...' Also **moylow** (Cork) in same sense.

make [n., *c*.1545–; 'since 1860 only dial. & Scot. & Dubliners' (DHS)]. Halfpenny in pre-decimal currency. **1942** *Barrack Variety*: 'SEE IRELAND FIRST IN SPITE OF THE EMERGENCY. Cruises by Canal Boat...First class cuisine — bacon and cabbage every day...See the native Kilcock boys diving for "wings" [q.v.] and "makes"...' **1982** Éamonn Mac Thomáis, *Janey Mack* (q.v.), *Me Shirt is Black*: 'This one took us on daylight treasure tours, digging up the Robber's Den, but we never found a make...' **1985** Máirín Johnston, *Around the Banks of Pimlico*: 'Bets were unlimited on the inner ring and as much as the tosser [see **tosser** 1.] put down had to be covered before the boxman [q.v.] looking after the tosser allowed the "makes" to be tossed.'

make (a) hare of see **hare** 1.

make-in, the [n., <*make* (q.v.)]. Street game played with halfpenny. **1981** Brendan Behan, *After the Wake*: 'We were...playing "the make-in" on Brennan's Hill down by the Mountjoy brewery when his approach was signalled...'

make wonder of [vb. phr., gen. in neg.]. Pay excessive attention to. **1995** Éamon Kelly, *The Apprentice*: 'The men didn't make much wonder of me. One man said to my father, "Is this Brian?" thinking that I was called after my grandfather.'

malavogue/malivogue [vb., nonce-word]. Beat, rough-handle.

malecyartin see **meelcartin**

malivogue see **malavogue**

mallacky [n., cf. Ir. *meallach* (adj.), globular, lumpy]. Cat-shit, as in **cats' mallacky, dogs' tobaccy** (Moylan).

malt [n., abbrev.]. (Malt) whiskey. **1955** J.P. Donleavy, *The Ginger Man*: "'Where's Catherine, the girl? Send her with two scalding malts and a spot of gin for the lady…'" **1977** Flann O'Brien, *The Hair of the Dogma*: 'Perhaps I had better translate the poem for the benefit of limey visitors who are over here drinking the malt intended for our good selves.' See also **ball of malt**.

mammy, the [colloq. *c.*1520–; in Hib.E gen. with def. art.]. Affect. children's term for mother; (iron.), mother or wife in adult usage. **1985** Gay Byrne in John Quinn (ed.), *Must Try Harder*: 'When my mother comes to collect me (All together — ahhh! the mammy collecting little Gaybo [q.v.] from school!)…' **1995** Tom Doorley, *Sunday Tribune*, 17 Dec: 'we were entertained [in Le Caprice restaurant] by a Brooks Brothers type trying to impress his girlfriend…and the Irish businessman desperately trying to engage the mammy in light conversation'.

mammy's boy [n. phr.]. S.o. excessively dependent upon maternal affection. **1995** Patsy McGarry, *Irish Times*: 'But was Shaw just a cry-baby, a mammy's boy? Michael Holroyd…speculated that the playwright's dislike of Wesley, "and later schools", appeared to have been "because they took him away from his mother".'

Man above, the [n. phr., cf. Ir. *an fear suas*, *idem*]. God. See also **your man**.

man a dear! see **man dear!**

manam a dioule!/monomundioul! [exclam., <Ir. *m'anam do'n diabhal!*, my soul to the devil!]. As thus. **1754** Thomas

Sheridan, *The Brave Irishman*: 'CAPTAIN Monomundioul! but when I go back to Ireland, if I catches any of these spalpeen [q.v.] brats keeping a goon [gun]…but I will have them shot stone-dead first, and phipt [whipped] through the regiment afterwards.' Also **thanum-on-dioul!** [<Ir. *d'anam d'on diabhal*, your soul to the devil!]. See **tare-an'-ouns**.

man (a) dear! [exclam., intens. of what follows; form of address in this sense] (Ulster). Good heavens! **1983** *John Pepper's Illustrated Encyclopaedia of Ulster Knowledge*: '"It's my jacket," he explained. "It fell in." "Man dear, sure it wudden' be worth wearin' if ye ivver got it out," his friend said.' **1995** Shane Connaughton, *A Border Diary*: '"Man, dear, I seen meself and Tommy Rennicks goin' up to Hillsborough to work for a big Protestant farmer."'

mancreeper see **mankeeper**

maneen [n., <'man' + Ir. dimin. *ín*]. Little man (gen. derog.). **1914** James Joyce, *Portrait of the Artist* (q.v.) *as a Young Man*: '"I was standing at the end of the South Terrace one day with some maneens like myself and sure we thought we were grand [q.v.] fellows because we had pipes in our mouths."' **1960** John O'Donoghue, *In Kerry Long Ago*: 'and before he knew where he was he saw a small maneen standing on the road beside him, showing his teeth in anger'. **1965** Lee Dunne, *Goodbye to the Hill*: '"He's got nothing to shave," Billy snorted. "He's only a maneen, trying to be big."'

mangy [adj., <OF *manjue/mangeue* (vb.), itch + y]. Beggarly, mean. **1981** Brendan Behan, *After the Wake*: 'people looking out the windows at the footballers and screaming advice and abuse to young Coughlin not to be so mangy with the ball'.

man in the gap [n. phr., <king's champion deputed to hold the *bearna baoil*, Ir. gap of danger]. One who 'courageously and successfully defends any cause or any position' (PWJ). **1922** James Joyce, *Ulysses*: '…Stephen was blissfully unconscious that, but for that man in the gap turning up at the eleventh

hour, the finis might have been that he might have been a candidate for the accident ward'. **1925** Percy French, *Prose, Poems and Parodies*, 'The Queen's After-Dinner Speech' (on occasion of Victoria's visit to Ireland, 1900): '"So drink to the min," sez she, "That have gone in to win," sez she, "And are clearin' the way," sez she, "To Pretoria today," sez she. "In the 'Gap o' Danger'," sez she, "There's a Connaught Ranger," sez she...'

mankeeper/mancreeper [n., <Sc. *idem*, newt]. As thus. **1979** Jack McBride, *Traveller in the Glens* (of Antrim): 'the story goes that a man who had drunk from a mankeeper-infested pool felt strange movements in his tummy shortly afterwards...no less than seven very thirsty newts hopped out of his inhospitable inside'. See also **arklooker**, **athlukard**.

manners see **put manners on s.o.**

manswear [vb., <OE *man* (n.), wickedness + *swerian* (vb.), swear]. Commit perjury.

man, your/your only see **your man, your only man**

mar [n., <Sc. *idem*, impediment, defect] (Ulster). Barrier or hindrance (YDS).

marafastot!/marragh frofat! [exclam., <Ir. *marbhthásc ort*, death tidings (curse) on you (Bliss)]. A curse on you! **1630** Thomas Dekker, *The Honest Whore Part II*: 'BRYAN Slawne laat [Ir. *Slán leat*, goodbye], fare de well. Ah marragh frofat boddagh [q.v.] breen.'

Marble City [nickname, <occurrence of marble in the area]. Kilkenny. **1965** Colm Ó Lochlainn, *More Irish Street Ballads*, 'James Stephens, the Gallant Fenian [q.v.] Boy': 'Born in the Marble City, ere Stephens grew sixteen/His warm blood in fountains flowed most proudly for the green.' **1995** *Irish Times*, 2 June: 'audiences will be treated to the best of comedy from 47 class acts, who will give 72 shows in six venues in the Marble City'.

market see **past one's market**

market house [n.]. Premises licensed to open before normal hours to facilitate a specific business/industrial clientele. **1995** Brian Farrell in Seán Power (ed.), *Those were the Days, Irish Childhood Memories*: 'the still closed doors of the "market houses", pubs that were licensed to open early to meet the needs of the market workers but which were oases drawing early-morning drinkers from all over the city [of Dub.]'.

markins [n. pl., cf. Ir. *máirtín*, vampless stocking] (Ulster). Socks without toes.

marksman [n.]. Individual who cannot sign his name and has to make his mark.

marley/marlie [adj. & n., cf. Sc. *marl* (vb.), mottle, OF *merelolé* (adj.), speckled] (Ulster). 1. [adj.]. Mottled like marble. 2. [n.]. Child's marble. **1951** Sam Hanna Bell, *December Bride*: '"Will he be let out tae play marlies wi' me?" "Son, Con's a papish [q.v.]."' Hence **his head's a marlie** he is not thinking straight (CUD).

marragh frofat! see **marafastot!**

marrow see **morrow**

mart/mort/morth [n., <ON *mergth* (n.), many]. Great deal. **1943** George A. Little, *Malachi Horan Remembers*: '"Ay, Mr Fitzgerald, breeding and training can do a mart to a man or dog."'

martyr [n., <OF *martire* (vb.), torment]. Tormentor. **1943** George A. Little, *Malachi Horan Remembers*: '"Green, the tinker, was his enemy. They were the hard pair of martyrs. They were never in twist [q.v.]."'

Mary banger [adj.]. Said of dowdy female, dowdier than Mary hick (q.v.).

Mary hick [adj.]. Said of dowdy female. See also **Mary banger**.

masey, the see **the Ma**

mask [vb., <OE *masc* (n.), mash, cf. Ger. *meisch* (n.), mash for beer] (Ulster). Draw (of tea).

ma's plaster [n. phr.]. Whinger. See **the Ma**.

mass see **meas**

massacree/massacrate [adj. & vb.]. [adj.]. Term of abuse. [vb.]. Massacre. **1913** W.M. Letts, *Songs from Leinster*, 'The Unbiddable Child': 'He's after upsetting the Widow Foy's pail —/She'll murder him yet, Widow Foy!/An' he's pulling the massacree dog by the tail...'

massive [adj.]. Huge, impressive, excellent. **1996** Joe Carroll, *Irish Times*, 30 Nov: 'you need to get up your strength to face the shopping malls the next day when the sales are only massive'. **1996** Christy Kenneally, *Maura's Boy, A Cork Childhood*: '"Yerra [q.v.] dat one's a cod [q.v.] boy; dere's no shootin'!" That was out. "Me sister said de wan in de Palace [cinema] is massive."'

mate/meat [n., *mate* <Hib.E pronun.]. Food in general. **1951** Sam Hanna Bell, *December Bride*: 'He pushed his plate away and studied the faces round the table as he spoke. "To tell ye the truth," he said at last, "I don't feel like meat."' Also **mate–house** (Ulster). Simple restaurant. See also **meal's meat**.

materials/matts [n. pl.]. Ingredients for a tumbler of punch.

mather [vb., cf. Sc. *idem* (n.), dish for holding meal (CSD)]. Mix, stir into. **1922** James Joyce, *Ulysses*: 'he thinks he knows a great lot about a woman's dress and cooking mathering everything he can scour off the shelves into it'.

matts see **materials**

Maud Gone Mad [nickname]. Maud Gonne MacBride (1865–1953), revolutionary. **1993** R.F. Foster, *Paddy & Mr Punch*: 'Charlotte Despard, Maud Gonne's companion in arms...is another [convert]. Dubliners knew them as "Maud Gone Mad and Mrs Desperate".'

maughie/maughy/mogh [adj., cf. Sc. *maughsome*, loathsome] (Ulster). Humid, mouldy. **1932** *Ulster Hiker* (Cushendall, Co. Antrim), 'The Ulster Dialect', June: '"It's a maughie sort of day" refers to warm, close temperature.' Hence **mogh** [n.]. Sultry, moist atmosphere (MON).

mauser [n., <Ir. *más*, buttock]. Fleshy woman. Hence **mausey** [adj., <Ir. *másach*, having large buttocks]. As thus.

1939 James Joyce, *Finnegans Wake*: 'plays gehamerat when he's ernst but misses mausey when he's lustyg'.

mavourneen/avourneen [exclam., <Ir. *mo mhuirnín*, my love/voc. of *muirnín*]. Term of affection, gen. applied to females. **1907** J.M. Synge, *The Shanachie* (q.v.), 'People of the Glens': 'I told a little about the poverty I had seen in Paris. "God Almighty forgive me, Avourneen," she went on, when I had finished, "we don't know anything about it."' **1922** James Joyce, *Ulysses*: '"Come round to Barney Kiernan's," says Joe. "I want to see the citizen." "Barney mavourneen's be it," says I.' See also **Kathleen Mavourneen**.

mawgabraw [exclam., <Ir. *magh go brách*, the field for ever]. Parting shot directed at individual leaving in high dudgeon over some real or imagined offence (OTF).

mawkin [n., cf. Sc. *idem*, 'half-grown girl' (CSD)] (Ulster). Simpleton (MON).

may-fayner [n., <Ir. *mé féin*, myself alone]. Selfish individual.

maygrum/maigrum [n., <Ir. *meadhrán*, dizziness, giddiness]. Dizziness/ noise in the head. **1907** Joseph Guinan, *The Soggarth Aroon* (q.v.): '"He wants your reverence to come round after the station [see **the stations**] and cure the 'maygrum' in his head..."' **1948** George Fitzmaurice, *Dublin Magazine*, 'There are Tragedies and Tragedies', July/Sept: 'MAURA ...she only got to the end of the boreen because having a gumboil she balked at navigating the slippery steps for fear of a maygrum rising in her head'.

maypole [n.]. House dance. **1993** Mick McInerney in Joe O'Reilly & Sixth Class, Convent School, Edenderry, *Over the Half Door*: 'There was nearly a maypole every Sunday night. There used to be one out in Colgan's in Ballindoolin. Pat Mooney had another one a few years after that. They used come from near and far for the Maypoles.'

mealacreeshy/mealycreeshy [n., <'meal' + 'greasy'] (Ulster). Oatmeal fried in fat. **1951** Sam Hanna Bell,

December Bride: 'Now he pushed his plate away after mopping up the last of the *mealycreeshy* which had been their evening dish.'

meal's meat [n. phr.] (Ulster). 'Food taken at one meal' (Patterson). See **mate**.

mealycreeshy see **mealacreeshy**

meas/mass [n., <Ir. *meas*, estimation, judgment, opinion]. As thus, as in 'I have no mass in clothes or them things' (Todd).

measle [vb., <Du. *maschelen* [n. pl.], red blotches on legs from heat of fire] (Ulster). Cause legs to speckle by sitting too close to fire. Also **maisled** [p. part.]. See also **ABC**.

meat [n.]. 1. Human body. **C.1780** Anon., *Luke Caffrey's Kilmainham Minit*: 'But when dat we come to de Row [New Row, Dub., site of prison],/Oh, dere was no meat in de market.' 2. See **mate**.

me-awe see **mí-ádh**

meb [n., <?]. 1. Child's marble. **1995** Gerry Fehily in Mary Ryan et al. (eds.), *No Shoes in Summer*: 'There were always marbles too; the large ones were called TAWS and the small ones MEBS, but we only played during the Marble Season.' 2. [n. pl.]. Testicles, hence fool, unpleasant person (cf. bollix (q.v.)). See also **taws**.

me daza [adj., <?] (Cork). Perfect, esp. in appearance. **1966** Séamus Murphy, *Stone Mad*: '"Danno, I certainly appreciate the excellent cuisine of your good woman." "Yeah, it's me daza! Ye can't beat a good tightener [see **tighten**] in the middle of the day."' **1990** Cecil Hurwitz, *Cork Holly Bough*: 'As we would say in Cork, I was "Me Daza", togged out from head to toe...'

meddle [vb. trans.] (Ulster). Hurt or annoy (s.o.).

medium [n.]. 1. (Kerry). Indeterminate measure of stout. Also **meejum** [<local pronun.] (Cork). Half-pint of stout. **1993** Frank Casey in Michael Verdon, *Shawlies* (q.v.), *Echo Boys* (q.v.), *the Marsh and the Lanes* (q.v.): *Old Cork Remembered*: 'the women would slip into the snug [q.v.] for a quiet drink. They drank the "meejums", the half-pints. Some of the shawlies used to cover their mouths with their shawls, they were so shy about it.' **1994** Con Houlihan, *Rose of Tralee Souvenir Programme*, 'The Wine of the Country': 'It had no legal existence; it wasn't a standard measure but it was very popular a generation ago. When you entered a pub you hardly ever called for a medium as your first drink. You called for a pint. When you had finished it, you proffered your glass and said "throw a medium into that". The quantity poured depended upon the person behind the bar.' 2. The Ir. language (slightly derog.). Most commonly as in **through the medium** (of Ir., understood). **1944** 'Puss' (M.J.F. Matthews), *TCD, A College Miscellany*, 'Moryah' (q.v.), 9 Mar: 'What, you did your Christmas shopping through the medium?/You were under your O'Dearest [brand-name of pop. mattress] in '16 [1916, date of the Easter rising)?' **1991** Tony Gray, *Mr Smyllie, Sir*: 'a scheme to encourage the use of Irish in the home by the payment of an annual bonus of £2 to parents who succeeded in persuading their children to conduct their everyday lives "through the medium", as we used to say'.

mee-aw see **mí-ádh**

meejum see **medium** 1.

me elbow! [exclam., euphem. for 'me arse!', poss. infl. by 'not knowing one's arse from one's elbow']. Expression of disbelief/incredulity. **1920** Conal O'Riordan, *Adam of Dublin*: 'Mrs Macfadden had a proper pleasure in telling her husband, commenting on this catastrophe: "I warned you that he had the Castle [Dublin Castle, former seat of Brit. rule] behind him." "Castlemiyelbo!" was that strong man's undaunted answer.'

meelcartin/malecyartin [n., <Ir. *míol ceartáin*, crab louse] (Ulster). Chilblain, sore on the foot.

Meeting of the Waters [nickname, <song by Thomas Moore, 1779–1852, in praise of eponymous Co. Wicklow beauty spot] (Dub.). Public urinal, College St, Dub., in front of which stood

statue of Moore. **1922** James Joyce, *Ulysses*: 'He crossed under Tommy Moore's roguish finger. They did right to put him up over a urinal: meeting of the waters.'

me granny! see **granny**

mehawn! [exclam., <?, cf. Ir. *mo thón!* my arse!] (Ulster). Expressing disbelief. **1937** *Irish Times*, 10 Mar: 'The man from Belfast was in scathing mood..."Come to Belfast and have a look at our trams if you want to see real stream-lining. Stream-lining, mehawn!" The closing expletive, I might mention, is more or less spelt as it is pronounced. It is the Belfast equivalent of "moryah!" [q.v.]'

mehil/meitheal [n., <Ir. *meitheal*, working party]. As thus. **1988** Alice Taylor, *To School through the Fields*: 'It took large supplies to feed the hungry *meitheal* (the group of neighbours who had come to work with us)...' **1995** Shane Connaughton, *A Border Diary*: '"That season there was only one other farm done before us. Us two and a whole mehil of men worked there."' **1996** Tom Widger, *Sunday Tribune*, 17 Nov: 'The idea of "A Day on the Bog" (RTÉ Radio 1)...was to set up a meitheal that would have impressed Marx...At a meitheal everyone is supposed to muck in, cut, carry, store. Here, only one man worked. The others had a wonderful time.'

melder [n., <Sc. *idem*, quantity of meal etc., <ON *meldr*, *idem*] (Ulster). 1. Dirty mess, heap. 2. Large quantity, as in **eat a melder** [vb. phr.]. Eat too much.

melia/millia murder! [exclam., <Ir. *míle murdar* (lit. thousand murders), 'horror of horrors!' (Dinneen)]. 'A general expression of surprise, alarm or regret' (PWJ). **1866** Patrick Kennedy, *Legendary Fictions of the Irish Celts*: 'He trod on the dog's tail, and if he did he got the marks of his teeth in his arms, and legs, and thighs. "*MILLIA MURDHER* (thousand murders)!" cried he...' **1908** Lynn Doyle, *Ballygullion*: '...Michael in the middle av thim, an' the wimmen hanging round, pullin' the skirts av men's coats, an' cryin' melia murdher.' **1977** Flann O'Brien, *The Hair of the Dogma*: 'But there

was sacred holy melia murder about it afterwards.' See also **murdersheery!**

melodion loaf [nickname, <similar shape to melodeon (accordion)] (Ulster). A type of loaf. See **sore head**.

melt [n., <'milt', spleen; roe, spawn, <OE *milt*, spleen, spawn]. 1. Tongue, as in **keep in your melt** [exclam. & vb. phr., <tongue's similarity in shape to spleen] (Ulster). Hold your tongue. 2. Spleen, indeterminate internal organ. See also **break one's melt**. **1914** George Fitzmaurice, *The Pie-Dish*: 'JOHANNA ...what foolery was on me to leave my good home in Glounasroan to meet this shame — the melt broke in me from the boiling sun of June...' Hence **I'll knock your melt in!** 3. See **hoor's melt**.

mense [n., <Sc. *idem*, discretion, good manners] (Ulster). As thus, modest behaviour. Hence **menseless** [adj.]. Ill-bred. **1817** James Orr, *The Posthumous Works of James Orr of Ballycarry*, 'The Irish Cottier's Death and Burial': 'Though here and there may sit a menseless loun [q.v.],/The thoughtfu' class consider poor folks' need...'

merciful hour! [exclam.]. Mild oath. **1995** RTÉ TV serial, *Upwardly Mobile*, 27 Oct: 'Merciful hour, would you look at the state of ya!' **1996** Eanna Brophy, *Sunday Tribune*, 7 July: '"Well, here we are at last. Merciful hour! What do you mean we've to jump on that platform [on the USS *John F. Kennedy*]? If I'd known we were going to be doing this I'd have kep up me aerobics."'

merdle [n., <Sc. *idem*, cf. Fr. *merdaillon*, dirty, disagreeable child]. Large family of children.

merra/merrow [n., <Ir. *murúch/ muruach*, mermaid]. Young woman; 'the place do be full of half-naked Dutch and Swedish merras in the Summer' (Sligo man, quoted DOM).

merries [n. pl., <'merry-go-round']. Fairground amusements in general. **1996** Christy Kenneally, *Maura's Boy, A Cork Childhood*: 'At the start of every holiday, I measured out my money for the merries.'

merrow see **merra**

merry begotten [n.]. Love child. **1797** *Memoirs of Mrs Margaret Leeson, Written by Herself, Vol. III*: 'Elinor West was a merry begotten, of R[obert] A[rmstrong] of Capel-street, who when nine years old bound her to a ribbon-weaver...'

Merry-dancers [nickname] (Ulster). Aurora borealis.

meskin/miskin [n., <Ir. *meascán*, lump]. Lump of butter. **1925** Louise McKay, *Mourne Folk*: 'Mary Anne was not slow in noticing that there was a miskin of butter carefully rolled in a cloth in the woman's basket.'

messages [n. pl.]. (Small) purchases, groceries, etc. for domestic use. **1970** Christy Brown, *Down All the Days*: 'They grabbed the messages he was bringing around to the houses from the butcher's shop where he worked as a messenger boy...' **1987** Lar Redmond, *Emerald Square*: 'In the afternoon she got me out of bed and sent me for the messages to our local grocer...' **1995** Margaret Duffy in Mary Ryan et al. (eds.), *No Shoes in Summer*: 'When I was young most women did not carry shopping bags. All the messages or shopping would be carried in a big apron tied around the waist.'

messen [n., <Sc. *idem*, small dog; small, insignificant person] (Ulster). Cur, contemptible individual (MON).

messer [n.]. Seriously incompetent and/or irresponsible individual, gen. male. **1975** John Ryan, *Remembering How We Stood*: 'At this time...he [Brendan Behan] was also quite an appalling messer. One would have to rifle the annals of Bacchus to find a more determined messer.' **1987** Vincent Caprani, *Vulgar Verse & Variations, Rowdy Rhymes & Rec-imitations, 'My Grandfather's Pint'*: 'Similarly he [the Grandfather] frowned upon cider-sippers, crossword doodlers, mots [q.v.], backslappers, young wans [q.v.]... Such "messers" and insufferable triflers were the curse of any decent pub.' **1991** Roddy Doyle, *The Van*: '"He's only there to stop messers from comin' in..."

"Me bollix [q.v.]," said Jimmy Sr, "How does he tell they're messers?"' Hence **messing** [pres. part. & n.] in same sense; [joc.] as in **only messing**, only joking.

Methody [adj., n. & nickname]. 1. [adj. & n.]. Methodist. **1841** S.C. Hall, *The Fate of the O'Learys*: '"Miss Milly Naylor is going to be married to — guess who?" "Guess, how should I guess? A methody parson?"' **1925** Louise McKay, *Mourne Folk*: '"He tould us a yarn about an ould fella that went to his chapel. I think it was a Methody chapel."' **1931** Shan F. Bullock, *After Sixty Years*: 'What religion Mr Bean and his family observed I cannot say. None of them went to church. Perhaps they were Methodys, as we called them...' 2. [nickname]. Methodist College, Belfast. **1969** Robert Greacen, *Even without Irene*: 'I stopped running, for the chances were now less that a "peeler" [q.v.] would stop me and ask me to explain myself. How could a "Methody" boy explain that he had wanted to kill his father?' **1985** John Boyd, *Out of my Class*: 'Only one scholarship boy from Mountpottinger chose Methody and I assumed that that was because nobody had told him that girls went there.'

mí-ádh/mee-aw/me-awe [n., <Ir. *mí-ádh*, ill-luck, misfortune]. 1. As thus. **1994** Gabriel Byrne, *Pictures in my Head*: '"There's some class [q.v.] of a mí ádh on him, doctor," my father says, looking at me...' 2. 'General name for the potato blight' (PWJ).

michaar/michear/micheer [n., <OF *muchier/mucier* (vb.), hide]. Thief. **1663** Richard Head, *Hic et Ubique*: 'I came in wid my pishfork, thou knows't, and I see a greasy guddy hang [q.v.] upon my wife, and I did creep in like a michear...and there I did see him putting the great fuck upon my wife...' See also **mitch**.

Mick see **Mickey**

mickey/micky [n., Hib.E, mid C19]. 1. Penis. **1922** James Joyce, *Ulysses*: 'I'll put on my best shift and drawers let him have a good eyeful out of that to make his micky stand for him...' **1993** Roddy Doyle, *Paddy Clarke Ha Ha Ha*: 'She [the nurse] was the one with the ice-pop stick. The one down on her knees staring at our mickeys. She didn't look that way. She looked nice.' **1995** Djinn Gallagher, *Sunday Tribune*, 1 Oct: (on Disneyland Paris) '...I hope you appreciate the fact that I have so far managed to avoid the cheap laughs available to anyone who will stoop so low as to joke about "Mickeys" and "rides" [q.v.]...' 2. [rarer; cf. Austral. usage thus]. Female genitalia. **1991** Bob Quinn, *Smokey Hollow*: '"There was an old lady, God bless her,/ Who threw a leg over the dresser./The dresser was sticky,/And stuck to her mickey,/And no one could dress her, the messer [q.v.]."'

Mickey/Mick [nickname; **Mick** is more freq. non-Ir. usage] (Ulster). Catholic, derog. **1966** Robert Harbinson, *No Surrender*: 'But the mountain was inaccessible because to reach it we had to cross territory held by the Mickeys. Being children of the staunch Protestant quarter, to go near Catholic idolaters was more than we dared...' **1993** R.F. Foster, *Paddy & Mr Punch*: 'those nineteenth-century Irish emigrants who went to England and made a good thing of it: especially those aspiring careerists and *arrivistes* who may be referred to as "micks on the make"'. See also **Morning Mick**.

mickey-dazzler [n.]. Ladykiller. See **mickey** 2.

Mickey Mack [n., <'mishmash'] (Cork). Mess, failure.

Mickey Murphy Mikie Murphy [cant phr.]. Six of one and half a dozen of the other.

micky see **mickey**

middle man [n. phr.]. One who took large farms on long leases from landed gentry and set them in small portions at exorbitant rents to under-tenants. **1800** Maria Edgeworth, *Castle Rackrent*: 'The agent was one of your middle-men, who grind the face of the poor, and can never bear a man with a hat upon his head...'

midge's knee-buckle [n. phr.] (Ulster). Very small article.

mig [n., <Ir. *míog*, cheep, cry as of plover] (Ulster). Screech, squeal.

miggie [n., <?] (Ulster). Cap too big for the wearer; cap resembling beret; woollen nightcap.

mighty [adj. & adv.]. Outstanding, wonderful, great, as in **the crack** [see **crack** 1.] **was mighty** [cent. phr.].

mighty coonagh [adj. phr., <?]. Said of couple that are 'very great [q.v.], going strong or walking out' (PO'F).

Milkmaid's Way [nickname] (Ulster). Milky Way.

mill into [vb., cf. Brit. sl. *mill*, beat, thrash (DHS)]. Attack physically.

millia murder! see **melia murder!**

millye-hip [n., <Ir. *milleadh*, act of breaking + *teip*, failure]. Unfortunate occurrence, injury, disastrous attempt (OTF).

mim/mimsey [adj., onomat., as s.o. talking through pursed lips] (Ulster). Prim, prudish.

Mincemeat Joe [nickname, <consignment of dried fruit he bought from the Greek government and resold to Britain as mincemeat]. Joe Griffin, businessman & racehorse owner. **1990** Raymond Smith, *Vincent O'Brien, The Master of Ballydoyle*: 'Mincemeat Joe was one of the most colourful characters [see **character** 1.] ever to hit the racing scene ...When Royal Tan beat Tudor Line by a neck in 1954...he danced an Irish jig and threw his hat in the air as the 8–1 winner [of the Grand National] was being led in.' **1996** Andrew Baker, *Independent on Sunday* (London), 29 Dec: 'Great gamblers of the past, like "Mincemeat Joe" Griffin and Terry Ramsden, have been undone by a flutter too far.'

mind [vb.] (Ulster). Remember.

minding mice at a/the crossroads [catchphrase]. Engaging in any nugatory or undemanding activity; also, conversely, undertaking a task demanding patience and cunning. **1970** Christy Brown, *Down All the Days*: 'Not far from the wrong side of the border. You could always tell by their canny little ways, famous for the minding of mice at the crossroads.' **1977** Flann O'Brien, *The Hair of the Dogma*: 'The majority of the members of the Irish parliament are professional politicians, in the sense that otherwise they would not be given jobs minding mice at a cross roads.' **1995** Deaglán de Bréadún, *Irish Times*, 7 Oct: 'The modern spin doctor is ...a combination of "cute hoor" [q.v.] and master strategist, someone who can mind mice at the crossroads and write an election manifesto at the same time.'

mingi man [n. phr., <Swahili *mingi* (adj.), much, many] (army). Itinerant trader. **1980** Bernard Share, *Cara*, 'South Lebanon: The Spring Turns Sour', Sept/Oct: 'We were to hear a lot about the Mingi men...Mingi men began with the Irish UN contingent in the Congo, and the word has not only followed the Irish around but has gained international currency...Mingi men sell everything they think a soldier might need — and a number of things he can probably do without.'

minging [adj., <?] (Ulster). Child's term for very dirty.

Minister's coat [nickname]. Garda (police) greatcoat. **1995** Renagh Holohan, *Irish Times*, 21 Oct: 'The law — stopping plain-clothes gardaí from being on duty in dance halls — is alleged to have arisen from an incident in a Tipperary town in the 1930s when a young garda got a local girl pregnant after a dance...The naive girl told her family that she was invited by the garda to "lie down on the Minister's coat"...another garda, awaiting transfer for years, warned his superiors that if he did not get his move he would resort to the "Minister's coat method"...'

mint [vb., <OE *myntan*, intend, think] (Ulster). 1. Intend, endeavour. 2. Insinuate, hint. 3. Beat, hurt.

mint-hog [n., see **hog**, C19–20]. Pre-decimal shilling.

minyeric [n., <?, cf. Ir. *meann*, blemish + *oighreach*, sores from cold or chafing]. Variously defined as 'disease of the blood,

consumption, fever' (RTÉ Radio, *The Odd Word*, 31 July 1995). **1995** Alice McGuinness, RTÉ Radio, *The Odd Word*, 24 July: 'Ah wisha [q.v.], sure she had the minyeric.'

miscall [vb., <Sc. *idem*, denounce, slander] (Ulster). Call (s.o.) names; scold. **1951** Sam Hanna Bell, *December Bride*: '"I'm searching the nettle thickets like an ould wife these days." "Aye, I remember your mother miscalling the fowl. It was a bad blow when she went, Fergus."' **1983** W.F. Marshall, *Livin' in Drumlister*, 'The Runaway': 'He miscalled me for all the oul' thurfmen,/All iver ye heerd he went through...'

mischancy [adj.] (Ulster). Unlucky, risky.

misdoubt [vb.] (Ulster). Disbelieve, doubt. **1938** Seumas MacManus, *The Rocky Road to Dublin*: '"...I've made up my mind to marry." "Oh! — Do I know her?" "I misdoubt me if you do. I don't know her meself."'

Misery Hill [nickname]. Earth formation resulting from excavation of Ringsend Basin, Grand Canal, Dub., 1790s. **1996** Lorna Siggins, *Irish Times*, 8 May: 'The great mound of soil unearthed at the Dodder mouth became a refuge for the homeless during the Famine years and earned the nickname "Misery Hill".'

misery-moany [n.]. Habitual complainer. **1944** Francis MacManus, *Pedlar's Pack*: 'The sour face of a poor misery-moany that never saw a good day in his life.'

misfortunate [adj.]. Unfortunate.

misgeegle/misgiggle [vb., <Sc. *misgoggle/misgoogle,* spoil, mar, mismanage, bungle] (Ulster). Disfigure, spoil, upset.

mishanter [n., <Sc. *idem*, bad luck, mischance] (Ulster). As thus.

miskin see **meskin**

mislippened [p. part. as adj., <Sc. *mislippen* (vb.), neglect] (Ulster). Said of individual coarsened by neglect.

mislist [vb., <Sc. *idem*, molest] (Ulster). As thus.

mismake [vb., <Sc. *idem*, trouble, disturb, unsettle, blush] (Ulster). Betray oneself by showing surprise.

mismorrow [vb., <see **morrow** 1.] (Ulster). Take an article by mistake. Also **mismorrowed** [adj.]. Ill-matched (of a couple).

mismoved [p. part. as adj.] (Ulster). Worried, upset. **1899** Seumas MacManus, *In Chimney Corners*: '"...I'm goin' to get even with ye at last, boy-o [q.v.]." "Good morra, and good luck," says Willie, not the laist thrifle mismoved, seemin'.'

mister-me-friend [n. phr.]. Form of semi-derisive address. **1977** Flann O'Brien, *The Hair of the Dogma*: 'that class [q.v.] of talk was excitin' me, crippled with corns all me life and mister-me-friend this doc standing there as bould as brazen brass'. Similarly **mister-me-man**. See **looka'**.

mitch [vb., <palat. form of OE *mycan*, steal, obsolete in Std Eng. 1650–; or <OF *muchier/mucier*, hide]. Play truant. **1993** Jack Glennon in Joe O'Reilly & Sixth Class, Convent School, Edenderry, *Over the Half Door*: 'You'd be surprised that they [the priests] could slap you for not answering a question. But they didn't bother me — I wasn't into divilment [q.v.] and I never mitched.' **1996** Paul Cullen, *Irish Times*, 24 May: 'Responding to TDs' questions on the problems of truancy Mr [Austin] Currie confessed that in his own day, he too had "mitched".' Also as in **on the mitch** [adj. phr.].

mither [vb., poss. <perceived characteristics of Sc. *idem* (n.), mother] (Ulster). Nag, scold.

mizzle [n. & vb., <Du. *miezelen*, drizzle]. As thus.

mná na hÉireann [catchphrase, Ir. *idem*, women of Ireland]. As thus. Came into vogue at time of election of President Mary Robinson (1990), in which women's votes were crucial; subsequently often iron./applied to articulate women in general. **1995** Brian Boyd, *Irish Times*, 15 Dec: 'When Mary Robinson ushered in the concept of a "fifth province" of Ireland, she probably didn't realise that the Nualas [pop group] had got there before her — this particular brand of Mná na hÉireann exists on the interface between rural Ireland and Hollywood...' **1995** Philomena O'Brien, *Irish Times*, 16 Dec: 'When are Mná na hÉireann going to realise that not all mná are exactly the same? The woman's movement is simply going to have to grow up and stop this internecine squabbling...' **1996** Lise Hand, *Sunday Tribune*, 27 Oct: 'And Mná na hEireann turned out in numbers for the launches of Maureen Gaffney's work, *The Way we are Now*...and to toast Mary Cummins' collection of her brilliant columns...'

moan [vb., <OE *maenan*, mourn] (Ulster). Pity.

mockeen [n., <Ir. *maicín*, pet, spoilt child]. As thus.

mockeyah [adj., <'mock' + endearment suffix] (Cork). Not serious, not for real.

mock man [n. phr., <Ir. *fear bréige*, false man]. Scarecrow (Moylan). See also **Fir Bréaga**.

Model County [nickname, <its progressive approach to agriculture/model farms. First agricultural school in Ire. founded at Bannow mid-1850s.]. Wexford. **1987** Lar Redmond, *Emerald Square*: 'Electricity had come with the advent of the Shannon scheme...The "model county", as always, went forward quickly.' **1996** Headline, *Irish Times*, 3 Sept: 'Model county greets return of hurling victors'.

mogh see **maughie**

moider/moidher/moither [vb., obsc., cf. Ir. *modartha* (adj.), dark, murky, morose]. Perplex, worry, fatigue. **1900** Moira O'Neill, *Songs of the Glens of Antrim*, 'Corrymeela': 'There's a deep dim river flowin' by beyont the heavy trees,/This livin' air is moithered wi' the bummin' [buzzin'] of the bees.' **1938** Seumas MacManus, *The Rocky Road to Dublin*: 'His father and mother were upbraiding him for two things — wasting his weekends on the bogs and mountains, and moidherin' his head and murdering himself...with idle tales.' **1995** Alan Fahy, *Irish Times*, 15 July: 'My grandmother, born in Mayo in 1903...used this word frequently in her conversation. Indeed, a cry of "don't be moidherin' me!" was generally taken as a stern enough warning not to try further grandparental...patience.'

moilly/mooly [adj. & n., cf. Ir. *maol* (adj.), bald]. 1. [adj. & n.]. Hornless (goat etc.). **1938** Seumas MacManus, *The Rocky Road to Dublin*: 'while there was fun to be sure at the bargaining for pigs and mooly cows, far more was the joy of beholding light-hearted crowds come together [at the fair]'. 2. [adj. & n.]. Bald (individual). **1951** Sam Hanna Bell, *December Bride*: 'a great lumbering fellow, Robbie Art, nicknamed Moiley, because of his high bald forehead, had selected the men from Banyil'. 3. [n., derog.]. Slightly effeminate man.

moither see **moider**

Moll Doyle [n. phr., <Moll Doyle's Daughters, C18–19 secret agrarian society]. Ref. to this society/its members. **1867** Patrick Kennedy, *The Banks of the Boro*: 'Some folk, however, owed him a spite for the taking of the land, and Moll Doyle and her daughters were hired to pay him a visit.' Hence **give s.o. Moll Doyle** [vb. phr.] administer a severe reprimand, as wife to husband; **by the powers of Moll Doyle!** [exclam.] mild oath (PWJ).

mollocker see **mullacher**

Molly [n., <'Miss Molly', milksop, effeminate fellow, *c*.1750–(DHS)]. 1. 'A man who busies himself about women's affairs or does work that properly belongs to women' (PWJ); cissy. **1961** Frank O'Connor, *An Only Child*: 'The whole group jeered me, and called me "Molly" (our word for "sissy"...' See also **piteog**. 2. Young girl. **1966** Patrick J. Flanagan, *The Cavan & Leitrim Railway*, 'The Narrow Gauge': ''Twas my intention much more to mention/Though half its praises I haven't sung./Big babies bawling and Mollies calling/With click-click-click telegraphic tongue.' **1982** Éamonn Mac Thomáis, *Janey Mack* (q.v.),

Me Shirt is Black: 'I've known Mollys with bikes, Mollys with skates...and men who claimed that they were in the "Molly Maguires" [q.v.].'

Molly Bán [n. phr., <?, cf. Samuel Lover (1797–1868), 'Molly Bawn' (pop. ballad)]. 1. Concern, confusion. **1916** Willie Ryan, letter to his brothers Clem & Hugh: 'They [the Brit. milit.] were drawing a cordon round the city [of Dub.] and splitting up different areas as rebels were freely moving about in mufti. This caused "Molly Bawn" with us — we were trying to finish off the [whiskey] stills and shut down...' Also as in **the times of Molly Bán** [n. phr.]. Life of leisure/luxury. **1992** Brian Leyden, *Departures*: '"Why should they [Ir. men] get married when Mammy [q.v.] does it all? They have the times of Molly Bán, with mothers dancing attendance on them."'

Molly Maguires [nickname, <?]. 1. Agrarian movement active in Leitrim, Longford & Roscommon, *c*.1844. **1922** James Joyce, *Ulysses*: 'his tall talk to the assembled multitude in Shanagolden where he daren't show his nose with the Molly Maguires looking for him to let daylight through him for grabbing the holding of an evicted tenant'. 2. [*c*.1890–]. Followers of John Redmond (1856–1918) as opposed to All-for-Irelanders. **1961** Frank O'Connor, *An Only Child*: 'The Redmond supporters we called Molly Maguires, and I have forgotten what their policy was — if they had one...' **1980** Colm Lincoln, *Steps and Steeples*: '[attempting] to hold a public meeting in [Cobh]...[James] Connolly was knocked from his soapbox as the mob charged to cries of "up de Mollies"'.

Molly Malones [nickname, <song, 'In Dublin's Fair City': 'In Dublin's fair city,/Where the girls are so pretty,/I first set my eyes/On sweet Molly Malone']. Dubliners. **1987** Christopher Nolan, *Under the Eye of the Clock*: 'The Meehans were moving to the Big Smoke. The rednecks [q.v.] were going to meet the Molly Malones.' See also **Dub** 1.

Monaghan [prop. n. as common n., obsc.]. Clown, fool. **1689** Anon., *The*

Irish Hudibras: 'And today make Holy-day/When all de Monaghans shall play/Ordain a statute to be drunk,/And burn tobacco free as spunk [q.v.].' **C.1735** Jonathan Swift, *A Dialogue in Hybernian Stile*: 'B. ...I have seen him often riding on a sougawn [straw saddle]. In short he is no better than a spawlpeen [see **spalpeen**], a perfect Monaghan.'

moneyball [n.] (Munster). Children's sweet. **1995** Mary Lodge in Mary Ryan et al. (eds.), *No Shoes in Summer*: '...O'Neill's Moneyball shop, the most famous shop in Waterford at that time [*c.*1910–30] as you might win a halfpenny if you bought a halfpenny moneyball there.'

mongler [n.]. Mongrel. **1948** John O'Connor, *Come Day — Go Day*: '"You'd better take that ould mongler of yours away out of that, Kelly," Neilly said. "It bit another young girl last week."'

mongrel fox [n. phr., derog., <unscripted comment by Liam Cosgrave (1920–) at Fine Gael party Ard-Fheis (annual conference), May 1972: 'I don't know whether some of you do any hunting or not, but some of these critics and commentators are like mongrel foxes, they are gone to ground and I'll dig them out...']. Gen. term of abuse, esp. in relation to the media. **1991** Garret FitzGerald, *All in a Life*: 'These enemies of the [Fine Gael] party, whom, in a hunting metaphor that came easily to him, he described as "mongrel foxes"...' **1996** RTÉ Radio, commercial, 19 Dec: 'Remember Liam Cosgrave when he faced down the Mongrel Foxes? Read *The Cosgrave Legacy*...'

moniker/monicker/monniker [n., poss. <Shelta *manik* <Ir. *ainm*, name (reversed) — this deriv. not gen. accepted]. Personal name.

monomundioul! see **manam a dioule!**

monross [adj., poss. <'morose'] (Ulster). Rude, surly, boorish (MON).

Monto [nickname, <abbrev. + endearment suffix]. Montgomery St, C19–20 Dub. red-light district. **1961** Dominic

Behan, *Teems of Times and Happy Returns*: 'They created a dream world inhabited only by Al Jolsons and Rudolph Valentinos. Their homes were really situated not in the slums of Monto, but far away on the Pacific seaboard...' **1994** Mary Corbally in Kevin C. Kearns, *Dublin Tenement Life*: 'I don't feel any shame in coming from the Monto, but the reputation was there cause of the girls. In them years they was called "unfortunate girls" [q.v.]. We never heard the word "whores"...very rarely you'd hear of a brothel, it was a "kip" [q.v.]...'

mooch [vb. & n., <*mitch* (q.v.)] (Munster). Play truant. 'A great claim to fame was to go on the "mooch" from school...' (EW).

moocher [n., professional beggar, *c.*1855– (DHS)]. Beggar, not necessarily professional. **1994** Noel Hughes in Kevin C. Kearns, *Dublin Tenement Life*: 'Then I had a row with another fella...He was "Pig's Eye" O'Hara's son and his nickname was "Turkey Hole" O'Hara — he was a moocher.' Also **on the mooch** [adj. phr.] in same sense.

moolicking [pres. part. as n.] (Ulster). Sound thrashing (YDS).

moolock/mullack [n. & vb., <Ir. *múnlach* (n.), liquid manure, putrid water]. As thus; work or walk in mud. **1995** Edmund Pierce, *Waterford News & Star Christmas Supplement*, 'Wordy Waterford': 'In winter when roads were muddy and grey-green with runny cowdung...no solid citizen would soil his polished boots with the *moolock*, unless he was a dealer.'

mools [n. pl., <Fr. *mules*, slippers] (Ulster). Broken chilblains.

mooly see **moilly**

moon see **go to the moon**

Mooney's apron [nickname] (cardplaying) (Ulster). Ten of clubs.

moonlighter [n.]. Rustler, esp. of landlords' cattle, C19. **1914** George Fitzmaurice, *The Moonlighter*: 'SYNAN ... you dare go against the rules while I am the Captain of the moonlighters! But we aren't sure of the grabber [q.v.] yet...' **1966** Patrick J. Flanagan, *The Cavan & Leitrim Railway*: 'despite the forthright condemnation of the priests a "Captain Moonlight" roamed the Leitrim hills and "moonlighting" became a common pastime'.

moonshlay [n., <Ir. *maidhm shléibhe*, eruption (of mountain etc.) (Dinneen)]. Flash flood in river.

moot [vb., cf. Sc. *idem*, moult] (Ulster). Waste away by slow degrees (MON).

mope [n., cf. Brit. milit. sl. *moper*, deserter]. Term of contempt. See **yahoo**.

mopsy [n., cf. *mopsey*, 'a dowdy or homely woman' (Grose)]. Forward, impudent girl (Moylan).

Morning Mick [nickname, see **Mickey**]. *Irish News* (Belfast) newspaper, predominantly Catholic/nationalist. **1979** John Morrow, *The Confessions of Proinsias O'Toole*: 'taking their lead from what Prods [q.v.] call "The Morning Mick", whose editor had cried out for an independent inquiry into the tragic deaths of five young husbands and fathers'.

morrow/marrow [n. & vb.] (Ulster). 1. [n., <Sc. *marrow*, match, equal, facsimile]. As thus; husband/wife; one of a matching pair (shoes etc.). 2. [vb., <ME *morwe* (n.), day after]. 'Borrow a horse for the day on the understanding that one lends a horse in return the next day' (EDD).

mort see **mart**

mortal/mortial [adv., intens., <Sc. *mortal*, very, extremely]. As thus. **1925** Louise McKay, *Mourne Folk*: '"I cud see nothin'; it was a mortial dark night; but just then at Glenoughlan schoolhouse the moon came out of the clouds..."' **1943** George A. Little, *Malachi Horan Remembers*: 'Everywhere the old man moved, the girl moved further. After a while you could see he was getting mortal tired.' Hence **mortally** [adv.]. **1996** *Leinster Leader* (Naas, Co. Kildare), 10 Oct: 'Solicitor Conal Boyce said the pair had been drinking very heavily and were now "mortally contrite".'

mortaller [n., <'mortal' + endearment suffix]. Mortal sin, as defined by the Catholic Church. **1996** *Sunday Tribune*, 25 Feb: 'In his time Montgomery banned more than 1800 films in 17 years. "Sex was a mortaller back in those days," one of the contributors [to RTÉ Radio's *Bowman's Saturday 8.30*] said...' **1996** Eanna Brophy, *Sunday Tribune*, 24 Mar: '"oh shaggin' hell, I'm nearly after denting the Beamer [q.v.], trying to steer past that oul' one [q.v.] in her clapped-out Lada. Oh God, I suppose that's two or three more mortallers I've clocked up."'

morth see **mart**

mortial see **mortal**

moryah!/moya!/muryaa! [exclam., <Ir. *mar dhea*, forsooth]. Expression of strong disbelief or dissent; in sense of 'supposedly'. **1914** James Joyce, *Dubliners*, 'Ivy Day in the Committee Room': 'And the men used to go in on Sunday morning before the [public] houses were open to buy a waistcoat or a trousers — moya! But Tricky Dicky's little old father always had a tricky little black bottle up in a corner.' **1970** Christy Brown, *Down All the Days*: 'Women was all they ever thought of. The opening between the thighs. Gateway to paradise. Moy-ah.' **1977** Flann O'Brien, *The Hair of the Dogma*: '"He come up every now and again to the digs to see how I was muryaa..."'

mosey [n., <?]. Bull. **Late C18** Anon., *Lord Altham's Bull*: '"I being de fust in de field, who should I see bud de mosey wid his horns stickin in de ground. Well becomes me, I pinked up to him, ketched him by de tail, and rode him dree times round de field, as well as ever de master of de tailor's corporation rode de fringes [q.v.]."' See also **ankle–spring warehouse**.

moss [n., <OE *mos*, bog] (Ulster). Worked bogland. **1982** Henry Glassie, *Passing the Time*: '"The moss land is better than the upland for growin'," Bob Armstrong explained. "It has no rocks."' **1986** Charles McGlinchey, *The Last of the Name*: 'The sappers were telling him

their pay came to half-a-crown a day, and that was thought to be a great pay entirely, for working men at that time [1835] were paid 6d a day, or 10d for a day in the moss.'

mossa see **amossa**

mossy diemens [exclam., poss. <Ir. *an mbás an deamhain*, (by) the demon's death]. Mild expletive, as in **by the mossy diemens!** (OTF).

mot/mott [n., <*mort*, girl, harlot, *c.*1785 (Grose, DHS; but cf. 'Ask the Experts', *Evening Press*, 16 Sept 1965: 'An expert from Dublin tells us that he always thought the word "mort" came from Romany-Shelta and he quoted "To every rogue his gentry mort" (to every young man his gentle girl). Although most authorities ignore the Romany origin it has some support...' Commonly with def. art. Not infrequently rendered as **moth**, <common Hib.E confusion of spoken *t* and *th*; cf. thread/tread etc.] (Dub.). Affect. term for girlfriend, wife. **1965** Lee Dunne, *Goodbye to the Hill*: 'I couldn't understand fellas who chased snotty-nosed mots and tried to give them a kiss and all the rest of it.' **1970** Christy Brown, *Down All the Days*: '"Isn't that right, missus?" he said, grabbing her cardigan sleeve. "Wasn't it me dancing feet that made you be me mot?"' **1995** Arnold J. O'Byrne in Seán Power (ed.), *Those were the Days, Irish Childhood Memories*: 'Naturally, we only paid thruppence. You only went to the soft seats [of the cinema] when you got older and if you were taking a "moth" (girl).' Also **motting** [pres. part.]. Courting, doing a line (see **line** 2.). **1934** Sean O'Casey, *Windfalls*, 'A Gentle Wind': '"He'll be bringing Mary Timmons to th' pictures to-night, if he doesn't get too dhrunk...He must be motting her now, for six months."'

Mother Machree [prop. n., <title of Rida Johnson Young's pop. C19 Ir.-US ballad, <Ir. *mo chroí*, my heart]. Term of endearment, latterly ironic. Hence **Mother Machree-ish** [adj.]. **1993** John A. Murphy in Seán Dunne (ed.), *The Cork Anthology*: 'At the vulgar end of the spectrum the Irish songs were "stage" or

syrupy, or Mother Machree-ish, brought home by returned Yanks.'

mother naked [adj. phr.]. Stark naked.

mother of all souls/St Patrick [n. phr.]. Vagina (Grose).

mott see **mot**

mouldy/mowldy [adj.]. Drunk. **1939** James Joyce, *Finnegans Wake*: '...Haubernea's livliest vinnage on the brain, the unimportant Parthalonians with the mouldy Firbolgs and the Tuatha de Danaan googs'. **1977** Wesley Burrowes, *The Riordans*: 'The cast gives me an inscribed silver medal...Anne D'Alton gives me antique gold cufflinks. We move to Benny McDonnell's pub in Clonee and get mowldy.' **1987** Vincent Caprani, *Vulgar Verse & Variations, Rowdy Rhymes & Rec-im-itations*, 'How Jem the Dancer Fought and Died for Ireland', '"It was as plain as a pikestaff that he was mouldy drunk and that the drink had risen the hate and temper in him so that he was swearing to cleave the head off anyone that came within an ass's roar [q.v.] of him."'

mountain dew [nickname]. Illicit whiskey, poteen (q.v.). **1824** Thomas Moore, *The Memoirs of Captain Rock*: 'On the third evening of my stay, however, the influence of the genial "mountain dew", which my Reverend host rather bountifully dispensed, so far prevailed over my fears and my prudence, that I sallied forth, alone...' **C19** Pop. ballad, 'The Hackler from Grouse Hall': 'When I was young I danced and sung and drank good whiskey too,/Each shebeen [q.v.] shop that sold a drop of the real old mountain dew...'

mountainy [adj.]. Of rural upland dweller/mountain land, freq. mildly derog. **1932** Seán O'Faoláin, *A Nest of Simple Folk*, 'A Broken World': '"now that the gentry are gone, won't the people, the mountainy people, and so on, begin to make a complete world of their own?"' **1969** Frank O'Connor, *Collection Three*, 'A Great Man': 'In the next bed was a dying old mountainy man who had nothing in particular wrong with him except old age and a broken heart.' **1996**

Kathryn Holmquist, *Irish Times*, 28 Oct: 'A scheme to sell one acre of "mountainy" land in west Kerry for $1.4 million was reported by the *Kerryman*.'

mounthagh/mounthaun [n., <Ir. *mantach, mantachán*, gap-toothed, gap-toothed person]. As thus (PWJ).

mouth [n., cf. *idem*, 'noisy, prating, ignorant fellow; late C17–mid 19' (DHS)]. Term of great contempt. **1961** Tom Murphy, *A Whistle in the Dark*: 'HARRY Our intelligent brother wants it seven to three. Our intelligent brother is warning him to keep away from us trash. Well, mouth, what about the eighth Mulryan?' **1970** Christy Brown, *Down All the Days*: '"Want to be on that, you mouth?" answered Charlie, getting red and indignant...' **1976** R.M. Arnold, *The Golden Years of the Great Northern Railway*: 'Best known Enniskillen signalmen were George Henderson...and Jimmy Compton who would respond to criticism from the shunters with "Ye mouth ye!"' See also **have a mouth on one**.

move [vb.]. Pick up (a girl), click (q.v.). **1996** Dermot Healy, *The Bend for Home*: 'Drank the sherry before the pictures, passed by Sheila without a word and moved Emer.' See also **shift** 1.

mow [vb., <Sc. *idem*, copulate with] (Ulster). As thus.

mowl [n., <?]. Children's street game played by lifting open the cover of a water hydrant and aiming coins or flat stones into it.

mowldy see **mouldy**

moya! see **moryah!**

mozzy [n., <?] (Ulster). Large stone, esp. as projectile (TT).

muck savage [n. phr., <rugby football]. One addicted to robust play; rough/uncouth individual. **1996** David Hanly, *Sunday Tribune*, 25 Feb: 'One jury says [Peter Clohessy's] a muck savage who should never be allowed near a rugby pitch again, the other that he is a good man who lost the head [q.v.]...'

mug [n.] (Ulster). Sulky individual.

muggered/muggy [p. part as adj./adj., <'muddled'] (Ulster). 'Muddled with drink' (Traynor); half-drunk (CUD).

mul/muller [n., cf. Brit. colloq. *mull*, muddle, failure]. Fool, useless object. **1952** Bryan MacMahon, *Children of the Rainbow*: 'An awkward old muller that same boat was! After a struggle we succeeded in getting her to ride the almost silent tide.' **1976** Tom Murphy, *On the Outside*: 'JOE   And she'll say, "Who did you come with?" And you'll say — oh, Mickey Ford or someone... What's all the fuss about this one for anyway, she's only a mul.'

mulchie [n.] (Dub.). Culchie (q.v.) from urban rather than rural background.

mulderoy see **mulldy**

mullacher/mollocker [n., cf. Ir. *mullachán*, stout, strongly built boy; Austral. *mullock*, ignorant/worthless person]. Rough, unskilled individual; rough, heavy object. **1951** Patrick Kavanagh, *Envoy*, 'Diary', Mar: '"It needs to be bottomed with big mollockers of stones," says Owney as he picks up the crow-bar.'

mullack see **moolock**

mulldy/mulderoy [n., <?] (Ulster). Fat/stupid person.

muller see **mul**

Mullingar heifer see **beef to the heels like a Mullingar heifer**

mulvather [vb., <Sc. *malvader*, stun by a blow, injure]. Bamboozle, confuse. **1891** Bram Stoker, *Snake's Pass*: 'He was so much mulvathered at the shnake presumin' to stay, that...for a while he didn't think it quare that he could shpake at all.'

mundge [vb., <'munch'] (Ulster). Chew slowly with the mouth closed. 'It seems to be nearly the opposite of munch' (MON).

Munster plums [nickname]. Potatoes (Grose).

mur [n., <?] (Ulster). Light, misty drizzle (YDS).

murder machine [n. phr.]. Educational system as perceived by P.H. Pearse (1879–1916). **1996** *Irish Times*, 9 Apr: 'The values of Dickens' Mr Gradgrind and the ghost of Easter present are rampant, not the spirit of Padraig Pearse, who condemned the then education system as a "Murder Machine".'

murdersheery! [exclam., <Ir. *murdar síoraí*, eternal murder] (Ulster). 'Expression of acute disappointment or anguish' (YDS). See also **melia murder!**

murial [n., with epenthetic vowel]. Mural, by extension any wall decoration. **1968** RTÉ TV serial, *The Riordans*: 'JOHNNY A murial. That's the name for a painting on a wall. An awful lot of the Lounges now have murials. EAMON What would it be a picture of? JOHNNY Anything at all...'

Murphia [nickname, conflation of 'Murphy' and 'mafia']. The Ir. diaspora, specifically in Britain, and esp. high-profile professionals. **1995** Rachel Borrill, *Irish Times*, 6 Mar: 'A leading member of London's "Murphia", the group of high-profile Irish who have made good...' **1996** Oliver Bennett, *Independent on Sunday* (London), 17 Mar: 'In Britain, the Irish who benefit from such affirmative reinforcement tend to be white-collar workers, particularly those who work in high-profile liberal-minded professions: they have been tagged "the Murphia"...' **1997** Bernice Harrison, *Irish Times*, 11 Jan: 'The opening night...at the National Theatre on London's South Bank this week was like a Murphia magnet — the small theatre was packed with Irish people.'

murphy [n., <common surname, reflecting prominence in Ir. diet, more gen. non-Ir. usage]. Potato. **1995** Éamon Kelly, *The Apprentice*: 'When you sat down to such a meal there was a mountain of laughing [q.v.] Murphies in the middle of the table...'

muryaa! see **moryah!**

musha see **amossa**

music [n., see **heads or harps**]. '[A]n Irish term, to express, in tossing up, the harp side, or reverse, of a farthing or halfpenny...' (Grose).

muskin [n., <Sc. *idem*, 'A measure equal to an English pint' (CSD)] (Ulster). Half-pint of whiskey.

mutton dummies [n. pl., <?] (Ulster). Plimsolls, gym shoes.

myam [n. & vb., onomat.] (Ulster). Mew (of cat).

my friend [n. phr.]. Menstrual period.

my hat [expletive]. Expressive of dismissal, disbelief, negation. **1995** Éamon Kelly, *The Apprentice*: 'nothing would convince the old man but that the Blessed Virgin had put money in his pocket..."I am sure and certain," he said, "I had no money. It was a miracle!" "Ah, miracle my hat," the parish priest replied...' Also **in my hat** in same sense. **1996** Dermot Healy, *The Bend for Home*: '"So what are you doing here?" "We're on holidays," said Matti Donnelly. "You are in my hat. Do you think I'm a gom [q.v.]?"'

Myles the Slasher [nickname]. Myles O'Reilly, C17 rebel leader. **1950** Richard Hayward, *This is Ireland: Ulster and the City of Belfast*: 'and that famous O'Reilly, *Myles the Slasher*, another great Confederate warrior, came here [to the Franciscan friary in Cavan town] for his long rest after his death-blow at Finea [Co. Westmeath]'. **1996** Dermot Healy, *The Bend for Home*: 'At the green pump outside Kit Daley's in the middle of the village [of Finea] there is a monument raised to Myles the Slasher.'

my lord see **lord**

my pulse see **macushla, pulse**

N

nab/knab [n.]. 1. [cf. Sc. *idem*, person of consequence; pretentious, conceited person] (Ulster). 'A knowing old-fashioned little fellow (Derry)' (PWJ); man of importance, conceited person. 2. [euphem.]. The Devil. 3. Joker (cards). Hence **nabby** [adj.]. Natty. 4. [cf. 'navvy']. Working man. **1994** John V. Morgan in Kevin C. Kearns, *Dublin Tenement Life*: 'we were all nabbies. A nabbie is a working man, a man that works on shovels or hard work...' Also **nabs** [n. pl.]. One in authority, cf. 'his nibs'. **1950** Brian Nolan (Myles na gCopaleen), *Envoy*, 'The Martyr's Crown', Feb: '"What do you think, only two lurries [*sic*] packed with military, with my nabs of an officer hopping out and running up the steps to hammer at the door..."'

naboclesh [interj., <Ir. *ná bac leis*, never mind]. As thus.

nacket/neachlett [n., <Sc. *idem* <Fr. *naquet*, ballboy at tennis] (Ulster). Precocious child; mean, sneaky person.

nadger [n., <?] (Ulster). 1. Young boy (SH). 2. Ill-tempered person (Traynor).

nadiums [n. pl., <?] (Ulster). Non-sensical ideas/notions; unconvincing excuses; backchat.

nag/niag [n., <Ir. *cnag*, ball]. Ball used in hurling.

nager/nagur/nayger/nigger [n., <ON *hnoggr*, mean person] (Ulster). Niggardly person. Hence **nagerliness** [abst. n.] etc.

naggin/neggin/noggin [n., <Ir. *noigín*, 'vessel made of wood, and holding nearly a quart' (Dinneen)]. Measure (variable) of alcohol; latterly applied to small bottles of whiskey. See **Baby Power**. **1718** John Durant Breval, *The Play is the Plot*: 'MACHONE Tree noggans [*sic*] of usquebaugh [q.v.], Joy [q.v.], fat [what] tink you? All in one jug...we shall be a great while drinking out this half Crown in plain drink.' **1806** Anon., *Ireland in 1804*: 'Our driver is a furious presbyterian

of the Calvinistic sort...Though aspiring to uncommon sanctity, he passed no liquor-house on the road (and there were multitudes) without drinking a *neggin* [*sic*] (two bumpers) of raw whiskey...'

nagur see **nager**

nail see **go off at the nail, pay on the nail**

nailer's chimney [nickname]. Half-tall felt hat. **1943** George A. Little, *Malachi Horan Remembers*: 'There were those who, instead of a "nailer's chimney", wore a "Bailen's hat", so called from the maker of that name who lived at Ballyfolan, near Brittas [Co. Dub.].'

naller/Naller, the [nickname]. Grand Canal, Dub. **1988** Peter Sheridan in Dermot Bolger (ed.), *Invisible Cities*, 'Childhood in Abercorn Road and Seville Place': 'When we crossed the bridge to Seville Place...another waterway came to dominate — the "naller"...' **1994** Greg Dalton, *My Own Backyard, Dublin in the Fifties*: 'Winters were something else on the Naller. When it froze over, we all thought we were Hans Christian Andersen without the skates.'

nallion [n., cf. Sc. *noll*, large piece of anything] (Ulster). Lump, bump.

Nancy [nickname]. Gun, employed by Robert Emmet's associates in rising of 1803. **1943** George A. Little, *Malachi Horan Remembers*: '"Three hours I lay bleeding,/My Nancy by my side,/'Till early the next morning/I shot G— from Malahide."'

nancyballs [n. pl., corruption of 'aniseed'] (juvenile). Aniseed sweets. **1991** Bob Quinn, *Smokey Hollow*: 'There were also many consolation prizes of a farthing, the coin with the kingfisher which was pretty but could buy only two aniseed sweets, better known as Nancyballs.' **1995** Phil O'Keeffe, *Down Cobbled Streets, A Liberties Childhood*: 'the audience lined up at our back gate after school. The fee expected was a jelly-baby, a honey-bee toffee or a Nancy ball...'

nap [vb., <Sc. *idem*, knock, hammer]. Knock softly.

Napoleonise [vb., <'Napoleon Bonaparte', nonce-word?]. Inflate, exaggerate. **1841** Charles Lever, *Charles O'Malley, The Irish Dragoon*: 'The bulletin, believe me, is not Napoleonised into any bombastic extravagance of success. The thing was splendid: from the brilliant firework of the old pump itself to the figure of Perpendicular dripping with duckweed...'

napper [n., cf. Eng. dial. *nap* (adj.), expert, clever] (Ulster). 'Anything large or good of its kind' (Patterson).

narration/norration [n., <'oration'] (Ulster). Great noise, row, uproar.

narrow [adj.] (Ulster). Miserly, mean.

Narrowback [n., <?] (Munster). Person of Ir. parentage born in America, esp. one who returns to Ire. to live.

narrow-nebbed [adj.] (Ulster). Sharp-nosed. See **neb** 1.

narsum [n., <'arse']. As thus. **1663** Richard Head, *Hic et Ubique*: 'PATRICK ...then wid my pishfork I clap him upon the narsum, and I did make sharge for him in the King's name, thou knows't, to stay dere til I fetch the Cunt— stable...'

nary a one [n. phr., <'never']. Not a one. **1968** J.P. Donleavy, *The Ginger Man*: '"They think nothing of living between dirty sheets and carrying on indiscriminately. With nary a thought of the consequences stored up with God."' See also **ne'erawan**.

nass [vb., <?] (Munster). Roll (hoop).

nat [n., <Sc. *idem*, person of short stature] (Ulster). As thus.

natarnal [adj., intens., <'eternal']. Expressing disgust.

national [adj. as n., poss. <'national collection' (political usage)]. Collection among colleagues for worker down on his luck. **1966** Séamus Murphy, *Stone Mad*: 'It was a case for a "national" so every week one of the men collected threepence a man for me.'

national handler [n.]. Frontman for politician. **1986** Gene Kerrigan, *Magill*, Apr: 'Realising, he [Garret FitzGerald]

said, the depths to which the economy had sunk, he had asked his most efficient National Handler...to devise an emergency plan to give the economy some immediate buoyancy.' **1988** 'Wigmore', *Magill*, Mar: 'He [Pádraig Ó hAnnracháin] pre-dated the National Handlers and was himself a one-man team. Unlike the Handlers, Pádraig was merely heard and rarely seen...'

National Literary Prize [nickname]. Said of a book banned under the Censorship of Publications Act 1929. **1993** Seán Joyce in Michael Verdon, *Shawlies* (q.v.), *Echo Boys* (q.v.), *the Marsh and the Lanes* (q.v.): *Old Cork Remembered*: 'As soon as Dev [q.v.] took over you got a whole new attitude to literature. Books that were classics in other countries were suddenly banned here...The writers used to call that ban the National Literary Prize. If the government decided for some reason to ban his book, the author would say: "I won the National Literary Prize."'

native [n.]. Illicit whiskey, poteen (q.v.). **1797** *Memoirs of Mrs Margaret Leeson, Written by Herself, Vol. III*: '...I was not sorry to get rid of that exalted lady, as she became extremely troublesome, and was beside too fond of the native'.

natural draft [n. phr.] (Ulster). Living; spit (see **spit** 2.) and image.

nature [n.]. Natural feeling, kindliness. **1943** George A. Little, *Malachi Horan Remembers*: 'Ay, she had very little nature in her. Maybe that was on the head of her being a widow.' **1991** John B. Keane, *Love Bites and Other Stories*: 'Said he with a baleful eye and a voice rendered mellifluous by alcohol "there is no nature in a love-bite from false teeth".' **1994** Christy Murray in Kevin C. Kearns, *Dublin Tenement Life*: 'People in them days were great. They had more feelings, more nature.' Also **natural** [adj.] in same sense.

nauky/nawky/knacky/knawky/ knackety etc. [adj., cf. Sc. *knaw* (vb.) <OE *cnawan* (vb.), know] (Ulster). Cute, cunning; skilful, resourceful.

nayger see **nager**

neachlett see **nacket**

near/nearbegone [adj.] (Ulster). Miserly, tight-fisted. **1939** Patrick Gallagher ('Paddy the Cope' (q.v.)), *My Story*: 'He was a very nice man and absolutely honest, but very near.' **1983** W.F. Marshall, *Livin' in Drumlister*, 'Sarah Ann': 'Did ye iver know wee [q.v.] Robert? Well, he's nothin' but a wart,/A nearbegone oul' divil with a wee black heart...'

nearhand [adv., <Sc. *nearhaun*, almost] (Ulster). As thus.

neather [adj., <Ir. *n'fheadar/ní fheadar*, I don't know]. **1824** Thomas Crofton Croker, *Researches in the South of Ireland*: 'This "up entirely" [q.v.]...seems to imply beyond reach or knowledge, and is frequently used instead of "I don't know", to which the Irish cottager has a peculiar aversion, perhaps from the phrase being applied as a term of reproach to any stupid or simple person, coupling it with the Christian name, as Shane Neather...'

neave see **nieve**

neb [n. & vb., <Sc. *idem*, snout, <ON *nef*, beak, derog.] (Ulster). 1. [n.]. Nose. **1966** Patrick Boyle, *At Night All Cats are Grey*, 'Odorous Perfume her Harbinger': '"Nothing satisfies her. Mooching around from Billy to Jack with a neb on her like a wet week (q.v.)."' See also **black neb**, **narrow-nebbed**. 2. [vb.]. Pry, poke one's nose into. **1951** Sam Hanna Bell, *December Bride*: '"D'ye want the countryside filled wi' polis, nebbing intae everybody's business?"' Hence **nebby** [adj.]. Over-inquisitive. **1932** *Ulster Hiker* (Cushendall, Co. Antrim), 'The Ulster Dialect', June: 'I should advise the "nebby" (forward) hiker to have a "crack" [see **crack** 1.] with the first "knowin'" Ulster "gaudsman" (plough-driver) he meets.' **1979** John Morrow, *The Confessions of Proinsias O'Toole*: '"Houl' hard [see **hold hard!**], Duncher, houl' hard," I pleaded. "I don't want you to think I'm being nebby, but I have to get things straight..."' 3. [vb.]. Put a point on a pencil.

neck as in **he is in his neck/me neck** [vb. phr.]. Expression of disbelief. **1939** Sean O'Casey, *I Knock at the Door*: '"Let's have a go at Duck on the Grawnshee [q.v.]," Touhy would say, "an' I'm first." "That me neck!" Kelly would cry.'

nedcullion [n., <Ir. *nead cailleach*, wood anemone (Dinneen)]. As thus.

needle [vb., cf. Brit. sl. *idem*, irritate, annoy]. Scrounge. See **put to the pin of one's collar, be**.

ne'erawan [n. phr.]. Not a one. See also **nary a one**.

neevy navy nick nack [n. phr., <ON *hnefi*, fist] (Ulster). Children's game involving concealment of small articles in the hand. See **nieve**.

neeze [vb., <Norweg. dial. *njosa* <ON *hnjosa*, sneeze] (Ulster). As thus.

neggin see **naggin**

neighbour [adj.] (Ulster). OK, all right.

neighbour's childer (q.v.) [n. phr.] (Ulster). Children particularly close to each other though not related.

neigher/nicker/nicher [n. & vb., <Sc. *neigher* (vb.), whinny] (Ulster). Snigger, laugh.

neither one's arse nor one's elbow [n. phr.]. Neither one thing nor the other. **1914** James Joyce, *A Portrait of the Artist* (q.v.) *as a Young Man*: '"Do you know what limbo is?" he cried. "Do you know what we call a notion like that in Roscommon...Neither my arse nor my elbow!" Temple cried out scornfully.'

neither popular nor profitable [cant phr.]. **1996** Justin Comiskey, *Irish Times*, 17 May: 'The phrase "neither popular nor profitable" was uttered quite often by some people in political circles during the 1940s and 1950s. When [Brian] O'Nolan [Myles na gCopaleen] began to use it as a pillar of phoneydom in some of his satire, the phrase quickly disappeared from the politician's diction.'

Nelly's room as in **up in Nelly's room behind the wallpaper** [catchphrase]. Presumed location of missing or misplaced objects etc. **1995** Pat Ingoldsby in Seán Power (ed.), *Those were the Days, Irish Childhood Memories*: 'There are certain things you know as a child without anybody ever telling you. Certain things and places. Places like "Up in Nelly's room behind the wallpaper". You knew exactly were this was...It was a safe place.'

neuck see **nyuck**

newance/new'ins [n. & adj.]. Novelty, (something) unexpected. **1927** Peadar O'Donnell, *Islanders*: '"It's new'ins to see ye on this island," he greeted them, "an' ye're welcome."' **1951** Sam Hanna Bell, *December Bride*: '"There's a bit of a blow on, but that's no newance in these parts."'

next nor near [prep., intens.]. Near. **1952** Michael McLaverty, *Truth in the Night*: '"You never go next nor near her house and her mother feels she isn't wanted."'

niag see **nag**

Niall of the Nine Sausages [nickname, <'Niall of the Nine Hostages', High King, AD 380–405]. Niall Boden, presenter of pop. sponsored RTÉ Radio programme for Donnelly's sausages (1950s).

nice as ninepence [adj. phr.] (Ulster). Very nice (Traynor).

nicely [adj.]. The worse for drink. **1968** John Healy, *The Death of an Irish Town*: 'the board was put across the sideboards of the cart and Himself [q.v.], with the reins in his hand and "nicely", called out "Come on, woman."' **1996** Nell McCafferty, *Sunday Tribune*, 27 Oct: 'Norma [Cotter] was "nicely" was how her friend described Norma's condition after what seemed like a respectable, quiet party.'

nice one [n. phr.]. Fit or appropriate person (iron.). **1913** George A. Birmingham, *General John Regan*: '"If you talked that way to Billing when he was trying to run away without paying —" "You're a nice one to talk about paying," said Doyle.'

nick [n., 'late C19–20 or perhaps far older' (DHS, of the phrase 'in the nick');

Hib.E gen. with adj., as in **in good/great nick**]. Condition. **1975** John Ryan, *Remembering How We Stood*: 'as venerable buildings went, it [the Bailey pub] was in good heart; in a word — the premises was in sound "nick"'. **1995** Maeve Binchy, *Irish Times*, 25 Mar: 'There must even be a way of thinking that if you have to tear the house to pieces every spring, then it can't have been in great nick the rest of the time...'

nick an' go [n. phr.] (Ulster). Close shave.

nicker see **neigher**

nickie cakes! [exclam., <Sc. *nickit bake*, biscuit with indentations on top] (Ulster). 'Very easy!' (TT). See also **wee buns!**

nieve/neave [n., <ON *hnefi*, fist] (Ulster). Hand, handful. See **neevy navy nick nack**.

niff-naff see **nyiff-nyaff**

nigger see **nager**

night train [n. phr.]. Night post-detoxification programme for drug users. **1996** Kitty Holland, *Irish Times*, 10 Sept: 'Nora is now on the "night train". After numerous failed detoxes...she would have to work with her doctor to get back on the day programme.'

nicher see **neigher**

nikko [n., <Brit. sl. 'nix', nothing + endearment suffix, poss. <Romany *nisser* (vb.), avoid (DHS)] (juvenile) as in **keep nikko** [vb. phr.]. Keep watch. **1991** Bob Quinn, *Smokey Hollow*: 'All they could do was turn up the radio full blast and continue smoking rolled-up brown paper fags, taking turns to keep nikko for their mother...'

nim [vb., <OE *niman*, take, capture, steal] (Ulster). Steal.

ninny-hammer [n., cf. Sc. *ninycumpook*, nincompoop; *hammer*, clumsy person]. Idiot. **1879** Charles J. Kickham, *Knocknagow*: '"Blur-an-agers [q.v.], have sinse, sir — have sinse." "Have sense yourself — and that's what you'll never have, you ninny-hammer," retorted the master...' **C.1914** (first published 1969) George Fitzmaurice, *The Ointment Blue*:

'TEIG ...the neighbours laughing at us and we going in a pair of ninny-hammers knowing nothing...'

nip [n., <?] as in **in one's/the nip** [adj. phr.]. Stark naked. **1991** Roddy Doyle, *The Van*: '"You'd be better off going around in your nip," said Jimmy Sr.'

nippit [adj., <Sc. *nip* (vb.), pinch] (Ulster). Tight-fitting.

nirls [n., sing., <Sc. *idem*, chickenpox] (Ulster). As thus.

nivel [vb., <Norman dial. *nifler*, sniff noisily] (Munster/Leinster). Turn up one's nose at something.

nixer [n. & (rarely) vb., <colloq. Germ. *nix* (<*nichts*), nothing + endearment suffix]. Work undertaken outside of normal paid employment and usually clandestinely. **1970** Christy Brown, *Down All the Days*: '"Don't be worrying, Ma. Joe's in the way of doing a few nixers. He's doing an extension for Mattie Madigan."' **1987** Vincent Caprani, *Vulgar Verse & Variations, Rowdy Rhymes & Rec-im-itations*, 'Gough's Statue': 'and by payday of that week there were a couple of hundred "nixered" broadsheets of the ballad being passed from hand to hand'. **1995** *Sunday Tribune*, 22 Oct: 'Closer inspection indicated it [the book] was all about *Japanese Shinto Shrine Architecture*. Is our minister [Ruairí Quinn] seeking some oriental contracts as a nixer?'

nobber [n., cf. Brit. sl. *nob* (vb.), copulate, from *(k)nob* (n.), penis] (Cork). One having sexual relations. **1991** Teddy Delaney, *Where we Sported and Played*: 'the two of us saw a couple hurrying up Beale's Hill, a well-known nobbers' haunt: your wan [q.v.] was wriggling her chest enticingly'.

no better man [concessive phr.]. Implying appropriateness/suitability. **1994** Greg Dalton, *My Own Backyard, Dublin in the Fifties*: 'When he [the confessor] asks me about bad language, no better man, so I give him a demonstration as requested.'

noble call [n. phr., <?]. Invitation to perform/sing at social gathering. **1995** Phil O'Keeffe, *Down Cobbled Streets, A Liberties Childhood*: '"Noble call now!" And in the silence that ensued while a noble call was passed on, we laid bets as to the identity of the next performer.'

noddy [n., <nodding motion]. One-horse conveyance. **1847** John Edward Walsh, *Ireland Sixty Years Ago*: 'The Ringsend car [q.v.] was succeeded by the "noddy", so called from its oscillating motion backwards and forwards. It was a low vehicle, capable of holding two persons, and drawn by one horse. It was covered with a calash, open before, but the aperture was usually filled by the "noddy boy", who was generally a large-sized man...'

no empty skite [n. phr., invar. neg., <Sc. *skite* (n. & vb.), shoot, splash] (Ulster). Very full.

noggin see **naggin**

no goat's toe [adj. phr.] (Ulster). Sensible, no fool.

noit/knoit/nudyan etc. [n., cf. Sc. *knoit*, large piece of anything] (Ulster). Insignificant person (Patterson); blockhead, idiot; bunion.

noody-nady [adj. & n., <Ir. *niúidí neáidí*, hesitant in speech or manner; annoying individual]. As thus. **1939** James Joyce, *Finnegans Wake*: 'But Noodynaady's [*sic*] actual ingrate tootle is of come into the garner mauve...'

nooks [n. pl., <Shelta *niuc*, penny] (Cork). Money.

norration see **narration**

no sooner calved than licked [adj. phr.]. Dealt with/disposed of peremptorily. **1995** Dersie Leonard in Mary Ryan et al. (eds.), *No Shoes in Summer*: 'every time he'd come to town he'd give me two shillings and sixpence which, I may say, was no sooner calved than licked'.

not a child/wean (q.v.) **in the house washed** [adv. phr.]. Nothing accomplished: protest at having been overtaken by events. **1966** Patrick Boyle, *At Night All Cats are Grey*, 'The Betrayers': '"Ten o'clock," she said. "The spuds still in their jackets and not a wean in the house washed."'

not a word of a lie [n. phr.]. The whole truth. **1953** *The Stories of Frank O'Connor*, 'The Miser': '"Wouldn't you be better off in hospital?" "I won't tell you a word of a lie, father...I couldn't afford it."'

note [n., <OE *notu*, related to OE *neat*, bullock, cow, heifer] (Ulster). Time of calving (of cow), as in 'when is she at her note?' (Patterson).

notice box [n. phr., cf. *nous-box*, head (Grose)]. S.o. inclined to seek attention, put on airs (q.v.). **1995** Aidan Higgins, *Donkey's Years*: 'Maeve Healy is now coming downstairs in shorts. Mumu says she is a minx, a slithery article [q.v.], Miss Notice Box.' **1996** Nuala O'Faolain, *Are You Somebody?*: 'the same influences I came under affected more people than me. Teachers used to say "Miss Noticebox! You're nothing but a noticebox!"'

notion [n.]. 1. [n. & n. pl., <Lat. *noscere* (vb.), know; fancy for something, 1746]. Sexual inclinations; and as in **have a notion of** [vb. phr.] be amorously attracted to. **1979** Seán O'Faoláin in David Marcus (ed.), *Body and Soul*, 'The Talking Trees': 'she said they didn't want any girls in their school who had notions. The three gazed at one another, and began at once to discuss all the possible sexy meanings of notions.' **1995** Michael 'Gossie' Browne in Mary Ryan et al. (eds.), *No Shoes in Summer*: 'It's a hard bind when a dacent woman has a notion of you and does you a good turn...unless of course you get a notion of her as well!' 2. [n. pl.]. Pretensions, inflated opinion. **1921** Lennox Robinson, *The Whiteheaded Boy* (q.v.): ''Tis too high notions William always had.' **1948** George Fitzmaurice, *Dublin Magazine*, 'There are Tragedies and Tragedies', July/Sept: 'KYTIE Even the loss of cash can't stop him from boobying, for boobying is what I call his fashionable notions.'

not while pussy's a cat [adv. phr.] (Ulster). Never.

not wise [adj.] (Ulster). Insane.

'nough/'nuff [n., <*a nough*, corruption of 'enough', supposed. indef. art. replaced by possessive]. Sufficiency. **1908** Lynn Doyle, *Ballygullion*: '"Poor Jer went

to Kilkishen mass an' after mass he went into the pub. He drank his 'nuff there."'

nought and carry one [adj. & nickname]. Lame, nickname for person so afflicted.

nourished [p. part. as adj.]. Having drink taken (q.v.). **1970** Christy Brown, *Down All the Days*: '"Ah, that's a powerful [see **power**] smell, Essie," he says, coming in well nourished from the pub and taking a look at the big pot bubbling like bejasus [q.v.] on the gas.'

no-user [n., cf. Austral. 'no-hoper']. Useless individual. **1993** Sam McAughtry, *Touch & Go*: '"He was put up to me as a bit of a no-user; watch him, Dicky."'

nudger [n., <?]. Term of abuse. **1994** Gabriel Byrne, *Pictures in my Head*: 'She called us names like heartscalds [q.v.] and nudgers and guarlyas [q.v.]...and say [*sic*] that we took the biscuit and the tin hat [see **put the tin hat on**].'

nudyan see **noit**

'nuff see **'nough**

nuitna [n., <?]. Mistake-prone person (EW).

nun with a price on her head [nickname]. Five-pound note. See **holy show**.

nur/nurr/knurr [n., <Sc. *nurr*, decrepit person] (Ulster). As thus; 'small, insignificant thing' (Patterson). See **chancy**.

nurg [adj., poss. cogn. with *nur* (q.v.)] (Ulster). Miserly, stingy (Patterson).

nurr see **nur**

nurse-child [n.]. Fostered child of (gen.) unmarried mother. **1985** Máirín Johnston, *Around the Banks of Pimlico*: 'I knew some "nurse-children", as they were called, who were very happy with their foster-mothers, but they lived in dread of being taken away and sent somewhere else...' **1989** Hugh Leonard, *Out after Dark*: 'The town's verdict was that if you were eejit [q.v.] enough to adopt a nurse-child, I, in the heel of the hunt [q.v.], was what you were liable to end up with.'

nurse-tender [n.]. Hired nurse.

nyaah/nyaa, the [n., onomat.]. Strong nasal intonation/enhancing quality in singing. **1993** John A. Murphy in Seán Dunne (ed.), *The Cork Anthology*, 'The Piano in Macroom': 'Sean-nós [singing in traditional Ir. style] was alive, if not altogether well, and living down the road, and known to outsiders as "having the nyaah".' **1996** Frank Patterson, *Irish Times*, 5 Dec: 'Pavarotti's is the most natural voice...Domingo's is huge, much bigger than Pavarotti's, but it doesn't have his "nyaa".'

nyafflin' [pres. part., onomat.] (Ulster). Eating noisily with one's mouth open (SH).

nyam!/knyam! [exclam. & vb., onomat.] (Ulster). Cat's cry, hence whinge, complain (of children).

nyarley fry [n. phr., <?] (Ulster). 'Well-cooked fry of eggs, sausages, bacon and soda bread' (Pepper).

nyerp/nyirp [n., <Sc. *nyarb*, peevish complaint] (Ulster). Unpleasant, complaining person. Also as in **give one the nyerps** [vb. phr.]. Annoy, irritate.

nyiff-nyaff/niff-naff [n. & vb., <'knick-knack'] (Ulster). 1. [n.]. Trifling thing; small person. 2. [vb.]. Potter about.

nyimf/nyimp [n., <Sc. *nimp*, tiny bit] (Ulster). As thus.

nyinger [n., <?] (Ulster). Spittle (SH).

nyirm [vb., <OE *gyrmane* (vb.), lament] (Ulster). Nag or whine.

nyirp see **nyerp**

nyitter [vb., cf. 'natter'] (Ulster). Nag.

nyuck/nyuk/neuck [n. & vb.]. 1. [vb., <Brit. sl. 'nick', steal] (Ulster). As thus. 2. [n., <?]. Person of little account. **1995** May O'Connor, RTÉ Radio, *The Odd Word*, 28 Aug: 'Not out of the top drawer, or the middle, or the bottom.' 3. [n., <Sc. *neuck/neuk*, nook, recess] (Ulster). Plug of tobacco; small bit of anything.

O

Oakboys [nickname]. Protestant secret society in Ulster, 1763–. **1973** Maureen Wall in T. Desmond Williams (ed.), *Secret Societies in Ireland*, 'The Whiteboys' (q.v.): 'There seems little doubt...that the Whiteboys and Rightboys [q.v.] had their origin, as had the Oakboys and Hearts of Steel [q.v.] in Ulster, in stated grievances that were largely economic.' **1988** R.F. Foster, *Modern Ireland 1600–1972*: 'the "Oakboy" movement in the north sprang up against taxes levied for road-building...it mobilised Catholics as well as lower-class Presbyterians and Anglicans'.

oanshagh/oonshugh/ownshuck/óinseach/unshook etc. [n., <Ir. *óinseach*, foolish woman; fool]. As thus. **1866** Patrick Kennedy, *Legendary Fictions of the Irish Celts*: '"Musha [q.v.], Jack, but you're the devil's quare [see **quare** 1.] youth...to be makin' a horse of my pot-rack. Come down, you onshuch, and go to bed."' **1879** Charles J. Kickham, *Knocknagow*: '"Don't be makin' an oonshugh uv yourself," said Phil.' See also **amadaun**.

oashin [n., <Ir. *óinsín*, dimin. of *óinseach*, fool, foolish woman]. Weakling. See also **oanshagh**.

oberins [n., cf. Sc. *obering*, hint, inkling] (Ulster). Trifling work, as in **wee** (q.v.) **oberins** (Patterson).

obligement [n.] (Ulster). Favour.

O'Brien's dog [n. phr.]. One who is all things to all men. **1996** Peter Cassells, RTÉ TV, *Prime Time*, 23 Jan: '[The Minister for Finance was] Trying to be like O'Brien's dog, goes a bit of the way with everyone.' See **Billy Harran's dog**, **Lanna Macree's dog**, **Lanty McHale's dog** for similarly disposed canines.

och! [exclam., <Ir. *idem*, 'expressing sorrow, regret, weariness, impatience, etc.' (CUD). As thus.

och-hanee-o/och och an a nee o! [exclam., <Sc. Gael. *ochan-i*, extension of *och* (q.v.), expressing sorrow, weariness] (Ulster). As thus. **1913** Alexander Irvine, *My Lady of the Chimney Corner*: '"We shall meet again, mother," I said. "Ay, dearie, I know rightly [see **right** 1.] we'll meet, but ochanee [*sic*], it'll be out there beyond th' meadows an' th' clouds."'

ochone!/ohone! [exclam., <Ir. *ochón!* alas!]. As thus. **1698** John Dunton, *Report of a Sermon*: 'Now, Christians, if greatness, or riches, or hollyness, or strent [strength] could not keep does peoples now reshted from deat's all-dewouering mout, ohone, fwy vould he spare any of us?' **1922** James Joyce, *Ulysses*: 'OLD GUMMY GRANNY (*Rocking to and fro.*) Ireland's sweetheart, the king of Spain's daughter, alanna [q.v.]. Strangers in my house, bad manners to them! (*She keens with banshee* [q.v.] *woe.*) Ochone! Ochone! Silk of the kine!'

odd clod, the see **clod** 1.

odds [n. pl.] (Dub.). Loose change. Also **odjins**.

odious/odjous see **ojus**

O'Donnell's gallon [n. phr., <Ir. *galún Uí Dómhnaill*, a full bumper (Dinneen)]. Large quantity (of drink). See **gallon**.

officer-toed [adj.] (Ulster). Having turned-out feet.

off one's bap [adj. phr., see **bap** 2.] (Ulster). Astray in the head (q.v.).

often as fingers and toes [adv. phr., cf. Ir. *comh is atá méireanna coise agus láimhe orm*, as often as I have fingers and toes (Dinneen)]. Frequently.

ogenagh [n., cf. Ir. *óigeantacht*, youthfulness] (Ulster). Simpleton (Patterson).

ohone! see **ochone!**

oil/ile [vb., cf. Sc. *oil of aik* [n. phr.], 'beating with an oaken cudgel' (CSD)]. Beat severely.

óinseach see **oanshagh**

Oirish [adj., Paddyism: see also Appendix]. Connoting excessive or exaggerated display of perceived national characteristics. Hence **Oirishness/Oirishry** [abst. n.]. **1996** Pat Cotter, *Irish Times*, 28 Aug: '[John] Boland's own sensitivities regarding Paddywhackery [q.v.] and Oirishness suggest to me that he is one of those very metropolitans I accuse of being embarrassed about their origins.' **1996** Harry Browne, *Irish Times*, 3 Sept: 'presenter Michael O'Donnell set the scene at Westport House, Co. Mayo, with a bit of Oirishry — "The west of Ireland, where the inevitable rarely happens", etc. etc.'

ojus/ojous/odious/odjous [adj. & adv.] (Ulster). Very. **1995** Shane Connaughton, *A Border Diary*: '"I mind [q.v.] the time the uncle was buried. It was an ojous cold day. A thin skite [q.v.] of snow lay over the country."' **1996** Dermot Healy, *The Bend for Home*: '"The ladder was dangled out of the door of the plane till it reached the ground. It was an ojus height and then I had to climb down."'

olagon/ullagon [n. & vb., <Ir. *olagón* (n.), wail, lament]. As thus. **1929** Daniel Corkery, *The Stormy Hills*, 'The Ruining of Dromacurig': 'He stopped up his rambling hullagoning [*sic*], and when I glanced up at him I saw his big mouth and it hanging open...like you'd see the clab [q.v.] of an idiot.' **1989** Hugh Leonard, *Out after Dark*: 'I would eat my grandmother's soapy potatoes before seeing it again, this time with Jeanette MacDonald ullagoning about the little brown road winding over the hill.' **1992** Sean O'Callaghan, *Down by the Glenside, Memoirs of an Irish Boyhood*: 'She started olagoning and screeching, "Mickey me darlin' son."'

old for words and phrases beginning thus see also under **oul', ould**

old dog for the hard road [n. phr.]. Said of one inured by experience. **1946** Myles na gCopaleen, *Irish Writing No. 1*, 'Drink and Time in Dublin', May: 'I was supposed to be staying with the brother-in-law, of course, when the wife was away. But sure it's the old dog for the hard road. Drunk or sober I went back to me own place.' **1966** Patrick Boyle, *At Night All Cats are Grey*, 'Meles Vulgaris': 'A murmur of appreciation went round. "Sound man [q.v.]." "The old dog for the hard road."' See also **pad**.

old-fashioned [adj.]. Precocious. **1939** Sean O'Casey, *I Knock at the Door*: '"This comes of letting him go to the funeral," complained Michael. "He's getting twice too old-fashioned for his years."'

old God's time [n. phr.]. Time immemorial. **1961** Dominic Behan, *Teems of Times and Happy Returns*: '"sure even the strongest of us can't live for ever, an' these same places have been standin' since oul God's time"'. See also **little God's time**.

Old Lady of Westmoreland Street, the [nickname]. The *Irish Times* newspaper, founded 1859. The address is now that of the former rear entrance in D'Olier St. **1991** Tony Gray, *Mr Smyllie, Sir*. 'an incredible enclave of Dickensian squalor and Victorian respectability...It was not for nothing that until some time during the Second World War the *Irish Times* was always known in Dublin as "The Old Lady of Westmoreland Street".' **1996** John Cooney, *Sunday Tribune*, 18 Aug: '[Malcolm] Harris hurls colourful verbal abuse at RTÉ, *The Sunday Tribune* and even the stately Old Lady of D'Olier Street...'

Old Mon [nickname, <'monastery']. Patrician Brothers' school, Market St, Galway. **1996** *City Tribune* (Galway): 'A book to be launched later this year will recall schoolboy memories for thousands of Galwegians. The book, on the history of the "Old Mon"...is being written by former pupil and city historian James Casserley.'

Old Red Socks [nickname] (Ulster). The pope.

old sod [nickname & term of affection]. 1. [nickname, affect./Paddyism]. Ire., esp. from an 'exile's' viewpoint. **1879** Charles J. Kickham, *Knocknagow*. 'The mere suspicion that the landlord wished to get rid of them has driven many an Irish family far away from the "old sod".' 2. [term of affection]. **1980** Emma Cooke, *Female Forms*: '"Take your pick, oul' sod, either check into the hospital or get away from it all."'

old son see **oul' son**

old stock see **oul' stock**

Old Toughs [nickname]. Royal Dublin Fusiliers, former regiment in Brit. army. **1939** Sean O'Casey, *I Knock at the Door*: '"The Royal Dublin Fusiliers," he said a little thickly, "the Old Toughs, by the right, quick march for foreign lands..."' See also **Dub** 2.

Old Wife [nickname] (Ulster). Ballan wrasse (*Labrus maculatus*).

olé, olé, olé, olé! [exclam.]. Soccer chant adopted by supporters of Republic of Ireland team, 1980s–1990s. See **Jack's Army**. **1995** Gerard Lee, *Irish Times*, 22 Dec: 'Sir — Before Ireland qualify for the next World Cup, could we please clear up what it is exactly we are singing to the lads on the pitch. As Gaeilge [in Irish] we are singing "Drink it, drink it, drink it" (ól é). In French we are singing "With milk, with milk, with milk" (au lait)...'

Oliver's summons [n. phr., <name of C19 Co. Limerick landlord]. Said of an idle individual driven to work by necessity or other circumstances; from Oliver's habit of seizing the goods of those whom he wished to work for him and impounding them until the work was completed (PWJ).

one see **wan**

one and one see **wan and wan**

one for everyone in the audience [cant phr., <Gay Byrne (see **Gaybo**), RTÉ TV, *Late Late Show*, passim, goods etc. provided by commercial interests for distribution to studio audience]. Eclectic distribution of goods, services, etc., gen. mildly derog. **1997** Pat Rabbitte, *Irish Times*, 25 Feb: 'As soon as you come up with a good idea...everyone around the Cabinet table puts their hand up and says "I want one too." So you end up with measures that were designed for unemployment areas, but there has to be one for everyone in the audience.'

onehandled adulterer [nickname, <'one-handed']. Admiral Horatio Nelson, with ref. to his representation on Nelson's Pillar, O'Connell St, Dub. (1818–1966). **1922** James Joyce, *Ulysses*:

'"And settle down on their striped petticoats, peering up at the statue of the onehandled adulterer." "Onehandled adulterer!" the professor cried. "I like that. I see the idea. I see what you mean."'

one thing, the [n. phr.]. Sexual intercourse. **1989** Hugh Leonard, *Out after Dark*: 'the tide of English summer visitors, all of them only after the One Thing'. See also **the other**.

on leg [adv. phr.] (Ulster). Out of bed, up.

only trotting after [vb. phr., cf. Ir. *ag sodar i ndiaidh duine*, trotting after s.o.]. Unable to keep up with, outfaced, outsmarted. **1952** Anon. (Patrick Kavanagh?), *Kavanagh's Weekly*, 'I Went to the Fair', 21 June: 'Sometimes the third party is the actual owner [of the cattle for sale] who is there to carry the play further. The three-card lads are only trotting after these men.' **1995** Eanna Brophy, *Sunday Tribune*, 17 Sept: 'But he [David Copperfield] was only trotting after the show I saw in the RDS the previous weekend. One wave of two hands, and a whole company with 600 jobs disappeared.'

on one end's errand see **errand**

on one's keeping see **keeping, on one's**

onset [n., cf. Sc. *idem*, outhouse, farmstead] (Ulster). Small cluster of houses.

on the batter see **batter**

on the blanket [vb. phr., <'blanket protest' by nationalist prisoners in Long Kesh, Belfast, 1976–, who refused to wear prison clothing and wore a blanket instead]. **1983** Bobby Sands, *One Day in my Life*: '"How long have you been on the blanket now?" he [the warder] enquired, and added immediately, "Don't you think you'd be as well packing it in?" "No, I don't," I answered him dryly.' **1986** Derek Dunne, *Magill*, 'McFarlane, The Inside Story', Apr: 'Brendan McFarlane had his clothes taken from him and was told to do prison work. He refused and joined others "on the blanket".'

on the hop [adj. phr.]. Playing truant. **1993** John O'Keefe in Michael Verdon, *Shawlies* (q.v.)*, Echo Boys* (q.v.)*, the Marsh and the Lanes* (q.v.)*: Old Cork Remembered*: 'When I used to go to school, I was a wild character [see **character** 2.] I used to go on the hop. Wouldn't go to school at all.'

on the leg [adj. phr.] (Ulster). Gadding about.

on the pig's back see **pig's back**

on the tear see **tear**

ooh ah Paul McGrath! [exclam.]. Fan greeting for pop. member of Republic of Ireland soccer team, 1980s–1990s, esp. in the 1990 World Cup matches. **1996** Uinsionn Mac Dubhghaill, *Irish Times*, 18 Mar: 'Paul McGrath gave a nonchalant thumbs-up to the chants of "ooh-ah" as he headed the [St Patrick's Day] parade...' **1996** Headline, profile of Paul McGrath, *Sunday Tribune*, 1 Sept: 'This could be the last ooh-aah'.

oonshugh see **oanshagh**

oorie/oorey/oory [adj., <Sc. *oorie*, languid, sickly-looking] (Ulster). As thus; hung-over.

oosha! [interj., onomat.]. Accompanying action of hoisting child in the air. **1975** Eilís Brady, *All In! All In!*: 'Sally go round the moon/Sally go round the stars/Sally go round the chimney pot/And an oosha! Mary Ann.'

ort [n. & vb., <Sc. *oarts* (n.), refuse] (Ulster). 1. [n. pl.]. Scraps, leftovers. Also **ortins/oartins** in same sense. 2. [vb.]. Pick out the best (of food) and leave the rest.

oshin [n., <Ir. *oisín*, fawn] (Ulster). 'A weakly creature who cannot do his fair share of work' (PWJ).

ossified [p. part. as adj., pun on 'stoned']. Intoxicated. Hence **ossification** [n.]. Process of becoming intoxicated. **1975** John Ryan, *Remembering How We Stood*: 'If we could have delayed this ossification to the "Circe" episode it would have been more in accordance with the structure of *Ulysses*...'

other, the [euphem.]. Sexual intercourse. **1997** Brendan Glacken, *Irish Times*, 'Times Square', 10 Apr: '...I explained to Naomi what "the other" (as in "a bit of") meant in my home country. She was not amused.' See also **the one thing**.

other morrow [n. phr.] (Ulster). Day after tomorrow.

other side, the see **side, the other**

ottercop see **attercap**

oul', ould for words and phrases beginning thus see also under **old**

ould boy [n. phr., euphem.]. The Devil. **1909** Canon Sheehan, *The Blindness of Dr Gray*: '"The ould boy must have something to say to you, you blagard; and shlipped in the black blood somehow or other..."'

ould wan see **oul' wan**

oulfella [n., <Dub. pronun. of 'old fellow' and gen. written thus] (Dub.). Old man; more specifically father. **1961** Dominic Behan, *Teems of Times and Happy Returns*: '"Yer oulwan's [q.v.] a lavatory cleaner,/Yer oulfella's terrible mean./They sit in the pub drinking porter [q.v.],/Yer washin' has never been clean."' **1987** Lar Redmond, *Emerald Square*: 'It was a sign of the times that he was no longer "Dad". "The Oul' Fella" was good enough these days.' **1995** RTÉ TV serial, *Upwardly Mobile*, 27 Oct: 'Not like the Mansions: you knew you were home when you saw your oulfella's underpants blowing on the line.'

oul' flower [term of address, <?] (Dub.). Expression of sentimental affection, more usu. between males, as in **me oul' flower**. **1966** Liam Ó Cuanaigh, *Evening Press*, 21 Nov: 'A hard ticket [q.v.]...can take fivepence from a nun with the comment "Five dee [q.v.] is dead [q.v.] right — there y'are — God bless you, me oul' flower...' **1987** Lar Redmond, *Emerald Square*: '"Wait a minute me oul' flower," he said to me, "hold on, it's not that bad."' **1995** National press advertisement, 18 Sept: 'SAM [q.v.], ME OUL FLOWER, You're welcome home. Congrats to the Dubs [see **Dub** 1.] from KIRWANS [florists].'

oul granny grunt [n. phr.]. Precocious child.

oul' one see **oul' wan**

oul' shAbbey [nickname]. Abbey Theatre, Dub., before 1951 fire and rebuilding. **1967** Sean McCann, *The Story of the Abbey Theatre*: 'the [new] Abbey opened in 1966...No longer could the Dubliners make a date with their favourite remark "See you at the oul' shAbbey tonight."'

oul' son/old son [n. phr.]. Affect. form of address between males. **1996** Tom Humphries, *Irish Times*, 29 Jan: '"Now Kenny, oul son, suppose you are two nil down, you are playing away and they are putting a lot of crosses in. Ten minutes left. What would you do?"'

oul' stock [exclam.]. Affect. form of address between males. **1979** Frank Kelly, *The Annals of Ballykilferret*: '"Begod [see **begob**] he will. I never seen him bet [beaten] yet. Me life on ye Mr G. oul' stock!"'

oul' wan/ould wan/oul' one [n. phr., representing Dub. pronun. of 'one', and freq. spelt thus]. Old woman; more specifically and familiarly mother, wife. **1965** Lee Dunne, *Goodbye to the Hill*: 'The oul' ones used to smile among themselves...They said it was the size of her tits that did it with the apprentice...' **1982** Éamonn Mac Thomáis, *Janey Mack* (q.v.), *Me Shirt is Black*: 'Carrying cases was tough work. I think some ould wans had cases full of turnips...' **1994** Ferdia Mac Anna, *The Ship Inspector*: 'The only problem is that my Ould One always votes Fine Gael.' See also **wan**.

oussie [adj., <?] (Ulster). Too curious by half.

outby [adv., <Sc. *idem*, out of doors, at a distance] (Ulster). Just beyond the immediate environment (YDS).

outfall [n., <Sc. *idem*, quarrel] (Ulster). As thus.

out-going Sunday/Monday [n. phr.]. Days following a wedding when wedding party went to church/market together.

outlong [adv. & prep.]. Beyond immediate (urban) area. **1996** Christy Kenneally, *Maura's Boy, A Cork Childhood*: 'Coming nearer to Christmas he organised trips "outlong" to gather moss so that we could clad the walls [of the crib]...'

out-mouthed [adj.] (Ulster). Having protruding teeth.

out of pain [adj. phr.] (Munster). Having survived initial shock of cold water when swimming. **1996** Christy Kenneally, *Maura's Boy, A Cork Childhood*: 'Paddy and Michael loved the water and couldn't wait to be togged off [see **togs**] and "out of pain".'

out of the face [adv. phr.] (Ulster). From first to last without stopping (Patterson).

outsider [n.]. 1. Two-wheeled horse-drawn vehicle, 'outside car'. **1914** James Joyce, *Dubliners*, 'Grace': 'When they came out into Grafton Street, Mr Power whistled for an outsider...Mr Kernan was hoisted onto the car...' 2. Mentally impaired individual. **1960** John O'Donoghue, *In Kerry Long Ago*: 'sunstroke made a sudden change in him, poor fellow, and upset his mind...he was brought down to the chapel with others called "outsiders" for instruction in Catechism'.

outsleep [vb.] (Ulster). Oversleep. See also **sleep it out**.

over [vb., gen. neg.] (Ulster). Survive, overcome, recover from. **1979** John Morrow, *The Confessions of Proinsias O'Toole*: '"Some oul' goat of a Priest up in that posh school gave her a rub of the relic [q.v.] and she says she's niver overed it..."'

overhand [n.] (Ulster). Upper hand (Traynor).

overlook [vb.]. Afflict with the evil eye, bewitch. **1942** Seán Ó Súilleabháin, *A Handbook of Irish Folklore*: 'Was "overlooking" sometimes accidental rather than done by design? Did some people possess the "evil eye" without being aware of the fact?'

overright [prep., <Ir. *os comhair*, opposite, <confusion with *cóir*, right, decent, honest (PWJ)]. Opposite, in front of.

overseen [p. part. as adj.]. Bewitched. See **overlook**.

owl-light [n.]. Dusk. **1951** Sam Hanna Bell, *December Bride*: 'In the owl-light there appeared over a rise in the road the piper followed by twenty or thirty lads and girls.'

ownshuck see **oanshagh**

ox see **ucks**

oxo [n., <*Oxo*, proprietary beef extract preparation, & poss. by analogy with 'OK'] as in **the job's oxo** [catchphrase]. Expression of affirmation. (See also **game ball**.) **1996** Nell McCafferty, *Sunday Tribune*, 21 Jan: '[Princess] Anne pulled a cord, the curtains swished, there was a plaque and that was that. Not one word did she utter. Not even "The job's oxo."' **1996** RTÉ TV serial, *Glenroe*, 10 Mar: 'MILEY   ...and why shouldn't I worry about the cattle? DINNY Don't you worry about that. It's all right. The job's oxo.'

oxter/oxther [n. & vb., <OE *ohsta* (n.), armpit]. [n.]. As thus. [vb.]. Go arm in arm. **1966** Patrick Boyle, *At Night All Cats are Grey*, 'The Metal Man': '"About the last thing I can remember is Cleary oxtering Kreuger out the bar door."' **1992/3** R.G. Morton, *Five Foot Three* (Belfast), 'Slag Heaps by the Shannon': 'Suddenly a coal-miner appeared behind us...He stalked away, helmet perched at a jaunty angle, tin under his "oxter", along the Arigna road.' Also **oxtercog** [vb., <ME *cogge* (n.), armpit]. Go arm in arm.

oyster [n.]. Gob of phlegm/spittle. **1922** James Joyce, *Ulysses*: 'The citizen said nothing only cleared the spit out of his gullet and, gob, he spat a Red bank [Dub. oyster bed] oyster out of him right [see **right** 1.] in the corner.' See also **belch an oyster**.

P

pachal/pachle see **pauchle**

pack [adj., <Sc. *idem*, intimate, familiar, friendly]. As thus. **1966** Patrick Boyle, *At Night All Cats are Grey*, 'The Betrayers': '"I just thought you might know," he said. "You and she being so pack."'

pad/padroad [n., <OE *paeth*, footway] (Ulster). Narrow path. **N.d.** Proverb: 'The old dog for the hard road [q.v.] and the pup for the pad.' **1995** George Sheridan in Mary Ryan et al. (eds.), *No Shoes in Summer*: 'Ketty was in Legolagh [Co. Fermanagh] when she got ill. She was able, with help, to walk the padroad to our house...' Also **out on one's/the pad** [adj. phr.]. Out for a stroll/walk; gadding about. **1956** Sam Hanna Bell, *Erin's Orange Lily*: '"Come on in, the two of ye —" "Ach now, Alec, we wouldn't like to do that! I was just out on my pad wi' James Orr here..."'

paddle [vb.] (Ulster). Walk with short steps.

paddocksteel [n., <Sc. *paddock*, toad + *steele*, stool] (Ulster). Mushroom. But see **puddockstool**.

Paddy Brophy as in **the colour of Paddy Brophy** [n. phr., <Waterford character (see **character** 1.)]. Unhealthy colour. **1995** Edmund Pierce, *Waterford News & Star Christmas Supplement*, 'Wordy Waterford': 'What mother today would say to her daughter when she looks pale as a fading primrose, "Are you feeling alright, you've the colour of Paddy Brophy on you"?'

paddy frog [n. phr., <OE *pada*, toad] (Ulster). Frog.

paddy hat [n. phr., see **paddy frog**] (Ulster). Toadstool. See **puddockstool**.

Paddy of the Bog [nickname]. Heron (Moylan).

Paddy's eye-water [n. phr.]. Illicit whiskey, poteen (q.v.).

Paddy's milestone [nickname]. Island of Ailsa Craig, Irish Sea.

Paddy the Cope [nickname, <local pronun. of 'co-op']. Patrick Gallagher (1873–1964), founder of the pioneering Templecrone (Co. Donegal) Co-operative Society, 1906. **1916** *Irish Homestead*, 11 Nov: '"Paddy the Cope" was not only a good fighter but a man of business of the type which is not infrequently born on an Irish bog and ends his days as an American millionaire...'

Paddy Ward's pig [n. phr.]. **Late C18** Anon., *Lord Altham's Bull*: '...Madame Stevens [Steevens's Hospital, Dub. (1733)] was the word, where I lay for seven weeks in lavendar, on de broad of me back, like Paddy Ward's pig, be de hokey [q.v.]'. **1847** John Edward Walsh, *Ireland Sixty Years Ago*: 'Who Paddy Ward was, we believe, has eluded the inquiries of historians and antiquaries. He was, however, very eminent for his sayings and doings...'

paddy whack/paddywhackery [n., 'a paddy-whack; a stout brawney Irishman' (Grose), <mid C19 Cork character (see **character** 1.), 'Paddy Whack' (nickname); but many other attribs.]. Stage-Ir. goings-on; exaggeration of national characteristics, customs or behaviour; employment of such alleged characteristics in a racist context. **1889** *Event* (Cork): 'About thirty-five years ago there lived...a few miles out of Carrigaline, a celebrated character, nicknamed Paddy Whack. He earned the alias by frequent rows he got into...' **1995** Kim Bielenberg, *Irish Times*, 3 Aug: 'As a result of this outbreak of Euro-paddywhackery, the Irish bar is set to become as familiar an institution on every continental high street as the Chinese restaurant...' **1996** Eamonn Sweeney, *Sunday Tribune*, 4 Feb: '..."The Drinker", the story [by Michael Collins] of an alcoholic who despite drinking 30 pints a day still holds down a job on the railways, is a ludicrous wallow in some never-never land of pub Paddy-whackery'.

padroad see **pad**

pag [n., derog., <?] (Ulster). Useless individual.

paghil/pahil/pahle see **pauchle**

paik [vb., <Sc. *idem*, beat, chastise] (Ulster). Beat up, thrash.

pair of drawers [n. phr.] (Ulster). Chest of drawers.

Pa-Joe [nickname]. Private soldier, 'Tommy', in use in 1st Western Division, 1920s–. **1931** Patrick Crowe, *An t-Óglach*, 'The Capers of a Kerry Blue', Dec: 'A Free State soldier on service in Kerry, during the disturbances of 1922, returned one day with a Kerry Blue as a present for Mary Lane, his best girl. She married John Malone, and kept the dog in memory of Pa-Joe.'

palatic see **parlatic**

palaver [vb., <Sc. *idem*, gossip, talk over] (Ulster). Talk idly. **1913** Alexander Irvine, *My Lady of the Chimney Corner*: '"Och [q.v.], don't spake s'downmouthed, Anna," says I. "Sure ye'll feel fine in th' mornin'." "Don't palaver," says she, and she lukt terrible serious.'

pallion/palyeen/palleen [n., <Sc. *pillions*, rags, tatters; cf. Ir. *pillín*, small cushion, pad, pillion]. 1. Bundle of clothes/rags. 2. Unfashionable garment. 3. Person dressed in too many clothes/in rags. Hence **in paleens** [adj. phr.]. In rags.

palltog see **polthogue**

palyeen see **pallion**

pampootie [n., <Ir. *pampúta*, simple leather shoe]. As thus. **1906** E.Œ. Somerville & Martin Ross, *Some Irish Yesterdays*: 'Men and women alike wear "pampooties" — slippers of raw cowhide, with the hair outside...' **1967** Sean McCann, *The Story of the Abbey Theatre*: 'that long catalogue of "contacts with daily life", stretching from the Aran "pampooties" and red petticoats...to the frying sausages in "Juno [and the Paycock]"'.

pan, the [n., metonym] (Ulster). Fry, food cooked in a frying pan. **1983** *John Pepper's Illustrated Encyclopaedia of Ulster Knowledge*: '"When he comes in from the brew [see **broo** 1.] he's the happy man when he smells the pan."'

Pana/Pa'na [nickname, <abbrev. + endearment suffix] (Cork). Patrick St, Cork's main thoroughfare. **N.d.** Pop. ballad: 'All the Echo boys [q.v.] in Pana/Had bunches of banana/On the night the goat broke loose upon the Parade.' Also **doing Pana** [vb. phr.]. **1971** Seán Beecher, *The Story of Cork*: 'Before the advent of the cinema and television, the principal recreation of the people was "doing Pana", a form of Celtic Paseo, walking up and down Patrick Street meeting friends and acquaintances.' **1993** Maisie Flynn in Michael Verdon, *Shawlies* (q.v.), *Echo Boys, the Marsh and the Lanes* (q.v.): *Old Cork Remembered*: 'On Monday night, when we'd have the money for dancing, we used to go down Patrick Street...No one knew it as Patrick Street, only *Pa'na*. There used to be loads of people on Pa'na on a good night...My father used to say "Raz as me daz ah [see **me daza**], I'm going down Pa'na."'

panada/panady/pandy/paneda [n., <Sp. *panada*, Fr. *panade*, bread and butter boiled to a pulp] (Ulster). Bread pudding.

pancrocked [p. part. as adj.] (Ulster). Exhausted, worn out (YDS).

pandy [n. & vb.]. 1. [n. & vb., <Lat. *pande palma* (adv. phr.), with open hand]. Blow on the hand, beat thus. **1944** James Joyce, *Stephen Hero*: 'He had sometimes watched the faces of the prefects as they "pandied" boys with a broad leather bat...' Hence **pandybat** [n.]. Instrument for inflicting corporal punishment as above. **1916** James Joyce, *A Portrait of the Artist* (q.v.) *as a Young Man*: 'The pandybat made a sound too. The fellows said it was made of whalebone and leather with lead inside.' 2. [n.]. Little pan/pot. **1921** (first published 1983) Patrick MacGill, *Lanty Hanlon*: 'He came and wanted to know if Neal wanted a kettle mended, a pot legged or a pandy made...' 3. [n.] (Ulster). Mashed potatoes with butter and scallions (YDS). 4. [n.]. See **panada**.

paneda see **panada**

pang [vb., <Sc. *idem*, stuff full, cram] (Ulster). As thus.

pant [n., <?] (Ulster). 'A great deal of talk' (SH); absurd activity; rumour; s.o. with a lot of news. **1927** Peadar O'Donnell, *Islanders*: '"I followed him meself over to Dan Rogers'. Me father was wild with me for leavin' me work, but I knew Dan'd be a pant."'

paper, the see **de paper**

paper the moon see **hand me down the moon**

Papish/Paypish [adj. & nickname, derog.] (Ulster). Roman Catholic. **N.d.** Pop. ballad, 'The Relief of Derry': 'The vessel strikes the traitrous boom, does pitch and reel and strand,/Our Papish foes cry out our doom and OPEN GATES demand.' **1849** Pop. ballad, 'Dolly's Brae': 'And when we came to that great hill they were ranked on every side/And offering up their papish prayers for help to stem the tide/But we loosed our guns upon them and we quickly won the day/And we knocked five hundred papishes right over Dolly's Brae.'

pappit [n., <ME *popet/te*, poppet, small/dainty person] (Ulster). Very tiny person.

Paraic [adj., rhym. sl., Padraig Pearse, politician and revolutionary (1879–1916)]. Fierce (q.v.). **1989** Roddy Doyle, *War*. 'TOMMY (sitting down; to NOEL and ANGELA) The smell in the jacks [q.v.] is Paraic. NOEL (sardonically) Go 'way! [See **get away ou' that!**]'

parcel [n., <?] (Ulster). Troublesome/peculiar individual.

parch [n., <'perch', measure of length]. As thus. **1983** W.F. Marshall, *Livin' in Drumlister*, 'The Runaway': 'Well, boys, he was frothin' with anger,/The spittles flew from him a parch...'

parisheen [n., <'parish' + Ir. dimin. *ín*]. Foundling; 'one brought up in childhood by the parish' (PWJ).

Park, the [prop. n., metonym, <Phoenix Park, Dub., location of Áras an Uachtaráin, residence of the President of Ireland]. President's residence; appurtenances and/or office of the presidency. **1989** John Healy, *Magill*,

Nov: 'Brian in the Park would be a very welcome breath of fresh air. There is little fear of Lenihan dressing himself up in a protocol-style suit...' **1996** Jack Norton, *Sunday Tribune*, 21 Jan: 'With the prospect of a vacancy in "The Park" in the not too distant future, I hope there will not be any "cosy little cartels" deciding this issue...' **1996** John Horgan, *Irish Times*, 11 May: 'the Fianna Fáil party...is at a cross-roads now, just as it was when de Valera [see **Dev**] went to the Park in 1959'. See also **Uncle Tim's Cabin**.

parlatic/palatic [adj., Hib.E var., by syncope and metathesis, of 'paralytic']. Seriously intoxicated. **1977** Flann O'Brien, *The Hair of the Dogma*: '"He was after givin' himself the devil of a toss althegither and he couldn't get up, he was like a man parlatic a Saherda night.' **1977** James Plunkett, *Collected Short Stories*, 'Finegan's Ark': '"The majority up there," he said, "is young blades getting parlatic on the smell of a cork..."' **1983** *John Pepper's Illustrated Encyclopaedia of Ulster Knowledge*: '"Had he drink on him?" aims to establish if someone was (a) palatic (b) bluthered [q.v.]...'

parley [interj. & n.]. 'Home' in children's games. See **barley play**.

parliamentary side [n. phr.]. Decorous/respectable aspect as in **parliamentary side of one's arse** [n. phr.]. **1922** James Joyce, *Ulysses*: '"Three cheers for Israel!" "Arrah [q.v.], sit down on the parliamentary side of your arse for Christ's sake and don't be making a public exhibition of yourself."'

parliament whiskey [nickname]. Legal whiskey, as opposed to illicit whiskey or poteen (q.v.). **1988** John McGuffin, *In Praise of Poteen*: 'One important result of this [introduction of new government regulations, 1780s] was that the quality of legal (or "parliament whiskey" as it was called) declined as distilleries were forced to work faster and faster.'

pass [n., cf. Ir. *spéis*, interest, as in *níl spéis agam ann*, I am not interested in it] as in **put no pass on someone/something** [vb. phr.]. Ignore, take no interest in.

1945 Sean O'Casey, *Drums Under the Windows*: '"An' if you were with us, comrade," said the gaunt one…"you'd make one more." "I thought you said you didn't put any pass on numbers?"'

pass oneself [vb.] (Ulster). Behave in the manner expected. See **like oneself**.

Passover, the [nickname, <Jewish faith of Cork Lord Mayor]. Trinity Bridge over the Lee, Cork city, opened by Gerald Goldberg during his mayoralty, 1977. **1993** John Goodby in Seán Dunne (ed.), *The Cork Anthology*: 'and the fly-/Over opened by Lord Mayor Goldberg was rumoured/To have been rechristened by locals/The passover'.

passremarkable [adj.]. 1. Worthy of comment. **1989** Hugh Leonard, *Out after Dark*: 'To Father Kearney, everyday mayhem…was not in the least passremarkable.' 2. (Of individual) Given to passing cheeky/tactless remarks. **1996** Christy Kenneally, *Maura's Boy, A Cork Childhood*: 'When she left, I was crucified for being "passremarkable". These women were the heart of the house…' In this sense also **passremarkin'** (Ulster).

past oneself [adj. phr.] (Ulster). Silly, insane.

past one's market [adj. phr.] (Ulster). Past marriageable age, on the shelf. **1983** W.F. Marshall, *Livin' in Drumlister*, 'Sarah Ann': 'Ay she fell till the cryin', for ye know she isn't young,/She's nearly past her market, but she's civil with her tongue.'

pateen [n., <'Pat' + Ir. dimin. *ín*]. Term of contempt. **1922** Anon., *Tales of the RIC*: 'the poor Pateens were kept as a labour platoon by the gunmen, and made to do all the dirty work'. See also **podgreen**.

Patrick's pot [n. phr.]. Drink on the house on St Patrick's Day (Moylan).

patternavy [n., <*Pater* (*noster*) + *Ave* (*Maria*), Catholic prayers]. Prayers featured among the trimmings (q.v.) of the rosary.

pattha/peata [n., <Ir. *peata*, pet; cf. *peata beag a mháthar*, his mother's little

darling]. Pampered child. **1988** John Healy, *Magill*, 'The Wild One', Apr: 'in most families, there'd be "the peata", the weakest of the family, whom a protective mother would "keep at home"'.

patty-fingers [n. phr. & adv. phr.]. Finger contact in holy water font. **1952** Frank S. Nugent, from story by Maurice Walsh, *The Quiet Man* (film): 'MICHAELEEN OGE FLYNN And who taught you to be playing patty-fingers in the holy water?…Maybe you don't know that it's a privilege reserved for courting couples and then only when the banns 'as been read.' **1990** Lord Killanin, quoted in Gerry McNee, *In the Footsteps of 'The Quiet Man'*: 'The holy water font was taken from outside the Catholic Church and placed at the door of the Church of Ireland for the patty-fingers scene.'

pauchle/pachal/pachle etc. [n. & vb., <Sc. *pauchle* (n.), bundle; & cf. Ir. *pachaille* (n.), bunion] (Ulster). 1. [n.]. Stout/thickset/fat/lazy/clumsy/awkward person; incompetent, useless person, as in **the paughle fra Ahoghill** (Co. Antrim); untidy person; timid person; badly done job. **1951** Sam Hanna Bell, *December Bride*: 'The old man, whose eyes had been fixed on the rowers, turned to her …"Pah! That pachel — he's only an ould jinny [q.v.] of a man!"' 2. [vb.]. Walk clumsily/with difficulty; (of child) shuffle about on the bottom.

pauderins [n., <Ir. *paidrín*, rosary]. Rosary beads.

paut [vb., <Sc. *idem*, 'push out the feet alternately when one is lying down; move about gently or leisurely' (CSD), <OE *potian* (vb.), push with the foot] (Ulster). Go about leisurely in stockinged feet (Traynor).

pavee [n., derog., <?]. Itinerant Jewish trader. **1996** Dermot Healy, *The Bend for Home*: 'some of the older fuckers shouted "There's a smell of Healy the pavee. Jew lover! Are you with the pavees now, Healy?"'

pawky [adj., <Sc. *idem*, shrewd, sly] (Ulster). 1. As thus. 2. Easygoing, lazy.

pawny [n., poss. <Hindust. *pani*, water, <returning soldiers in Brit. army, esp.

Munster Fusiliers; or <Shelta *pawnee*, water] (Cork). As thus; rain (Beecher).

pay [n., <Sc. *idem*, pea]. Roe of fish. **1995** Phil O'Keeffe, *Down Cobbled Streets, A Liberties Childhood*: 'Herrings, with the backbone yanked out and the creamy white pay still inside, made crispy eating on Fridays.'

pay on the nail [vb. phr.]. Pay when due. 'This expression had its origin in a custom formerly prevailing in Limerick city...The purchaser of anything laid down the stipulated price or the earnest *on the nail...*' (PWJ). **1967** Seán Jennett, *Munster*: 'in the [Limerick] town museum in Newtown Pery is a pedestal known as the "Nail" on which money was placed to conclude a bargain, a custom from which the saying "pay on the nail" has come; the custom was not confined to Ireland, however'.

peaswisp/beeswisp [n., <Sc. *beeswisp*, 'wild bee's nest on the surface of the ground' (CSD)] (Ulster). 'Small bundle of anything tossed together like a wisp of pea straw' (Patterson). 'Tangled, confused mess' (YDS) as in **your head's like a peaswisp**.

peat [n.] (Ulster). Sod of turf. **1951** Sam Hanna Bell, *December Bride*: '"Sure I've been going to Belfast market ever since I was the height av two peats."'

peata see **pattha**

pech/pegh [vb., <Sc. *idem*, pant, puff, sigh heavily] (Ulster). As thus; breathe heavily; grunt. **1983** W.F. Marshall, *Livin' in Drumlister*, 'John the Liar': 'But there was John, he had his two han's up,/Scared like [q.v.] an' peghin', with no hat or coat...'

peck [vb.]. Eat. **1968** John Healy, *The Death of an Irish Town*: '"We went back to the doss house and there was a meal. I couldn't peck it, cove [q.v.]; anyway I had a rake [see **rake** 1.] of sandwiches me mother made and I pecked them and went to bed."'

peeble [vb., cf. Sc. *wheeple*, 'try to whistle' (CSD)]. Whistle tunelessly.

peedy/peedie [n., <Sc. *peerie* (adj.), small] (Ulster). Small boy's penis. **1992**

Michael Longley, *Irish Review* (Belfast), 'Massive Lovers', Spring/Summer: 'I was the philosopher watching a pair of butterflies/Until massive lovers exposed my peedie and grey hairs'.

peeled egg [n. phr.] (Ulster). Soft job, easy number (CUD).

peeler [n., <Robert Peel, C19 organiser of Brit. and Ir. (1818) police forces. Archaic except in Hib.E, usu. derog.]. Policeman; esp. member of Brit. security forces in Northern Ire. **1989** Tommy McCourt, *Magill*, Aug: 'the cops made a big charge up Rossville Street followed by the Paisleyites. Whole flats just emptied out stuff used as missiles rained on the peelers...' **1994** Dermot Healy, *A Goat's Song*: '"And what I want to know is whether Shamey Coyle shot this peeler?"'

peelgarlic see **pillgarlic**

peely-wally [adj., <Sc. *idem*, pale and sickly-looking] (Ulster). As thus.

peenthrug [n., <?] (Ulster). Nonsensical talk (Traynor).

peeodler [n., cf. Ir. *péadóir*, meddler, trickster, busybody (Dinneen)] (Ulster). Mischievous person. 'He's a peeodler all right. He doesn't know what to be up to...' (Todd).

pee pee! [exclam.]. Call to peafowl, turkeys.

Peep o' Day Boys [nickname, <their daybreak arms searches on Catholics]. Protestant peasant movement, formed at Markethill, Co. Armagh, 4 July 1784. **1973** Hereward Senior in T. Desmond Williams (ed.), *Secret Societies in Ireland*, 'The Early Orange Order 1795–1870': 'More serious were the Peep o' Day Boys who appeared in the 1780s when non-enforcement of the penal code made it possible for Catholics to acquire the arms of disbanded Volunteers.' **1988** R.F. Foster, *Modern Ireland 1600–1972*: 'the government was evidently incapable of disciplining the Protestant "Peep o' Day Boys", who claimed they were simply enforcing the Penal Laws reneged upon by the gentry.'

peerie/peery [n., <Sc. *idem*, pegtop] (Ulster). As thus. **1913** Alexander Irvine,

My Lady of the Chimney Corner: "'M' head's spinnin' 'round like a peerie!" he exclaimed. "Whin did ye ate anything?" asked the sweep. "Yesterday.'"

peetney [n., <'pee']. Urine. **1979** Michael O'Beirne, *Mister, A Dublin Childhood*: 'it seemed awful the day mother had to hold Meg over the pot, and say in a coaxing tone, "Now do your peetney." And "ta [q.v.], ta. Do your ta.'"

peg [n. & vb.]. 1. [n.]. Step. **1980** Séamus de Faoite, *The More we are Together*, 'Pictures in a Pawnshop': "'I wouldn't travel another peg of the road with a fraud. You can see as good as I can," Joe Jack growled.' 2. [vb. trans., cf. *idem*, intrans., move/go vigorously or hastily; 'aim at with a peg or pegtop 1740' (OED)]. Throw; hammer, beat. **1960** John O'Donoghue, *In Kerry Long Ago*: 'He was away from school this day and spent half his time pegging stones at crows...' **1993** Joe Langan in Joe O'Reilly & Sixth Class, Convent School, Edenderry, *Over the Half Door*: "'Who did that to you?" "Miss O'Sullivan." "Well, that's the last time she'll stop with us," and he pegged her suitcase out the door.' Also **pegged** [adj.] (Ulster). Annoyed; in a huff.

Peggy's/Peggie's leg [n., <Eng. dial. *peggy*, wooden implement for stirring washing in a tub]. Stick of boiled sweet. **1943** George A. Little, *Malachi Horan Remembers*: 'Out came the apples and the Peggy's-leg. She chewed, while he stared at his boots.' **1980** Emma Cooke, *Female Forms*: 'The establishment had been the same since the days when he and Carrie used to buy its homemade Peggy's leg.' **1995** Phil O'Keeffe, *Down Cobbled Streets, A Liberties Childhood*: "'A ha'penny bag of Peggie's leg, please."... "No Peggie's leg today," the woman behind the counter peered at me...'

pegh see **pech**

peloothered [p. part. as adj., poss. <play on *floothered* (q.v.)/*polluted* (see **pollute** 3.)]. Intoxicated. **1914** James Joyce, *Dubliners*, 'Grace': "'Yes, yes," said Mr Kernan, trying to remember..."How did

it happen at all?" "It happened that you were peloothered, Tom," said Mr Cunningham gravely. "True bill [q.v.]," said Mr Kernan, equally gravely.'

pelt [n., <*idem*, human skin, joc. & dial. 1605]. As thus; esp. as in **in one's pelt** [adj. phr.]. Stark naked. **C.1830s** Michael Moran, aka Zozimus (q.v.), 'Pharo's Daughter': 'In Agypt's land contaygious to the Nile/Old Pharo's daughter went to bathe in style,/She tuk her dip and came unto the land/And for to dry her royal pelt she ran along the strand...' **Late 1940s–1950s** Trinity College, Dub. lecturer Ernst Scheyer to female student wearing a passremarkable (see **passremarkable** 1.) fur coat: 'Ah, I see you in your pelt!' **1970** Christy Brown, *Down All the Days*: 'no roasting horse-chestnuts on sticks, or lying in their pelts on the big flat boat-shaped slab of rock in the middle of the river'.

penny boy [n. phr.] (Ulster). One at the beck and call of another. **1930** Peadar O'Donnell, *The Knife*: "'Do you think I am a penny boy for Dan Sweeney?" Father Burns said angrily. "You wouldn't be a son of your father if you were."' **1966** Patrick Boyle, *At Night All Cats are Grey*, 'Odorous Perfume her Harbinger': "It beats out," he says, shaking his head slowly. "You'd make a penny-boy out of Solomon himself."' See also **ha'penny boy**.

penny rush [n. phr.]. Cheap children's admission to matinée cinema performances. **1981** Paddy Crosbie, *Your Dinner's Poured Out!*: 'Some people say that the Penny Rush was originally a South [Dub.] City feature in the Abercorn. I do not dispute that, but I can tell them that THE Penny Rush took place every Saturday in the late Teens and early Twenties at the Phoenix Cinema on Ellis Quay...For a penny you were put into either the "Woodeners" [q.v.], the "Cushioners" or the "Upstairs" according to your place in the queue.' See also **twopenny rush**, **fourpenny rush**, **sixpenny rush**.

people's bank [n., euphem.]. Pawn-broker. **1994** Thomas Lyng in Kevin C.

Kearns, *Dublin Tenement Life*: 'It was always called the "people's bank" here in Dublin because the ordinary person could come in and get a few shillings just like that, just by taking off their coat or anything.'

perrigle/perrigal/peoracle [n., <?] (Ulster). 1. Sickly child. 2. Woman who looks a 'sight'.

pet [adj. & n.]. 1. [adj., cf. Ir. *peata* (n.), 'fine day in bad weather' (Dinneen)]. As thus, as in **a pet day**. **1995** Éamon Kelly, *The Apprentice*: 'I like to think of it as a sunny day; a pet day coming to brighten up the countryside after a lot of rain.' 2. [n., <?]. Crust. **1995** Phil O'Keeffe, *Down Cobbled Streets, A Liberties Childhood*: 'We watched carefully as the shop assistants broke the batches of loaves apart, the pet of the bread swelling as the steam escaped and slowly settling back into position.'

Pete Briquette [nickname/stage name]. Pat Cusack, member of the Boomtown Rats rock group, 1975–. **1986** Bob Geldof, *Is That It?*: 'We changed Pat Cusack's name because we thought it sounded too Irish. We made it more Irish. We changed it to Pete Briquette, which was a pun on the fuel cakes made in Ireland from compressed peat.'

Peter the Packer [nickname, <his practice of packing juries]. Peter O'Brien (1842–1914), Lord Chief Justice. **1932** Edward Marjoribanks, *The Life of Lord Carson*: 'Peter O'Brien gained for himself the title "Peter the Packer" by his extensive exercise of the Crown right, under an Irish Juries Act, of directing jurors summoned for criminal cases, when called, to stand aside, and so excluding from the jury-box those who, it was believed, would not under any circumstances convict a prisoner...' **1936** Oliver St John Gogarty, *As I Was Going Down Sackville St*: 'He and I were not on very friendly terms since I had offered in answer to his advertisement for a shooting brake to hold twelve, a seven-seater limousine. "But — " said the agent. "If Peter the Packer can't get twelve into it, who can?"'

Pettigo [prop. n., village, Co. Donegal] as in **go to Pettigo!** (Ulster). Go to Jericho!

pevelling [vb. n., <?] (Ulster). Beating, hammering.

peysle/pisel/picell [vb., cf. Sc. *peist*, work feebly] (Ulster). Work half-heartedly, pretend to work; dither.

phthrough! [exclam.]. Call to a donkey. **1938** Seumas MacManus, *The Rocky Road to Dublin*: 'They posed one another with their prize posers...the spelling of the turf-boy's halt-call to his donkey, Phthrough!...'

piana [n., <Dub. pron. of 'piano'] (Dub.). Cash register. **1977** Flann O'Brien, *The Hair of the Dogma*: '"Sairtantly," the curate [q.v.] said, taking the cheque and walking up with it to the "piana"...' Also **piano** [n.]. Barrel organ. **1945** Patrick Campbell, *Irish Times*, 'An Irishman's Diary', 1 Feb: 'Once he [Mr Royal] hired out "a piano, with a barra [barrow] and an ass, and two birds and a thousand fortunes". It seems the birds handed out the fortunes in their beaks...'

picell see **peysle**

pick [n., <'peck' (vb.)]. 1. Quantity a bird could peck, hence small portion or amount. As in **not a pick (on him)** said of s.o. preternaturally thin. **1993** Sam McAughtry, *Touch & Go*: 'When I tried it [the suit] on she went narrow-eyed, womanlike, studying me. "There's not a pick extra on you and you should be big-made [q.v.]," she said...' 2. Bite (of a fish). **1995** Hannah Mulhall in Mary Ryan et al. (eds), *No Shoes in Summer*: 'He [my father] would let me hold a fishing rod and if I got a pick he would have it in and oh the excitement to get a fish.'

pick and dab [n. phr.] (Ulster). Potatoes and salt. Also **have neither pick nor dab with** [vb. phr.]. Have nothing to do with.

pickering [pres. part., <?]. Expressing amorous interest in (girl) (Moylan).

pickle [n., <Sc. *idem*, grain] (Ulster). Small portion or amount. **1925** Lynn

Doyle, *Dear Ducks*: "'Curse the misbegotten little brute, if it had carried its tail decently out behind like an ordinary dog the divil a pickle [of shot] it would ha' got..."' **1973** Sam Hanna Bell, *A Man Flourishing*: "'He tells me the crop was poor." "Poor?" echoed his uncle. "A jenny-wren [see **jenny**] could have sat on her haunches and ate the top pickle o' grain. It was *that* poor."' See **pick**.

picky [adj., <Ir. *pioc* (vb.), pick, as in *ag piocadh ar an mbia*, picking at food]. Fussy about food; hence **picker** [n.]. Also **pukey** [adj.], **puke/pyock** [n.] (Ulster) in same sense.

picky beds see **piggybeds**

piece [n.] (Ulster). 1. Worker's packed lunch; sandwich etc. **1969** Robert Greacen, *Even without Irene*: 'I went into the scullery, poured out a cup of buttermilk and made myself a big "piece".' **1979** John Morrow, *The Confessions of Proinsias O'Toole*: '[the children] gathered round us on the pavement, howling such unscripted refrains as "Who stole the cheese outa the gravedigger's piece? Francie O'Toole, Francie O'Toole, Francie O'Toole!"' Hence **piece-plate** [n.] sandwich plate; **piece-time** [n.] lunchtime. 2. Person, as in **sore piece** (Ulster). Troublesome person.

pigeon-footed [adj.] (Ulster). Sly, cunning.

pigeon's pair [n. phr.] (Ulster). Family of two children only (Patterson).

pigging [adj.] (Ulster). Very dirty.

piggybeds/picky beds [n. pl.]. Children's street game, played on chalked geometrical designs on pavements by hopping on one foot kicking the 'piggy' from 'bed' to 'bed'. **1975** Eilís Brady, *All In! All In!*: 'An empty shoe-polish or ointment tin makes an ideal piggy. The tin is filled with moist clay to give it weight and then the lid is stamped well down...so that it won't open during play.' **1982** Vincent Caprani, *Rowdy Rhymes and 'Rec-im-itations'*, 'Rememberin'': 'And the freckly mot [q.v.] with the pigtails, and the one called "Bright-eyed Sal"?/'Member them chalkin' their

piggy-beds, and how they raised our hopes/With their easy way of dancin' through the skirl of their skipping ropes?' Also **pickey/pickie (beds) beddies, beds**.

pig-ignorant (q.v.) [adj., intens.]. Very stupid; very boorish. **1965** Lee Dunne, *Goodbye to the Hill*: 'I didn't want him to think I was pig ignorant altogether, even though that's exactly what I was.'

pig iron [n.] as in **just for pig iron** [adv. phr., <low value of a pig or ingot of cast iron first reduced from the ore]. For the hell of it. **1995** Tom Stopford, *Irish Times*, 12 Sept: 'I did attempt to make and bake a fruit cake, just for pig iron, so to speak; and fruit cake is the appropriate term, because the process drove me bananas.'

pig's back [n. phr.], gen. as in **on the pig's back** [adj. phr., <Ir. *ar dhrom na muice*, *idem*, reflecting former importance of the animal as 'the gentleman that pays the rint' — cf. Austral. sl. *on the sheep's back* in same sense]. Enjoying good fortune. **1969** Robert Greacen, *Even without Irene*: 'Someone remarked: "Henry's on the pig's back now." It did not seem to me to be a particularly enviable position, but they seemed to imply that Father had just had a stroke of luck.' **1989** Hugh Leonard, *Out after Dark*: 'I had never in my life experienced such sophistication. It was the sweet life, easy street, clover, the pig's back.' **1995** Michael Finlan, *Irish Times*, 4 Dec: '"If we're given this money, we're on the pig's back," says Joe Kelly...He envisages some 20 or more music students coming into Kiltimagh [Co. Mayo]...'

pig's whisper [n. phr.] (Ulster). Measure of distance; stage whisper.

pillaloo! see **fuillaloo!**

pillgarlic/peelgarlic [n., <clove of garlic]. 1. Bald-headed individual. 2. Gen. term of contempt. **1995** RTÉ Radio, *The Odd Word*, 31 July: 'I was left sitting there like the pillgarlic.' 3. (Ulster). Yellow-complexioned, half-starved/shabbily dressed individual.

pin [n.]. Pioneer (q.v.) pin.

pincher [n.]. Pincers, pliers.

pindy [adj., <?]. Musty, as in **pindy flour** [n. phr.]. 'Flour that has begun to ferment slightly on account of being kept in a warm moist place' (PWJ).

pinhooking [pres. part., <?] (horse racing). Buying foals and selling them as yearlings. **1990** Raymond Smith, *Vincent O'Brien, The Master of Ballydoyle*: 'the little village of Kilsheelan where...he [Phonsie O'Brien] today successfully combines breeding with pinhooking'.

Pink [nickname]. Dublin University sporting colours, abolished 1936. **1936** *Irish Times*, 4 May: 'The "Pink" was instituted in 1927, chiefly through the agency of Mr Terence Millin...It was an effort to get something that would correspond to the "Blue" of Oxford and Cambridge...'

pinkeen [n., <Ir. *pincín*, minnow]. As thus. **1980** Emma Cooke, *Female Forms*: 'Knots of farming people hoping there would be a breeze near the water. A gang of kids chasing pinkeens.' **1986** Padraic O'Farrell, *'Tell me, Sean O'Farrell'*: 'Fishing for pinkeens, using a humble sally rod, twine, bent safety-pin and maggot, provided hours of fun.' See **leebeen**.

Pinkindindies [nickname; 'Lit. a "turkey-cock given to pinking with a rapier"' (DHS)]. Association of C18 bucks (see **buck** 3.). **1795** *Memoirs of Mrs Margaret Leeson, Written by Herself, Vol. II*: 'At that time, Dublin was infested with a set of beings, who, however they might be deemed *gentlemen* by their birth, or connexions, yet, by their actions, deserved no other appellations than that of RUFFIANS. They were then called *Pinking-dindies* [*sic*]...' **1847** John Edward Walsh, *Ireland Sixty Years Ago*: 'Others were known by the soubriquet of Sweaters and Pinkindindies. It was their habit to cut off a small portion of the scabbards of the swords which every one then wore, and prick or "pink" the persons with whom they quarrelled with the naked points...'

pinner [n.]. Gaoler. See **boozle**.

pintle [n., <OE *pintel*, penis, cf. Brit. sl. 'prick'] (Ulster). 'Small, annoying person' (SH).

pioneer [n., <Total Abstinence League, founded 1889, later Pioneer League]. Total abstainer from alcohol. **1994** Dermot Bolger, *A Second Life*: '"The bastard!" my father screamed. "The tight-arsed Pioneer...lapsed–Pioneer, drunken and alcoholic!"' Hence **pioneer pin** [n.]. Insignia of membership. **1997** *Irish Times*, 14 Feb: 'From Clongowes he [Anthony Murphy] brought home two precious things: the coveted Pallas medal for mathematics and a Pioneer pin from a holy man, John Sullivan.' **Put in the pin** [vb. phr.]. Become total abstainer. **1897** *Nenagh Guardian*, Feb: 'Defendant produced a six months' pledge, but the chairman [of Roscrea Petty Sessions] told him the bench did not recognise short certificates. On Cussen promising to "put in the pin" for twelve months, he was let off with a fine of one penny.' Also **pioneer's pour** [n. phr.]. Generous libation of alcohol resulting from lack of practical experience. **1996** Christy Kenneally, *Maura's Boy, A Cork Childhood*: 'Relations bowled in at all hours and reeled out after a sherry or whiskey from Dave's heavy hand. He had a "pioneer's pour".'

piper's invitation, come on the [vb. phr., <Ir. *cuireadh píobaire*, piper's invitation, <welcome traditionally accorded to itinerant pipers]. Come uninvited.

pirta [n., <Ir. *práta*, potato, by metathesis] (Ulster). As thus. **1913** Alexander Irvine, *My Lady of the Chimney Corner*: '"Go on now, guess [what we have for dinner]!" said he. "Pirtas an' broth!" said I. "Yer blinked [see **blink**], ye cabbage head, we've got two yards ov thripe forby!"'

pisel see **peysle**

piseog/pishogue [n., <Ir. *piseog*, charm, spell]. As thus. **1979** Frank Kelly, *The Annals of Ballykilferret*: 'Formerly it was the custom to put hen eggs in a man's haycock to bring him bad luck. This was really the placing of a kind of curse or "pishogue" on the man and his goods.' **1982** Edmund Lenihan, *Long Ago by Shannon Side*: '"There was an old woman

...an' she was steeped in piseogs. She could nearly take the cream out o' the milk...without a separator or anything like that."' **1995** Frank Harte in Mary Ryan et al. (eds.), *No Shoes in Summer.* 'Certain days and dates...one had to be careful about. The 1st of May, "May Day", had quite a list of pishogues attached to it.'

pish [n., <Fr. *pisser* (vb.), urinate] (Ulster). As thus; rain heavily.

pishmire [n., <ME *pissemyre*, ant, <urinous smell of anthill] (Ulster). Irritable individual.

pishogue see **piseog**

piss and vinegar [adj. phr.]. 'Very enthusiastic about your job' (EW).

pissing–time [n. phr., cf. *pissing-while*, C16–mid C19 (DHS), very short time]. As thus. **1995** Brendan O'Carroll, *The Chisellers* (q.v.): '"Mind you, these suites won't last pissing–time," Sean added. "They're not supposed to..."'

piteog [n., <Ir. *idem*, effeminate man]. Man who prys into women's affairs. See also **Molly**.

pitter [n., cf Ir. *práta*, potato] (Ulster). As thus.

pizawn [n., <Ir. *padhsán*, delicate/ complaining person] (Cork). '[S]mall, scrawny individual' (Beecher). **1909** Canon Sheehan, *The Blindness of Dr Gray*: '"what can the childre [*sic*: see **childer**] learn with a *pizawn* like that... who'd rather be oilin' his hair an' gallivantin' wid the girls"'.

plaak [n. & vb., cf. Sc. *playock*, plaything] (Ulster). Antics to amuse children; behave thus.

plabbery [adj., cf. Ir. *plab* (n. & vb.), splash, *plabar/clábar* (n.), mud]. Sloppy. **1922** James Joyce, *Ulysses*: '...Id just go to her and ask her do you love him and look her square in the eyes she couldnt fool me but he might imagine he was and make a declaration with his plabbery kind of manner'.

plack [n., <Sc. *idem*, small Sc. coin, C15–16, poss. <Flem. *placke/plecke*, small

coin]. 1. Farthing, something of low value. **1689** Anon., *The Irish Hudibras*: 'What though of ready [money] ne'er a plack/ Yet many a plugg of good toback/ It cost me to come to dis port.' 2. (Ulster). Mouthful. **1804** James Orr, *Poems on Various Subjects*, 'To the Potatoe': 'With *them* galore, an' whyles a plack/To mak' me frisky,/I'll fen [fend], an' barley freely lack —/Except in whisky.'

plain [n., abbrev. of 'plain porter']. Single strength stout. **1994** Nancy Cullen in Kevin C. Kearns, *Dublin Tenement Life*: 'she had a begging can [see **bagging can**] with a lid on it and she'd say, "Go down to Mr Quinn and tell him to give you a nice creamy gill of plain — and tell him to give me good value"'. See **porter, your only man**.

Plain People of Ireland, the [n. phr.]. Originally without iron. connotation but subverted thus by Myles na gCopaleen (Flann O'Brien). **1919** Eamon de Valera (see **Dev**) to Sinéad de Valera, 19 July: 'the plain people at any rate accept and recognise the Irish Republic.' **1968** Myles na gCopaleen, *The Best of Myles*: '*Myself*:...What trade is that at which a man will succeed only by sticking it? *The Plain People of Ireland (eagerly)*: What is it? *Myself*: Bill-posting. *The Plain People of Ireland*: O HA-HA-HA-HA-HA! (Sounds of thousands of thighs being slapped and the creak of coarse country braces...)' **1991** Tony Gray, *Mr Smyllie, Sir*: 'Anyone in the country who considered a book unsuitable for perusal by the Plain People of Ireland could send it, with the offending passages marked, to the Censorship Board.' **1995** Mr Justice O'Hanlon at UCD seminar, 13 May: '[Fine Gael and Fianna Fáil] had been ready and willing to sell out the moral and religious values of the plain people of Ireland in return for a promise of support from the promoters of the "liberal agenda"...'

plámás/plaumausy [n. & vb., <Ir. *plámás*, flattery, soft talk]. As thus. **1960** John O'Donoghue, *In Kerry Long Ago*: '"God help your head, the man [the priest] had little time for their *plaumausy*

any more than his like do have today when calling on the people that have nothing in their pockets..."' **1969** Tom Mac Intyre, *The Charollais*: "'we are, in no sense, boasting." "Shur I know ye're not, m'lord — I always knew ye'd go places, an' I'm not just plawmassin' ye now."' **1991** Teddy Delaney, *Where we Sported and Played*: 'I was as reluctant as any young fledgling to fly the nest, and when the *plámás* had no effect was told to "shut up outa dat..."'

planet-rain [n., <misunderstanding of Eng. dial. 'rain by planets', rain in one area and not another, as if under planetary influence (CUD)] (Ulster). Short, heavy shower.

plank [n. & vb., cf. *idem* (vb.), 'put down, deposit, plant, colloq. 1859' (OED)]. Cash etc. hidden away for subsequent use; hide away thus. **1996** Christy Kenneally, *Maura's Boy, A Cork Childhood*: 'This [the glass case] was the great untouchable, opened only by adults ...whenever we had visitors. My mother had a "plank" there, a secret stash of cash in a yellow teapot.'

plant [vb., deliver a blow, colloq. pugilistic sl. 1808; cf. also Grose, bury]. **1994** RTÉ TV serial, *Glenroe*, 14 Nov: 'BIDDY Miley, I swear to God if you don't go to sleep I'll plant you.'

planter [n., <plantation of Ulster, C17–18, by Scots & English] (Ulster). Outsider.

plarry [n., cf. Sc. *plorie*, 'piece of ground converted into mud by treading, etc.' (CSD)] (Ulster). Unappetising mess of food.

plasham/playsham/plaisham [n., cf. Ir. *pléiseam*, fool]. Term of abuse. **1927** Peadar O'Donnell, *Islanders*: "'Plasham on ye," Mary Manus retorted: "yer couple of years away in 'Merica spoiled ye..."' **1921** (first published 1983) Patrick MacGill, *Lanty Hanlon*: "'Ye plaisham ye, Manus!" she roared. "It's at home ye should be, tied up with the cows."'

plaster [n.] (Ulster). 1. Unpleasant individual, hypocrite. **1938** Seumas MacManus, *The Rocky Road to Dublin*:

"'To do that [keep him out]," said Long John's Nelly, "we'd have to build up both the doors and the windows." "Well," replied her indignant adviser, "if I was in your place, and afflicted with that plaster, I *would* build them up."' **1966** Patrick Boyle, *At Night All Cats are Grey*, 'The Betrayers': 'the pony sniffed and nuzzled at Cassie's face. "Don't be trying to get round me, you old plaster," she said...' 2. Encumbrance, esp. wife/child, as in **a plaster to one's arse** (Moylan). See also **ma's plaster**, **poultice**.

plastered [p. part. as adj.]. Drunk. **1990** Mary Farragher, quoted in Gerry McNee, *In the Footsteps of 'The Quiet Man'*: 'When I look out of the kitchen window I swear I can still see Barry [Fitzgerald] standing there as though he was plastered with the drink, rocking backwards and forwards on his heels.'

Plastered Saints [nickname, see **plastered**, <their frequently meeting in pubs; play on 'plaster saints']. Group of Dub.-based individuals (Fr Austin Flannery, Seán Mac Réamoinn, Louis McRedmond *et al.*) interested in post-Vatican II Catholic theology, ecumenics, etc., 1960s.

plastic Paddies [nickname]. Children of first-generation Ir. immigrants in Britain. **1996** Nuala O'Faolain, *Irish Times*, 17 Feb: 'There are many kinds of London-Irish — the ones who came with cardboard suitcases and broken hearts in the old days; the modern ones, who happen to be in London but might be in Paris or New York; and the "plastic Paddies"...who are mostly like the urban young anywhere.'

plausey/plauzy/plossey [n. & adj., <Ir. *plásaí* (n.), flatterer, plausible individual, wheedler]. [n.]. As thus. [adj.]. Flattering, cajoling. **1943** George A. Little, *Malachi Horan Remembers*: 'After bedding the horse, and the women had got shut of the plausey talk, Kitty found herself sitting down...'

play-boy/playboy [n.]. Fun-loving scamp. **1879** Charles J. Kickham, *Knocknagow*: 'Phil Lahy commenced to laugh...."Mat," said he, " you wor always a play-boy." "The divil a much of a play-boy in id," returned Mat, "I'm only tellin' you to keep your eyes open."' **1960** John O'Donoghue, *In Kerry Long Ago*: 'playboys were often said to pour strong tobacco water into the porter [q.v.] at such a time as this, to put a hurry on the strawboys' [see **straw**] journey home...'

play puck [vb. phr., see **puck** 1.]. Cause confusion, havoc. **1995** 'Drapier', *Irish Times*, 23 Dec: 'Already, however, the battle lines for the next election are being drawn up...though events, as we all know, can play puck with the best-laid plans.'

playsham see **plasham**

pleesbeen [n., <Ir. *plispín*, insignificant, worthless person/thing]. As thus. **1914** George Fitzmaurice, *The Pie-Dish*: 'JOHANNA Don't be giving me talk, you little pleesbeen, and your grandfather in a settle-bed on the kitchen floor!'

plenish [vb., <OF *plenir*, fill]. Furnish a house. Hence **plenishing/plenishment** [n.]. Sticks of furniture; domestic supplies. See **gowpen**.

plerauca [n., <Ir. *pléaráca*, revelry, high jinks]. As thus.

plocker see **plugher**

ploid as in **ploid on you!** [exclam., cf. Ir. *piolóid ort*, deuce take you (Dinneen)]. As thus. **1927** Peadar O'Donnell, *Islanders*: '"Mush [see **amossa**], ploid on ye, Manus, but yer clean gone! He's fair light in the head [q.v.] smokin' tay [tea]," his wife pleaded...'

ploodacha [adj., cf. Ir. *plodaigh/plódaigh* (vb.), crowd, throng] (Ulster). Full (of drink).

plossey see **plausey**

plout [n. & vb., <Sc. *idem*, splash, fall] (Ulster). [n.]. Dip, swim; bubbling of boiling water; sudden heavy shower. [vb.]. Take a dip; boil vigorously.

plouter/plowter [vb., <Sc *plowter*, wade through mud, walk awkwardly or slovenly (CSD)] (Ulster). As thus.

pluck [n., <Ir. *pluc*: (n.) (rounded) cheek; (vb.) stuff, puff one's cheeks, cram]. (Rounded) cheek; mouthful, snack, light meal. **1922** James Joyce, *Ulysses*: 'Cissy Caffrey bent over him to tease his fat little plucks and the dainty dimple in his chin.'

plugher/plocker [n., cf. Ir. *plúch* (vb.), choke; *plúchadh* (n.), asthma] (Ulster). 1. Noisy clearing of the throat. **1948** John O'Connor, *Come Day — Go Day*: '"There you are," he cried. "Sixty-five in a lock [q.v.] of days and as supple" — a plocker of coughing seized him...' 2. Smoke-filled atmosphere.

plump [n. & vb.] (Ulster). 1. [n. & vb., <Sc. *idem*, heavy shower, rain heavily, <ME *plompe* (vb.), fall down]. As thus. 2. [n. & vb., onomat.]. Act of boiling vigorously: 'I gave the pratas [see **praties**] a plump' (CUD); boil vigorously. Hence figurative. **1938** Seumas MacManus, *The Rocky Road to Dublin*: '"Chile, dear, while I'm selling this baste take care if you open your mouth again not to put both your feet in it, and then plump yourself afther."' 3. [vb. onomat.]. Shoot a marble.

plunk [vb., poss. <'flunk'] (Ulster). Fail an examination.

Plunket-street [prop. n.] as in **strip a peg in Plunket-street** [catchphrase, <location of old clothes market] (Dub.). Dress in second-hand clothes. **Late C18** Anon., 'Lord Altham's Bull': 'De Mosey [q.v.] took down Plunket-street/Where de clothes on de pegs were hanging...'

pock [n.] (Ulster). Smallpox.

podger [n., poss. <'podge'/'pudge', 'anything short and thick' (OED) + endearment suffix]. Short, thick cudgel. **1887** Anon., quoted by R. Henchion in *Cork Centenary Remembrancer 1887–1987* (1986): 'The glint of sunshine on [a sword] was the spark that fired the tinder under the simmering cauldron of emotionalism, for hidden podgers and shillelaghs [q.v.], ash plants and paling posts were uncovered...to flay the peelers [q.v.].'

podgreen [n., <Ir. *Pádraigín*, little Patrick]. Term of contempt. **1903**

George Moore, *The Untilled Field*: "'Is it Jimmy Welsh you are asking — the podgreen at the other side of Michael?'" See also **pateen**.

podion ball [n. phr., obsc.] (Ulster). Large hard ball.

podreen [n., <Ir. *paidrín*, rosary beads, 'bead string of any kind' (Dinneen)]. Small potato (on a stalk) (OTF).

pogled/poggled [p. part. as adj., originally milit. sl. <Hindust. *pagal* (n.), madman, idiot] (Ulster). Crazy; very tired.

póg mo thón [catchphrase, Ir. *idem*, kiss my arse]. See also **K.M.R.I.A.**

point [n.] as in **potatoes and point** [n. phr., joc.] (Ulster). Meal of potatoes only: 'each person, before taking a bite, *pointed* the potato at a salt herring or a bit of bacon hanging in front of the chimney: but this is mere fun' (PWJ).

poitín see **poteen**

poke [n. & vb.] (Ulster). 1. [n., <ON *poki*, bag]. Bag, sack, wallet, pocket. Hence **poke-shakings** [n.]. Last pig in litter; youngest child of large family. See **shake of the bag**. 2. Ice cream cone; cone-shaped bag for sweets etc. **1948** John O'Connor, *Come Day — Go Day*: 'In about quarter of an hour they emerged again onto the footpaths, carrying four penny, brown paper pokes of chips.' **1996** Ulster TV, commercial for Schuster's (US) ice cream, June: '*[American voice:]* Now you can even get it from the store in a poke — whatever that is.' Hence **poke-man**, **poke-van** for ice cream seller, van. See also **to-sheen**. 3. [n. & vb., <?]. Stoop.

police clothes [n. phr.]. Free second-hand clothing distributed by the police to the poor. **1994** Mary Doolan in Kevin C. Kearns, *Dublin Tenement Life*: 'And police clothing, I got them meself. You went to an old stable for them...and they'd hand it out to you. They'd look at them (children) and say, "Here, that'll fit him." A jumper and old shirt and trousers... dirty. *Horrible* dirt.'

polish [n.]. 'Speech smacking of insincerity' (Moylan).

pollock [vb., <?]. Cheat, trick. **1797** *Memoirs of Mrs Margaret Leeson, Written by Herself, Vol. III*: 'A Mr S—t—y, a hungry-looking dog, son of a Cabinet-maker, lived with me on the Rock road [Dub.] for a few months as my favourite Paramour; during which time he by degrees *pollocked* (to use a new phrase for cozening or tricking one), me out of considerable sums of money...'

poll talk [n. phr., <ME *polle*, nape of the neck, 1671]. Backbiting.

pollute [n. & vb.]. 1. [n.] (Ulster). Visitor who comes too often. 2. [vb.]. Pester. 3. [p. part. as adj.]. Very drunk. **1991** Roddy Doyle, *The Van*: '"All ages," he told them. "Polluted out of their heads."'

polly [n., <'poll']. Hornless cow. **1927** Peadar O'Donnell, *Islanders*: 'That very evening Mary Manus came over to say they were going to sell their polly: they were short of grass for her.' See also **pow**.

pollywoggle [n., cf. Sc. *pollywag*, tadpole]. As thus. **1995** Aidan Higgins, *Donkey's Years*: 'The tadpoles devour one another indiscriminately, feeling no pain, working up from the tail...Rita Phelan calls them pollywoggles.'

polter/poulter/powter [vb., <Sc. *pouter/powter*, work in a careless manner, potter about] (Ulster). As thus. **1991** Shane Connaughton, *The Run of the Country*: '"So she wants me to stay with her. I'm going to. I don't mind. I like polterin' about the place."'

polthogue/palltog [n. & adv., <Ir. *paltóg*, blow, thump, poss. <Eng. dial. *poult* (vb.), beat, strike (DOM)]. [n.]. As thus. [adv.]. Hell for leather. **C.1948** Michael Tunney, 'The Rollicking Boys around Tandragee': 'Have you e'er seen an Irishman dancing palltog/How he faces his partner and turns up his brog...'

poly [vb., <?] (Ulster). Shoot a marble by flicking the thumb over the forefinger (CUD).

poms [n. pl., <?]. Dancing shoes. **1995** Phil O'Keeffe, *Down Cobbled Streets, A Liberties Childhood*: 'we slung our black dancing poms over our shoulders and set off for our lesson. As we walked through

the dark brooding streets around the Guinness complex, the clatter of our black chrome-buckled hornpipe shoes echoed off the frowning buildings.'

ponny [n., <?] (Cork). Enamel or tin mug used in primary schools for free milk. **1996** Christy Kenneally, *Maura's Boy, A Cork Childhood*: 'When we went to the yard for our break, we got an aluminium "ponny" of watery milk and a dry bun.' Also **ponger** (Ulster) in same sense. **1991** Shane Connaughton, *The Run of the Country*: 'In the house, to quench their thirst they drank buttermilk in pongers...'

pooch/pouch [vb., <'poach', <palat. form of 'poke']. Poke around, idle. **1925** Liam O'Flaherty, *The Informer*: '"Then I began to pouch about makin' ready to go to bed..."' **1985** Máirín Johnston, *Around the Banks of Pimlico*: 'There was usually someone able to pooch around and find a shop that had just got in paraffin oil, tea or butter...' **1986** Padraic O'Farrell, *'Tell me, Sean O'Farrell'*: 'If she heard you had stopped working, she shouted: "If you go sweep, sweep, but if you go pooch, come down."'

poogh [n., <?, poss. onomat.] (Ulster). Puff.

pook [n.] (Ulster). 1. [<Sc. *idem*, 'pull with nimbleness or force; pull gently' (CSD)]. Nudge to attract attention. 2. [<?]. Grain of wood. Also **short in the pook** [adj. phr.]. Quick to burn, hence quick-tempered.

pookapyle [n., <Ir. *púca*, see **pookey**]. Toadstool, poisonous fungus.

pookawn [n., <Ir. *púcán*, open boat carrying mainsail & jib]. As thus. **1945** Robert Gibbings, *Lovely is the Lee*: 'He might be for part of a day with Pat Corcoran in his pookawn...'

pookeen [n., <Ir. *púic*, blind over the eyes]. Game of blind man's buff.

pookey/pookie (man) [n., <Ir. *púca*, pooka, malignant spirit]. 1. Bogey man; fairies in general. **1960** John O'Donoghue, *In Kerry Long Ago*: 'These brown robed-figures [monks] moved silently from one place to another like animated mummies...Their habits looked exactly like the ones I had seen upon the dead laid out at wakes. "Now at last I am among the pookies," I thought...' **1992** Brian Leyden, *Departures*: '"Off with you now, before it gets dark," she would gesture with her stick. "Before the pookey man gets you."' 2. Term of contempt. **1961** Tom Murphy, *A Whistle in the Dark*: 'HARRY ...I could tell him stories better than that about what we done. He's not like you pookies. Eh, Dessie?'

pooley/poolie [n.] as in **do pooley** [vb. phr.]. Urinate. **1939** James Joyce, *Finnegans Wake*: 'Lynd us your blessed ashes here till I scrub the canon's underpants. Flow now. Ower more. And pooleypooley.' **1981** Paddy Crosbie, *Your Dinner's Poured Out!*: 'Mr Dooley/Done his pooley/Up against his sister's garden wall.' **1995** Aidan Higgins, *Donkey's Years*: 'I draw stick-men with straight lines for arms and legs...with vacant expressions stamped on their faces. "Can you do pooley?" Nurse O'Reilly asks us.'

poor mouth [n. phr., <Ir. *béal bocht* (q.v.), *idem*]. Persistent complaint of poverty. **1908** Lynn Doyle, *Ballygullion*: 'Ye had only to go an' make a poor mouth to Sammy and he'd ha' give ye the coat off his back.' **1982** Éamonn Mac Thomáis, *Janey Mack* (q.v.), *Me Shirt is Black*: 'Willie [Walsh] and Johnny [Claudius Beresford] got drinking one night and began making the poor mouth to one another. "Lookit [see **looka'**]," said Johnny, "I brought over James Gandon to build the Custom House..."' **1995** Declan Lynch, *Sunday Independent*, 3 Dec: 'They [the anti-divorce faction] argued that the entire political establishment was against them...They played the poor mouth despite mounting a well-funded, highly devious, and very effective campaign...'

pooshie see **pushie**

Pope, the [nickname]. Eoin O'Mahony (1904–70), one of the last of the great eccentrics. **1951** 'The Bellman', *Bell*, 'Meet the Pope', Jan: '"The Pope" halts abruptly in his *monologue extérieur*. For a full ten minutes he has been utterly unconscious, it seems, of the fact that it has been snowing so thickly that he is now so like a subfusc silver-spangled Santa Claus that children are crowding round us...' **1981** Brendan Behan, *After the Wake*: '...*The Marseillaise* sung by the choir of Trinity scholars in the version attributed to its distinguished alumnus known as The Pope'. **1988** Henry Boylan, *A Dictionary of Irish Biography*: 'of the various accounts of how he acquired the nickname, probably the most reliable ascribes it to a remark he made while a schoolboy at Clongowes... taken (mistakenly) to show an ambition to be Pope'.

popehead [n.] (Ulster). Roman Catholic, derog. **1994** Dermot Healy, *A Goat's Song*: 'Then the girls learned at school how their father had been teaching manners to the popeheads.'

poppy [n.]. 1. Hole in stocking. **1995** Phil O'Keeffe, *Down Cobbled Streets, A Liberties Childhood*: '"You've a poppy in your stocking." The poppy would have grown bigger as we struggled home, the hand-knitted stitches loose and rambling.' 2. (children's usage). Potato. **1996** Christy Kenneally, *Maura's Boy, A Cork Childhood*: '"Maura, will you call to Billy's for me? Three chump chops and two centre loins...The poppies in Annie's are like balls of flour.' Also **pop-pop** in same sense.

poreen/poureen [n., <Ir. *póirín*, small potato]. As thus.

porridge [n.]. Confusion, mix-up. **1995** Seán O'Rourke, RTÉ Radio news, 12 Sept: 'In Wicklow something of a porridge took place yesterday in Fianna Fáil...'

porter [short for 'porter's ale', 'porter's beer', from association with porters and other labourers]. 'Single X' Guinness, formerly a weaker, and cheaper, brew than Guinness XX. Colloq. applied to stout in general. **1966** Patrick Boyle, *At Night All Cats are Grey*, 'Oh Death Where Is Thy Sting-aling-aling': '"There'll be no porter posing as stout in this house if I can help it."' Also **loose porter** (Munster). Draught stout. **1994**

Con Houlihan, *Rose of Tralee Souvenir Programme*, 'The Wine of the Country': 'At a small farmer's threshing, this [the drink] usually consisted of bottled stout; a big farmer might have a few barrels; the drink was served in mugs and was called "loose porter", though of course it was stout.' Also known as plain (q.v.), abbrev. of 'plain porter'. See also **your only man**.

poss out [vb. trans., <*idem*, beat or stamp clothes in water 1611, <OF *pousser*, push]. Wash. **1970** Christy Brown, *Down All the Days*: '"Sean — you blondey bastard — keep out while I poss out the floor! You have me heart broke..."' **1995** Phil O'Keeffe, *Down Cobbled Streets, A Liberties Childhood*: 'She was a generous and loving person and did not mind at all all the slopping and possing out of baby clothes...' Hence **possing wet** [adj.]. Very wet. **1922** James Joyce, *Ulysses*: 'when she undid the strap she cried out, holy saint Denis, that he was possing wet and to double the half blanket the other way under him'.

potash [n., <Fr. *potage*, soup, confused with 'potash' (common fertiliser)]. Stew. **1942** Eric Cross, *The Tailor and Ansty*: 'the wife had brought up a grand [q.v.] "potash" of pig's head and cabbage and potatoes'.

potato trap [n.]. 'Mouth. Shut your potatoe trap and give your tongue a holiday' (Grose).

poteen/poitín [n., <Ir. *poitín*, little pot]. Illicit whiskey. **1933** (of incident in the 1820s) Eamonn O'Tuathail (ed.), *Munterloney Folk Tales*: 'Up in the morning early and off to Mass. And when we came back we invited a few of the neighbours in and we had the two quarts of poitín and all in all we had some crack [see **crack** 1.] that Christmas.' **1942** Eric Cross, *The Tailor and Ansty*: 'There was this man who was bringing a load on a cart from Cork to Macroom and it must have been a ton weight. And he saw that his horse...was failing, but he really wanted to get to Macroom that night. Well, he had a bottle of poitín with him, and he put it back into the horse,

and she was as lively as could be for another piece of the road.' **1978** John McGuffin, *In Praise of Poteen*: 'County Antrim was the scene, in 1965, of two deaths attributed to poitín. This has led to the kind of hysterical generalisation that is frequently made by the popular press that "if you drink poitín you'll go blind or die or both".' Also **poteen-twang** [n. phr.]. Lie; ability to lie persuasively. See also **mountain dew**.

pothologue [n., cf. Ir. *potúil* (adj.), pot-like]. Fat child. **1960** John O'Donoghue, *In Kerry Long Ago*: '"The same *pothologue* of a child grew up a fine young man by all accounts."'

pot-walloper [n.]. Female domestic servant, slavey, derog. **1948** Patrick Kavanagh, *Tarry Flynn*: '"The dirty pot-walloper," she was referring to Molly now, "sure it's not that I'd care a hair [see **hide nor hair**] if you had to keep away from her."' **1965** Lee Dunne, *Goodbye to the Hill*: 'Doogan was already up there, drinking orange with a mot [q.v.] who was a pot-walloper if ever I saw one.' Hence **pot-wallop** [vb.] in same sense. **1921** (first published 1983) Patrick MacGill, *Lanty Hanlon*: 'All the pot-walloping scum of the market gurgled in.'

pouce/pouse [n., <Fr. *pousse*, dust] (Ulster). Flax-dust. Hence **poucy** [adj.]. Dusty, untidy, gen. derog. term. **1966** Florence Mary McDowell, *Other Days Around Me*: 'there were still those who preferred a hard life out-of-doors to being condemned to a "poucy" indoor life'.

pouch see **pooch**

poulter see **polter**

poultice [n.] (Ulster). Hypocrite; 'unwelcome person who sticks around' (YDS). **1977** Sam McAughtry, *The Sinking of the Kenbane Head*: '...I approved of her. She was brisk and matter-of-fact and she wasn't a poultice, like the other girls in our street.' See also **plaster**.

pounder [n.] (Ulster). 'Person who sold pounded freestone' (CUD) as in **plain as a pounder** [adj. phr.]. Very unhandsome. **1995** Shane Connaughton, *A Border Diary*: 'Their looks didn't help.

They were as plain as pounders. Men came from England to court them, but they never stayed long.'

poundies [n. pl.]. Potatoes mashed with butter. **1927** Peadar O'Donnell, *Islanders*: 'He went in. The mother was peeling potatoes, making poundies for the supper.'

poureen see **poreen**

pouse see **pouce**

pow [n., <'poll'] (Ulster). (Bald) head. See also **polly**.

power [n., <*idem*, large number or quantity 1661 (OED)] as in **a power of**. Large quantity of; great deal of. **1907** J.M. Synge, *The Shanachie* (q.v.), 'The People of the Glens': '"I had a power of children," an old man, who was born in Glenmalure, said to me once.' **1946** Mervyn Wall, *The Unfortunate Fursey*: '"It's a fine building," said the friar, adding thoughtlessly, "it must have cost a power of wealth to build."' Hence **powerful** [adj.]. **1943** George A. Little, *Malachi Horan Remembers*: '"Talking of coaches a minute ago brings to my mind the old steam-trams that took their place. They were a powerful invention."' Also **more power to your elbow!** [exclam. phr.]. Expression of approval/admiration/ encouragement; good on you! (q.v.).

powter see **polter**

pracus/prackus/prockus [n., <Ir. *prácás*, hotchpotch, mess]. As thus, esp. of food on a plate. **1913** Alexander Irvine, *My Lady of the Chimney Corner*: '"M' legs an' feet wor as stiff and shtrait as th' legs ov thim tongs in yer chimley. Och [q.v.], but it's the prackus I was from top t' toe!"'

praties [n. pl., <Ir. *práta(i)*, potato(es)]. As thus. Also **preys** (Ulster).

prawb [n., <Ir. *práib*, soft mass, mush]. As thus. **1991** James Kennedy, *The People who Drank Water from the River*. 'There was a lot of prawb (a messy job with the hands) in filling [black] puddings.'

prawg see **prog**

pree [vb., <Sc. *prieve*, prove, taste] (Ulster). Partake of, taste. **1844** Robert

Huddleston, *A Collection of Poems and Songs on Rural Subjects*, 'The Lammas Fair (Belfast)': 'Here's yellow-man [q.v.] an' tuffy sweet,/Girls will ye taste or pree it...'

Premier County, the [nickname, poss. <prominence of resident Butler family]. Tipperary, esp. in GAA games context. **1996** Enda McEvoy, *Sunday Tribune*, 7 July: 'Having failed in the recent past to win Munster titles with some indisputably talented teams, the Premier County now stand more or less an even chance...'

price of as in **the price of me** [n. phr.]. Just deserts, all I am worth/good for. **1980** Bernard Farrell, *Canaries*: 'FERGUS Is this really Marie's father? RICHARD Yes. An absolute wizard at cards. TOMMY They're going to call the police — it'll be the price of him if he's jailed.' **1989** Hugh Leonard, *Out after Dark*: '"Well, that's the price of me," she said, "oul' eejit [q.v.] that I am, for being soft with you..."' **1996** Brendan Glacken, *Irish Times*, 25 Jan: 'It will be the full price of the critic quoted above if he begins to hear Kon's "disembodied mutterings"...'

Prick with the Stick, the [nickname]. Statue of James Joyce, Dub. See **the Hags with the Bags**.

prickles [n. pl.] (Ulster). Gooseflesh.

priested [p. part.]. Ordained in the Roman Catholic Church.

priesteen [n., <'priest' + Ir. dimin. *ín*]. Little priest, derog. **1995** Tom Widger, *Sunday Tribune*, 22 Jan: 'We are told, for example, that in the early 1930s she [Caitlín Thomas] danced at ceilidhs [q.v.] with "no knickers under her skirt and did cartwheels". Now that was bound to attract attention, if it was true. But where, I hear you ask, was the prieshteen with the hawthorn shtick?' See also **sogarteen**.

priest's share [n. phr.]. Soul (PWJ).

prig [vb., <?, originally thieves' cant, pilfer] (Ulster). 1. Haggle, bargain. 2. Pilfer.

prime [adj. & adv.] (Ulster). First class, excellent.

privities [n. pl.]. Private parts. **1797** *Memoirs of Mrs Margaret Leeson, Written by Herself, Vol. III*: 'poor C— found his *privities* extremely chilled, which caused him in a paroxism of rage to throw the well sluced peruke [which had been pissed in and thrust into his breeches] into a running brook at the bottom of the garden'.

prockus see **pracus**

Prod/Proddie/Proddy [abbrev. (+ endearment suffix), derog.]. Protestant. **1963** Leslie Daiken, *Out Goes She* (Dub. street rhymes): 'Proddy Proddy ring the bell/Call the soupers [q.v.] back from Hell.' **1994** Ferdia Mac Anna, *The Ship Inspector*: '...Mrs Donovan appeared in front of me, expression grim and knowing. "Trust a Proddie to come back from the dead," she said.' Also **Proddie-dog/Proddywoddy/Proddywhoddy** in same sense. **N.d.** Cork children's rhyme: 'Proddy Woddy Green Guts/ Never said a Prayer,/Take him by the long coats/And throw him down the stairs!' **1961** Dominic Behan, *Teems of Times and Happy Returns*: 'All Protestants were rich and wore good clothes and didn't play in the streets. They were sissies, and when the fellas saw them coming over the bridge from Jones Road they used to shout "Proddie Dog"...' **1970** Christy Brown, *Down All the Days*: '"Proddywhoddy, go home!" they chanted ...Bloody poxy Proddywhoddy! He doesn't believe in the Virgin Mary, boys!"' **1989** Hugh Leonard, *Out after Dark*: '"Only don't let them know you're a Catholic. If they [the Orangemen] ask you, say you're a Proddy-dog."'

prog/prawg [n. & vb., cf. Sc. *idem*, probe, prod, prick & Eng. sl. *idem* (vb.), 'poke about for food' (DHS)] (Ulster). 1. [n. & vb.]. As thus. **1908** Lynn Doyle, *Ballygullion*: '"What's to be done?" sez he, afther he'd progged it for five minits. "I'm clane bate."' 2. [vb.]. Look for a bargain (SH). Hence **on the prog** [adj. phr.] looking around for something, esp. food; **progger** [n.] scrounger. 3. [vb.]. Steal apples from an orchard.

proogy! [exclam., <Sc. *proochy*, call to young calf] (Ulster). As thus.

proper order [catchphrase]. Just right/ I should think so. **1989** Hugh Leonard, *Out after Dark*: '"Proper order," Holy God said..."It may be only a tenner, but it's one bit of hookery [see **hook**] he won't be let get away with..."'

Protestant herring [n. phr.] (Munster). 'Originally applied to a bad or stale herring: but in my boyhood...applied, in our neighbourhood, to almost anything of an inferior quality: "Oh that butter is a Protestant herring"' (PWJ).

prough/prugh/pruck [n. pl., cf. Sc. *pruch*, perks] (Ulster). Material possessions, esp. illegally come by; free gifts.

proughal/proughle [n. & vb., <?] (Ulster). 1. [n.]. **1983** Polly Devlin, *All of us There*: 'a derisive term for a person who has failed to do something he or she has boasted to do'. 2. [vb.]. Move about awkwardly.

pruck/prugh see **prough**

prug prug! [exclam.]. Call to cows to come in for milking. See **chook chook!**

pubickers [n. pl., <'pubic' + endearment suffix]. Pubic hair. **1995** *Sunday Tribune*, 5 Nov: 'He [Niall Toibín] acknowledges Dublin wit by way of a claim made by Jimmy Bourke, who ran a theatrical costumiers, that [Micheál MacLiammóir's: see **the Boys** 2.] mysterious wig "was made from his own pubickers".'

puce pencil [n., <perceived colour of lead]. Indelible pencil. **1953** Frank O'Connor, *The Stories of Frank O'Connor*, 'My Da': 'He had a little twopenny [notebook] he wrote his commissions in with a bit of puce pencil he wet with his tongue...'

puck [n. & vb.]. 1. [n. & vb., <Ir. *poc*, short, sudden blow, esp. of ball in hurling]. As thus. **1979** Frank Kelly, *The Annals of Ballykilferret*: 'The account of the aforegoing happenings was passed between the philosophers and wits of Ballykilferret to the accompaniment of sniggers and sharp little pucks in the ribs, which are known as "puckin".' **1991** James Kennedy, *The People who Drank Water from the River*: 'Few days passed without a puck around [with a hurley] in the paddock or on the road in front of the house.' See also **play puck**. 2. [n., <Ir. *poc*, 'bag, pack or "puck"' (Dinneen)]. Large quantity, ample sufficiency. **1965** Lee Dunne, *Goodbye to the Hill*: '"Like the two pound you gave me when you told that cock–and–bull story about the suit you brought back from your holiday, and you with pucks of money in your pocket.' See also **tucks**.

Puck [nickname, <Ir. *poc*, billy goat]. Annual festival, Killorglin, Co. Kerry, at which a goat is crowned king of the revels; the goat itself. **1932** Seán O'Faoláin, *Midsummer Night Madness and Other Stories*, 'The End of the Record': 'I often walked from Dublin to Puck, and that's a hundred miles, without ever disturbing anything but a hare or a snipe.'

puckawn [n., <Ir. *pucán*, small billy goat]. Man who smells.

pucker [n.]. 1. [<*idem*, 'state of agitation or excitement (colloq.) 1741' (OED)]. 1. Panic, contretemps. **1991** John B. Keane, *Love Bites and Other Stories*: 'He was a strong hardy fellow, a relation of my wife's. Just as he drew abreast of us, I seized him by the belt of his overcoat and allowed myself to be dragged out of an otherwise imponderable pucker.' **1995** John James McManus in Mary Ryan et al. (eds.), *No Shoes in Summer*: 'By the time he arrived I was in a bit of a pucker ...My wife said to pour a glass of whiskey for myself and my brother...' 2. [cf. Ir. *pocaire*, fragment]. Minnow, small fish. See **gubog**.

pudding, break a see **break a pudding**

puddockstool/paddockstool/puddock-steel [n., see **paddocksteel**, with which it is confused] (Ulster). Toadstool. **1979** Jack McBride, *Traveller in the Glens* (of Antrim): 'If you are in the Nine Glens at mushroom time, you may be warned not to pull "puddockstools"...but you may be excused for not knowing the difference between a "puddockstool" and a "puddocksteel" [*sic*] (mushroom).' See **paddy hat**.

pudge [n., <?]. Pulp. '"As soft as pudge" is a common expression' (OTF).

puithernawl [vb., cf. Ir. *púitseáil* (n.), act of rummaging]. To be busy with trifles. **1960** John O'Donoghue, *In Kerry Long Ago*: "'He's not inclined to do a single thing in his spare time only *puithernawling* with old music boxes when 'tis cutting a handful of litter he should be...'"

puke/pyock [n., <Ir. *pioc* (vb.), pick, as in *ag piocadh ar an mbia*, picking at food]. 1. (Ulster). Supercilious person. 2. 'Poor, unhealthy-looking person' (PWJ). 3. See **picky**.

pullaloo! see **fuillaloo!**

pull a stroke see **stroke** 3.

pulling a/the cord [vb. phr.]. Courting. **1879** Charles J. Kickham, *Knocknagow*: "'An' so far as goin' on goes, I'd say 'tis Miss Anne an' himse'f that's pulling the coard.'"

pulling the devil by the tail [vb. phr.]. Living on one's wits; existing at the margins; surviving/getting by. **1914** James Joyce, *Dubliners*, 'Two Gallants': 'He was tired of knocking about, of pulling the devil by the tail, of shifts and intrigues.' **1995** Shane Connaughton, *A Border Diary*: 'Like all actors, David [Kelly] put a poor mouth [q.v.] on it. "Oh you know, just pulling the divil by the tail."'

pullogue [n., <Ir. *poll*, hole + dimin. *óg*]. Apples stolen and hidden (PWJ).

pulse [n.] as in **my pulse** [term of endearment, <Ir. *mo chuisle, idem*]. My dear/darling. **1924** Liam O'Flaherty, *Spring Sowing*, 'Going into Exile': "'Now mother, what's the good of this work?" "No, you are right, my pulse," she replied quietly.' See **macushla**.

pumpture [n. & vb.] (Ulster). Puncture, tyre trouble. **1991** Shane Connaughton, *The Run of the Country*: "'The feckers [see **feck** (vb.) 2.]. Last time they pumptured all our bicycles.'"

punkawn [n., <Ir. *poncán*, Yankee (derog.)]. Talkative, self-assertive person. **1943** George A. Little, *Malachi Horan Remembers*: "'They were a comical sight. I remember well, and I only a 'punkawn' of a chap, seeing them pass and I at the head of the gravel pit.'"

puntam [n., <Ir. *idem*, 'lively person, esp. a woman of low stature' (Dinneen)]. As thus.

purty [adj., <'pretty' by metathesis]. As thus. **1960** Edna O'Brien, *The Country Girls*: 'What do you think of, Hickey, when you're thinking?" "Dolls. Nice purty little wife. Thinking is a pure cod [q.v.].'" Hence **purties** [n. pl.]. Little gifts for a girl.

push [n.]. 1. Scrape, difficulty. 2. Assistance, encouragement. **1990** John McGahern, *Amongst Women*: "'Would you like us to tie the sheaves, Daddy?" Mona asked. "That'd be a great push,"' he said.'

pusheen [n.]. 1. [<'puss' + Ir. dimin. *ín*]. Kitten; affect. term for cat. 2. [n. pl., <pushing motion associated with use]. Slippers. Also **pushers** in same sense.

pushie/pooshie [n.] (Ulster). 1. [<Ir. *pus*, mouth, see **puss** 1.]. One who takes offence easily; timorous person. **1966** Patrick Boyle, *At Night All Cats are Grey*, 'Oh Death Where Is Thy Sting-aling-aling': "'Your sister is a right [see **right** 1.] pooshey," he said. "The clergy have the living daylights frightened out of her."' 2. [<'puss', cat + endearment suffix]. Call to a cat; effeminate man.

puss [n., vb. & nickname]. 1. [n., <Ir. *pus*, mouth; sulky expression]. As thus; sulk. **1960** John O'Donoghue, *In Kerry Long Ago*: 'trying to console him, while on the verge of sulking at the same time ...I went west to the hayshed with a puss on me and pulled a handful of hay.' **1988** John Waters, *Magill*, Sept: 'He [the Taoiseach (Prime Minister)]...apparently amuses himself by looking out the window at them [members of the Doheny & Nesbitt School of Economists (q.v.)] arriving in to work and shouting out things like "Wouldya look at the long puss on that fellow?"' **1991** Roddy Doyle, *The Van*: "'But then you put this puss on yeh — it's not my fault we've no fuckin' money for your fuckin' Christmas cards!'" Hence **pussful** [n.]. Mouthful. 2. [nickname, <*idem* in same sense, <?, 1668 (OED)]. Hare. **1996** 'Y', *Irish Times*, 30 Jan: 'The French have various

nicknames for the hare. Our usual one is puss. But the French call him or her variously "Le Capuchin", the Capuchin, "le bossu", the humpback, "le oreillard" (Big Ears)...'

puss music [n. phr., see **puss** 1.]. Mouth music, style of traditional singing. **1952** Bryan MacMahon, *Children of the Rainbow*: 'Then we heard passages of "puss music", a kind of lilting-humming [see **lilt** 2.] that some countrymen are adept at.'

Puss Sunday [nickname, see **puss** 1.]. First Sunday in Lent. **1986** Padraic O'Farrell, *'Tell me, Sean O'Farrell'*: 'This was "Puss Sunday", so called because the girls that didn't get married before Lent couldn't marry till Easter so they went round with a "puss" on them.' See also **Chalk Sunday**.

pussy four corners [n. phr.]. Children's game. **1995** Phil O'Keeffe, *Down Cobbled Streets, A Liberties Childhood*: 'I had fallen while playing Pussy Four Corners, a game we played at speed, running from one corner to another without being caught.'

pusthaghaun [n., cf. Ir. *pusachán*, pouter, sulky person]. Conceited person (PO'F).

put a foot under one [concessive phr., gen. in neg.]. Exhibit Terpsichorean ability. **1995** Patrick Boland, *Tales from a City Farmyard*: 'Although, as the fella said [see **fellow**], I couldn't put a foot under me, nevertheless I loved going to dances.'

put a tooth in it [concessive phr., invar. neg.] as in **not to put a tooth in it**. Come directly to the point. **1938** Seumas MacManus, *The Rocky Road to Dublin*: 'the older Masters were yet truly, even if condescendingly, kind to him...Without putting a tooth in it, they admired him...' **1996** Bertie Ahern, RTÉ Radio news, 17 June: 'I am afraid, not to put a tooth in it, that the confidence in the RUC is lower than it has been any time in the last 20 years.'

put it up to s.o. [vb. phr.]. Attack, menace, force a response. **1995** *Leinster Leader* (Naas, Co. Kildare), 21 Dec: 'the defendants continued to hurl abuse...At this point she called for assistance. "They refused to go home and they put it up to us," she said.'

put manners on s.o. [vb. phr.]. Discipline, induce to conform. **1987** Lar Redmond, *Emerald Square*: 'I have never forgotten this ill-starred creature, who put manners on at least one most un-Christian Brother.' **1996** Frank Millar, *Irish Times*, 17 Feb: 'Hopeful theories were polished and refined. Perhaps it [the IRA bomb at Canary Wharf, London] was a "one off" — an attempt to "put manners" on the Brits.'

put on [vb.]. 1. inver. (Ulster). Get dressed. 'The wife's upstairs puttin onner' (Pepper). See **getonye**.

put on airs [vb. phr.]. Assume an attitude of superiority.

put pass on s.o. [vb. phr.] (Ulster). Give heed to s.o.

put past [vb.]. 1. [invar. neg. & cond., <Ir. *cuir thiar* (vb.) as in *Ní chuirfinn tharat é*, lit. I wouldn't put it past you]. Expressive of belief that s.o. is capable of anything. **1970** Christy Brown, *Down All the Days*: '"I think the oul cow did it on purpose...I'd put nothing past that wan [q.v.], let me tell you."' **1996** RTÉ TV serial, *Glenroe*: 'DINNY She's serious! MILEY I tell you one thing now, I wouldn't put it past her.' 2. (Ulster). Lay aside, discard.

put the bag on [vb. phr. intrans.] (Ulster). Take to begging.

put the boots on [vb. phr. trans.]. Bring to an end. **1944** James Joyce, *Stephen Hero*: '"The first day I came here I saw some bills up about a concert." "O, that's off. Father Lohan put the boots on that..."'

put the bush in the gap! [exclam.]. Close the door!

put the heart across/crosswise [vb. phr., cf. Ir. *d'fhág an croí a áit aige*, lit. his heart left his place at him]. (Of event, happening, etc.) Alarm exceedingly. **1925** Liam O'Flaherty, *The Informer*: '"Where have ye ben [sic]?" she whispered. "O Lord! Ye put the heart crosswise in me."' **1986** David Marcus, *A*

Land Not Theirs: "'She's a widow, you know, and these raids always put the heart across her, so I keep her company if I'm here.'"

put the spake/speak on s.o. [vb. phr., <Ir. *forrán a chur ar dhuine*, lit. put (an) attack on s.o.]. Address. See **spake**.

put the tin hat on [vb. phr. trans.]. Finish for good. **1939** Sean O'Casey, *I Knock at the Door*: "'if you can only manage to give him a few homers in the higher bit of his belly, I'll dance in then and put the tin hat on him'".

puttiby [n.] (Ulster). Snack. **1913** Alexander Irvine, *My Lady of the Chimney Corner*: 'Sunday breakfast was what she called a "puttiby", something light to tide them over until dinner-time. Dinner was the big meal of the week.'

put to the pin of one's collar, be [vb. phr.]. Be stretched to the limit. **1966** Patrick Boyle, *At Night All Cats are Grey*, 'The Metal Man': "'he makes bloody few mistakes as far as needling for drink is concerned, even the Scroggyman would be put to the pin of his collar to best him'". **1996** Dermot Ahern, TD, RTÉ TV, *The Week in Politics*, 12 Oct: 'Fianna Fáil has 69 TDs, and even at that we are put to the pin of our collar to attend all these committee meetings.'

put years on [vb. phr.]. Cause distress/fatigue/anxiety etc.

pyock see **puke**

Q

quagh [n., <Sc. *quag*, quagmire] (Ulster). As thus.

Quaker [nickname, <characteristics of religious society] (cricket). **1922** Maurice J. Wigham, *The Irish Quakers*: 'Quaker honesty has often come in for comment, and in the days when local cricket teams were more frequent, the straight ball of no pretensions which simply removed your middle stump used to be known as a "Quaker".'

quality, the [n., vulgar or archaic in Std Eng.]. The Anglo-Ir. and their imitators; gen. superior social class. **1920** W.M. Letts, *Songs from Leinster*, 'The Fair': 'The quality will stare when they see the way we're driving,/The polis stand in wonderment to watch the cart arriving...' **1992** John M. Feehan, *My Village, My World*: '"The ladies and gents of the town, the quality, priests, nuns and Christian brothers," he declaimed, "don't have to relieve themselves at all. That's only for the likes of us. That's why God made plenty of grass in the countryside and none at all in the town."' **1995** Phil O'Keeffe, *Down Cobbled Streets, A Liberties Childhood*: 'They [the Huguenot weavers] dressed the fashionable ladies of Dublin, and Dublin was rapidly gaining a reputation as an exciting city now, for the quality were having one long, glorious ball.'

quality toss [n. phr.]. Attributes/bearing of the quality (q.v.). **1921** (first published 1983) Patrick MacGill, *Lanty Hanlon*: '"look at him the day with his quality toss and his wife in silks and satins and his girl that won't come out on the street unless she's in shoe-leather"'.

quare [adj. & adv., <Hib.E pronun. of 'queer']. 1. Good, nice, very, and as intens. **1927** Peadar O'Donnell, *Islanders*: '"A quare ould grin he had on him, and, be me sowl, Biddy, nobody noticed any huff on yerself."' Also **quarely** [adv.]. 2. Strange, peculiar. **1995** Tom Widger, *Sunday Tribune*, 22 Jan: 'By west of Ireland standards her [Caitlín Thomas's]

carry on [q.v.] — attacks on police, wrecking pubs — would have been looked on as "a bit quare, alright".'

quare an' [adj. phr.]. Very. But **quare an' saft** (Ulster). Not soft (daft) at all (of person).

quare fella/fellow [n. phr.]. 1 Individual distinguished by eccentric/unusual conduct/situation. **1993** William Trevor, *Excursions in the Real World*: '[Sean O'Casey] was a Protestant among Catholics, proud, rigid and idealistic, immediately an outsider...In Dublin parlance he was "a quare fella".' 2. Prisoner condemned to hang. **1954** (first production) Brendan Behan, *The Quare Fellow* (title of play).

quare harp/hawk [n. phr.]. Odd individual. **1989** Hugh Leonard, *Out after Dark*: 'My father...made matters worse by nudging me and saying "Oh, young Gunger is a queer harp!"'

quare man m'da! [exclam.] (Ulster). Expression of disbelief.

quare place, the [n. phr.]. Hell. **1970** Christy Brown, *Down All the Days*: '"I hope you're with God in heaven tonight, but I know in me heart it's down in the quare place you are..."'

quare stuff, the [n. phr.]. Illicit whiskey. **1978** John McGuffin, *In Praise of Poteen* (q.v.): 'Tourists seeking Irish souvenirs are not infrequently sold rot gut and told that it's "a drop of the quare stuff". The only quare stuff likely to be in it is Parazone or Bluestone.'

queef/quiff [n., poss. <Anglo-Indian *idem*, 'idea, fancy, movement, suggestion' (DHS)] (Ulster). Crafty move, dodge (YDS).

queenie [n.]. Children's throwing game ('Queenie case/Queenie-i-o, who has the ball?'). **1995** Phil O'Keeffe, *Down Cobbled Streets, A Liberties Childhood*: 'I threw the ball back, but the game of Queenie was abandoned — the next challenge was on.'

queer see **quare**

queeralities [n. pl.] (Ulster). Peculiarities.

quickened [p. part. as adj.] as in **quickened with drink** [adj. phr.]. Under the influence. **1947** Frank O'Connor, *Irish Miles*: "'Sure, man,' said the poet, 'don't you see 'tis the way I'm so quickened with drink? Why do you be always at me when you know I'm so sensitive?'"

quick of oneself [adj. phr.] (Ulster). Fast and accurate (of workman etc.).

quick time [n. phr., <OE *cwic* (adj.), fast] (Ulster). Daylight saving (summer) as opposed to standard time.

quiff see **queef**

quilt [n. & vb.]. 1. [n., <?]. 'Old woman' (of a man); rascal, contemptible/mean individual; fool who behaves against his own interests (rarely female); timid, effeminate man. 2. [vb., <?]. Run away, take to one's heels (Moylan). 3. [vb.,

<Sc. *idem*, thrash]. As thus. Hence **quilting** [n.].

quim [adj., <Sc. *queem*, pleasant, neat] (Ulster). Affectedly nice, prim; moving with ease and precision (CUD).

quingled [p. part. as adj., <Ir. *cuingeal/ cuingir* (n.), yoke; pair, couple] (Munster). Married.

quirk [n.] (Ulster). 1. [<?]. Curl of a pig's tail. 2. [cf. Sc. *idem*. (vb.), cheat]. Untrustworthy individual.

quit [vb., imper.] (Ulster). Stop, as in **quit girnin'** (q.v.).

quo'hes/shes [nickname, <their freq. use of the phrase 'quo(th) he/she'] (Ulster). Derry people (men/women) as seen from the Inishowen peninsula, Co. Donegal. Hence **the quo'he/she side of the water** [n. phr.].

R

Ra, the [nickname, abbrev.]. Irish Republican Army (Provisionals). **1995** Sam McAughtry, *Sunday Tribune*, 27 Aug: 'Neither the Ra nor the army was much interested in the effects of the bombing. The game was the thing.' **1995** Philip MacCann, *The Miracle Shed*, 'Grey Area': '"Ring up on Saturday morning, right?" Vomit was verifying. "Say Turner's recruiting for the Ra."'

raany/ranny [n., <Ir. *ranaí*, thin, lank person or animal] (Ulster). Small, stunted, emaciated person/animal; 'thin, delicate, sneaky-looking cat, cow or girl' (CUD).

rabbit–sheaf [n.]. Last corn-sheaf cut (Moylan).

rabblach [n., cf. Ir. *raiple*, noise, bustle; *raipleachán*, worthless person; Sc. *rabblach*, nonsense, incoherent speech; *rabbling*, act of mobbing] (Ulster). 1. Nonsensical talk. 2. Gathering of persons. 3. Rabble, mob.

rabble [n., see **rabblach**] (Ulster). Hiring fair.

racan [n., <Ir. *racán*, rake (implement)]. Lanky, raw–boned individual.

race [n.] (Ulster). Brief visit, journey.

rachlie [adj., <Sc. *idem*, dirty, disorderly] (Ulster). As thus.

rack/rake [n. & vb., <Ir. *raca* (n.), comb]. Coarse hair comb; comb the hair. **1913** Alexander Irvine, *My Lady of the Chimney Corner*: 'My preparation was to wash my feet, rake my hair into order, and soap it down...' **1985** Máirín Johnston, *Around the Banks of Pimlico*: 'After washing and dressing herself she would let down her hair and "rack" it with a big comb.' **1991** John B. Keane, *Love Bites and Other Stories*: 'No great notice was taken when an unfortunate member of the opposite species [male] passed away. I'll grant you he received a rough and ready shave from the corpse dresser and his hair might have been racked as the saying goes...' Hence **rack one's poll** [vb. phr.]. Comb one's hair.

1893 E.Œ. Somerville & Martin Ross, *Through Connemara in a Governess-Cart*: 'the mermaid, when not decoying sailors to their fate, is incessantly "racking her poll" as they say in the County Cork'.

racker [n.]. 1. [<Ir. *reacaire*, reciter of poems, newsmonger] (Leinster). Professional jester. 2. [cf. Ir. *ragaire*, late-night rambler]. 'Kind of horseboy possessed of speed, stamina and knowledge of a district in which he operates' (OTF).

raddle [n. & vb., <OF *reddale* (n.), stout stick or pole]. As thus. **1995** Michael 'Gossie' Browne in Mary Ryan et al. (eds.), *No Shoes in Summer*: 'he took out a tenner and a fiver and handed them to me and he took out his raddle and raddled him [the bullock]'.

raft [n., <Norweg. dial. *idem*, thin stick] (Ulster). Tall, thin person.

raging [pres. part.]. Very annoyed.

rag on every bush, have a [adj. phr.]. Said of a 'Young man who is caught by and courts many girls but never proposes' (PWJ).

rag order, in [adj. phr.]. In dire straits; in an untidy/disorganised state. **1991** Roddy Doyle, *The Van*: 'She had the look of a dipso about her all right; another year and she'd be in rag order.' See also **skee-ball order, in**.

rags and jags, in [adj. phr.]. In tatters.

ráiméis/ramas etc. [n. & vb., <Ir. *ráiméis* (n.), nonsense, senseless talk, <'romance']. As thus; talk thus. **1922** James Joyce, *Ulysses*: '"Some people," says Bloom, "can see the mote in others' eyes but they can't see the beam in their own." "Raimeis," says the citizen.' **1953** Frank O'Connor, *My Oedipus Complex and Other Stories*, 'Uprooted': '"You were ramaishing so I woke you up."' **1996** Joe Walsh, TD, RTÉ TV, *Questions and Answers*, 11 Mar: 'We're now going to listen to the same old ráiméis as ever: blame Fianna Fáil...'

rain bullock sturks [vb. phr., <Sc. *stirk* (n.), OE *stírc/stíorc* (n.), steer] (Ulster). Come down in torrents.

rain cats and dogs [vb. phr.]. Come down in torrents. **1738** Jonathan Swift,

Polite Conversation: 'I know Sir John will go, though he was sure it would rain cats and dogs' (first recorded usage). **1996** Eanna Brophy, *Sunday Tribune*, 25 Feb: '"But what's the story in Cork this morning?" "Yerra [q.v.] 'tis raining cats and dogs here, boy!"'

rair see **rare** [vb.]

rake [n. & vb.]. 1. [n., cf. Ir. *reic*, lavish spending]. Large number/quantity. **1996** Elaine Keogh, *Irish Times*, 30 Aug: 'Mrs B says there are other teenagers involved [in prostitution]. "There's a rake of them doing it; the health board knows about it and they told me they told the guards about it."' 2. [n. & vb., cf. Sc. *gang a rocking*, visit neighbour's house with *rock* (distaff) and spindle for friendly gathering] (Ulster). Friendly visit; ceilidh (q.v.); pay such a visit. **1938** Seumas MacManus, *The Rocky Road to Dublin*: 'Rambling [q.v.] was done to neighbouring houses, homes within a mile's distance of the rambler's own, and was an every-night occurrence. When on occasion, the rambler took it into his head to visit a house three miles or six from his own, that was raking.' Hence **raking pot of tea** [n. phr.]. Female gossip session following a ball etc. **1800** Maria Edgeworth, *Castle Rackrent*: 'there were grand dinners...and then dances and balls, and the ladies all finishing with a raking pot of tea in the morning'. 3. [n. & vb.]. Turf fire banked up to burn overnight; bank up such a fire. Hence **read the rake** [vb. phr.]. Tell fortunes. **1964** Michael J. Murphy, *Mountain Year*: 'they [old women] claimed they could read fortunes and the future from the hieroglyphics of embers, or in ashes raked with the fingers: "reading the rake", as they called it'. Also **rake-fire** [n.]. Visitor who outstays his welcome. 4. [n. & vb.]. See **rack**.

rallagh [n. & vb., <'rollick'] (Ulster). Loud laugh; laugh loudly (MON).

rallianach [n., <Ir. *railliúnach*, strong clumsy fellow]. As thus. **1938** Seumas MacManus, *The Rocky Road to Dublin*: 'He was a *rallianach* of a fellow — big, lumpy, untidy, uncultivated, loud-voiced, and with a shock of straggly red hair like

a thatch-roof after an October hurricane.'

rallion see **rullion**

ram! [exclam., euphem.]. Damn! Hence **rammed** [p. part. as adj.]. **1938** Seumas MacManus, *The Rocky Road to Dublin*: '"Where's the other scoundrels, you rammed wee [q.v.] rascal?" he yelled...' Hence **rammee!** [exclam.]. Damn me!

ramas see **ráiméis**

ramatracks [n., nonce-word] (Ulster). Aimless wandering (YDS).

ramble [n. & vb.]. Friendly visit to neighbour's house at night. **1938** Seumas MacManus, *The Rocky Road to Dublin*: 'Almost every man, and many boys, rambled on every night the winter round — ramble being the term for the leisured night visit to a neighbour's house where, around a gay fire, the family and the rambler...sat and talked and listened from dayli'gone [q.v.] till rosary time.' See **rake** 2. Hence **rambler** [n.], **rambling-house** [n.]. **1995** Éamon Kelly, *The Apprentice*: 'in winter our house became a visiting-place, what was known in our locality as a rambling house...The men who rambled to our house were the married men of the locality.'

ramguntchagh [adj. & n., <Sc. *ramgunshoch* (adj.), rugged; morose; rough; rude (CSD)] (Ulster). Excessively rude (person) (MON).

rammelgarry [n., cf. Sc. *rammelin* (pres. part. as adj.), rambling, talkative] (Ulster). Long, senseless story (SH).

ramp/rampy [adj., <Sc. *ramp*, rank, rancid, strong-smelling (CSD)] (Ulster). Unpleasant-tasting, bitter (YDS).

ramscootrify [vb., <Sc. *ramscooter*, send flying in a panic (CSD)] (Ulster). Beat up, defeat s.o. in argument.

ramstam [adj. & adv., <Sc. *idem*, headlong, impetuous] (Ulster). As thus. [adj.]. **1908** Lynn Doyle, *Ballygullion*: 'a bigger ould dundherhead niver went out wi' a gun in his fist. Between his short sight, an' his ramstam way av runnin' at things, it was the danger av your life to go within a mile av him.' [adv.]. 'I tole him not to go at it ramstam' (Pepper).

rander see **ranner**

randle [n., cf. Sc. *raird*, backward breaking of wind]. 'A set of nonsensical verses, repeated in Ireland by schoolboys ...who have been guilty of breaking wind backwards before any of their companions…' (Grose).

randy [n., <Sc. *idem*, frolic; wild, reckless person] (Ulster). Wild individual; scold, 'coarse, romping woman' (CUD).

rann [n., <Ir. *idem*, verse, stanza]. Angry speech. 'He put a rann out of him' (Moylan).

rannel [vb.] (juvenile) (Ulster). Pull the hair (Patterson).

ranner/rander [n. & vb., poss. <Flem. *randen* (vb.), rant; or *rann* (q.v.)] (Ulster). [n.]. Person who talks nonsense; wild, indistinct dream. [vb.]. Ramble, talk incoherently. **1983** *John Pepper's Illustrated Encyclopaedia of Ulster Knowledge*: '"That's the Reverend John James Gilmore, the best and finest wee [q.v.] meenester we've had for a lang time," he said firmly. The wife gave the minister a look. "I told you he was randerin', Mr Gilmore," she said.'

ranny see **raany**

rant [vb., cf. Ir. *ranteir* (n.), rambler, rover]. Court. **1921** (first published 1983) Patrick MacGill, *Lanty Hanlon*: 'The ranting season was in full swing now. Every holly-bush in the parish sheltered a pair of lovers nightly.'

ran-tan [n., see **ramstam**] as in **on the ran-tan** [adv. phr.]. On the spree, on the batter (q.v.). **1986** Padraic O'Farrell, *'Tell me, Sean O'Farrell'*: 'one morning a local lad struggled into Mass having been on the ran-tan all night in Prosperous'.

rantered (up) [adj., <Sc. *ranter* (vb.), work hurriedly and carelessly; darn, cf. Fr. *rentraire*, fine-draw a seam] (Ulster). Dishevelled.

ranty-berries [n. pl., <Sc. *rantry*, mountain ash] (Ulster). Rowan-berries.

rap [n., <?]. Counterfeit coin; anything of little worth. **1930** *Irish Times*, 14 May: 'That very expressive phrase, "I don't care a rap", suggests a query as to its origin. It would appear that Dublin may claim credit for adding this word to current speech about the beginning of the eighteenth century when the counterfeit halfpence then in circulation were dubbed "raps". The earliest printed reference is to be found in one of the famous "Drapier's letters" [1724] in which Swift writes of "many counterfeits passed under the name of raps".'

rapid! [exclam. & adj.]. Term of praise. **1990** Roddy Doyle, *The Snapper*: 'He wheeled it out, and wheeled in the real present. Larrygogan followed it in. "Ah rapid! Da — Ma —, thanks. Rapid. Ah deadly."' **1991** Ferdia Mac Anna, *The Last of the High Kings*: '"I'll borrow me Pa's Jag. We'll have a rapid time." Maggie told Davy to fuck off.' Also **caught rapid!** [catchphrase]. Caught in the act.

rap or run [vb. phr., cf. Sc. *rap*, Middle Low Ger. *rappen*, seize, snatch] (Ulster). Obtain by fair or unfair means (MON); scrape together, as in **all one can rap or run with**.

rapparee [n., <Ir. *ropaire*, violent person, robber, scoundrel, <C17 dispossessed Catholic landlords who acted thus for survival and revenge]. Rebel, robber. **1705** John Michelburne, *Ireland Preserved*: '*Enter five Rapparees*...3 RAP. We be does, de Rebels call Rapparees, we be de Kings gued volunters.' **1920** Daniel Corkery, *The Hounds of Banba*, 'On the Heights': 'I felt sure that anyone who keeps the "authors" in his thoughts would not refuse a corner of his bed to a rapparee.' **1922** James Joyce, *Ulysses*: 'Then he rubs his hand in his eye and says he: "What's your opinion of the times?" Doing the rapparee and Rory of the hill [title of rebel song by Charles J. Kickham, 1828–82].'

rare [adj., freq. as intens.]. Exceptional, outstanding. As in **rare oul'/ould time/s** [n. phr., catchphrase]. 1. Intense enjoyment. **1994** Ferdia Mac Anna, *The Ship Inspector*: 'A quantity of recently deceased Department of Agriculture officials were in process of being fricasseed. The refuse operatives were having a rare ould time.' 2. [n. pl.]. Idealisation of the past. **1995** Patrick Boland, *Tales from a City Farmyard*: 'Family pride today is not what it used to be in the Dublin of the rare old times.'

rare/rair [vb. trans., <OE *raeran*, rear]. Bring up, rear. Hence **rairin** [n.] in same sense. Also **it's far from...you were raired/raised** [catchphrase]. Implying s.o. has 'come up in the world', often mildly derog., or has pretensions. **1997** *Irish Times*, subhead to article 'Sir Paul Arises', 5 July: 'Sir Paul McCartney: it's far from that he was raised — and far from it he raised his own'.

rare/rear up [vb.] (Ulster). Get angry, scold. **1996** *Sunday Times* (London), 24 Nov: 'Sean Duignan, his [Albert Reynolds's] former press secretary, says he "reared up" when it was suggested that he donate the money...to charity.' Also **rarin' to** [adv. phr.]. Very eager to.

rasher [n.] (Dub.). Sexual intercourse, hence **Rasherhouse** [nickname]. Women's prison at Mountjoy (see **the Joy**). **1997** Alan Roberts, *The Rasherhouse*: '"Ay Betty," a voice Mags had not heard before, shouted from a window. "Who's the new bit of stuff in the Rasherhouse?"' Also **rub of the rasher** [n. phr.] in same sense. See also **rub of the relic**.

rasper [n., <Sc. *idem*, 'one who speaks in an exasperating manner'] (Ulster). Rough or sharp expression or person.

rat's arse as in **give a rat's arse** [vb. phr., invar. neg.]. Care a damn. **1996** 'Sam', quoted in *Irish Times*, 21 Sept: 'You're in a small rural environment where you're the king of the castle. Then you come to Dublin where no one gives a rat's arse and you're nobody.'

rats under cover [nickname, <initials] (Ulster). Royal Ulster Constabulary. **1996** (unpublished) Gavin Gallagher, *Perceived View*: 'The process of Ulsterisation meant that you got hassled quite a bit from your local police force, the RUC. Rats under cover was what we called them...'

rattle [vb., onomat.] (Ulster). Work or act with speed/energy.

rattle–can [n.] (Ulster). Noisy child.

rattler [n., <Ir. *reachtaire*, steward]. As thus. **1995** Norman Mongan, *The Menapia Quest*: 'his granduncle, Thomas "Rattler" Monahan (1843–1910) was herdsman for Colonel Bolton, a Louth land–owner'.

rattlie/rattly [n.] (Ulster). 1. Child's rattle, as in **get s.o.'s rattlie up** [vb. phr.] rouse to anger. See also **slasher** 2. 2. [n. pl.]. Broken china used for playing shops. See **chaney**.

rave [vb., <OF *raver*, dream; be delirious] (Ulster). Ramble in the mind, dote.

ravel [vb.]. Talk childishly/incessantly/nonsensically. **1914** George Fitzmaurice, *The Pie-Dish*: 'JOHANNA ...and 'tisn't taking notice of him you would be and he ravelling in his talk as the like of them [old men] do, ever and always.'

raven's bit [n. phr.]. Beast that is about to die.

rawny [adj. & n., <Ir. *ránaidhe*, thin, lank (person/animal) (Dinneen)]. Thin, sickly (person). Also **rawly** (poss. error for **rawny**) (Ulster). **1969** Robert Greacen, *Even without Irene*: 'And every boy jack of them was crammed with city lore... wheedlers who could take the last "wing" [q.v.] from a rawly innocent country lad.'

rawser/razzer [n., <Brit. sl. 'rozzer', policeman] (Dub.). As thus. **1982** Éamonn Mac Thomáis, *Janey Mack* (q.v.), *Me Shirt is Black*: 'Policemen, among other things, were known as *Bobbies*, *Peelers* [q.v.], *Poliss*, *Cops*, *Rawsers*...' **1985** Máirín Johnston, *Around the Banks of Pimlico*: 'Someone was always sure to go to Newmarket for the police and as soon as the lookouts saw them coming they would shout "Here's the Razzers"...'

rawsie/rossie [n., <Ir. *rásaí*, vagrant]. 1. Female tinker/itinerant/traveller. **1989** John Banville, *The Book of Evidence*: 'I was surrounded suddenly by a gang of tinker girls, what my mother would have called *big rawsies*.' 2. Brazen woman.

1939 James Joyce, *Finnegans Wake*: 'and there she's for you, sir, whang her, the fine ooman, rouge to her lobster locks, the rossy...' **1985** Máirín Johnston, *Around the Banks of Pimlico*: '"Wait till I get you outside the gate, ye common rossie ye. I'll lave ye suckin' yer blood."'

rawsiner see **rozener**

Raytown [nickname, <fishing association]. Ringsend, Dub. **1988** Vincent Caprani, *Cara*, 'Raytown', Mar/Apr: 'the locals have left the scholars to their disputations and have happily settled for the time-honoured appellation of "Raytown". That nickname pays affectionate tribute to their rich ancestry...'

razoring [pres. part.]. Spoiling for a fight (Moylan).

razz, on the [adv. phr., <Brit. sl. 'on the razzle' <*razzle-dazzle* (nickname), fairground roundabout 1890s]. On the spree. See **wojious**.

razzer see **rawser**

read (up) [vb., <practice of reading names of alleged moral/financial defaulters from the altar in Catholic churches] as in **he read me**. He censured me severely. **1993** Michael Boland in Michael Verdon, *Shawlies* (q.v.), *Echo Boys* (q.v.), *the Marsh and the Lanes* (q.v.): *Old Cork Remembered*: 'You wouldn't back-answer the parish priest. Oh no. He'd read you from the pulpit.' Also **read from a height** (q.v.) [intens.] in same sense.

reader [n.]. Newspaper. **1994** Mary Corbally in Kevin C. Kearns, *Dublin Tenement Life*: 'In them years they called the paper a "reader". So you'd say you were going out to sell your readers. They were only a penny each at the time.'

ready–come–at [n.]. Skimpy female garment (Moylan).

real stuff, the [n. phr.]. Illicit whiskey, poteen (q.v.). **1954** George Fitzmaurice, *Dublin Magazine*, 'The Terrible Baisht', Oct/Dec: 'AUCTIONEER There's two 5-star bottles of Sandeman under the seat ...I've put a pint bottle as well of the real stuff [*slyly to* STUDENT] chin, chin!'

Real Taoiseach, the [nickname] (esp. Cork). Jack Lynch, Taoiseach (prime minister) 1966–73 and subsequently, on his replacement by Liam Cosgrave (1973–7). **1996** Michael Ryan, RTÉ TV, *Nationwide*, 11 Nov: 'It is thirty years since Jack Lynch was appointed Taoiseach. Indeed, down in Cork he's still known as "the Real Taoiseach".'

rear up see **rare up**

Rebel County, the [nickname, <'Rebel Cork', characterisation attrib. to the fact that the mayor of the city and his son were executed (1499) with Perkin Warbeck, pretender to Eng. throne]. Cork, esp. in GAA games context.

reck [n. & vb., <OE *reccan* (vb.), care, heed, mind, <ON *raekja, idem*]. Look, acknowledgment, as in 'your man [q.v.] wouldn't give you a reck' (EW); acknowledge.

red [adj., <Sc. *idem*, willing, skilful, <ON *hrathr*, quick, agile] (Ulster). Generous, liberal.

red-belly [n.]. 1. Char (fish), *Salvelinus alpinus*. 2. Any small fish caught by children in pools. **1986** R. Henchion, *Cork Centenary Remembrancer 1887–1987*: 'the thornies [see **thorneen**] turning out to be the little fish known as tittlebat [q.v.], red-bellies, belly-busters, etc.'.

redd (up) [vb., <Sc. *redd*, set in order, cf. OE *raedan*, put in order; MDu. *reddan* in same sense] (Ulster). As thus. **1908** Lynn Doyle, *Ballygullion*: 'an' before ye could say "Jack Robinson" the two av thim was at it hammer an' tongs ...Divil a thought av reddin' them was in his mind.' **1956** Sam Hanna Bell, *Erin's Orange Lily*: 'when the house had been redd up and the animals and fowls provendered for the day, all the family would pack into the trap and drive out to the main road'. **1983** Polly Devlin, *All of us There*: 'All through meals we hold onto our plate lest it be whipped away and the table redd-up to her satisfaction.' Also **red out** in similar sense. **1995/6** Dermot Mackie, *Five Foot Three* (Belfast), 'Whitehead Report': '...August was a month for cleaning out water tanks. Whitehead,

Lisburn, Ballymena and Portrush all got a good "red out"...'

reddans [n. pl., see **redd**] (Ulster). Odds and ends.

reddin'-up [n. phr., see **redd**] (Ulster). Criticism of s.o. in his/her absence.

red lead [nickname, <colour]. Luncheon sausage (EW).

redneck [n., derog., cf. US sl. *idem*, southern rural white (ODMS)]. Country yokel, culchie (q.v.). See **Heffo's Heroes**, **Molly Malones**.

red-nelly [n.]. Child's marble. **1994** Vonnie Banville Evans, *The House in the Faythe*: 'a line was drawn where we knelt and flicked our biggest and best "red-nellies" trying to remove the taws from the circle'.

red shank [nickname, <legs reddened from exposure]. C18–19 rebel.

ree [adj., <Sc. *idem*, crazy, delirious, wild; high-spirited (of horse), cf. OE *rethe*, fierce, cruel, furious] (Ulster). Enraged, wild, wanton, drunk, high-spirited (of horse).

reed [n., cf. Sc. *idem*, 'fourth stomach of a ruminant' (CSD)] (Ulster). Vital organs, life. As in **put out one's reed** [vb. phr.]. Give of one's utmost.

reedilums [n. pl., cf. Sc. *reed* (adj.), fierce, wild, drunk]. Staggers. **1960** John O'Donoghue, *In Kerry Long Ago*: 'and Biddy, the craythur [see **craythur** 2.], getting reedilums and darting pains across her eyebrows from twisting on an empty stomach like a hawk above a chicken'.

reef [vb., cf. Icel. *rjúfa*, break, burst, violate]. Attack violently; tear, remove forcibly. See **lower**. Hence **reefer** [n.] (Ulster). Heavy blow or slap (YDS). **1966** Patrick Boyle, *At Night All Cats are Grey*, title story: 'I watched her grow old again...and I wondered could I get away before she started reefing me.'

reek [n. & vb., cf. Icel. *rjúka* (vb.), Ger. *rauchen* (vb.), etc., smoke] (Ulster). Act of smoking; whiff of a pipe; smoke. **1979** Paddy Tunney, *The Stone Fiddle*: 'a neighbour who was making his ceili [q.v.] suggested to my father that there

was firewood enough on his lands in Rossmore to keep both our chimneys reeking'.

reel [n. & vb., cf. Sc. *idem*, romp (vb.)] (Ulster). 1. [n.]. Joke, trick. 2. [vb.]. Chaff, make fun of. Also **off the reel** [adj. phr.] odd, eccentric; **right/straight off the reel** [adv. phr.] at once.

reel-footed/fitted [adj., <Ir. *reilig*, grave, <early belief that the condition was induced by walking when pregnant over a grave]. Club-footed.

reenawlee [n., <Ir. *righneálaí*, lingerer, dawdler, loiterer]. As thus.

ree-raw see **rí-rá**

reeve [vb., <Sc. *idem* (n. & vb.), rivet, clinch] (Ulster). Close (a door). **1983** Polly Devlin, *All of us There*: 'As we go past she slams a door. "She can reeve a door the best I ever knowed," Francey MacAllister says...'

reever [n., see **reeve**] (Ulster). Hit, thump.

Reilly [prop. n.]. Synonym for excellence, success, as in **life of Reilly** [n. phr.]. **1968** John Healy, *The Death of an Irish Town*: 'we couldn't go wrong if we grew beef and produced milk, and both by the ton, and the job was Reilly'.

relics of auld/old dacency/decency [n. pl., catchphrase]. Preserved memorials of a more fortunate era, personal or gen.; latterly freq. ironic. **1977** Wesley Burrowes, *The Riordans*: 'Mrs Howard represented an old, almost anachronistic part of rural life, the relic [*sic*] of oul dacency...' **1994** Vonnie Banville Evans, *The House in the Faythe*: 'He was a fine tall man who bore, as my mother used to say, "the relics of auld dacency". He had obviously seen better days...' **1996** Tom Doorley, *Sunday Tribune*, 30 June: 'Over the years I've been asked to poke around in a few country house cellars in the hope that these relics of auld dacency might yield up some interesting finds.'

relievers [n. pl.]. Comfortable slippers/shoes.

relievio [n.]. Children's game involving two teams, a member of one trying to run through the other uncaught to 'release' a team member.

relish cake [n. phr.]. Baked patty containing blood added to other ingredients (mushrooms, cabbage, etc.). **1982** Thomas Gallagher, *Paddy's Lament*: 'the owners of the bled animals would carry the blood home and add it as a fortifier to various other foods. Some made "relish cakes" with it...'

rench see **wrench**

renegade [n., derog.] (Ulster). Apostate; one who has abandoned his/her (gen. Catholic) religion.

rensh see **wrench**

rent [vb., <'rend'] (Ulster). Vomit (Pepper).

residenter [n.] (Ulster). Old inhabitant; old fixture or feature. **1966** Patrick Boyle, *At Night All Cats are Grey*, 'Myko': 'This was a real old residenter, long enough on the premises to claim squatter's rights. There was no need to unscrew the coffin lid to put a name on the tenant.'

reth see **wreath**

rhoo! [exclam., <Ir. *arú*, ah!]. As thus. **1663** Richard Head, *Hic et Ubique*: 'PATRICK O yea, between me and God achree, my Moistare [master] will make mad for my shelf [self]. Upjack and supjack [object and subject]; rhoo fuate de Deole ale thee [what the Devil ail (q.v.) thee].'

rib [n., <Ir. *ribe*, single hair (of the head)]. As thus.

ribber [n., <'rub'] (Ulster). Hessian bag worn as apron to protect clothes in farm work (SH).

Ribbonmen [nickname, <insignia of organisation]. C19 agrarian movement pledging itself 'To destroy Protestant kings, to burn churches, to destroy heretics and to spare no man but a Roman Catholic.' **Early C19** Jeremiah O'Ryan, 'The Peeler [q.v.] and the Goat': 'I am no rogue, no Ribbonman,/ No Croppy [q.v.], Whig, or Tory, O...' **1988** R.F. Foster, *Modern Ireland 1600–*

1972: 'The early nineteenth century saw the proliferation of rural protest movements, the "banditti" or "Whiteboys" [q.v.] of contemporary accounts, who can be categorized, often according to locality, as Whitefeet, Threshers, Terry Alts, Rockites, Carders [q.v.], Caravats [q.v.], Shanavests [q.v.] or Ribbonmen — the last term applicable to an organization with a more generalized political view than many of the others.'

ribe [n., <Sc. *idem*, cabbage which does not grow properly] (Ulster). Very thin individual; animal in poor condition. Hence **riby**, **ribish** [adj.] in same sense.

rickle/ruggle [n., cf. Ir. *ricil*, pile of turf; Sc. *rickle*, loose heap or pile] (Ulster). Very thin person or animal, also **rickle/ruggle o'banes** (bones) [n. phr.] in same sense; unsteady building etc.

rickmatick [n., <Sc. *idem* <'arithmetic', collection, lot, crowd] (Ulster). As thus, esp. as in **the whole rickmatick**. **1948** Patrick Kavanagh, *Tarry Flynn*: '"It's a poor thing that I can't have one day's peace with the whole rick-ma-tick of yous [q.v.]."'

ride [n.]. Woman (more rarely man) generous with sexual favours; sexually attractive woman, less commonly man, fine thing (q.v.). **1939** Sean O'Casey, *I Knock at the Door*: '"On the way home," said the man wearing the bowler hat, "we met two lovely big-diddied [see **diddy**] rides, and they were all for us going home with them..."' **1991** Roddy Doyle, *The Van*: 'A ride, she was. It was weird thinking his son was going out with a ride; but it was true.' **1996** *Irish Times*, 19 Mar: 'Though you [female teachers] dress and move like Attila the Hun, this is no protection from...being called names like slag, fat-arse, droopy-boobs or ride.'

rider [n.] (Cork). Gaming term employed in feck (see **feck** [n.] 2.) schools. **1996** Seán Beecher, RTÉ Radio, *Sunday Miscellany*, 16 June: 'When a coin finished up landing against a jack [q.v.] it was called a rider.' See also **boxman**, **jockey**, **tosser** 1.

riding the fringes [vb. phr.] (Dub.). Riding the franchises, ceremony carried out by the city corporation in procession, lapsed late C18. **1847** John Edward Walsh, *Ireland Sixty Years Ago*: 'The principal civic ceremony which still continued within that period with unabated splendour was the triennial procession of the corporation, vulgarly called "riding the fringes".'

rift [vb., cf. ON *rypta*, break]. Belch. **1966** Patrick Boyle, *At Night All Cats are Grey*, 'The Metal Man': 'He gives one more porter [q.v.] rift and makes across the street to the barracks...' **1992** Brian Leyden, *Departures*: 'I suffered her weight and her cold touch...and waited with her each time she told me she had to stop to "rift gas".' **1995** Aidan Higgins, *Donkey's Years*: '"The Bowsy [q.v.] just let out a rift," I informed Lizzy Bolger. Mumu called belching a rift; rifting was rude...'

rig [n., <Sc. *idem*, half-castrated animal/ one with imperfectly developed male organs]. As thus; man similarly afflicted. **1994** Stephen Mooney in Kevin C. Kearns, *Dublin Tenement Life*: 'Now her husband, a fine cut [see **cut** 1.] of a fella, it was commonly known to the menfolk around there that he was a "rig", a man with one ball...*unserviceable*.'

riggie/riggy [n., <Sc. *idem*, cow with a white stripe along her back] (Ulster). As thus.

right [adj.]. 1. [gen. as intens.]. **1988** Roddy Doyle, *The Commitments*: 'There was a young guy who worked in the same shop as Jimmy...he seemed like a right prick...' Also **right-looking** [adj.], **rightly** [adv.] in same sense. See also **rightly** [adv. used as adj.]. **1960** Edna O'Brien, *The Country Girls*: '"Of course we're paying. It's nicer when you pay. You're a right-looking eejit [q.v.]."' 2. [gen. neg.] (Ulster) as in **not right in the head**. Deranged.

Rightboys [nickname]. Secret agrarian society, *c*.1785. **1973** Maureen Wall in T. Desmond Williams (ed.), *Secret Societies in Ireland*, 'The Whiteboys' (q.v.): 'The third major outbreak of violence...seems to have started on the borders of Cork and Kerry — where people began taking an oath to obey Captain Right — hence the name Rightboys, which was applied to them during this phase.'

rightify [vb.] (Ulster). Rectify.

rightly [adv. used as adj.] (Ulster). 1. In good health. **1995** Shane Connaughton, *A Border Diary*: 'Across the Border the Cavan drawl shakes off the dust and picks up a biblical clip. "Howya? How's she cuttin'? [q.v.]" becomes "Are ye rightly?"' 2. Under the influence of alcohol. **1951** Sam Hanna Bell, *December Bride*: 'Carspindle reached up and took the bottle from his hand. "Are ye rightly, Hami?" he asked.' **1994** Susan McKay, *Sunday Tribune*, 6 Nov: 'It [the pub] is crowded, and, at seven in the evening, a lot of people are "rightly"...'

right one [n. phr.] (Ulster). Unpredictable individual.

ringle-eyed [adj., <Sc. *idem*, wall-eyed, <OE *hring* (n.), ring]. Having a light-coloured iris in a dark outer circle (PWJ); with different-coloured eyes.

ring o' day [n. phr., cf. Ir. *fáinne an lae*, lit. 'ring of the day', dawn]. As thus. **1938** Seumas MacManus, *The Rocky Road to Dublin*: 'After Tuathal each, in turn, told his own tale — until the ring of day formed in the east, and came light to carry them home.'

ring papers [n. pl.]. Brit. army pension book. **1993** Con O'Donoghue in Michael Verdon, *Shawlies* (q.v.), *Echo Boys* (q.v.), *the Marsh and the Lanes* (q.v.): *Old Cork Remembered*: 'Though expressly against the law, there was a very profitable trade in pension books. The ring papers, they used to call them since they had the dates stamped in little rings.'

Ringsend car [nickname, <Ringsend, Dub.]. One-horse hackney vehicle. **1773** Theophilus Cibber, *Epistle to Mr Warburton*: 'There straddles he over the buttocks of the horse with his pedestals on the shafts, like a driver of a Ringsend car furiously driving through thick and thin...' **1847** John Edward Walsh, *Ireland Sixty Years Ago*: 'The earliest and rudest of these [one-horse vehicles] were the

"Ringsend cars", so called from their plying principally to that place and Irishtown, then the resort of the *beau monde* for the benefit of sea-bathing. This car consisted of a seat suspended on a strap of leather, between shafts, without springs.' See also **noddy**.

Ringsend uppercut [n. phr., <Ringsend, Dub.]. Kick in the groin. **1991** John B. Keane, *Love Bites and Other Stories*: 'the most devastating of all blows in the common street confrontation was the Ringsend Uppercut. This was simply a kick between the legs.'

riotery [n.] (Ulster). Noise, hubbub.

rip [n., <Sc. *idem*, 'slovenly-dressed girl' (CSD)]. 'A coarse, ill-conditioned woman with a bad tongue' (PWJ). **1932** Seán O'Faoláin, *Midsummer Night Madness and Other Stories*, 'Childybawn' (q.v.): '"I wonder could it be something that ould jade Ma Looney said to me ...She was always a bad-minded ould rip."' **1990** Roddy Doyle, *The Snapper* (q.v.): '"Mammy," said Linda, "it's stupid." "I don't care," said Veronica. "I spent hours making those skirts for you two little rips —"' **1991** Bob Quinn, *Smokey Hollow*: '"Them nuns are mean rips," said Slag Kelly... "They wouldn't give you the steam off their piss."'

rip, on the see **tear**

rippit [n., <Sc. *rippet/rippart/rippit*, noisy disturbance] (Ulster). Row.

rí-rá/ree-raw [n., <Ir. *rí-rá/rírá*, hubbub, uproar]. As thus. **1995** *Irish Times*, 12 Jan: 'Two animated characters, Rí and Rá, feature in an Irish-language series for children which starts next Thursday...' **1995** Phil O'Keeffe, *Down Cobbled Streets, A Liberties Childhood*: 'I rose on my elbow and watched as someone in great distress was led out from the waking-room. My father saw me and told me to lie down and everything would be all right. "It's only a bit of a *rí-rá*," he said. "They always happen at funerals."' **1996** RTÉ Radio, *News at One*, 8 Feb: 'Rí-rá, raic [Ir., racket, uproar] and ruaille buaille [q.v.] was the order — or rather the disorder — of the Dáil today...'

rise [vb. trans.]. Rouse, stir up, provoke. **1994** Vonnie Banville Evans, *The House in the Faythe*: 'Being more than a bit of a mischief-maker he never failed to try to rise Bill...' **1996** *Irish Times*, 17 Aug: '"I was cross, you'd be cross too," says Bob Graham. "I'm very short-tempered, don't you rise me or I'll fly."' See **riz** 2.

rise out of [vb. phr., <Ir. *éirigh as*, lit. *idem*, give up, relinquish]. As thus.

risharrig [n., <Ir. *rith searraigh*, lit. foal's run; short run, unsustained effort (Dinneen)] as in **in a risharrig** [adv. phr.] (Cork). Clumsily, awkwardly (DOM).

risk it for a biscuit [vb. phr.]. Take a chance, esp. with sexual connotation. **1995** Brendan O'Carroll, *The Chisellers* (q.v.): '"Hey, Mark," Mrs Williams called. "Would you risk it for a biscuit?" "Go on outa that [see **get away ou' that!**], Mark Browne," Mrs Troy called. "Wiggle your arse when you go by us, yeh fine thing [q.v.]!"'

rit [n. & vb., <Sc. *idem*, scratch, chasm, groove; furrow, score, scratch, <OE *rittan* (vb.), cut, slit] (Ulster). [n.]. Edge. [vb.]. Mark a line on turf bog with spade before cutting.

riz [vb. as adj., solecistic p. part. of 'rise']. 1. Up out of bed. 2. Very angry. **1977** Wesley Burrowes, *The Riordans*: 'when he [Tom] heard that Jude had been propositioned by John-Joe, the landlord, he was riz, as only he *can* be riz.' **1983** W.F. Marshall, *Livin' in Drumlister*, 'Me an' me Da': 'Consarnin' weemin, sure it wos/A constant word of his,/"Keep far away from them that's thin,/Their temper's aisy riz."' See **rise**.

roadeen see **rodden**

roan [n., cf. Sc. *rone/ronn*, spout for carrying off rainwater] (Ulster). Roof gutter.

roast beef [n. phr., <?] (printing) (Belfast). Work not charged for at time of commission. **1826** 'A Compositor', *The Text-Book, or Easy Instructions in the Elements of the Art of Printing*: 'When a journeyman has wrought more work than he has charged in his bill, and which

he intends to charge at a future time, it is called roast beef.'

roaster [n.]. Potato kept hot on the coals for serving at the end of the meal. **1995** Éamon Kelly, *The Apprentice*: 'My mother had kept the dinner for us with some roasters...sitting on the red embers.'

robin–run–the–hedge [nickname]. Gorse grass (*Galium aparine*). **1996** 'Y', *Irish Times*, 10 June: 'A reader from Sligo puts in a gentle reminder-cum-rebuke that in an item on cleavers...the most expressive of its names was left out: robin-run-the-hedge.'

rocket [n., <Fr. *rochet*, OE *rocc*, outer garment]. Little girl's dress or frock (PWJ).

rodden/roadeen [n., <Ir. *róidín*, little road]. As thus. **1893** E.Œ. Somerville & Martin Ross, *Through Connemara in a Governess-Cart*: 'From the use of the affectionate diminutive "roadeen" I knew that my cousin was trying to engage my sympathies...'

rodney [n., <?, colloq., *c.*1865–1910, '(very) idle fellow' (DHS)]. Fool, no-hoper. **1948** Patrick Kavanagh, *Tarry Flynn*: '"I thought it might be this rodney of an uncle of yours who was threatening to come back to lie up on us..."'

rog [n., <?]. 'Mongrel pigeon, recognised by its eye, hence the insult "Go away with your rog's eye"' (EW).

roitery [n., cf. Sc. *roit*, 'forward, disorderly person' (CSD)] (Ulster). 'Assortment of utter rubbish' (YDS).

rolling [pres. part. as adj., <unsteady gait] (Ulster). Drunk and incapable. **1978** John Hewitt, *The Rain Dance*, 'The True Smith of Tieveragh': 'And when he came back, *rolling*, from the town/they'd tug his coat the way he had to go,/or see him happed [see **hap (up)**] and safely bedded down.'

Roman collar [nickname, <Roman Catholic priest's garb]. Generous head on pint of draught stout, suggestive to serious drinkers of publican's reluctance to give full measure. **1966** Patrick Boyle, *At Night All Cats are Grey*, 'The Metal Man': 'We all sat watching Jonty put the Roman collars on the pints with a few skites [see **skite** 1.] of fresh porter [q.v.] from the barrel.'

roney [n., <Ir. *ruánach*, (adj.), reddish]. Red calf or cow.

Ronnie Delany, do a [vb. phr., <winner of gold medal in 1,500 metres, 1956 Olympics]. Travel rapidly. **1996** Maeve Binchy, BBC Radio 3 interview, 22 Mar: 'Do a Ronnie Delany to the airport.'

rook [n.] (Ulster). Cantankerous individual; 'industrious but ungenerous person, anxious to "get on"' (YDS).

rookied [p. part. as adj., cf. Sc. *rook* (vb.), plunder, devour]. Wrecked.

rooky–rawky [n. & adj., cf. Ir. *rúcach*, rustic, boor & Ir. *rúcaí*, 'the country summer visitors to Kilkee [Co. Clare]' (Dinneen)]. Term of contempt. **1932** Seán O'Faoláin, *Midsummer Night Madness and Other Stories*, title story: 'And an old devil he was, living up there all alone, in what she used to call his rooky-rawky house.'

roolie–boolie/roolye–boolye   see **ruaille buaille**

room/Room, the [n. + def. art.]. Applied to drawing-room, parlour, etc. freq. kept for visitors. **1800** Maria Edgeworth, *Castle Rackrent*: 'He was at the table in *the room*, drinking with the exciseman and the gauger, who came up to see his honor...' **1994** Vonnie Banville Evans, *The House in the Faythe*: 'The Room, with capital letters, was on the right-hand side. It would, in our anglicised or Americanised modern times, be referred to as the lounge-cum-dining-room. To us it was The Room, pure and simple.' **1996** Anon., *Irish Times*, 24 Sept: 'I was taking a shower when my then five-year-old son shouted to me that there was a girl waiting for me downstairs. "Bring her into the room...," I roared back at him. He took me at my word.'

roopy/roupy [adj., <Sc. *roup* (vb.), shout, cry hoarsely] (Ulster). Hoarse.

rosiner see **rozener**

rossie see **rawsie**

Roto, the [nickname, <abbrev. + endearment suffix]. Rotunda maternity hospital, Dub. (opened 1757). **1981** Brendan Behan, *After the Wake*: "'It's Rochford's baby," said I. "Out of upstairs. He's only new out of the Roto this week.'"

rotto [adj., <abbrev. of 'rotten' + endearment suffix]. The worse for drink. **1939** Sean O'Casey, *I Knock at the Door*: "'The both of us were rotto," went on the driver wearing the bowler hat, "the two of us strugglin' together, him helpin' me and me helpin' him...'"

rough-heads [n. pl.]. Low-grade sods of turf from the top of the bank.

roughness [n., <Sc. *rough* (adj.), plentiful] (Ulster). Abundance.

roul see **heart of the roul**

rounds [n. pl.] as in **put rounds on oneself** [vb. phr., cf. Ir. *cuirim timpeall orm féin*, lit. I put a round/detour on myself]. Go out of one's way to help/oblige.

rounds of the kitchen, the [n. phr.] (Ulster). Good beating.

round the world for sport see **around the world for sport**

roup [n., cf. *roopy* (q.v.)] (Ulster). Auction.

roupy see **roopy**

rout/rowt [n. & vb., <ON *rauta* (vb.), shout] (Ulster). Bellow.

rowdly-dow/rowdy-dow/rowdle-dee-dow [adj. & n., onomat.]. Informal celebration. **1987** Vincent Caprani, *Vulgar Verse & Variations, Rowdy Rhymes & Rec-im-itations*, 'Wayzgoose': "'Is it fanciful and formal?" I next asked Rent-a-Row./"Ah dhivil the bit [q.v.] of formal — more of a 'rowdy-dow'...'" **1996** *Leinster Leader* (Naas, Co. Kildare), 11 July: 'the flip-side, the live recording of "Sunday Papers", a raucous and rowdle-dee-dow romp through the Sunday "rags" cataloguing the pleasures to be gleaned by the serious amateur perv in ads for naughtie [*sic*] knickers'.

rowl see **heart of the roul**

rowt see **rout**

Royal County, the [nickname, <Tara, former seat of kings & high kings]. Co. Meath, esp. in GAA games context. **1996** Colm Murray, RTÉ TV news, 28 July: 'This was Meath's day. The hungry Royal County hung on to win by two points.' **1996** Frank McNally, *Irish Times*, 12 Sept: 'Back in the 1950s and early 1960s, a government resettlement programme introduced farmers from the west to available land in Meath. Since then, there have been little pockets of the Royal County which are forever Mayo.'

rozener/rosiner/rawsiner etc. [n., <?, cf. Ir. *raisín*, ration, snack]. (Generous) measure of drink, gen. spirits. **1908** Lynn Doyle, *Ballygullion*: 'whin he turned round to his writin' desk, the wee [q.v.] man poured himself out a rozener would ha' made a cat spake'. **1934** Samuel Beckett, *More Pricks than Kicks*: "'And the rosiner," said Mrs Tough, "will you have that in the lav too?" Reader, a rosiner is a drop of the hard [see **hard stuff**].' **1981** Brendan Behan, *After the Wake*: 'Going past a pub on the corner of Eccles Street...My granny and Long Byrne and Lizzie MacCann all said they'd be the better of a rozziner.'

ruaille-buaille/roolie-boolie/roolye-boolye [n., <Ir. *ruaille buaille*, commotion, tumult, ruction]. As thus. **1938** Seumas MacManus, *The Rocky Road to Dublin*: 'the mighty hubbub of people shouting, cows rowting [q.v.], pigs squealing, sheep bleating...hucksters yelling — *roolye-boolye* such as never before on earth was heard, and never could again'. **1986** Padraic O'Farrell, *'Tell me, Sean O'Farrell'*: 'When dawn broke, every crow, sparrow and jackdaw from Daingean to Bracknagh congregated around the roof making "rúille-búille" [*sic*]...' **1996** John S. Doyle, *Sunday Tribune*, 17 Mar: 'Much as we may like to cod [q.v.] ourselves that we are an exuberant, fun-loving race, bubbling over with the crack [see **crack** 1.] and the *ruaille-buaille*, the truth is different.'

rubber [n., <'rub' (vb.)]. Housemaid's dusting cloth.

rubber dollies [n. pl., <Brit. dial. *dollies*, rags (EDD)] (Cork). Plimsolls, track shoes. **1978** T. Hallisey, *Cork Holly Bough*: 'I was dressed in an old sports' coat...a pair of rubber dollies and a skullcap.' **1993** Isabel Healy in Seán Dunne (ed.), *The Cork Anthology*, 'A Cork Girlhood': 'Going barefoot in summer was a painful affectation more than a necessity, for there were always ...Rubber Dollies (the white t-strap canvas shoes made at the Dunlop factory) in which every Cork child was reared.'

rubberies [n. pl., <?] (thatching). Thin laths (of bog fir). **1982** Edmund Lenihan, *Long Ago by Shannon Side*: '"Well, then, on top of them [the rafters] there were what old people used to call rubberies. They were branches about as round as a man's arm and they were split..."'

rub fat into the fat sow's arse [vb. phr.]. Gild the lily.

rub of the relic [n. phr.]. Sexual congress. **1982** Mervyn Wall, *Hermitage*: '"After all," he added heavily, "she's not in the first flush of her youth." "Well, you look out. She's just dying for a rub of the relic."' **1988** Clare Boylan in Máirín Johnston (ed.), *Alive, Alive O!*: 'Eason's was a real Dublin place. The girls in there were real Dublin and the discussion in the canteen at the break was who had had a rub of the relic.' See also **rasher**.

ruckawn [n., <Ir. *racán*, racket, rumpus, brawl; *lucht racáin*, brawlers, rowdies]. Noisy/boisterous/quarrelsome group of people.

rucky-up see **ruggy-up**

ruction [n., poss. <'the Insurrection of 1798' (PWJ)]. Disturbance, fight, uproar, gen. pl., as in **there will be ructions**. There will be trouble/war. **C19** Ulster ballad: 'In the county Tyrone near the town of Dungannon/ There's many a ruction meself had a hand in...' **1931** Shan F. Bullock, *After Sixty Years*: 'I never heard of any serious ructions between the parties in our territory...and quite obviously it would have been a foolish thing for Mr Bean's Roman Catholics to make trouble, say, with Derry's Protestants.' **1991** John B. Keane, *Love Bites and Other Stories*: '"You'll fall out with a black-haired woman," she [the fortune-teller] said, "and there will be ructions."'

rue-rub [n., <'rue' (vb.) <OE *hreowan* (vb.), repent, grieve] (Ulster). Of the scratching of an itch that breaks the skin (PWJ).

rug [vb., cf. Ir. *idem*, p. tense of *beir*, bring, take; Sc. *rug/rugg*, pull forcibly] (Ulster). Pull, tug (the hair).

ruggle see **rickle**

ruggy-up/rucky-up [n., cf. Ir. *racán*, racket, rumpus, brawl]. Street fight. **1985** Máirín Johnston, *Around the Banks of Pimlico*: 'As Saturday night wore on a carnival atmosphere was generated as the pubs filled up, the hooleys [q.v.] began and the "ruggy-ups" erupted.' **1995** Phil O'Keeffe, *Down Cobbled Streets, A Liberties Childhood*: 'The sight of a police car or a lone bobby on a bicycle was enough to send us all racing for the safety of our garden gates in case there was a rucky-up.'

rullion/rallion [n., <Sc. *idem*, rough shoe of untanned leather, <ON *hriflingr*, *idem*] (Ulster). Lout; dirty person/animal.

rumble see **rummle**

rummagumption/rummelgumption [n., <Sc. *rummelgumptions*, flatulence]. As thus; imaginary illness.

rummle/rummel/rumble [vb., <Sc. *idem*, shake about] (Ulster). As thus; wash clothes/potatoes by stirring in water; stir up fish in water. **1939** Patrick Gallagher ('Paddy the Cope' (q.v.)), *My Story*: 'there was a flood in the river that morning, and John Charlie and my father rummelled it, and got a creel full of trout'. Also as in **put that in your jug and rummle it** [catchphrase] put that in your pipe and smoke it, injunction to accept a given situation; **rummlegarey** [n., <Sc. *idem*, rambling, roving person] (Ulster) restless person; nonsensical story/talker.

rump and a dozen [n. phr.]. 'A rump of beef and a dozen of claret; an Irish wager,

241

called also buttock and trimmings' (Grose).

rumplety thump [adv.] (Ulster). Untidily, in a muddle.

run [vb. trans.]. See off, chase away. **1987** Lar Redmond, *Emerald Square*: '"That's run that one [q.v.]," she said with satisfaction. "I've been waitin' for a chance teh nail that hussy."'

runagate [n., <Sc. *idem*, <'renegade' <Lat. *renegare*, renegade, deserter] (Ulster). Wanderer, s.o. always on the go.

runchy [adj., cf. Sc. *runch* (vb.), crunch any harsh edible substance] (Ulster). Tough, fibrous.

runion [n., cf. Ir. *ruidín*, small article/amount] (Ulster). 'Small, relatively worthless belonging' (YDS).

runjey [adj., <Sc. *runchy/runchie*, large, raw-boned] (Ulster). 'Of a structure or make-up nearly answering to the poetical description "Half muscle, half bone"' (MON).

runner [n.]. 1. as in **do a runner** [vb. phr.]. Engage in a precipitate departure. **1995** Gene Kerrigan, *Sunday Independent*, 31 Dec: 'When Bishop Brendan Comiskey did a runner this year it was inevitable that his parishioners would be deliberately misled about the reason for his abrupt flight.' **1996** Renagh Holohan, *Irish Times*, 2 Nov: 'The accused [MEPs] maintained they weren't doing a runner from the daily grind but were off to important parliamentary business elsewhere.' 2. See **runner-in**.

runner-in/runner [n.]. Recent arrival in a locality — or so considered. **1977** Wesley Burrowes, *The Riordans*: 'the viewers, as honorary members of the Leestown community, were beginning to resent outsiders; to mistrust the runners, the blow-ins [q.v.].' **1980** Bernard Farrell, *Canaries*: 'MADALENE ...I've spent more of my life in Dublin than I have in Navan. That's where I'm from. FERGUS (*Teasing*) She's a runner-in.' **1994** Ferdia

Mac Anna, *The Ship Inspector*. 'Even families who have lived in Redrock for over a hundred years are regarded as mere "runners-in".'

runners [n. pl., noted in Green as 'Aus. use' but not in Wilkes]. Plimsolls, track shoes, usu. black, brown or white. **1970** Christy Brown, *Down All the Days*: 'helpless to stop themselves, the urine ran down their bare cold legs into their mucky runners'. **1985** Máirín Johnston, *Around the Banks of Pimlico*: 'Shoes were polished with Nugget or Cherry Blossom and in summer runners were washed and given a good coat of Snoween to spruce them up.'

run-race [n.] (Ulster). Leap. **1908** Lynn Doyle, *Ballygullion*: '...I took a run-race an' got up on the ditch, thinkin' I felt the baste's teeth in me leg ivery minit'.

run rings round [vb. phr., <Austral. sl. −1891, poss. <Austral. Rules football or rugby (DHS)]. Bamboozle, beat hollow.

runt [n.] (Ulster). Cabbage stalk.

rust [vb., <Eng. dial. *rusty*, stubborn, <'restive', infl. by 'rust' (waste away by idling, OED)] (Ulster). Refuse to work or go forward (of horse etc.); sulk. **1908** Lynn Doyle, *Ballygullion*: '"we've got out av our road, and the mule is rusted and won't go a fut furdher than your gate. And we're all destroyed [q.v.] with rain an' wind."' **1983** W.F. Marshall, *Livin' in Drumlister*, 'The Runaway': 'I wos puddlin' at shirts in a bucket,/I was baffled with sarvints an' fowl,/An' wan night with me feet in the ashes/I rusted — I did, be me sowl.' Hence **rusty** [adj.] stubborn; **take the rust** [vb. phr.] refuse to work.

rustic [n.] (Leinster). Type of baker's loaf; turnover (Moylan).

rut [n., poss. <'runt']. Smallest pig in litter; term of abuse. **1939** Sean O'Casey, *I Knock at the Door*. '"Come in you little rut, when you're told," shouted the woman at the door, "and don't be keepin' every one waitin'."'

S

sack-em-ups [n. pl.]. Grave-robbers. **1943** George A. Little, *Malachi Horan Remembers*: "'There were in those days men who went by the name of 'sack-em-ups' — what you would call resurrection men. They used to rob the graveyards and sell the bodies to the doctors.'"

SAG [acronym]. St Antony Guide, pious inscription on back of letter etc. **1990** John McGahern, *Amongst Women*: 'Eventually when the letter came in its blue envelope with the pious SAG printing across the seal, the hand so firm holding a gun or tool shook as he took it.'

saibies [n. pl., cf. Ir. *síobhas*, chive] (Ulster). Scallions.

said and led, be [imper. phr.]. Take (my) advice. **1909** Canon Sheehan, *The Blindness of Dr Gray*: "'Be said and led by me, Dick Duggan. Leave Kerins alone.'" Hence **said by** [adv. phr.]. Willing to consider, be advised. **1948** Patrick Kavanagh, *Tarry Flynn*: "'Still, if you'd be said by, I have a little plan of me own and if all goes well we might do better than so.'"

sally wattle [n., <Ir. *saileach*, willow] (Ulster). 'Branch of a thorn hedge with the thorns removed' (Pepper). Hence **sally picker** [n.]. 1. Chiffchaff (*Phylloscopus collybita*). 2. Sedge warbler (*Acrocephalus schoenobaenus*). 3. Willow warbler (*Phylloscopus trochilus*).

Sam [nickname, abbrev. of 'Sam Maguire', Gaelic sportsman and republican activist, d. 1927]. The Sam Maguire Cup, trophy for the senior All-Ireland football championships, first presented 1928. (Kildare beat Cavan 2-6 to 2-5.) **1995** Donal Dineen, *Irish Times*, 3 Aug: 'I also managed to...discover a cluster of green and gold tents surrounding a flagpole waving "Donegal for Sam" in the breeze...' **1996** *Irish Times*, 16 Jan: '"And is that Sam then?" he asks, pointing to Paul Bealin. His pal beside him saved me the trouble. "That's Paul Curran," he said authoritatively. "The cup's called Sam Hire. That's his name just like my crisps are called Sam Spuds." I left this four- or five-year-old professor to explain the rest.'

same difference, the [adj. phr.]. Identical.

same man with his knee bent [n. phr.]. Identical or very similar article, individual or event.

sanacan [n., cf. Ir. *can chan* (adv.), hither and thither (Dinneen)]. 'A farm labourer who was hired for a year and boarded and lodged by an employer was, if at the expiration of that period he sought another situation, termed a Sanacan' (OTF). Hence **Sanacan Sunday** [nickname]. First Sunday in May and the day after such service was terminated.

sancy see **sonsy**

sang! as in **by my sang!** [exclam., <Fr. *sang*, blood] (Ulster). Mild oath.

sanger [n., <abbrev. of Dub. pronun. *sangwitch* + endearment suffix] (esp. Dub.). Sandwich. **1995** Tom Doorley, *Sunday Tribune*, 21 May: 'If you're charging £4.75 for sangers, your customer will assume they are not made from white sliced pan...'

santer [vb., poss. <'saunter'] (Ulster). Talk ramblingly.

Santy [prop. n., <abbrev. + endearment suffix]. Santa Claus. **1965** Lee Dunne, *Goodbye to the Hill*: 'you smiled sardonically, even though you didn't know that's what you were doing, whenever anyone talked about Santy Claus'. **1995** Helen Rock, *Sunday Tribune*, 24 Dec: 'She [Mrs Claus] took me on a tour of the workshops — bright, cosy underground caverns staffed by busy smiling elves with Santy himself as gaffer...'

sapling [n.]. Young animal, esp. greyhound. **1977** Wesley Burrowes, *The Riordans*: 'Father Sheehy bought a pair of greyhound saplings and asked Johnny Mac to train them. This was rather like locking an alcoholic in a distillery...'

Saraft see **Shraft**

Sassenach [n., <Ir. *Sasanach*, Eng. person, Protestant]. As thus, gen. derog. **1961** Dominic Behan, *Teems of Times and Happy Returns*: 'it's one thing announcing to all and sundry that you intend killing every Sassenach...but quite a different matter is the business of getting them within shooting distance'. **1984** John McGahern, *Oldfashioned*: '"I hear we are about to have a young Sassenach on our hands, an officer and a gentleman to boot, not just the usual fool of an Irishman who rushes to the railway station at the first news of a war..."'

sauncy see **sonsy**

sausenger [n., <'sausage' + endearment suffix] (Ulster). Sausage.

sauvaun [n., <Ir. *sámhán*, nap, doze]. As thus. **1986** Padraic O'Farrell, *'Tell me, Sean O'Farrell'*: 'He [the priest] used gallop down off the altar and charge down to where the boyos [q.v.] would be having a sauvaun (rest) or a collogue [q.v.] (chat) in the porch.'

sawney [n., cf. Ir. *saonta* (adj.), naive, gullible] (Cork). Fool. **1993** Seán Beecher in Michael Verdon, *Shawlies* (q.v.)*, Echo Boys* (q.v.)*, the Marsh and the Lanes* (q.v.)*: Old Cork Remembered*: 'When he was shown the gononstrips [q.v.], and not being a sawney, he spotted a way for doing foxers [q.v.] and soon he had loads of lops [q.v.].'

Saxon shilling [n. phr., term of contempt]. Payment made to those recruited in Ire. to the Brit. army, esp. 1914–18 war. **1995** Ned Gilligan in Mary Ryan et al. (eds.), *No Shoes in Summer*: 'the volunteer was given a shilling. This made it a binding contract, and even years after if the soldier was lucky enough to return home from war service he would always be referred to as "Oh! He took the Saxon shilling."'

scad [n., <Sc. *idem*, 'a colour obliquely or slightly seen as by reflection' (CSD), cf. OE *sceadu*, shadow] (Ulster). As thus.

scaddan keek [n. phr., <Ir. *scadán caoch*, 'salt water used as kitchen [see **kitchen**

1.] with potatoes' (Dinneen)]. Poor substitute.

scad-the-beggars [n. pl., <'scald'] (Ulster). Leeks fried in a pan.

scaith see **scath**

scald [n. & vb.]. 1. [<Ir. *scal* (n.), hot tea]. Tea (as beverage); make tea. **1995** Phil O'Keeffe, *Down Cobbled Streets, A Liberties Childhood*: 'Turning to Madge he said, "When the dinner's finished, take them down to Mrs Tierney. You can play there till it's time to scald the tea."' **1995** Lise Hand, *Sunday Independent*, 3 Dec: 'After an interminable wait, without as much as a cup of scald on offer...a deep male voice boomed out of nowhere: "Ladies and (somewhat unnecessarily) gentlemen — the First Lady of the United States...' 2. [<Ir. *scall* (vb.), scald, fig. grieve bitterly]. 'To be *scalded* is to be annoyed, mortified, sorely troubled, vexed' (PWJ). **1920** Seumas O'Kelly, *The Leprechaun of Kilmeen*: '"Tom," she says, "was there ever such a scald put into the country since the first day it was made, as that leprechaun?"' **1995** Geoffrey O'Shea in Mary Ryan et al. (eds.), *No Shoes in Summer*. 'Tipperary beat us. We were scalded after all the hardship [of the journey to Dub. from Kilkenny]. We booked in at Stoke's Guest House for the night.' See also **heart-scald**.

Scalder [nickname, <?]. Native of Enniscorthy, Co. Wexford. **1994** Vonnie Banville Evans, *The House in the Faythe*: 'I don't know why she felt that way. Probably because of her own harsh childhood and the fact that she was an "Enniscorthy Scalder" among all the "Yellow Bellies" [q.v.].'

scaldy [n., <Ir. *scalltán*, fledgling, nestling, <ON *scalle*, bald head]. Unfledged bird; hence person with little or very short hair. **1996** Arthur Houston, *Irish Times*, 12 Apr: 'Sir...growing up in Belfast in the 1930s a baby in the nest was always a scaldy — what else could one have called it.' (Contribution to a correspondence which also located the word in Galway, Louth, Mayo, Monaghan, Sligo and Wexford.)

scallion-eater [nickname]. Inhabitant of Co. Carlow.

scalteen/scolsheen [n., <Ir. *scall* (vb.), scald]. 'Made by boiling a mixture of whiskey, water, sugar, butter and pepper (or caraway seeds) in a pot: a sovereign cure for a cold' (PWJ). **1943** George A. Little, *Malachi Horan Remembers*: 'They always had "scalteen" ready at the Jobstown Inn. Men in weather like this ...would be coming in with the mark of the mountain on them.'

scam [vb., <Sc. *idem*, singe, scorch, <ON *skam* (n.), shame, injury] (Ulster). Burn/overheat (food).

scammel [n., <*idem*, trade name] (Ulster). Large articulated lorry (YDS).

scanger [n., <?] (Connacht). Group of students at a bar (University College, Galway).

scantlin [n., <OF *escantillon*, sample, small amount (Mod.F *échantillon*] (Ulster). Pattern, appearance, type, build, breed. [n. pl.]. Scraps. **1938** Seumas MacManus, *The Rocky Road to Dublin*: 'Both of them [the two women]...had forgotten when they cut their wisdom teeth, but they were what he called "a hardy scantlin"' that could not be harmed by the toughness of his townland.'

scapper [vb., poss. <'scarper', make off in a hurry; cf. It. *scappare*, escape, get away]. As thus. **1961** Tom Murphy, *A Whistle in the Dark*: 'MUSH But they seen us coming, and they're scappering lively, and Des is dropping...'

scarlet [adj.] (Dub.). Flushed with embarrassment; 'mortified'. **1989** Roddy Doyle, *War*: 'LORRAINE Yeh dirty bitch, yeh, Yvonne. *She then realises how loudly she has spoken*...LORRAINE (*laughing, embarrassed*) Oh Jesus, I'm scarlet.'

scath/scathe/scaith [n. & vb., <OE *scethhan* (vb.), injure; Sc. *skaith* (n.), injury, loss] (Ulster). Injury, loss; damage. **1901** George Francis Savage Armstrong, *Ballads of Down*: 'Nor fear wound or scath from hand of mine'.

scatter [n. & vb.]. 1. [n., cf. Ir. *scaradh gabhail*, bandiness] (Cork). Irregular gait.

1966 Séamus Murphy, *Stone Mad*: 'what used to amuse me was the scatter of him coming towards you, his two feet being jerked out sideways and one hand in the overcoat pocket and the shoulders moving up and down'. 2. [n., <?] (Cork). Appearance, as in **cut a scatter**. Dress well (Beecher). 3. [vb.] (Ulster). Knock to the ground, flatten. 'Employed widely at football matches or in pubs...' (YDS).

sceach [n., <Ir. *idem*, prickly, quarrelsome person]. As thus.

scéal/skeal [n., <Ir. *scéal*, news, story]. As thus. **1689** Anon., *The Irish Hudibras*: 'Ycome like fool, ygo vidout/My skeal, vid finger in my mout.' **1983** Bobby Sands, *One Day in my Life*: 'Wasn't it all just living from one stinking cold meal to the next, creating false hope for oneself, clinging to every rumour that came your way? *Scéal, Scéal, Scéal!* The Irish word for news or story was now so worn out that even the screws used it.'

scew-ways see **skew-ways**

scheme [vb., <Sc. *idem*, play truant] (Ulster). As thus. **1938** Seumas MacManus, *The Rocky Road to Dublin*: 'he was strongly tempted to scheme school rather than provide the fun that the scholars [q.v.] were ever hungering for. Often, boys did so scheme...'

scholar [n.]. School pupil. **1907** Joseph Guinan, *The Soggarth Aroon* (q.v.): 'the "scholars" — as school children were always called'. **1938** Seumas MacManus, *The Rocky Road to Dublin*: 'Many of the scholars — for scholar was the modest title bestowed on every pupil from his first school-day — came distances of four, and even five, miles to school...' **1996** Pat Smyth, *Irish Times*, 29 Mar: 'Sir — Vere Foster, that wonderful educationalist of bygone days, provided copybooks for poor scholars learning to write.'

school dance [n. phr.]. Series of house dances. **1991** Seán Ó Ciaráin, *Farewell to Mayo*: 'Every winter, one or more "school dances" would be held in the district. By way of explanation, a "school dance" as we knew it had nothing whatsoever to do with school. It was a chain of dances lasting a whole fortnight, with dancing in a different house every night...'

scib [n., cf. Ir. *idem*, basketful, small load]. Very small object; puny, emaciated individual (OTF).

sciddin [n., <Ir. *sceidín/scidín*, small potato]. As thus.

scilleán/sciollán [n., <Ir. *sciollán*, 'portion of potato containing an "eye" or seed for planting' (Dinneen)]. As thus. **1991** James Kennedy, *The People who Drank Water from the River*: 'But the [potato] pit is a long way from the spring day when Auntie Nonie would come to cut the scilleáns.' **1995** Éamon Kelly, *The Apprentice*: 'The precious small piece holding an eye and maybe a young shoot was called a *sciollán*. There were many things in our district for which there was no English word and that was one.'

scobe [vb., <Sc. *idem*, scoop out roughly] (Ulster). Eat fruit with the front teeth (Todd).

scollop [n. & vb., <OF *escalope*, escallop] (Ulster). [n.]. Badly cut lump of bread, meat, etc. [vb.]. Cut something thus.

scolsheen see **scalteen**

sconce [n. & vb.]. 1. [n., <?] (Cork). Glance, look (Beecher). 2. [vb., <?]. Banter, tease. 3. [vb. & n., <Sc. *idem* (vb.), avoid, cheat, trick out of]. Shirk work or duty, avoid paying one's debts; one who acts thus.

scooch [n., nonce-word?]. Lift in a car. **1994** Vonnie Banville Evans, *The House in the Faythe*: 'we took no notice of the ones [cars] that stood here and there since we very seldom had any likelihood of getting a "scooch", as we called it, in any of them'.

scoops [n., invar. pl. as in 'a few scoops']. A few (or more) drinks. **1991** Roddy Doyle, *The Van*: 'There was nothing like it, the few scoops with your mates.' **1993** Brendan Glacken, *Irish Times*, 'Times Square', 11 Oct: '*The Ma* [q.v.]: Ah fer jaysus [q.v.] sake Anto — what I wanta know is, whattye going to do abourra? Can we sue de Corpo [q.v.] or wha? *The Da* [q.v.]: Do? I'm goin down to de Anchor for a few scoops, dat's what I'm doin fer starters. Jaysus [q.v.], it's not every day a fella hears he's goin to be a granda, wha? *The Ma*: No — not a granda of bleedin cygginets [q.v.] anyway, ye fekkin [see **feck** (vb.) 2.] eejah [see **eejit**]!' **1995** Gene Kerrigan, *Sunday Independent*, 3 Dec: 'He [Raymond Smith] has now written his memoirs, recounting a life spent enjoying scoops (both journalistic and the other kind).'

scoosh [n., <Sc. *idem*, rush of water] (Ulster). Gush.

scoot [n. & vb.] (Ulster). 1. [n.]. Diarrhoea; tiny amount of liquid. 2. [vb., <Sc. *idem* <OE *sceotan*, shoot]. Squirt water. 3. [n., <Sc. *idem*, term of gross contempt]. Inconsequential person/thing.

scoot-eye [n.] (Cork). Eye with a cast, or person so afflicted.

score [n.]. 1. (road bowling) (esp. Ulster/Cork). Match. **1948** John O'Connor, *Come Day — Go Day*: '"There's a score starting, boys," Neilly called, and they raced up eagerly to see the first shots being broken.' **1993** Mick Barry in Michael Verdon, *Shawlies* (q.v.), *Echo Boys* (q.v.), *the Marsh and the Lanes* (q.v.): *Old Cork Remembered*: 'The score is the equivalent of a match in other games. The origin of the score was derived from the fact that the match took approximately twenty throws.' 2. [<?] (Cork). Stroll, as in **go for a score**.

scorrick [n., cf. Sc. *scurroch*, the least particle] (Ulster). Odds and ends in a pocket.

Scotch convoy [n. phr.] (Ulster). Walk home with a visitor who then walks back with one.

Scotch lick [n. phr.]. Cleaning job half done. See also **cat's lick**.

scour [n.]. 1. [poss. <conflation of 'scour' & 'sour'] (Cork). Sour look or behaviour (Beecher). 2. [<Sc. *idem*, shower] (Ulster). Thick drizzle.

scout [n., <Sc. *idem*, 'term of contempt for man or woman' (CSD)]. 'Bold, forward girl' (PWJ).

scouther see **scowder**

scove [n., <?] (Cork). Walk. **1950** J.C. Coleman, *Journeys into Muskerry*: 'The Lee fields, favourite walking ground of Corkonians, flank the river from Carrigrohane to the city. A "scove"...up the fields is a Sunday morning constitutional going back to distant times.'

scowder/scouther [n. & vb., <Sc. *idem*, 'a hasty toasting' (CSD), scorch, singe, brown toast] (Ulster). Oaten cake baked only on the outside; hence something unfinished, half done; an unqualified tradesman; half-educated person; scraps of food thrown to dogs etc. **1833** William Carleton, *Traits and Stories of the Irish Peasantry*, 'Going to Maynooth': 'He's but a scowder, not a finished priest in the larnin'.' **1983** Polly Devlin, *All of us There*: '"What's this scowder?" he says, peering at anything that is not utterly familiar.'

scrab/scraub/scrawb [vb., cf. Du. *schrabben*, scratch, scrape]. 1. As thus; put the marks of ten fingernails down s.o.'s face (PO'F). **1985** Máirín Johnston, *Around the Banks of Pimlico*: 'there was the danger of getting involved in gang warfare and some of the regulars would scrawb or reef [q.v.] you to bits if you looked crooked at them'. **1985** Phil O'Keeffe, *Down Cobbled Streets, A Liberties Childhood*: 'My instinct always was to run; run from the shadowy corners and uncertain gateways...and the noise of scrawbing cats as they fought at the corners of the grainstore...' 2. Gather potatoes left after main picking.

scradin [n., <Ir. *scráidín*, worthless little person or thing]. As thus. **1952** Anon. (Patrick Kavanagh?), *Kavanagh's Weekly*, 'I Went to the Fair', 21 June: 'This would embarrass any normal man, but it was seldom it embarrassed any of the hungry *scradins* of farmers who were to be found guarding donkey carts full of bonhams [piglets]...'

Scraff see **Shraft**

scram [n., cf. Ir. *scramaire*, big, gaunt, useless man]. Old useless horse (OTF).

scrammely [adj., cf. Ir. *screamh* (n.), crust, scum]. Knitted together. **1991** James Kennedy, *The People who Drank Water from the River*. 'When the haw was heavy and "scrammely"...I'd hear the sergeant-major's voice of my father urging "Shake it out well..."'

scran/scrant [n., <Sc. *idem*, food, cf. Norweg. *skran* (adj.), lean, shrivelled]. Inferior food, scraps, as in **bad scran to you!** Bad luck to you! **1925** Lynn Doyle, *Dear Ducks*: '"I'm the makin's of a good shot...but I'm unfortunate at it, bad scran to it, I'm unfortunate."' **1927** Peadar O'Donnell, *Islanders*: '"An' amn't I pullin' against Mason?" Charlie persisted. "Musha [q.v.], bad scrant to the same Mason; he's a plague..." she said.' **1989** Hugh Leonard, *Out after Dark*: '"The coward wouldn't stand his ground...But he heard me right enough, bad scran to him."'

scrape [n.] (Cork) as in **a good scrape**. A sexually obliging female. See also **court, hoult.**

scrapings [n. pl.]. 1. (Ulster). Of s.o. who is excessively thin, delicate, as in 'she's away to scrapin's...' (Pepper). 2. Leftovers.

scraps [n. pl.]. Coloured cut-out pictures collected by children. **1995** Phil O'Keeffe, *Down Cobbled Streets, A Liberties Childhood*: 'We bought marbles in Granny Redmond's shop...She sold marbles, scraps — cut-out figures of people and animals — pencils, sticks, sweets and lollipops.'

scratcher [n.]. 1. [<reaction induced by the presence of fleas or bugs, or both]. Bed. **1977** Sam McAughtry, *The Sinking of the Kenbane Head*: '"Two o'clock," Jack would mutter to himself savagely, "Two o'frigging clock." Ripping his clothes off he would hurl himself back into the scratcher...' **1991** Roddy Doyle, *The Van*: 'Bertie turned around to the young one [q.v.]. "Are you like tha' in the scratcher?" he said.' 2. Lottery scratch card. 3. ['Anglo–Irish, C19' (DHS)]. Toe.

scraub/scrawb see **scrab**

screagh/skraik/skreigh etc. [n., <Sc. *skraich/skraigh/skraik* etc., screech, scream] (Ulster). As thus, as in **screagh**

o'dawn/day [n. phr.]. Cockcrow; dawn. **1925** Lynn Doyle, *Dear Ducks*: 'But the mother-in-law let a skreigh out of her an' fell on her knees. "It's a miracle!" sez she...' **1951** Sam Hanna Bell, *December Bride*: '"Ye must ha' rose at the skraik o'dawn!" shouted Purdie, his arms hanging loose.'

scree/screed [n., <OE *screade*, fragment, shred; *scriod*, as below, appears to be an unverified Ir. deriv.]. Long roll or list; last drop/fragment. **1907** Joseph Guinan, *The Soggarth Aroon* (q.v.): '"hard enough we're getting it to support a *scriod* o' childre [*sic*: see **childer**]"'. **1943** George A. Little, *Malachi Horan Remembers*: 'He had drunk every scree about the house, and would have drunk the stock too, but his wife baffled him...' **1986** Padraic O'Farrell, *'Tell me, Sean O'Farrell'*: 'I remember one fellow, and every time he got the price of a drink he would duck into Scally's pub. Before the day was over he had drunk every scree in the bar.'

screenge/scringe [n. & vb., <noise of fingernail on glass etc.]. [n.]. S.o. always on the lookout for a bargain/opportunity. [vb.]. Scrape, scour; search thoroughly. **1938** Seumas MacManus, *The Rocky Road to Dublin*: 'they spent hours tramping, screenging among rocks, firing into caves — but the devil a dorcu [mythical animal] did they find'.

screw [n.]. 1.[<?, –1827]. Bottle of wine (DHS). 2. [<Ir. *scrúdaigh* (vb.), examine]. As thus, as in **take a screw at** [vb. phr.]. Look at, examine. **1968** Myles na gCopaleen, *The Best of Myles*: 'of a Sunda the Frenchmen do be walkin' around the gardens having a screw at the statues'.

screwmoose [n., <Sc. *screw*, shrewmouse] (Ulster). As thus.

scringe see **screenge**

Scripturian [prop. n.]. Man respected for his learning. **1938** Seumas MacManus, *The Rocky Road to Dublin*: 'Two or three great Scripturians were in the parish, who boasted the ownership of a book or books...'

scrocky [adj., cf. Ir. *scraith* (n.), scurf]. Flaky (of skin).

scroof/scruff [n., <'scurf' by metathesis, <OE *scruf/sceorf*, poss. <OE *sceorfan* (vb.), gnaw] (Ulster). 1. Dandruff. 2. Thin crusts of bread. **1913** Alexander Irvine, *My Lady of the Chimney Corner*: '"These wather-mouthed gossoons [q.v.] who pray air jist like oul' Hughie Thornton wi' his pockets bulgin' wi' scroof..."' 3. People of no account, scum.

scrub [n., cf. *idem*, 'shabby fellow' (DHS)] (Ulster). Untrustworthy individual. **1983** W.F. Marshall, *Livin' in Drumlister*, 'The Lad': 'I knowed a scutcher that wrought [q.v.] in Shane,/He was a drunken scrub...'

scrubber [n., cf. Brit. sl. *idem*, tart/prostitute; Hib.E usage, though retaining female ref., does not usu. imply sexual liberality]. Common woman of working class. **1965** Lee Dunne, *Goodbye to the Hill*: 'and I feel sure that some of them scrubbers that know more than they should about men look for it [an erection] when you get up off the seat [of the bus]'.

scruff see **scroof**

scrunt [n., <Sc. *idem*, stunted, insignificant/mean, miserly person] (Ulster). As thus; small apple. Hence **scrunty** [adj.] in same sense.

scud [n. & vb., <Sc. *idem*, blow; beat] (Ulster). [n.]. Curse, jinx; smack (on bare buttocks) with open hand; stroke, blow; small quantity (of manure thrown on the ground); gen. term of abuse. [vb.]. Strike thus, beat. **1969** Tom Mac Intyre, *The Charollais*: '"So ye'd have the scud o'tay, m'lord?" "No — thankyou — we don't feel like tea — at the moment — thankyou."' **1979** John Morrow, *The Confessions of Proinsias O'Toole*: '"You really can misjudge people, can't you?" "He's a friggin' scud, for my money," I said...' **1995** Shane Connaughton, *A Border Diary*: 'I don't know why John is known as "The Scud". There's an expression round here: "I'll hit you a scud."'

scuddler [n., <Sc. Gael. *sguidilear*, scullion, drudge, mean fellow] (Ulster). Young person who helps out in the home.

scullogue [n., <Ir. *scológ*, small farmer]. As thus. **1939** James Joyce, *Finnegans Wake*: 'old bagabroth, beeves and scullogues, churls and vassals'.

scumber/scumble [vb., cf. OF *descombrer*, relieve of a load; 'produce something foul', 1596 (OED); poss. confused with 'scumble', overlay thinly with semi-opaque colour]. Make a mess of a painting job.

scunder see **scunner**

scunge [n. & vb., <Sc. *idem* (vb.), slink about] (Ulster). [n.]. S.o. always on the make. [vb.]. Gallivant.

scunner/scunder [n., <Sc. *idem*, dislike, disgust] (Ulster). As thus. **1908** Lynn Doyle, *Ballygullion*: 'So they went to Coort, an' afther a power [q.v.] of law, Hughey was bate, an' lost five or six times the value av the lamb; an' that gave him a scunner again law and lawyers...' **1951** Sam Hanna Bell, *December Bride*: '"You've taken a very sudden scunner at the Dineens." "I've taken no scunner at the Dineens..."' **1983** Polly Devlin, *All of us There*: '"Bad cess [q.v.] to him, and his breed, seed and generation, wouldn't he give you the scunder looking at him..."' Hence **scunnered** [p. part. as adj.] in same sense. **1991** Shane Connaughton, *The Run of the Country*: 'He was scunnered. It had got into the bed. A rat in the bed. The bastard.'

scureechting [pres. part., cf. Ir. *scoraíocht* (n.), 'gossiping visit to a neighbour's house' (Dinneen)]. As thus. **1960** John O'Donoghue, *In Kerry Long Ago*: '"What fright is on you tonight?" asked my mother..."I'm going *scureechting*," said I, as calmly as I could, to put her off the track.'

scut [n. & vb.]. 1. [n., cf. Ir *sciota*, scut, snippet]. Contemptible individual. **1939** Sean O'Casey, *I Knock at the Door*: '"You young scut," she said, giving him a slight shake. "If you try to make fun of your mother, I'll give you a welt [q.v.] that you won't be the better of for a week."' **1958** Frank O'Connor, *An Only Child*: 'Oh, that unspeakable scut, George Crosbie [Cork newspaper proprietor].' 2.

[n. & vb., poss. <rabbit's scut]. Free ride on the back of a lorry etc.; avail of such a ride. **1975** Eilís Brady, *All In! All In!*: 'Little boys love to boast about the great scut they got after the milk-car or the laundry-van...' **1982** Éamonn Mac Thomáis, *Janey Mack* (q.v.), *Me Shirt is Black*: 'We went to the funeral by scutting on the backs of cabs...' **1991** Roddy Doyle, *The Van*: 'one of them kicked the van. Jimmy Sr knew they were scutting on the back, the fuckers.'

scutch [n., poss. <rabbit's scut; or cutty-pipe (see **cutty** 1.)]. Clay pipe. **1994** John-Joe Kennedy in Kevin C. Kearns, *Dublin Tenement Life*: 'Women all in their shawls and you'd see them smoking, it'd be underneath their shawl. A small little clay pipe, a "scutch" they used to call it. It was cut down like [q.v.] to a small little thing they could hold in their hand.'

scutch (grass) [n., <OE *cwice*, quick]. Couch grass. **1991** James Kennedy, *The People who Drank Water from the River*: 'The problem, we agreed, was the "scutch" grass which after I had gone through the S section of various dictionaries turned out to be "couch" grass.'

scutter [n. & vb., <Ir. *sciodar* (n.), scour, diarrhoea; cf. ON *skita* (n.), excrement]. Excrement; defecate. **1991** Teddy Delaney, *Where we Sported and Played*: 'I glanced around furtively and...wiped the scutter that ran down the back of my leg with the grease-proof paper...' **1987** Vincent Caprani, *Vulgar Verse & Variations, Rowdy Rhymes & Rec-im-itations*, 'How Jem the Dancer Fought and Died for Ireland': '"And when I think of all that I did for him! The big fucker oughta be tied to a cow's tail and scuttered to death!"' Also **scutters** [n. pl.]. Diarrhoea. **1977** Wesley Burrowes, *The Riordans*: 'Who else could tell Father Sheehy that the baby had the scutters...or call Murph a hairy hoor [q.v.]?' Also as expletive. **1922** James Joyce, *Ulysses*: 'Buck Mulligan frowned at the lather on his razorblade..."Scutter," he cried thickly.'

scuttered [p. part. as adj., cf. *scutter* (q.v.) and Ir. *sciotarálaí* (n.), silly talker]. Having drink taken (q.v.). **1966** Patrick Boyle, *At Night All Cats are Grey*, title story: "'It's my belief, Missus, that the bowsie [q.v.] in that car was rightly [see **right** 1.] scuttered.'" **1995** Joe O'Connor, *Sunday Tribune*, 8 Oct: 'All you younger people ever think about is getting scuttered on cheap drink and committing lewd acts of an unnatural nature.'

scut the whip [exclam., <children's game, see **scut** 2.]. Warning to driver of scutters aboard. **1987** Lar Redmond, *Emerald Square*: 'got a free ride up the hill...on the back axle of a cab, until some louser [q.v.] shouted "Scut the whip!" and we had to jump off in a hurry...' **1991** Bob Quinn, *Smokey Hollow*: 'kids hung on to the back of the cart. Those for whom there wasn't room at the back would fall away yelling "Scut the whip, scut the whip" to spoil it for the successful ones.'

scuttle [vb., <?] (Cork). Smoke cigarette butts (Beecher).

Scut under the Butt, the [nickname, <scut 1. & Butt Bridge, Dub.]. Statue of James Connolly (1868–1916). **1996** Eanna Brophy, *Sunday Tribune*, 26 May: 'Within days of the unveiling of the (smallish) new James Connolly statue opposite Liberty Hall, we heard it referred to as "The Scut under the Butt".' **1996** Renagh Holohan, *Irish Times*, 1 June: 'Suggestions reaching Quidnunc this week for the new addition to the capital's landscape include the Scut under the Butt, the Marxist under the Arches or...the Agitator with the Rotavator. This last...is because he is depicted standing in front of a backdrop of a bronze starry plough [flag of Citizen Army].'

seanachie see **shanachie**

Seán Citizen [prop. n.]. Archetypical man in the street. **1977** Wesley Burrowes, *The Riordans*: 'Benjy and Gillian were found in a compromising position, changing out of clothes and provoking a phone call from my old friend Sean Citizen...'

segotia [n., <?; the etym. <Ir. *seo dhuit-se*, this [is] for you, is not gen. accepted]

as in **old segotia** [n. phr.]. Close friend (male usage). **1977** Myles na gCopaleen, *The Hair of the Dogma*: 'a side door [in the Scotch House]...through which shall be admitted all persons being...Old Segotias of the said Myles na Gopaleen'. **1987** Vincent Caprani, *Vulgar Verse & Variations, Rowdy Rhymes & Rec-im-itations*, 'Wayzgoose': "'Fair dues [q.v.] to all the members what don't forget old mates;/ But I have one final question, if you'll bear with me awhile..." "Oh fire away, sagosha [*sic*]," he answered with a smile.' **1995** Aidan Higgins, *Donkey's Years*: "'Ah cummere to me now me old shegoshia [*sic*]," Grogan coaxed me in the yard...'

semmit see **simmet**

sent back [n. phr.] (Ulster). S.o. who is apparently 'returned' after death. **1913** Alexander Irvine, *My Lady of the Chimney Corner*: 'There were several interpretations of Hughie. One was that he was a "sent back". That is, he had gone to the gates of a less cumbersome life and Peter or the porter at the other gate had sent him back to perform some unfulfilled task.'

sent for [adj. phr.] (Ulster). Marked for death: 'When I swalleyed that bone I was sure I was senfer' (Pepper).

septic [adj., <?] (Cork). Affected, vain (Beecher).

sevendable [adj., <Sc. *sevendle/sevennil*, strong, secure, sufficient, proparoxytonic accent on *ven*] (Ulster). Excellent; great; strong. Hence **sevendably** [adv.] in same sense. **1979** Paddy Tunney, *The Stone Fiddle*: 'the two O'Connors fell upon their Protestant friends and trounced them sevendably'.

sevener [n., <?] (Dub.). Fainting fit. **1987** Lar Redmond, *Emerald Square*: "'hurry an' get a small whiskey on me book [on credit]...this woman has "done a sevener"' — the Liberties equivalent of a lady out the Ballsbridge way having the vapours'.

shaad [n., <Ir. *sead*, louse, parasitical animal]. Term of abuse. See **feist**.

shade [n.]. 1. [<OE *sceadan* (vb.), part, divide] (Ulster). Hair parting. 2. [<Shelta

séideóg, policeman]. Garda (policeman).
1967 Bryan MacMahon, *The Honey Spike*
(q.v.): '"*Shades!*" urgently from Breda.
The whispered warning made Dickybird
freeze over his card table.' **1968** John
Healy, *The Death of an Irish Town*: '"The
shades! Screw the shades!" was the dialect
to warn the combatants that the guards
were here.' See **shidogue**.

shag boss [n. phr., <?] (printing). 'A
"clicker", under-foreman, often one
with inflated notions of imagined status
and power, etc.' (WS).

shagger [n., <'shag' (vb.), copulate with
(gen. male); 'he is but bad shag' (Grose)].
Term of contempt, not necessarily with
sexual connotation. **1991** Teddy
Delaney, *Where we Sported and Played*:
'my maths exercise copy that some
shagger stole on the way to school on
Monday morning'. **1995** RTÉ TV serial,
Upwardly Mobile, 22 Sept: 'My wife loves
him. I on the other hand think he's a
shagger of the first order.'

shagger's back [n. phr., see **shagger**;
'Austral. use' (Green)]. Painful male
condition iron. assumed to result from
excessive sexual activity.

shake/shakings of the bag [n. phr., cf.
shake-bag, female pudend (DHS)]. Runt
of the litter; unprepossessing person.
1939 Sean O'Casey, *I Knock at the Door*:
'This had been the shake of the bag, and
she knew she would never have another
child.' **1995** Patrick Boland, *Tales from a
City Farmyard*: 'My mother was in her
forties when I arrived, the only child
from the second marriage, and "the
shakings of the bag" as I was often
described.'

sham [n., cf. Shelta *sam*, boy; but see
1996 below] (Connacht). Townie,
derog.; individual, derog.; [voc.] mate,
friend; citizen of Tuam (Co. Galway),
gentleman. **1961** Tom Murphy, *A
Whistle in the Dark*: 'MUSH It's the fly
shams I'm talking about. You have to
keep watching them all the time. HARRY
What fly shams? MUSH Them smiling
shams that start doing you favours
because they want something off you.'
1968 John Healy, *The Death of an Irish*

Town: 'One sham wheezed he was
bleeding badly and the cove [q.v.] with
the razor said: "you're not Jesus Christ."'
1996 *Tuam Herald*, 6 Jan: '"We invented
the word sham. It came from a short
serial film that used to be screened at the
old Odeon, in which one of the main
characters was a witch called Shamba."
The late Noel Fallon, on the occasion of
his first visit to his native Tuam in 40
years, explaining how he and a few
friends had coined the word sham, made
famous by the plays of Tom Murphy and
the songs of the Saw Doctors.' Also **buff
sham**, **rager sham** [n. phr., derog.].
Country boy. **1968** John Healy, *The
Death of an Irish Town*: 'They were, in the
current slang of the town, "the buff
shams", "rager coves [q.v.]"...The "rager
shams" were not supposed to be as smart
as us "townies"...'

shammier [n., <?] (Dub.). Tennis ball.
1979 C.S. Andrews, *Dublin Made Me*:
'We continued the game with the
shammier along the footpath after school,
varying it with the usual boyish
horseplay...'

shamrock tea [n. phr., <the three
leaves, implying a very weak brew]
(Ulster). Weak tea.

sham-shite [vb.]. Skulk, hide away. **1948**
Patrick Kavanagh, *Tarry Flynn*: '"Only
pretending to be hurted, that's all," said
the blacksmith. "You don't worry, sham-
shiting behind the hedge he is."'

shan [n., poss. <Ir. *seang*, thin, lean,
emaciated person]. Dwarf in family/litter
of otherwise well-grown persons/animals
(OTF).

shanachie/seanachie [n., <Ir. *seanchaí*,
traditional storyteller]. As thus. **1966**
Sean O'Sullivan, *Folktales of Ireland*,
Introduction: 'On the Aran Islands he
[Synge] met a shanachie who had talked
with Sir William Wilde...' **1980** David
Marcus, *Irish Short Stories Vol. 2*,
Introduction: 'the importance of the
seanachie (storyteller) as a pivotal figure in
rural Irish life...must account for the
predisposition of the twentieth century
Irish writer towards the short story'. See
also **shanachus**.

shanachus/shanagh [n., <Ir. *seanchas*, act of storytelling]. Chat, conversation. See also **shanachie**.

Shanavest [nickname, apparently <Ir. *sean* (adj.), old + 'vest', but origin obsc.]. Agrarian secret society, C18–19. **1824** R.H. Ryland, *History, Topography and Antiquities of the County and City of Waterford*: 'The Shanavests were called Paudeen Car's party. Q. Why were they called Shanavests? A. Because they wore old waistcoats.' See also **Caravat**, **Ribbonmen**.

shandanagh [n., <Ir. *seanduine*, old man/person]. As thus. See **doll**.

shandrydan [n., <?; PWJ suggests <Ir. *sean* (adj.), old; but poss. <Eng. dial. *shan* (adj.), paltry; 'chaise with a hood' (1820) (OED)]. Decrepit, old-fashioned conveyance. **1899** E.Œ. Somerville & Martin Ross, *Some Experiences of an Irish RM*: '"Did you see that old shandrydan of hers in the street a while ago, and a fellow on the box with a red beard on him like Robinson Crusoe."'

shank [vb.] (Ulster). Walk.

Shankill Butchers [nickname, <brutal nature of killings]. Loyalist murder squad operating in Belfast, 1970s–1980s. **1995** Shane Connaughton, *A Border Diary*: 'Like people of all persuasions, he had to box clever to live during the Troubles [q.v.]. He told me he'd had a drink with the Shankill Butchers.' **1996** BBC Northern Ireland TV, *Newsline*, 28 Oct: 'Nearly all the 19 people murdered by the Shankill Butchers were Catholics. Most were tortured before being killed.'

shannagh see **shanachus**

shanty [n., <Ir. *sean tí*, old house; US 'shanty town', 1882–]. Small/poor-quality house.

Shan Van Vocht [nickname, <Ir. *sean bhean bhocht*, poor old woman]. Personalisation of Ire. **C19** Pop. ballad: '"Oh! the French are in the bay,/They'll be here by break of day,/And the Orange will decay,"/Says the Shan Van Vocht.' **1916** Eoin MacNeill, memorandum to Irish Volunteers: 'There is no such person

as Caitlin Ni Uallachain [see **Cathleen ní Houlihan**] or Roisin Dubh or the Sean-bhean Bocht, who is calling us to serve her. What we call our country is a concrete and visible reality.' **1988** R.F. Foster, *Modern Ireland 1600–1972*: 'The small but influential Irish feminist movement used Gaelicist channels, too: through the journal *Shan Van Vocht* founded in Belfast by Alice Milligan and Anna Johnston...'

shape [n. & vb.]. 1. [n.]. (Romantic) approach. **1908** Lynn Doyle, *Ballygullion*: 'The father an' mother, too, was always bummin' [q.v.] up Pether's money... when they seen him makin' a shape afther her.' 2. [vb.]. Put on airs, show off. **1939** Sean O'Casey, *I Knock at the Door*: '"Yah," sneered Connor, "you're shapin'. Just because your father's dead you think you're big in your black suit."' **1958** Frank O'Connor, *An Only Child*: 'when I behaved in the simple, manly way recommended in the school stories, they said I was mad or that I was "shaping" (the Cork word for swanking)'. **1992** Sean O'Callaghan, *Down by the Glenside, Memoirs of an Irish Boyhood*: 'My mother had bought me a white shirt and a red tie...so John the Sur's grandson certainly "shaped".' In the same sense **throw shapes** [vb. phr.], used esp. in physical description, also with connotations of aggression. Hence also **shaper** [n.].

sharee/sharoy/shiroy [n., <Fr. *soirée*, evening] (Ulster). Rowdy, boisterous gathering; ostentatious show. Hence also **sharee dance** [n. phr.]. Supper dance. See also **swarry**.

shaugh/shough [n. & vb., <Ir. *seach*, turn, spell (Dinneen)]. 'Turn or smoke of a pipe' (PWJ). **1898** Seumus MacManus, *The Bend of the Road*: 'Himself and the Playboy [q.v.] shoughed out of the same pipe.'

shaughraun [n., <Ir. *seachrán*, wandering, aberration, derangement]. 1. As thus; wanderer, esp. as in **on the shaughraun** [adj. phr.], of one wandering seeking work. **1922** James Joyce, *Ulysses*: 'We'll paralyse Europe as Ignatius Gallaher used

to say when he was on the shaughraun, doing billiardmarking in the Clarence.' **1961** Flann O'Brien, *The Hard Life*: '"Well the dear [q.v.] knows I think you are trying to destroy my temper, Father, and put me out of my wits and make an unfortunate shaughraun out of me!"' 2. Fairy influence which causes travellers to lose their way. See **stray** 3.

Shaun bautha [prop. n. phr., <Ir. *Seán báite*, watered whiskey]. Anything watered down or reduced to fragments. **1960** John O'Donoghue, *In Kerry Long Ago*: '"Away she went over hill and dale, shivering like an ivy leaf for fear she'd fall off and be killed alive where not a mother's son could find her till the ravens made *Shaun Bautha* of her corpse."'

shawlie/shawly [n., <shawl, the distinguishing dress, late C19–20]. 'An Irish fisherwoman, esp. of Dublin' (DHS); female street seller in general. **1944** Francis MacManus, *Pedlar's Pack*: 'I lean back and turn to see the reflected face of the shawly whom I take to be one of those hard-working women who sell fruit and fish and vegetables in the street.' **1958** Frank O'Connor, *An Only Child*: 'I hated the very sight of that shawl; it meant an immediate descent in the social scale from the "hatties" to the "shawlies" — the poorest of the poor!' **1987** Vincent Caprani, *Vulgar Verse & Variations, Rowdy Rhymes & Rec-imitations*, 'The Shawlie': 'one of those little old women — or oul' wans [q.v.] — habitually enveloped in a big black shawl and who used to frequent the Dublin streets...right up until the early 1960s'.

shebeen [n., <Ir. *síbín*, illicit whiskey]. An unlicensed drinking place, hence any disreputable public house etc. **1847** John Edward Walsh, *Ireland Sixty Years Ago*: 'a low public-house, where a weak small-beer was sold for a farthing a quart. It was in high request, as connected with the family of St Patrick, for we are told in the song — "His mother kept a shebeen shop/In the town of Enniskillen."' **1906** E.Œ. Somerville & Martin Ross, *Some Irish Yesterdays*: 'he would complete, at the always convenient shebeen, the

glorious fabric of intoxication, of which the foundation had been well and duly laid at the funeral'. Also **shebeeners** [n. pl.]. Habitués of such premises.

shebinock [n., <Ir. *seibineach*, large plump person or animal]. As thus.

sheddins [n. pl., <Sc. *shedding*, crossroads] (Ulster). As thus.

sheebone/sheebow [n. & vb., <Ir. *síobadh* (n.), blow, drift]. Blizzard; snow falling thus. **1983** W.F. Marshall, *Livin' in Drumlister*, 'Sarah Ann': 'But I'm for tacklin' Sarah Ann, no matter if the snow/Is iverywhere shebowin' [*sic*], when the morra comes I'll go.'

sheefra [n., cf. Ir. *síofra*, precocious child; Ir. *síofróir*, know-all, gossip]. As thus.

Sheela [n., <Ir. prop. name *Síle*]. Man or boy who takes an interest in 'affairs properly belonging to women' (PWJ).

sheelafeeka [n., <Ir. *síle an phíce*, earwig]. Term of abuse.

sheeogue [n., <Ir. *sí*, fairy + dimin. *óg*]. Fairy, changeling. **1866** Patrick Kennedy, *Legendary Fictions of the Irish Celts*: '"God send it's not one of the sheeoges [*sic*] you are nursing, instead of poor wild Rickard!"'

sheep's eyes, make/throw [vb. phr.]. 'When a young man looks fondly and coaxingly on his sweetheart he is "throwing sheep's eyes at her"' (PWJ).

sheilamaid [n.]. Clothes dryer formed of wooden bars slotted into metal holders, raised by pulleys to the ceiling. **1995** Aidan Higgins, *Donkey's Years*: 'Or behind the mangle under the sheilamaid, where the cats made their stinks.'

Sheila Wee [nickname, <?]. Cannon used by William III of Eng. in siege of Limerick. **1991** James Kennedy, *The People who Drank Water from the River*: 'In 1690 Patrick Sarsfield and "Galloping" Hogan [q.v.]...blew up the William siege-train and its famous big gun the "Sheila Wee"...'

shellickeepookie/shillig-a-booka [n., <Ir. *seilide*, snail + Ir. *púca* <ON *pukí*, imp]. Snail. **1879** Charles J. Kickham,

Knocknagow: '"what have you under the crib to tempt the birds to go into it?" "A bit of boiled pueata [potato], sir," Tommy answered readily, "an' a shillig-a-booka, and a few skehoshies [rose-hips]."'

shellityhorn/shellydyhorn [n., <Ir. *seilide*, snail + horn (of snail)]. Snail. **1966** Séamus Murphy, *Stone Mad*: 'He moved around like a shelldyhorn [*sic*] with his grievances tucked in as part of his kit.' **C20** Children's rhyme: 'Shellity, shellity-horn/Stick out your two black horns.'

shenanigan/s [n. & vb., poss. <Ir. *sionnachuadh*, 'act of playing the fox, japing' (Dinneen), though Cornish and East Anglian origins have been suggested (DHS), also <American Indian or prop. name 'Seán Hannigan', identity unknown. 'From middle 1800s Western [US]' (DAS).]. Tricks, trickery, japes; behaving thus. **1987** Lar Redmond, *Emerald Square*: '"he's too bloody freemakin'. I soon cut him off the day he tried his oul' shinanickin' [*sic*] with me! I never deal there now."'

sherral [n., <?]. Mean, unprincipled fellow. **1986** Padraic O'Farrell, *'Tell me, Sean O'Farrell'*: 'I remember a trick played on an old sherral (mean man) who was as cross as a bag of cats.'

sheugh/shuch/shugh [n., <Sc. *idem*, ditch] (Ulster). As thus. **1991** Shane Connaughton, *The Run of the Country*: '"Flat Fermanagh," said his father, "and lookit [see **looka'**] will you at Cavan — a humpy oul' horse knee-deep in a sheugh."'

shidogue [n., <Shelta *séideóg*, policeman]. As thus. **1952** Bryan MacMahon, *Children of the Rainbow*: 'he cupped his hands about his mouth and called out in a loud voice: "The shidogues! The shidogues!"…The word terrified the tinkers. The law was their hereditary foe.' See **shade** 2.

shift [vb. & n.]. 1. [vb. & n.]. Pursue girls for amatory purposes; indulge in French kissing; have sexual intercourse with. **1996** *Irish Times*, 8 May: 'the accused boy told his mother he had kissed her. His mother asked if that was all and he replied "I shifted her." Asked to explain, he continued, "I went all the way but I

didn't force her."' **1996** Carmel Wynne, *Irish Times*, 21 May: 'Clearly no 11- or 12-year-old is emotionally ready to deal with the sexual feelings aroused by "shifting", "meeting" or "getting off" [q.v.] — the slang terms widely used for "a Frenchie" [French kiss].' See also **move**. 2. [vb.] (Ulster). Change one's clothes.

shiggy-shoo see **shugglyshoe**

shilcorn/shillcorn [n., <Sc. *chillcorn/ shillcorn*, blackhead] (Ulster). Facial pimple, sore (YDS).

shillelagh [n., <oak forests of Síol Éalaigh (Shillelagh), Co. Wicklow]. Oak cudgel.

shillig-a-booka see **shellickeepookie**

shingerleens [n. pl., cf. Ir. *singirlín*, *Fuchsia globosa* (Dinneen)]. 'Ornamental tags and ends — or ribbons, bow-knots, tassels, etc. — hanging on dress, curtains, furniture, etc.' (PWJ).

Shinner [nickname, abbrev. of 'Sinn Féin']. Applied by loyalists and the British to the republican political party of that name (1905–) and its sympathisers. **1987** Lar Redmond, *Emerald Square*: 'He was a member of the guerilla force that broke the power of the British in the twenty-six counties, a "Shinner".' **1995** *Irish Times*, 25 Feb: 'What Arthur Griffith and Michael Collins [see **the Big Fella**] thought as they gazed down from the wall at the "shinners" trooping up the stairs can only be imagined.' Hence (Ulster) Catholics in general. **1997** Eamonn McCann, *Irish Times*, 22 Feb: 'He [John Taylor] called Catholics "Shinners". He said there were decent Shinners in Tyrone and Fermanagh but once you moved to the cities…there was a different breed of Shinner altogether.'

shinny [n., <Sc. *idem*, 'the game resembling hockey' (CSD), similar to hurling, otherwise *shinty*] (Ulster). Game of hurling; stick used in the game. **1818** John Dickey, *Poems on Various Subjects by John Dickey*, 'Address to Parkgate': 'Now coos the woodquest in the rising grove/Where I have often with the warping drove/Of Shinny Players, ended many a

hail...' **1913** Alexander Irvine, *My Lady of the Chimney Corner*. 'Despite my fistic encounters, my dents in the family loaves, my shinny, my marbles, and the various signs of total, or at least partial, depravity...'

shipyard ear [n. phr., <Belfast yards]. Deafness. **1979** John Morrow, *The Confessions of Proinsias O'Toole*: 'A victim of "Shipyard Ear," I diagnosed, that industrial ailment caused by excessive noise...'

shipyards [n. pl.] (Ulster). Large feet/ shoes (YDS).

shire [vb., <Sc. *idem*, drain water off] (Ulster). As thus, as in **shire one's head** [vb. phr.]. Rest, relieve pressure on. **1948** John O'Connor, *Come Day — Go Day*: '"take yourselves off now and let me get my head shired. I'll cut you a piece of bread for the time being."'

shiroy see **sharee**

shish [vb., gen. imper., <'shush' by fronting of vowel]. Cease making a noise. **1995** Phil O'Keeffe, *Down Cobbled Streets, A Liberties Childhood*: '"You're all good childer [q.v.], every one of ye," she said..."Just shish now, not a word, while I go and see to your mother."'

shite [n. & exclam., more gen. in Hib.E than 'shit', excrement, cf. Ger. *scheiss* etc.]. Term of contempt; expression of disgust. Also **to have one's shite** [adj. phr.]. Retort indicating rejection. Cf. glue, to have one's (q.v.). See **Jem**. Also **you will in your shite!** [exclam.]. Retort implying there is no chance that you will. **1992** Roddy Doyle, *Brownbread*: 'JOHN I have to have a shite — I'm goin' in the corner here, Donkey; okay. DONKEY (to JOHN) Yeh will in your shite! No way! — Go ou' to the jacks [q.v.]!...'

shitehawk [n., <*shite* (q.v.) + 'hawk' on analogy with *gobhawk* (q.v.)]. Contemptible individual, gen. male. **1979** John Morrow, *The Confessions of Proinsias O'Toole*: 'a straightforward Military Intelligence plan for the extermination of two flocks of dangerous shitehawks with the one stone'. **1991** Roddy Doyle, *The*

Van: 'Jimmy Sr would throw the little shitehawk out on his ear if he turned up now.' **1996** Brendan Glacken, *Irish Times*, 'Times Square', 17 Oct: 'It is not hard to thrill to the paper's [*Western People*, Mayo] regular court reports of people battling with bar stools or beer mugs...casting powerful tribal accusations like "shitehawk" and "bog-dwarf bollocks [see **bollix**]" at one another...'

shit from a shool, like see **shot off a shovel, like a**

shloother [n., cf. Ir. *sluaiste*, layabout (DOM)]. As thus.

shlowny [adj., <Ir. *sleamhnaigh* (vb.), slide, slip] (Cork). Slippery (Beecher).

shoggle [vb., cf. ME *shogge*, shake, jolt] (Ulster). As thus.

shoneen [n., <Ir. *seoinín*, aper of foreign ways, poor Protestant (Dinneen), <*Seon*, John, esp. John Bull, archetypical Englishman + dimin. *ín*]. Ir. person aping Eng. ways; 'would-be gentleman who puts on superior airs' (PWJ). **1914** James Joyce, *Dubliners*, 'Ivy Day in the Committee Room': '"Hasn't the working-man as good a right to be in the Corporation as anyone else — ay, and a better right than those shoneens that are always hat in hand before any fellow with a handle to his name?"' **1995** Frank Kelly, *Irish Times*, 3 Oct: 'Throughout most of my schooldays, I was constantly berated by my Irish language teachers for not being able to speak my "native" tongue and of [*sic*] being a "shoneen".' **1996** Tom Humphries, *Irish Times*, 3 Feb: 'The damage done by the shoneens and the gombeens [q.v.] will take quite a while to repair. Consolation lies in the thought that the [soccer] national team should be serviceable again pretty soon.'

shook [vb., p. tense & solecistic p. part. as adj.]. [p. tense]. Shaken, surprised, as in **that shook you!** Expressing aggressive response or retaliation. **1977** Flann O'Brien, *The Hair of the Dogma*: '"Smart boy wanted," she said coarsely. "That's your breakfast. Ate it and shut your gob." This, to use slang parlance, "shook" me.' **1982** Éamonn Mac Thomáis, *Janey Mack* (q.v.), *Me Shirt is Black*: 'we'd have been dead only for the war. "Sorry, no cigarettes." We used to kick the shop counters and say, "That shook them."' **1994** Ferdia Mac Anna, *The Ship Inspector*: 'When she had her back to him, he slipped a piece of soggy bread down the back of her neck. "Now. That shook you," Rory said.' [solecistic p. part. as adj.] as in **very shook-looking**. Frail, unwell after illness.

shooler/shuiler [n., <Ir. *siúlóir*, wanderer, vagrant]. As thus. **1866** Patrick Kennedy, *Legendary Fictions of the Irish Celts*: '"...I didn't make them crowns at all; it was a big *shuler* [*sic*] (vagrant) of a fellow that took employment with me yesterday"'. **1938** Seumas MacManus, *The Rocky Road to Dublin*: 'His mother had particular interest in all *shuilers*. There was never wanderer or beggar, tinker or pedlar, crossed her threshold without finding themselves seated...'

shoot the boots off s.o. [vb. phr.] (Ulster). Extirpate.

shop teeth [n. phr.]. False teeth, dentures.

short twelve [nickname]. Brief Sunday midday mass.

shot off a shovel, like a [adv. phr.]. With great rapidity. **1922** James Joyce, *Ulysses*: '[Bloom ascended] to the glory of the brightness at an angle of forty-five degrees over Donohoe's in Little Green Street, like a shot off a shovel.' **1992** Brian Leyden, *Departures*: 'And the race is on. The shopkeeper's assistant is out the door like a shot off a shovel.' Also **like shit from a shool** [<Sc. *shool/shuil/shule*, shovel] (Ulster) in same sense.

shough see **shaugh**

show out [vb.] (Ulster). 'Appear in public as man and wife shortly after the wedding' (YDS). Hence **Showing Sunday** [n. phr.]. First appearance thus at mass.

Shraft/Saraft/Shraff/Scraff [n., <'Shrove']. 'Shrovetide: on or about Shrove Tuesday' (PWJ). **1867** Patrick Kennedy, *The Banks of the Boro*: 'I was in Insiscorfy [Enniscorthy], you see, on Sraft [*sic*] Tuesday...'

shraums [n. pl., <Ir. *sram*, matter running from the eyes]. As thus.

shtal/shtall [n., cf. Romany *chal*, man, fellow]. Husband, partner. **1942** Eric Cross, *The Tailor and Ansty*: '"Will you look at my ould shtal? Will you look at the puss [see **puss** 1.] on him?"'

shuch see **sheugh**

shuggly-shoe/shuggy-shoo/shuggety-shoo/shiggy-shoo etc. [n. & vb.] (Ulster). 1. [n. & vb., <Sc. *shoggie* (vb.), swing back and forth like a pendant, cf. Middle Low Ger. *shocken* (vb.), swing]. [n.]. Suspended rope used as a swing; act of swinging child in the air; (game of) see-saw. [vb.]. Play on see-saw; act thus. **1908** Lynn Doyle, *Ballygullion*: 'if he ever did get near makin' up his mind, ould Jemmy the stone-mason would throw in some objection that would set his head shuggelty-shooin' again'. 2. [n., cf. Sc. *shog-bog*, quaking bog]. Quagmire; 'soft place in a bog where a person can jump up and down without breaking the surface' (CUD).

shugh see **sheugh**

shuiler see **shooler**

sichin/sichan/siccan [adj., intens.] (Ulster). Such, such a. See **glam**.

sick [n.] (Ulster). Invalid. **1983** *John Pepper's Illustrated Encyclopaedia of Ulster Knowledge*: '"We make the best poteen [q.v.] and give the sick a glass. If that doesn't work we give him another..."'

side, the other [n. phr., periphrasis]. Britain as viewed from Ireland. **1793** Charles Macklin, *The True-Born Irishman*: ''O'DOGHERTY   O aye, you politicians promise us the devil and all [q.v.] while you are among us, but the moment you get to t'other side, you have devilish bad memories.' **1991** Tony Gray, *Mr Smyllie, Sir*: 'It is October 1940, and it is dark outside in Westmoreland Street. On the other side, as we used to say in those days, the Battle of Britain is at its height...'

sign [n., <Ir. *rian*, trace, small quantity]. As thus. **1960** John O'Donoghue, *In Kerry Long Ago*: '"We'll give you shelter

all right, my good man..." says MacGrane, says he, "but the devil carry the sign have we in the house for you to eat."'

sign's/signs on (it) [concessive phr., <Ir. *tá a rian air*, lit. 'the mark of it is on him', he looks it]. 'Used to express the result or effect or proof of any proceeding' (PWJ). **1936** Frank O'Connor, *Bones of Contention and Other Stories*, 'The Majesty of the Law': 'Dan had looked after his mother while the life was in her, and after her death no other woman had crossed the threshold. Signs on it, his house had that look.' **1963** John McGahern, *The Barracks*: '"Pass the exams. That's what gets people on. That and swindlin'. I didn't do much of either meself. More's the pity. And signs are on it!"'

simmet/semmit [n., <Sc. *semmit*, poss. <OF *samit*, samite] (Ulster). Man's vest/ singlet. **1948** John O'Connor, *Come Day — Go Day*: 'Kitty took dry shirt, socks and semmit from the line across the fire and threw them on the sofa beside him.' **1979** John Morrow, *The Confessions of Proinsias O'Toole*: '...I, down to simmit and jock strap, crept stealthily in beside Steffers'.

Simon Pure [nickname, <?]. Good-quality poteen (q.v.). **1908** Lynn Doyle, *Ballygullion*: '"Here's somethin'll console ye. This is the rale Simon Pure this time."'

singleton [nickname]. 'Corkscrew, made by a famous cutler of that name, who lived in a place called Hell [passage leading from Christchurch Lane to Christchurch Yard, now vanished], in Dublin; his screws are remarkable for their excellent temper' (Grose).

singlings [n.]. Strong first distillation of whiskey or poteen (q.v.). **1845** William Carleton, *Tales and Stories of the Irish Peasantry*, 'Bob Pentland': 'Even this running was going on to their satisfaction, and the singlings had been thrown again into the still, from the worm of which projected the strong medicinal *first-shot* [q.v.] as the doubling commenced — the last term meaning the

spirit in its pure and finished state.' **1978** John McGuffin, *In Praise of Poteen*: 'The practice had been common for years of selling off "singlings"...to people suffering from sprains, hacks and cuts. "Just rub the singlings on and the pain will disappear like magic," it was widely believed.'

sink the black [vb. phr., <snooker term]. Consume pints of stout. **1995** RTÉ Radio news, 14 Apr: 'the men who were sinking the black in Dublin's Beggar's Bush pub'.

sinnery [adj. & adv., cf. Sc. *idem* (adj.), sundry, several] (Ulster). Sundry, various. Hence **in sinnery** [adv. phr.]. In bits.

sis [n., <Eng. dial. *siserary* <Lat. *certiorari*, form of legal writ] (Ulster). Long-winded, pointless story/excuse.

sitting-down [n.] (Ulster). House and land. **1938** Seumas MacManus, *The Rocky Road to Dublin*: '"My friend Billy's house and farm will be a good sittin' down for any woman."'

six and tips [n. phr., 'elaboration of *six*, six-shilling beer' (DHS)]. 'Whiskey and small beer' (Grose).

six-pack [n., <bottles/cans of drink] (Ulster). Paramilitary punishment shooting of informers etc. See **knee-cap**. **1994** Paddy O'Gorman, *Queuing for a Living*: '"A 6-pack?" "That there's the hands, the knees, the ankles."'

sixpenny rush [n. phr., <price of admission]. Cheap children's admission to matinée cinema performances, *c*.1950s–1960s. **1988** Gabriel Byrne, *Magill*, Mar: 'I have rowdied in lines of bedlam on Saturday afternoons outside picturehouses all over Dublin for the sixpenny rush and remember standing with my two jam jars, the price of admission to the Tivoli in Francis Street.' See also **penny rush**, **twopenny rush**, **fourpenny rush**.

skail [vb. intrans., <Ir. *scaoil* (vb. trans. & intrans.), release, discharge]. As thus. **1938** Seumas MacManus, *The Rocky Road to Dublin*: 'As a hero he was led back to school, and when school skailed that day, all of the children walked

around and around him in fascinated wonder...'

skalp [vb., cf. Ir. *scealpaire* (n.), pilferer] (Cork). Cheat (Beecher).

skeal see **scéal**

skee-ball order, in [adj. phr., <?]. In first-class order. **1973** Noël Conway, *The Bloods* (q.v.): 'just to satisfy himself personally that the battalion had all the equipment it was supposed to have and that it was in skee-ball order'. See also **rag order, in**.

skeedeen [n., <Ir. *sceidín*, any small thing]. As thus; 'small potato' (PWJ).

skeek [n., cf. Sc. *skeeg*, drop] (Ulster). Pouring of tea (SH).

skeeory [n., <Ir. *sceachóir/í*, haw/s]. Haw, fruit of dog rose.

skeet [vb. intrans., <*skit* poss. <ON *skjóta*, shoot]. Shy. **1995** Geoffrey O'Shea in Mary Ryan et al. (eds.), *No Shoes in Summer*: 'Was a quarter mile gone, when the mare started to skeet. I untackled. Went between the shafts, guided her and shoved the cart most of a mile.'

skeeter [n., <?]. Agricultural implement. **1995** Mick Doyle in Seán Power (ed.), *Those were the Days, Irish Childhood Memories*: 'The other horse was tackled to a wooden rake called a "skeeter" which brought the hay to exactly the correct spot for each wynd [see **wynde** 1.].'

skeeze [vb., <?]. Peep. **1922** James Joyce, *Ulysses*: 'Old Garryowen started growling again at Bloom that was skeezing round the door. "Come in, come on, he won't eat you," says the citizen.'

skelf [n., <Sc. *idem*, splinter, cf. Ir. *scealp* in same sense] (Ulster). As thus; piece chipped or cut off. **1966** Séamus Murphy, *Stone Mad*: 'I remember a figure carver from Dublin who was always taking skelfs off his knuckles.'

skelly [n. & vb., <Sc. *idem* <ON *skjelga*, OE *sceolh*, squint] (Ulster). As thus. **1908** Lynn Doyle, *Ballygullion*: 'some of the red-hot Nationalists kept takin' quare

[see **quare** 1.] skellys at a flag in the corner wi' King William on it'. **1913** Alexander Irvine, *My Lady of the Chimney Corner*. 'He was charged — rumour charged him — with having blinked [q.v.] a widow's cow. It was noised abroad that he had been caught in the act of "skellyin'" at her.'

skelp [vb. & n., <Sc. *idem*, beat (vb.)]. Strike with the open hand, whip, beat; such a blow. **1920** Lynn Doyle, *Ballygullion*: '"I didn't tell ye to hit me such a skelp," sez he. "You've loosened every tooth in me head..."' **1968** Myles na gCopaleen, *The Best of Myles*: '"Begob [q.v.] the poor landlady gets the windup in right [see **right** 1.] style. Then the brother starts tappin' her chest and givin' her skelps on the neck."' **1979** Frank Kelly, *The Annals of Ballykilferret*: 'the attention of the central figure is distracted to allow one of the local cailíns [see **colleen**] to sneak from her chair and give him a "skelp" on the head with the ash plant..."Skelpin'" is believed to have had its origin in the days of landlordism, when the landlord's agent was known as a "tricky boy" [see **trickie**] or a "go boy" [q.v.] in the Ballykilferret area.'

skeugh [n., <Ir. *scoth*, chip, splinter (of rock)]. As thus. **1995** Phil O'Keeffe, *Down Cobbled Streets, A Liberties Childhood*: 'One, two, sometimes three dogs ran out to challenge us, and we were no Cuchulainns as we picked stones and skeughs from the ditches.'

skew-ways/skeow-ways/scew-ways [adv., <Ir. *sceabha* (n.), slant, obliquity, <'skew' (vb.) <OF *eschuer/eschever* (vb.), eschew]. (Awkwardly) slanted, tilted. **1991** Teddy Delaney, *Where we Sported and Played*: 'the fella who started in the left lane...could end up going scew-ways in a circle round the cat's eyes'.

skhone [n., <?] (Ulster). Humorous story/yarn (YDS).

skiboo [n., cf. Sc. *skybal*, low, worthless person] (Ulster). Nobody in particular (Todd).

skidder [n. <Ir. *sciodar*, broken sour milk] (Munster). As thus.

skillet [n.]. Cooking receptacle. **1986** Padraic O'Farrell, *'Tell me, Sean O'Farrell'*: 'The house where we stayed had skillets in the gardens for sanitation. Girls got stung by nettles in the most delicate places when using them.'

Skillingers, the [nickname]. 6th Iniskilling Dragoons of the Brit. army, raised 1690. Its badge is the castle of Enniskillen, Co. Fermanagh.

skilt [n. & vb., poss. <ME *skelt* (vb.), hasten]. [n.]. Cheeky/irresponsible/ flirtatious girl; small girl. [vb.]. Move about quickly; run away, run wild (in). **1951** Sam Hanna Bell, *December Bride*: '"Since when hae ye taken to skiltin the fields on a Sabbath?"'

skimf [n., cf. Sc. *scimp* (adj.), small, scanty] (Ulster). Tiny amount.

skimpit [adj.] (Ulster). Tight-fitting.

skin, [n.] as in **decent skin** [n. phr., synecdoche]. Term of affection, gen. between males. **1966** Liam Ó Cuanaigh, *Evening Press*, 21 Nov: 'Skins. Usually decent, mellowing with the years to become decent oul' skins; never see you caught for the price of a smoke, a read of the paper or the loan of a pump for your bike...' **1977** Myles na gCopaleen, *The Hair of the Dogma*: 'ask any guard to direct you to Keating's of Store Street. John is a very decent skin.' **1989** Hugh Leonard, *Out after Dark*: 'his crippled boss had, like a decent skin, lent him forty pounds, enough for a new start in London'.

skin a louse [vb. phr.]. Be very stingy and grasping.

skinny-eight [n.]. Narrow oblong section in children's game of pickie or piggybeds (q.v.). **1995** Phil O'Keeffe, *Down Cobbled Streets, A Liberties Childhood*: 'I was negotiating the problem of hopping on one leg and kicking the pickie into the skinny-eight, when Jenny hissed at me, "She's coming."'

skinnymalink [n., extended form of 'skinny']. Tall, preternaturally thin individual. Also **skinnymalink melodeon legs** (Ulster). '[O]ld-time expression of irreverence...used by small boys

concerning an elder' (Pepper). **N.d.** Children's rhyme: 'Skinnymalink melodeon legs big banana feet/Went to the pictures and couldn't get a seat.'

skin on one's face [n. phr., gen. neg.] (Ulster). Respect. **1993** Sam McAughtry, *Touch & Go*: '"Christ, that's the worst I ever heard. The man's in for murder and you're tapping him. Have you no skin on your face?"'

skins as in **for skins** [adv. phr., invar. neg., cf. US sl. *skin*, dollar; Eng. sl. *idem*, sovereign (DHS)]. At all; in any way. See **court**.

Skin-the-Goat [nickname, <?]. James Fitzharris, car driver involved in the assassination by the Invincibles (q.v.) of Brit. government officials Burke & Cavendish, May 1882. **1922** James Joyce, *Ulysses*: '"Skin-the-goat," Mr O'Madden Burke said. "Fitzharris. He has that cabman's shelter, they say, down there at Butt bridge."' **1979** C.S. Andrews, *Dublin Made Me*: 'A poorly dressed old man passed the time of day with my uncle and I was told, as if it was a great secret, that the man was "Skin the Goat"...' **1996** Éamonn Mac Thomáis, RTÉ Radio rebroadcast, *The Song and the Story*, 6 Feb: 'James Fitzharris was known as Skin the Goat, but you wouldn't call him that to his face. Though you could call him Skin. For some reason he didn't seem to mind that.'

skip [n.]. 1. [poss. abbrev. of *skip-kennel*, lackey or manservant, 1668– (OED)] (Trinity College, Dub.). A college servant. (Last male skip, Larry Kelly, d. Jan 1974.) **1948** 'Simplex', *TCD, A College Miscellany*, 'Petulant Poem', 13 May: '"I wonder why I am a skip,"/He said, ignoring heaps of dust,/And leaving cocoa on the cups/ And, stuck to plates, much hardened crust...' Also **skippery** [n.]. Rudimentary kitchen in sets of college rooms, the skip's domain. 2. [Anglo-Ir. colloq., late C19–20 (DHS)]. Dance. 3. [<?] (Ulster). Soccer 'strip'. **1977** Sam McAughtry, *The Sinking of the Kenbane Head*: 'he started up a football team once called North Star. A publican called McEldowney bought them their skip — red jerseys, white pants and red and white socks.'

skit [n. & vb., <*idem*, ridicule or caricature, 1781–, poss. <ON *skjóta* (vb.), shoot]. Taunt, make game of. **1985** Máirín Johnston, *Around the Banks of Pimlico*: 'he could be very abusive with strangers passing by and the children going to school in Francis Street were forever jeering him for a bit of a skit'. **1986** Tom McDonagh, *My Green Age*: 'she skitted with me, saying that if I was good she would give me a kiss'. **1995** *Leinster Leader* (Naas, Co. Kildare), 27 July: 'She denied a suggestion from Mr Williams' solicitor...that she and staff at Abrakebabra were "in the habit of having a bit of a skit at his expense".'

skite [n. & vb.]. 1. [cf. Sc. *skit* (n.), a slight shower; 'a small quantity of any liquid' (CSD), <ON *skjóta* (vb.), shoot] (Ulster). [n.]. As thus; splash of water (see **Roman collar**); frivolous, talkative person. Also **on the skite** [adj. phr.]. Engaged in serious drinking. [vb.]. Splash with muddy water; slip, slide; skim (a stone); squirt. 2. [<OE *scitan* (vb.), shit/shite]. [n.]. Useless, unreliable individual, esp. as in **empty skite**. [vb.]. Void excrement.

skite-the-gutter [n. phr.] (Ulster). Person of no account. See **skite** 2.

skitter [n.] (Ulster). 1. [cogn. with *skit* (vb.); cf. Sc. *skit*, vain, frivolous or wanton girl 1572] (Ulster). As thus, but of both sexes. **1948** John O'Connor, *Come Day — Go Day*: '"I'll tell your father, you wee [q.v.] skitter ye," he yelled at young Kelly.' **1983** Polly Devlin, *All of us There*: 'Any child who offends her strict territorial sense of propriety is called a "skitter".' **1996** Martina Devlin, *Sunday Tribune*, 'Confessions', 2 June: 'My father wondered how did I ever get hooked up with a "quare [see **quare** 1.] skitter" like that, and me a BA.' 2. [<ON *skita*, excrement]. Diarrhoea (see **scutter**); term of abuse. Also **skin off your skitter** [n. phr.]. Least of things.

skraik see **screagh**

skree [n., <?]. Large number of small things (PWJ); sizeable quantity.

skreigh see **screagh**

skull [n., <shape] (Cork). Loaf of bread similar to a 'duck' loaf.

sky farmer [nickname, <'their farms being *in nubibus*, "in the clouds"' (Grose)]. Farmer who, having lost his land, keeps 'a cow or two grazing along the roadsides' (PWJ).

slabber [n. & vb., poss. <Du. *slabberen* (vb.) or Low Ger. *slabbern* (vb.), befoul with saliva] (Ulster). Untidy/talkative individual; excessive eloquence; act thus. **1993** Seamus Heaney, *The Midnight Verdict* (translation of Brian Merriman, *Cúirt an Mheán Oíche*): 'Their one recourse is the licensed robber/With his legalese and his fancy slabber.' **1993** Sam McAughtry, *Touch & Go*: '"let him slabber away there, sure anybody that needs to have the soles of their feet tickled before he can get a stand-on [q.v.] deserves nothing but sympathy"'.

sladdy [n., <Ir. *sleaidí*, 'cooked *cnuasach* (edible seaweed)' (Dinneen)]. As thus. **1996** Leslie Matson, *Méiní, The Blasket Nurse*: '"Sladdy...was classed along with butter, meat and fish as *anlann* or "kitchen" [see **kitchen** 1.]...'

slag [vb., cf. Brit. sl. 'slag off', abuse verbally]. Taunt, criticise, denigrate, take a rise out of. **1971** Seán Beecher, *The Story of Cork*: 'But "slagging", the art of badinage, is an integral part of [Cork] city life and finds its expressions in the cinemas, at games, but not unfortunately any more in the theatres...' **1979** Frank Kelly, *The Annals of Ballykilferret*: 'The increased availability of drink created an ambience highly favourable to the "shlaggin" competition. "Shlaggin", which can best be described as a sort of prolonged verbal duelling, is a fiercely competitive activity...' **1995** Jackie Bourke, *Irish Times*, 14 Mar: 'However, they "slagged" each other a lot about girls at school and some boys in the class claimed to have dated...' Also **slagger** [n.] in same sense.

slake [n., <Sc. *slaik*, lick] (Ulster). Quick, inefficient cleaning; layer of jam etc. spread on slice of bread (YDS).

slammick [n., <Ir. *slaimice*, untidy person, probably <Brit. dial. *slammock*, *idem*]. Messy, untidy individual.

slap [n.]. 1. [poss. <*slap*, blow, C18–early C19]. Booty, swag. **C.1780** Anon., *Luke Caffrey's Kilmainham Minit*: 'For Luke he was ever the chap/To boozle [q.v.] de bull-dogs [sheriff's officers] and pinners [q.v.],/And when dat he milled [made] a fat slap/He merrily melted [spent] de winners.' 2. (Ulster). Large number or quantity. **1995** Shane Connaughton, *A Border Diary*: '"Don boy's no daw [q.v.]. He sells Bingo tickets and no one'll go by him without buying. He's ropes of money. Slaps of it."' 3. [<Sc. *idem*, gap] (Ulster). Gap in hedge.

slasher [n.]. 1. 'Bullying, riotous fellow' (Grose). 2. [<action of striking] (Ulster). Lambeg drum. **1995** Fintan Vallely, *Irish Times*, 12 July: 'According to Richard Sterrit...one Davis from nearby Glenanne originated the drum in the last century. Locally they are fondly called "slashers", "rattlies" or "tibbies", while in Moy, Co. Tyrone...they are called "Killymans" after a local village.'

slates, away for see **away for slates**

slat mara [n. phr., cf. Ir. *slad-mhara*, murder and robbery; *slad-mharóir*, freebooter (Dinneen)]. Term of contempt. **1927** Peadar O'Donnell, *Islanders*: 'Arrah [q.v.], damn on ye! It's not the nerve to hoult [q.v.] a girl ye'd have yerself, ye poor slat mara," Biddy said...'

slavvers [n., <Sc. *slaver* (n. & vb.), slobber, Icel. *slafra* in same sense] (Ulster). Shower of spittle/saliva 'issued by s.o. in great agitation' (YDS).

slawher [vb., <Ir. *soláthair*, provide, supply]. As thus, as in **slawher for oneself**.

sleekit/sleeked [adj., <Sc. *idem*, unctuous] (Ulster). Devious, sly. **1951** Sam Hanna Bell, *December Bride*: '"Look at her now, keeking [see **keek** 1.] at us through the window. Heth [q.v.], but she's a sleeked one that."'

sleep it out [vb. phr.]. Sleep in. See also **outsleep**.

sleeveen [n. & (more rarely) adj., <Ir. *slíbhín* (n.), sly individual]. As thus; term of abuse. **1965** Lee Dunne, *Goodbye to the Hill*: '"You bastard. You sleeveen bastard," he yelled into my face.' **1968** Myles na gCopaleen, *The Best of Myles*: '"You don't hesitate to...denounce me to your even weightier wife as a thief, a fly-by-night, a sleeveen and a baucagh-shool [q.v.]."' **1989** Hugh Leonard, *Out after Dark*: '"That fellow's a sleeveen," he said. It was a pejorative word meaning a little mountainy fellow, as treacherous as he was unpredictable.'

sleuter/slooter/sluter/slitter etc. [n. & vb., <Sc. *slooter/slutter/slotter* etc. (n. & vb.), filthy mess, sloven, eating or drinking in slobbering manner, working or walking in slovenly manner; lumpish inactive person; act in slovenly manner, gobble food noisily, slobber, engage in wet, dirty work, etc.; cf. Ir. *sliútar* (n.), big, clumsy foot] (Ulster). As thus; person with badly fitting clothes; person who sneezes carelessly; wet mud; pretend to work; do laundry carelessly; cook badly; etc.

slice off the legs [n. phr.]. Sexual intercourse with female. **1965** Lee Dunne, *Goodbye to the Hill*: 'he'd had a row with the missus or something. Probably wanted a slice off the legs before his porridge...'

sliddher [vb., <Ir. *sliodarnach*, act of sliding]. Skip or glide (OTF).

slider [n.]. Ice cream wafer. **1995** Tom McCaughren in Seán Power (ed.), *Those were the Days, Irish Childhood Memories*: 'On presenting our thrupenny bit, we received what we called a slider, or wafer, and then it was off to some sunny spot again...'

sliggin [n., <?]. Light indoor shoe, slipper. Hence **slig** [vb.]. Walk with a shuffle, as if in slippers. **1995** Phil O'Keeffe, *Down Cobbled Streets, A Liberties Childhood*: '"at the rate you're springin' up your feet could grow a whole size bigger. And we can't chance getting them too big. We don't want you sliggin' your shoes to the chapel if they're not the right size."'

slim [n.] (Ulster). Small griddle scone, soda bread or potato. **1997** George O'Brien, reviewing Maurice Hayes, *Black Pudding with Slim: A Downpatrick Boyhood, Irish Times*, 3 Jan: '...Mrs Hayes' home-made black pudding and Aunt Lil's "slim" (potato pancake) sound delicious'.

sling [vb.] as in **sling a calf** [vb. phr.]. Abort (of cattle). **1977** Wesley Burrowes, *The Riordans*: 'The animal that Tom had bought in September slung her calf.'

slinge/slunge [vb., <Sc. *slinge*, skulk]. 1. Walk slowly and lazily. **1908** Lynn Doyle, *Ballygullion*: 'ould Jemmy was no way fond av work, an' as long as he was dhrawin' his pay for slungein' about the yard...he was as happy as a sow in a sheugh [q.v.]'. **1991** Bob Quinn, *Smokey Hollow*: 'With a black look at Joe he slinged up his garden path. They saw him disappear into the kitchen and waited despondently for the indignant sounds of refusal from Mrs Lynch.' 2. Play truant. **1997** RTÉ Radio rebroadcast, *The Boy from Bruree*, 19 Apr: 'EAMON DE VALERA [see **Dev**] He was younger than I was...and he was leeching and slingeing — these were words that used to be used if you were — what's this the regular word for it was — mitching [q.v.].'

slipe [n. & vb., <Sc. *slype*, sledge used in agriculture; 'move freely, as a weighty body drawn through mud' (CSD), cf. Low Ger. *slepen* (vb.), drag] (Ulster). 1. [n.]. Rude cart or sledge without wheels. **1845** William Carleton, *Tales and Stories of the Irish Peasantry*, 'Bob Pentland': 'From the mill it [barley] was usually conveyed to the still-house upon what were termed *slipes*, a kind of car that was made without wheels, in order the more easily to pass through morasses and bogs...' **1951** Sam Hanna Bell, *December Bride*: '"Away and fetch the slipe, Geordie," he said to the man, and when it was dragged out the ram was tied and laid upon it.' 2. [n.]. Ungainly/awkward, thin person. 3. [vb.]. Drag along roughly. **1983** W.F. Marshall, *Livin' in Drumlister*, 'The Runaway': 'They dhregged her out over the tailboard,/She scramed, but I darn't intherfair,/An' they sliped her —

aw lominty [q.v.] father,/They sliped her right [see **right** 1.] in to the stair.'

slippier [n.] (printing). 'The act of "slipping in or out of one's...work area unknownst to the overseer' (WS).

slippy tit [n. phr.]. Sly/untrustworthy individual. **1983** *John Pepper's Illustrated Encyclopaedia of Ulster Knowledge*: '"He's a slippy tit — even comes into the house like a drop of soot."'

slitter see **sleuter**

slob [n., <Ir. *slaba*, mud; slovenly person (cf. Yidd. *zhlub/shlub*, uncouth person)]. Harmless, soft individual; latterly more derog.

slobberdegullion [n., cf. Ir. *slapar*, worker in muck, sloven, *c.* 1615– (DHS)]. A despicable individual; 'a dirty, nasty fellow' (Grose). **1969** Tom Mac Intyre, *The Charollais*: 'Cromwell's curse [see **curse of Cromwell**] and [Henry] Ireton's ire on the slobberdegullion who dared disturb him.'

slock/slog/slough [vb. & n., children's sl. *c.*1800–, <?] (Cork). [vb.]. Steal apples. [n.] as in **go for a slock** [vb. phr.]. Raid an orchard.

slooter see **sleuter**

sloothering/slouthering [adj., cf. Ir. *sliúdrálaí* (n.), slippery individual]. Coaxing, sly. **1946** Donagh MacDonagh in Robert Greacen (ed.), *Irish Harvest*, 'Duet for Organ and Strings': 'Oh, a villain she was, the same Mrs Teevan, with a sloothering smile for his reverence you could butter your bread with...'

slope [vb., <Brit. dial. *idem*, trick, cheat]. As thus. **1993** Frank Casey in Michael Verdon, *Shawlies* (q.v.)*, Echo Boys* (q.v.)*, the Marsh and the Lanes* (q.v.): *Old Cork Remembered*: 'There's great sport in trying to slope the publican, cheat him out of a drink or two.'

slough see **slock**

slouster [n. & vb., <Ir. *slusaí* (n.), dissembler, flatterer] (Ulster). As thus, 'flatterer who lacks the art of flattering successfully' (Todd).

slouthering see **sloothering**

slow on the draw [adj. phr.]. Reluctant to buy one's round of drinks. **1975** John Ryan, *Remembering How We Stood*: 'Behan, though generous in many ways ...was notoriously tight-fisted when it came to buying a round in the company of his coevals — "slow on the draw", as they used to say...'

slow stamp [n. phr.] (Northern Ire.). Ordinary postal rate, as opposed to first class.

slug [n. & vb., <Ir. *slog*, swallow, cf. US *slug down* (vb. phr.); *slug* (n.), 'sl., some kind of strong drink (obs.)' (OED)]. Act of drinking; consume liquid.

slunge see **slinge**

slunk [n. & vb., cf. Sc. *slonk*, mire, ditch; 'noise made by...walking with shoes full of water' (CSD); wade through a mire] (Ulster). [n.]. Deep rut in a road, hence **slunky** [adj.] in same sense. See **heatherbleat**. [vb.]. Of loose shoes that move up and down on the feet.

sluter see **sleuter**

smacht [n., <Ir. *idem*, rule, regulation]. As thus. **1960** John O'Donoghue, *In Kerry Long Ago*: 'I play *All the Way to Galway Town*, putting what vigour I can into it through sheer defiance of Brother Isaac, himself and his *smacht*.'

smack [n.] (Ulster). Attraction towards s.o. of the opposite sex.

smahan [n., <Ir. *smeachán*, small amount]. Taste or small quantity, usu. of drink. **1961** Flann O'Brien, *The Hard Life*: '"Will you join me in a smahan?" "Now, Mr Collopy, you should know me by now. Weekends only..."' **1975** John Ryan, *Remembering How We Stood*: 'I remember thinking it strange that he [Dylan Thomas] should be swilling beer when all the odds were that he should have graduated to smatháns [*sic*] of malt [q.v.] by this stage.'

smalliking [pres. part. (as n.)] (Ulster). 1. [pres. part. as n., <Ir. *smailc* (vb.), smack]. Beating. 2. [pres. part., <?]. Eating noisily with one's mouth open.

smather [vb., cf. Ir. *smearadh* (n.), daub] (Cork). Spread, as of butter, blood, etc.

smell of oneself as in **have a smell of oneself** [vb. phr., cf. Austral. *have tickets on oneself*]. Have a high opinion of oneself. **1989** Hugh Leonard, *Out after Dark*: 'that my Uncle Sonny was right about me having a smell of myself: that Gentleman Jack had become too grand for the likes of my father'.

smiddy [n., <'smithy']. Dirty house, hovel.

smidgin [n., see **smithereens**]. Small fragment. **1988** John Waters, *Magill*, Mar: '...Gerry McGuinness...was smoking a cigar which was at least a foot long — without as much as a smidgin of the sense of irony which is required to do this successfully'.

smig [n., <Ir. *idem*, chin; cf. Icel. *idem*, beard] (Ulster). As thus.

smit [n. & vb., <OE *smitte* (n.), spot]. Infection; infect. **1943** George A. Little, *Malachi Horan Remembers*: 'make the Sign of the Cross with the first two fingers on the right hand, then point the two fingers at him you are afeared of. No smit can fall on you or yours then.' **1951** Sam Hanna Bell, *December Bride*: 'she thought she knew the truth of her mother's words "Like a leper smits you with leprosy, a drunkard smits you with misery."' Hence **smittle** [adj.] (Ulster). Infectious.

smithereens [n., <Ir. *smiodar*, fragment + dimin. *ín*, 1841–; or poss. <Brit. dial. *smithers*, fragments]. Small broken fragments (lit. & fig.). **1958** Frank O'Connor, *An Only Child*: 'I suspect that she was one of those dreamy, romantic women whose marriage, to be successful, must first make smithereens of their personality...' **1966** Séamus Murphy, *Stone Mad*: 'wan crack and down they came, smashed in smithereens after all a man's trouble'. **1993** Sam McAughtry, *Touch & Go*: '"You were a cheeky bastard with brains," she said. "Christ, I loved you to smithereens, the way you stood up to the teachers."'

smoor [n. & vb.]. 1. [<Ir. *smúr* (n.), ash, dust, soot, grime]. As thus; cover in ash etc. **1957** E. Estyn Evans, *Irish Folk Ways*: 'Before the fire is raked [see **rake** 3.] and "smoored" (buried in peat-ash) a spark

should be dropped into the foot-water...'
2. [<Sc. *idem*, cf. Low Ger. *smoren* (vb.), smother, drown]. Fine mist; smother, drown. **1844** Robert Huddleston, *A Collection of Poems and Songs on Rural Subjects*, 'The Cobbler': 'Whan ower the traveller piles the heap/O' smoorin' snaw, or splashy sleet.'

smug [vb., <?]. Engage in homosexual activity. **1916** James Joyce, *A Portrait of the Artist* (q.v.) *as a Young Man*: 'Stephen looked at the faces of the fellows...He wanted to ask somebody about it. What did that mean about the smugging in the square? Why did the five fellows out of the higher line run away for that?'

smullock [n. & vb., <Ir. *smalóg*, fillip, flip]. [n.]. Flip of the finger; rap with the knuckles. [vb.]. Thrash.

smush [n.]. 1. [<Ir. *smaois*, snout]. Mouth, face. 2. [<'mush']. Small pieces; something reduced to pulp.

snafoo [n. & vb., modified version of Brit. (Green) or US (ODMS) WWII milit. acronym: Situation Normal All Fucked Up]. Impossible or disastrous situation; induce such a situation. **1973** Noël Conway, *The Bloods* (q.v.): '"We'll never make soldiers of them," was Milligan's comment after a morning of "As you WERE" commands, every time one of the newcomers snafood a simple right or left turn...'

snag see **snig**

snailer [n.]. Trail of mucus. **1993** Roddy Doyle, *Paddy Clarke Ha Ha Ha*: 'He had two snailers coming out of his nose even though it wasn't all that cold.'

snap-apple [n.]. Game played at Hallowe'en, hence **Snap-Apple Night**. **C.1833** William Maginn, *Frazer's Magazine*, quoted in Davis & Mary Coakley, *Wit and Wine* (1975): 'While I'm waiting for my chop, I'll try and describe some of the humours of Snap-Apple Night for you.' **1996** *Irish Times*, 29 Oct: 'However, it was good, too, for those of us engaged in Snap Apple and Ducking — some of the messier traditions of Samhain [1 Nov, autumn festival in Celtic calendar].'

snapper [n.]. Infant. **1990** Roddy Doyle, *The Snapper*: 'Bimbo put his glass down. "Sure, that's wha' we were put down here for. To have snappers." "You should know," said Jimmy Sr.' See **breadsnapper**.

snatch-the-bacon [n.]. Children's street game. **1995** Úna Claffey in Seán Power (ed.), *Those were the Days, Irish Childhood Memories*: 'There were also, of course, marbles along the footpaths, "snatch-the-bacon", cards and all the other street games we played in the pre-television age...'

snawshil [vb., <Ir. *cnáimhseáil* (n.), (act of) grumbling, complaining]. Grumble, complain. **1968** Myles na gCopaleen, *The Best of Myles*: 'Did Arthur start jumpin' and scootin' about an' roarin' out of him? Did he start bitin' and snarlin', snawshilin' and giving leps [q.v.] in the air with excitement?'

sned [vb., <?] (Ulster). 'Have carnal knowledge of a woman' (YDS).

snell [adj., <Sc. *idem*, sharp, quick, <OE *idem*] (Ulster). As thus.

snicket [n., <?] (Ulster). Penis.

sniffer [n.] (Mountjoy prison, Dub.: see **the Joy**). One who derives pleasure from the aroma of women's knickers. **1993** Pat Tierney, *The Moon on my Back*: 'The lads used to lower string down to the windows below them and, in exchange for cigarettes, etc., some of the women used to tie their knickers on to the string and send them up. Anyone caught or suspected of involvement in this type of carry on [q.v.] were slaggingly [see **slag**] referred to as "sniffers"...'

snig/snag 1. [n. & vb., <'snick']. [n.]. Cut, cutting remark; small piece, undersized thing; term of endearment for baby. Also (Ulster) 'a child who cuts the string of another child's kite in order to steal it' (CUD). **C.1780** Anon., *Luke Caffrey's Kilmainham Minit*: 'We tipped him a snig as he said,/In de juggler [jugular], oh dere where de mark is...' [vb.]. Cut, slash, cut awkwardly; snick, cut, chop; trim turnips. **1992** Sean O'Callaghan, *Down by the Glenside*,

Memoirs of an Irish Boyhood: 'it was time for "snigging" — pulling the turnips from the soil and cutting the tops and roots off them'. See **turnip-snagger**.

snip [n., <Sc. *snib*, small bolt for fastening a door, cf. Dan. *snibbe* (vb.), check by repressive action]. Safety catch on door lock. **1992** Pauline Bracken, *Light of Other Days, A Dublin Childhood*: 'At night the "snip" was put on the lock and security was assured for the wee [q.v.] hours.'

snipe [n.] (Ulster). Person with long nose. Also **healthy as a snipe** [adj. phr.]. Very well, in good form.

snirt [n. & vb., <Sc. *idem*, laugh in a suppressed manner (CSD)] (Ulster). As thus; stifled laugh. **1908** Lynn Doyle, *Ballygullion*: '"So I tould him the first wan or two stories come intil me head, an' he was well plazed. Ivery now an' thin he'd break out in a snirt av a laugh..."'

snoke/snook [vb., <Sc. *idem*, smell about like a dog] (Ulster). Sniff around for news/gossip. **1939** Patrick Gallagher ('Paddy the Cope' (q.v.)), *My Story*: '"Just say that you heard there was bad stuff in Brennan's, you know how that Anna one would be snooking for news..."'

snool [n. & vb., <Sc. *idem*, abject, cringing person; weak fool, anything mean or paltry; submit tamely; act meanly; cringe; sneak; overbear; snub; etc.] (Ulster). Sly, secretive person/ animal; sneak; coward; dejected person; sneering person; intimidate; sulk; complain. Hence **snooly** [adj.] in same sense. Also **snooly** [n. & vb.]. S.o. who lets his/her hair grow down over the eyes; act thus.

snoot-cloot [n., <ME *snut*, nose; OE *clut*, piece of cloth] (Ulster). Handkerchief. **1854** Edward L. Sloan, *The Bard's Offering*, 'The Weaver's Triumph': 'He hemmed and he ha'd, and he swore it was shameless,/Syne [then] oot wi' his snoot-cloot and dighted [wiped] his nose.'

snore see **take snore**

snot/snotter [n., <ME *snotte*, mucus of the nose] (Ulster). 1. Impudent/dirty/ despicable person. 2. Nose. **1991** Shane Connaughton, *The Run of the Country*: '"Hit him a slap on the snotter if he comes near you."' Also **snotterbox**.

snottery [adj., <'snot'] (Ulster). Nasty; 'pompously indignant' (CUD).

snowball [n.]. Cumulative prize in bingo game. **1995** Brendan O'Carroll, *The Chisellers* (q.v.): 'The room was a-buzz with anticipation as everyone realised that the early call on a line meant that most probably the Snowball would go.'

snow broth/broo [n., <Sc. *snaw-bree*, melting snow, slush] (Ulster). As thus.

snuff at a wake see **like snuff at a wake**

snuffe [n., cf. *in high snuff* (adj. phr.), 'in "great form", elated' (DHS)]. Fit of passion. **1675–95** Anon., *Purgatorium Hibernicum*: '"I, Nees [Aeneas]" sayes she in mighty snuffe,/"And be! Is tink it warm enough..."'

snug [n., <'snuggery', bar-parlour of public house 1837]. Small area of pub partitioned from the view of the gen. clientele but with direct access to the bar counter. **1993** Snowball Brereton in Joe O'Reilly & Sixth Class, Convent School, Edenderry, *Over the Half Door*: 'The crack [see **crack** 1.] was good as Josie said. The children weren't allowed in the pub and the women used to drink in their own "snug". In my time women weren't seen in pubs.' **1995** Phil O'Keeffe, *Down Cobbled Streets, A Liberties Childhood*: 'Women and children were not allowed into a public bar except for a little place called a snug, where women could be served drink while in the company of a man or have a jug filled to take home.'

socdollogher [n., 'Perhaps a composite Anglo-Irish provincialism, from "sock", to strike a hard blow, and "dallacher", blindness, the act of blinding, dazing' (Little, as below)]. Mighty blow. **1934** Samuel Beckett, *More Pricks than Kicks*: '"Plato!" sneered the P.B. "Did I hear the word Plato? That dirty little Borstal Boehme!" That was a sockdologer [*sic*] for someone if you like.' **1943** George A. Little, *Malachi Horan Remembers*:

'...Cooper went down for the ninth and last time. Dan [Donnelly] had hit him a socdollogher that broke his jaw like you would a match.'

Sodom and Begorrah (q.v.) [catchphrase]. Characterisation of the difference between the Dub. Gate and Abbey Theatres respectively in the 1930s, with ref. to the sexual orientation of Hilton Edwards and Micheál MacLiammóir (see **the Boys** 2.), directors of the Gate, vis-à-vis the Abbey's predilection for rural drama. **1990** Micheál Ó hAodha, *The Importance of Being Micheál*: 'When a caustic wit described the difference between the two theatres as being between "Sodom and Begorrah" knowing heads nodded.' (Attributed by Ó hAodha to James Montgomery, then film censor.) **1979** C.S. Andrews, *Dublin Made Me*: 'It is said that asked by his wife how they should celebrate their wedding anniversary he suggested two minutes silence and it is to the same character [unidentified: see **character** 2.] that the description of the Gate and Abbey Theatres as "Sodom and Begorrah" is attributed.' Or *alternatively*: **1996** Anthony Cronin, *Samuel Beckett, The Last Modernist*: 'Nor was [Dylan] Thomas taken by the book's [*Murphy*] humour, which he characterised in a phrase soon to obtain wide currency in Ireland, but nearly always attributed to various local wits, as "Sodom and Begorrah".'

soft day [n. phr., euphem.: anything between sequential showers and a downpour]. As thus and commonly as a salutation. **1913** W.M. Letts, *Songs from Leinster*, 'A Soft Day': 'A soft day, thank God!/A wind from the south/With a honeyed mouth;/ A scent of drenching leaves...' **1922** Anon., *Tales of the RIC*: 'a "saftday" — a day of heavy drizzling rain and a mild west wind off the Atlantic'. **1995** Shane Connaughton, *A Border Diary*: 'The downpour gives way to squalls, then a drizzle. "A soft class [q.v.] of a day," someone says.'

soften the cough [vb. phr.]. Reduce (s.o.) to size; take down a peg. **1996**

Denis Coughlan, *Irish Times*, 13 Dec: '...Mary Harney's brave boast that they could win 15 seats in the next general election was dismissed as hyperbole. The latest [opinion poll] figures will, however, soften a few political coughs.' **1997** Maeve Binchy, *Irish Times*, 11 Jan: 'there is now a number you dial and, lo and behold, don't you get the number of the friend who has just hung up. That will soften the cough of those people who can't be bothered to leave a few short and courteous words on the answering machine...'

soft eye, have a [vb. phr.]. Have an amorous inclination. **1962** M. O'C. Bianconi & S.J. Watson, *Bianconi* (see **Bian**)*, King of the Irish Roads*: '...James was now a resplendent footman, soon to become butler, and had begun "to have a soft eye" for...Eliza's personal maid'.

soft spot [n. phr.]. Indulgent attitude. **1947** Frank O'Connor, *The Common Chord*, 'The Holy Door': 'he'd never see her short of anything. He meant it too, because he was a warm-hearted man and had always kept a soft spot for Molly...' **1996** Anthony Cronin, *Samuel Beckett, The Last Modernist*: 'Beckett had what would in Ireland be called "a soft spot" for Trinity [College, Dub.] and a continuing sense of guilt about it.'

sogarteen [n., <Ir. *sagart*, priest + dimin. *ín*, freq. slightly derog.]. Little priest, priesteen (q.v.). **1960** John O'Donoghue, *In Kerry Long Ago*: '"and what was worse, the Sogarteen Aroon [see **Soggarth Aroon**] forgot the whiteness of his collar, and turned parish bailiff for the gathering of his dues"'.

Soggarth Aroon [nickname, <Ir. *sagart*, priest + *a rún*, see **aroo**]. Term of affection for Catholic priest.

soirée see **swarry**

Soldiers of Destiny [lit. translation of Ir. *Fianna Fáil*, latterly usu. iron.]. The FF political party (founded 1926) and its members. **1995** Michael Finlan, *Irish Times*, 3 Aug: 'I managed to get into the tent where the patrons were being slowly broiled...all in the cause of giving a financial leg-up to the Soldiers of Destiny.'

Soldiers of the Rearguard [nickname]. Veterans recruited for service in the Emergency (WWII). **1961** Dominic Behan, *Teems of Times and Happy Returns*: '...I should really say a word or two about the "Soldiers of the Rearguard", or, as they were officially called, "The Twenty-Sixth Battalion". This force was composed of men who had fought in the Easter Rising and the War of Independence, and the average age must have been about fifty...'

sonny jim [n. phr., semantic shift <'Sunny Jim', cartoon character in 'Force' cereal advertising, 1930s ('High o'er the fence leaps Sunny Jim,/FORCE is the food that raises him')]. Term of affection, gen. from parent to son; also ironic. **1993** Roddy Doyle, *Paddy Clarke Ha Ha Ha*: '"Bedtime, sonny jim." I didn't mind. I wanted to go.'

sonsy/saucy/sunsey/sancy [adj., <Ir./Sc. Gael. *sonas* (n.), happiness, good luck, good fortune] (Ulster). Lively, full of fun; pleasant; buxom; lucky, auspicious; comely, pleasant (of female). **1913** Alexander Irvine, *My Lady of the Chimney Corner*: '"If I catch myself thinkin' aanythin' saucy ov that aul' haythen baste I'll change me name!" he said...' **1977** Sam McAughtry, *The Sinking of the Kenbane Head*: 'Mother was small, like Dad, and sonsy. At the least excitement a round spot would glow on each of her cheeks.' **1983** W.F. Marshall, *Livin' in Drumlister*, 'The Talking Flea': 'An' there on the stroke of eleven/His sonsy big Rosie he seen,/With Fairies before an' behine her/An' her cocked up like a queen.'

sookey [n., <*sukey*, kettle; 'low, –1823' (DHS)] (Travellers). As thus.

sooleymander see **suleymander**

sooner [n., <'sooner or later']. 'Lazy, useless dog that would sooner defecate in the house than outside' (YDS); lazy animal in general. **1995** Tom Glennon, *Irish Times*, 3 Nov: 'The problem with our ferret was that he was spoilt or a "sooner". Instead of terrifying the rabbits

...our ferret was satisfied to catch one rabbit, dine off it and fall asleep.'

soorlick [n., <Sc. *idem*, common sorrel] (Ulster). As thus.

soorlucking [pres. part., cf. Ir. *súr* (n.), act of searching for; *súlach* (n.), dirty water, liquid manure, farmyard filth]. Searching for food in dirty water. **1960** John O'Donoghue, *In Kerry Long Ago*: 'and indeed it was no surprise at all to see the ducks *soorlucking* about the water in holes of his mud floor'.

soot [n., cf. Ir. *sotal*, pride, arrogance; gen. in neg. sense] (Cork). Pleasure, satisfaction. **1996** Christy Kenneally, *Maura's Boy, A Cork Childhood*: 'Actually it wasn't so bad but I wouldn't give her "the soot of it".'

soother [n. & vb.]. [n.]. Baby's dummy. **1985** Máirín Johnston, *Around the Banks of Pimlico*: 'We never used milk in tea, only sweetened condensed tinned milk which had a notice in big type, UNFIT FOR BABIES. This stern warning didn't prevent mothers from dipping the babies' rubber soothers into the tin and scooping up a big dollop...' **1996** Nuala Haughey, *Irish Times*, 6 Feb: 'The adults took turns to nurse Alexei on a couch while he sucked on his blue soother to relieve his teething pains...' [vb.]. Pacify, in same sense. See **alanna**.

sootherer [n., cf. Ir. *suthaire*, dunce, cheat (Dinneen) but poss. corruption of *slootherer* (see **sloothering**)]. Plausible individual with the gift of the gab. **1935** *Irish Times*, 13 Nov: 'He [the broadcasting politician] is in direct touch with the feminine section of the community, which is specially liable to be influenced by the kind of speaker whom Mr James Stephens would call a "sootherer".'

sore [adj.]. Absolute, utter, complete.

sore hand [n. phr.] (Ulster). Very thick sandwich; 'large piece of bread with butter and jam' (TT).

sore head [nickname] (Ulster). Type of loaf. **1990** Harry Currie, quoted in Walter Love, *The Times of our Lives*: 'So I spent some time becoming an expert in

Melodion loaves, Turnovers, Sore heads, Donkey's Lugs, Paris Buns and the lot.'

sorra [n. & interj., <OE *sorg* (n.), sorrow]. [n.]. Euphem. for the Devil. **1839** William Carleton, *Fardorougha the Miser*: 'She doesn't give herself many airs [see **put on airs**] but her people were as proud as the very sarra'.' [interj., with neg. sense]. As 'devil' in *devil a bit* (q.v.) and similar. **1925** Louise McKay, *Mourne Folk*: 'an' when I got a handle after me name...the sorra bit of me would know myself at all...' **1961** Dominic Behan, *Teems of Times and Happy Returns*: '"No wonder she was pregnant when her honeymoon was over, sorra much else was there to do."' Also **sorra loss o' ya** (Connacht). Pity about you; expressive of iron. sympathy/concern. See also **hate**.

sorrow go by me! [exclam.]. '[C]ommon expletive used by the presbyterians in Ireland' (Grose).

sotherer [n., cf. Sc. *sotter*, scorch or burn; sound made in boiling or frying] (Ulster). Blow or slap. **1979** Jack McBride, *Traveller in the Glens* (of Antrim): '"She landed me a 'sotherer' of a 'dunner' [q.v.] on the 'lug' and made it 'bizz' for half an hour after..."'

sotter [n., see **sotherer**]. Bubbling noise made by saliva in pipe stem.

sough [n., <Sc. *idem*, sigh, sound of wind, rumour; *souch*, deep sigh (CSD)] (Ulster). As thus. **1908** Lynn Doyle, *Ballygullion*: 'The net took him on the shin-bone, an he riz about two feet in the air, an lit on his belly on the plantin' ditch wi' a sough.'

soult [n., <Ir. *samhailt*, spectre, apparition]. Term of contempt.

sound man! [exclam.] (esp. Cork). Expression of approval. **1980** Séamus de Faoite, *The More we are Together*, 'Pictures in a Pawnshop': 'the faces that tiered all the way to the roof at the back came alive in cheers and shouting when the pair came in sight. "Sound man, Joe Jack!... My life on you, Jack..."' **1986** David Marcus, *A Land Not Theirs*: '"Good boy. Sound man. Honour thy father and thy mother — isn't that right?"'

souper [n., <'taking the soup', said of those who induced Catholics by the offer of sustenance to convert to Protestantism at the time of the Great Hunger (q.v.) or famine; also those who accepted it]. As thus, and gen. term of contempt, esp. as applied to Protestants. **1963** Leslie Daiken, *Out Goes She* (Dub. street rhymes): 'Proddy [q.v.] Proddy ring the bell/Call the soupers back from Hell.' **1995** Martha Reid in Mary Ryan et al. (eds.), *No Shoes in Summer*: 'He [my grandfather]...was originally RC but changed to C of I during the Famine not because he was a "souper" as was common practice then, but because he didn't agree with the Pope's infallibility.' Hence **soup** [vb.] in same sense. **1975** Peter Somerville-Large, *The Coast of West Cork*: 'The question of souping is a delicate and emotional one; many proselytising clergymen have been unjustly accused of this unpleasant form of pressure.'

souse [adv. & vb.] (Ulster). 1. [vb., poss. onomat.]. Fall heavily with some weight. 2. [adv., <1.]. Suddenly, without warning. **1908** Lynn Doyle, *Ballygullion*: '"Chew, Chew, sir!" shouts the brother-in-law [to the dog], jumpin' back off the road; and wi' that he steps, souse! intil Pether's half-made well.' 3. [vb.]. Dig sods from a furrow between ridges and add to ridge. **1979** Paddy Tunney, *The Stone Fiddle*: 'The coping or sousing of an acre of lea, when the keen cutting edge of the McMahon [spade] was thrust through rush roots...'

sow [vb., poss. <*idem* (n.), female pig] (Clongowes Wood College, Co. Kildare). Engage in homosexual relations. **1995** Aidan Higgins, *Donkey's Years*: 'to spoon (to court), to sow (to love), to sigh, to sin-o; it was nature...'

sowans/sowens/sowins/sugeen [n., <Ir. *Samhain*, 1 Nov (PWJ); or Ir. *suán*, Sc. Gael. *sùghan*, drink of water in which oatmeal has been steeped]. 'A sort of flummery or gruel usually made and eaten on Hallow Eve' (PWJ). **C.1735** Jonathan Swift, *A Dialogue in Hybernian Stile*: 'A. ...And what breakfast do you take in the country? B. Why, sometimes sowins, and sometimes stirabout [q.v.]...'

spa [n. & adj., abbrev.]. Gen. derog., implying serious ineptitude. **1990** Roddy Doyle, *The Snapper* (q.v.): '"He's not tha' bad." "I suppose he isn't. He's still a spa though." Sharon laughed again. "You're a terrible fuckin' wagon [q.v.], Jackie."' **1995** *Irish Times*, 24 Oct: 'one of his more mature and articulate pupils informed him that the current meaning — in young people's parlance — of the word "spa" is crazy, mad, daft, and that it derived from an abbreviation of the medical term "spastic"'.

spacer [n.]. 1. (Dub.). Streetwise youth, esp. of the Liberties. **1987** Lar Redmond, *Emerald Square*: '[I] identified with and loved the characters [see **character** 1.] I had been reared alongside. "Spacers" they call them now, but I preferred one spacer to a dozen of these college types...' 2. [cf. US/Brit. sl. *spaced out* (adj. phr.)]. Crazy/eccentric person; header (q.v.).

spadger/spadgy [n., cf. Ir. *spideog*, robin, small bird (Dinneen)]. Sparrow. **1996** Christy Kenneally, *Maura's Boy, A Cork Childhood:* 'Our brown spadgies were drab compared to finches, linnets, robins and thrushes.'

spag see **spaug**

spake [n., <Hib.E pronun. of 'speak']. Speech; say. **1954** Benedict Kiely, *Honey Seems Bitter.* 'One of the two commercial men, ending his meal and sluicing his pipes with porter [q.v.] said: "A good spake, Butler, boy."' **1968** RTÉ TV serial, *The Riordans*: 'EAMON ...If you're painting people with clothes on, you don't paint them the same as what you would if you wanted them with no clothes on and had to turn round and put clothes on after. JOHNNY (*As Eamon goes off to clean a brush.*) That's the longest spake I ever heard him making.' **1996** Tom Widger, *Sunday Tribune*, 25 Aug: 'Just as they [RTÉ] began broadcasting live from the regions, letting the locals have their own spake, local and community radio was doing that very thing.'

spalpeen [n. & adj., <Ir. *spailpín* (n.), seasonal hired labourer, scamp]. As thus; 'The word spalpeen is now used in the sense of a low rascal' (PWJ). **1754** Thomas Sheridan, *The Brave Irishman*: 'there ishn't one of these spalpeens that has a cabin upon a mountain, with a bit of a potatoe-garden at the back of it, but will be keeping a goon [gun]'. **C.1910** Anon., *Irish Wit and Humour.* 'The spalpeen is carrying away more shot than would sit [set] up an ironmonger in Skibbereen.' **1950** Liam O'Flaherty, *Insurrection*: 'This penniless spalpeen that I found wandering about the streets and brought home with me...' Also **spulpin** (Ulster) in same sense.

spalter [vb., cf. Sc. *idem*, sprawl] (Ulster). Walk unsteadily in large strides.

span [adj., cf. Brit. sl. *spange*, new, dressy (DHS)]. Brand-, as in brand-new. **1991** John B. Keane, *Love Bites and Other Stories*: 'Looks were exchanged. We had heard them all and here was a span new one concocted by a Decies man.'

spang [n. & vb., <Sc. *idem*, leap, bound] (Ulster). 1. [n. & vb.]. As thus; long stride. **1908** Lynn Doyle, *Ballygullion*: 'Just as he was up on it [the ditch], we hears a yell from behind; and the wee [q.v.] man gives a spang an' over.' 2. [vb.]. Take s.o. aback.

sparabill [n., <'sparrow'] (Ulster). Flat-sided, headless shoemaker's nail (YDS).

spare [n.] (Ulster). Buttoned fly of man's trousers. **1979** John Morrow in David Marcus (ed.), *Body and Soul*, 'Beginnings': 'homely bespectacled Mrs Poots...ripped open my fly! (I should say "spare", for in those days zips were a laughable Yankee eccentricity...)'

spark [n.]. Boy/girlfriend, object of romantic interest. **1909** Canon Sheehan, *The Blindness of Dr Gray*: '"the sooner you get back to your wife's company, the better for you and her. Her old spark might be hanging around."' Hence **sparking** [vb. n.]. Romantic dalliance. **1920** Seumas O'Kelly, *The Leprechaun of Kilmeen*: '"I told you," says the leprechaun, "that Tom'd find us out some fine day! We'll be having to be giving up our little bit of sparking now!"'

sparrow-fart [n.]. Insignificant or contemptible individual; also said of a child who is crabby (see **crab** 1.). **1992** Sean O'Callaghan, *Down by the Glenside, Memoirs of an Irish Boyhood*: 'His assistant was a tiny, sparrow-fart of a man...'

spatchcock [n., abbrev. of 'dispatch cock', hen killed and immediately cooked]. 'An Irish dish upon any sudden occasion' (Grose).

spaug/spag [n. & vb.]. 1. [n., <Ir. *spág* (n.), big, clumsy foot]. As thus; [pl.] sensible walking shoes. **1922** James Joyce, *Ulysses*: 'Look at the young guttersnipe behind him hue and cry...Taking off his flat spaugs and the walk. Small nines.' **1979** Jack McBride, *Traveller in the Glens* (of Antrim): '"There he sut in the bare spaags [*sic*], wan fut on every hab [hob] maizlin' [see **measle**] his shins..."' 2. [vb.]. Walk barefoot.

spay/spey [vb., cf. Sc. *spaer* (n.), fortune-teller, <ON *spa* (vb.), foretell] (Ulster). Predict, tell. **1913** Alexander Irvine, *My Lady of the Chimney Corner*: '"She speyed I'd live t'see ye," he said. "She speyed well," I answered.' **1983** Polly Devlin, *All of us There*: '"You couldn't be up to [q.v.] what she'd say. She'd spay fortunes, that one."' Hence **spay-woman** [n.].

speed as in **come speed** [vb. phr.] (Ulster). Have success, make progress, prosper. **1951** Sam Hanna Bell, *December Bride*: 'The girl rushed out impatiently. "Well, did you come any speed?" "Aye, girl dear, I did indeed! And with the first bid too!"'

speel/speely [vb., <Sc. *idem*, climb] (Ulster). Climb agilely.

spelder [vb., <Sc. *idem*, rack the limbs in striding (CSD)] (Ulster). Pull muscles.

spell job [n. phr., <'spell', turn of work taken in relief of others]. Job of uncertain/indefinite duration. **1983** *John Pepper's Illustrated Encyclopaedia of Ulster Knowledge*: '"If only I'd known it was a spell job," he said, "I'd nivver have taken it."'

spey see **spay**

spider's wemix [n. phr., <?] (printing). Additive for softening printing ink. 'Not

in general use, but common among machinemen, Alex Thom's [Dub., *c*.1950s]...' (WS).

spiflicated [p. part. as adj., poss. fanciful formation on 'suffocate', <Brit. sense of handle roughly, crush, destroy, etc.; <which fig. Hib.E sense]. Highly intoxicated. **1968** Myles na gCopaleen, *The Best of Myles*: 'elephants; fluthery-eyed [see **fluthered**]; spiflicated; stewed; tight'.

spike [n., casual ward (tramps' sl., DHS)]. (Maternity) hospital. **1967** Bryan MacMahon, *The Honey Spike*: '"There's spikes is poxed with bad luck, an' the children out of 'em are born in bits. An' there's honey spikes, full of good fortune."'

spink [n., <Ir. *speanc*, crag, cliff]. As thus. **1938** Seumas MacManus, *The Rocky Road to Dublin*: 'Our lad went out, climbed the spink above the still-house, and spied around him.' **1939** Patrick Gallagher ('Paddy the Cope' (q.v.)), *My Story*: 'When we came near the fairies' home we heard a fiddle up in the spink playing the most beautiful music.'

spit [n., <OE *spittan* (vb.), spit, colloq. 1825]. 1. Measurement of distance. **1961** Dominic Behan, *Teems of Times and Happy Returns*: '"But sure it's only four miles," argued Da. "A good spit," agreed Mr Devoy.' 2. Close likeness, esp. as in dead spit (q.v.) of.

Spite Terrace [nickname]. Fairview Crescent, Dub. **1996** Mary Russell, *Irish Times*, 29 May: 'When James, Earl of Charlemont, discovering the joys of sea-bathing, restricted access to his Marino estate in Clontarf a local developer built a row of six-storey buildings smack in front of the same estate...It was a Pyrrhic victory for the builder, however, for Fairview Crescent (aka Spite Terrace) had neither a water supply nor gardens.'

spitting at the tongs [adj. phr.] (Ulster). Pregnant.

splah [n., <'splay'] (Ulster). Flat/splayed foot; splaying of feet when walking.

spleece [vb., poss. <MDu. *splissen*, splice, <splitting rope ends beforehand]. Split. **1675–95** Anon., *Purgatorium*

Hibernicum: '"Swoop, swoop! *a callagh* [Ir. *a chailleach*, o hag], oh!," sayes Nees [Aeneas],/"De devill may dee coller spleece."'

splink [n., <Ir. *splinc*, gleam, glimmer]. As thus. **1960** John O'Donoghue, *In Kerry Long Ago*: '"That fellow hasn't a splink of sense, God help him..."'

splughins [n. pl., cf. Ir. *spliuchán*, pouch; blister] (Ulster). Heavy boots.

splurt [n. & vb.]. Spurt, splutter. 'A neighbour's child who had poured half a bottle of ketchup over her dress explained that it had splurted out' (DOM).

spogger [n., <?] (Cork). Peaked cap (Beecher).

spoiled five [n. phr.] (Ulster). Card game. **1908** Lynn Doyle, *Ballygullion*: 'times is changed since thin, an' ye dare hardly take a hand av spoiled five at the back av a ditch now-a-days'.

spoiled priest [n. phr.]. Postulant who fails to continue to ordination; man who leaves the priesthood. Also **spoiled nun** in same sense.

spoileen [n., Ir. *spóilín*, small piece of meat; *-aonaigh*, ditto used at a fair (Dinneen)]. Coarse soap made from scraps of grease and meat, sold at fairs.

spoof [vb., cf. Brit. sl. *idem*, hoax, humbug (DHS)]. Tell lies; embellish facts. Hence **spoofer** [n.].

spook [vb., <*idem* (n.) <Ger. *spuk* (n.), ghost]. Alarm, scare. **1995** Charlie Swan in Seán Power (ed.), *Those were the Days, Irish Childhood Memories*: 'a dog came sniffing around the sweets on the ground. Joe shouted at the dog to "shoo, shoo!" but of course he spooked the horse instead.' **1996** Donal Lunny, interview, *Irish Times*, 19 Sept: '...I was trespassing on farmers' property. I used to spook cattle and rob orchards, catch fish. That's how I spent my youth.'

sports-king [n., <?]. Loud-mouthed, incompetent individual. **1975** John Ryan, *Remembering How We Stood*: '"We'll charter a whole bloody plane! There must be enough sports-kings left in Dublin to fill a plane." "Sports-king" was an echo of Dublin small talk, nineteen-thirty vintage — the nearest contemporary expression would be "piss-artist".'

spother [n., <Ir. *spadar*, 'wet, heavy turf, as last year's turf left on the bog exposed to the weather' (Dinneen)]. As thus. **1996** Michael Longley, *Irish Review* (Belfast), 'A Sprig of Bay', Spring/ Summer: 'In the abandoned schoolhouse I shelter from the rain/With hundreds of pupils and look beyond boreen and hollow bog (the "spother" in these parts...'

sprachle/sprauchle [n. & vb., <Sc. *idem*, scramble, struggle towards, sprawl, cf. Ir. *spreachall* (n.), spatter] (Ulster). As thus; trip, tumble; stretch out lazily. **1908** Lynn Doyle, *Ballygullion*: '"Give me a help out, Brian," sez he, after a sprauchle or two, "I can't manage it."'

sprags [n. pl., cf. Sc. *sprague*, 'long, lean, clumsy finger, toe, hand or foot' (CSD)] (Ulster). Feet (SH).

sprassy see **sprazzy**

sprauchle see **sprachle**

sprazzy/sprassy [n., cf. Shelta *sprazi*, sixpence] (Cork). Pre-decimal sixpence (Beecher). See also **tack** 4.

spreety [adj., cf. Sc. *spreet* (n.), sprite, disembodied spirit (OED)] (Ulster). Thin, weedy-looking.

sprick/spricklybag [n., <Sc. *spreckled* (adj.), spotted] (Ulster). Stickleback spawn. **1983** W.F. Marshall, *Livin' in Drumlister*, 'The Lad': 'So he thrinneld [see **thrinnle**] his hoop and waded the burn/An' ginneld [see **ginnle**] for spricklybags.' **1995** Catherine McAleavey in Mary Ryan et al. (eds.), *No Shoes in Summer*: 'the beech trees came into leaf and the children who lived near the river...brought in jam-jars of spricks [to school]'. Hence **sprickled breid** [n. phr.]. Rich fruit bread. See **barmbrack**.

sprissaun [n., <Ir. *spreasán*, worthless individual]. As such.

spruss [n., <Ir. *brus/sprus*, broken, crumbled pieces; dust]. As thus. **1907**

Joseph Guinan, *The Soggarth Aroon* (q.v.): 'a lot of old spruss of straw'.

Spud [nickname, <*murphy* (q.v.)]. Generic nickname for anyone with surname 'Murphy'. **1949** Tom Barry, *Guerrilla Days in Ireland*: 'Immediately the action started I sent Jim Murphy (Spud) and eleven riflemen to reinforce Kelleher.'

spunk [n., <Ir. *sponc*, tinder]. As thus, match, hence spirit, mettle.

spunkie [n., <Sc. *idem*, lively young fellow] (Ulster). As thus. See **gleg**.

sputrach [n., cf. Ir. *spruadar*, crumbled matter]. Mass of worthless rubbish.

spy farley [n., <*farley* (q.v.)] (Ulster). Inquisitive gossip. Also **spy farleys** [vb.]. Nose around for news.

Squad, the [nickname]. Assassination gang in War of Independence, founded 19 Sept 1919. **1990** Tim Pat Coogan, *Michael Collins* (see **the Big Fella**): 'The Squad was a group of assassins, a specially-selected hit-squad directly under Collins' orders.' See also **the Twelve Apostles**.

squatter [n.] (Ulster). Voyeur. **1993** Sam McAughtry, *Touch & Go*: 'When we kids spotted one of these [men] watching a heaving, panting pair of lovers, we would forego our own thrill and raise the alarm: "Look out — squatters!"'

squaver [vb., intens. of 'quaver'] (Ulster). Throw the arms about; square up as if to box; manoeuvre (a vehicle) with many changes of direction.

squelch [n.]. Fall. 'Formerly a bailiff caught in a barrack-yard in Ireland, was liable by custom to have three tosses in a blanket, and a squelch; the squelch was given by letting go the corners of the blanket, and suffering him to fall to the ground' (Grose).

squint [vb., <?] (Ulster). Provide for (Todd).

squireen [n. & adj., <'squire' + Ir. dimin. *ín*]. 'An Irish gentleman in a small way who apes the manners, the authoritative tone, and the aristocratic bearing of the large landed proprietors. Sometimes you can hardly distinguish a squireen from a half sir [q.v.] or from a shoneen [q.v.]' (PWJ). **1997** Nuala O'Faolain, *Irish Times*, 14 July: 'Why did he [Charles J. Haughey] go into the low-paid trade of politician when he was already... building towards a squireen lifestyle?'

squirt [n.]. Small addition of stout. **1993** Frank Casey in Michael Verdon, *Shawlies* (q.v.), *Echo Boys* (q.v.), *the Marsh and the Lanes* (q.v.): *Old Cork Remembered*: 'you had to have two barrels to make the one pint. The high barrel and the flat barrel. You'd put the high stuff in first and then came a bit from the flat. The squirt, they called it. That'd give it a fine creamy head.'

stabber [n., <'stub out']. Remaining portion of a cigarette that has been stubbed out. **1982** Éamonn Mac Thomáis, *Janey Mack* (q.v.), *Me Shirt is Black*: 'At lunch-hour break football conversation was mixed with questions. "Hey Mack, any fags, any weeds, any butts, any stabbers, any coffin nails?"' **1986** Bob Geldof, *Is That It?*: 'They hover about the entrance [of the church] and stub out their cigarettes before the consecration...then the "stabber" is re-ignited and the dash to the pub begins.' Also **stab** [vb.]. Stub out a cigarette.

Stab City [nickname, <reputation for violence]. Limerick. **1995** Diarmuid Doyle, *Sunday Tribune*: '"I liked hurting people," he said...before going on to tell us about his motto in the 1970s and 1980s when he was one of the people responsible for creating Limerick's reputation as Stab City.'

stacan [n., cf. Ir. *stocán*, idler, lounger]. As thus. **1927** Peadar O'Donnell, *Islanders*: '"There's a hardness about her. A young girl that has no nature [q.v.] in her for a man's Sunday trousers is only a stacan."'

stag [n. & vb.]. 1. [n. & vb., <Ir *staig* (n.), informer]. One such who betrays his comrades; inform. **1845** William Carleton, *Tales and Stories of the Irish Peasantry*, 'Bob Pentland': 'The two worst informers against a [poteen (q.v.)] distiller, barring a *stag*, are a smoke by day and a fire by night.' 2. [n., <?]. Inedible potato. 3. [n., <?]. Cold-hearted, selfish woman (PWJ).

staggeen [n., <Ir. *staig*, old nag + dimin. *ín*]. As thus.

staggering bob [nickname]. Abortive or premature calf; its flesh as food. **1802** Maria & Richard Lovell Edgeworth, *Essay on Irish Bulls*: 'she is the one that never denies herself the bit of *staggering bob* when in season'.

staghey see **stughie**

stall [n., cf. Ir. *stail*, stallion, gay spark, paramour (Dinneen)] (Cork). Sexual encounter. **1993** Seán Beecher in Michael Verdon, *Shawlies* (q.v.), *Echo Boys* (q.v.), *the Marsh and the Lanes* (q.v.): *Old Cork Remembered*: 'On the way home, they went up to Bob and Joan's [?], and he got a great stall.'

stall-fed [adj.]. Pampered. **1970** Christy Brown, *Down All the Days*: '"I keep telling you to come here. You won't be stall-fed, but you'll get your share of what's going."' **1996** Elaine Crowley, *Cowslips and Chainies* (q.v.): 'a lazy bastard, lying on his arse morning noon and night when he wasn't in his mother's being stall-fed'.

stampey [n., <Ir. *steaimpí*, potato cake]. As thus; credited with aphrodisiac properties. **C.1914** (first published 1969) George Fitzmaurice, *The Ointment Blue*: 'TEIG ...A strange thing occurred to myself a Friday night through taking more than my share of the stampey for supper, and 'twould rise the hair on your head the tallyho [q.v.] I had with a mad cat...'

stand [n., poss. <*idem* (vb.) as in 'stand a round'] (Cork). Reward, tip (Beecher).

standing [n.]. 1. Second-hand clothes stall. **1968** John Healy, *The Death of an Irish Town*: 'You were dressed in cast-offs or remakes. Or from "the standings"...set up on the back of a lorry where glib-tongued salesmen harpooned a farmer's wife...' 2. as in **fall out of one's standing** [vb. phr.]. Collapse with exhaustion, hunger. **1995** Phil O'Keeffe, *Down Cobbled Streets, A Liberties Childhood*: '"God love them all," I heard her say..."but it's hard times to be out on the streets, and some of them nearly

fallin' out of their standin'."' Also to convey amazement, as in **I nearly fell out of my standing**.

stand-on [n., cf. Brit. sl. *hard-on*; *cock-stand* in same sense]. Erection. See **slabber**.

stapple see **stopple**

starve [vb., <OE *steorfan*, die] (Ulster). [intrans.]. Suffer from extreme cold. [trans.]. Make extremely cold. **1939** Patrick Gallagher ('Paddy the Cope' (q.v.)), *My Story*: 'She said, "I do not keep any beer. If I did I would not give it to you as it would starve you with the cold."'

stashy [adj., <?] (Ulster). Fancy (SH). Also **stashied up** [adj. phr.]. Dressed to kill.

Stater [nickname, abbrev.]. Member of Irish Free State forces supporting Treaty side in Civil War, 1921–2. **1965** Lionel Fleming, *Head or Harp* (see **heads or harps**): 'The streets themselves were full of "Staters", rather uncouth young men in British uniforms which had been hurriedly dyed green...'

stations, the [n. pl., <succession of places visited by clergy on fixed days]. Mass held in the home in rural areas remote from a church, occasion of large concourse and generous hospitality. **1938** Seumas MacManus, *The Rocky Road to Dublin*: 'Held twice a year, at the end of harvest and Easter, the Stations were a legacy from the Penal Days, those centuries when...the priest was a hunted man who...heard confession in a hidden glen or in some remote cottage, gathering the people to him there.' **1991** Seán Ó Ciaráin, *Farewell to Mayo*: 'Stations were held on a rotary basis — a different house was chosen each time until the whole townland was covered, and then they started again at the first one.' **1996** RTÉ TV serial, *Glenroe*, 13 Oct: 'BIDDY The stations are Dinny's idea, not mine, not Miley's but Dinny's — but you wouldn't think it to look at all this.'

Statue, the [nickname] (Cork). Statue of Fr Mathew, the Apostle of Temperance

(1790–1856), by John Henry Foley (1817–74), transport nexus and meeting point in Patrick St. See **jag** 1.

stave [n., metonym, <musical notation]. Song. See also **bar** 2.

steall/stawl/styall [n., <Ir. *steall*, dash, poured-out quantity]. As thus. **1939** Patrick Gallagher ('Paddy the Cope' (q.v.)), *My Story*: 'Sally made a stawl of tea for us.'

steamer [n.] (Cork). 1. [cf. Shelta *stima*, tobacco pipe]. Cigarette (Beecher). 2. [<?]. Male homosexual (Beecher).

Steelboys/Hearts of Steel [nickname]. Agrarian secret society in Ulster, *c*.1760s, aka Hearts of Steel. **1973** Hereward Senior in T. Desmond Williams (ed.), *Secret Societies in Ireland*, 'The Early Orange Order 1795–1870': 'transitory agrarian secret societies like the Steelboys protested that Catholic tenants were threatening their living standards by offering higher rents in bidding for leases'.

steeler [n., <'steel' + endearment suffix]. Metal ball used in game of marbles. **1994** Vonnie Banville Evans, *The House in the Faythe*: 'The coloured taws were treasured and the steelers (probably ball-bearings) were an especial prize.' See also **chalk** 1., **glasser**.

steeped [adj.]. 1. [<'steep' (vb.), imbue (with some quality)]. Fortunate (steeped in good fortune). 2. [<'steep' (vb.), soak, saturate] (Ulster). Drenched, soaked with rain.

steerinah [n., <'steering' + endearment suffix] (Cork). Child's homemade toy cart.

steever [n., <'steeve' (vb.), stow (cargo etc.)] (Ulster). Hard kick, as in **a good steever**.

stem see **stim**

stepmother's breath [n. phr.] (Ulster). Cold draught of air, keen wind.

steps see **up the steps**

steugh [n., <Sc. *steuch*, bad smell] (Ulster). As thus.

stevin [n., <OE *stefn*, period, time] (Leinster). As thus. '"Wait your stevin,

boy!" said an elderly lady in a pub...to a young fellow who had lost the run of himself [q.v.] and burst into song...' (DOM).

stewmer/stumer [n., poss. <Yidd. (DHS); but cf. Swed. *stum* (adj.), dumb, mute. In Brit. sl. 'a sham, anything bogus or worthless' (DHS).]. Individual of limited intelligence. **1966** Patrick Boyle, *At Night All Cats are Grey*, 'Go Away, Old Man, Go Away': 'Dancing and jack-acting [q.v.] is all that one [q.v.] cares for. Oh, a nice stumer of a wife I let myself in for!' **1966** Liam Ó Cuanaigh, *Evening Press*, 21 Nov: 'Stewmers are the next best thing to goms [q.v.], but whilst a countryman was once pointed out to me as being a stewmer, you'll find few culchies [q.v.] who are goms.' **1987** Lar Redmond, *Emerald Square*: '"Deasy," said the Kipper, "stand up." Deasy, the biggest, thickest [see **thick** 1.] "stumer" in class, lurched to his feet.'

Stick/Stickie [nickname, <adhesive employed on identity badge]. Member of the Official Sinn Féin, following the split which led to the formation of the Provisionals, 11 Jan 1970. **1993** Brendan O'Brien, *The Long War*: '"there were a lot of 'Sticks' here...you had fucking 'Sticks' running Belfast. Hadn't pulled a trigger since fucking '72."' **1995** Tim Pat Coogan, *The Troubles* (q.v.): 'The Provisionals, also known as "Provos", "Provvies" and, sometimes, "Pinheads", used to fix their labels to their lapels with pins. The Officials used gum, hence the term "Stickies".'

stick-in [n.] (Ulster). Knockout drumming competition. **1995** Fintan Vallely, *Irish Times*, 12 July: 'Today the major focus is weekend "stick-ins"...These will have from five to 10 drums taking part, in bigger ones as many as 40...'

sticking out [pres. part. as adj.] (Ulster). Impressive, prominent; obvious. **1969** Tom Mac Intyre, *The Charollais*: '"we have, in fact, been blessed with courage of a high order." "Stickin' out, m'lord — an' there's nothin', m'lord, a woman admires more nor courage in a man."'

stife [n., <'stifle' (vb.) <ME *stufle* (vb.), OF *estouffer* (vb.), stifle, smother]. Smoky atmosphere.

still an' all [adv. phr.]. Nevertheless. **1925** Liam O'Flaherty, *The Informer*: '"Can ye find no better man to arrest ...than me, that's dying on me feet o' consumption. An' havin', still an' all, to work me hands off at me trade..."' **1968** RTÉ TV serial, *The Riordans* (of a murial (q.v.)): 'EILY   That's a terrible old-fashioned suit. EAMON Sure what does it matter? They're all Pagans do you see. EILY   Still an' all...would you not put them into something more casual?' **1969** Robert Greacen, *Even without Irene*: 'He never really liked farming...Still and all — as we said in the local [Belfast] idiom, he had ventured back, with the proceeds of the insurance money...'

stim/stime/stem [n., <Ir. *steamar*, jot or tittle; also cf. Sc. *styme*, glimpse, glimmer]. Very small quantity or item. **1830** William Carleton, *Traits and Stories of the Irish Peasantry*, 'The Lianhan Shee': '"Did any of you see a strange woman lavin' the house...?" she enquired. "No," they replied, "not a *stim* of any one did we see."' **1938** Seumas MacManus, *The Rocky Road to Dublin*: 'At midnight the pair of them would head for home... through the black dark following paths where the boy couldn't see a stim.' **1969** Frank O'Connor, *Collection Three*, 'Masculine Protest': 'Up to that day I never felt a stime of sympathy with my neurotic patients...'

stir [n. & vb., <OE *styrian* (vb. trans.), move, stir up. In reflexive sense rare or obsolete in Std Eng.]. 1. (Ulster). Plan, intention; fun, 'crack' (see **crack** 1.). **1948** Patrick Kavanagh, *Tarry Flynn*: '"I was talking to Mary Callan last night." "I see," said Eusebius..."Had she any stir?"' 2. [vb., reflexive, or by implication] as in **don't stir (yourself)!** Also **stir one's stumps** [vb. phr.]. Get moving. **1966** Patrick Boyle, *At Night All Cats are Grey*, 'Myko': '"Come out to the shed," he says, "and you'll soon see what's eating me. And stir your stumps," he shouts back at me from the yard.'

stirabout [n., Hib.E 1682–]. Oatmeal porridge. **1913** Alexander Irvine, *My Lady of the Chimney Corner*: '"Tay" that evening consisted of "stir-about", Sonny Johnson's unearned bap [see **bap** 1.] and buttermilk.' **1993** Mrs Carter in Joe O'Reilly & Sixth Class, Convent School, Edenderry, *Over the Half Door*: 'I remember the time of the war and the ration books when food was very scarce ...We had to eat this Indian stirabout or yellow meal.'

stocious [adj., poss. <Sc. *stot* (vb. & n.), stagger (Todd)]. Intoxicated. **1983** Polly Devlin, *All of us There*: 'We knew them all, the singers and the songs, but we thought of them as the embarrassing outbursts of men stocious with drink.' **1991** Bob Quinn, *Smokey Hollow*: '"For God's sake, woman, have a bit of sense ...Of course it was an accident. He was probably stocious when he came in."' **1993** Sam McAughtry, *Touch & Go*: '"Mary and me pushed you into the snug [q.v.] and from then on your man [q.v.] Dan was part of the round. We knocked him stocious."'

stocker [n. pl., <?] (Leinster). Uncommon fish found among main catch in boat's hold, divided between all hands (DOM).

stocking [n., <*idem*, store of money kept in stocking, Eng. dial. & colloq., C19] (Cork). As thus. 'Dealers on Coal Quay [q.v.] invariably kept paper money inside their stockings...' (Beecher).

stog [vb., cf. Sc. *idem*, 'drive in a tool too deeply when working with wood' (CSD)]. Bury. **1922** James Joyce, *Ulysses*: 'A porter[q.v.]-bottle stood up, stogged to its waist, in the cakey sand dough.'

stone stout [n. phr.] Container. **1995** Guinness drip mat: 'Bottled Guinness once came in what were known as "stone stouts" — bottles made from stoneware.'

stookawn [n., <Ir. *stuacán*, fool]. As thus.

stoon/stoun/stound [n. & vb., <Sc. *stoun/stound* (n. & vb.), ache, numb with pain] (Ulster). As thus. **1951** Sam Hanna Bell, *December Bride*: 'Suddenly he turned to his cousin and shouted: "That woman

near killed me! I was stooned for days after it!''"

stoor [n. & vb., <Sc. *stour*, (raise) a) dust, <Anglo-Fr. *estur* (n.), storm] (Ulster). [n.]. Whirling dust. [vb.]. Travel/move rapidly.

stople [vb., cf. Sc. *stopple* (n.), tube of small bore]. Penetrate sexually. See **fozy**.

stoppage [n.] (Ulster). Speech impediment, stammer.

stopple/stapple [n., <MDu. *stapel*, stem, stock]. Stem of a pipe; stalk of grass; icicle.

stop-the-clock [n., <'custom of stopping the clock when there is a death in the house' (Pepper)] (Ulster). S.o. who always expects the worst.

store see **asthore**

stoun/stound see **stoon**

stour [n., <Sc. *idem*, dust, dust in motion, smoke-like fog] (Ulster). Dust, smoke.

stove [n., cf. *idem* (vb.), fumigate with sulphur] (Ulster). Bad or strong smell; smell of drink. Hence **stoving** [pres. part. as adj.]. Drunk.

straddy [n., <Ir. *sráid*, street]. 'Idle person always sauntering along streets' (PWJ).

strap [n.]. 1. [<Ir. *straip*, harlot (Dinneen)]. As thus, and as gen. term of abuse. **1675–95** Anon., *Purgatorium Hibernicum*: 'Amongst this traine, who (thinke you) espied he/But his old mistress, Madam Dydy? —/That pin'd to death, the fawnening strapp!/Some say for love, some of a clapp...' **1842** Samuel Lover, *Handy Andy*: '"You infernal old strap!" shouted he, as he clutched a handful of bottles...and flung them at the nurse.' **1989** Hugh Leonard, *Out after Dark*: 'Gloria was the kind of strap who could look after herself in a pit of snakes.' See also **streepach**. 2. [<Ir. *strapaire*, vigorous, well-built girl (Dinneen)]. Strong girl. 3. [<*idem*, credit, Eng. dial., C19] (Cork). As thus (Beecher), as in **he is good for strap**.

stravage/stravaige/stravege [vb., <Sc. *stravaig* (n. & vb.), saunter, poss. <OF

estravaguer, wander; cf. Sc. *stravaiger* (n.), one who leaves a religious community]. Roam, wander. **1913** W.M. Letts, *Songs from Leinster*, 'Little Peter Morrissey': 'You'll see him in the winter time stravagin' through the wet;/ He's not so wishful to go home where likely he'll be bet [beaten].' **1989** John Banville, *The Book of Evidence*: '...I, who for ten years had stravaiged the world like a tinker, never doing a hand's turn of work'. **1994** Gabriel Byrne, *Pictures in my Head*: 'Out straveging the roads by the look of you. Well I hope she was worth it...'

straw [vb.]. **1960** John O'Donoghue, *In Kerry Long Ago*: 'Strawing is an old Kerry custom in which uninvited people pay a friendly visit to a wedding dressed in straw suits for disguise. They dance and drink when they arrive.' **1995** Éamon Kelly, *The Apprentice*: '"It will be a great wedding...There'll be no shortage there." "What good is that to us," Old Scanlon replied, "when we won't be invited? Unless we'd straw. Did you ever straw, Ned?" he asked my father.' Hence **straw boys** [n. pl.]. **1991** Seán Ó Ciaráin, *Farewell to Mayo*: 'A highlight of the wedding evenings, and something which, as far as I know, existed only in West Mayo, was the attendance of "straw-boys" at weddings.'

straw-farmer [n.]. Poor/inefficient farmer, derog. **1943** George A. Little, *Malachi Horan Remembers*: 'About a hundred years ago the next farm to mine here was owned by a man by the name of Frank Lynam...he was no straw-farmer, but an honest man.' See **strong farmer**.

strawk-hawk [vb., <Ir. *strácáil* (n.), (act of) striving, struggling, dragging along (Dinneen); gen. as pres. part.] (Cork). As thus. 'Expression of good-humoured resignation' (Beecher).

stray [n.]. 1. (Ulster). S.o. who differs markedly from other members of the family (YDS). 2. Casual sexual congress. **1965** Lee Dunne, *Goodbye to the Hill*: 'there was just no getting away from it, I loved a gargle [q.v.] and a bit of stray'. 3. Fairy influence causing travellers to lose their way. **1979** Paddy Tunney, *The Stone

Fiddle: 'Johnnie McGee was once as straight as a yard of pump-water until the stray came on him at the back of Breen Mountain.'

streak of misery see **long streak of misery**

streal see **streel**

stredlegs [adj. & adv., <'straddle'] (Ulster). Astride, esp. of woman astride horse. **1983** W.F. Marshall, *Livin' in Drumlister*, 'The Runaway': 'Got a shawl an' whusked it about her,/Got stredlegs behin' on the cowlt./Ay, stredlegs, for that's the way weemin/Bees ridin' the horses all now...' See also **striddle** 2.

streel/streeler/streal/strool [n. & vb., <Ir. *sraoill* (n.), slattern]. [n.]. As thus. **1920** Seumas O'Kelly, *The Leprechaun of Kilmeen*: '"I suppose his streel of a wife," says he, "couldn't be trusting him with it..."' [vb.]. Drag along untidily (of dress etc.). **1952** Oliver St John Gogarty, *Collected Poems*, 'Ringsend': 'I will live in Ringsend/With a red-headed whore... And listen each night/For her querulous shout,/As at last she streels in/And the pubs empty out.' **1991** Bob Quinn, *Smokey Hollow*: 'As they streeled to school in the mornings they would be overtaken by purposeful men in good suits...striding to catch the tram in Rathgar.' Hence **streely/strealy** [adj.]. Of a tall, thin individual; unkempt, straggly (of hair). **1995** Tom Humphries, *Irish Times*, 4 Dec: 'So there we were, late in the game [of hurling]...when the wonder point came about. A long strealy lad by the name of Finn...went to take a 70.'

streepach/streepo [n., <Ir. *striapach*, whore]. As thus. **1605** Anon., *Captain Thomas Stukeley*: 'Zee [I] am afraid Brian Mac Phelemy is wyd his streepo, and forgeats to hang a siegne [sign] or let us in.' **1991** Bob Quinn, *Smokey Hollow*: 'It [the horse] had a long tail that whipped at their faces while their Granda cursed it, "Will you hup outa that, you lazy streepach."' See also **strap** 1.

street [n., <Ir. *sráid*, level ground around a house]. As thus. **1948** Patrick

Kavanagh, *Tarry Flynn*: 'Through the thick hedge he could see into Brady's street and when the door was open hear the talk within the house.' **1995** Mamie McDermott in Mary Ryan et al. (eds.), *No Shoes in Summer*: 'The "street" was the word for the space immediately in front of each house in our locality [Cooley Peninsula, Co. Louth].' **1995** Shane Connaughton, *A Border Diary*: 'They play the scene on the "street" in front of the house. Then Marie Conmee as Mrs Prunty comes out...'

strib [vb., <'strip'] (Ulster). Drain the last drops from a cow when milking. **1799** Samuel Thomson, *New Poems*, 'To a Hedgehog': 'If that thou stribs the outler cow,/As some assert,/A pretty milkmaid, I allow/Forsooth thou art.' **1966** Florence Mary McDowell, *Other Days Around Me*: 'nine-quart cans for buttermilk, two-quart tins for dippers or for "stribbing" cows, one-quart cans for sweet milk...tea-drawers [q.v.], workers' tea cans...theirs [the tinkers'] was a glorious stock-in-trade'.

striddle [vb.] (Ulster). 1. [cf. Sc. *idem* (n.), 'gait of a man with bent legs' (CSD)]. Walk with abnormal gait. 2. [<'straddle']. Sit astride. See also **stredlegs**.

striffin [n., <Sc. Gael. *sreabhainn*, thin, membranous film, thin skin (CSD)] (Ulster). Thin film inside eggshell; small length of anything.

string of misery see **long streak of misery**

stripe [n. & vb.]. Land division. **1968** John Healy, *The Death of an Irish Town*: 'They [Mayo farmers] do not understand why, when a farm is taken over, it is not "striped" and parcelled out among what's left...They are sure that a "stripe" of a neighbour's farm will give them an economic holding...'

stripper [n., see **strib**]. Cow which is running dry. Hence **strippings** [n.]. '[L]ast of the milk...at milking — always the richest' (PWJ).

stroke [n.]. 1. (thatching). Measurement. **1985** Olive Sharkey, *Old Days Old Ways*: 'Jack, like most other thatchers...worked a width of approximately three feet at a time. Known as a stroke, this was said to be a comfortable width and was more or less standard.' 2. (Cork). Appetite (Beecher). 3. [not as Brit. sl. *idem*, underhand trick (ODMS)]. Successful and spectacular (political) ploy, not necessarily underhand. **1988** John Healy, *Magill*, 'The Wild One', Apr: 'He [Donogh O'Malley] loved the stroke. He loved going into the local school unannounced and asking for a day off for the students...' Hence **pull a stroke** [vb. phr.]. Get away with something. **1993** Paddy Tyrrell in Joe O'Reilly & Sixth Class, Convent School, Edenderry, *Over the Half Door*: 'So he said, "Well, you'll have to apply to the County Council for permission for that tapping [of the main sewer]." I never heard another word from that day to this. Well, that happened on a Patrick's morning — and you'd think you'd be pulling a stroke.' Also **stroker** [n.] in same sense.

Stroke City [nickname]. Derry/Londonderry. **1994** Michael Palin, *Great Railway Journeys*, 'Derry to Kerry': 'The schizoid nature of the city remains in the firm retention of its two names, both of which are loaded with significance. There have been attempts to have it both ways — Londonderry-stroke-Derry — which merely led to it being risibly referred to as "Stroke City".'

strone [n., <Sc. *idem* (vb.), urinate; pour] (Ulster). Pour (of tea/milk).

strong farmer [n. phr.]. Prosperous farmer with large acreage etc. **1951** Sam Hanna Bell, *December Bride*: 'It was pleasant, thought Sara, to sit up here beside Hamilton, a strong farmer going to market.' **1977** Wesley Burrowes, *The Riordans*: 'What the audience saw was a family living on the outskirts of Leestown, a village near Kilkenny. Tom Riordan, a strong farmer; his wife Mary, absorbed in her family...' **1996** Anthony Cronin, *Samuel Beckett, The Last Modernist*: '*Autumn Fire* [T.C. Murray] has for its hero a "strong" farmer who has a young wife but is rendered impotent by an accident.' See **straw-farmer**.

strool see **streel**

stroop/stroup [n., <Sc. *idem*, spout; cf. Swed. *strupe*, throat] (Ulster). Spout; lip of jug. **1993** Seamus Heaney, *The Midnight Verdict* (translation of Brian Merriman, *Cúirt an Mheán Oíche*): 'Yet who gives a damn at the end of it all/For them and their dribbling stroup and fall?'

strunt [vb. & n., cf. Sc. *idem*, 'to walk about in a sullen mood' (CSD), sulky fit] (Ulster). Sulk, sulks, as in **take the strunts** [vb. phr.]. Huff, withdraw in anger.

stuccour/stucker [vb., cf. Ir. *stocaire* (n.), interloper, sponger (Dinneen)]. Cadge. **1907** Joseph Guinan, *The Soggarth Aroon* (q.v.): 'to "stucker" for a drink'.

stuff [n. as adj., cf. Brit. sl. 'hot stuff']. Excellent or outstanding individual. **1927** Peadar O'Donnell, *Islanders*: 'Ruth's hand was in Charlie's. "I wanted a dip, and I got it," she said. "By the Lord, she's stuff," Manus O'Donnell commented.'

stughie/staghey/styaghie, etc. [n., <Sc. *stughie*, 'anything that fills to repletion; satisfying food' (CSD)] (Ulster). Unappetising mess of food, leftovers, mess in general.

stugue [n. & vb., <Ir. *stua* (n.), arch, arc; 'anything arched or curved' (Dinneen)]. As thus. **1867** Patrick Kennedy, *The Banks of the Boro*: 'He began to think that his inside would be all gone, and that he'd fall in a stugue on one of the big diamond-shaped flags of the floor.'

stum [n., <Sc. *idem*, blockhead]. Sulky, taciturn individual; gen. term of abuse. **1986** Padraic O'Farrell, *'Tell me, Sean O'Farrell'*: 'A passer-by one day asked the old stum for some "griosach" [q.v.] to light his pipe. He looked over the door and saw a child's hand sticking out of the pot.'

stumer see **stewmer**

stummle [n. & vb., <ON *stumla* (vb.), stumble, trip] (Ulster). Attempt.

stump [n.] (Ulster). (Apple) core.

stunt [n.]. Military engagement, War of Independence/Civil War. **1922** P.F.

Quinlan, diary: 'Crossley [tender] going with Corporal G when stunt came on then off for we knew not where terrible secrecy.'

sturk [n., <Ir. *stiorc*, short, stocky individual]. As thus.

styaghie see **stughie**

styall see **steall**

suck/suckie [n.]. 1. First-year schoolboy. **1996** Dermot Healy, *The Bend for Home*: 'The sucks from the first year ran errands for the seniors to the shop...' 2. Pet name for cow. **1927** Peadar O'Donnell, *Islanders*: 'A cow greeted the woman's appearance with an eager low. "Poor suckie," she said.'

Suds [nickname]. Peter Sutherland (1946–), politican, European Commissioner. **1989** John Healy, *Magill*, Jan: 'You have to be out of your crazy tiny mind to follow "Suds", otherwise the departing Peter Sutherland, Europe's best known Irish man.'

sugawn/sughan [n., <Ir. *súgán*, straw-rope]. As thus; apron. **1945** Robert Gibbings, *Lovely is the Lee*: '"Take with you a halter of sugawn," he said; "a straw rope it must be, and throw it over the mare's head and the enchantment will be broken...' Also as in **sugawn chair** [n. phr.]. Chair with woven straw seat.

sugeen see **sowans**

sugh [n., <Sc. *idem*, stroke] (Ulster). Slap.

sughan see **sugawn**

suleymander/sooleymander/syla-mander [n. & vb., <?]. [n.]. Heavy blow/thump; large quantity/number of anything. [vb.]. Strike a blow with open hand.

summachaun [n., <Ir. *somachán*, plump youngster]. As thus; (Connacht) 'big ignorant puffed-up booby of a fellow' (PWJ).

sunburstry [n., <symbol of rising sun's rays associated with C19–20 national movement; cf. device on badge of national army]. Excessive/exaggerated patriotism. **1931** A.W. Kward, *An t-Óglach*, 'Tales of a Flying Column

[q.v.]', June: 'His son Frank did not fling frothy Sunburstry in the face of any man: he was concerned with unemotional essentials...' **1968** Austin Clarke, *A Penny in the Clouds*: 'All through my early years, the word "Nationalism" shone in my mind, despite those who mocked at patriotic speeches and denounced them as "sunburstry".'

sunsey see **sonsy**

Swaddler [nickname, 1745–; 'a "Protestant" account of its origin is that a Dublin priest, hearing an early Methodist speak of "the babe in swaddling clothes", gave the name to the sect (Wall)]. 1. Methodist preacher. **1922** James Joyce, *Dubliners*, 'An Encounter': 'and so we walked on, the ragged troop screaming after us "*Swaddlers! Swaddlers!*", thinking that we were Protestants...' **1961** Flann O'Brien, *The Hard Life*: 'You won't find Quakers or swaddlers coming out with any of this guff [q.v.] about suffering.' 2. Catholic who converts to Protestantism for material reward. **1970** Christy Brown, *Down All the Days*: '"And who took charity from any so-so minister, will you tell me?" cried Magso. "I'm no bloody swaddler!"'

swarry/soirée [n., <Fr. *soirée*, evening social gathering] (Ulster). As thus. **1951** Sam Hanna Bell, *December Bride*: 'The soirée of which Fergus had spoken was really the "treat" and sports that followed the yearly religious examination of the Presbyterian children of the townlands.' **1972** Florence Mary McDowell, *Roses and Rainbows*: 'the children's year followed that of the calendar. December was the end of the year. December was Christmas. December was the school swarry.' See also **sharee**.

sweat [vb.]. Deprive of. **1829** Gerald Griffin, *The Collegians*: '"Pink him! Sweat him! Pink the rascal!" cried another horseman, riding rapidly up...' **1847** John Edward Walsh, *Ireland Sixty Years Ago*: 'As they passed the house of a publican...on Ormond quay, they determined to amuse themselves by "sweating", i.e. making him give up all his fire-arms.'

sweat drink [n. phr.]. After-work drink given to catering staff in compensation for steamy working conditions and antisocial hours. **1995** *Irish Times*, 9 Dec: 'Unions and management in a Dublin hotel are at odds over the so-called "sweat drink". Management at Jurys Hotel had called time on the traditional after work drink...However, attempts to scrap the 33-year-old scheme...have left it with more than a headache.'

sweel [vb., <Sc. *idem*, swaddle, wrap round, cf. Icel. *sveipa*, envelop, shroud] (Ulster). As thus. 'She was that sweeled in her jeans it's a wonder the zip went up' (SH).

sweeney, on one's [adv. phr., <rhym. sl. 'on one's Tod Sloan', US jockey C19]. Alone, on one's own. **1996** Richard Marsh, RTÉ Radio, *Sunday Miscellany*, 21 July: 'In Ireland "on your tod" is taken to refer to the legendary Sweeney Todd, so "on your tod" becomes "on your sweeney".'

Sweep, the [nickname, abbrev.]. Sweepstakes, linked to major horse races, set up by Joe McGrath's Hospital Trust Ltd under Act of 1930. **1996** David Hanly, *Sunday Tribune*, 3 Nov: 'You will remember the Lottery's predecessor, the Irish Hospitals' Sweepstake, once a part of our culture...The "Sweep" made some

families fabulously wealthy (and the winners didn't do too badly either).'

sweetener [n.]. One who bids at auctions, with no intention of buying, to put prices up.

switch [n.]. 1. [<?] (Cork). Dislike, as in **get a switch about s.o.** 2. [see **scutch (grass)**]. Couch grass. **1986** Padraic O'Farrell, *'Tell me, Sean O'Farrell'*: 'Scutch, called switch here in Kilkenny, was a deadly weed to get into a garden.'

swither [n. & vb. <Sc. *idem* (vb.), hesitate, cf. OE *swithrian* (vb.), weaken, destroy]. Vacillation; vacillate. **1913** Alexander Irvine, *My Lady of the Chimney Corner*: 'the two men stood looking at each other — speechless. "Ye can do switherin' as easy sittin' as standin'," Anna said, and Billy sat down.' **1943** George A. Little, *Malachi Horan Remembers*: 'She was in a woeful swither waiting there, straining her ears to catch what she was frightened of her life to hear.' **1983** W.F. Marshall, *Livin' in Drumlister*, 'Me an' me Da': 'So I swithered back an' forrit/Till Margit got a man;/A fella come from Mullaslin/An' left me just the wan.' Also **in swithers** [adj. phr.] in same sense.

swope [n. & vb., <OE *sopa*, mouthful (n.)]. Drink (DOM).

swotty [adj.] (Ulster). Well-dressed.

sylamander see **suleymander**

T

ta [n.]. Bowel motion. See **peetney**.

Taca [n., <Ir. *idem*, prop, support; freq. capitalised as if an acronym]. Fund-raising scheme for Fianna Fáil party, 1960s–1970s. **1986** Gene Kerrigan, *Magill*, Jan: 'They [Fianna Fáil] had survived the Taca scandal, which involved a naive attempt to formalise and give a social dimension to the financing of the major parties by business interests.' **1987** T. Ryle Dwyer, *Charlie*: 'Taca was "a fairly innocent concept", according to Haughey. "In so far as it had any particular motivation it was to make the party independent of big business and try to spread the level of financial support across a much wider spectrum of the community."' **1996** Deaglán de Bréadún, *Irish Times*, 27 Jan: 'The event was organised by Fianna Fáil's support group in the business community, Forum 2000. This was founded in February last year with a membership fee of £1,000 a year (no snide remarks about TACA please)...'

tack [n.]. 1. [<?]. Bad, rancid taste in food. Hence **tacked** [adj.]. Rancid (of butter/bacon). 2. [gen. neg.]. Least possible amount (of work, clothing). See **tap** 2. 3. [poss. <ON *taka*, revenue, tenure of land]. Spell of fine weather; situation, steady job. 4. [<?] (Cork). Pre-decimal sixpence (Beecher). See also **sprazzy**.

tackle [n.] (Ulster). Difficult child/person; a 'handful'; scolding woman. See **blade**.

tacklings [n. pl.]. Equipment for making poteen (q.v.). **1979** Paddy Tunney, *The Stone Fiddle*: 'he lured me into his kitchen to see the complete "tacklings". There was a still on the huge turf fire, a still-head...a wonderful copper pipe with many bends, known as a worm, and a huge wooden barrel filled with water.'

Taig see **Teig**

tail [n., <*idem*, harlot, *c.*1780–1850 (DHS)] (Ulster). Loose woman, prostitute.

taildraft [n.] (Ulster). S.o. who holds back; useless worker.

tailer/tailor see **taylor**

tail o' the day [n. phr., cf. Ir. *eireaball an lae, idem*]. Late evening.

Taj Micheál [nickname, <Micheál Browne (1896–1980), Bishop of Galway]. The new and architecturally eclectic Galway Roman Catholic cathedral, opened under the bishop's patronage in 1966.

take a box [vb. phr.] (Clongowes Wood College, Co. Kildare). Defecate. **1995** Aidan Higgins, *Donkey's Years*: 'To slash (to piss), to take a box (to crap)...'

take a feather out of s.o. [vb. phr., invar. neg.]. Faze (q.v.) s.o.

take a hand (out of) see **hand**.

take a trick out of [vb. phr., cf. Ir. *feidhm a bhaint as rud*, make (lit. take) use of something] (Ulster). As thus.

taken in at, be [adj. phr.] (Ulster). Be surprised by. **1908** Lynn Doyle, *Ballygullion*: 'the dog set up the horridest howlin' ye iver heard, an' I was that taken in at him I dhropped the chain and let him go'.

take-on [n.] (Travellers). Second husband. **1994** Paddy O'Gorman, *Queuing for a Living*: '"He's not your father. He's a take-on. An' it'll always be thrown in my face."'

take one off the wrist [vb. phr.]. Masturbate (male). **1965** Lee Dunne, *Goodbye to the Hill*: 'and there wasn't a picture house. So all they could do was drink or play pitch and toss, or take one off the wrist.'

take one's end [vb. phr.] (Ulster). Die with laughter. **1908** Lynn Doyle, *Ballygullion*: 'Ye'd ha' taken your end at her. It was "another cup av tay, Misther O'Hare," an' "thry a bit av toast"...as foolish-lookin' as an ould cat playin' wi' a spool.' Also **take one's fair end** in same sense.

take snore [vb. phr.] (Ulster). Huff, sulk (SH).

take s.o.'s toe [vb. phr.] (Ulster). Affect, 'get into' s.o., as in **what has taken her toe?** What has got into her?

take the needle [vb. phr., cf. Brit. sl. 'get the needle', become angry (DHS)]. As thus. **1981** Brendan Behan, *After the Wake*: '"No need to take the needle over it. Just answer a civil question."'

take the soup [vb. phr., see **souper**]. (Of a Catholic) Convert to Protestantism (at time of the Great Hunger (q.v.)).

take to the fair [vb. phr., gen. reflexive]. Amaze, fascinate, surprise. **1966** Patrick Boyle, *At Night All Cats are Grey*, title story: '"What would take you to the fair," he said, "is the way a decent modest girl could make such a disgrace of herself. To be found stretched out in your pelt [q.v.] on the floor of an old deserted hut..."' **1968** Myles na gCopaleen, *The Best of Myles*: '"But I'll tell you what takes me to the fair. Your men [q.v.] above in the park. The fellas that's tryin to hunt the deer into a cage."' Also **take things to the fair** [vb. phr.]. Exaggerate, overreact. **1951** Frank O'Connor, *Traveller's Samples*, 'This Mortal Coil': '"You take things to the fair, Dan," I said to him once. "All I ask...is that bloody idiots will keep their opinions to themselves..."'

take your hour! see **hold your hour!**

talk from the teeth out [vb. phr.] (Ulster). Speak hypocritically.

tallamacka/tallymackey/telemachus [n., cf. Ir. *tailmeálaí*, banger, thumper]. Clamour, noisy disagreement.

tally-boy see **tarry-boy**

tally-ho [n., poss. <Fr. *tayaut*, deer hunting cry]. Confusion, fuss. **1967** Bryan MacMahon, *The Honey Spike* (q.v.): '"...I wouldn't be surprised with all this tallyho if I dropped a kid myself the minute we reached that bloody Spike"'. **1996** Eoghan Harris, *Irish Times*, 26 Oct: 'Surely David Hanly...would have heard people like Seán Ó Riada using the word, as in "What's the tally-ho?"'

tallymackey see **tallamacka**

tallywagger see **trallywagger**

tangle [n.]. Bunch. See **gripe**.

tangler [n.]. Middleman in cattle dealing. **1952** Anon. (Patrick Kavanagh?), *Kavanagh's Weekly*, 'I Went to the Fair', 21 June: 'At this point a third party turns up. Sometimes that third party is the actual owner...Generally, however, the deal was on the level and the middleman, the "tangler", was authentic too. Enter the tangler. "What's atween yous [q.v.]?"' **1973** Noël Conway, *The Bloods* (q.v.): 'He asked for two bob, but with the "Hooker" acting as "tangler" a compromise was reached: one-and-a-tanner.' **1995** Hannah O'Donnell in Mary Ryan et al. (eds.), *No Shoes in Summer*: 'At long last they reach the village, the place is a hive of activity, the drovers and tanglers are moving about, testing udders and flanks.'

tanglers three! [exclam.]. Used in game of conkers when strings of opposing chestnuts become tangled. First to shout thus claims advantage. **N.d.** (unpublished) Maurice J. Wigham, *A History of Newtown School* (Waterford) *1798–1998*: 'The Autumn term began with chestnuts ...It was not long before "Conkers 4" was being compared with "Conkers 15", and the prowess of "Seasoners". Shouts of "Tanglers 3" were heard on the gravel...'

tanker [n., <?] (Ulster). Cheeky girl.

Tans see **Black and Tans**

tantitherum [n., <Ir. *teach an tsughtraim/súraim*, lit. house of 'worthless liquid/overdrawn tea' (Dinneen)] (Leinster). Unlicensed drinking premises, shebeen (q.v.). **1943** George A. Little, *Malachi Horan Remembers*: '"the inns in Rathfarnham were great places, surely...Different entirely they were to the little mountain places that used to be around here. Tantitherums we called them. Eh? A tantitherum was a public house and it wanting a licence.'

tap [vb. & n.]. 1. [vb.]. Wheedle money/ drink out of s.o. See **skin on one's face**. Hence **tapper** [n.]. One who acts thus. 2. [n.]. Small quantity of work. See **tack** 2.

tappany see **tepeny**

tare [n.]. 1. [cf. Sc. *treaing* (pres. part. as adj.), excessive, very great] (Ulster). Great quantity (YDS). 2. See **tear**.

tare/tear an' ages/agers [expletive, euphem., corruption of '[Christ's] tears + aches' (DHS)]. Sacrilegious oath. **C.1830s** Michael Moran (Zozimus (q.v.)), *Pharo's Daughter*: 'A bull-rush tripped her, where-upon she saw/A smiling babby in a wad of straw,/She took it up and said in accents mild:/Tare an' ages, girls, which of yez [see **youse**] owns the child?'

tare-an'-ouns [expletive, euphem., corruption of '[Christ's] tears and wounds', C19–20]. Sacrilegious oath. **1831** Samuel Lover, *Legends and Stories of Ireland*, 'Ye Marvellous Legend of Tom Connor's Cat': '"Now no more of your palaver, Misther Connor," says the cat; "just be off and get me the shoes." "Tare and ouns!" says Tom, "what'll become o' me if I'm to get shoes for my cats?"' **1879** Charles J. Kickham, *Knocknagow*: '"It is past four, Barney." "Thanum-on-dioul [see **manam a dioule!**], can it be late so early?" he exclaimed. "Tare-an'-ouns, I'll be kilt [q.v.].'" **1922** 'Pink Ox', *TCD, A College Miscellany*, 'Dan O'Connell v. Biddy Moriarty', 15 June: '"Oh, tare-an-ouns," ses she. "Oh, be the hokey [q.v.], the disgrace!/An honest woman called parrylellygrum to her face."' See also **thunder-an'-ouns**.

targe/targer [n., <Sc. *targer*, virago, <OE *tergan* (vb.), irritate]. Scolding woman; bold, brazen woman. **1979** John Morrow in David Marcus (ed.), *Body and Soul*, 'Beginnings': 'She was twenty-seven then, a fine looking targe of a woman...skirt tucked up in the legs of her drawers and me perched on her shoulders...' **1979** Michael O'Beirne, *Mister, A Dublin Childhood*: 'The forewoman, Miss Helena Molony, was a proper targer, Maggie said.' **1985** Máirín Johnston, *Around the Banks of Pimlico*: 'Her mother was a forewoman in Todd Burns factory in Mary Street and was locally called "a right [see **right** 1.] oul' targe".'

tarra [adj. & n., <local pronun. of 'terror'] (Ulster). Terrible; terror. **1983** W.F. Marshall, *Livin' in Drumlister*, 'The Runaway': 'The gowls [see **gowl** 1.] of wee [q.v.] Robert wos tarra,/The veins riz like coards on his skull...' **1995** Shane Connaughton, *A Border Diary*: '"I had to bring him [the horse] home and put him in a shed. He kicked up a horrid pile. A holy tarra [see **holy terror**]."'

tarry see **torry**

tarry-boy/tally-boy [n., cf. Sc. *tarry-fingers*, dishonest person] (Cork). Male of questionable behaviour; randy individual (Beecher).

tartles [n. pl., <Sc. *tartle* (vb.), rend, scatter] (Ulster). Ragged clothing; hanging pieces (of manure etc.).

Tart with the Cart, the [nickname]. Dub. street sculpture of Molly Malone. See **the Chime in the Slime**.

Tá Sé's [nickname, <Ir. *tá sé*, lit. 'it is']. First (Ir.-speaking) Battalion, Ir. army. **1973** Noël Conway, *The Bloods* (q.v.): 'Among those who had come to say "good-bye" to the "Bloods" at this time [1940] was Lt. Seán Collins, who had come to the Battalion a decade earlier from the "Tá Sé's"...'

tashpy [n., <Ir. *teaspach*, ardour, tendency to gad]. As thus. **1906** E.Œ. Somerville & Martin Ross, *Some Irish Yesterdays*: '"Now as for the foxy mare ...she'd have as much thricks and *tashpy* on her...as a lad that'd be goin' to a fair."'

taste [n.]. Small quantity. **1993** Joe Langan in Joe O'Reilly & Sixth Class, Convent School, Edenderry, *Over the Half Door*: 'They were like concentration camps, the schools, in them days. I only got a taste of learning, an idea, but I didn't really learn till I left school.'

tat [n., <Ir. *táth*, tuft, bunch; Sc. *tat*, tuft of wool etc. (CSD) related to *tatter*, cf. Icel. *toturr*, tatters] (Ulster). Tangled or matted hair on a girl or animal. Hence **tatty/tautie/teuted/tauted** [adj.], tan-gled, matted; and thus **tats and taws** [n. phr., pleonasm] in same sense. **1944** Mary Lavin, *The Long Ago and Other Stories*, 'The Will': '"we knowing all the time the old clothes you were likely to be wearing, and your hair all tats and taws, and your face dirty"'.

tatie/tattie/tatty [n., <Sc. *idem*, potato] (Ulster). As thus. Hence **tattie cake** [n. phr.]. Potato bread/cake. **1971** John Moore, quoted in *Irish Booklore*, 'John Moore, A Donaghadee Poet': 'Craigavon spoke of "tattie" cake,/Admittedly rich and rare,/ Producing rose-pink-white skin/On colleen [q.v.] sweet and fair.' Also **tatie/tattie/tatty-hoker** [n., <Sc. *tatie-howker*, potato digger; cf. Swed. *halka* (vb.), hollow out]. Ir. seasonal potato harvesters in Scotland. **1991** Seán Ó Ciaráin, *Farewell to Mayo*: 'Others went to Scotland to work at the potato harvest, men, women and children — the tattie-hokers they were known as, but they were not in the same league as the beet men.' **1994** Christopher Fitz-Simon, *The Boys* (see **the Boys** 2.): 'the *new Irish*, the Harrys who have made money...and who have forgotten that their fathers were tatty-hokers in Scotland'.

taws [n. pl., <'taw', child's marble]. Testicles.

tay-drawer/tea-drawer [n., *tay*-<Hib.E pronun.] (Ulster). Large tin mug with lid in which tea was left to draw by the fire. **1908** Lynn Doyle, *Ballygullion*: 'The leg straightened out wi' a snap, lit ould Pether on his back, an' the toe av it just took the wee [q.v.] tay-drawer that was simmerin' on the hob.'

taylor/tailer/tailor [n., <?]. Spirit measure. **1935** *Irish Times*, 27 July: 'Even three ounces of whiskey — what Ireland calls a "taylor" and England a "double" — are sufficient, according to the Committee, "to affect appreciably the mental processes and neuro-muscular co-ordination"...' **1946** James Stephens, *The James Joyce I Knew*: 'The barman brought the refreshment that I ordered — it was called a "Tailor of Malt [q.v.]". It was larger than a single, and it only escaped being a double by the breadth of a tram-ticket...'

Tay Pay [nickname, <Hib.E pronun. of initials]. T[homas] P[ower] O'Connor, 1848–1929, journalist and politician, proprietor of *T.P.'s Weekly*, 1902–. **1922** James Joyce, *Ulysses*: '...Paddy Hooper worked with Tay Pay who took him on

to the *Star*. Now he's got in with Blumenfeld. That's press. That's talent.' **1968** Austin Clarke, *A Penny in the Clouds*: 'Con O'Leary...had worked on *The Manchester Guardian* and at this time was "ghosting" the memoirs of "Tay Pay"...'

tea-drawer see **tay-drawer**

Teague see **Teig**

tear/tare [n.] as in **on the tear/tare** [adj. phr., see **tare** 1.]. Engaging in bout of extended drinking; on the spree. **1925** Liam O'Flaherty, *The Informer*: 'He went noiselessly up the stairs without attracting the attention of the revellers who were still "on the tear".' **1927** Peadar O'Donnell, *Islanders*: '"It's because Neil is goin' that yer Aunt Mary is goin', for she knows fine he'll go on the tare."' **1977** Sam McAughtry, *The Sinking of the Kenbane Head*: 'But of course, with his weakness, the money did him more harm than good in the long run, for it only put him on the tear for days.' Hence **on the rip** in same sense.

tear an' ages see **tare an' ages**

tear-lathers [n. pl., lit. 'tear-leathers'] (Ulster). Shreds, tatters.

tears/teers [n. pl. <'tear' (vb.), move violently, hence rushing gallop or pace, 1838] (Ulster). As thus. 'Ye shudda seen the tears of him down the road' (Todd).

teasy-whacker [n., cf. *teasle*, female pudend (DHS)]. Slut. **1970** Christy Brown, *Down All the Days*: '"O a lovely woman, and that bloody little teasy-whacker over there destroying her mother's memory!"'

teathens/teathins [n. pl., cf. Sc. *tathe*, luxuriant grass grown on droppings] (Ulster). As thus.

teddy bear [n.]. Woman's shawl. **1994** Tommy Maher in Kevin C. Kearns, *Dublin Tenement Life*: 'A good shawl, a big brown shawl was called a "teddy bear". My mother had one of them.'

Ted Head [nickname, <series title]. Fan of TV series *Father Ted*. **1996** Brian Boyd, *Irish Times*, 4 June: 'the President, Mrs Robinson, might herself be a Ted

Head as she has requested a meeting with the show's writers, Arthur Matthews and Graham Linehan, during her visit to London this week'.

teehee/teehie [vb., <ME *tehee* (n.), derisive laughter] (Ulster). Make fun of.

teem [vb., cf. Ir. *taom*, empty of water, bail; ON *taema*, empty]. Pour water off boiled potatoes; bail water. **1948** Patrick Kavanagh, *Tarry Flynn*: 'Teeming the pot into a bucket...holding one of the legs of the pot with his right hand and the pot lid with his left...' Hence **teeming** [pres. part.]. Pouring rain.

teers see **tears**

tee-tee [n., <?]. Lemonade bottle top, pierced and used as cover for clay pipe to enable it to be smoked upside down (EW).

Teig/Taig/Teague [nickname & adj., <Ir. *Tadhg*, proper name]. 1. Irishman. **1718** John Durant Breval, *The Play is the Plot*: 'CARBINE Thou has the brogue a little sure. JEREMY As well as any Teague of 'em all Sir, if that can do your honour any kindness.' 2. (Ulster). Term of disparagement for Roman Catholics (Ir., and others by extension, cf. colloq. Austral. *tike/tyke* in same sense). **1979** John Morrow, *The Confessions of Proinsias O'Toole*: '"total withdrawal, you said, an' there's still a full company of them Scotch Teigs protectin' that holy kiphouse [see **kip**] down there"'. **1994** Dermot Healy, *A Goat's Song*: '"Sorry," said the youth. "It's all right," said Jack. "Taig cunt," said the youth.'

Tele, the [nickname, abbrev.]. *Belfast Telegraph* newspaper, founded 1870. **1969** Robert Greacen, *Even without Irene*: 'a man might well be unhappy if, after a hard day's slogging, he had to sit down to his tea without having his "Tele" for moral support'. **1995** Ken Gray, *Irish Times*, 22 July: 'Unusually for an evening paper, the *Tele*, as it soon became known, set out to be a primary source of information...'

telemachus see **tallamacka**

tell a picture [vb. phr.]. Recount the plot of a film seen, *c.*1950s. **1979** John

Morrow in David Marcus (ed.), *Body and Soul*, 'Beginnings': 'They sang hymns... and passed the time challenging one another on Biblical texts rather than "telling" pictures or swapping dirty yarns.' **1995** Patrick Boland, *Tales from a City Farmyard*: 'Not everyone could get to see all the pictures around in those times before television arrived. and so, if one kid saw a picture that none of the others had seen, he would be booked to tell that picture...All of the gang were good picture-tellers...'

ten commandments [n. pl.]. Fingernails (PWJ).

tent [n., <OF *atente*, attention] (Ulster). Heed, attention, as in **take tent** [vb. phr.]. Take notice. **1900** Thomas Given, *Poems from College and Country by Three Brothers*, 'A March Storm in Different Ways': 'The clouds in darkest ragements flung/Kept singin' as they went,/But whether Psalm or Hymn they sung/I didna then tak tent.'

tepeny/toppony/tappany [adj. & n., <'top'] (Ulster). [adj.]. Crested. [n.]. Crested fowl; timid, cowardly individual (MON).

terr [n., <?]. 'Ignorant, presumptuous individual' (PWJ). **1986** Padraic O'Farrell, *'Tell me, Sean O'Farrell'*: 'A likeable terr (provocative man) in spite of all, he was killed when a lean-to where he slept over near Millicent collapsed on him.'

terror see **holy terror, tarra**

tester [n., <*Teston*, silver coin of Henry VIII of Eng.]. Pre-decimal sixpence. See **hog**.

thacka/thackeen/thuckeen [n., <Ir. *toicín*, pert girl, hussy]. As thus. **1842** Michael & John Banim, *Father Connell*: '"Thackeen, thackeen, hearken to me," said a whispering voice almost above her.' **1944** Patrick Purcell, *A Keeper of Swans*: '"Surely to God you don't mean he's in earnest with that thuckeen of Andy Gorman's...?"'

that shook you! see **shook**

thaulach [n., <Ir. *tálach*, cramp, swelling in wrist]. 'Pain or cramp in the muscles due to heavy manual work' (OTF).

thauloge [n., <Ir. *táilleog*, small loft]. 'Boarded-off square enclosure at one side of the kitchen fireplace...where candle-sticks, brushes, wet boots, etc. are put' (PWJ).

thaveless [adj., cf. Sc. *thieveless/thowless*, listless, spiritless, lacking energy, etc. (CSD)] (Ulster). Incompetent.

theeveen [n., <Ir. *taobh*, side + dimin. *ín*]. Patch on side of boot/shoe (OTF).

thereaway [adv., <Sc. *thereawa'*, thereabouts, about that time] (Ulster). As thus.

thick [adj. & n.]. 1. [adj. passing into n., 1597]. Stupid, obtuse. **1965** Lee Dunne, *Goodbye to the Hill*: '"who are you going to meet if you work in the building line? A load of bogmen [q.v.] that don't know any better, and after a few years of it you'll be as thick as they are."' **1970s** TV cartoon commercial for Erin Thick Chicken Soup: 'One and one is three? You're the thickest chicken I've ever met!' **1991** Roddy Doyle, *The Van*: 'The dog was no thick. He could nearly talk...' Also **thicko** [n.] in same sense. **1997** Maeve Binchy, *Irish Times*, 11 Jan: 'What kind of thicko will make a nuisance call any more when he knows that the frightened recipient only has to dial three or four digits and the number of the nuisance caller will be revealed.' Also **thick as two short planks** and (Ulster) **thick as poundies** (q.v.) [adj. phr.] in same sense. 2. Close to, closely acquainted (PWJ). See **great**. 3. [adj.]. Angry. **1996** Dermot Healy, *The Bend for Home*: '"How was it different?" "That was then. This is now." "All right," I said. "Now you're thick." "No I'm not," I said.'

Thing, the see **the Tomb of the Unknown Gurrier**

think long [vb. phr.] (Ulster). Be homesick (SH).

thirteen/er [n., <difference in value — in pence — between Ir. & Brit. currencies pre-1826]. Ir. shilling. **1965** Colm Ó Lochlainn (ed.), *More Irish Street Ballads*, 'Billy O'Rourke': 'I gave the captain six thirteens,/To carry me over to Margate,/

But ere I got on half the road,/It blew at the devil's own hard rate.'

this weather see **weather, this**

thivish [n., <Ir. *taibhse*, ghost, spectre]. As thus.

thole [vb., <OE *tholian*, suffer, endure] (Ulster). Put up with (something). **1951** Sam Hanna Bell, *December Bride*: '"There's pain and evil in me now!" cried the girl, the tears springing to her eyes. "But I'll thole it — and it won't be on my knees!"' **1966** Patrick Boyle, *At Night All Cats are Grey*, 'Go Away, Old Man, Go Away': 'She would come round some time. He would just have to take her easy and thole a while longer.'

Thomond see **like Lord Thomond's cocks**

thon way [adj., <OE *thon*, that] (Ulster). Pregnant.

thoolermawn [n., cf. Ir. *tuathalán*, blunderer, tactless person]. Blundering fool. **1977** Flann O'Brien, *The Hair of the Dogma*: 'I warned and I double warned that thoolermawn of an ownshuck [q.v.] that he'd get nothing at the heel of the hunt [q.v.].' **1989** Hugh Leonard, *Out after Dark*: 'the thoolermawns who had drafted the bye-laws had omitted to insert a clause making it an offence for strollers in public places at night time to slow down to a standstill'.

thorneen [n., <Ir. *tairngín/tairnín*, small nail; thornback (Dinneen)]. Small fish caught in pools by children. **1995** Daithí Healy, *Cork Holly Bough*: 'Before the Corporation built their massive estates, we used to go out "The Rocks"...fishing for thorneens with our handkerchiefs and jampots.' Also **thornie**, **thornyback**, **tittleback**, **tittlebat** in same sense. **1953** Frank O'Connor, *My Oedipus Complex and Other Stories*, title story: '"I want to go down the Glen and fish for thornybacks with my new net..."' See also **red-belly**.

thountabock [n., <Ir. *teann tabac*, strong tobacco]. Good beating (PWJ).

thran see **thrawn**

thraneen/thrauneen/thrawneen [n., <Ir. *tráthnín*, slender grass stalk]. 1. As

thus. **1995** Aidan Higgins, *Donkey's Years*: 'I imagined that he would...blow all his foulness into me, his badness, as you would blow up a frog by sticking a sharp thrawneen through its skin.' 2. [cf. *Ní fiú tráithnín é*, 'it's not worth a thraneen' (Dinneen)]. Insignificant amount. **1943** George A. Little, *Malachi Horan Remembers*: 'She was given the best of everything, and was not above asking for what she thought was left out. She did not care a thraneen for anyone.' **1960** John O'Donoghue, *In Kerry Long Ago*: 'the hens didn't care a *thrauneen*, for, like myself, they came when they were hungry, without bothering whether it was "Tick, Tuck or Hurish [q.v.]" as long as they got the food!' **1989** John Healy, *Magill*, Oct: 'Here let me say there's not as much as a thraneen of difference on this matter between [Alan] Dukes and [Charlie] Haughey: it merely depends who is in and who is out of office.'

thrape/threep [vb., <OE *threapian*, Sc. *thrape/threep*, insist on, wrangle, browbeat] (Ulster). As thus.

thrapple see **thropple**

thrauneen see **thraneen**

thravally/trevally/travally [n., <Sc. *trevally/trevaillie*, disturbance, scolding, quarrelling, cf. Fr. *réveiller* (vb.), rouse, stir up] (Ulster). As thus; 'noisy gathering of people come together for some common purpose' (YDS); outburst of cursing/scolding. **1866** Patrick Kennedy, *Legendary Fictions of the Irish Celts*: 'An' there was such a *thravally* ruz in the kitchen about it at last, that the young king came to hear the rights of it.' **1983** W.F. Marshall, *Livin' in Drumlister*, 'Sarah Ann': 'Man, he let a big thravalley [*sic*], an he sent us both — ye know,/But Sarah busted cryin', for he seen we maned till [to] go.' **N.d.** Children's rhyme: 'But in yearly jubilation all Ulster people join/For a Dutchman bate a Scotchman at the Battle o' the Boyne./An we're towl to keep the mem'ry green or orange, strong and hot/Of that long-ago threvally [*sic*] when a Dutchman bate a Scot.'

thrawn/thran/trawn [p. part as adj., <Sc. *thraw* (vb.) <OE *thrawan* (vb.), throw] (Ulster). Cross-grained, stubborn, contrary. **1908** Lynn Doyle, *Ballygullion*: '"Hiven send him some dacent girl... before he meets the widow, for there's no tellin' what he'd do, he's that thrawn."' **1925** Richard Rowley, *County Down Songs*, 'Up in the Mountains': 'Thrawn folk are lovers,/Foolish lad an' lass,/But won't the heart grow kind again/As the days pass?'

thrawneen see **thraneen**

thraws [n. pl., cf. Sc. *thraw*, reverse of fortune; OE *trea*, misery, calamity] (Ulster). Extremity, misery. **1908** Lynn Doyle, *Ballygullion*: 'The wee [q.v.] man takes a good pull at it, an' all at once begins chokin' as if he was in the last thraws.'

three-na-haile/threena-halah see **tre na ceile**

threep see **thrape**

three prices, the [n. phr., <?]. Excessive amount. **1927** Peadar O'Donnell, *Islanders*: '"Arrah [q.v.], for heaven's sake, Mary, not a tay [tea] I'll have. They charge ye the three prices."'

Three Steeples, the [nickname]. Triple spires of St Finnbar's Cathedral, Cork city. **1987** Pat Daly, *Cork Holly Bough*: 'Here's down the lads from "the Three Steeples" — a reference to the most prominent landmark associated with French's Quay...'

thresh [vb.]. 1. [<'thrash'] (Ulster). As thus. 2. [<?] (Maynooth College). Walk on the outside of a group. See **chub**.

thrill [n.]. 1. Derog. term for woman. **1987** Vincent Caprani, *Vulgar Verse & Variations, Rowdy Rhymes & Rec-imitations*, 'Goldilocks and the Three Teddy Boys 1956': 'Now up round Summerhill there lived this grand [q.v.] ould "thrill"/(What might be termed a gamey sort of soul)/She was fond of winin', dinin', and on her back reclinin'...' 2. Euphoria. **1993** Frank Casey in Michael Verdon, *Shawlies* (q.v.), *Echo Boys* (q.v.), *the Marsh and the Lanes* (q.v.): *Old Cork Remembered*: 'They usually came in groups for a quick pint after work. Now and again what was called a "thrill" would come over one of them, and feeling a big man he'd buy a pint for all his friends.'

thrilled skinny [adj. phr.]. Very excited/enthusiastic, delighted. **1996** Liam Griffin, *Irish Times*, 15 July: 'especially George (O'Connor) and Billy (Byrne). They are the father figures within the [Wexford hurling] squad...Of course I'm thrilled skinny for the supporters...'

thrimmle [n. & vb.] (Ulster). Tremble. **1908** Lynn Doyle, *Ballygullion*: 'For his hands was in such a thrimmle wi' narvousness that he could hardly snap the breech.'

thrinnle [vb., <Sc. *trinle*, trundle] (Ulster). As thus. See **sprick**.

throat [n.]. as in **have a throat on one** [vb. phr.]. Be afflicted with a severe thirst. **1990** Roddy Doyle, *The Snapper* (q.v.): '"Go on." "No, I'm goin' up to bed." "I'd go up with yeh only I've a throat on me." Veronica smiled.'

throng [adv., <OE *gethrang* (n.), throng, crowd]. Crowded, occupied. **1906** E.Œ. Somerville & Martin Ross, *Some Irish Yesterdays*: '"Thim that was before us cursin' black and blue for the way ourselves was squeezin' thim. 'Faith [q.v.]! We are throng as three in a bed!' says Dan..."' **1938** Seumas MacManus, *The Rocky Road to Dublin*: 'Because Billy had had no help *footering* [*sic:* see **fother**.] with his farm, and wrestling with cattle, he had been "too throng" ever to go courting.' Hence **throng day** [n. phr.]. **1908** Lynn Doyle, *Ballygullion*: 'an' the market-day bein' a throng day for the polis in Ballygullion, 'twas ginerally Billy's throng day outside av it, delivering a wee [q.v.] keg here and there'.

thropple/thrapple [n., <Sc. *idem*, windpipe, <OE *throt-bolla*, gullet, windpipe] (Ulster). Throat. **1951** Sam Hanna Bell, *December Bride*: '"...Tammie Gilmore tried tae blow Hami's head off, and Hami got him by the thrapple"'. **1983** W.F. Marshall, *Livin' in Drumlister*, 'The Runaway': '"Ye unsignified ghost!" sez his mother,/An' with that jist before he cud wink/She ketched Sarah Ann be

the thrapple/An' whammeld [see **whammel** 2.] her right [see **right** 1.] in the sink.' Hence **open-throppled** [adj.] addicted to drink; **thropple-deep (in)** [adj. phr.] up to the neck (in).

through oneself [adj. phr.] (Ulster). Confused, mixed-up.

throughother [adj. & adv., <Ir. *tré n-a chéile/trí chéile*, mixed up, confused, see **tre na ceile**]. 1. [adj. & adv.]. As thus. **1909** Stephen Gwynn, *Holiday in Connemara*: 'He told me...about the awful hours he had endured, taking our ladies and gentlemen whose talk he only understood imperfectly, how he passed the day with his wits going *trí chéile* — through other as we say...' **1948** John O'Connor, *Come Day — Go Day*: '"Will we keep on these ould shirts too, da?" "No, you'll not keep on these ould shirts too, da! Man, but you're a through-other being..."' 2. [adj.]. Within same family or group, as in 'they're all married throughother' (Todd). 3. [adj.] (Ulster). Untidy, disorderly, unmethodical. **1990** Tom O'Kane, quoted in Walter Love, *The Times of our Lives*: 'The roads was let out to local people to keep them, in them days...But there were throughother people as well.'

through the medium see **medium** 2.

thuckeen see **thacka**

thulk [n., <Ir. *tolg* (n. & vb.), attack, thrust]. Butt/blow with the head (OTF).

thullabawn [n., poss. as *thoolermawn* (q.v.)]. Fool. **1977** Flann O'Brien, *The Hair of the Dogma*: 'continually presenting the Irish people as even worse cornerboys [q.v.] than they are, in plays written by thullabawns'.

thumb [vb., cf. *idem*, possess (a woman), C18–19 (DHS)]. Masturbate (of women). **1997** *Irish Times*, 9 May: 'The accused agreed he had told gardaí he had no interest in women but he was incorrectly recorded as adding "I'd always let them thumb themselves."'

thunder and lightning [n. phr., 'ex the effects' (DHS), C19]. Mixture of shrub and whiskey.

thunder-an'-ouns [expletive, cf. Ger. use of *Donner*, thunder, as in *Donner und Blitzen!* etc.; *ouns* — euphem. for '[Christ's] wounds']. Mildly sacrilegious expression. **C.1910** Anon., *Irish Wit and Humour*: "'Thunder an' ouns! but they've cotched [caught] it!...There's three [birds] wounded, anyhow, for they had hardly strength to fly over yon hedge...'" See also **tare-an'-ouns**.

thundergob/gub [n., <Ir. *gob*, mouth] (Ulster). Noisy and/or incessant talker.

thundering disgrace [cant phr.]. Derog. expression widely applied subsequent to original use. **1984** Bruce Arnold, *What Kind of Country*: 'The Minister for Defence, Paddy Donegan, opening a new cookhouse...in Mullingar on Monday, October 18 [1976], departed from his scripted speech to describe President Ó Dálaigh, with additional expletives, as "a thundering disgrace" for having referred the Emergency Powers Bill to the Supreme Court.'

thunder up the gulley [n. phr.] (Cork). Children's game involving stuffing a cast-iron pipe with paper and lighting it, producing a loud roaring sound (Beecher).

thurmus/thurrumus [vb., <Ir. *toirmisc*, prohibit, prevent, hinder] (Munster). 'Sulk from food' (PWJ), i.e. refuse food in petulant manner (of children).

Tibb's Eve [n. phr., <'St Tibb's Eve', evening of last day, Day of Judgment]. Day that will never come. **1866** Patrick Kennedy, *Legendary Fictions of the Irish Celts*: "'When will you marry me?" says the giant. "You're puttin' me off too long." "St Tibb's Eve," says she.' **1938** Seumas MacManus, *The Rocky Road to Dublin*: 'but the boy minded little the cold passage, or the time she took, even if it was to Tibb's Eve — because he had found lying in a window, a wonderful book'. **1944** Francis MacManus, *Pedlar's Pack*: "'Do you know you could keep running from this until Tibb's Eve without striking Christian country!'"

ticket, hard see **hard ticket**

tickieman/tickman [n.] (Ulster). Salesman offering credit. **1979** John

Morrow, *The Confessions of Proinsias O'Toole*: "'It's an ill wind, Francie; a far cry from the peaceful days when tickmen were wearing out my doorstep.'"

ticky [n., poss. <South African sl.]. Threepenny piece. **1995** Aidan Higgins, *Donkey's Years*: "'You won't believe this, Lil, but that bloody bitch has given me the wrong change again." He was a tanner short. Two tickies.'

tiddleyhoy [n., euphem., <?]. Private parts. Also **tiddlypush** in same sense. **1934** Samuel Beckett, *More Pricks than Kicks*: 'He wore a belt/Whenever he felt/A pain in his tiddlypush...'

tiddrer [n., poss. var. of *tay-drawer* (q.v.)]. Teapot.

tie on one [vb. phr.] (Ulster). Dress oneself. See **getonye**.

tierce [n., <cask and its contents 1531 (OED)]. As thus. **1982** Pádraig Ó Clára, *Cork Holly Bough*, 'The Cork Shawlies [q.v.]': 'They also got a "sup out of the tierce". They were shy about this and usually held a corner of the shawl in front of their faces while they downed the half-pint in one swig.'

tiff [n., <?]. Cheap liquor. **C.1687** Anon., *Bog Witticisms*: 'And we will shing [sing] curds and crame by Chreest, and buttar and eggs, bony-clabber [see **bonny-clabber**], and tiff, untel de coow shall have cauf...'

tighten [vb.]. 1. [cf. *tightener* (n.), large amount of liquor (DHS)]. Fortify with alcohol/food. **1841** William Carleton, *The Misfortunes of Barney Brannigan*: "'...I ever an' always had a distaste agin wather, unless whin there was something to tighten it; ha, ha!'" Hence **tightener** [n.] in same sense. **1948** John O'Connor, *Come Day — Go Day*: 'many's the time he had seen the two of them over in her house, drinking her aleplant, and sitting down to a tightener of potatoes and brown-gravy...' 2. (Ulster). Get s.o. into shape; hence **that'll tighten you!** 'That is just what you deserve' (CUD). Also **tightener** [n.]. Tough job, spell of hard work.

tilly [n., <Ir. *tuilleadh*, addition, increase]. 1. Small added measure, gen. of milk, given to customers; container for such a measure. **1922** James Joyce, *Ulysses*: 'He watched her pour into the measure and thence into the jug rich white milk, not hers...She poured again a measureful and a tilly.' **1991** Bob Quinn, *Smokey Hollow*: 'it [the milk] seemed mostly all right to Mrs Toner who always insisted on a "tilly" or an extra splash when he had filled the pint container'. **1995** Brendan Cantwell in Mary Ryan et al. (eds.), *No Shoes in Summer*: 'the milkman would again dip into his milk churn, take out a sizeable measure and top up Julia's four pints. This extra quantity of milk was known as a "tilly"...' 2. Attachment to digging spade. **1991** James Kennedy, *The People who Drank Water from the River*: 'Thump the spade went into the ridge, driven deep by my father's hobnail boot on the tilly.'

timbering [vb. n.] (Ulster). Beating.

Time in the Slime, the see **the Chime in the Slime**

timer [n.]. One who beats the rhythm for a set dance while lilting (see **lilt** 2.). **1990** Mick Matthews, quoted in Walter Love, *The Times of our Lives*: 'Often the set dances were accompanied by a lilter, known as the "timer", who kept his foot going all the time.'

tin [vb., <?] (Ulster). Scold, reprimand.

ting [vb., <Sc. *idem*, overeat] (Ulster). As thus, stuff oneself. Hence **tinged (up)** [p. part as adj.] in same sense.

tinges [n. pl., <?]. Goods remaining long on drapers' hands (PWJ).

tinker's fart [n. phr.]. Nugatory amount. **1969** Tom Mac Intyre, *The Charollais*: 'The Charollais...had never looked more mundane, sprawled there, chewing a head of the national vegetable, and, by all appearances, not giving a tinker's fart what happened.'

tinker's time, at [adv. phr.]. Very slowly.

tinned [p. part. as adj., cf. Brit. sl. 'tin', money, cash]. Wealthy. **1922** James Joyce, *Ulysses*: 'Provost's house. The reverend Dr Salmon: tinned salmon. Well tinned in there.'

tin-pandy [n., see **pandy** 2.]. Tin mug. **1938** Seumas MacManus, *The Rocky Road to Dublin*: 'they were very poor people without a bowl or a mug on their dresser — although there were a couple of plates there, and a few tin-pandies filled with milk'.

tint [n., <*tinct* (obsolete), tincture]. Indeterminate measure of alcoholic drink. **1954** George Fitzmaurice, *Dublin Magazine*, 'The Terrible Baisht', Oct/Dec: 'If Hollyhocks saw us taking our little tint it's a scandal he'd be making of it. He's a holy show [q.v.] for remarking on women drinking.' **1995** Éamon Kelly, *The Apprentice*: 'The men accepted a bowl of porter [q.v.] from a large bucket. There was a tint of wine for the ladies.'

Tintown [nickname, <corrugated iron construction]. Prison camp at the Curragh, Co. Kildare, used by the British during the War of Independence and subsequently by the Free State authorities in the Civil War. Served as internment camp for IRA members during WWII. **1973** Noël Conway, *The Bloods* (q.v.): 'some 80 Bloods had been attached to the Engineers to assist in building the internment camp, later to be known as Tintown'. **1994** T. Ryle Dwyer, *Guests of the State*: 'Over 500 suspected members [of the IRA] were rounded up and interned for the duration of the war at the Curragh in Hare Park — or Tintown...'

tip around [vb.]. Do odd jobs. **1991** James Kennedy, *The People who Drank Water from the River*: 'Tipping around for us happened in unsettled weather. A pike could be got here and there where the hay was light or a few grass cocks made... The bank of the river could be mowed between showers.'

tipcat [n.]. Children's game. **1986** Padraic O'Farrell, *'Tell me, Sean O'Farrell'*: 'Tipcat was played by paring a small piece of stick until it had two pointed ends. This was thrown on the ground, the Cat, and it was tipped by a longer stick and belted as far as possible.'

Tipperary fortune [n. phr., 'two townlands, stream's town, and ballinocack, said of Irish women without fortune' (Grose)]. Breasts, pudenda and anus.

Tipperary lawyer [n.]. Cudgel.

tissic/tisick [n., <'phthisic']. Cough. **1943** George A. Little, *Malachi Horan Remembers*: 'Whiskey cures the gout/The colic and the tissic./There's not the slightest doubt/It's the very best physic.' Hence **tizicky** [adj.]. Fastidious about food; self-conscious (Moylan).

titter of wit/sense [n. phr., poss. <'titre', measure of dilution]. Common sense. **1961** Dominic Behan, *Teems of Times and Happy Returns*: '"Well," said Granny, "will they ever get a titter of sense? Twelve an' six to see a crowd of eejits [q.v.] kick a ball away from them an' then run after it."'

tittle [vb.] (Ulster). Walk in mincing fashion (SH).

tittleback/tittlebat [n., <'stickleback'] (children). See **thorneen**.

tobar [n., cf. Romany *tober*, road]. Camping ground. **1996** Péigín Doyle, *Irish Times*, 30 Apr: '"The days of going to an area and just pitching the tent are over," says Jennifer [Johnson]. "Lots of the old Tobars (the traditional circus word for a camp ground) are gone."'

tober [vb. trans., cf. Sc. *toober*, beat, strike] (Ulster). Settle, calm down s.o. (SH).

togs [n. pl., cf. Brit. usage, clothes in gen.]. Swimming costume or trunks. **1992** Pauline Bracken, *Light of Other Days, A Dublin Childhood*: 'Catholics just didn't seem to achieve this style with their "bathing costumes" or "togs".' **1995** Patrick Boland, *Tales from a City Farmyard*: 'In the middle of the farmyard there was a huge round wooden water barrel where we sailed our home-made boats, and jumped into in our bathing togs on hot summer days.'

toisheen see **to-sheen**

toly [n., <Sc. *toalie*, 'small, round cake of any kind of bread' (CSD)] (Ulster). Baker's dough.

Tomb of the Unknown Gurrier (q.v.), **the** [nickname, play on 'Warrior', with ref. to monuments in Paris and elsewhere] (Dub.). Concrete trough with plastic 'flame' erected on O'Connell Bridge to mark first An Tóstal ('Ireland at Home' festival) 1953. **1991** Tony Gray, *Mr Smyllie, Sir*: 'the whole contrivance was so vulgar and nasty that a crowd of engineering students tore the plastic flame from its fixings after a few months and threw it into the Liffey. Myles [na gCopaleen] had already christened it the Tomb of the Unknown Gurrier.' Also referred to, somewhat less imaginatively, as **the Thing**. **1996** Adrian Sinclair, *Irish Times*, 31 Jan: 'Sir...I am prompted to ask what is happening in this country in the business(?) of celebrating the Millennium — other than the clock in the river? (One is reminded of the fate that befell the An Tóstal "thing" on O'Connell Bridge in 1951 [*sic*] in this respect.)'

Tom the Devil [nickname, <his torturing of victims during 1798 rising]. Thomas Homann, sergeant, North Cork Militia. **1996** Patrick Comerford, *Irish Times*, 2 Sept: 'the greatest abuse [by Wexford hurling teams] was reserved ...for Cork. And this was so because the memory of "Tom the Devil" was alive in Wexford a century after the rising.'

Tonehenge [nickname, <Theobald Wolfe *Tone* (1763–98), revolutionary leader + *Stonehenge*, Brit. prehistoric monument]. Memorial to Tone on St Stephen's Green, Dub., by Edward Delaney (1967). **1987** E.E. O'Donnell, *The Annals of Dublin*: 'On account of its monolithic design, it is promptly nicknamed "Tonehenge".' **1993** Vincent Caprani in *The Berlitz Travellers* [*sic*] *Guide to Ireland*: 'Tone's statue, against a background of giant granite plinths, was no sooner unveiled when some Dublin wag christened it "Tone-henge" (the nicknaming of the city's statues being something of a traditional pastime).'

tongue [vb.] (Ulster). Scold, abuse.

tootn-egg [n., <?]. 'A peculiar-shaped brass or white-metal button...I have seen it explained as *tooth-and-egg*; but I believe this to be a guess' (PWJ).

top of the morning [salutation]. Greeting, latterly Paddyism. **1879** Charles J. Kickham, *Knocknagow*: '"The top of the morning to you, Miss Grace," suggested that Father Hannigan affected the phraseology of the peasantry.'

topper [n.] (school). Pencil sharpener.

toppony see **tepeny**

torry/tarry [n.]. 1. [abbrev.] (Ulster). Dormitory. **1973** R.M. Arnold, *NCC Saga, The LMS in Northern Ireland*: 'This old [locomotive] driver appears to have had a curious preference for the men's "torry" to that of his own bed at home.' **1996/7** Dermot Mackie, *Five Foot Three* (Belfast): 'If the locomotive workshop gets the go-ahead in 1997 the carriage shop and the old NIACRO tarry will have to be moved...' 2. See **tory**.

tory/torry [n., <Ir. *tóraí*, bandit, outlaw; 'Advocate for absolute monarchy and church power; also an Irish vagabond, robber, or rapparee [q.v.]' (Grose)] (Ulster). Rascal, said of lively, likeable child (YDS).

tory-top [n., <?]. Seed cone of a fir tree as in **spinning like a tory-top** [adj. phr.]. Suffering from dizziness.

to-sheen/toisheen [n., <Ir. *toisín*, small measure (Dinneen)]. 1. (Cork). Conical paper container. **1993** Johnnie Barrett in Michael Verdon, *Shawlies* (q.v.), *Echo Boys* (q.v.), *the Marsh and the Lanes* (q.v.): *Old Cork Remembered*: 'The shopkeepers had *to-sheens*, a conical container that looked like an ice cream cone. It was made up of paper. You could put anything into that.' See also **poke** 2. 2. Small measure of drink. **1980** Julia O'Faolain in David Marcus (ed.), *Irish Short Stories*: 'The least she might have done was ask the man in for a drink. "A wee [q.v.] toisheen," thought Condon with Celtic graciousness "— and a chat..."'

tosser [n.]. 1. (game of pitch-and-toss, cf. Austral. two-up). Individual who tosses or spins the coins when all bets have been laid. **1985** Máirín Johnston, *Around the Banks of Pimlico*: 'Two ones, head and a harp [see **heads or harps**], meant that the tosser had to toss again. Two heads meant that the tosser had won so everyone placed bets again. Two harps meant that the tosser had lost his bet.' See also **boxman**, **feck** [n.] 2., **jack**, **jockey**, **rider**. 2. [n., poss. <pitch-and-toss, gen. in neg.]. Small low-value coin. **1966** Séamus Murphy, *Stone Mad*: '"...I'll give the company some sidelights on Maisie... For all your scraping, you never had a tosser left after her."' **1980** Emma Cooke, *Female Forms*: 'She came home, sleepy-eyed, to porridge...she had no money. Not a tosser.'

tossicate [vb., <'intoxicate' + 'toss'] (Ulster). Agitate, disturb, disquiet. Hence **tossication** [n.]. Disturbance, disruption.

toss the cups [vb. phr.] (Ulster). Tell fortunes by reading tea leaves. **1913** Alexander Irvine, *My Lady of the Chimney Corner*: '"Now that ye're in sich fine fettle, Anna," Jamie said, "jist toss th' cups for us!" She took her own cup, gave it a peculiar twist, and placed it mouth down on the saucer.'

Tottenham in his Boots [nickname]. Charles Tottenham (1685–1758), politician. **1952** Maurice Craig, *Dublin 1660–1860*: '[In 1731] A dispute had arisen between the Government and the patriotic party...When it came to a division the numbers were exactly equal. But at the crucial moment in came Colonel Tottenham...covered with mud and still wearing a huge pair of jack-boots. He had ridden all through the night, nearly sixty Irish miles, to cast his vote for the patriots. For many a long year after that "Tottenham in his Boots" was a standing toast in patriotic circles.'

totty-twigging [vb. phr., poss. <*totty*, 'a high-class whore' (DHS) + *twig* (q.v.)] (Rockwell College, Co. Tipperary). Girl-watching. **1993** Tim Pat Coogan, *Dev* (q.v.): *Long Fellow* (q.v.), *Long Shadow*: '...Jack and Mike Ryan invited him [de Valera] to share their home and pastimes — shooting, fishing, card playing and "totty-twigging", the local slang for girl watching'.

toty [adj., <Sc. *tottie*, snug, warm] (Ulster). As thus.

touch [n.] (Ulster). Moment, short space of time. Also **touchous** [adj.]. Quick to take offence.

tout [n.] (Ulster). Informer. **1997** Anthony McIntyre, *Sunday Tribune*: 'Marty [McGartland], always eager to call a spade a shovel, maintains the glorified fiction throughout the book that he was an agent rather than a tout.'

tove [vb., cf. Sc. *idem*, talk familiarly and at length] (Ulster). Boast. Hence **tovey/tovy** [adj., cf. Sc. *tovie*, babbling, garrulous in liquor]. Boastful, stuck-up.

traich/trake [n., <Sc. *traik*, long, tiring walk] (Ulster). 1. As thus. 'You gave me a great trake for nothing' (PWJ). **1951** Sam Hanna Bell, *December Bride*: '"When you are lifting the praties [q.v.] from the lough field it'll be a long traich up to Rathard.' 2. Diarrhoea and vomiting (SH); undefined illness or debility that's 'going round'. 3. Big ungainly person. Hence **traiky** [adj.]. '[S]low-moving and apparently unwell' (CUD).

trail the wing [vb. phr.] (Ulster). Seek sympathy through sulking.

traipse [vb., poss. <MDu. *trappen*, tread]. Walk till wearied under adverse conditions (OTF).

trake see **traich**

trallywagger/tallywagger [n., poss. <tail (of dog) <OE *taegl*, tail + intrusive *r*]. Loose thread hanging from hemline of clothing.

trance [n., <?]. Children's game also known as piggybeds (q.v.).

trasby [n., cf. Ir. *trasnaigh* (vb.), contradict, interrupt, heckle] (Ulster). Row, argument.

travally see **thravally**

travel [vb.] (Ulster). Go on foot, walk. Hence **traveller** [n.]. Tinker, itinerant. See **shooler**.

trawn see **thrawn**

tray [n.]. Light wheelless conveyance for bringing turf down from upland bogs. **1920** Daniel Corkery, *The Hounds of Banba*, 'On the Heights': 'They were the

marks of a "tray", as peasants of that place call it both in Irish and English...'

treacle billy [n., cf. Brit. sl. *treacle-man*, commercial traveller]. Lodging house. **N.d.** Anon., *The Twangman* (see **twang**): 'He loved a lovely maiden/As fair as any midge/And she kept a treacle billy depot/One side of the Carlisle Bridge.'

treble [vb., cf. *idem* (n.), kind of step dance, measure or music for this, Eng. dial. 1805–(OED)]. Dance. **1995** Phil O'Keeffe, *Down Cobbled Streets, A Liberties Childhood*: '"When can I have taps on my shoes? I could treble a hornpipe a lot better if I had.'" Hence **trebler** [n.].

tre na ceile/three-na-haile/threena-halah [adv. phr. & adj., <Ir. *trí/tré na chéile*, mixed up, confused]. 1. [adv. phr.]. As thus. **1833** Michael Banim, *The Ghost-Hunter and his Family*: '"This is the night that sends [spirits] over an' hither, threenah-halah, up an' down.'" **1938** Seumas MacManus, *The Rocky Road to Dublin*: 'the good Dean, always equal to an emergency, ordered the twenty-four matrimonial aspirants on their knees, higgledy-piggledy, *tre na ceile*, bestowed on them, in bulk, the marriage blessing, and then commanded, "Now, boys and girls, get up and sort yourselves."' 2. [adj.]. Dirty/sloppy (woman).

trevally see **thravally**

trice [n. & vb., <'tryst'] (Ulster). Arrangement, bargain; make agreement or bargain.

trick [n.] as in **do the trick** [vb. phr., <*idem*, get a woman with child, *c*.1830–]. Engage in sexual intercourse. **1978** Tom Murphy, *On the Inside*: 'MALACHY Sure. Jasus [q.v.], I'd be afraid of that one! Does she do the trick?'

trick-acting [pres. part.]. Messing about, showing off. **1952** Bryan MacMahon, *Children of the Rainbow*: 'Trick-acting the girls were, with little attention for the coursing field.' **1994** Mary Corbally in Kevin C. Kearns, *Dublin Tenement Life*: 'Just stand at the corner and be talking. You'd see them laughing and joking and trick-acting...cause they'd no money to go in and get a pint.' **1995** Proinsias de Rossa in Seán Power (ed.), *Those were the Days, Irish Childhood Memories*: 'the street was teeming with people of all ages...the youngsters playing "pickie" [see **piggybeds**] and "relievio" [q.v.], the youngfellas [q.v.] trick-acting with youngwans [q.v.]'. See also **act the maggot**, **cod**, **jack-act**, **jig-act**.

trickie/tricky [n., cf. *trick*, 'person who is alert and amusing: Austral. and NZ colloq., late C19–20' (DHS)]. As thus, but more gen. derog. See **caffler**, **waxy**.

tricking hall [n. phr.]. Communicating hallway in tenements. **1994** Stephen Mooney in Kevin C. Kearns, *Dublin Tenement Life*: 'if the police were chasing you this is where the tricking halls in the tenements come into being. It might be six houses of halls all with the rear yards back-to-back and you'd run in through number 1, we'll say, and you'd bee-line it all the way to number 6...'

tricky see **trickie**

trig [adj., <Sc. *idem*, smart, active, tidy, trim, spruce, <ON *tryggr*, true]. As thus. **1983** W.F. Marshall, *Livin' in Drumlister*, 'Our Son': 'Trig and dacent he went away,/His fortune for to win,/With a good warm suit an' a muffler gay,/And a wee [q.v.] round trunk of tin.' Hence **trigged out** [adj. phr.]. Dressed in one's best.

trimmings [n. pl.]. Additional prayers attached to the saying of the rosary. **1993** Margaret O'Donovan in Michael Verdon, *Shawlies* (q.v.), *Echo Boys* (q.v.), *the Marsh and the Lanes* (q.v.): *Old Cork Remembered*: 'They had this thing called "the trimmings", whereby you prayed to this saint and that saint and all the saints. Eventually you'd fall asleep saying the trimmings.' **1995** Éamon Kelly, *The Apprentice*: 'When we touched our breasts, calling on the Sacred Heart to have mercy on us, my mother launched into the trimmings...' See **patternavy**.

trinket [n., cf. Sc. *trinkie*, narrow channel between rocks (CSD)] (Ulster). Gutter.

trog [vb., <Sc. *trogg*, barter, exchange]. Bargain, swap. See **bit**.

troithín [n., <Ir. *idem*, 'a soleless stocking worn without shoes, a spat' (Dinneen)]. Old woman.

trokey [n., cf. Sc. *trolie*, slovenly girl or woman] (Ulster). As thus (SH).

trolleyed [p. part. as adj., <?]. Drunk. **1996** Paul Howard, *Sunday Tribune*, 12 May: '"Half a bottle of Pernod and a naggin [q.v.] of Paddy," said Fionnuala, her backside sticking out of the drinks cabinet..."Good," Róisín said. "Bring them over. You can't really do this properly unless you're trolleyed."'

trot [n.]. Restlessness. **1927** Peadar O'Donnell, *Islanders*: '"It's under her the trot is, always running to the mainland."'

trot a mouse [vb. phr.] as in **you could trot a mouse across/on it**. Said of strong tea etc. **1979** Paddy Tunney, *The Stone Fiddle*: 'She brewed him a mug of good strong tea, the kind you could trot a mouse on...' **1983** *John Pepper's Illustrated Encyclopaedia of Ulster Knowledge*: 'Two extremes in tea-making are covered by the statements, "I like tea you could trot a mouse across" and "It was that wake [weak] you could read the paper through it."'

troth and soul/sowl [exclam., <'truth']. Indeed, in truth. **1948** Patrick Kavanagh, *Tarry Flynn*: '"there's three pictures here and the likes of them is not in the parish...troth and sowl they'll not be shifted while I'm here"'.

trotting after, only see **only trotting after**

Troubles, the [prop. n., euphem.]. Applied to Ir./Brit., Pro-/Anti-Treaty, Republican/Loyalist war, civil war and violence, 1920s and 1969–. **1973** Noël Conway, *The Bloods* (q.v.): 'the destructive capabilities of armies had advanced quite a bit since the Bloods had first foregathered in Boyle around the time of "The Troubles"'. **1988** John Healy, *No One Shouted Stop!* (previously published as *The Death of an Irish Town*, 1968): 'Ireland became a two-sided country once again as "The Troubles", that happy Irish euphemism for civil war, grew more murderous by the year...'

trouncer [n., <'trounce'] (Ulster). Attractive girl, 'smasher'.

trousered [p. part. as adj., <?]. Drunk. **1996** Paul Howard, *Sunday Tribune*, 5 May: 'I had a dream once that I was out on the batter [q.v.] with Alex Higgins, Oliver Reed, Richard Harris, George Best and the late Richard Burton. Completely trousered we were...'

trout in the well, (have a) [adj. & n. phr.]. Be pregnant. **1948** Patrick Kavanagh, *Tarry Flynn*: '"Ah, a trout in the well!...And worse can happen to a woman. The mother was a hot piece [see **piece** 2.].'"

trucer/trucilier [analagous with 'volunteer'/'fusilier']. Soldier of fortune in 1920s period. **1971** Margery Forester, *Michael Collins* (see **the Big Fella**), *The Lost Leader*: 'many fair-weather soldiers now flocked to join local units; "Truciliers", as they became known'. **1979** C.S. Andrews, *Dublin Made Me*: 'These old hands were also inclined to belittle the recruits who had joined [the army] since the Truce. The word "Trucer" was coined even at this early stage and it was to have a devastating significance later on.'

true bill [catchphrase]. Assertion of veracity. **1946** Myles na gCopaleen, *Irish Writing No. 1*, 'Drink and Time in Dublin', May: '"I'll tell you a damn good one. You won't believe this but it's a true bill. This is one of the best you ever heard."'

true for you! [catchphrase, <Ir. *is fíor duit*, lit. *idem*, you are right]. As thus (with emphasis on 'for').

truff [n., cf. Sc. *idem* (vb.), pilfer, steal] (Ulster). Stolen goods.

trummicky [adj., <Ir. *tromach*, topsy-turvy]. As thus, back to front, upside down.

tryst [vb., <Sc. *idem*, engage to meet] (Ulster). As thus.

tube [n., cf. Brit. sl. *idem*, prison officer who seeks information from informers (Green)] (Ulster). Term of contempt. Hence **tubed** [p. part. as adj.]. Worn out, useless (YDS).

tucks [n. pl.]. Plenty, as in **tucks of time**. **1961** Tom Murphy, *A Whistle in the Dark*: 'IGGY (*calling Harry*) C-c-come on, sham [q.v.]! HARRY (*off, coming downstairs*) Tucks of time, tucks of time.'

tugger [n., <?] (Dub.). (Female) old-clothes dealer. **1982** Éamonn Mac Thomáis, *Janey Mack* (q.v.), *Me Shirt is Black*: 'The *Tuggers* was the nickname for the women who collected old clothes in big wicker boxcars and gave out cups and saucers.' **1985** Máirín Johnston, *Around the Banks of Pimlico*: 'There were always women who traditionally worked such as dealers, tuggers and paper-sellers...' **1994** Elizabeth 'Lil' Collins in Kevin C. Kearns, *Dublin Tenement Life*: 'Oh, he had about thirty or forty tuggers bringing him stuff, women and men tuggers. They used to call the people that went around with the basket cars to the doors "tuggers".'

tullock [n., cf. Ir. *tolg* (n. & vb.), attack, buffet, jolt] (Cork). Blow (Beecher).

tully eye [n. phr., cf. Sc. *tuilyie* (n. & vb.), quarrel, fight, in sense of one eye 'fighting' the other] (Ulster). Squint. Hence **tully-eyed** [adj.]. **1979** John Morrow, *The Confessions of Proinsias O'Toole*: 'And what better way to rattle even a moderately brave man than to make him the target of a tully-eyed sniper?'

tumble [vb. trans., <OE *tumbian*, cf. Fr *tomber*, fall]. Bring down a bird. **1879** Charles J. Kickham, *Knocknagow*: 'He took out his powder-horn to load again, feeling comfortably sure of "tumbling" — it is to *feathered* bipeds we apply the word — every bird he pointed his gun at...'

tumbling paddy [n. phr.]. Horse-drawn (wooden) rake for turning hay. **1988** Alice Taylor, *To School through the Fields*: 'A contraption called a tumbling paddy was used to collect the rows of hay into big heaps...It was like a giant comb with two handles at the back...'

tuppenny rush see **twopenny rush**

Turfburner, the [nickname]. Last steam locomotive built in Ire., powered by turf (peat). **1992** Tom Ferris, *Irish Railways in Colour*: 'The locomotive, officially numbered CC1, but widely known as the Turfburner, was completed at Inchicore in the summer of 1957...'

turf patrol [n. phr., <euphem. for hashish]. Hashish-smoking session. **1992** Shay Healy, *The Stunt*: '"Let's go on turf patrol." "I'm your man," Sean said. "Where's the pipe?"..."You get the pipe and I'll get the turf."'

turn [n. & vb.]. 1. [n.] (Leinster). Entertainment, crack (see **crack** 1.); one who supplies such, as in **a quare** (see **quare** 1.) **turn**. **1996** Ronan Kelly, RTÉ Radio, *Morning Edition*, 2 July: '"the turn" — that's the local word for the crack' (describing drive-in bingo at Ballymanny, Co. Wexford). 2. [vb.]. Change one's religion, as between Christian sects (gen. derog.). **1987** Lar Redmond, *Emerald Square*: '"Well, if she 'turns' with you, she'll lose her family an' if you 'turn' with her you'll lose yours."' **1996** Robert Saulters (Grand Master of the Orange Order), quoted *Irish Times*, 'This Week They Said', 14 Dec: 'It was disloyal of Mr [Tony] Blair to have married a Roman Catholic. I think if he can turn one way, he can turn in the management of the country.' See **jump**.

turnip-snagger [n., see **snig**]. Term of denigration, esp. as applied to rural dwellers. Given currency by Myles na gCopaleen in his *Irish Times* column, 1939–66. **1991** Tony Gray, *Mr Smyllie, Sir*: '"it is not *you* that we object to. It is the nocturnal activities of that gang of turnip-snaggers and potato pickers employed...to run the [newspaper censorship] service in your absence."' **1995** B.L., *Irish Times*, appreciation of Mary King, 20 July: 'But even her legendary sympathy failed her the stormy evening she saw the inebriated writer [Flann O'Brien] land on all fours... "Unhand me, you vulgar turnip-snaggers!" he ungraciously admonished his two rural rescuers.'

turrey [n., dimin. or affect., <Sc. *torr!* (exclam.), call to pigs, cf. Ir. *taraigí!*, come!] (Ulster). Pig (MON).

twang [vb. & n., poss. onomat.]. Fuck a woman; woman seen as sexual object. Hence **twangman** [n.]. Pimp. **N.d.** Anon., *The Twangman*: 'Come listen to my story,/'Tis about a nice young man./ When the militia wasn't wanting/He dealt in hawking twang.'

twarthy [adj.] (Ulster). Two or three (SH).

Twelfth, the [nickname, <date]. Orangeman's Day, 12 July, commemorating the Battle of the Boyne, 1690. Also **the Twalfth** in imitation of Ulster pronun.

Twelve Apostles, the [nickname]. Hit squad recruited by Michael Collins (see **the Big Fella**) during War of Independence, 1920. **1990** Tim Pat Coogan, *Michael Collins*: 'in January 1920 Collins added Tom Keogh, Mick O'Reilly and Vincent Byrne. The expanded Squad [q.v.] became known as the "Twelve Apostles".' **1996** Stephen Collins, *Sunday Tribune*, 18 Aug: 'He [Michael Collins] built up a group known as "the 12 apostles" who carried out a series of killings which horrified many in Ireland as well as in Britain. The most notorious was Bloody Sunday [see **Bloody Sunday** 1.]...'

twig [vb., <Eng. sl. *idem*, understand, confused with Ir. *tuig*, with same sense]. Look at; catch on, understand. **1754** Thomas Sheridan, *The Brave Irishman*: 'CAPTAIN O'BLUNDER ...Oh Cangrane, that's not it, but it was next door — Arrah [q.v.], go ask phat [what] sign my cousin Tradwell lives at next door to it. *Enter a mob, who stare and laugh at him*. 1. MOB. Twig his boots. 2. MOB. Smoke his sword, &c &c...' **1922** James Joyce, *Ulysses*: 'Give's a shake of the pepper, you there. Catch aholt. Caraway seed to carry away. Twig?'

Twirlies [nickname, <'Am I too early?'] (Dub.). Holders of free travel passes who attempt to board buses outside permitted hours.

twiss [n., <prop. name]. 'A jordan, or pot de chambre. A Mr Richard Twiss having in his "Travels" given a very

unfavourable description of the Irish character, the inhabitants of Dublin, by way of revenge, thought proper to christen this utensil by his name — suffice it to say that the baptismal rites were not wanting at the ceremony' (Grose).

twist [n.]. 1. [<stem *twi-*, division in two/uniting two in one]. Quarrel, disagreement. Also as in **bad/good twist** [n. phr.] bad/good spirits; **in twist** [n. phr.] in agreement, on good terms; **out of twist** [n. phr.] in a state of disharmony/disagreement. **1943** George A. Little, *Malachi Horan Remembers*: "'Dan MacLoughlan, of Ballinascorney, took a wife to his house. She was a neat-looking wench, so at first all went well with them. But in a short while they got out of twist.' 2. Turn, as in **my twist**. **1973** Noël Conway, *The Bloods* (q.v.): 'One mixed-up semi-soldier from civvie-land, doing his first twist of the two-on and four-off, successfully challenged the visiting Orderly Officer but when asked to repeat his orders replied: "To halt all aircraft approaching my post between dusk and dawn."' **1990** Roddy Doyle, *The Snapper* (q.v.): "'I don't believe I'm hearin' this," said Paddy. "Ah fuck off, Paddy," said Jimmy Sr. "Anyway, it's your twist."'

twist and twine [vb. phr.] (Ulster). Whine, be peevish.

twisted [p. part. as adj., cf. Brit. sl. *idem*, hanged (<twisting of rope) (DHS)]. Drunk.

two-double [adj.] (Ulster). Very stooped (YDS).

two ends of, the [adj. phr.]. Complete, utter.

two foot thicker than Butt Bridge [adj. phr., <bridge over River Liffey, Dub., built 1932 and newest crossing before 1970s/1980s.]. Very stupid. See **thick** 1.

twopenny/tuppenny rush [n. phr.]. Cheap children's admission to matinée cinema performances. **1961** Dominic Behan, *Teems of Times and Happy Returns*: 'It [the Drumcondra Grand] was better than the Sunday twopenny rush at the "Plaza" because they were mostly big people and you didn't get anyone shouting "Look out, mister!" when the crook came behind the chap [q.v.].' **1982** Éamonn Mac Thomáis, *Janey Mack* (q.v.), *Me Shirt is Black*: 'I used to buy my suits at five shillings a week in the Volta Picture Palace in Mary Street...and many's the time getting a fitting I could see [James] Joyce with the silver flashlamp trying to quieten down the Tuppenny Rush!' **1995** Billy French in Mary Ryan et al. (eds.), *No Shoes in Summer*: 'the Sundrive [cinema, Dub.], or the "bower", as we called it, had its "tuppenny rush" where, when the doors were opened, one was physically carried in on the backs of young screaming demons'. See also **penny rush**, **fourpenny rush**, **sixpenny rush**.

U

ubbabo! [interj., <Ir. *ababú*, heavens!].
Exclam. of wonder/surprise. **1866**
Patrick Kennedy, *Legendary Fictions of the
Irish Celts*: '"...I'll give you out the very
things that are wanted in the morning."
"Ubbabow!" says the smith, "are you in
earnest?"'

ucks/ux/ox [n., <?] (Cork). Apple
core, as in **have you on the ux!**, **I'm up
the ucks! first on your ucks!** [exclam.].
Used to claim or 'bags' the core of an
apple s.o. is eating. **1993** Maisie Flynn in
Michael Verdon, *Shawlies* (q.v.), *Echo
Boys* (q.v.), *The Marsh and the Lanes* (q.v.):
Old Cork Remembered: 'we'd waste
nothing. Even the core of an apple. If
you were eating an apple now, I'd say,
"First on your ox." That meant the core
was mine.

uhlan see **holyawn**

ullagon see **olagon**

ullilu! [exclam., cf. Ir. *uileacán*, alas].
Expression of sorrow. See **fuillaloo!**

umberstick [n., <Lat. *umbra*, shade]
(Ulster). Umbrella (Todd).

umper/umperin' [n., <Ir. *iompair*,
transport]. Lift. **1826** John Banim, *Tales
of the O'Hara Family*, 'Crohoore of the
Billhook': '"fen [when] 'tis so very asy to
get an umperin all de way home for
nothing"'.

unbeknownst [adj.]. Unnoticed/
unobserved. **1966** Patrick Boyle, *At
Night All Cats are Grey*, 'Oh Death
Where Is Thy Sting-aling-aling': '"Now,
father, you surely didn't think that the
clatter of the bottles went unbeknownst?"'

unbethink [vb.] (Ulster). Think
something not to be the case. 'They
unbethought them they'd ever see
Belfast' (CUD).

unca see **unco**

Uncle Arthur [nickname, cf. Sp. *tío*,
uncle, in same affect./respectful sense].
Arthur Guinness (1725–1803), revered
founder (1759) of the eponymous Dub.
brewery, and by extension his heirs and
successors. **1970** Nicky Furlong, *Harp*,
'Ty o' Letch, Nypore?' ('A small beer,
neighbour?' — Forth dial., south-east
Wexford): '...Wexford, a city which has
close and blissful relations of an
impeccable moral standard with our
Uncle Arthur to this day'. **1995** *Irish
Times*, 27 June: 'An unfamiliarity with the
proper Dublin-brewed pint from Uncle
Arthur is probably to blame for some of
their [Eng. visitors'] condition.' **1995** Paul
O'Kane, *Irish Times*, 1 Sept: 'Mr Meaney
[of Caffrey's Ale]...realises that with a
dominant position in the market,
Guinness will be a tough opponent. "You
can't challenge Uncle Arthur head-on,
you'll lose every time. So you've got to
go around him or over him."'

Uncle Paythur [n., <Peter Flynn,
character in Sean O'Casey, *The Plough
and the Stars* (1926): '*His face invariably
wears a look of animated anguish, mixed with
irritated defiance, as if everybody was at war
with him, and he with everybody*'].
Querulous complainer. **1989** John Healy,
Magill, Oct: 'not since Dr Conor Cruise
O'Brien [see **the Cruiser**] condemned
the Labour Party as "poltroons" and
"Uncle Paythers" [*sic*] and then joined
the party will we have seen so great a
switcheroo'.

Uncle Tim's Cabin [nickname, pun,
<Tim Healy (1855–1931), first Governor-
General of the Irish Free State, 1922].
Former Viceregal Lodge, Phoenix Park,
Dub., subsequently the residence of the
Presidents of Ireland. **1979** Peter
Somerville-Large, *Dublin*: 'At the
Viceregal Lodge Tim Healy...took over
from the Lord Lieutenant as Governor
General. [Oliver St John] Gogarty,
lamenting "the spacious days of Lord
Wimbourne", called the rechristened
Arus an Uachtaráin "Uncle Tim's
Cabin".' See also **the Park**.

unco/a [adj. & adv., <Sc. *unco*: (adj.)
strange, foreign, unknown; (adv.) very,
extremely, <OE *uncuth* (adj.), unknown]
(Ulster). As thus. Hence [iron.] **unco
guid** (good), describing a hypocrite
(Traynor).

298

Uncrowned King of Ireland, the [nickname]. Charles Stewart Parnell, statesman/politician (1846–91). **1977** S.F. Pettit, *This City of Cork, 1700–1900*: 'As the procession wound down Shandon Street and North Main Street the people would come out in crowds... to savour the excitement of seeing the "Uncrowned King of Ireland" go by.'

underboard [adj.] (Ulster). 'Describes a dead person, in a coffin, not yet buried' (SH).

under-foot salve [n. phr.] (Ulster). 'Filth as applied as a poultice in the case of horses, etc.' (Traynor).

Undertakers [nickname]. C18 aristocratic power-brokers who controlled borough politics with the connivance of the government. **1936** Edmund Curtis, *A History of Ireland*: 'Townshend was commissioned by George [III of Eng.] to end the corrupt rule of the "undertakers", and the corruption and jobbery of the Irish government...' **1966** J.C. Beckett, *The Making of Modern Ireland 1603–1923*: 'The influence of these parliamentary managers (nicknamed "undertakers" since they "undertook" to see parliamentary business through the house of commons) was partly personal... and partly derived from their control of patronage.'

unfaithful [adj.]. Unreliable, lacking in commitment. **1995** Shane Connaughton, *A Border Diary*: 'Talking about a blacksmith he said, "He got ojus [q.v.] unfaithful. He hated shoeing a horse in the end. He was afeered of them."'

unfordersome [adj., cf. Sc. *unfurthersome*, unpropitious, difficult] (Ulster). Unmanageable.

unfortunate girl [n. phr., euphem.]. Prostitute, 'so termed by the virtuous and compassionate of their own sex' (Grose). **1795** *Memoirs of Mrs Margaret Leeson, Written by Herself, Vol. II*: 'They [the pinkindindies (q.v.)] ran drunk through the streets...and, with great valour, broke open the habitations of unfortunate girls...and treated the unhappy sufferers with a barbarity and savageness, at which,

a gang of drunken coal-porters would have blushed.' **1994** Bridie Chambers in Kevin C. Kearns, *Dublin Tenement Life*: 'Now there was a red lamp lodging house over there, Lynch's, and they were all unfortunate girls. Mostly girls from the country who were after being in (domestic) service and went wrong...'

United Arthritis Club [nickname] (Dub.). United Arts Club. **1975** John Ryan, *Remembering How We Stood*: 'Amongst its considerable accomplishments was to have "blackballed" Patrick Kavanagh. It was generally known around town as the United Arthritis Club.'

Unknown Gurrier, the see **the Tomb of the Unknown Gurrier**

unshook see **oanshagh**

untholable [adj., see **thole**] (Ulster). Unbearable.

up a tree in Rosemount [adj. phr., <Derry/Londonderry (see **Stroke City**) city suburb] (Ulster). 'Missing but not missed' (TT).

upcast [vb., <Sc. *idem*, reproach, cast in the teeth] (Ulster). As thus.

up entirely [adv.]. Altogether. See **neather**.

up in Nelly's room behind the wallpaper see **Nelly's room**

up in one's hat [adj. phr.]. Overjoyed. **1927** Peadar O'Donnell, *Islanders*: '"I can't get over Statia Byrne winning that half-mile...Statia will be up in her hat."'

up in the lift [adj. phr., <OE *lyft* (n.), sky, heavens]. In high spirits.

upon my song! [exclam.]. Expressive of astonishment, surprise; used gen. to add emphasis. **1996** Dermot Healy, *The Bend for Home*: 'Upon my song,' said my mother, 'but you were the right [see **right** 1.] blackguard.'

up on one's end [adj. phr.] (Ulster). Ready for a fight. See **backspang**.

uppity [adj., cf. US usage, s.o. who does not 'know his place', as in 'uppity nigger']. Above oneself, putting on airs. '"Just because her son's a civil serpent she's that uppity ye'd think she was roilty'" (Pepper). **1995** Phil O'Keeffe, *Down Cobbled Streets, A Liberties Childhood*: 'Visiting the neighbours with the newly-christened child was an old Dublin custom which my mother could not ignore. If she did, she knew she would be charged with being uppity.' Hence **uppie** [n.] (Ulster). Self-important person.

upsetting [pres. part. as adj., <Sc. *idem*, proud, stuck-up] (Ulster). Self-important; putting on airs (q.v.). **1864** John Boyce, *Mary Lee or the Yank in Ireland*: 'Many's the little up settin' squireen [q.v.] and purse-proud budagh [see **boddagh**] threw themselves in her way.'

up the country people [n. phr.] (Ulster). 'Persons from any part of Ireland, except the north-east of Ulster' (Patterson).

up the steps [n. phr., <steps of Cork Courthouse] (Cork). In court. **1995** *Irish Times*, 14 July: 'Mr Sweeney said he then told Garda Kiernan that he wanted no trouble at all and that he would have him "up the steps", meaning the courthouse.'

up the wall/s [adj. phr., <US sl., 'crazy, wild' (DAS)]. Agitated, angry, emotional, extremely anxious. **1948** John O'Connor, *Come Day — Go Day*: '"...Shemie, you better go home with your Uncle Tommy. Your mother will be up the walls."' **1993** Seán O'Neill in Joe O'Reilly & Sixth Class, Convent School, Edenderry, *Over the Half Door*: 'I had a manager at the time, Mattie

Gilmore. He was up the wall over my coming back [from America]. I didn't live it down for about two years...'

up to [adj. phr.]. Capable of, as in **I wouldn't be up to it**. I wouldn't be able for it.

urchin see **horchin**.

Urination Once Again [nickname, <poem by Thomas Davis, 'A Nation Once Again', published 1846] (Dub.). College Green statue of Davis by Edward Delaney (1966) and its intermittently eructating fountain.

'usha [interj., contraction of *musha* (see **amossa**)]. **1914** James Joyce, *Dubliners*, 'Ivy Day in the Committee Room': '"Mean little tinker! 'Usha, how could he be anything else?"'

usquebagh/usquebaugh [n., <Ir. *uisce beatha*, water of life]. Whiskey. **1616** Ben Jonson, *The Irish Masque*: 'PAT Tey [they] drinke no bonny clabbe [see **bonny-clabber**], i'fayt, now./DON It is better ten [than] usquebagh to daunsh [dance] wit, Patrick.' **1718** John Durant Breval, *The Play is the Plot*: 'MAC ...Are you brewing the Usquebaugh you little Rogue, that makes you be such a long while?' **1806** Anon., *Ireland in 1804*: 'Of the celebrated liquor, known by the name of usquebaugh, there are two sorts, a green and a yellow; the former made with angelica, and the latter dyed with saffron. The only genuine usquebaugh is manufactured in Drogheda...'

ux see **ucks**

V

vag [n., abbrev. of 'vagrant', cf. Austral. sl. *idem*]. Vagabond, itinerant. **1938** Seumas MacManus, *The Rocky Road to Dublin*: '"I'm going to have something to say to them vags, that day, that will raise blisters on their conscience..."'

vardie [vb., cf. Brit. sl. *vardo*, see, look at, observe]. As thus. **1997** Joe O'Donnell, *Independent on Sunday* (London), 'Seraphim Preening', 9 Mar: 'He vardied the cell. Saw the paper figures for the first time. Picked one up. "What's all dis?"'

veggie [nickname, <'vegetable']. Physically/mentally disabled child, derog. **1996** Sheila Beckett, *Irish Times*, 9 Apr: 'Already it is common for children who avail of the services of a remedial teacher in ordinary schools to be known as the "veggies". You can just imagine what children with a serious disability would be called.'

Vincents, the [nickname]. Members of the Society of St Vincent de Paul, charitable organisation. **1995** Harry Browne, *Irish Times*, 14 Nov: 'a woman he met just after she'd been mugged in Ballybough [Dub.]; the poor woman was on her way to a funeral, he said, and would you believe she actually goes into the flats there for the Vincents?'

vis-a-vis [n., <position of passengers]. Horse-drawn conveyance. **1847** John Edward Walsh, *Ireland Sixty Years Ago*: 'This [the jingle (q.v.)] was finally succeeded by the jaunting-car, which still holds its place, and was, *Hibernice*, termed a *vis-a-vis*, because the company sit back to back.'

voteen [n., <'devotee', cf. Ir. *deabhóideach* (adj.), devout, devotional]. Said of one ostentatiously pious; crawthumper (q.v.).

W

waarsh see **warsh**

wad [vb.] (Ulster). Wager.

wadge [n., <'wedge'] (Ulster). Thick slice of bread (YDS).

waff [n., <Sc. *idem* (vb.), flutter, flap] (Ulster). Puff at a pipe; rumour, idea, inkling.

wag [n., cf. Sc. *idem*, 'contemptuous designation of a fellow' (CSD)] (Ulster). S.o. without firm opinions, yes-man (YDS).

wag/wag-at-the-wall [n., <Sc. *wag-at-the-wall*, wall-clock]. As thus. **1908** Lynn Doyle, *Ballygullion*: 'The ould wag-at-the-wall was goin' "tack-tack, tack-tack", very slow an' steady...' **1966** Patrick Boyle, *At Night All Cats are Grey*, title story: 'Wait a moment! What was this nagging memory of a wag-o'-the-wall [*sic*]? Ticking away remorselessly.'

wagon [n.]. Pejorative term for woman, esp. one with an unpleasant/bitchy streak. **1991** Roddy Doyle, *The Van*: '"I told yeh," said some oul' wagon. "A cod an' a small chips."' **1994** Ferdia Mac Anna, *The Ship Inspector*: 'Ground stewardesses are snooty-nosed wagons and all pilots think they're God's gift to women.' **1995** Brendan O'Carroll, *The Chisellers* (q.v.): '"Go on outa that [see **get away ou' that!**], yis [q.v.] pair of fuckin' drunken wagons," another voice called from the group...'

wain/wean [n. phr., <Sc. *wee ane*, small one, child] (Ulster). As thus. **1979** Jack McBride, *Traveller in the Glens* (of Antrim): 'To the "weans" their father is "our oul' fella [q.v.]" and their mother "the oul' lady".' **1990** Iris Brennan, quoted in Walter Love, *The Times of our Lives*: 'I used to tell me mother if it wasn't for the war I'd have had a tribe of weans.' **1996** Kitty Holland, *Irish Times*, 10 Aug: 'Natalie Clements holds a pretty little girl of about nine by her side. "I am afraid to bring my wains into the town [Derry] ...our bandsmen can't go into the shops

and still they are selling tricolours."' Also **weans dear!** [exclam.] (Ulster), emphasising what follows; **not a wean in the house washed** see **not a child in the house washed**.

wairsh see **warsh**

waited on [pres. part. as adj., <Sc. *wait on*, 'watch beside those near death' (CSD)] (Ulster). Dying, expected to die.

wakerife [adj., <Sc. *idem*, wakeful, sleepless] (Ulster). As thus.

walings [n. pl., <Sc. *wale* (vb.), choose, select] (Ulster). Leavings, refuse.

walk [vb.] (Ulster). Participate in politico-religious procession, esp. of members of Orange Order on 12 July (see **the Twelfth**). **1997** Renagh Holohan, *Irish Times*, 12 July: 'One [Oliver Crilly] cartoon features a Northerner at a street crossing in New York. He is looking at the pedestrian sign "Don't Walk" and comments "I came over here to get away from that."'

Walking Day/Sunday [nickname] (Dub.). Viewing day, Donnybrook Fair, C19. **1996** Con Costello, *Leinster Leader* (Naas, Co. Kildare), 6 June: 'Crowds of people flocked there [Donnybrook] on Walking Sunday (a custom also adopted at Punchestown where the first meeting was held in 1850) to see the booths...' Also Sunday before Rathfarnham Fair, 10 June. **1943** George A. Little, *Malachi Horan Remembers*: '"The Sunday previous to the fair was called 'Walking Sunday', as it was on that day that the people who lived at a distance commenced walking their stock."'

walking-woman [n., <Ir. *bean siúil*, strolling woman, beggarwoman (Dinneen)]. As thus. **1943** George A. Little, *Malachi Horan Remembers*: '"we had cures, and good ones too. It was the old walking-woman that would be bringing them (or the knowledge of them) around the country."'

wall-falling [adj., <?]. Exhausted. **1979** Michael O'Beirne, *Mister, A Dublin Childhood*: '"I got my separation, Michael — we're in town! Now we'll all have a nice cup of tea, I'm only wall-fallin'."'

wallop [n. & vb., <Sc. *idem* (vb.), dangle loosely; move fast, shaking the body or garments] (Ulster). 1. [n.]. Loose-limbed horse or individual. **1908** Lynn Doyle, *Ballygullion*: 'He was a thin wallop av a fellow wi' limbs that loose ye'd ha' thought he was hung on wires...' 2. [n. & vb.]. Fast movement 'with much fluttering of arms, legs, clothes' (Traynor); move thus.

wallstead [n.] (Ulster). Ruin with only the remains of the walls standing. **1978** John Hewitt, *The Rain Dance*, 'Garron Top': 'And no more mark of man than, long since passed,/a ruined *wallstead* with its sheltered trees...'

walter [vb., <Sc. *idem*, roll back and forth on the ground] (Ulster). As thus. Hence **waltered** [p. part. as adj.]. Mired in boggy ground (Patterson).

wan/one [n., *wan* <Hib. E pronun., slightly derog.]. Female; see **oul' wan**, **young wan**, **your man**.

wan and wan/one and one [n. phr., *wan and wan* <Dub. pronun.]. A portion of fish and chips. **1940s** Cathal Mac Garvey, *The Green Line and the Little Yellow Rod*: 'Jamesy's build was round about, such was anything but stout,/Tho' in height he topped his butty by a span./ Lingering ever near a pub, they would seldom dream of grub,/Save their nightly *table d'hote* of "wan and wan".' **1986** Vincent Caprani, *A View from the DART*: 'Giuseppe Cervi arrived in Dublin in the 1880s...Signora Cervi, with very little English at her command, helped behind the counter and generally processed the take-away orders by pointing at the selection of fried fish — "uno di questo, uno di quello" (one of this, one of that). This was soon shortened to "uno e uno", then "one and-a one", and in less than a decade Dubliners in general were ordering their portion of chips and one fish as "wan and wan".' **1995** Moya Ní Éilí, *Irish Times*, 7 Oct: 'A chara — "One and One" in Tahiti. The chips are down. The fish are fried to a crisp [by French nuclear testing].'

wanchancy [adj., <Sc. *idem*, unlucky, boding evil, <OE *wan*, lacking] (Ulster). As thus.

wangle [n., <'handful of straw a thatcher grasps in his left hand from time to time' (PWJ)]. Lanky, weak young fellow.

wangrace/wangrease/wangress [n., <Sc. *idem*, light oatmeal gruel for invalids] (Ulster). As thus.

want [n., <*wanting* (adj.), weak-minded, dial. 1877, <ON *vant*, deficiency]. Mental weakness, as in **a little/wee** (q.v.) **want**. **1987** Lar Redmond, *Emerald Square*: '...Lil whispered to me that he had had a nervous breakdown, there was a "little want" in him'. Also **wanting** [adj.]. Mentally deficient.

wap [n., cf. Eng. dial. *idem* (vb.), throw quickly or with violence]. Bundle of hay/straw. See **fother**.

wapper [n., <Sc. *idem*, something excellent of its kind] (Ulster). As thus (MON).

Ware [prop. n., cf. Ir. *earrach*, (season of) spring]. As thus. **1938** Seumas MacManus, *The Rocky Road to Dublin*: 'In Donegal, then, the sheep in Ware (Spring) were sent up to the mountains, and taken down to the lowlands again after the crops were harvested.'

war-hawk [n., cf. Sc. *idem* (exclam.), beware! take care!] (Ulster). Bailiff or summons-server (Patterson).

warlish see **worldish**

warm [adj.] (Ulster). Well-to-do.

warm s.o.'s ear [vb. phr.] (Ulster). Deliver slap to the side of the head. Gen. an unexecuted threat (YDS).

warrant [n.] as in **a good/great warrant** [n. phr.]. A good hand, a safe bet. **1906** E.Œ. Somerville & Martin Ross, *Some Irish Yesterdays*: 'She was described at the time of her marriage as "fine and fair and freckled, and a great warrant to fatten turkeys".' **1914** George Fitzmaurice, *The Pie-Dish*: 'JOHANNA ...I'd never make this cabin this day but for meeting with Marse Quilter of the sheebeen [see **shebeen**], that forced a bottle of porter [q.v.] on me, and a good warrant she always had to give it'. **1995** Éamon Kelly, *The Apprentice*: 'They talked about the age he had reached,

about his farm and the great warrant he
was to work.'

warsh/waarsh/wairsh/wersh/worsh
[adj., <Sc. *warsh/warsche*, tasteless]
(Ulster). As thus, insipid. Hence **warsh-
looking** [adj.] sickly pale; **warshness**
[n.] sickish feeling.

wasp [n., <colour of uniform] (Dub.).
Traffic warden.

was–was [n., <?]. Water (EW).

watch-pot [n.]. 'A person who sneaks
into houses about meal times hoping to
get a bit...' (PWJ).

water-brash [n., <Sc. *brash* (poss.
onomat.), slight attack of sickness]
(Ulster). Sick feeling caused by sour
stomach.

water-guns [n.] (Ulster). 'Sounds as of
gunshots, said to be heard around the
shores of Lough Neagh by persons sailing
on the lake' (Patterson). **1896** W.S.
Smith, *Nature* (London), Jan: 'For many
years after my settlement here from
England, I heard at intervals, when near
Lough Neagh, cannon-like sounds...'
1995 Brendan McWilliams, *Irish Times*,
23 Oct: 'the water guns are generally
recognised to be a local manifestation of
a relatively common phenomenon called
the "Baristal guns"...which first came to
general notice in the last century near the
town of Baristal on the Ganges Delta'.

water rat [nickname] (Ulster). Customs
official. **1995** Catherine McAleavey in
Mary Ryan et al. (eds.), *No Shoes in
Summer*. 'Every child paraded in fairy
dress [q.v.]. I wonder does Cathal
Gamble remember being a Water Rat
(Customsman) with white uniform cap
and real car.'

waumish [adj., <Sc. *idem*, uneasy,
squeamish] (Ulster). Said of an
uncomfortable sensation before illness.

wax a/the gaza see **gaza**

waxy [n., <use of wax-end for stitching]
(Dub.). Cobbler. **1982** Éamonn Mac
Thomáis, *Janey Mack* (q.v.), *Me Shirt is
Black*: '"Leather isn't the same now as it
was years ago or are the waxies using
cardboard to make boots and shoes?"'

Also as in **Waxies' Dargle** [nickname,
*c.*1890–]. Annual gathering at Irishtown
Green, near Ringsend. **N.d.** Pop. ballad:
'Says my oul' wan [q.v.] to your oul'
wan,/Will you come to the Waxie's
Dargle?/Says your oul' wan to my oul'
wan,/"Sure I haven't got a fardel [see
fardel 1.]."' **1922** James Joyce, *Ulysses*:
'"Two old Dublin women on the top of
Nelson's pillar..."That's new," Myles
Crawford said. "That's copy. Out for the
waxies' Dargle. Two old trickies [q.v.],
what?"' **1936** *Irish Times*, 25 Mar: 'At
that time [late C19] the Dargle in
Wicklow was, if possible, more popular
as a holiday resort...than it is at present,
and "Dargle" has passed into popular
speech as synonymous with "holiday
resort". In Dublin slang of the period a
cobbler was known as a "waxy". Not
being able to get as far away from town
on their days off as the better-class
Dubliners...they had to be content with a
run to Irishtown and Merrion sands.'
1981 Brendan Behan, *After the Wake*:
'"Why can't you write about something
natural? Like the time we all fell into the
water at the Waxie's Dargle."'

way [n.] (Ulster) as in **be in a great way
about s.o.** [adj. phr.] be in love with;
have a poor way on one [adj. phr.] be
in poor circumstances.

wean see **wain**

wear [n. & vb., <?]. French kiss. **1986**
Bob Geldof, *Is That It?*: 'You could get a
"wear", a kiss with open mouth; a "feel";
a "dry ride", a crunching of pubic bones,
or a "ride". Sex was a competitive event
in those days...' **1991** Ferdia Mac Anna,
The Last of the High Kings: 'On Saturday
nights, they went to the tennis club hops.
What'dye get? What'dye get? they asked
each other afterwards. Just a wear,
Frankie lied. No use, I got a feel, Nelson
boasted. Well, I got me hole, little Cyril
McLean bragged.'

Wearie/Weary [prop. n., <Sc. *idem*, the
Devil] (Ulster). As thus.

weather-bleat/blade [n.] (Ulster). Male
snipe.

weather-gaa/gall [n., <Sc. *idem*, lower
part of rainbow, <*gall*, sore, wound,

<OE *gealla*, sore on a horse] (Ulster). Broken rainbow; low, thick part of a rainbow seen in broken weather.

weather, this [adv. phr., cf. Ir. *aimsir*, time, weather]. The present time.

weaver's kiss [n. phr., <Sc. *weaver*, spider] (Ulster). Touch of a spider when hanging from its thread.

web-toed [adj.] (Ulster). Said of a good swimmer.

wedgie [n.]. Type of bullying assault. **1996** Kathryn Holmquist, *Irish Times*, 5 May: 'The *Wexford People* said that two Wexford "bullies" were sent home from the Gaeltacht for inflicting "wedgies". A "wedgie" is a type of punishment, often meted out by bullies in boys' schools, whereby perpetrators inflict pain by catching the victims' underwear and yanking it upwards.'

wee [adj. & n., <Sc. *idem*, small (adj.), <OE *weg* (n.), weight, small quantity] (Ulster). [adj.]. As thus. [n.] as in **in a wee**. In a short time.

wee buns/onions! [exclam.] (Ulster). No bother! See also **nickie cakes!**

weechie see **weeshy**

weechil/witchel [n., <'wee (q.v.) child'] (Ulster). Child, 'stout lump of a boy' (Traynor).

wee folk/people [nickname] (Ulster). Fairies. **1995** George Sheridan in Mary Ryan et al. (eds.), *No Shoes in Summer*: 'if Ketty had to leave the house to go out for turf, she would put the tongs on the side of the cradle in case the wee people would take or exchange the child'. See also **little people**.

Wee Free [nickname] (Ulster). Member of Free Presbyterian Church.

week see **wick** 1.

weekly insult [n. phr.] (Cork). Wages. **1939** James Joyce, *Finnegans Wake*: 'and a decent sort of the hadbeen variety who had just been touching the weekly insult'.

wee onions! see **wee buns!**

wee palaces [n. phr.] (Belfast). Workers' houses. **1996** Richard Roche, *Irish Times*, 8 Nov: 'Although the old Shankill,

with its "wee palaces"...its factories and family-run shops, has largely disappeared, the loyalties that distinguished its inhabitants still pertain.'

wee people see **wee folk**

weeshy/weechie [adj., cf. Sc. *weeshie*, delicate, watery] (Ulster). Tiny. **1907** Joseph Guinan, *The Soggarth Aroon* (q.v.): '"my little weechie gossoon [q.v.] that died"'.

Wee Six [nickname] (Ulster). The six counties of Northern Ireland.

wee still [n. phr.] (Ulster). Illicit whiskey, poteen (q.v.).

weethin/wee thing [n. (phr.)] (Ulster). Little. **1951** Sam Hanna Bell, *December Bride*: '"My good man," said Sarah, leaning out of the trap, "would ye kindly move a weethin till I read that board behind ye?"'

weet-weet! [exclam.]. Call to ducks. **1995** Shane Connaughton, *A Border Diary*: '"How do you talk to ducks?" she asks. "Chuck-chuck-chuck" [q.v.] for hens. "Beep-beep-beep" for turkeys. But I can't remember what you say to ducks."..."Weet-weet-weet-weet-weet-weet-weet. That's how you call ducks."'

wee wasp [n. phr.] (Ulster). Sharp-tongued person.

we had one (of them) but the wheel came off it [cant phr.]. Satiric response to long or pretentious statement. **1946** Donagh MacDonagh, *Happy as Larry*: '5TH TAILOR ...And tell us it wouldn't rate a line/In Boston or New York, Vienna, London, Cork, Would make no delicate cheek incarnadine. LARRY We had one of them but the wheel came off it!/You don't need words that length to tell me straight...'

weigh–de–te–bucketty [n.] (Ulster). See-saw.

well-got [adj.]. Affluent; enjoying an advantageous position/influence. **1965** Lee Dunne, *Goodbye to the Hill*: 'Not that there weren't a few "well-got" families in the flats. It was just that they seemed so out of place that it was difficult to think of them belonging there.'

well-mended [p. part. as adj.] (Ulster). Improved in health.

well-put-on [adj.] (Ulster). Well-dressed. See **put on**.

well up [adj.]. Tall. **1993** Joe Langan in Joe O'Reilly & Sixth Class, Convent School, Edenderry, *Over the Half Door*. 'There was one great character [see **character** 1.] in them days and he only a young lad...he was a huge big fellow and he still only going to school but he was horrible well up.'

well wear! [exclam.]. Congratulatory wish, esp. in relation to new suit of clothes etc. **1975** John Ryan, *Remembering How We Stood*: (quoting Denis Guiney, proprietor of Clery's department store, Dub.) '"whether 'twas blue mink or tom cat 'tis all the wan to me. Good luck to ye — and well wear."' **1995** Éamon Kelly, *The Apprentice*: '...I wore the suit going to mass, and the new cloth cap I got to go with it. Everyone I knew took notice of me with words of greeting like "Well wear!" or "You're a man now!"'

welly-coat see **wylie-coat**

Welsh parrot [nickname] (Ulster). Puffin.

welt [n. & vb., <?]. Blow, stroke; beat. Hence **welt the floor!** [imper. phr.]. Encouragement to dancers.

werra! werra!/wirra! wirra! [exclam., <Ir. *a Mhuire*, lit. O (Virgin) Mary!]. Mild oath. **1909** Canon Sheehan, *The Blindness of Dr Gray*: '"Tisn't I'm dishturbin' yere pace [peace], John Duggan...but thim that's brought shame into this house. Oh, wirra! wirra!" she cried...'

wersh see **warsh**

West Briton [nickname, gen. derog., esp. in contraction **West Brit.**]. Ir. man or woman professing, or assumed to profess, loyalty to the Republic's former occupiers, or apeing their manners. **1934** 'Colyn' (R.P. McDermott), *TCD, A College Miscellany*, 'An Appeal for National Unity (An Address to the Historical Society [by Eamon de Valera: see **Dev**])', 15 Nov: ''Tis with pleasure I confess that I rise now to address/This gathering of aliens and traitors,/And if what I say to you is unpleasant it is true;/Those who praise you are at best prevaricators./West Britons though you be,/Listen carefully to me...' **1945** *Irish Times*, 8 May: '...50 young men attacked the doors of the Wicklow Hotel to cries of "Give us the West Britons" and "Put out the traitors"'. **1995** Ronnie Drew, *Irish Times*, 4 May: 'It [Dún Laoghaire, Co. Dub.] was a very strange place, sort of colonial...There was a West Brit feel about the place.'

wet [n. & vb.]. 1. [n.]. (Alcoholic) drink. **1961** Dominic Behan, *Teems of Times and Happy Returns*: '"It's not every day a man gets the chance of buyin' a wet for such as yourself, Mr Kearney, sir. An' you after writin' such a bloody fine song ['The Soldier's Song'].''' **1966** Séamus Murphy, *Stone Mad*: 'the *Cheerful Maid* moved out from the quay an' the rest of us moved off for a wet to discuss the voyage'. **1993** Sam McAughtry, *Touch & Go*: '"Where you heading?" He tried to make the question casual..."I'm heading for a wet. Coming?"' 2. [vb.] as in **wet the tea** [vb. phr.]. Make tea. **1913** Alexander Irvine, *My Lady of the Chimney Corner*: '"When we were alone, alone with Withero, Mary "wet" a pot of tea, and warmed up a few farrels [see **fardel** 2.] of fadge [q.v.]..."' **1980** Harriet O'Carroll in Máire Mhac an tSaoi (ed.), *A Dream Recurring*, 'The Day of the Christening': '"Don't you feel it's close, Rosy?" "I didn't notice it," said Rosaleen. "Will you have some tea if I wet it?"'

wet and dry [adj. phr., 'has its origin in constant work of the kind not interrupted by the notoriously fickle Irish weather' (Wall)]. Constant, stable, steady. **1922** James Joyce, *Ulysses*: 'How much did I spend? O, a few shillings. For a plump of pressmen. Humour wet and dry.'

wet-my-foot [nickname, onomat. of call] (Ulster). Quail.

wet week [n. phr.]. Short period of time. **1997** Deirdre O'Kane, *Irish Times*, 21 May: 'Sure, women have only been out of the kitchen a wet week if you think about it.' Also as in **he wasn't a wet week in the job**; **he had a face on him like a wet weekend**.

wezel [n., <?]. Artificial vagina used for sexual gratification. **1979** C.S. Andrews, *Dublin Made Me*: 'There must have been a very long underground tradition of sex erudition where boys of fourteen could talk of soixante neuf and of wezels (merkins) and of cunnilingus and fellatio.'

whack [n.]. 1. [cf. Sc. *idem*, large portion of food or drink]. Food, sustenance (PWJ); good allowance of drink. 2. Pickpocket (DHS). Also **not the whack** [adj. phr.]. Not up to the mark.

Whacker [nickname, <*paddy whack* (q.v.)]. Generic nickname for anyone with first name 'Paddy'.

whale [vb., <US dial. *idem*, hit, thrash, trounce, poss. <OE *wael* (n.), slaughter (DAS); or <OE *wale* (n.), weal]. Beat. **1966** Patrick Boyle, *At Night All Cats are Grey*, 'The Betrayers': '"I never whaled a horse yet. And I've put a brave [q.v.] few through my hands."' Also **whale away** [vb. phr., derog.]. Apply oneself with indifferent results.

whammel/whemmle etc. [n. & vb., <Sc. *idem* <ME *whelm*, turn (a hollow vessel) upside down] (Ulster). 1. [n.]. Blow or thump. 2. [vb.]. Upset, turn upside down. **1983** W.F. Marshall, *Livin' in Drumlister*, 'Secrets': 'An' round the world I'll brag/How I whammeld the moon in Bernish/An' fetched her home in a bag.'

whang [n. & vb.]. 1. [n., <Sc. *idem*, thong, leather boot, lace, <OE *thwang*, thong]. Leather bootlace, long strip of leather; long, lanky person. **1913** Alexander Irvine, *My Lady of the Chimney Corner*: 'His boots looked as if a blacksmith had made them, and for whangs...he used strong wire.' **1938** Seumas MacManus, *The Rocky Road to Dublin*: 'little Master MacGrath of the mountains who, wet day or dry day.. showed himself never in public without an umbrella bound midway by a black-leather whang...' **1977** Myles na gCopaleen, *The Hair of the Dogma*: 'He

[Aodh de Blacam] invented a fabulous world of whangs...boxty [q.v.], poundies [q.v.], crubeens [q.v.], sheelamagoorlas, fairy mounds, crassogues, patterns, the Mountains of Mourne...' 2. [n.]. Large piece or quantity of anything. 3. [n.] (Ulster). Muscle. **1951** Sam Hanna Bell, *December Bride*: 'A week after the attack Hamilton could raise his arm stiffly from his side. "Gie the whangs o' your shoulder time to supple up," counselled Petie...' 4. [n., confused with 'tang'] (Ulster). Rancid taste in milk/butter. 5. [vb., onomat.] as in **whang away** [vb. phr.]. '[H]ide, or secrete some object (tool, paper, scarce sorts of type [individual metal characters], etc.) for safe-keeping' (WS).

whassah [n. & vb., <Ir. *fásach* (n.), wilderness, deserted place]. Food given to cows in some unusual location; feed cows thus, 'such as along a lane or road' (PWJ).

whatever you're having yourself [catchphrase, cf. Ir. *agus mar sin de*, and so forth]. *Idem*; et cetera, in dismissive sense. **1988** John Waters, *Magill*, 'Every Good Boy Deserves Favour', Sept: 'His [Seán Doherty's], they alleged, were the politics of the stroke [see **stroke** 3.], the fixer, the parish pump, of graft, hookery [see **hook**], crookery and whatever you're having yourself.' **1995** Willie O'Kane, *Irish Times*, 18 Mar: 'Beckett is certainly a great writer; he is also a unique writer, but we must also grant this quality to Rushdie, Rider Haggard, Barbara Cartland and, as Myles [na gCopaleen] used to say, "whatever you're having yourself".' **1995** J.P. Duggan, *Irish Times*, 29 Nov: 'She [Britain's Princess Diana] wants to be Queen of Hearts and Marilyn Monroe rolled into one. Queen of Tarts more like, the palace mutters. There will always be an England: Rule Britannia: whatever you are having yourself.'

whaup [n., <Sc. *idem*, curlew] (Ulster). As thus.

whee! [exclam.]. Call for horse to stop.

wheeble [vb., <*whibble*, lie (Donegal, EDD), poss. <'quibble'] (Ulster). Argue oneself out of a tricky situation.

wheek [n. & vb., onomat.] (Ulster). [n.]. Nimbletwist. [vb.]. Snatch, steal, twist nimbly. **1959** Padraic Gregory, *Collected Ulster Ballads*, 'The Winding Roads o' Down': 'I work my days in city streets/ Where hustlin' men wheek by...'

wheeker [adj. & n., see **wheek**] (Ulster). (Something) exceptionally good. **1993** Sam McAughtry, *Touch & Go*: '"John has a hell of a peeper [eye]," Dicky Walters said. "A real wheeker."' **1996** *Irish Times*, advertisement for Northern Ireland Tourist Board, 30 May: 'why not consider taking a Belfast City Break. Apart from picking up the odd useful phrase for your next cocktail party, you'll have a "wheeker" of a time.'

wheeler [n.]. Horse used in pulling hearse. **1995** Patrick Boland, *Tales from a City Farmyard*: 'The two horses harnessed side by side on the shaft nearest the hearse were known as "wheelers", the ones that really did the pulling...'

wheen [n., <Sc. *idem* (n.), several, <OE *hwaene* (adj. & n.), (a) few] (Ulster). Small or large number. **1889** W.G. Lyttle, *The Royal Visit to Ireland* (letter from 'Robin' — pseudonym of W.G.L. — to Prince Albert Victor of Eng., subsequently Duke of Clarence): 'The dear [q.v.] na, if ye wud cum doon to Bangor for a day but the fowk wud like it. Ye cud hae a birl [q.v.] on the Switchback Railway, and then ye cud see the Masonic Hall...an' a wheen ither places.' **1925** Louise McKay, *Mourne Folk*: '"You needn't smile," said Mary Anne, "I've given this cure to a good wheen of people..."' **1945** Sir Basil Brooke, speech at Stormont banquet for Field-Marshals Sir Alan Brooke and Sir Harold Alexander, 17 Oct: 'If Britain wants any more Field-Marshals they can have a wheen of them from us.'

wheep/whoop [n., vb. & exclam., cf. Sc. *wheep* (n. & vb.), sharp, shrill cry] (Ulster). [n. & vb.]. As thus. [exclam.]. Expressive of surprise. **1908** Lynn Doyle, *Ballygullion*: '"What would ye think av Brian O'Connor's daughter?" sez he, wi' a narvous kind av a titther. "Whoop," sez I to meself, "the widow's done."' **1926** Richard Rowley, *Apollo in Mourne*, 'On

Slieve-na-Man': 'Up on the mountainside/There's only the whin–chats cheepin'/ Or high in the hedge at dusk/A rogue of a blackbird wheepin'...' Hence **wheeper** [n.]. Fife. **1844** Robert Huddleston, *A Collection of Poems and Songs on Rural Subjects*, 'The Lammas Fair (Belfast)': 'The red coat boys now on parade,/They shake the grun they're gaun on:/An' clout the sheepskin yet extends,/An' wheeper's louder blawin'...'

wheeple [vb., <Sc. *idem*, utter sharp, short cries; whistle, attempt to whistle] (Ulster). Whistle (badly).

wheesht! see **whisht!**

wheet!/wheetie! [exclam. & n., <Sc. *wheety*, call to poultry] (Ulster). Call to ducks; the duck itself. **1951** Sam Hanna Bell, *December Bride*: 'As he approached the farm he heard the boy's voice call "wheet-wheet! wheet-wheet!" and saw the bobbing line of ducks come at his bidding...'

wheezle [vb., <Sc. *idem*, breathe with difficulty, <ON *hvaesa*, hiss, wheeze] (Ulster). As thus.

whemmle see **whammel**

where Aughrim was lost [n. phr., <battle of Aughrim, 12 July 1691, a Williamite victory]. Where the trouble began/disaster occurred. **1962** Brendan Behan, *Brendan Behan's Island*, 'The Confirmation Suit': 'The waistcoat was all right, and anyway the coat would cover it. But the coat itself, that was where Aughrim was lost.'

whid/whud [n., <Brit. sl. *whid*, word, Sc. *idem*, lie, fib, poss. <OE *cwide*, speech] (Ulster). Hint, sign, rumour.

whiffle [vb., cf. 'waffle'; Sc. *whiffle*, play the fife or flute] (Ulster). Give an evasive answer (MON).

whigmaleeries [n. pl., <Sc. *idem*, odd fancies, wild ideas] (Ulster). As thus (MON).

whillalew/loo! see **fuillaloo!**

whip [n. pl. & vb.] (Ulster). 1. [n. pl.]. Plenty. **1952** Bryan MacMahon, *Children of the Rainbow*: '"Her breedin' right an' left," I said, "for four generations back.

The whips of brains her cousins had will be mentioned."' 2. [vb.]. Move quickly.

whipster [n.]. 1. [cf. Sc. *whippy*, term of contempt applied to a young girl]. 'A bold forward romping impudent girl' (PWJ). **1920** Seumas O'Kelly, *The Leprechaun of Kilmeen*: '"Sure, the decent man," says he, "is as innocent as a child unborn, but it's that whipster Maura Lally that's on for the ruination of him!"' 2. (Munster). 'A girl inclined to *whip* or steal things' (PWJ).

whisht!/whist!/wheesht! [exclam. & n., <Ir. *tost* (n.), silence, with initial aspiration, cf. *bí i do thost*, be silent, shut up]. Silence! **1908** Lynn Doyle, *Ballygullion*: '"Wheesht, Pat," sez he, risin' on his elbow and spakin' in a whisper. "I'll get it back yet."' **C.1910** Anon., *Irish Wit and Humour*: '"This isn't where I ordered you to stop," said I. "Whist! your honour, whist!" ejaculated Paddy; "I'm only desaving [deceiving] the baste..."' Also **hold one's whisht** [vb. phr.]. Be silent. **1986** Gene Kerrigan, *Magill*, Aug: 'There was a petulant whine in P.J. Mara's voice. "But you *can't* just tell Charlie [Haughey] to hold his whisht. *Nobody* tells CJH to hold his whisht."' **1995** Phil O'Keeffe, *Down Cobbled Streets, A Liberties Childhood*: '"Mary, they've brought the puddings." "Hould your whisht, can't ye, and let the children down."'

whisper! [exclam., <Ir. *cogar!*, idem, 'a word with you!' (Dinneen)]. Listen! **1914** George Fitzmaurice, *The Pie-Dish*: 'JACK   Ah, 'tisn't a coolness we'll be having, Eugene, over a thing of nothing. Whisper — what turned me in again was this: the cows were tied up in the stall by me...' **1929** Daniel Corkery, *The Stormy Hills*, 'The Emptied Sack': '"Whisper," he said, "did you ever hear this?" and he hissed out an Irish saying...'

whist! see **whisht!**

whistler [n.]. 1. [<?] (Leinster). Newcomer, 'blow-in' (q.v.). **1992** Michael O'Toole, *More Kicks than Pence*: 'There seemed to be more than the usual small-town resentment of outsiders (in Naas outsiders were termed "whistlers")...' 2. [onomat.]. Broken-winded horse.

Whit [abbrev.]. Public holiday falling on first Monday in June, replacing that formerly coincident with the Monday after Whitsun.

Whiteboys [nickname]. Secret agrarian society, first active 1761. **1936** Edmund Curtis, *A History of Ireland*: 'In these troubles both sides formed themselves into what were in fact "peasant trade unions", the "White-boys" being the Catholic, and the Ulster presbyterians calling themselves "Steel-boys" [q.v.] and "Oak-boys" [q.v.].' **1973** Maureen Wall in T. Desmond Williams (ed.), *Secret Societies in Ireland*, 'The Whiteboys': 'At first they were called "Levellers" [q.v.], but soon grievances with regard to rent and tithes were added...and they took to wearing white shirts. They then became known as Buachaillí Bána or Whiteboys...' **1983** Steve McDonagh, *Cork Holly Bough*: 'At the time of the land agitation many of the Whiteboys and other groups dressed in straw as disguise.'

Whitefeet [nickname]. Secret agrarian society, C19. **1943** George A. Little, *Malachi Horan Remembers*: '"It was at the head of this path that my father was near put to the loss of his life by the Whitefeet...Some of the Whitefeet were angry with him either for standing apart, or perhaps they were like many another, just land-grabbers itching to have him out of the way."' **1973** Joseph Lee in T. Desmond Williams (ed.), *Secret Societies in Ireland*, 'The Ribbonmen' (q.v.): 'The Whitefeet asked in Leix [Laois] and Offaly in 1831, only two years after Catholic emancipation, "What good did emancipation do us? Were we better clothed or fed...?"'

white-headed boy [n. phr., <'the very fair hair of babies and young children' (DHS); <Celtic preference for fair hair (Traynor)]. Favourite, one who can do no wrong. **1800** Maria Edgeworth, *Castle Rackrent*: '"As for me, he was ever my white-headed boy — often's the time when I would call at his father's...he would slip down to me in the kitchen..."' **1906** 'Centre', *Age* (Melbourne): 'Mallee Johnston, the white-headed boy who strides across the sward in 3½ steps, added

still more shine and polish to his already brilliant career.' **1916** Lennox Robinson, *The Whiteheaded Boy*: 'You'd have to pity her. Denis was always her white-headed boy, and this is a blow to her.' Also (Ulster) **whitehead**.

White Sergeant [prop. n., cf. Grose: 'A man fetched from the tavern or ale house by his wife, is said to be arrested by the white serjeant'] (Ulster). Mythical figure invoked to scare children into doing as adults wish.

whitteret/whittrick [n., <Sc. *idem*, weasel] (Ulster). Stoat (there are no weasels in Ire., but the name is often misapplied to the stoat); weaselly, bad-tempered person (YDS).

who-began-it [n.]. 'If you were going to put manners on someone [q.v.], you would say "I'll give him who-began-it"' (EW).

wholesome [adj.] (Ulster). Healthy, vigorous.

whoop see **wheep**

whoor's get see **hoor's get**

whoor's melt see **hoor's melt**

whore's get see **hoor's get**

whore's ghost [n. phr.]. Pejorative term for intractable/obnoxious object. **1973** Noël Conway, *The Bloods* (q.v.): '"Now the properly laid out [commando] course is a whore's ghost. I've seen the one at Gormanston...Everything is done at the double and they wear fatigues all the time, even the officers."'

whore's melt see **hoor's melt**

whottle [vb., onomat.]. **1979** Paddy Tunney, *The Stone Fiddle:* 'she leant out and emptied her glass into a cavity between the flags where a flock of ducks were whottling.'

whud see **whid**

whuddin' [pres. part., <Sc. *whud* (vb.), frisk] (Ulster). 'Applied to a hare when it is running about as if to amuse itself' (Patterson).

whush! see **hush!**

whyfor? [interrog., intens.]. Why? **1942** Eric Cross, *The Tailor and Ansty*: '"Whyfor should I get tidied?" she asked with surprise.'

wick [n. & adj.] 1. [n., <ON *vik* as in *munnvik*, corner of the mouth]. As thus. Also **week**. 2. [adj., <ME *wike/wyk*, wicked] (Ulster). Useless (SH).

wicked [adj.] (Ulster). Powerful, energetic.

wife-swapping sodomites [n. phr., derog.]. Media supporters of 'Yes' vote in the 1996 divorce referendum; hence gen. term of abuse. **1996** Eddie Holt, *Irish Times*, 6 July: 'It's got to be the soundbite of the year. "Go way, ye wife-swappin' sodomites," hissed No Divorce campaigner, Una Bean Mhic Mhathúna ...Una Bean's rebuke to reporters was a revealingly hostile end to a campaign which had opened with a little prayer.' **1996** Brenda Power, *Sunday Tribune*, 6 Oct: 'I expect to be reduced to far less coherently quotable insults than "You're only a shower of wife-swapping sodomites" when you all vote in approval of the daftest notion ever to escape from a cabinet discussion.'

wig [n. & vb.]. 1. [n.]. Second-sod turf, under top layer (Moylan). 2. [vb., <*idem*, scold or censure, sl. & colloq. 1829 (OED), cf. 'wigging']. As thus; pull s.o.'s hair (Moylan).

wigger [n.]. Derog. term for female.

wigs on the green [n. phr., <C18 practice of removing wigs before duelling]. Trouble, altercation. **1979** John Morrow, *The Confessions of Proinsias O'Toole*: 'His little eyes glittered evilly. "Wigs on the green, Francie! We'll have them Prods [q.v.] swimmin' for the Mull of Kintyre in a week!"' **1987** Lar Redmond, *Emerald Square*: '"There'll be wigs on the green," he said, "skin and hair flying...You are all," he added chattily, "being punished for copying your exercises..."' **1995** Eanna Brophy, *Sunday Tribune*, 2 July: '[Terry] *Wogan's Ireland*. Well, sure, here it is. The ould sod [q.v.] again. That's what some call me anyway. But there'll be wigs on the green if ever I catch them.'

wild [adv.] (Ulster). Very (cold, hungry, warm, etc.). 'That bull's wild tame' (Todd).

Wild Flowers of Tullahogue [nickname, derog.]. Jurymen newly qualified for service under the 1871 Juries Act. **1932** Edward Marjoribanks, *The Life of Lord Carson*: 'About that time an enterprising manufacturer of perfume had brought out a scent which he called "The Wild Flowers of Tullahogue". When [Lord] O'Hagan carried his Act, which lowered the qualification for jurymen, and admitted to the jury-box a class of peasants largely illiterate and quite unfitted for the discharge of judicial duties, his new juries were immediately called "The Wild Flowers of Tullahogue".'

Wild Geese [nickname]. Soldiers and scions of leading families who left after the broken Treaty of Limerick (3 Oct 1691) for the European mainland, where many served in continental military forces. **1903** George Moore, *The Untilled Field*: '"Do you remember, Ellen, the night you told me that after the siege of Limerick 'the wild geese' went to fight the stranger abroad when they could not fight him at home any longer."' **1914** W.B. Yeats, *Responsibilities*, 'September 1913': 'Was it for this the wild geese spread/The grey wing upon every tide'. **1938** Seán O'Faoláin, *King of the Beggars*: 'The flying Irish, down the Shannon or down the Lee with Sarsfield, looked up at the skies, and took the name, The Wild Geese. It was the end of a period. It was all but the end of a race.'

wiley-coat see **wylie-coat**

willick [n.] (Ulster). Whelk.

willie-hawkie [nickname] (Ulster). Little grebe (*Tachybaptus ruficollis*). Also known as **drink-a-penny** (Patterson).

Willie Week [nickname, <multi-instrumentalist (1918–75) who encouraged young people to play Ir. traditional music]. Willie Clancy Summer School. **1996** Theresa Judge, *Irish Times*, 8 July: 'More than 10,000 people are expected this week in the west Clare town of Miltown Malbay for "Willie Week"... Now in its 24th year, it is well established

as Ireland's biggest summer school in traditional music and dance.'

win [vb.] (Ulster). Defeat (in race etc.).

windy stool [n.] (Ulster). Window sill. **1983** *John Pepper's Illustrated Encyclopaedia of Ulster Knowledge*: '"A fella fell aff a windy stool" is as commonly used an example of dialect speech as "a fella felaff a larry [lorry]".'

wing [n.] (Dub.). Pre-decimal penny. **1922** James Joyce, *Ulysses*: 'Up to you, matey. Out with the oof. Two bar [see **bar** 1.] and a wing.' **1991** Bob Quinn, *Smokey Hollow*: 'he was trusted to bring the go-kart home on his own. He met an older child who offered him a "wing" for it...He handed over the family's entire transport system and took the penny home proudly to present to his shocked parents.' **1995** Aidan Higgins, *Donkey's Years*: 'the Shuffler already surrounded by caddies calling out to be hired. The going rate in those days was half a crown a round with tips optional, a wing.' See also **make**.

winkers [n. pl.]. (Horse) blinkers. **1952** Bryan MacMahon, *Children of the Rainbow*: 'maybe a sprig of red-gold beech leaves in the brass-studded winkers to confound the late flies'. **1993** Jimmy Hamill in Joe O'Reilly & Sixth Class, Convent School, Edenderry, *Over the Half Door*: '...I had the pony tied to a pole a little bit away from the hall. I had to put the winkers around his neck because he was able to throw it off.' **1995** Patrick Boland, *Tales from a City Farmyard*: 'When I was about seven...I was trusted to take the horses to the forge, usually leading them by a rein to the winkers.'

winter Friday [n. phr.] (Ulster). Cold, wretched-looking individual.

wipe [n.]. 1. Small quantity. **1968** John Healy, *The Death of an Irish Town*: 'one of them [landlords], Lord Dillon, owned a wipe of land in East Mayo. At that point where it wedged itself between Roscommon and Sligo it was nothing but bog.' 2. [poss. <'swipe']. Blow. **1916** Daniel Corkery, *A Munster Twilight*, 'The Return': 'She was one of those who, though they might give a man a "wipe" across the mouth, never get on their dignity...'

wirrasthrue [adj., <Ir. *a Mhuire is trua*, O Mary it is a pity/sorrow]. Sorrowful. **1944** James Joyce, *Stephen Hero*: "'Doesn't he look a wirrasthrue Jaysus [q.v.]?" said Stephen pointing to the Tsar's photograph and using the Dublin version of the name as an effective common noun.'

wirra! wirra! see **werra! werra!**

wisha [exclam., <Ir. *más ea*, if so, even so]. 'A sort of assertive particle used at the opening of a sentence' (PWJ); latterly Paddyism. *C*.**1910** Anon., *Irish Wit and Humour.* "'Duck! roast ducks! and this a fast day of the holy Church!" "Wisha! I never thought of that...'"

wish for see **great wish for**

wit [n.] (Ulster). Sense. Hence **witless** [adj.]. Lacking in sense. See also **titter of wit**.

witchel see **weechil**

wobble [n. & vb., <action of shaving brush] (Ulster). Soap lather for shaving; lather the face before shaving. Hence **wobbling brush** [n. phr.]. Shaving brush.

wobbler [n., <'wobble' + endearment suffix; cf. Brit. sl. *wobbly*] as in **throw a wobbler** [vb. phr.]. Give vent to annoyance/anger. **1990** Roddy Doyle, *The Snapper.* "'I don't know," he said. "I should give ou' [see **give off**], I suppose. An' throw a wobbler or somethin'.'"

wocky [n., cf. Sc. *wacht*, guard, watch] (Ulster). Watchman (YDS).

wojious/wojus [adj., <'woeful' + 'atrocious']. As thus. **1987** Vincent Caprani, *Vulgar Verse & Variations, Rowdy Rhymes & Rec-im-itations*, 'How Jem the Dancer Fought and Died for Ireland': "'and then suddenly we turned into Smithfield and happened on the most wojious ructions [q.v.].'" **1995** Joe O'Connor, *Sunday Tribune*, 30 July: 'I was out on the razz [q.v.] with the mott [q.v.] and her auld wan [see **oul' wan**] last night, I have a hangover on me that would fell an ox, I feel only wojus...'

woodener [n., <'wood' + endearment suffix]. Cheap wooden seat at cinema. **1970** Christy Brown, *Down All the Days*: 'They had come early...to sit enthralled on the seemingly unending rows and terraces of "woodeners", slapping, clapping, whistling and applauding...' **1985** Máirín Johnston, *Around the Banks of Pimlico*: 'The queue for the Tivo [Tivoli] was an exercise in self-inflicted torture. We would all line up for the woodeners outside the lane in Francis Street.'

woodner [n., <abbrev. of 'wooden-head' + endearment suffix]. Fool, dolt. **1997** Maeve Binchy, *Irish Times*, 7 June: "'It's only woodners that don't care how their country is going to be run. And they're eejits [q.v.] as well if they don't watch it [the election coverage].'"

wool [vb.] as in **wool the head off s.o.** (Dub.). Pull the hair violently. **1987** Lar Redmond, *Emerald Square*: "'What did you expect him to do?" said my mother unexpectedly. "Stand there and let you wool the head off him?'"

woolly-bear [nickname]. Hairy caterpillar.

worsh see **warsh**

worda [n., <?] (Ulster). Father. 'I went for a wee [q.v.] walk with worda' (Pepper).

worldish/warlish [adj., <'world'] (Ulster). Old person still in possession of his/her wits.

worm-month [nickname, <incidence of many insect transformations] (Ulster). Fortnight before and after Lammas (July/ Aug).

wrap [n. & vb., <Sc. *idem*, knock, cf. 'rap']. As thus. Hence **wrap and run** [adv. phr.]. In great haste: 'I gathered every penny I could wrap and run' (PWJ).

wrap up [n. phr.]. Parcel of scraps. **1965** Lee Dunne, *Goodbye to the Hill*: 'And Jimmy the butcher was a decent skin [q.v.]. He always gave me a wrap up when I had finished, which meant we had a good stew at home on a Sunday...'

wreath/reth [n., <Sc. *idem*, snowdrift, <OE *wraeth* (vb.), twist, curl] (Ulster). As thus.

wren, the [n.] as in **go in/with the wren** [vb. phr.]. Take part in activities of the Wren Boys on St Stephen's Day (26 Dec), involving carrying a holly bush from house to house to the accompaniment of a song commemorating the wren's traditional betrayal of Christ. **1993** Joe Carthy in Joe O'Reilly & Sixth Class, Convent School, Edenderry, *Over the Half Door*: 'I went with the Wren in my young days and got very little out of it bar, maybe, a belt of a dishcloth!' **1995** Éamon Kelly, *The Apprentice*: 'On St Stephen's day we were never allowed out in the wren.' See **droleen**.

wrens, the [nickname]. Prostitutes servicing the Curragh milit. establishment, Co. Kildare, C19. **1996** Con Costello, *A Most Delightful Station*: 'The banishment of "the wrens"...by the resident magistrate was also mentioned by Michael Cahill, land agent to Lord Clifden. They were a nuisance to farmers, he said, as every ditch was crowded with them...they lived all the year round in the furze.'

wrench/rench/rensh [n. & vb., cf. Fr. *rincer* (vb.), rinse; OE *wrencan* (vb.), wrench; poss. confusion?] (Ulster). Hasty wash; rinse (MON).

wrought [vb., invar. p. tense, <Sc. *wrocht*, worked, laboured, struggled] (Ulster). As thus; 'You wrought hard and sore for them childer [q.v.]...' (Todd).

wullach [adj., <Ir. *uallach*, skittish, excitable]. As thus.

wylie/welly/wiley-coat [n., cf. Sc. *wylie*, 'kind of flannel used for skirts and petticoats' (CSD); otherwise obsc.]. Short báinín or other jacket.

wynde/wynd [n.]. 1. [cf. 'windrow', hay ready to be gathered into cocks]. Cock of hay. **1988** Alice Taylor, *To School through the Fields*: 'This was then used as the base for cocks of hay, or wyndes as they were called.' 2. [<Sc. *win/wind/wynd* (n.), turn to the left (of horses); termination] as in **from end to wynde** [adv. phr.]. From one end to the other.

Y

Y as in **up to the Y** [adv. phr.]. Up to the hilt. See **bread–earner**.

ya boy ya/ye! see **yeh–boy–yeh!**

yahoo [n., <Jonathan Swift, *Gulliver's Travels* (1726), derog.]. Individual of low intellectual and moral standard. **1923** Sean O'Casey, *The Plough and the Stars*: "'It 'ud be a nice derogatory thing on me conscience an' me dyin', to look back in rememberin' shame of talkin' to a word-weavin' little ignorant yahoo of a red flag socialist.'" **1961** Tom Murphy, *A Whistle in the Dark*: 'MICHAEL It's no use, Harry. The odds are too big this time. Seven to four now. Seven Mulryans. Not just seven ordinary yahoos just over.' **1982** Éamonn Mac Thomáis, *Janey Mack* (q.v.), *Me Shirt is Black*: 'Dean Swift was a terrible man for handing out nicknames. To him, nearly everyone was a yahoo or a mope [q.v.].'

yalderin [n., <OE *geolu* (adj.), yellow] (Ulster). S.o. of sallow complexion (YDS).

yalla buck [n. phr.] (Munster). Type of home-baked bread. **1995** Éamon Kelly, *The Apprentice*: 'My mother's soda cake was made from white flour but now and then she added Indian meal to make mixed bread. Locally this was called "yalla buck"...'

yammer [vb., <Sc. *idem*, complain, fret, <OE *geomerian*, mourn, complain] (Ulster). Cry, complain. Hence **yammerer** [n.]. Fractious child.

yap/yawp/yerp [n. & vb., <Sc. *idem*, nag, whine (onomat.)] (Ulster). [n.]. One who complains constantly; stab of pain. [vb.]. Nag, scold; cry peevishly, complain; throb with pain.

yappy [adj., <Sc. *idem*, hungry-looking, thin] (Ulster). As thus.

yard [n.] (Ulster). Toilet: 'it's hard gettin used to the yard bein upstairs' (Pepper). See also **get up the yard!**

Yard, the [nickname] (astronomy) (Ulster). Orion's Belt (Traynor).

yarkin/yerkin [n., <Sc. *yerking*, side seam of a shoe] (Ulster). Stiffening in a slipper (Todd); seam from top to toe of a man's leather boot (SH).

yarrib [n., <Sc. *yerb*, herb] (Ulster). As thus. **1938** Seumas MacManus, *The Rocky Road to Dublin*: 'No district was there without at least one woman wise in yarribs...'

yawp see **yap**

yeh–boy–yeh!/ya boy ya! etc. [exclam.]. Gen. expressive of admiration. **1995** Shane Connaughton, *A Border Diary*: "'The best man to dig a grave in the whole of Cavan is oul Hewitt out of Crubany. He's over eighty-five yah boya.'" **1995** Joe O'Connor, *Sunday Tribune*, 17 Sept: 'Their [bride and groom's] departure should be accompanied by merry cries of "gwan, yeh boy yeh"...it is at this point that the bride's mother should break down in tears... muttering to the priest, "yeh know, father, I never liked dat shower of miserly gombeen [q.v.] counter-jumpers" — meaning the groom's relations.' **1996** Donal Ó Celleachair, *Irish Times*, 15 June: 'Sir — Once again I throw my cap in the air, hug those nearest me and shout "ya boy ye Trevor". What eminent sense the man makes.' See also **hupyaboya!** Also **yeh-girl-yeh**. See **get up the yard!**

yell [adj., <Sc. *yeld*, ceasing to give milk] (Ulster). Dry (of cow).

yella- see **yellow-**

Yellow-bellies [nickname, <colour of football/hurling jersey]. Wexfordmen, esp. in GAA context. **1866** Patrick Kennedy, *Legendary Fictions of the Irish Celts*: 'Queen Elizabeth [I of Eng.] once witnessed a hurling match, the conquering party being Wexfordians, distinguished by yellow silk kerchiefs tied round their bodies. "Oh," cried her majesty, rapping out an oath, "what brave boys these *yellow bellies* are!"' **1989** John Maguire in Michel Sailhan (ed.), *Irlande*, 'Hurling Passion': 'A Cork, on raille sans pitié les "dégonflés" (yellowbellies) de Wexford, et les couleurs des uns désignent les ennemis des autres.' ('In Cork, they

jeer mercilessly the Yellowbellies of Wexford, and the colours of one designate the enemies of the other.'] **1996** RTÉ Radio commercial for *Examiner* newspaper, 13 July: 'Is this the year of the Yellow-bellies in Leinster or are Offaly on their way to another hurling final?'

yellow-hammer [n.]. Charity boy in yellow breeches, C19–20 (DHS). See **crawthumper**.

yellow kelters [n. phr., see **kelters**]. Gold coins, thus untold riches. 'That fellow has the yellow kelters and plenty — he is rich' (PO'F).

yellow man [n. phr., <colour] (Ulster). Sweetmeat associated with Ballycastle, Co. Antrim. **1923** Louis J. Walsh, *Glensman* (Cushendall, Co. Antrim), 'The Lammas Fair in Ballycastle', Jan: 'the old horses that once trotted proudly down the Ballymena Road on the Monday morning...have been replaced by ugly motor-lorries, and the "yellow man", the details of whose making a friend who once saw the process told me were too painful to relate, has been forced off the stalls by some ultra-hygienic imported toffee'. **1996** Michael Bateman, *Independent on Sunday* (London), 17 Mar: 'Y is for yellowman, a candy so curious it has never caught on far from its origins in Ballycastle, Co. Antrim, where it is made just once a year for Lammas Fair in August...It's a brittle toffee made with golden syrup, brown sugar, butter, vinegar and bicarbonate of soda. I'm sorry to say that my children thought it was the end.'

yellowpack [adj., <packaging of cheap 'own-brand' goods marketed by the Quinnsworth supermarket chain, 1980s]. Derog. term for low-paid employment of young people in a number of fields, replacing senior personnel; anything perceived to be inferior/cheaper. **1995** Renagh Holohan, *Irish Times*, 7 Oct: 'There has been much guffawing in Special Branch circles at the proposals by the Government cost-cutters that Garda ministerial drivers and minders be replaced by "yellow pack" chauffeurs and security people from the private sector.'

1996 Tim O'Brien, RTÉ TV, *The Week in Politics*, 30 Mar: 'Basically, [the Budget is] an attempt to create a yellowpack economy in the country...' **1996** Frank McDonald, *Irish Times*: 'The group [Bray Beachwatch] is supported by a local Labour councillor, Dr Tim Collins...He has described the current plan as "a yellow-pack scheme" which would be "very, very ugly".'

yellow yalderin (q.v.)**/yeldrick/yite/ yorn**, etc. [n.] (Ulster). Yellowhammer (*Emberiza citrinella*). **1947** Rosamund Praeger, *Old-Fashioned Verses and Sketches*, 'Hilltown': 'On each spray/By the roadway/Sits a yella-yite./An' the bees bum [buzz]/An' the clegs [q.v.] come/ An' bite.' Also **yellow yeldrick** as term of contempt.

Yeo [nickname, abbrev.]. Yeomanry corps under officers commissioned by Brit. Crown, established 1796. **1978** John Hewitt, *The Rain Dance*, 'The True Smith of Tieveragh': 'There is a ballad rooted in the Glens/about a rebel smith the Yeos pursued'.

yerkin see **yarkin**

yer man see **your man**

yerp see **yap**

yerra/dhera etc. [interj., <Ir. *dhera*, expressing disbelief, indifference, etc.]. As thus. **1713** *A Dialogue between Teigue and Dermot*: 'TEIGUE   Yerrou but how came dat about?/De Taughts of't makes my Tears burst out...' **1914** James Joyce, *Dubliners*, 'Ivy Day in the Committee Room': '"That'll be all right, Mr H," he said, "Yerra, sure the little hop-o'-my-thumb has forgotten all about it.' **1982** Edmund Lenihan, *Long Ago by Shannon Side*: '"Dhera, Father," sez I, "they were talking below, bedad [q.v.]."'

yer wan see **wan**, **your man**

yewk [vb., <Mid. High Ger. *jucken*, itch] (Ulster). As thus.

yinger [n., <?] (Ulster). Phlegm (SH).

yirree [n., <Ir. *a d'iarraidh*, trying to] (Ulster). Attempt, as in **make a yirree to** [vb. phr.] (Traynor).

yis/yiz see **youse**

yoke [n., placeholder, poss. <thatcher's tool, used either to carry a burden of straw or to hold it in position during thatching]. Unspecified object, as Fr. *machin*. **1916** James Joyce, *A Portrait of the Artist* (q.v.) *as a Young Man*: '"there was such a noise after the match that I missed the train home and I couldn't get any kind of a yoke to give me a lift"'. **1985** Máirín Johnston, *Around the Banks of Pimlico*: 'one day everyone was issued with a card to go up to Guinness's Dining Rooms to be fitted for gas masks. This was great fun for us and we came away with a cardboard box and a quare-looking yoke each...' **1995** Sean Jack O'Connell, *Irish Times*, 26 May: 'Sir — Cad é sort of a yoke an Milk Rás? An bhfuil sé like a milk race or like a Rás Bainne? Or bhfuil sé just pidgin Irish or Gaeilge pidgin?' Also **yokibus** [n., intens., affect.] in same sense. **1991** Ferdia Mac Anna, *The Last of the High Kings*: 'He liked to bounce the kids on his knee...Maggie was his blonde yokibus, Frankie was his little anarchist.'

yokkin [n., <'yoking' of horses] (Ulster). Spell of work.

yollick/yollick up [vb., <?] (Cork). Vomit.

yolp [vb., <?]. Bolt one's food (Moylan).

yorkie [n.] (Ulster). Common leech (*Hirudo medicinalis*).

yortlin [n., <Sc. *youdlin*, youth, stripling] (Ulster). Small, chirpy person (YDS). See **yowtlin**.

young fella [n.]. Young man.; son. See **young wan**.

young wan/one [n. phr.]. Young girl; daughter. **1965** Lee Dunne, *Goodbye to the Hill*: 'There was a right [see **right** 1.] load of young ones living in the flats, but I didn't like any of them very much.' **1982** Éamonn Mac Thomáis, *Janey Mack* (q.v.), *Me Shirt is Black*: 'Sometimes we'd get up enough courage to shout across the canal's green waters, "Youngwans here's youngfellas [q.v.]," and sometimes they shouted back, "Come on over here, youngfellas, here's youngwans."' **1996** John S. Doyle, *Sunday Tribune*, 1 Dec:

'You learn things from watching "Inspector Morse". Nobody under 40 wears a nightdress, for example...this had the authority of a gorgeous young one who nearly hypnotised the inspector into believing she was innocent of murder.'

your/yer man [n. phr.]. Individual whom it is considered unnecessary or undesirable, for a variety of reasons, to name directly. **1974** Éamonn Mac Thomáis, *Me Jewel and Darlin'* (see **jewel**) *Dublin*: '"Yer man — he has a face like a plateful of mortal sins."' Also **Your Man Upstairs** [n. phr.]. The Almighty. **1994** Ferdia Mac Anna, *The Ship Inspector*: '"The only thing to do is to go directly to Your Man Upstairs. Now. Our father who art in heaven..."' Also **your/yer wan** in same sense: see **wan**.

your only man [n. phr.]. The sine qua non, possessing a unique quality. **1939** Flann O'Brien, *At Swim-Two-Birds*: 'Do you know what I am going to tell you, he said with his wry mouth, a pint of plain [q.v.] is your only man.' **1995** Laurence Liddle, *Five Foot Three* (Belfast), 'Comments and Recollections': 'On an ordinary railway journey give me a centre corridor coach every time...but on a steam rail tour the compartment is your only man.' **1996** Mary Russell, *Irish Times*, 13 Aug: 'mine has taken me to Algeria and Georgia, not to mention Baltimore, Ballycastle and Burtonport... for there are times when the bike is your only man'.

your other eye! [exclam.]. Employed to express disbelief; nonsense! **1922** James Joyce, *Ulysses*: '"O!" shrieking, Miss Kennedy cried. "Will you ever forget his goggle eye?" Miss Douce chimed in in deep bronze laughter, shouting: "And your other eye!"'

your wan see **wan, your man**

youse/youze/yous/yis/yiz etc. [pl. pron.]. You (pl.). **1938** Samuel Beckett, *Murphy*: 'Wylie...had already seized Neary round the waist...and smuggled him halfway to the exit. "Howlt on there, youze," said the C.G.' **1991** Ferdia Mac Anna, *The Last of the High Kings*: 'the postman shouted from the bottom of the drive as Frankie and Ray held onto the barking, snarling family pet. "From now on, yiz can collect yer letters at the post office.'" **1993** Brendan Glacken, *Irish Times*, 11 Oct: 'THE DA [q.v.] How're yiz? Juss in time for de dinner, am I — nice timin', wha?' Also **yousens** (Ulster). See also **hiyis!**

yowder [n., cf. Sc. *youther*, 'steam or vapour arising from anything boiling or burning' (CSD)] (Ulster). Light drizzle (YDS).

yowtlin [n., see **yortlin**] (Ulster). 1. Infant. 2. Small thing.

yuk [n.]. Term of contempt. **1973** Noël Conway, *The Bloods* (q.v.): '"There's the boozers and the pictures for yuks like you who wouldn't be interested in libraries or museums.'

yuky [adj., <Sc. *yucky*, itching] (Ulster). As thus.

yup ya boy ya! see **hupyaboya!**, **yeh-boy-yeh!**

Z

Zozimus [nickname, <his recitation of history of St Mary of Egypt]. Michael Moran (1794–1846), blind Dub. balladeer. **1979** Peter Somerville-Large, *Dublin*: 'there was an attractive wild energy and wit about ordinary Dubliners, exemplified perhaps by Zozimus. The tall, gaunt, blind ballad singer wandered round the poorer quarters in his long frieze coat with its scalloped cape, his greasy beaver hat, corduroy trousers and "Francis Street brogues".' **1995** Sinéad Williams, *Ireland's Eye Christmas Annual*: 'Michael Moran, known as Zozimus...was a well known beggar and Dublin character [see **character** 1.]...he was also said to be talented at composing verse and his most popular works included "Whiskey and Water" and "Birth of Moses".'

Corrigenda and Addenda

Back of/Behind God Speed (q.v.). <screen placed in front of house door to act as wind-break.

cope (q.v.). Also (vb., Ulster), make lazy beds; harvest corn. See **souse**.

hood [n., <?] (Belfast). Streetwise youth. **1997** Gerry Moriarty, *Irish Times*, 2 Aug: 'Gerard, just turned 21, was popular among his age group. In Belfast parlance he was a "hood". He and his friends like to gather at street corners, party, chat up girls and steal cars... "UTH — Up the Hoods" is on many walls in west Belfast.'

Labour [n., <Labour Exchange, unemployment office] as is **on the labour** [adj. phr.]. On the dole, in receipt of social assistance. **1996** Nuala Ó Faoláin, *Are You Somebody?*: 'This woman was telling me the other day that where she lives nearly everybody is on the labour...And I said, automatically, "Well, what are they doing having big families, if they are on the labour?".'

motion [n., <Lat. *motio* (n.), movement] (Cork). Carnal inclination. **c19** *Pop. song*, 'The Girl from the Mill': 'We fell to drinking Beamish's porter [q.v.] to coax her motions in high display'. (DOM).

splank [n., <Ir. *splanc*, flash, spark]. Spark. **1979** Paddy Tunney, *The Stone Fiddle*: 'the crigs [q.v.] of hobnails on the flagstones set splanks flying to the rafters'.

Appendix

Racist Epithets

This listing embodies the perception of the Irish, as fostered largely — though not exclusively — by the former colonial power, as an inferior race of bungling peasants. Compare the French perception of the Belgians, the Canadian of the Newfoundlanders, and many other examples of contiguity and assumed superiority inducing racist prejudice. The phenomenon is, of course, alive and well in a domestic context in the form of 'Kerryman' jokes.

a bit Irish [adj. phr.]. Paradoxical, contradictory, gen. derog. **1997** *Examiner* (Cork), headline, 3 May: 'Old Head plan's a bit Irish' (of allegation that Ir. nationals were to be excluded from membership of Old Head of Kinsale Golf Club).

come the paddy over [vb. phr.]. Bamboozle, humbug.

Connemaras [nickname] (US). Immigrants from that area, derog. **1996** Uinsionn Mac Dubhghaill, *Irish Times*, 4 Nov: '[It was the practice] to slander the settlers as a people "born and trained as paupers...indolent, lazy and shiftless". The calumny persists to this day in Minnesota, where the word Connemara is still used as a term of abuse.'

Dear Joys [nickname]. 'Irishmen, from their frequently making use of that expression' (Grose).

Dublin dissector [n. phr., 'medical students *c*.1840–1900' (DHS)]. Cudgel.

Dublin University graduate [n. phr.]. Particularly stupid person (Green).

Irish apple/apricot/grape/lemon [n. phr.] (Brit.). Potato. 'It is a common joke against Irish vessels, to say that they are loaded with fruit and timber; that is, potatoes and broomsticks' (Grose).

Irish arms [n. phr.]. Thick legs. 'It is said of Irish women, that they have a dispensation from the pope to wear the thick ends of their legs downwards' (Grose).

Irish assurance [n. phr.]. 'A bold forward behaviour...it is said that a dipping in the river Shannon totally annihilates bashfulness; whence arises the saying of an impudent Irishman, that he has been dipt in the Shannon' (Grose).

Irish battleship [n. phr.] (naval) (Brit.). Barge.

Irish beauty [n. phr.] (Brit.). Woman with black eyes.

Irish buggy [n. phr.] (Brit.). Wheelbarrow.

Irish by birth but Greek by injection [n. phr.]. Male homosexual (Green).

Irish clubhouse [n. phr.]. Refined house of gay prostitution.

Irish confetti [n. phr.] (US). Stones, bricks, etc. employed as missiles; semen spilled extravaginally.

Irish dip [n. phr.]. Homosexual intercourse.

Irish draperies [n. phr.]. Cobwebs; drooping breasts.

Irish evidence [n. phr., late C17–mid-C19] (Brit.). False witness.

Irish fortune [n. phr., C19 (DHS)]. Vagina. See main entry for **Tipperary fortune**.

Irish hoist [n. phr.]. Kick in the arse.

Irish horse [n. phr.] (US). Tough corned beef; drooping penis.

Irish hurricane [n. phr.] (nautical). Flat calm with drizzling rain. Also **Irishman's hurricane** [1827– (DHS)] in same sense.

Irish lace [n. phr.]. Spider's web.

Irish legs [n. phr.]. Thick legs. See also **Irish arms**.

Irish local [n. phr.] (US). Wheelbarrow (DAS).

Irishman's dinner [n. phr.]. Fast.

Irishman's hurricane see **Irish hurricane**

Irishman's pocket [n. phr.] (US). One that is both capacious and empty.

Irishman's rest [n. phr.] (Brit.). 'Going up a friend's ladder with a hod of bricks' (DHS).

Irishman's ride [n. phr.] (Tasmania). Bicycle trip in which children take it in turns to ride.

Irishman's rise [n. phr., 1889–] (Brit.). Reduction in pay.

Irish marathon [n. phr.]. Protracted lovemaking.

Irish pennant [n. phr., 1883–] (Brit.). Frayed rope's-end blown by the wind.

Irish promotion [n. phr.] (gay use). Masturbation.

Irish rifle [n. phr., *c*.1840–]. Small comb.

Irish rise [n. phr.]. Detumescence.

Irish root [n. phr.]. Penis.

Irish screwdriver [n. phr.]. Hammer.

Irish shave [n. phr.]. Defecation.

Irish shift [n. phr.] (US). More than usually hypocritical political act.

Irish theatre [n. phr.] (milit.). Guardroom.

Irish toothache [n. phr.]. Penile erection; pregnancy. See also **Paddy's toothache**.

Irish toothpick [n. phr.]. Erect penis.

Irish toyles [n. phr.]. 'Thieves who carry about pins, laces, and other pedlars' wares, and under the pretence of offering their goods for sale, rob houses…' (Grose).

Irish turkey [n. phr.] (US). Corned beef and cabbage.

Irish wake [n. phr.]. Any boisterous celebration.

Irish way, the [n. phr., <belief that it substituted for contraception] (US). Heterosexual anal intercourse.

Irish wedding [n. phr.]. 1. ['gay use' (Green)]. Masturbation. 2. Emptying of a cesspool (DHS).

Irish whist [n. phr., C19]. Sexual intercourse.

Irish, you're [exclam.]. You're talking nonsense!

Mick see main entry

Oirish [adj.]. Attrib. of racist stereotype (see also main entry). Also **Oirishly** [adv.]. **1996** Hester Lacey, *Independent on Sunday* (London), 17 Nov: 'Terry Wogan could have been a bank manager by now — "if I'd played my cards right", he gurgles Oirishly.'

paddy [n.]. Rage, temper.

Paddy Doyle, do [vb. phr.] (naval/milit., C19–20] (Brit.). Be a defaulter.

Paddyland [nickname]. Ireland.

Paddy's funeral [n. phr.]. Any boisterous occasion.

Paddy's Opera [n. phr.]. Choral service at St Patrick's Cathedral, Dub. **1843** W.M. Thackeray, *The Irish Sketch Book*: 'Some of this class call the Cathedral Service *Paddy's Opera*; they say it is Popish — downright scarlet — and they won't go to it.'

Paddy's toothache [n. phr.]. Pregnancy. See also **Irish toothache**.

patsy [n., poss. <Patrick, but DAS suggests <It. *Pasqualino*, dimin. of *Pasquale*, 'used to designate a vulnerable, weak and small boy or man']. Fool, dupe, victim.

Teagueland [prop. n.]. Ireland. 'Teaguelanders: Irishmen' (Grose). See main entry for **Teig**.

Urinal of the Planets [nickname]. Ireland, 'so called from the frequent rains in that Island' (Grose).

weep Irish [vb. phr., 'Ex the copious lamentations of the Irish as at keening' (DHS)]. Shed crocodile tears.

References in the Text

The following authorities are referred to as indicated in the body of the work. Unless otherwise stated the date in brackets is that of the first edition.

Beecher Seán Beecher, *A Dictionary of Cork Slang* (Cork 1983)

Bliss Alan Bliss, *Spoken English in Ireland 1600–1740* (Dublin 1979)

CSD Alexander Warrack & William Grant, *Chambers Scots Dictionary* (Edinburgh 1974 reprint)

CUD C.I. Macafee (ed.), *A Concise Ulster Dictionary* (Oxford 1996)

DAS Robert L. Chapman, *The Dictionary of American Slang* (London 1987)

DHS Eric Partridge, *Dictionary of Historical Slang* (abridged edn, London 1972)

Dinneen Patrick S. Dinneen, *Foclóir Gaedhilge agus Béarla/An Irish-English Dictionary* (Dublin 1927)

DOM Diarmaid Ó Muirithe, 'The Words we Use', *The Irish Times, passim*

EDD Joseph Wright, *English Dialect Dictionary* (London 1896–1905)

EW Eddie Wymberry, *Spring Gardens* (Waterford 1995)

Green Jonathon Green, *The Macmillan Dictionary of Contemporary Slang* (3rd edn, London 1995)

Grose *A Dictionary of Buckish Slang, University Wit and Pickpocket Eloquence, Compiled Originally by Captain Grose* (London 1811)

MON Joseph Bigger (ed.), *Montiaghisms: Ulster Dialect Words and Phrases Collected by the Late William Lutton* (Armagh 1923)

Moylan Séamas Moylan, *The Language of Kilkenny* (Dublin 1995)

ODMS John Ayto & John Simpson, *The Oxford Dictionary of Modern Slang* (Oxford 1992)

Ó Dónaill Niall Ó Dónaill, *Foclóir Gaeilge-Béarla/An Irish-English Dictionary* (Dublin 1977)

OED *Oxford English Dictionary* (various edns)

OTF Rena Condrot, Pat Hurley & Tom Moore (eds.), *Old Tales of Fingal* (Dublin 1984)

Patterson W.H. Patterson, *Glossary of Words in Use in the Counties of Antrim & Down* (London 1880)

Pepper John Pepper's *Ulster-English Dictionary* (Belfast 1981)

PO'F Padraic O'Farrell, *How the Irish Speak English* (Cork 1981)

PWJ P.W. Joyce, *English as we Speak it in Ireland* (Dublin 1910)

S&R Gifford Lewis (ed.), *The Selected Letters of Somerville and Ross* (London 1989)

SH Rae McIntyre (ed.), *Some Handlin', The Dialect Heritage of North Ulster* (2nd edn, Limavady 1990)

Thorne Tony Thorne, *Dictionary of Modern Slang* (London 1990)

Todd Loreto Todd, *Words Apart, A Dictionary of Northern Ireland English* (Gerrards Cross 1990)

Traynor Michael Traynor, *The English Dialect of Donegal* (Dublin 1953)

TT Séamus McConnell, *Talk of the Town, A Derry Phrase Book* (Derry 1989)

Wall Richard Wall, *An Anglo-Irish Dialect Glossary for Joyce's Works* (Gerrards Cross 1986)

Wilkes G.A. Wilkes, *A Dictionary of Australian Colloquialisms* (Sydney 1978)

WS Vinnie Caprani, *A Whang of Slang* (Dublin 1989)

YDS William O'Kane, *You Don't Say?* (Dungannon, Co. Tyrone 1991)

Select Bibliography

This bibliography does not include those titles listed under References in the Text. Standard dictionaries have in general been omitted.

Bliss, Alan J. 'The Language of Synge' in *J.M. Synge, Centenary Papers, 1971* (Dublin 1972)

Brookes, Maureen & Joan Ritchie. *Tassie Terms — A Glossary of Tasmanian Words* (Melbourne 1995)

Bryson, Bill. *Mother Tongue* (London 1991)

Burgess, Anthony. *Joysprick, An Introduction to the Language of James Joyce* (London 1973)

Dolan, T.P. & Diarmaid Ó Muirithe (eds.). *Poole's Glossary...of the Old Dialect of the English Colony in the Baronies of Forth and Bargy* (Wexford 1979)

Edwards, John. *'Talk Tidy' — The Art of Speaking Wenglish* (Cowbridge 1985)

Flaherty, P.J. *The English Language, Irish Style* (Galway 1995)

Great Tuam Annual 2M (Tuam 1992)

Henry, Patrick L. 'English and its Varieties' in Victor Meally (ed.), *Encyclopaedia of Ireland* (Dublin 1968)

Irwin, P.J. 'Ireland's Contribution to the English Language' in *Studies*, vol. XX, no. 88 (1933)

McCrum, Robert, William Cran & Robert MacNeil. *The Story of English* (London 1986, rev. edn 1992)

Mac Énrí, Micheál. '"Ceant" agus Saoghal na dTincéirí' in *Béaloideas*, vol. 9, no. 2 (December 1939)

Mac Gréine, Pádraig. 'Irish Tinkers or Travellers' in *Béaloideas*, vol. 3, no. 2 (December 1931)

Mac Gréine, Pádraig. 'Further Notes on Tinkers' "Cant"' in *Béaloideas*, vol. 3, no. 3 (June 1932)

Marshall, W.F. *Ulster Speaks* (London 1936)

Milroy, James. *Regional Accents of English: Belfast* (Belfast 1981)

Norri, Juhani. 'Regional Labels in Some British and American Dictionaries' in *International Journal of Lexicography*, vol. 9, no. 1 (March 1996)

Ó Muirithe, Diarmaid. *A Dictionary of Anglo-Irish: Words and Phrases from Gaelic* (Dublin 1996)

Ó Muirithe, Diarmaid. *The Words we Use* (Dublin 1996)

Ó Muirithe, Diarmaid (ed.). *The English Language in Ireland* (Dublin & Cork 1977)

Panini, Dr. *Irish Up-to-Date* (Dublin 1933)

Partridge, Eric. *Shakespeare's Bawdy* (London 1955)

Paulin, Tom. *A New Look at the Language Question* (Belfast 1983)

Rees, Nigel. *Dictionary of Catchphrases* (London 1995)

Simes, Gary. *A Dictionary of Australian Underworld Slang* (Melbourne 1993)